All Manner of Murals

The History, Techniques and Conservation of Secular Wall Paintings

All Manner of Murals

The History, Techniques and Conservation of Secular Wall Paintings

Proceedings of the Secular Wall Paintings Symposia organised by the Icon Stone and Wall Paintings Group and supported by English Heritage, London 2004–5

Edited by Robert Gowing and Robyn Pender

Archetype Publications

ENGLISH HERITAGE

THE INSTITUTE OF CONSERVATION

In association with English Heritage and
The Institute of Conservation
First published 2007 by Archetype Publications Ltd. in association with English Heritage and the Institute of Conservation

Archetype Publications Ltd.
6 Fitzroy Square
London W1T 5HJ
www.archetype.co.uk

Tel: 44(207) 380 0800
Fax: 44(207) 380 0500

Cover images (clockwise from top left): Plas Mewydd, Llangollen (Wales) © M. O'Leary; 44 High Street, Bagshot (Surrey) © English Heritage Photo Library; Skinners' Hall, London © Crown Copyright. NMR; Civic Centre, Newport (Wales) © Downland Partnership Ltd.; Archer Pavilion, Wrest Park (Bedfordshire) © Paine and Stewart.

ISBN-10: 1-904982-11-5
ISBN-13: 978-1-904982-11-1

British Library Cataloguing in Publication Data
A catalogue record for this book is available from the British Library.

Printed on acid-free paper

Typeset by Kate Williams, Swansea
Printed and bound in Italy by Printer Trento srl

To the memory of Dr Giles Arthington Worsley 1961–2006

Contents

List of contributors

James Ayres
Freelance writer and consultant on historic buildings
c/o Bath Preservation Trust
1 Royal Crescent
Bath BA1 2LR

Caroline Babington
Freelance wall painting conservator
91 Canbury Avenue
Kingston, Surrey KT2 6JR

Ann Ballantyne
Private wall painting conservator
8 Saint Paul's Road
Richmond, Surrey
TW9 2HH

Dr Michael Bath
Emeritus Professor, University of Strathclyde
c/o 6 Roman Road
Balfron, Glasgow G63 0PW

Dr Roger Bowdler
Head of Territory Designation, Heritage Protection
English Heritage
1 Waterhouse Square, 138–142 Holborn
London EC1N 2ST

Tobit Curteis
Private wall paintings conservator
Tobit Curteis Associates
36 Abbey Road
Cambridge CB5 8HQ

Dr Jane Davies
Jane Davies Conservation
Lane End, Lockeridge
Marlborough, Wiltshire SN8 4EQ

Dr Kathryn Davies
Historic Buildings Inspector
English Heritage
Eastgate Court, 195–205 High Street
Guildford GU1 3EH

Kate Frame
Head of Conservation and Collections Care
Historic Royal Palaces
Apartment 59, Hampton Court Palace
East Molesey, Surrey KT8 9AU

Robert Gowing
Senior Wall Painting Conservator
Building Conservation and Research Team
English Heritage
1 Waterhouse Square, 138–142 Holborn
London EC1N 2ST

Elizabeth Holford
Private conservator
Elizabeth Holford Associates Ltd
Fine Art Conservation Studio
The Tobacco Factory
Raleigh Road
Southville, Bristol BS3 1TF

Kate Hunter
Project Leader
Newport Ship Project
Newport Museum and Art Gallery
John Frost Square
Newport, South Wales NP20 1PA

Dr Edward Impey
Director of Research and Standards
English Heritage
1 Waterhouse Square, 138–142 Holborn
London EC1N 2ST

Sophie Julien-Lees
Conservation and Collections Care
Historic Royal Palaces
Apartment 59, Hampton Court Palace
East Molesey, Surrey KT8 9AU

Andrea Kirkham
Private wall painting conservator
31 Silver Street
Norwich, Norfolk NR3 4TT

Alastair McCapra
Chief Executive
The Institute of Conservation
3rd Floor, Downstream Building, 1 London Bridge
London SE1 9BG

Ernestine McKay
Director
Frescoes Forever
78 March Court, Warwick Drive
London SW15 6LD

Marguerite O'Leary
Private conservator
95 Glengarry Road
London SE22 8QA

Tom Organ
Private wall painting conservator
The Wall Paintings Workshop
69 South Road
Faversham, Kent ME13 7LX

Stephen Paine
Private wall painting conservator
Paine and Stewart
66 Bradmore Park Road
London W6 0DT

Richard Pelter
Private conservator
International Fine Art Conservation Studios Ltd
43–45 Park Street
Bristol BS1 5NL

Pauline Plummer
Private wall painting conservator
19d, Kew Gardens Road
Richmond, Surrey TW9 3HD

Jane Rutherfoord
Private wall painting conservator
The Chapel, Milton Lilbourne
Pewsey, Wiltshire SN9 5LF

Peter Schmitt
Surveyor to the Fabric
Royal Academy of Art
Burlington House
London W1J 0BD

Sophie Stewart
Private wall painting conservator
Paine and Stewart
66 Bradmore Park Road
London W6 0DT

Anthony Wells-Cole
Senior Curator
Temple Newsam
Temple Newsam Estate
Leeds, West Yorkshire LS15 0AD

Dr Clare A. P. Willsdon
Reader
University of Glasgow
Room 307, 2nd Floor, 8 University Gardens
Glasgow G12 8QH

The late Dr Giles Worsley was a Senior Research Fellow at the Institute of Historical Research.

Foreword

Edward Impey, Director of Research and Standards, English Heritage *and Alastair McCapra,* Chief Executive, Icon, The Institute of Conservation

Of the properties under the care of English Heritage, more than 50 contain historic wall paintings. These span over 1700 years of secular decorative tradition: a 3rd-century fresco in the Roman Villa at Lullingstone in Kent, internationally significant late 14th-century wall paintings at Longthorpe Tower in Cambridgeshire, early 17th-century Baroque murals in the Archer Pavilion at Wrest Park in Bedfordshire, High-Victorian decorative paintings in Brodsworth Hall in Yorkshire, and a mid-20th-century painted stage within the battlements of Hurst Castle in Hampshire. These wonderful survivals not only enhance our enjoyment and appreciation of the sites, but they provide a unique insight into the ways these places were used and the people who used them. An integral part of each historic place, their value extends across many disciplines from the art enthusiast to the building professional.

As the government's statutory adviser on the historic environment for England, English Heritage is committed to working with all those with an interest in the historic environment, and who wish to improve our understanding of our collective past. Working with partners and professional colleagues such as the Institute of Conservation (Icon) creates a valuable synergy that can only increase the effective dissemination of our collective efforts, improve standards and raise public awareness.

The conference series from which this volume originates was a direct result of this collaboration, and English Heritage was proud to be able to support this valuable activity. It is equally proud that by making the material presented available through publication it can foster ongoing interest and awareness of this glorious part of our past.

Edward Impey

This volume has been published under the aegis of English Heritage and Icon's Stone and Wall Paintings Group. Icon was formed to make partnerships with other organisations more productive, to promote the sharing of knowledge between disciplines and specialisms, and to advance the understanding of the conservation community as a whole. The three symposia recorded in this volume embody these aims to an admirable degree.

The secular wall paintings symposia series exemplifies the forward-looking and multidisciplinary character of the conservation profession. Around one-third of Icon's 3000 members work on historic buildings and this volume will serve them well as a reference in years to come. It also points towards new challenges in scientific research and the need to develop closer cooperation between all the professionals involved in preserving our built heritage.

As well as co-publishing this volume, English Heritage has been most generous and supportive of the recent formation (in 2005) of Icon as a unified body for the conservation community. We are very grateful for its support and encouragement. I look forward to future opportunities to work together with English Heritage and commend to you the fruits of our current collaboration contained in this volume.

Alastair McCapra

Preface

Robert Gowing

Senior Wall Painting Conservator, Building Conservation and Research Team, English Heritage

This volume brings together a cross-section of the papers presented during the series of symposia on secular wall paintings held by the Stone and Wall Paintings Group committee of the former United Kingdom Institute for Conservation of Historic and Artistic Works (UKIC), since 2005 incorporated within the Institute of Conservation (Icon). The Group represents wall painting conservators across the UK, and its organising committee oversees an active programme of events including guided site visits and workshops as well as conferences and symposia. Subjects are chosen to reflect current activities and as a response to requests from membership, and this symposium series was no exception. As Senior Wall Painting Conservator at English Heritage, and Group Chair between 2002 and 2005, I was aware that there was much significant new research and many active and interesting conservation projects happening within the wall-paintings community. A number of issues directed our attention towards the subject of secular wall paintings in particular:

- Although secular wall paintings were being studied intensively across the UK, no forum existed to bring this diverse body of new knowledge together. Organisations such as the Vernacular Architecture Group, the Society for the Protection of Ancient Buildings, the Historic Houses Association and the Traditional Paint Forum have certainly supported and encouraged studies of secular painted decoration, and some of that material is published through their respective journals, but it has usually been incorporated with other subjects or too specialised to be able to raise awareness in the wider conservation community.
- Secular wall paintings, in particular domestic secular wall paintings, were not getting the same recognition, exposure, funding and even care as paintings in ecclesiastical sites.
- The popularity of domestic 'DIY' meant many new discoveries of historic interior decoration, but there was little guidance readily available for owners and local authorities.

A request for papers for a symposium dedicated to the history, techniques and conservation of secular wall paintings produced such an interesting and extremely diverse response that it was immediately clear a series of events would be needed. Three one-day symposia were therefore organised, and additional speakers invited to present their own research. Delegates spanned the profession and included conservators, art historians, curators, architects, archaeologists and conservation scientists. Three London venues were chosen to reflect the three periods being examined:

- *Illusions of Grandeur: English Baroque Wall Paintings* was held in the Fine Rooms of the Royal Academy of Arts in January 2004. Recent restoration of these rooms had resulted in the rediscovery of a painted frieze by William Kent (see the paper by Plummer and Schmitt, pp. 153–72).
- *Followers of Fashion: Renaissance Wall Paintings* in Britain was held at Carpenters' Hall in November 2004. This post-war building preserves rare surviving fragments of mid-16th-century wall paintings rescued from a fire which destroyed an earlier building in the 19th century.
- *Modern Traditions: 19th- and 20th-Century Secular Wall Paintings* was held at Skinners' Hall, in March 2005. The Banqueting Hall is decorated with a cycle of paintings by Frank Brangwyn, depicting scenes from the history of the guild (see the paper by Willsdon, pp. 89–101).

This volume reorganises the presented papers under the two main themes which emerged from the series:

- History, development and care of secular wall paintings
- Conservation and research case studies

Understanding wall paintings and their conservation needs demands a multidisciplinary approach. As well as a thorough knowledge of conservation materials and techniques, it is important to understand how materials and building systems behave, especially under challenging environmental conditions, and history must be researched not only in relation to the fine and decorative arts and architecture but also to socio-economics. The papers in this volume are fine examples of how all these disciplines can interact and inform each other while also illuminating a little known but utterly fascinating slice of vernacular life in the British Isles.

Robert Gowing
August 2006

Acknowledgements

I am grateful to all committee members of Icon's Stone and Wall Paintings Group for their unfailing support and commitment to the project. All three events were fully subscribed and well received: for this particular credit must go to Caroline Babington and John Burbidge, who put immense effort into arranging the conference bookings, the accommodation and the catering, and to David Odgers for chairing *Modern Traditions: 19th- and 20th-Century Secular Wall Paintings*. I would also like to thank the staff at the three venues: the Royal Academy of Arts, Carpenters' Hall, and Skinners' Hall; Gordon Audio Visual Ltd for providing the necessary technical equipment and support; and the reprographics department at English Heritage for the production of the delegate booklets.

The symposia and this publication owe much to the English Heritage Building Conservation and Research Team. Special thanks are due to Bill Martin, Head of Team, for generous financial and administrative support of the series and for co-funding this publication. Team members Sophie Godfraind and Clara Willett spent considerable time and effort assisting with the registration of delegates.

I am truly indebted to my co-editor, Dr Robyn Pender for unending support during the conferences and for her invaluable editorial skills and commitment towards this publication. Equal thanks go to Sophie Stewart, who took on the enormous task of collating the images and ensuring copyright approvals.

For the title of this volume, I must express thanks to Ernestine McKay, whose suggestion was inspired by the eccentric King and Queen in Lewis Carroll's *Through the Looking-Glass*.

Lastly, I wish to express my gratitude to Clive Aslet, editor of *Country Life* magazine, for kindly allowing the reproduction of an article by Giles Worsley that originally appeared in the 21 April 2005 issue. Giles was our first speaker at the Royal Academy in January 2004, opening the symposia series with a talk presenting his views on Baroque wall paintings, which sparked a lively and interesting discussion. These very ideas were subsequently published in *Country Life*, but his battle with cancer prevented him from contributing a paper to this volume. I am delighted to be able to include his *Country Life* article and honoured to be able to dedicate this volume to his memory.

Robert Gowing

Introduction: Designating the domestic – mural paintings and the Heritage Protection Review

Roger Bowdler

Head of Territory Designation, Heritage Protection Department, English Heritage

What do secular wall paintings and the reform of the government's systems of statutory heritage designations have in common? A reasonable question: and one which this introduction will seek to explain. The second conference of the series that took place in November 2004 at the Carpenters' Hall provided the opportunity to outline some of the issues that are being addressed by the Heritage Protection Review, and to make explicit the connection between designation and the way we recognise special interest in our historic environment. Listing buildings and scheduling archaeology are each ways of celebrating the notable, as well as ways of managing change within the planning process. What is afoot?

First, a word about the Heritage Protection Review (HPR). Formally opened by the Department for Culture, Media and Sport (DCMS) with a consultation document in July 2003, this review constitutes the most fundamental assessment of the way we have looked after the historic environment in England since the 1960s. Ambitious in its range and detailed in its approach, HPR aims to improve designation; to formally align separate approaches between buildings and archaeology; to review the methods of managing the historic environment through the consents system; and to promote positive management of buildings and sites through the promotion of management agreements. England's system of designation is widely admired internationally. Equally clear, however, is that the compartmentalised nature of our present dual buildings- and archaeology-focused approach requires attention and improvement. Responses to the proposals set out in the consultation were strongly in favour of reform.

Extensive consultation, practical testing of proposals through 'pilot projects', seminars, communicating with the sector; much has happened since 2003. The government is now working on the options for change: at the time of writing (July 2006), we are awaiting news of its decision as to whether to seek primary legislation (a 2005 Labour Party manifesto commitment) for the proposals outlined in HPR. Should a new Heritage Act be enacted, it is likely that we would see changes to the present system from around 2010 onwards. Listing and scheduling would be replaced with a new Register of Historic Sites and Buildings for England, onto which existing designations would migrate; consents systems would be overhauled, including the provision for management agreements; the role of local planning authorities may well change too. Few areas of the historic environment sector will be untouched as a result.

Designation leads to regulation and has a direct impact on an individual's freedom to enjoy his own property as he sees fit. If we are to maintain the levels of protection that listed and scheduled sites currently enjoy – on the basis that it is our duty to pass on our singular heritage to future generations – then we need to ensure that there is acceptance and understanding of the justifications and methods of our designations. But what has any of this to do with secular wall paintings? The answer can be summarised thus: HPR means rethinking the ways we view special interest in the historic environment. It means integrating landscapes and buildings; history and fabric; understanding and designation. In short, with reference to wall paintings, it asks that we review how we apply art history to issues of practical building conservation.

Wall paintings constitute one of the more sensitive overlaps between painting and buildings, art history and architecture. HPR is premised upon creating a sounder designation basis for the purposes of statutory control. It seeks to build upon the huge legacy of designations – scheduling has been with us since 1882, listing since 1947 – and bring a new emphasis on explaining special interest. Wall paintings are a case in point. Few other areas of our activity show how important it is to flag up special interest and ensure that future management is appropriately steered, through initial designation and through appropriate grading of the asset.

Expert conservators, art historians, building analysts and mural connoisseurs will rarely need statutory designations to provide interpretation of just why special claims are made for surviving instances of wall paintings. There is no disguising the fact that many of our inherited designations are bald in their briskness and less than comprehensive in their coverage. This should not surprise us: listing was originally intended to be just the flagging up of which buildings deserved retention and (from 1968 only) a special form of planning permission. List descriptions were intended solely to identify the building and not to interpret them or explain their claims to special interest. Those tasks were left to conservation officers and historic buildings inspectors. John Betjeman may have baulked at the creation of a cadre of state-funded, Courtauld-trained, inspectors back in the 1930s: but it is now recognised that there is a role for government guidance on ways of championing the appreciation and protection of our built heritage. At the heart of protecting the system of heritage protection lie more effective ways of communicating our own appreciation.

In the past, listing has always attempted to flag up wall paintings when known about: we continue this responsibility today and endeavour to recognise the great worth and value of this resource through appropriate designation and grading. Listing in the upper grades of I and II* (the terms themselves are curiosities, which HPR is reviewing) leads to the direct involvement of English Heritage in the planning process, and prioritises such designated entities for grant support. The more we know about wall paintings, the more precious they become; and their relative rarity becomes ever more apparent too. The possession of such survivals can be the crucial factor in making a building eligible for listing in the first place; it can also be the justification for a higher grade listing.

Murals, then, can make all the difference. Take the example of Wimbledon Public Library. Built in 1890, it remains a good example of the genre (if not a spectacular one). The factor that clinched the listing was the survival in the former children's library of post-war murals by students at the Wimbledon School of Art. Similarly, the former Trafalgar House in Portsmouth, a late Victorian YMCA building, might have fallen just below the threshold for listing had it not contained a spirited 1948 mural by Eric Rimmington showing service personnel disembarking at the station: this now forms a feature in the Wetherspoons pub that occupies the building (Fig. 1). Publications such as Clare Willsdon's *Mural Painting in Britain 1840–1940: Image and Meaning* (OUP 2000) have opened our eyes to the qualities of this hitherto neglected area of public art, and it is important that statutory designation not only keeps up with this development in perception, but does so in time to influence planning decisions. The interior decoration of historic vernacular buildings has also been gaining ground through seminal publications such as Ian Bristow's two-volume *Architectural Colour in British Interiors 1615–1840* (published by Yale University Press for the Paul Mellon Center for Studies in British Art 1996), and James Ayres' *Domestic Interiors: The British Tradition 1500–1850* (Yale 2003).

Grading can be crucial in helping to secure increased levels of technical guidance and support. Enhanced understanding can make all the difference in this regard. While access to most public buildings, and the bulk of the nation's churches, resulted in better appreciation of their interior decorative history (with

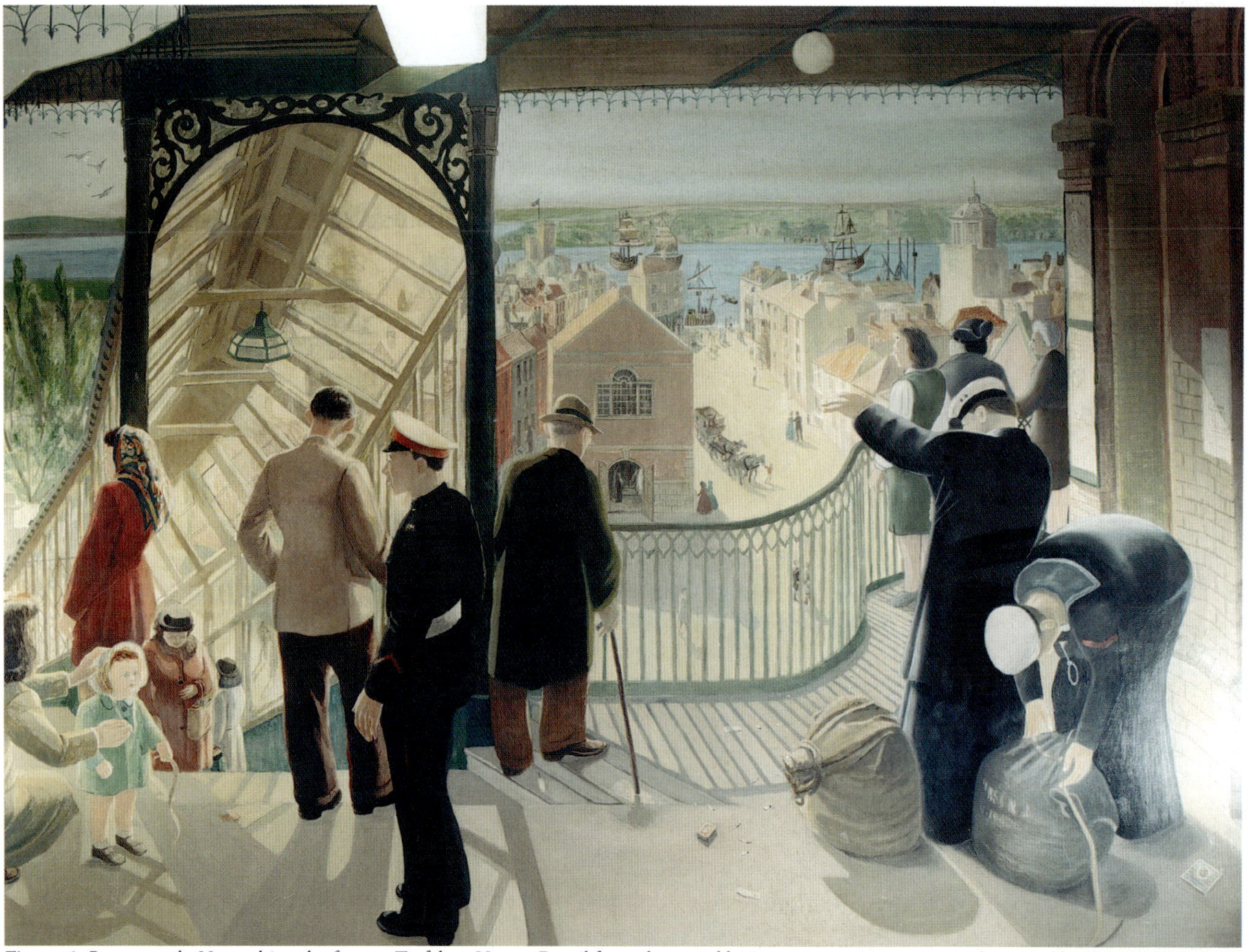

Figure 1 Portsmouth, Hampshire: the former Trafalgar House. Detail from the mural by Eric Rimmington, executed in 1949 for the committee of the Trafalgar Services' Club, and surviving as decoration within the pub which now occupies the building. *(© English Heritage. NMR)*

resulting higher numbers of grade I and II* listings), the interiors of the bulk of the smaller private vernacular buildings were never properly explored. It is therefore not surprising that we hear regularly of 'new discoveries' of wall paintings within these important yet humble dwellings, which necessitates their re-evaluation. One instance is to be found at 44 High Street, Bagshot, Surrey (see paper by Organ, pp. 43–51). An aisled open hall of the 14th century, re-fronted in the 18th century, the building itself is clearly of note. The recent upgrading was secured by the connection, established by Dr David Gaimster of the Society of Antiquaries, between the surviving mural decoration (found during building works), the related Bagshot House Lodge, used by James I's courtiers and the investiture of Prince Henry in 1610. This insight placed the house within the new context of Jacobean court culture and strengthened the building's claims to exceptional special interest. Nor do houses have to possess royal connections to make the cut. New Hall, near Ticklerton in Shropshire, is a decent enough Grade II 16th-century H-plan house. Detailed inspection of the interior, however, discovered three distinct schemes of late 16th-century wall painting including a monumental stag hunt in grisaille and an intriguing figure scene involving musicians and assorted animals (see paper by K. Davies, pp. 23–32) (Figs 2 and 3). These extremely rare survivals in themselves clearly warranted upgrading the building to Grade II*. Other outstanding examples, such as Thomas Barker's 1826 painting of the Massacre of Chios, in his Doric House in Bath, may warrant listing in the very highest grade of all.

Designation has been careful not to privilege the polite and courtly over the vernacular or popular: many humble vernacular buildings are listed as are many places or popular resort such as pubs, cinemas and institutes. Inevitably, grand set-pieces of the sort surveyed by Edward Croft-Murray will have been picked up in the earlier list surveys: no-one is likely to have omitted the Baroque embellishments of Moor Park or Reigate Priory, the Royal Society of Arts building with its epic James Barry cycle, or Sir Philip Sassoon's house at Port Lympne (with its Rex Whistler painted pavilion room) from their surveys. These splendours are, in one sense, obvious. Moreover, they were much more accessible during the initial listing inspections. But what do we do about the former Casbah Coffee Club in Haymans Green, Liverpool, with its pre-Beatles decoration by John and Cynthia Lennon and drummer Pete Best? Aesthetic merits are one claim to special interest, but we need to be mindful of popular culture

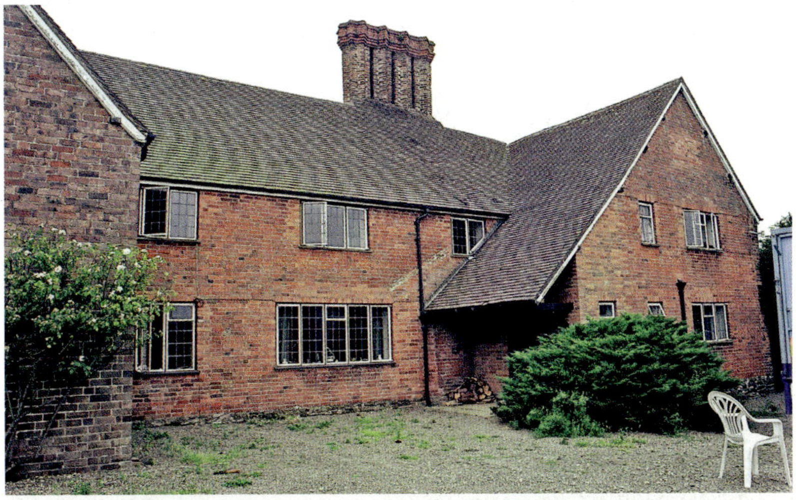

Figure 2 New Hall, near Ticklerton, Shropshire: general view of the front. The 16th-century H-plan house has clearly been altered numerous times. *(Photo: © R. Gowing)*

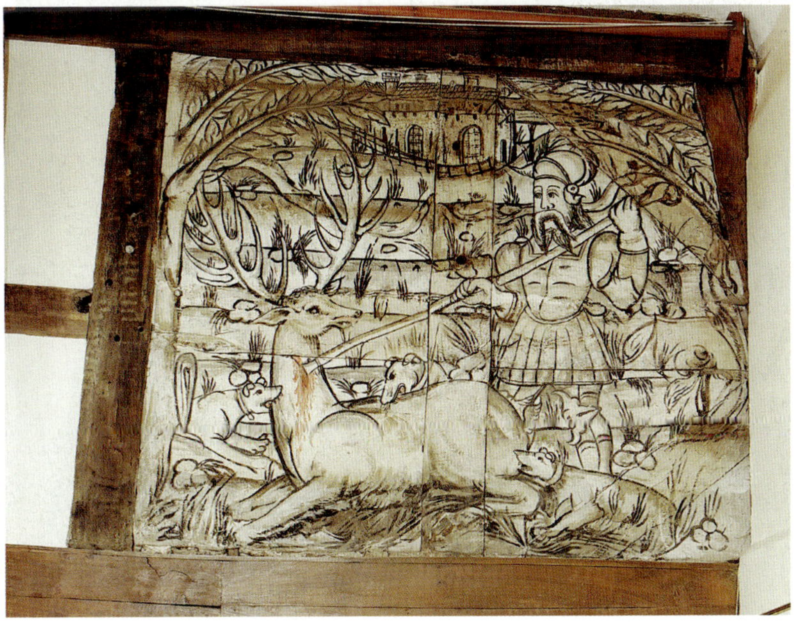

Figure 3 New Hall, near Ticklerton, Shropshire: view of the monumental wall painting within the main hall of the house. This painting of a stag hunt dates to the second half of the 16th century, and is predominantly grisaille, with only the blood accented in red. *(© English Heritage. NMR)*

too. Equally difficult is the recognition and understanding of the simpler decorative schemes such as those described in the paper by Andrea Kirkham (pp. 33–42).

One of the more marginal areas lies, inevitably, in relatively modern examples (the paper by McKay on pp. 103–12 certainly attests to their ongoing production). Judgement is invariably harder in such cases, which makes it all the more important to have publicly available criteria, against which we base our decisions. This quest for greater openness is another driver behind HPR. When do wall paintings cease to have automatic claims to special interest? What role should connoisseurship play? When is a socially committed but artistically inept daub of special interest? Just what is 'wall art'? Should we have protected the 1984 CND mural in Hackney? How can the undoubted significance of the wartime murals by Olga Lehmann in the underground factory at Corsham best be captured (Fig. 4)? What is the role of recording as an alternative to preservation *in situ*? Many issues demand attention and we are able to assure all concerned in the area of wall paintings (of whatever variety) that this attention will be given. Such creations tend to be one-offs and all the more important for that reason. Capturing current levels of understanding and appreciation is the basis of effective designation, and bodies such as the Institute of Conservation (Icon) play a crucial role in articulating these all-important claims to special notice.

Owners can sometimes be the most knowledgeable guardians of such survivals, as well as the proudest. This encourages proper care to be taken of these sensitive entities and feeds into the 'heritage cycle' of understanding, valuing, caring and enjoying. Enhanced designation entries have the potential to articulate more clearly the special interest of the buildings they describe, and to set out, in non-technical terms, the 'so-what' issues that designation seeks to capture. Observers of recent list descriptions will have noticed that they are expanded; they specifically seek to determine the claims to special interest and to communicate them more clearly. There remains much to do in this regard, and the challenge of revisiting the 380,000-odd existing descriptions (together with the 20,000 schedule entries, 1600 Register of Parks and Gardens and 43 Register of Battlefields entries) is considerable. Preparing a strategic programme for the Heritage Protection Department in the light of the anticipated White Paper is our current priority.

Recognising special interest in the historic environment is the primary role of designation. An enhanced designation basis is a prerequisite for effective management of our singular inheritance, and the Heritage Protection Review is determined to create such a basis. Wall paintings constitute one of our most enjoyable areas of activity: new discoveries, fresh insights and developing appreciation enable us to enrich designation entries and assign appropriate grades, thereby ensuring that appropriate care is devoted to this special and singular resource.

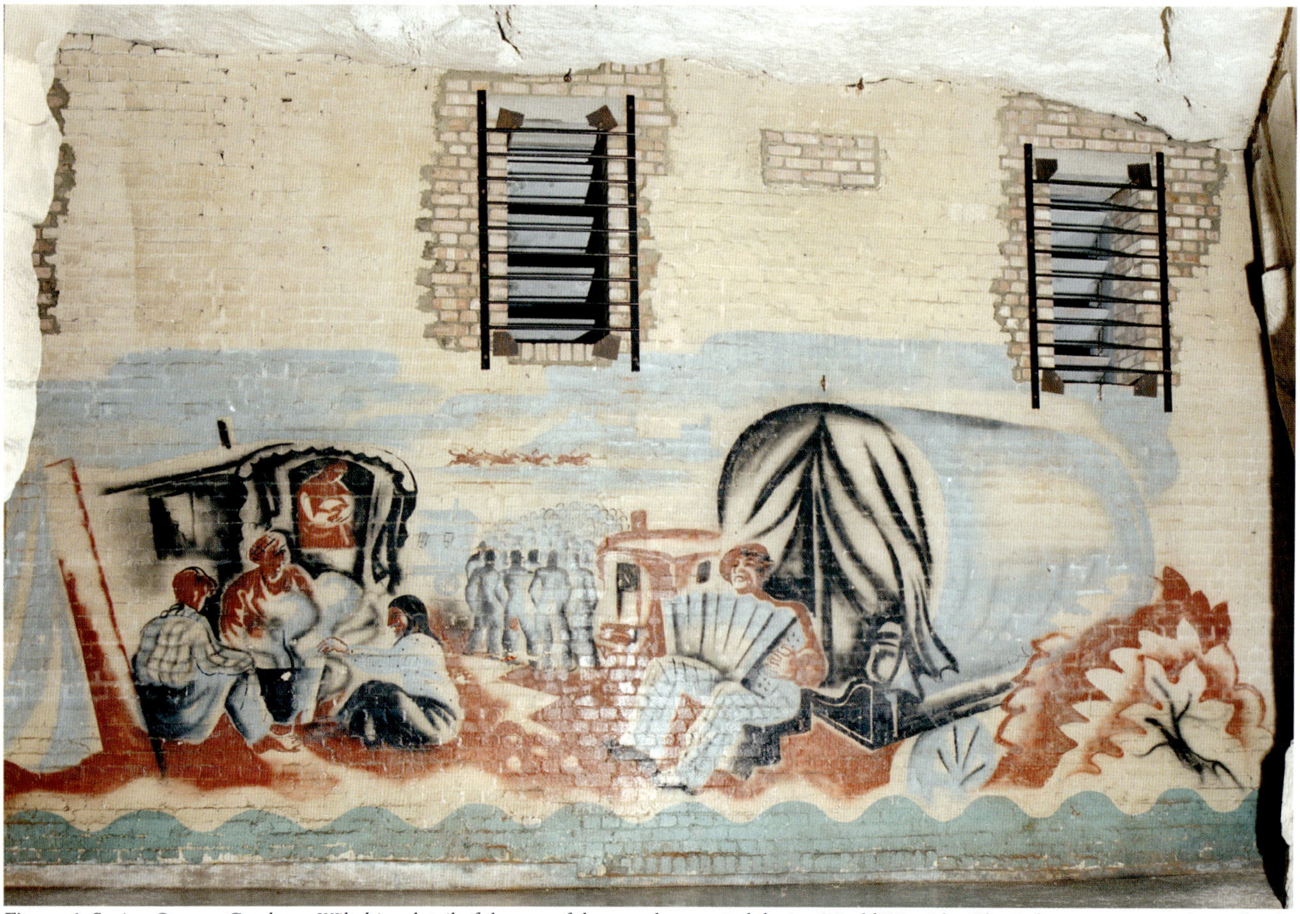

Figure 4 Spring Quarry, Corsham, Wiltshire: detail of the one of the murals executed during World War 2 by Olga Lehmann to cover the walls of the underground factory's canteen. *(© English Heritage. NMR)*

Part 1

History, development and care of secular wall paintings

Elusive sources for Renaissance wall paintings

Anthony Wells-Cole

There is only one central issue in art history it seems to me, and that is to try to understand, in as many ways as possible, how it is that works of art come to look the way they do. (John Shearman 1992)[1]

Understanding where an artist derived his inspiration – the core of artistic activity – must be among the most important ways of approaching a work of art. With artists of the 16th century, more than with earlier periods, it is necessary to ask whether inspiration came from within or was derived from elsewhere via the intermediate stage of a published image. For this period saw a development at least as revolutionary as the computer and the internet today: the application of printing to the dissemination of all sorts of images. Prints became 'the standard medium for the transmission of visual ideas across geographical distances'.[2] Assisted by the religious turmoil in Europe from the 1560s onwards, which brought an influx of continental artists and craftsmen flooding across the English Channel and North Sea, Renaissance and Mannerist prints transformed the appearance of architecture and decoration in England and Scotland during the early modern period.

Some years ago, when writing on the use of prints as sources of decoration in Elizabethan and Jacobean England, my concern then was to illustrate and discuss objects, and the print or prints on which they depended.[3] In other words, I was dealing with 'successes' – instances where I had been able to identify a print source – rather than failures, where I hadn't. The true picture is much less positive, for failures probably outnumber successes by a ratio of three, five, or even ten to one. A painting now in the Walker Art Gallery in Liverpool, depicting the *Story of Phaethon*, graphically illustrates both success and failure. Although executed on panel – and so not strictly speaking a wall painting – it is thought to have been commissioned for the decoration of Malpas Hall in Cheshire in the early 17th century. The painting combines several episodes from this well-known story. I found that a small subsidiary element in this picture had been copied by the artist from an engraving after Maarten de Vos, illustrating a completely different subject; however, I have been unable to discover a single print source for any of the other elements in this complex image. What is the explanation for this? Did the painter compose the remainder of his picture without reference to any other continental print? It seems highly improbable. Did he adapt a print so comprehensively that it cannot now be identified? Did he indeed use prints which survive as yet undiscovered? Or have they been lost altogether?

The same possibilities apply to wall paintings. Some, from their very appearance, are clearly independent of prints. These include painted versions of a textile or a textile-hung interior. The well-known late 16th-century paintings from Ivy House in Fittleworth, Hampshire (now in the Weald and Downland Open Air Museum, Singleton) and the 17th-century schemes discussed by Andrea Kirkham in this volume (pp. 33–42) are instances where it would not be profitable to search for a print source. Other paintings clearly imitate elaborate panelling. Examples are the Susanna Room at Little Moreton Hall, Cheshire, and paintings from Cumberland House in Ipswich (now at Christchurch Mansion, Ipswich). In the 16th century, there were indeed printed designs for panelling: they include patterns by an anonymous German artist with the initials *HS*, working in about 1530–40; by Michael Zimmerman, perhaps working in Vienna in about 1556; and by Jan Vredeman de Vries, published in the 1580s.[4] But these are too different to have provided the inspiration for the paintings.

A second possibility is that a painter was inspired by a print, but adapted it to a greater or lesser extent rather than copying it slavishly, feature by feature. This is a dangerous conclusion to reach for the simple reason that so many images were printed in the 16th century (the number certainly runs into the hundreds of thousands, if not millions of subjects) that one can never be sure that all the potential sources have been exhausted, as we shall see later. The same is true of a third possibility, that a painter followed a print source but the print is not known, either because it has not survived or because it has not yet been discovered. This must be the case with many decorative wall paintings imitating somewhat earlier continental design trends. Take Moresques, for example: at Cumberland House strapwork panels are combined with frieze panels of a continental-style Moresque ornament so sophisticated and idiomatic that no painter in England could have invented it for himself. These must depend on a print source. But although designs by Peter Flötner are very close in character, none has precisely the same arrangement of flowing stems. The actual source has not yet been identified.

So too with the many wall paintings that display convincing Italianate decoration, of the kind generally known in Britain as 'antiquework'. This is usually painted in black on white and is similar in appearance (if not in technique) to the *sgraffito* decoration of buildings in Italy and – north of the Alps – in towns under Italian influence, such as Prague or Innsbruck. English examples such as Shire Hall in Wilmington, Kent, have been illustrated by Francis Reader, but many others are recorded in East Anglia (for instance at Mildenhall Manor), and the south-east (as at Vernon House in Farnham, Surrey).[5] Harvington Hall in Worcestershire has examples that must have been derived from Italian or German ornamental prints or decorated page borders from the second quarter of the 16th century. Although one panel bears a generic similarity to a grotesque by Perino del Vaga dated 1532, neither this nor any other print found so far is close enough to be accepted as the actual source.

What of the spectacular examples of strapwork cartouches found in wall paintings? Here too the correspondence may be close. Strapwork panels from the Greenland Fisheries Building in King's Lynn, for instance, are similar to designs published by Johann Jacob Ebelmann in 1596. Other continental-style strapwork cartouches, like those in paintings at Vernon House in Farnham, Surrey, at Hengrave Hall in Suffolk, and in an early 17th-century house in Woodbridge, Suffolk, resemble Antwerp mannerist ornament designs so closely that printed sources must lie behind them. As no known ornament prints or book title pages have so far provided the answers, perhaps their source is to be found in title cartouches on maps or some other more obscure form of publication. Perhaps the originals have disappeared altogether.

Why should it be easier to identify the print sources for the many painted scenes derived from mythology or the Bible than it is for antiquework, or for other types of painted ornament? More than one answer suggests itself. Were the prints that were copied for antiquework simply used to destruction, where biblical prints were by their nature more highly valued and thus more likely to survive? Or could it be that, in the early modern period in Britain, painters developed an ability to devise convincing-looking continental-style ornament independent of prints, whereas they lacked any adequate training in figure painting and the composition of complete scenes, so that they were obliged to rely heavily on printed models? Or is it simply a question of the social status of a building, whereby a squire or an aristocrat had access to a source of prints not available to people of the middle class or below?

Knole in Kent is the epitome of a house built by a wealthy courtier who would have had easy access to sources of prints, if only through the artists and craftsmen he employed. Sir Thomas Sackville, who remade Knole from 1604 onwards as a 'place near London to retire to', had been appointed Lord Treasurer in 1599. This post carried responsibility not only for the administration of almost all the customs duty for the whole country, and for the sale of Crown lands (in which manner he acquired Knole), but also for the King's Works and its employees. The decoration of the Great Staircase, which I have explored elsewhere,[6] was executed by Paul Isaacson between 1605 and 1608. Isaacson depended on several suites of prints, including a series of *Maxims of the Wise Men of Greece* by Duetecum (Lucas or Johannes) after Cornelis Floris, published in 1554; *Virtues Conquering Vices* by Johannes Sadeler after Maarten de Vos (1579); *The Four Ages of Man* by Crispijn de Passe the Elder after Maarten de Vos (1596); *The Five Senses* by Pieter de Jode; and *The Virtues* by Crispijn de Passe the Elder.

Paul Isaacson was apparently paid £100 in March 1608 for a fascinating series of decorative paintings in the Matted Gallery (now called the Cartoon Gallery). Although aware of this series, I had not, in 1997, discovered any prints that could be accepted as their source. Some of the paintings are in vertical format, others horizontal. The vertical paintings take the form either of panels embellishing pedestals that support pilasters, or of panels bordered by carved (and painted) pilasters. The horizontal paintings consist of panels in the dado zone. Both formats display lively grotesques flanking a central cartouche which frames a figure, but the vertical paintings additionally contain elements of strapwork uniting the disparate features – the revolutionary contribution made by Raphael himself to the compositional process in Italy. Whether vertical or horizontal, the grotesques are particularly tantalising, for they look very familiar.

Stylistically they seem to postdate the grotesques of Leonard Thiry and Cornelis Bos (1540s) and Etienne Delaune and Jan Vredeman de Vries (1560s) on the one hand, but on the other they bear some resemblance to designs by Lukas Kilian (1607), Antonio Tempesta (1609), Wendel Dietterlin the Younger (c.1610), Georg Wechter the Younger (1619) or Georges Charmeton (1650s).[7] Examined in black-and-white illustrations, the fully polychrome Knole grotesques closely resemble engravings on precious metalwork, so it is perhaps not surprising that some of the designers of these prints were trained as engravers and medallists.

As no satisfactory source for the painted grotesques has yet been found, there may be other explanations for them. Was the painter skilled enough to devise them himself? Or was there another artist living in London at the time who might have supplied drawings as models? We know of at least one designer with the requisite ability living in London at the outset of the 17th century – Nicaise Roussel – and there must have been many others. Roussel was born in Bruges, possibly of French parentage, and settled in London in 1573, perhaps because of the worsening conditions in the Netherlands.[8] By trade he was probably a professional engraver of metalwork, and he has been credited with the decoration of several objects on the basis of comparison with a book containing a small selection (about a dozen) of Roussel's designs for grotesques. These were engraved by Johannes Bara and published in 1623 under the title *De grotesco ... Liber*. Most of these prints share the same kind of stylistic repertoire as the painted grotesques at Knole, raising the possibility that Roussel might have designed them for Paul Isaacson. Otherwise, Isaacson might have had just the same inventiveness as that shown by Roussel. We simply do not know.

What about the figures of the deities that populate the central cartouches at Knole? It is likely that all were based on suites of prints, some of which have not yet been identified as models. Five were indeed copied from a suite of engravings, shown here for the first time to be the suite known as the *Twenty Gods of Antiquity*, published in 1598 after designs

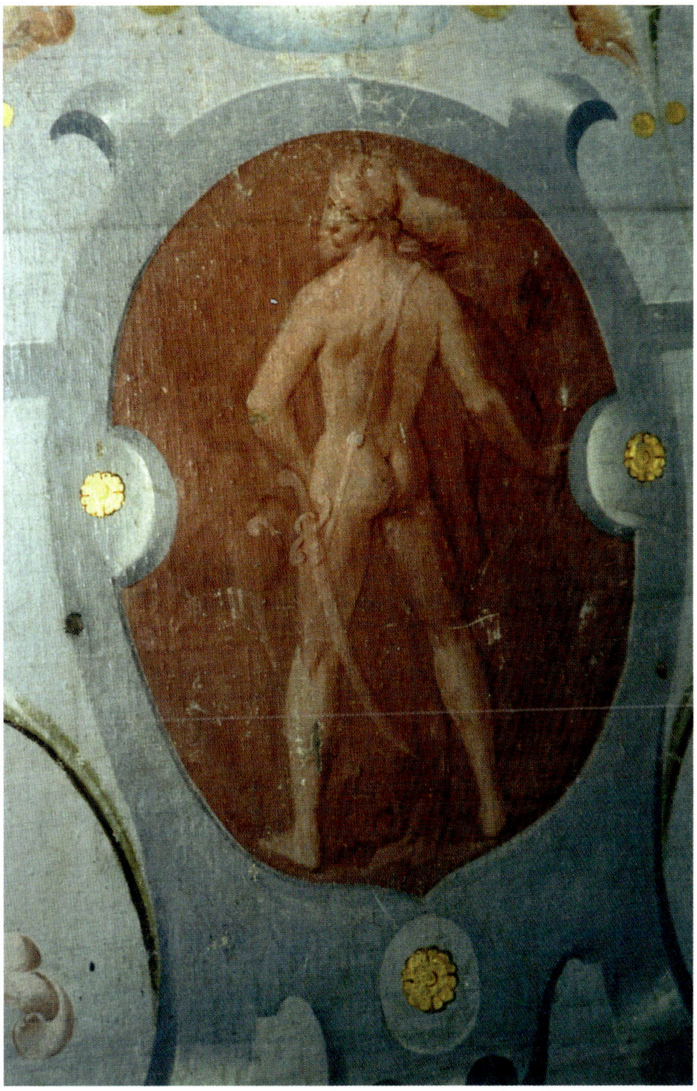

Figure 1 The Matted Gallery in Knole, Kent: *Mars*, perhaps by Paul Isaacson. *(© A. Wells-Cole, courtesy of the National Trust)*

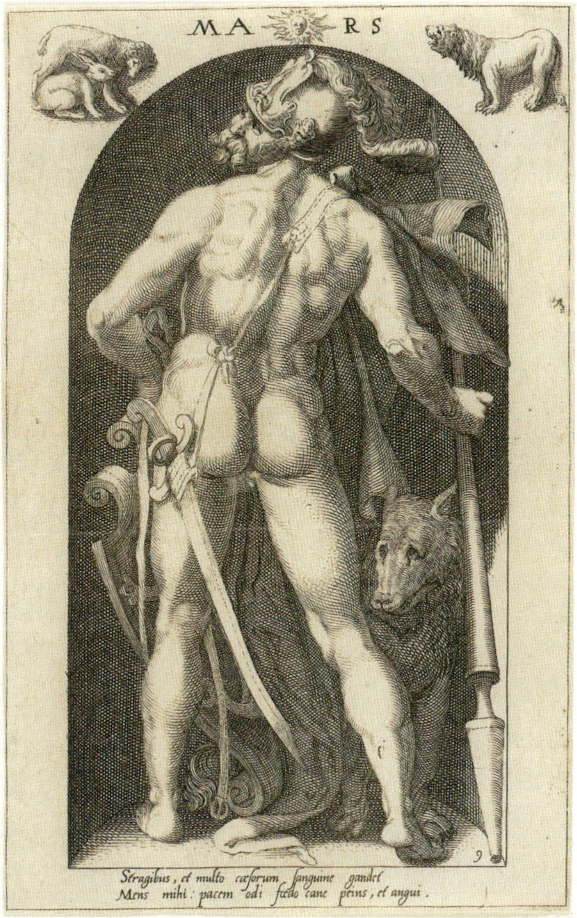

Figure 2 Nicolaus Breau after Karel van Mander: *Mars*, from the Twenty Gods of Antiquity, 1598. *(© Rijksmuseum, Amsterdam)*

by Karel van Mander (1548–1606). The figure of Mars, for instance, was copied from Nicolaus Breau's engraving after van Mander (Figs 1 and 2).

This is most significant. Karel van Mander was a friend of the painter Bartholomeus Spranger (1546–1611), who he met in Rome and later assisted in Vienna when Spranger was working on the triumphal arch for the entry of the emperor Rudolf II. In Haarlem he became acquainted with Cornelis Ketel (1548–1616), and the painter and engraver Hendrick Goltzius. Van Mander's designs for the *Twenty Gods of Antiquity* were based on engravings by Goltzius after Polidoro da Caravaggio, and were in turn engraved by Nicolaus Breau and Cornelis Drebbel.[9] They strongly recall Spranger's late-Mannerist style – a style that is hardly evident in Britain, and the paintings are the more important for that reason alone. But van Mander was also the author of the *Schilderboek* (or *Lives of the Painters*), the Netherlandish equivalent of Vasari's *Vite*, published in Alkmaar in 1604. This pioneering work was certainly known in England – Henry Peacham mentions that he used it – but no copy appears to have been listed in contemporary library catalogues.[10] So the use at Knole of van Mander's *Twenty Gods of Antiquity*, no more than ten years after the publication of the set, was the earliest evidence of the *direct* influence in the British Isles of this important figure that I had been able to discover, and until very recently it remained a solitary instance.

If the god-inhabited grotesques at Knole are evidence that a painter was able to devise for himself – or work with an engraver colleague to devise – satisfactory compositions in this mode, to what extent was this ability matched among painters elsewhere in Britain during the Renaissance period? My experience is that such ability seems to have been rare among makers in any medium: although painters might be thought to have been capable of greater independence than those who worked in other materials, this was the case only infrequently. Some paintings on panel from Edinburgh's Dean House (now shown in John Knox's House in Canongate, Edinburgh) demonstrate this point very clearly.

Dean House was bought by Sir William Nisbet in 1609; one of the paintings was said to be dated 1627. Michael Bath, who has made spectacular progress in explaining the wealth of decorative painting from the early modern period that survives in Scotland, argued that 'the painting [of Cain and Abel] is certainly based on the print from the Old Testament Series

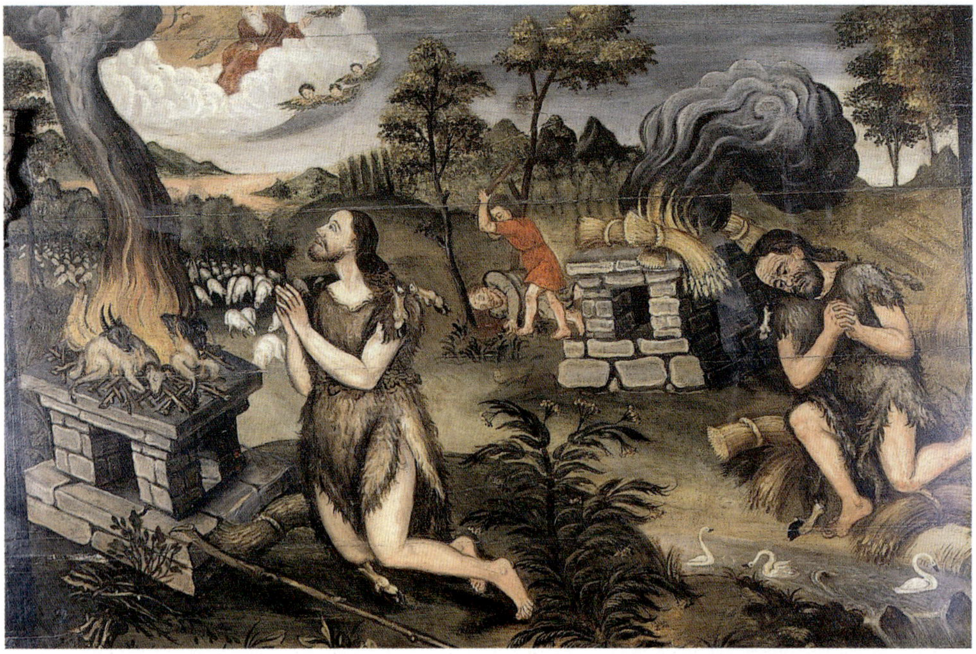

Figure 3 *Cain and Abel Sacrificing*, c.1627, from the Dean House in Edinburgh (now shown in John Knox's House, Canongate, Edinburgh).*(© John Knox House)*

by Johannes Sadeler after Maarten de Vos ... though the details are treated with some freedom'.[11] It is easy to see why he was led to this conclusion, for there are indeed many points of resemblance between painting and print. The painter in fact copied a different print altogether, however, almost without alteration. This print, by Adriaen Collaert after Joannes Stradanus, is the *Spiritus Pietatis*, from a set of seven Old Testament prints (Figs 3 and 4). His adaptation of the source material was limited to altering the figure of Cain, adding the murder scene in the background, and introducing the swans in the right foreground. The painter of *The Sacrifice of Isaac* from the same house perhaps selected passages from several prints, including Maarten de Vos's interpretation of the scene published in the *Thesaurus Veteris et Novi Testamenti* in 1579 and 1585, and Jost Amman's illustration in the *Biblia Sacra* or *Neuwe Biblische Figuren dess Alten und Neuwen Testaments* of 1564. Another possibility, of course, is that there was some intermediate print whose designer borrowed from both de Vos and Amman, arriving at the composition that was then copied by the Edinburgh painter. As yet, it is impossible to tell whether or not this was what actually occurred. If there is a moral to any of this, it is probably that the majority of Renaissance wall paintings in the British Isles do depend on a continental print source, which the painter copied as faithfully as his abilities allowed.

The value of searching widely for elusive sources is demonstrated by a series of painted cloths in the chapel of King's College, Aberdeen – not strictly wall paintings, of course, but subject to the same creative conditions. The set of five painted cloths is interesting because of their subject matter (they venerate the antiquity of kingship) and because of the circumstance of their commission (they were probably painted either for a visit of the future king Charles II in 1650 or 1651, or to mark the restoration of the monarchy in 1660). They may well have been farmed out to a number of different painters to meet a tight time deadline.[12] Supporting this possibility is the variety of their print sources, for at least three different suites must have been used: for *The Judgement of Solomon* Boetius Adam Bolswert's engraving after Peter Paul Rubens; for *Jephthah's Daughter* Matthias Merian's print from the *Icones Biblicae* published in Frankfurt in 1627; and for *David and Goliath* an as-yet unidentified print related to Virgil Solis's design in the *Biblische Figuren* of 1565.

Widely though I have cast my net in the search for sources even of biblical scenes, the models for many wall paintings remain enigmatic. Among these are the fascinating paintings at Kinneil House in Bo'ness, West Lothian. These represent the first of two phases of decoration of the east wing of the impressive house built by James Hamilton, second Earl of Arran, in 1553–4.[13] The South or 'Parable' Room contains six panels illustrating the parable of the *Good Samaritan*, *St Jerome in the Wilderness*, *Mary Magdalene* and *Lucretia*. The North or 'Arbour' Room includes four pictorial roundels of *Samson and Delilah*, *The Temptation of St Anthony*, *Abraham and Isaac*, and *David and Bathsheba*. It is impossible to believe that these could have been composed without the help of continental prints, but it is equally certain that, despite every effort, these prints have yet to be discovered. The same is true of the intriguing wall paintings at Canons Ashby in Northamptonshire, and of the unidentified scenes accompanied by texts from the Psalms of David discovered during the 1990s in a house in Micklegate, York.

Doubtless print sources for all will be found in time, for these paintings seem too sophisticated to be the unaided invention of the decorative painter. Two East Anglian wall paintings raise the interesting issue of the length of time that elapsed between the publication of a print and its adaptation for house decoration. Theoretically, with no part of Norfolk and Suffolk being geographically very far from the busy ports of King's Lynn, Yarmouth, Ipswich or Woodbridge, there would be no obstacle to a continental print or illustrated book being available within days of its arriving in England, provided that there was a demand for it. What happened in practice? A house in Hadleigh, Suffolk, recently investigated by Andrea Kirkham,

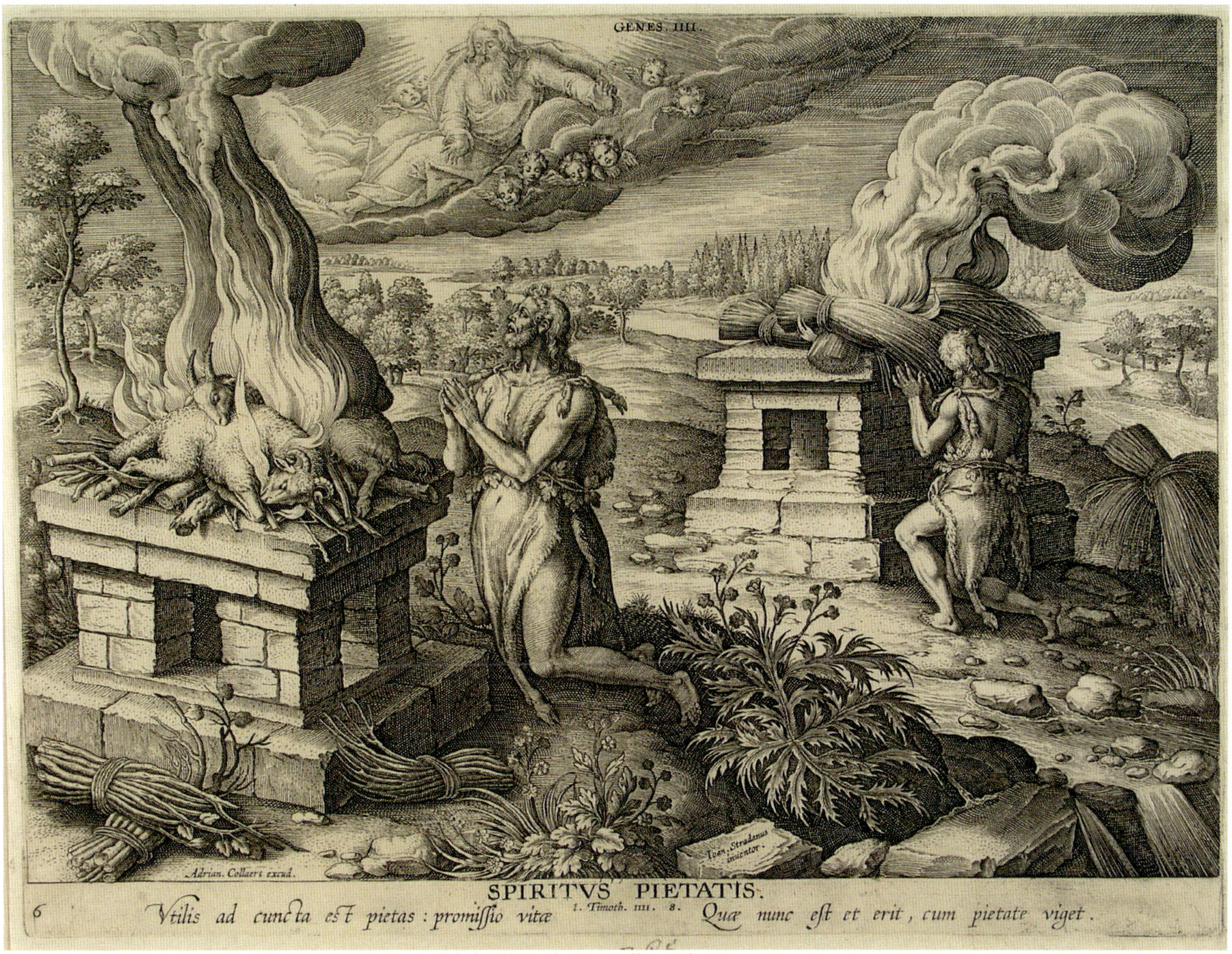

Figure 4 *Spiritus Pietatis* by Johannes Stradanus, published by Adriaen Collaert. *(© Boijmans Van Beuningen Museum, Rotterdam)*

has wall paintings which, from building evidence, should date from the second quarter of the 17th century. They depict two episodes in the story of Joseph: *Joseph Removed from the Pit and Sold* (from Genesis 37:28) and *Joseph and Potiphar's Wife* (from Genesis 39:12). In this case, the paintings must have followed their print source with relatively minimal delay, for they derive from the suite by Crispijn de Passe (perhaps after designs by Maarten de Vos) entitled *Liber Genesis*, published in 1612 (Figs 5 and 6).

That this was by no means always the case is proved by a fine wall painting which building evidence suggests was executed at very much the same date. This painting survives – albeit in rather poor condition – in a house near Stowmarket in Suffolk and depicts the *Sacrifice of Isaac* (Fig. 7). Employing a distinctive iconography, the figure of Isaac is shown prone on the sacrificial altar. Most German and Netherlandish artists (among them Virgil Solis, Jost Amman and Tobias Stimmer, Maarten van Heemskerck, Pieter de Jode, Maarten de Vos and Crispijn de Passe) – who were the ones most likely to provide the inspiration for decoration in England during the reigns of Elizabeth and James I – depicted Isaac kneeling, facing away from his father Abraham. One of the artists who departed from the norm was Matthias Merian, whose print bible the *Icones Biblicae* (copied for two of the decorative paintings in Aberdeen, as we have seen earlier), was published in 1627. Curiously, however, this convenient source of biblical illustrations was apparently very little used in the British Isles (although a version of this particular scene was engraved by Wenceslaus Hollar before 1644), and indeed the *Iconum Biblicarum* was not the source for this painting. Instead the artist copied a much earlier and more distinguished print, drawn from the *Historiarum Veteris Testamenti Icones*, first published by the Lyons firm of Trechsel and Frellon in 1538 and having woodcuts designed by Hans Holbein the Younger perhaps eight years before that (Fig. 8). These two East Anglian commissions demonstrate that the length of time elapsing between the publication of a print and its use was completely arbitrary, depending on circumstances which it is now impossible to discover.

A final example shows how the discovery of a print source can definitively resolve long-standing controversy over the date of a decorative scheme in a building. This is the case of an Edinburgh building once thought to have been the mid-16th-century palace of Mary of Guise. The building cannot have been decorated before 1587, however, as this was the publication date of *Patientia Christiana* (Christian Patience), the print engraved by Harmen Muller after Karel van Mander, on which the painting was based. Michael Bath explores the significance of this discovery more fully in this volume (pp. 11–21). From our point of view it is important also as being only the second identified instance of derivation from an engraving after Karel van Mander in the British Isles, the first being the decorative paintings at Knole, discussed above.

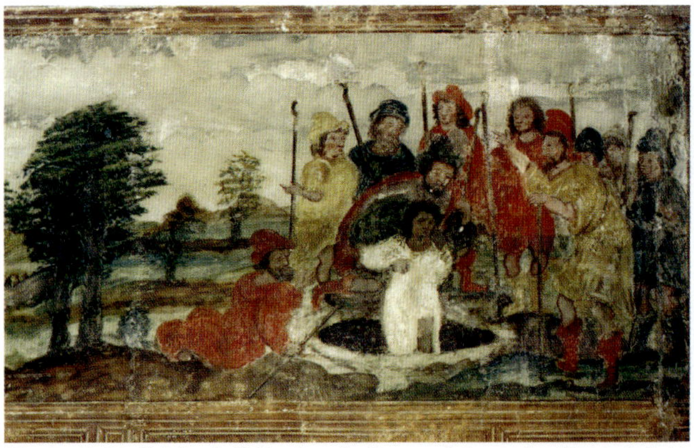

Figure 5 Hadleigh, Suffolk: *Joseph Removed from the Pit and Sold.* *(© A. Kirkham)*

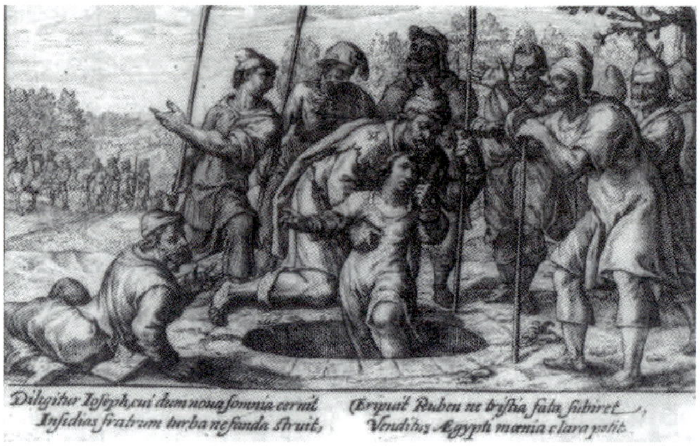

Figure 6 Crispijn de Passe (perhaps after Maerten de Vos), *Joseph Removed from the Pit and Sold*, from Liber Genesis 1612. *(© Rijksmuseum, Amsterdam)*

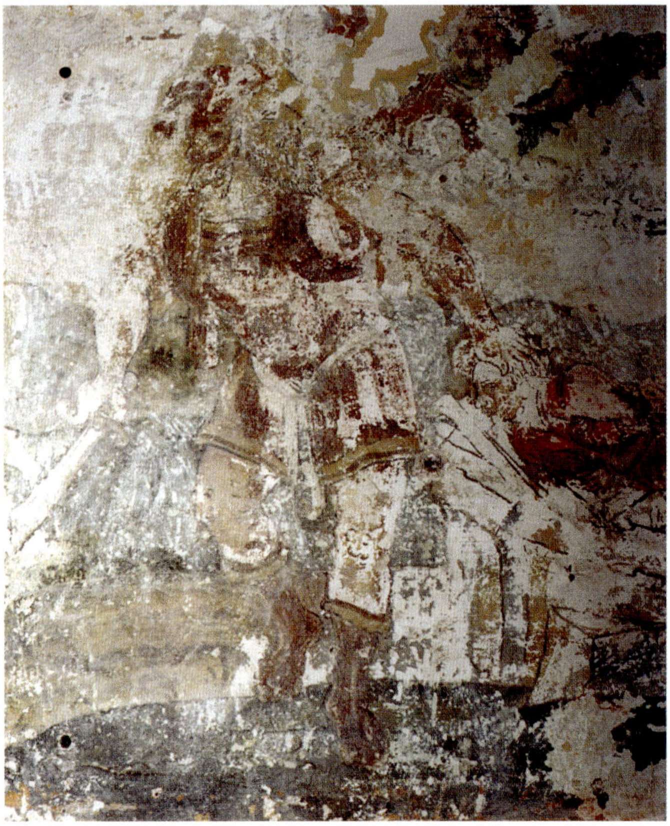

Figure 7 Stowmarket, Suffolk: *The Sacrifice of Isaac* c.1630. *(© A. Kirkham)*

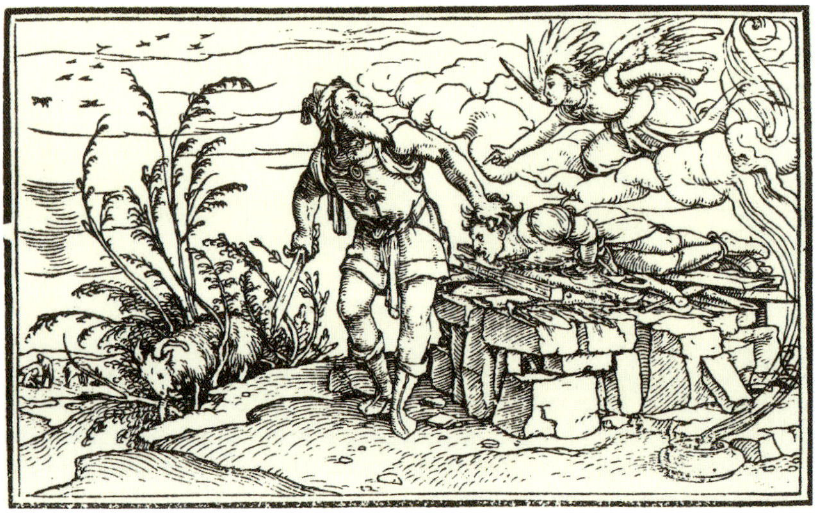

Figure 8 Hans Holbein the Younger, *The Sacrifice of Isaac*, from *Historiarum Veteris Testamenti Icones*, Lyons, 1538. *(© British Museum, Department of Prints and Drawings)*

Searching for possible print sources for works of art, as I hope to have demonstrated, is a crucial activity for, if they are identified, the core aspect of artistic creativity is illuminated. Comparison of a print and its painted derivation sheds invaluable light on the extent to which a painter was able to modify or transcend the original – in most cases, hardly at all – but also raises questions about the circumstances of the commission. Who decided on a particular print? Who owned the original? How did they come by it? How freely were prints in circulation? In the case of biblical subjects, what do they tell us about the religious inclinations of the patron? Or the extent to which biblical subjects were tolerated or openly allowed? Did one part of the British Isles differ from another in this respect? Were different artists' prints popular as sources in different parts of the country? If so, why? Other questions suggest themselves. How far down the social scale were prints used for domestic wall paintings? In particular, should we be surprised that a yeoman farmer's house near Stowmarket had a painting based on a Holbein woodcut?

Since during the reigns of Elizabeth and James I in England people did not often record in writing what works of art they were looking at, every new discovery of a print source can extend our knowledge of what prints were in circulation. The wall paintings discussed here (virtually all brought to my attention by specialists in other fields of activity) have produced a rich harvest in this respect, for in almost every case they represent – at least for me – the first identified instances of derivation from particular prints.

As the *Followers of Fashion* conference has shown, collaboration between wall painting specialists, art historians and conservators, print amateurs and literary historians can contribute significantly towards a fuller understanding of Renaissance wall paintings and their meaning.

Notes

1. Shearman 1992, p. 261.
2. Ivins 1969 cited in Watt 1994, p. 192.
3. Wells-Cole 1997.
4. Examples by these and other designers appear in Jervis 1974.
5. *Archaeological Journal* 1935.
6. Wells-Cole 1997, pp. 211–15.
7. For typical grotesque designs by these artists see Berliner and Egger 1981, nos. 447, 622, 498, 682, 853, 742, 889, 923 and 1079.
8. Oman 1978, pp. 4–8.
9. Leesberg *et al.* 1999, p. xxxiii.
10. Gent 1981, p. 68.
11. Bath 2003, p. 207.
12. Bracegirdle 2000, pp. 204–15.
13. Bath 2003, pp. 209 and 272–4.

References

Archaeological Journal 1935, xcii

Bath M. 2003, *Renaissance Decorative Painting in Scotland*, National Museums of Scotland, Edinburgh

Berliner R. and Egger G. 1981, *Ornamentale Vorlageblätter des 15.–19. Jahrhunderts*, Klinkhardt & Biermann, Munich

Bracegirdle L. 2000, 'Kings for Kings: the Old Testament painting', in Jane Geddes (ed.) *Kings College Chapel, Aberdeen 1500–2000*, Maney Publishing, Leeds

Gent L. 1981, *Picture and Poetry 1560–1620*, J. Hall, Leamington Spa

Ivins W.J. 1969, *Prints and Visual Communication*, MIT Press, New York

Jervis S. 1974, *Printed Furniture Designs before 1650*, W.S. Maney & Son for the Furniture History Society, Leeds

Leesberg M., Leeflang H. and Schuckman C. (eds) 1999, *The New Hollstein Dutch and Flemish Etchings, Engravings and Woodcuts, 1450–1700: Karel van Mander*, Sound and Vision, Rotterdam

Oman C. 1978, 'Nicaise Roussel and the Mostyn Flagons', *Leeds Arts Calendar* 83, pp. 4–8

Shearman J. 1992, *Only Connect: Art and the Spectator in the Italian Renaissance*, Bollingen Foundation, Princeton

Watt T. 1994, *Cheap Print and Popular Piety*, Cambridge University Press, Cambridge

Wells-Cole A. 1997, *Art and Decoration in Elizabethan and Jacobean England: The Influence of Continental Prints, 1558–1625*, Yale University Press, New Haven and London

The author

Anthony Wells-Cole is Senior Curator at Temple Newsam near Leeds, the house which he has been responsible for restoring since 1983. From 1969 to 1995 he was an honorary lecturer in the Fine Art Department of Leeds University; he is the author of *Art and Decoration in Elizabethan and Jacobean England: The Influence of Continental Prints 1558–1625* (Yale University Press 1997).

Was there a Guise Palace in Edinburgh?

Michael Bath

The Guise Palace in Edinburgh is what can only be called a historical gap site. John G. Dunbar makes no mention of it in his book, *Scottish Royal Palaces* (1999). One looks in vain for evidence of its construction or occupation in any of the usual state papers or standard historical documents such as the Master of Works' or Treasurer's Accounts.[1]

Mary of Guise/Lorraine married King James V of Scotland in 1538, and the four years of her marriage up until the king's death in 1542 saw the reconstruction of several of Scotland's royal palaces, with substantial work on both fabric and furnishings at Falkland Palace at Linlithgow, and at Stirling – where a new palace was constructed. This royal marriage to a French queen, raised in the dukedom of Lorraine and at the court of Francis I, undoubtedly had major consequences for court architecture and decoration in Scotland. Any building designed for occupation by Mary of Guise is likely to have confirmed those French influences on the iconography and architecture of the Scottish court which have often been noted.[2] Mary's daughter, Mary Queen of Scots, was born on 8 December 1542 and crowned eight days later, but during her long minority the regency of Scotland was held initially by James Hamilton, secondly by the Earl of Arran, and then (from 1554 to 1560) by the Queen Dowager, Mary of Guise, herself.

The earliest claim that Mary of Guise had a palace, or at least a chapel, in the old town of Edinburgh appears to be William Maitland's, whose *History of Edinburgh* appeared in 1753. It is not until 1825, however, that we find Robert Chambers, leading Scottish publisher, author and antiquarian, offering a description of the palace and oratory of Mary of Guise which includes a more detailed account of its antiquities. In *Traditions of Edinburgh* he describes a stone tenement in Blyth's Close, just below the castle in the Royal Mile, with the inscription *Laus et honor Deo* above the door, and the *MR* monogram of Mary of Guise. A flat in the upper floor had what he describes as a baptismal font and a niche for holy water; this and the room above had ceiling roundels with heraldic arms, fleurs-de-lis and an *HR* monogram (for Henry II of France?), which he takes to be stucco but which were later shown to be wood carving overlaid with successive coats of whitewash. Chambers records further apartments in a different range of buildings from the supposed oratory, which he identifies as state apartments of the palace, including a flat known as 'the Queen's Dead Room' apparently for no better reason than that it was painted black. Mary of Guise would have needed a new habitation, he speculates, after the palace at Holyrood (and much of the rest of Edinburgh) was burnt down by the English in 1544. As Chambers confesses, however, 'The Palace of the Queen Regent bears nowhere any date, and no records appear to exist, which could throw light upon its origin.'[3]

In 1845 the buildings in Blyth's Close, and others flanking two closes parallel with it but further up Castle Hill, were pulled down to make way for a new College of the Free Church of Scotland, and it was during this demolition that further pieces of carved stonework and wooden panelling were discovered, along with no fewer than four different painted ceilings. Shortly after their demolition Daniel Wilson, who was to become a leading archaeologist and secretary of the Society of Antiquaries of Scotland, published his *Memorials of Edinburgh* in which he gives the first detailed description of the various buildings and antiquities on this site, including the newly discovered painted ceilings.[4] Until recently, Wilson's *Memorials* remained our only guide to these painted ceilings and other decorative artefacts, many of which found their way into the hands of local antiquarians and collectors such as C.K. Sharpe. From Sharpe's collection some of them passed to the Museum of Antiquities, and hence to its successor the present National Museum of Scotland, where several are now conserved or on display in the museum's impressive collection of early modern wood carving.

Wilson identified four different apartments in various tenements that had painted ceilings of various sorts. One of these was decorated with eight emblems in ornamental borders, six of which evidently copied Claude Paradin's *Devises heroïques* (1551).[5] Some suggest a Protestant context with their emphasis on the doctrines of righteousness, sin, and affliction:

Gif thow wt. syn affleitit be,
Och than say Chryst cum thow to me
Swith the way, walk thow thairin,
Embrace the truth, abandoun ...

The last word, 'sin', has been omitted. Another fragment referred to 'The Trubilis of the Rightious'. A third apartment showed a figure kneeling at an altar with a 'vessel amid flames' into which a Hand of God was dipping a ladle, with the motto *Demum purgabitur* ('It will at length be purified'). The other compartment showed an aged man offering a heart to a bird with huge black wings, with the motto *Impossibile est* ('It is impossible'). The meaning of these images remains obscure and their iconography is puzzling.

Perhaps the most interesting of these painted ceilings, however, was in a tenement at the head of Blyth's Close on Castle Hill. This was evidently never part of the supposed palace, but was acquired – if not first built – in 1590 by two merchant burgesses, Robert McNaught and James Rynd, who inscribed the date 1591, the monogram *R.M.* (for Robert McNaught, not Maria Regina) and the motto *LAVS DEO* on the ashlar stonework of its front. This motto can still be read on Wilson's engraving after his own sketch, which was used as frontispiece to the 1891 edition of *Memorials* (Fig. 1). On the second floor was an apartment with a coved ceiling filled with strapwork cartouches framing five religious subjects: the Apostle John, Christ holding an orb, *Jacob's Ladder*, the *Baptism of Christ*, *Christ Asleep in the Storm*, the *Four Horsemen of the Apocalypse* and an allegorical picture (which Wilson describes as 'the most curious of all'[6]) showing a ship assailed by figures representing Death, the Devil and *Persecutio*.

Until recently, Wilson's description was the only record of most of these paintings, although two from the ceiling – Christ with the orb, and *Christ Asleep in the Storm* – have survived and are now in the Museum of Scotland. Consisting of five or six lengths of oak board, they are painted in the glue-based tempera medium commonly used in decorative painting at this period in Scotland (Fig. 2). A colour sketch of the first of these is also preserved among architect Thomas Bonnar's sketches of historical painted ceilings in the Historical Monuments Record in Edinburgh (and is reproduced in my book, *Renaissance Decorative Painting in Scotland*[7]). These 19th-century sketches were seemingly intended as potential patterns for new interior decoration in Victorian neo-baronial houses, by which Bonnar made his living.

Now a different set of colour sketches has come to light which corresponds exactly to the subjects described by Daniel Wilson in his Edinburgh *Memorials*. It is these 29 large watercolour and pencil sketches that are the subject for this article. The sketches are now in the National Monuments Record, and though unsigned, are preserved with a number of similar sketches of Scottish painted ceilings by the antiquary and architect A.W. Lyons. Lyons was an active Fellow of the Society of Antiquaries of Scotland, publishing scholarly papers in its

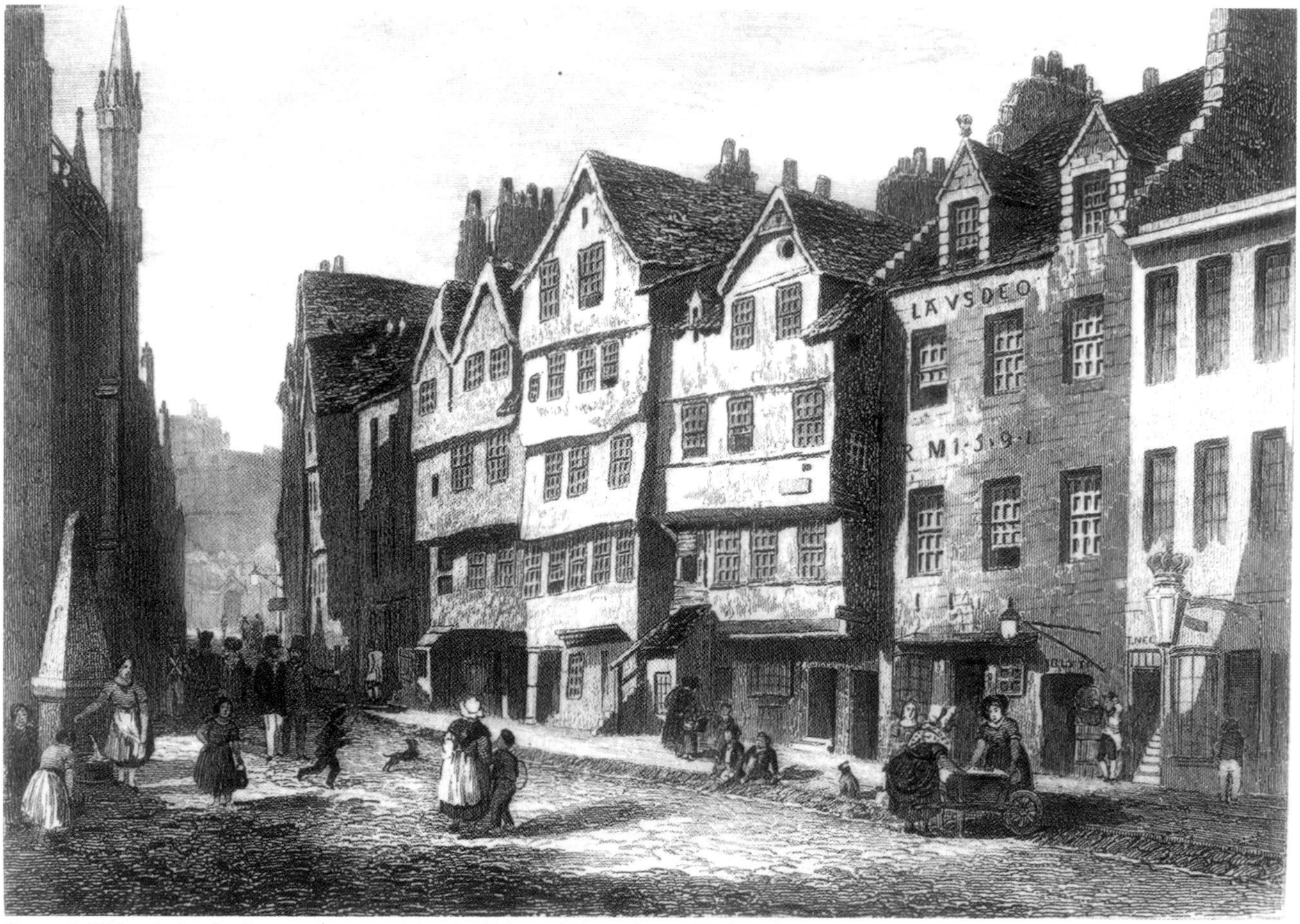

Figure 1 Wilson's sketch of tenements containing the 'Palace of Mary of Guise' before their demolition in 1845. From his *Memorials of Edinburgh*, 1891. *(© Glasgow University Library)*

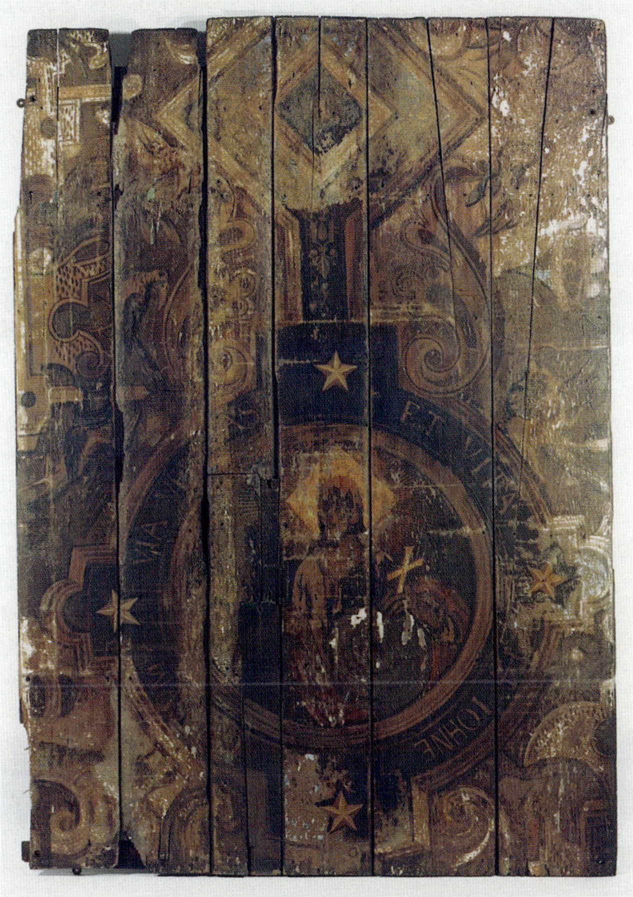

Figure 2 *Via, Veritas et Vita* panel from the supposed Guise Palace ceiling: tempera paint on boards. *(© National Museum of Scotland)*

Proceedings, and both his sketches and Bonnar's were almost certainly attempts to preserve a historical record (Fig. 3).

The belief that the decorative painting from this site came from the reputed palace of Mary of Guise was undoubtedly influenced by the fact that all the subjects are religious. Dowager Queen Mary was and (like her daughter) remained a Roman Catholic. At a time of brutal iconoclasm in Scotland, the period of John Knox, we might well suppose that such a ceiling could only have come from the apartments of the Catholic Queen Regent. As Daniel Wilson stresses, however, the supposed Guise Palace was surrounded by tenements occupied, at various times, by minor nobility or merchant burgesses. The structure of the multistorey tenements in the three closes which were pulled down in 1845 – Blyth's, Nairn's and Todd's – is extremely difficult to reconstruct, and it is not at all easy to work out from Wilson's description exactly where the various rooms of the supposed Guise Palace were in relation to the other tenements.[8] In his 1878 *Reminiscences of Old Edinburgh*,[9] Wilson makes it much clearer that the tenement containing these particular paintings was not part of the Guise Palace, but rather in McNaught and Rynd's house. As we shall see, that supports my central thesis in this paper: namely that these paintings could never have decorated the palace of the Catholic Queen Regent, but are much more likely to have been commissioned by the righteous Edinburgh merchant who put his *Laus Deo* motto over the public entrance to his tenement. Surrounding tenements belonged, at various times, to such burgesses as Edward Hope, who was a zealous anti-Catholic in the 1560s, and Alexander Achison and his wife Helen Reid, whose initials and heraldic arms were carved

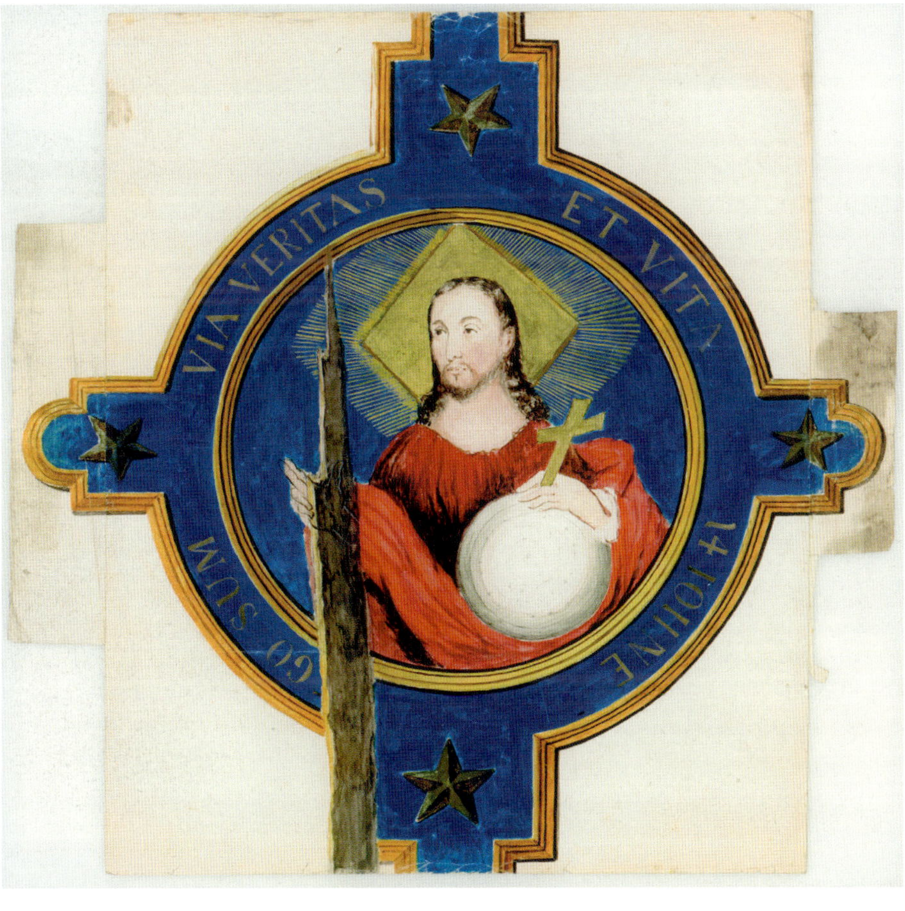

Figure 3 A.W. Lyons (attrib.): sketch of *Via, Veritas et Vita* panel from the 'Guise Palace'. *(Reproduced courtesy of the Society of Antiquaries of Scotland/ Royal Commission on the Ancient and Historical Monuments of Scotland)*

on one of the door lintels with the date 1557 and the motto *NOSCE TEIPSVM* ('Know thyself').

As I have stressed elsewhere,[10] the Reformation destruction of images was far less universal in Scotland than has commonly been supposed, strictly Protestant middle-class houseowners remaining quite capable of decorating their painted ceilings with biblical and religious subjects. These include not just relatively uncontroversial Old Testament histories and New Testament parables (such as those found in Regent Arran's house at Kinneil, or Edinburgh baillie William Nisbet's house at The Dean), but also images of the Godhead and even the Virgin Mary. Thus Matthew Lumsden, who later fought for the Covenanters, painted not only the *Nativity* and the *Crucifixion* but also the *Ascension* and the *Stigmata* on the ceiling of his house in the centre of Aberdeen, and there is good reason to believe that a merchant shipowner at Burntisland, just across the river Forth from Edinburgh, put both an *Agnus Dei* and a Virgin Mary on his ceiling.[11]

That these are all religious paintings perhaps calls into question their relevance to a symposium on 'secular' wall painting in Britain, even if they were all located in secular buildings. The Scottish reformation of images was arguably quite different from the English, however, and the fact that these are not wall paintings but painted ceilings is a reminder that they belong to a distinctive national tradition of Scottish decorative painting which has no counterpart in England. Decorating ceilings rather than walls is not a local or regional extension of any English fashion: its historical, national and doctrinal contexts are quite different.[12]

From the Lyons sketches, it is possible to work out that the elaborate strapwork cartouches in McNaught and Rynd's house framed seven or eight different compartments filled with religious subjects. Of the two central circular compartments, one shows the Apostle John. On either side of these compartments, lower down on the coved ceiling, were five or six rectangular compartments – presumably originally three on each side. These too are surrounded by rich strapwork and arabesques, with appliqué raised gilt stars and quite lavish use of what would appear to have been expensive blue azurite. The five rectangular compartments show three biblical subjects – *Jacob's Ladder*, the *Baptism of Christ*, and *Christ Asleep in the Storm* – and two allegorical subjects, which it is now possible to identify as *The Four Horsemen of the Apocalypse* and *Death, Persecution and the Devil* (Figs 4, 5 and 6).

The latter two pictures are complex allegories which are worth analysing in some detail, and they will occupy us for the remainder of this paper. The *Four Horsemen of the Apocalypse* is a subject widely represented in art, whose iconography was

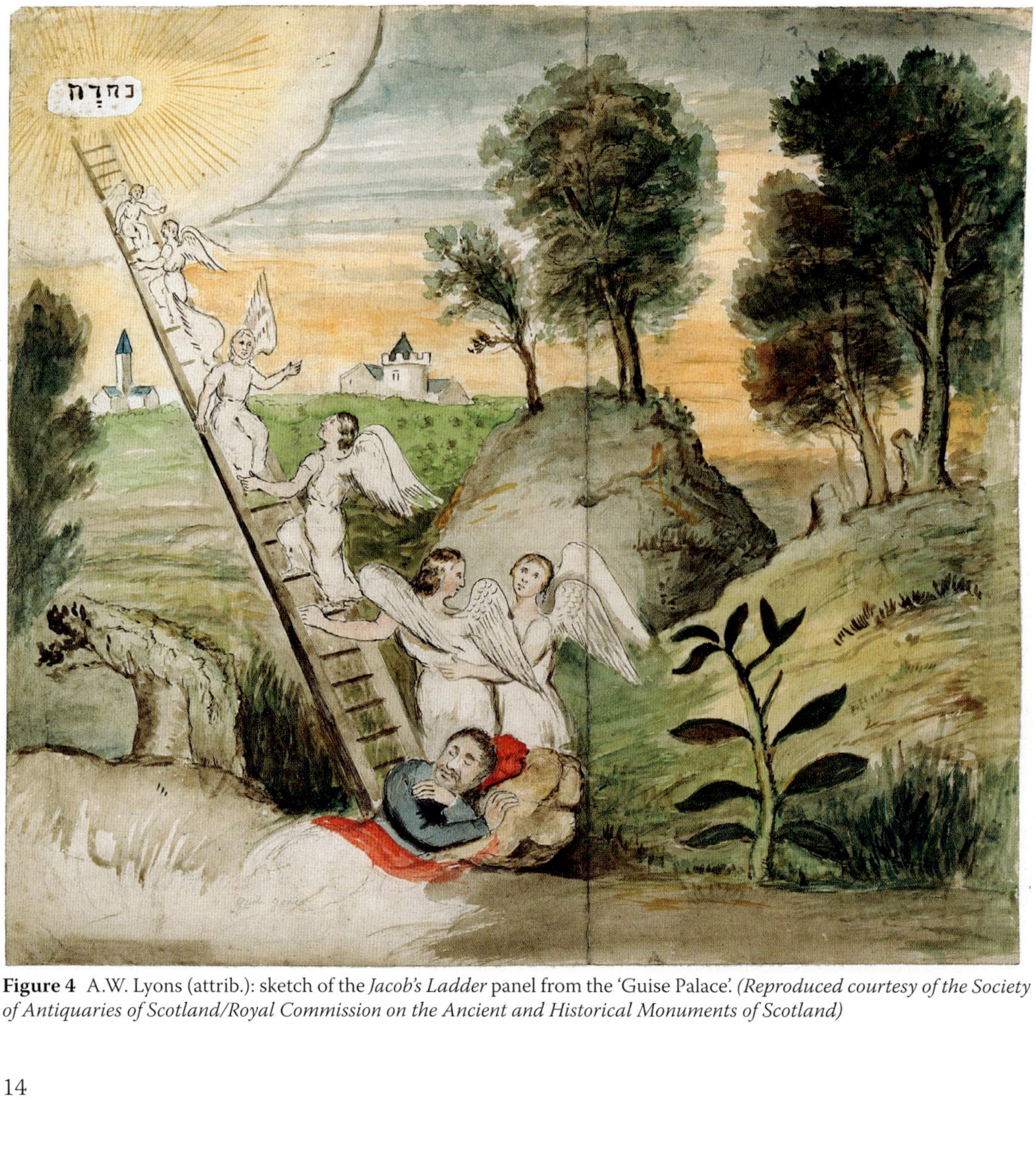

Figure 4 A.W. Lyons (attrib.): sketch of the *Jacob's Ladder* panel from the 'Guise Palace'. *(Reproduced courtesy of the Society of Antiquaries of Scotland/Royal Commission on the Ancient and Historical Monuments of Scotland)*

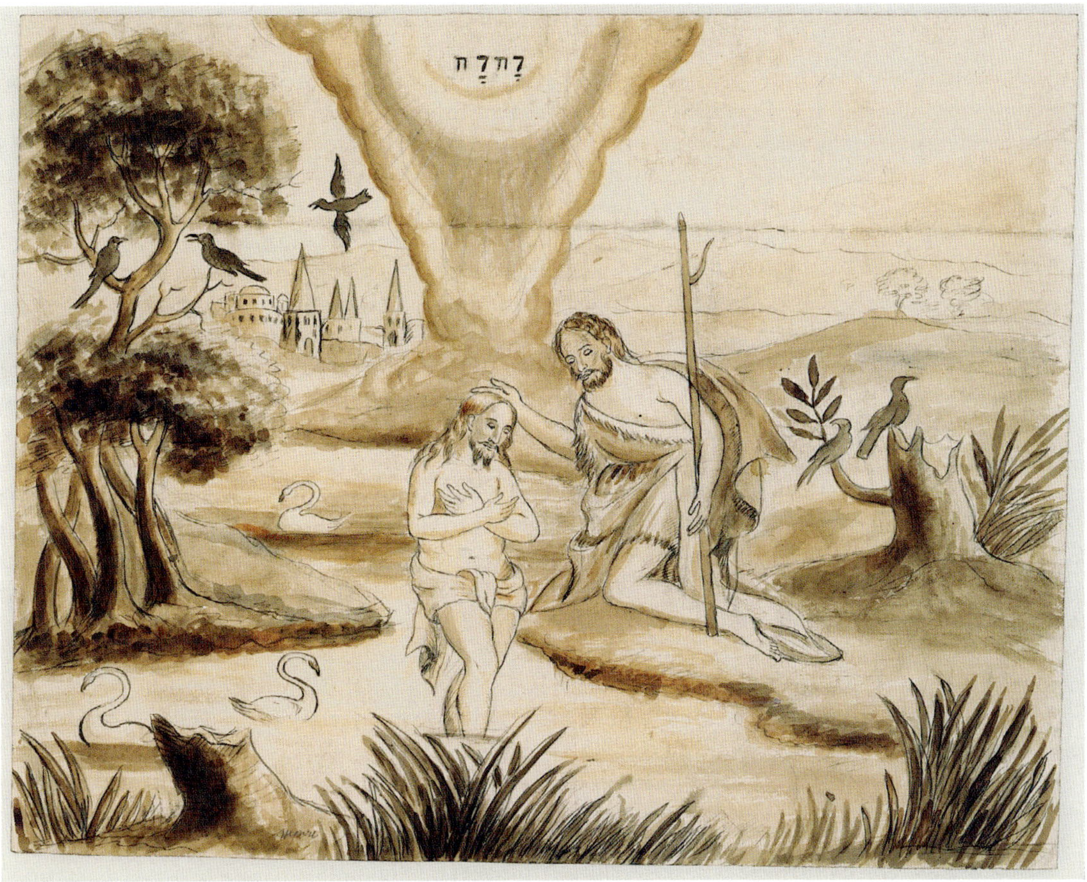

Figure 5 A.W. Lyons (attrib.): sketch of the *Baptism of Christ* panel from the 'Guise Palace'. *(Reproduced courtesy of the Society of Antiquaries of Scotland/Royal Commission on the Ancient and Historical Monuments of Scotland)*

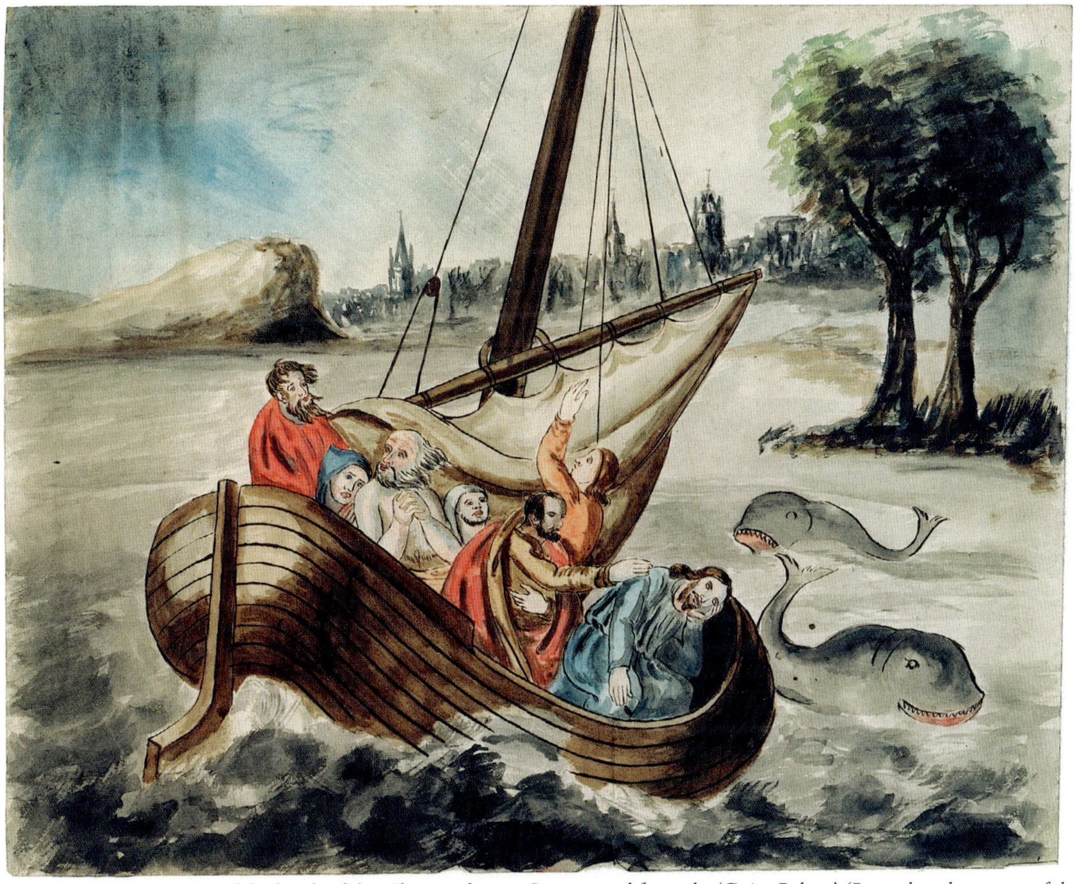

Figure 6 A.W. Lyons (attrib.): sketch of the *Christ Asleep in Storm* panel from the 'Guise Palace'. *(Reproduced courtesy of the Society of Antiquaries of Scotland/Royal Commission on the Ancient and Historical Monuments of Scotland)*

fixed by the detail of the biblical text (Revelation 6:1–8). They normally comprise:

1 A horseman sometimes described as *The Conqueror* wearing a crown and holding a bow, shown on a white horse;
2 *War* holding a sword and mounted on a red horse;
3 *Famine*, mounted on a black horse holding a pair of scales in his hand;
4 *Death* holding a spear or trident on a 'pale' horse, close to the mouth of Hell ('and Hell followed with him', Revelation 6:8).

This is precisely what we see in the Lyons sketch of this subject from the Edinburgh ceiling, where the *Four Horsemen* can be seen riding across the sky in their proper order on horses of appropriate colour and wielding their appropriate weapons; *Death* is shown on the shore of a seascape prodding a pile of three bodies with his spear, and with a flaming mouth of Hell behind him (Fig. 7). This detail is balanced on the opposite, right-hand side by a large building which, as we shall see, has to be interpreted as the City of God (over which the horsemen will not in fact triumph). The middle ground shows landscape details of a moored ship, and an island with a towered building.

Above each of the four horsemen is a winged beast in a roundel, representing one of the Four Evangelists: Mark a winged lion, Luke a winged ox, Matthew a winged quadruped with human face, and John an eagle. These images realise an iconography that goes back to early Christian art, based on Ezekiel 1:5–12, whose vision describes four beasts with faces 'and every one had four wings ... their wings were joined to one another' and their faces were those of a man, a lion, an ox, and an eagle, just as depicted in these roundels. The typological identification of the four beasts of Ezekiel with the four that surround the throne of God in Revelation 4:6–8 was conventional, and secured that association of the Four Evangelists with Apocalyptic iconography which was being exploited by this particular picture. Symbolically, they represent the real triumph of God and the Gospels over the darkness of Apocalyptic destruction. Shown on the ceiling in their bright yellow roundels (if we can trust Lyons' colouring) they contrast with the cloud-filled obscurity of the Apocalyptic landscape, prefiguring the eventual triumph of light over darkness and of each Evangelist over his corresponding horseman: offering what asks to be read finally as an optimistic interpretation of the providential end of things.

To see just how closely the Edinburgh painting conforms to the received iconography of this subject we have only to look at representations of it that appeared in early prints and engravings. The anonymous woodcut of 1536 that appeared in the Zurich Bible, for instance, shows just how faithfully the decorative ceiling realised this iconography (Fig. 8). *The Four Horsemen*, with *Death* and the mouth of Hell pursuing the three prostrate bodies in a clouded landscape, corresponds quite closely to the Edinburgh painting, though the woodcut is certainly not its immediate source; these features become generic in 16th-century Bible illustrations. The print does not show the seascape, the stately edifice, or the Four Evangelists, suggesting that the Edinburgh painting is at least realising a more complex typology than the print. Lyons' colour sketch confirms that the painter was aware of the way the biblical text established the different colours of the horses, something which the print medium cannot, by its nature, realise.

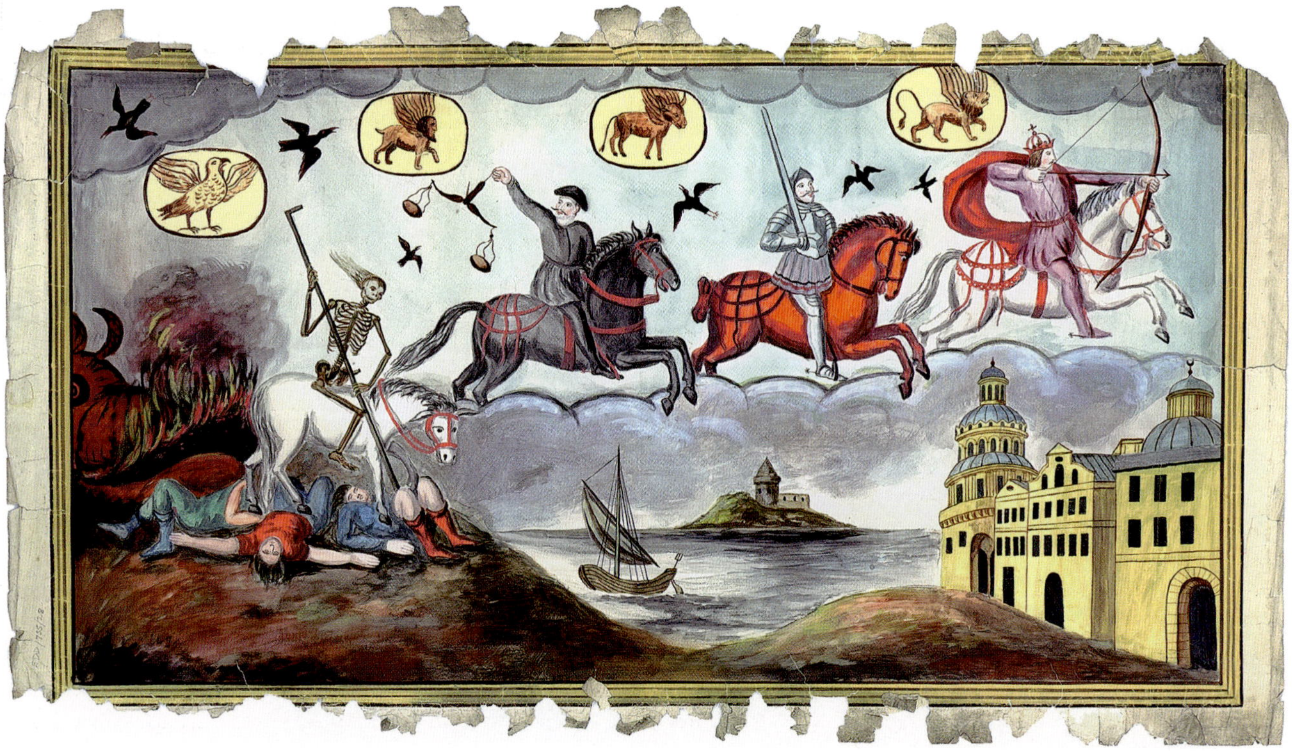

Figure 7 A.W. Lyons (attrib.): sketch of the *Four Horsemen of the Apocalypse* panel from the 'Guise Palace'. *(Reproduced courtesy of the Society of Antiquaries of Scotland/Royal Commission on the Ancient and Historical Monuments of Scotland)*

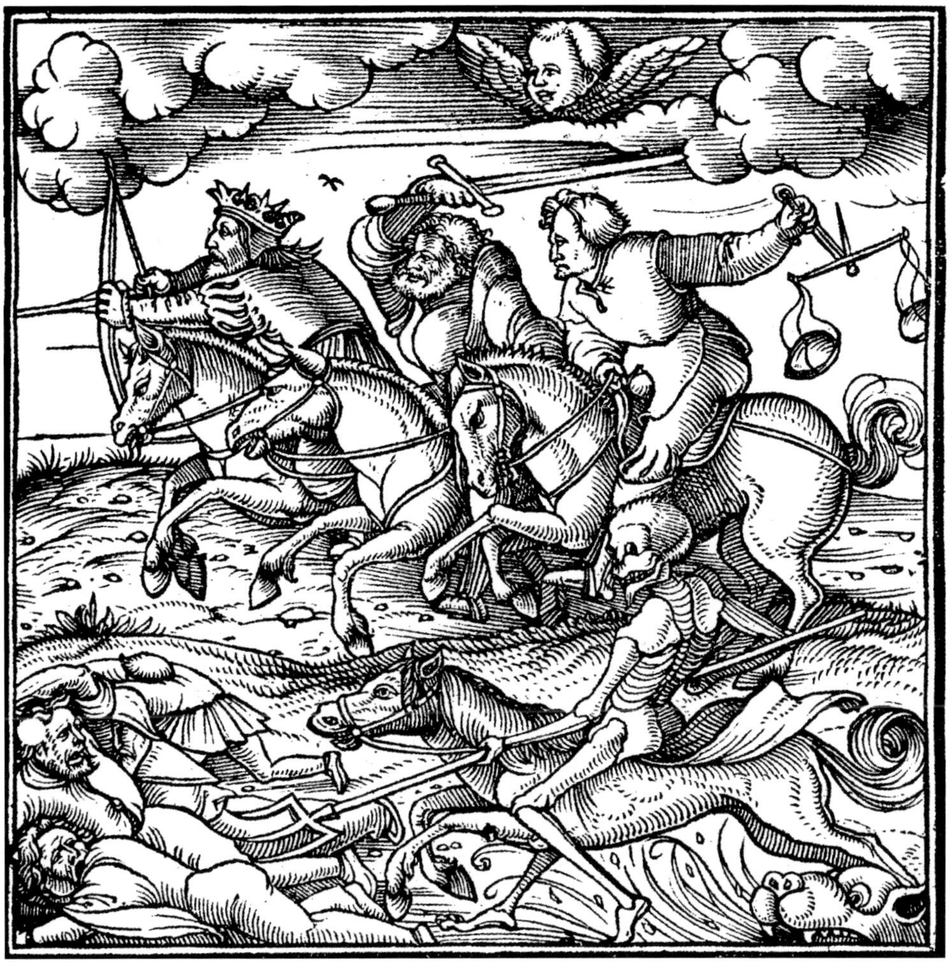

Figure 8 *The Four Horsemen of the Apocalypse*: anonymous woodcut from the Zurich Bible, 1536. *(© Glasgow University Library)*

Whatever the immediate source or pattern, it seems likely that the Edinburgh ceiling was executed by an artist, or for a patron, who had an informed interest in both the established iconography and the theology of his topic.

Much the same would seem to be true of the second of the allegorical subjects, which shows a large ship labelled *CARITAS* assailed by *Death*, *Persecution* and the Devil (Fig. 9). *Death* is unlabelled and rides a horse, but like the other two figures he is shooting arrows from his bow towards the ship. *Persecution* rides a serpentine, beaked monster. The ship is steered by a crowned helmsman, and has Christ's *IHS* monogram on its stern and flying from its mast; a Hand of God in the sky, labelled *MTATIO* (*sic*), holds a cord which is attached to the helmsman as if to guide him, and the ship is sailing towards a distant coast from which flames rise up below the label *VÆ* ('Alas!').

Anthony Wells-Cole has now identified the source for this painting and I am indebted to him for communicating this discovery, which strengthens the argument I proposed when this paper was first presented to the secular wall paintings conference in London. Karel van Mander's *Allegory of Christian Patience*, engraved by Harman Muller and published in Hamburg in 1587, is a more complicated allegory than the Edinburgh painting, though before we examine the way the Scottish painting adapts its source perhaps the first thing to note is the date. Mary of Guise died in 1560, almost 30 years before this print was published; it follows that the painting cannot possibly have decorated Mary's supposed palace.

Van Mander's allegory of *Patiencia Christiana* shows a female personification of *Patiencia* (which means 'endurance, suffering', rather than what we would call patience) steering a ship labelled *Humana caro* ('human flesh') with the help of a navigator's compass labelled *Verbum Dei* ('The Word of God') (Fig. 10). The ship is rigged with the shield of Faith, anchor of Hope and sail of Charity – the three biblical Virtues – and it sails away from the shore of *Patria* towards an opposite shore on which some sinners sit carousing at tables while others are being slain. A large siege-engine threatens a neighbouring city on which bodies hang from gallows below the word *Vae* (Alas!), and a more distant city is going up in flames beneath another *Vae* motto. A full-length figure of God the Father sits in clouds above the ship, holding three cords which run down to the three figures attacking the ship: the *World*, *Death* and the Devil. *Death* on a pale horse fires the arrows of Hunger, Sickness and Old Age; the Devil fires three arrows of Temptation, Sin and Avarice; while the *World* (the label *Mundus* can be found on his orb-shaped helmet) fires arrows of Treachery, Slander and Persecution. In the bottom margin, 20 lines of Latin verse explicate the allegory.

The way the Edinburgh painting handles its source can elucidate its own meaning and motives. Perhaps the most significant change is the figure of the crowned king replacing the female *Patientia* as helmsman of the ship. The full-length

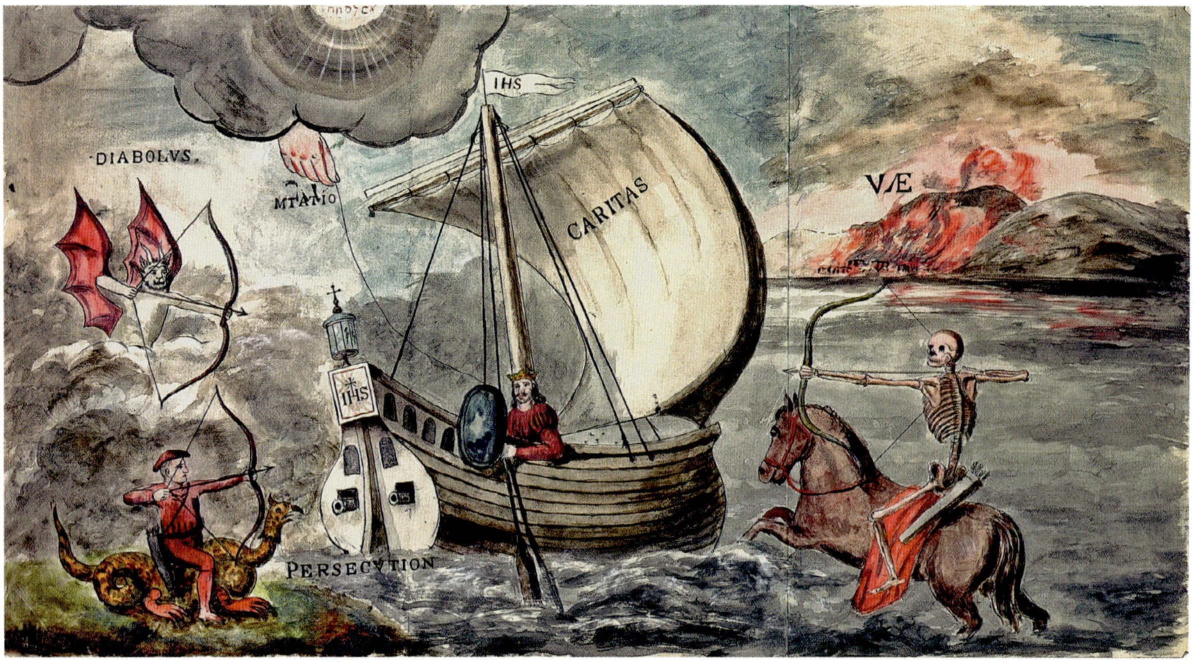

Figure 9 A.W. Lyons (attrib.): sketch of the *Death, Persecution and the Devil* panel from the 'Guise Palace'. *(Reproduced courtesy of the Society of Antiquaries of Scotland/Royal Commission on the Ancient and Historical Monuments of Scotland)*

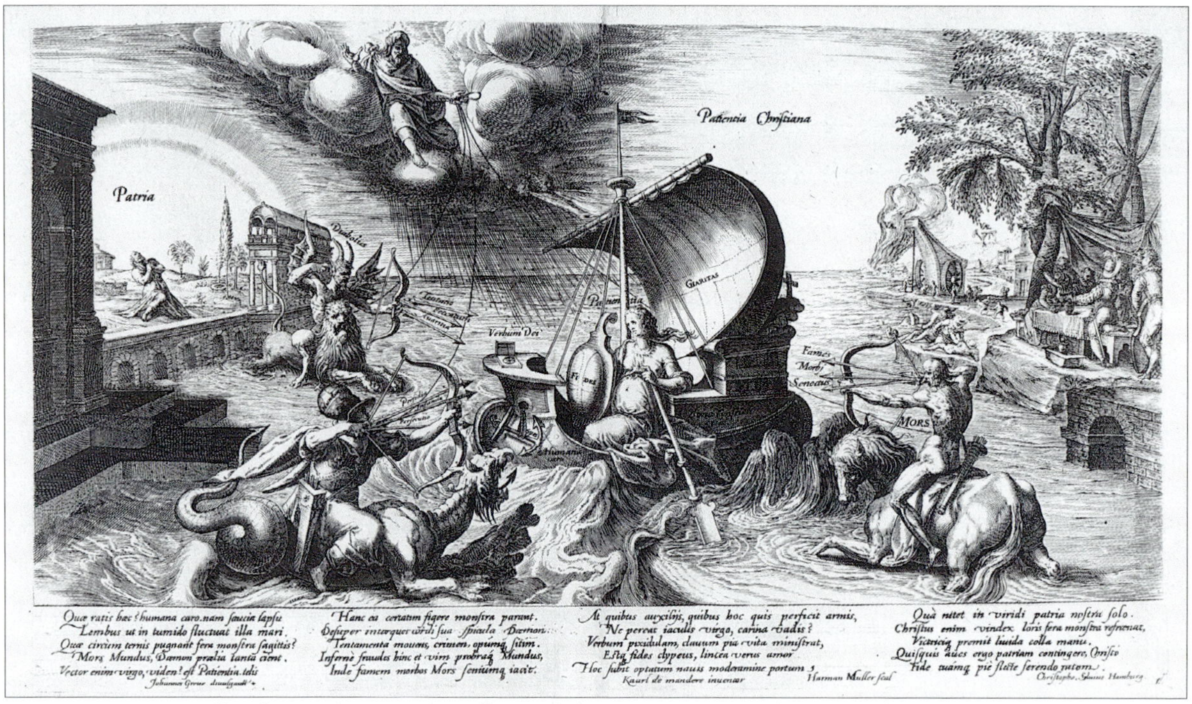

Figure 10 Harman Muller after Karel van Mander: *Allegory of Christian Patience*, Hamburg 1587. *(© British Museum, Department of Prints and Drawings)*

God the Father is changed to a Hand of God in a clouded radiance, holding a single cord which is attached to the ship's royal pilot with the added label *M[U]TATIO* ('Change'). The shore labelled *Patria* in van Mander's print design – with its kneeling figure in earnest prayer – disappears, and the opposite shore is much simplified, retaining only the burning city, now shown in a hilly landscape. The three archers assaulting the ship resemble those in the engraving so closely, however, as to leave no doubt that this was the artist's pattern, though they now have only a single arrow each, and van Mander's *Mundus* is relabelled *PERSECUTION*, evidently taking his name from the lowest of the three arrows in the print. This the Edinburgh painter might easily have mistaken for his name, though the triad of *World*, *Death* and the Devil is traditional in Christian morality if not in Christian art. The radical simplification of the detail illustrating the sinful activities on the far shore gives a new prominence to the burning City of Destruction with its *VÆ* inscription and imparts to the whole painting an Apocalyptic register that is much more pronounced than the complex allegory of van Mander's print. If the *MTATIO* label is indeed an abbreviation of *MUTATIO* (and it can surely not be anything else), then it must be suggesting divine guidance for a change of direction away from the burning City of Destruction and the arrows of *Persecution*. This must be read as a political, rather than simply a moral, allegory, and is most easily interpreted in a Reformation context as signalling a change of faith. The Ship of Faith, or the Church, was long established in Christian art, sometimes shown with a mast in the form of a cross, and this Ship of Charity marked with the monogram of Christ must be interpreted in this light. Although the Edinburgh artist omits the land labelled *Patria*, with its elegant classical buildings, he may well have taken the hint for interpreting the scene as a political allegory showing the Hand of God steering the nation away from the City of Destruction; indeed the Ship of Faith, or *CARITAS*, might easily also be read, given its new royal helmsman, as the Ship of State, and the relabelling of van Mander's *Mundus* as *Persecution* might, after all, be not so much a misreading of the print's somewhat confusing (not to say illegible) labelling as a deliberate reference to the persecution of the righteous, which threatens any nation that sails across to Roman Babylon.

Perhaps the most telling of the labels is the *VÆ* over the burning city on the far shore, for although it takes its hint from van Mander, this confirms its Apocalyptic register, i.e. to Revelation 18, where the city is Babylon. The translation in the 1611 Authorized Version supplies the full context for interpretation:

> Babylon the great is fallen ... and is become the habitation of devils, and the hold of every foul spirit, and a cage of every unclean and hateful bird ... she shall be utterly burned with fire ... And the kings of the earth ... shall bewail her, and lament for her, when they shall see the smoke of her burning ... saying, Alas, alas [Vulgate: *vae, vae*] that great city Babylon ... in one hour is thy judgement come. And the merchants of the earth shall weep and mourn over her; for no man buyeth their merchandise any more ... For in one hour so great riches is come to nought. And every shipmaster, and all the company in ships, and sailors, and as many as trade by sea, stood afar off. And cried when they saw the smoke of her burning (Revelation 18:2–18).

Although the painting's *Vae* is Latin Vulgate's exact word for the lamentation, at this time Babylon in Protestant discourse is always the Church of Rome. Moreover, if we wanted to fix the relevance of such a topic to the preoccupations of a merchant burgess in early 17th-century Protestant Edinburgh, the Bible's repeated reference to 'merchants', 'shipmasters' and 'the company in ships' would surely supply it, and if we were looking for biblical painting that entirely fitted the ideology of pious Protestant middle-class householders in early-modern Scotland, we could hardly do better.

Indeed we know quite a lot about the way Apocalypse iconography was used in Scotland at this period. As Arthur Williamson notes, 16th-century reformers 'emphatically believed that they were living in "the latter days" of the world and that their revolt from the Roman church enacted the eschatology portrayed at length in Daniel and Revelation' (Williamson 1979: 1). The Genevan exiles, Scottish and English, were intent on claiming that a Christian monarch would have a crucial role to play in the destruction of the Antichrist and the downfall of Babylon. The Geneva Bible cast Elizabeth I in this role, whereas the 1611 Authorized Version cast King James. For many Scots, particularly in the 1590s, and almost certainly for King James VI himself, it was the prospective Union of the Crowns that promised to fulfil this eschatology, but there was a profound difference between English and Scottish claims to be the elect nation that would fulfil God's plan for his reformed Church, as Williamson shows in some detail in his study, *Scottish National Consciousness in the Age of James VI*. In 1593, John Napier dedicated his

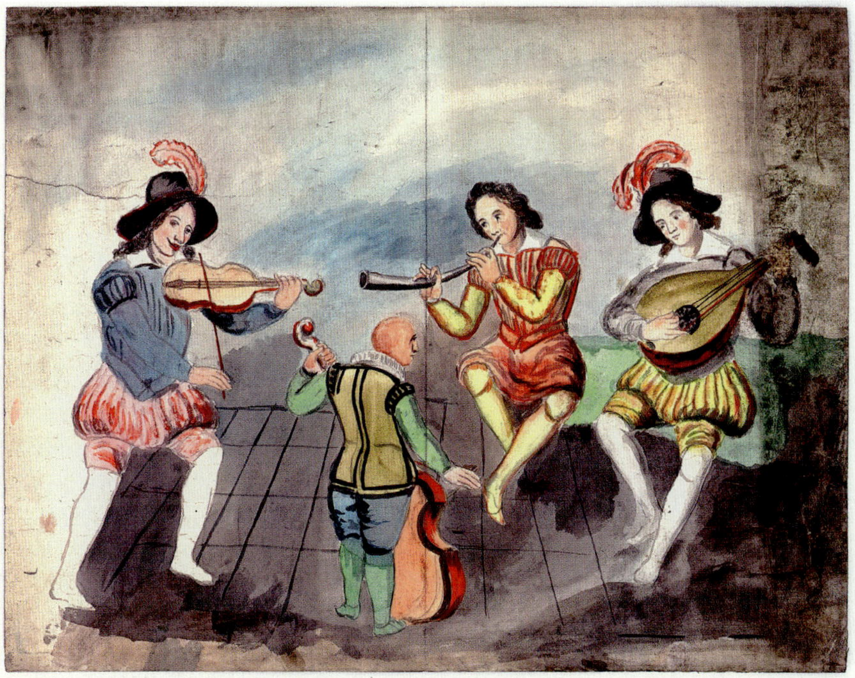

Figure 11 A.W. Lyons (attrib.): sketch of the *Four Musicians* panel from the 'Guise Palace'. *(Reproduced courtesy of the Society of Antiquaries of Scotland/Royal Commission on the Ancient and Historical Monuments of Scotland)*

A Plain Discovery of the Whole Revelation to King James, a dedication he removed from the second edition of 1611 in response to James's increasingly strident episcopalianism (as he promoted the English bishops under William Laud in blatant disregard of Scottish Presbyterianism). The need to produce a strict chronological framework for his eschatological narrative led Napier to study mathematics, and eventually to his invention of logarithms.[13]

It is probably impossible for us to determine the exact position of the Edinburgh Apocalypse paintings in relation to these political and doctrinal controversies, but we should be in no doubt that it is precisely such questions of Puritan eschatology, the elect nation, national identity and monarchical government, that supply the immediate context for any reading of this allegory on the Scottish painted ceiling, with its Hand of God guiding a crowned figure in the Ship of Christ away from the burning city of Babylon.

Finally, it is possible that the Book of Revelation might account for the one seemingly anomalous subject from the site, namely the panel showing *Four Musicians* (Fig. 11). Here at last it might look as if we have a secular, indeed a courtly, subject that would justify its inclusion in a royal palace and in the present studies of 'secular' wall painting in Britain. But I must rob myself of even that excuse, since I cannot help wondering if the *Four Musicians* (which C.K. Sharpe allegedly found at the back of a cupboard recess[14]) might have been suggested by verse 22 of the same Chapter 18 of Revelation, which forecasts the destruction of Babylon: 'And the voice of harpers, and musicians, and of pipers, and trumpeters, shall be heard no more in thee.' Could it be that this was read in context as a religious, rather than a secular, painting? And might it not originally have made up the missing sixth rectangular panel on the ceiling, which would be needed in order to balance the rectangular panels three-by-three on either side of the two central circular cartouches on the soffit showing Christ and the Apostle St John, who was, after all, traditionally seen as one and the same as St John the Divine, author of Revelation?

Conclusions

We now have most of what we might need to be able to read the iconography, not just of the individual images of this ceiling but of its overall programme. That programme was Protestant, militant and political. Clearly, these were never decorative surroundings of the Catholic Queen Regent, even if she did have a palace in Blyth's Close, but they are of a piece with painted ceilings from other tenements in this neighbourhood, with their insistence on sin, persecution, repentance, righteousness and salvation. Clearly Protestant iconoclasm in Scotland did not lead, as is sometimes supposed, to the wholesale destruction of all religious painting.[15]

Notes

1. References to the queen's lodgings in state papers at this period might easily be to Holyrood or to the Castle, whereas references in the burgh accounts (Adam 1899) are more likely to be to a townhouse. In 1552 there is a reference to men that cleaned the causeway between the queen's and the Lord Governor's lodgings (Adam 1899: 75); in 1554 boards and trestles were carried to the queen's lodging, and payments made for cleaning the queen's lodging outside the Tron 'with the convoy of the Moors' who performed in the *Corpus Christi* play there, and 'for the making of the Quenis grace house on the playfield, besyde the convoy house under the samyn, and the playaris hous', which were presumably temporary structures for viewing the performance (Adam 1899: 108–10). In 1556 payment was made to the 'ushers of the Queen's grace chamber door'. None of these records, however, identifies Blyth's Close as the location of the lodgings.
2. See for example Dunbar 1999, pp. 151–4. McKean (2001) takes the argument for French influence much further.
3. Chambers 1825, p. 87. Chambers' *Traditions of Edinburgh* was substantially revised and rewritten in 1846, and again in 1868 with a new introduction; the 1825 edition contains a fuller account of 'The Palace and Oratory of Mary of Lorrain' (pp. 74–87) than any of the later reissues. In 1833 Chambers also issued his *Minor Antiquities of Edinburgh* (William and Robert Chambers, Edinburgh) to cover material he had not found space for in his *Traditions*. 'These are now published as a third, or supplementary volume of *Traditions*' he writes; it nevertheless includes a brief account of the Guise chapel and palace (pp. 74–5) which adds nothing new, though its engraving by F.G. Bruce is the clearest illustration of Blyth's Close (a few years before its demolition) to have come down to us. Besides founding and running a leading publishing house, editing *Chambers' Journal*, writing and editing various books on Scottish letters, Chambers was also author of one of the most important pre-Darwinian theories of evolution, *Vestiges of the Natural History of Creation*, which Tennyson read before writing his stanzas on species extinction, with 'Nature, red in tooth and claw', in *In Memoriam*.
4. Wilson was an influential Fellow of the Society of Antiquaries of Scotland, who had trained as an engraver, providing his own drawings to illustrate *Memorials* – his first published work– in 1848. He later became a leading archaeologist, introducing the word 'prehistoric' into the English language and the periodisation into Stone, Iron and Bronze Ages, which had been proposed by the Scandinavian archaeologists with whom he was in contact. In 1853 he accepted the Chair of History and English Literature in Toronto, where he produced a pioneering ethnology of the native Canadian Indians (see Ash 1981).
5. Bath 2003, pp. 239–41.
6. Wilson 1848, p. 156.
7. Bath 2003, p. 125.
8. The National Monuments Record, RCAHMS Edinburgh, preserves a sketch plan of the site by John Sime, labelled *Rude sketch from memory of the buildings including Palace, &c of Mary of Loraine Queen Regent of Scotland during minority of Mary Queen of Scots, as they were AD 1832* (M/1/3v, John Sime Memorabilia). The sketch plan was executed to inform Wilson's 1848 description.
9. Wilson 1878, pp. 130–33.
10. Bath 2003, pp. 123–46.
11. *Ibid.*, pp. 124–7.
12. *Ibid.*, chapter 1.
13. Gribben 2000, p. 41.
14. Wilson states that this painting was the same as fragments of a larger, but much ruder, copy of the same design from Dean House, Edinburgh (1848, p. 157). For the Dean House paintings see Bath 2003, pp. 201–9 and 241–2. Now on display in the National Museum, Edinburgh, the surviving panels do not include the *Four Musicians*, but although executed in oil rather than tempera, they do use similar biblical subjects and could well be the work of the same artist. The best account of the notable antiquarian and eccentric, Charles Kirkpatrick Sharpe can be found in the 'Introductory Notice' to the 1868 revision of Chambers' *Traditions*: 'His thin effeminate figure, his voice pitched in alt – his attire, as he took his daily walks on Princes Street, a long blue frock-coat, black trousers, rather wide below, and sweeping over white stockings ... and a brown wig coming down to his eyebrows – had long established him as what is called

a character.' Sharpe's satirical sketch of Queen Elizabeth dancing a volta before the French ambassadors was well known, and he designed a calling-card for himself consisting of a musical stave with the single note of C# 'in jest upon his own peculiarity of voice' (Chambers 1868: i).

15. Much of the research for this paper was carried out in connection with my work on the Stirling Palace Academic Research Committee for Historic Scotland, and was greatly facilitated by the assistance of colleague Michael Pearce of Historic Scotland Conservation, who first drew my attention to A.W. Lyons' sketches and who identified key documents used in this paper.

References

Adam R. 1899, *Edinburgh Records: The Burgh Accounts, Vol. 1, 1544–1567*, printed for the Lord Provost and Council, Edinburgh

Ash M. 1981, 'David Laing, Daniel Wilson and Scottish archaeology', in A.S. Bell (ed.) *The Scottish Antiquarian Tradition*, John Donald, Edinburgh, pp. 86–113

Bath M. 2003, *Renaissance Decorative Painting in Scotland*, National Museums of Scotland Publishing, Edinburgh

Chambers R. 1925, *Traditions of Edinburgh*, W & C Tait, Edinburgh (revised 1846, 1868)

Dunbar J.G. 1999, *Scottish Royal Palaces*, Tuckwell Press, Edinburgh

Gribben C. 2000, *The Puritan Millennium: Literature and Theology 1550–1682*, Four Courts Press, Dublin

McKean C. 2001, *The Scottish Chateau: The Country House in Renaissance Scotland*, Sutton Publishing, London

Williamson A.H. 1979, *Scottish National Consciousness in the Age of James VI: The Apocalypse, the Union, and the shaping of Scotland's Public Culture*, John Donald, Edinburgh

Wilson D. 1848, *Memorials of Edinburgh in the Olden Time*, 2 vols, Hugh Paton, Edinburgh

Wilson D. 1878, *Reminiscences of Old Edinburgh*, 2 vols, David Douglas, Edinburgh

Wilson D. 1891, *Memorials of Edinburgh in the Olden Time*, revised edition, A & C Black, Edinburgh

The author

Michael Bath is Emeritus Professor of Renaissance Studies at the University of Strathclyde, where he taught English Literature until his retirement, co-authoring with Tom Furniss a book *Reading Poetry* (Longman) in 1996. Author of *The Image of the Stag: Iconographic Themes in Western Art* (Koerner 1992), he has worked extensively on Renaissance emblem books, serves as Chair of the Society for Emblem Studies and is co-editor of the journal *Emblematica*. His *Speaking Pictures* (Longman) came out in 1994 and the use of emblems in the hitherto little-known corpus of painted ceilings in Scotland led him into research on the applied arts in historic buildings, with a recent book, *Renaissance Decorative Painting in Scotland* (NMS 2003). He is currently working on a book, *Emblems for a Queen*, on the needlework of Mary Queen of Scots, and advising Historic Scotland on refurbishment of the Royal Palace in Stirling.

Secular wall paintings in the Welsh Marches

Kathryn Davies

Introduction

Why did George Jenkes choose to paint the walls of his parlour with a narrative featuring figures engaged in playing musical instruments? What was the story being told, and to whom was it being addressed? What was its significance? This paper considers how the answers to such questions can illuminate our understanding of the social and cultural aspects of people's lives in the late 16th and early 17th century. The wall painting in George Jenkes' home, at New Hall, Ticklerton in South Shropshire (one panel of which is shown in Fig. 1) will be used as a focus for the discussion.

New Hall is a typical hall with two cross wings dating from the second half of the 16th century. It was inherited by the Jenkes family in 1584, the same year George Jenkes was granted arms. In a first-floor chamber is a hunting scene that looks as though its source was a German print, since it depicts a hunting stag on foot, which is not typically English (see Figs 2 and 3 in the Introduction, p. xix). The musical scene, in the ground-floor parlour, was painted some time in the 1580s. It is part of a series of panels, probably originally running all around the room, of which only three survive. These depict figures with musical instruments, interwoven with symbolic motifs: a bird of prey (possibly an eagle), an ape or demon figure, and a hare running across the dado of one panel (Fig. 2). The dado, which is fragmentary, appears to be a well-executed form of black and white antiquework. The central panel has three figures, including a male figure and a female who is holding a lute, who seem to be the principal figures in the story. A second female, in a slightly subservient position, holds a Tudor rose in one hand and a gillyflower in the other, which is outstretched over the principal woman's head. All are in gentry 'best dress'. The other panels feature male figures with musical instruments. While the figures have the naivety of an amateur painter's work, the overall composition and the detailing suggest that someone more professional was involved in their execution.

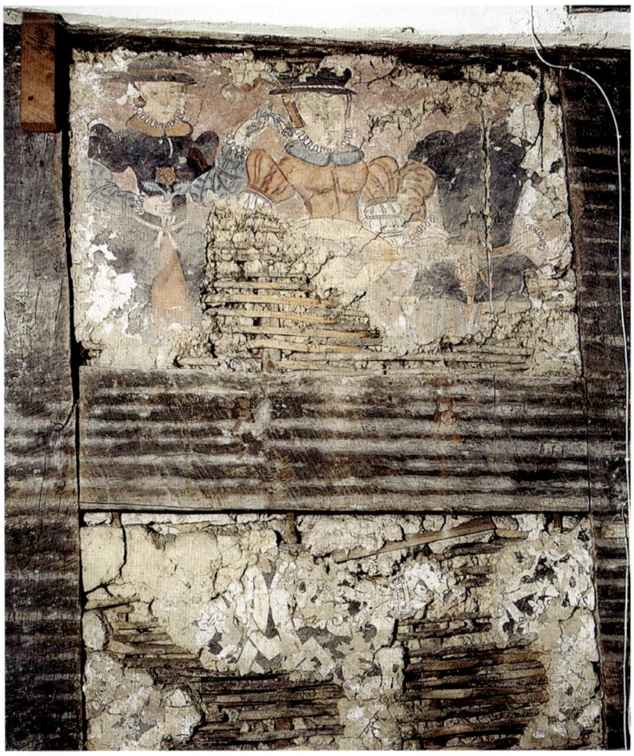

Figure 1 New Hall, near Ticklerton, Shropshire: panel 2 from the wall paintings located in the ground-floor parlour, showing three figures above a dado decorated in antiquework decoration. *(© English Heritage. NMR)*

This painting is not mere decoration. The iconography is very deliberate, suggesting that there are subtle and complex messages encapsulated in paintings such as these which reveal aspects of the social and cultural lives of the owners. The evidence for this claim emerges from the findings of my doctoral research into wall paintings in the Welsh Marches in the 16th and 17th centuries[1] which sought answers to the following questions:

- How common were wall paintings?
- Who painted them?
- When were they painted ?
- What was their significance?

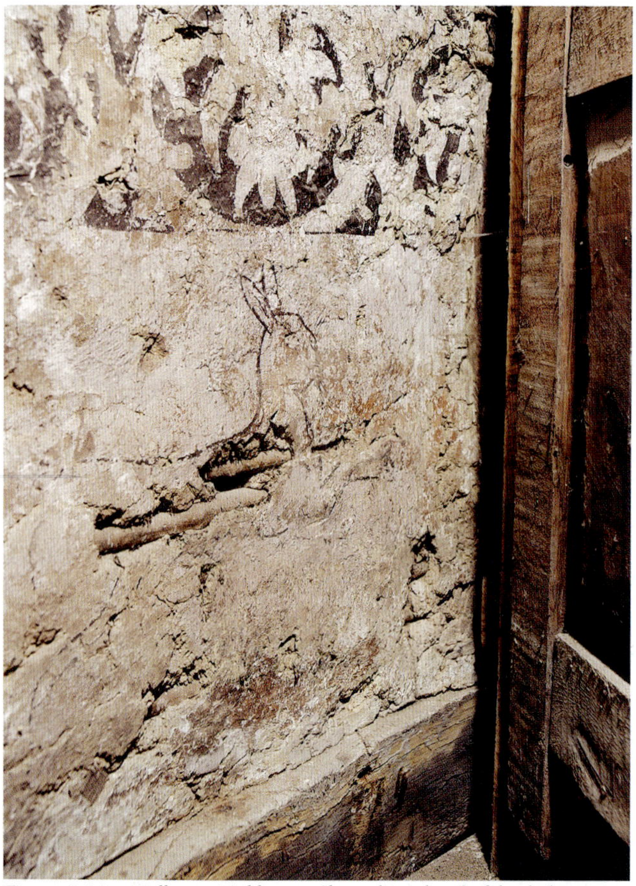

Figure 2 New Hall, near Ticklerton, Shropshire: detail of the dado section of panel 3 showing a fleeting hare. *(© English Heritage. NMR)*

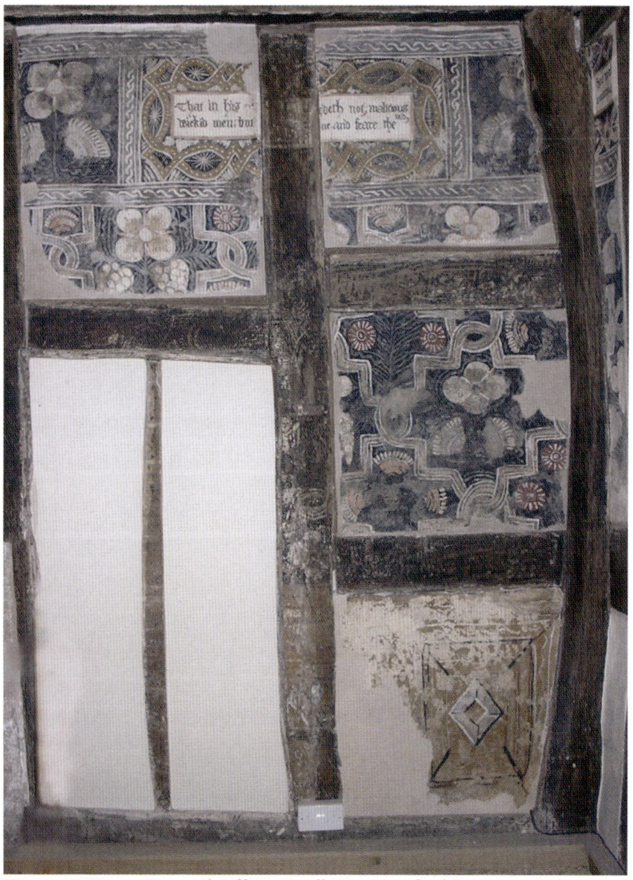

Figure 3 Town Council Offices, Ledbury, Herefordshire: general view of the wall painting in a first-floor chamber. *(© K. Davies)*

Sixteenth- and seventeenth-century vernacular wall paintings

Before progressing further, it is useful to look at what constitutes a typical wall painting in a vernacular building in the period of study. The fairly complete example surviving at the Town Council Offices in Ledbury, Herefordshire, illustrates the distinctive elements found in these paintings (Fig. 3). It covers the entire surface of the wall, infill panels and timbers (now faded) alike, and displays the typical tripartite composition of frieze, main panel and dado, reminiscent of the Renaissance organisation of architectural space. These elements are divided by bands or borders of contrasting decorative motifs such as guilloches. While not all paintings from the period include all three elements, most contain at least two.

The area of study, the Welsh Marches, lies between the Welsh mountains in the west and the lowlands of the Midland plain to the east, extending from the Dee estuary in the north to the Severn estuary in the south. It is an area that had some social, cultural and economic cohesion in the early modern period, when it had its own government under the President of the Marches. The research discussed here covers the Welsh counties of Denbighshire, Flintshire, Montgomeryshire, Radnorshire, Breconshire, Monmouthshire and Glamorganshire and the English counties of Cheshire, Shropshire, Staffordshire, Herefordshire, Worcestershire and Gloucestershire. This area was selected as it is not dealt with in any published work on wall paintings of the period, yet the indications are that both the original incidence and the survival of wall paintings in the Welsh Marches are high.

The fashion for wall paintings

To say that wall paintings were fashionable, true though that may be, is too simplistic and perhaps misses the point. Fashion is an expression of social and cultural values, and changes in fashion are symptomatic of underlying shifts in these values. Wall paintings in the Marches declined sharply in popularity during the course of the 17th century, being common only until around 1625. After this not only did they decrease in number, but they changed in character and became more restrained and architecturally conscious, as for example in painted overmantels. So what was happening in the world of ordinary people in the Marches to make them at first favour highly decorative wall paintings and what made them later change to other forms of decoration?

To set the context for the discussion it is useful to look at some of the wall paintings and the places in which they are found. From my research, looking at 233 paintings in 188 buildings, I concluded that they could be found in houses of all statuses except the poorest cottages, and that they were painted in both town and countryside throughout the Welsh Marches. Wall paintings are certainly found in high status houses such as Whitehall in Shrewsbury, where the painting is in a first-floor anteroom (Figs 4 and 5). Slightly lower down the social scale they survive in many houses of the minor gentry, such as Petsey, near Wem in Shropshire (Fig. 6). These houses typically display some form of external architectural expression of status, including features such as decorative timber framing or close studding, decorative chimney stacks, some form of ornamentation to windows and doors, and multistorey porches. The classical motifs incorporated into these are usually indicative of social aspiration. Additionally, many wall paintings were found in farmhouses typically occupied by yeomen. While these may have less architectural display, again there is usually some form of outward expression of status.

In towns, merchants' houses are among those exhibiting the greatest degree of decoration, and quite sophisticated wall paintings may be found here. Cotton's House in Market Drayton, Shropshire is a good example (Fig. 7), as are the Town Council Offices in Church Lane, Ledbury, Herefordshire (see Fig 3). Many wall paintings were recorded in Wales in buildings of a similar range in status. Although the accommodation of the Welsh gentry was typically much more modest, this is not reflected in the decoration of their homes.

It is worth noting that while most of the wall paintings surveyed in the Marches were found in higher status houses, it is likely that this reflects the pattern of survival of buildings from the period rather than the original incidence of wall paintings.

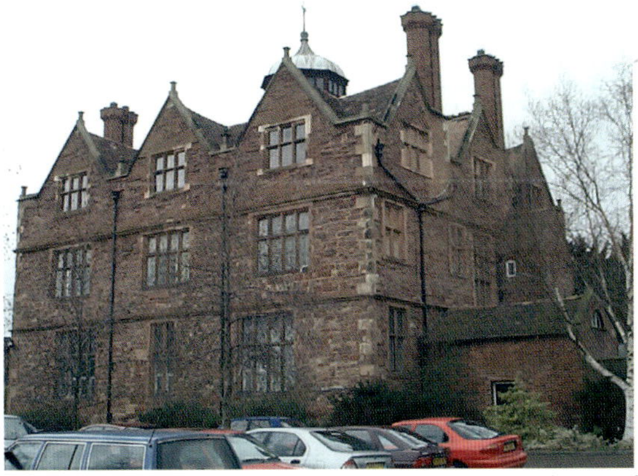

Figure 4 Whitehall, Shrewsbury, Shropshire: general view of the exterior. *(© K. Davies)*

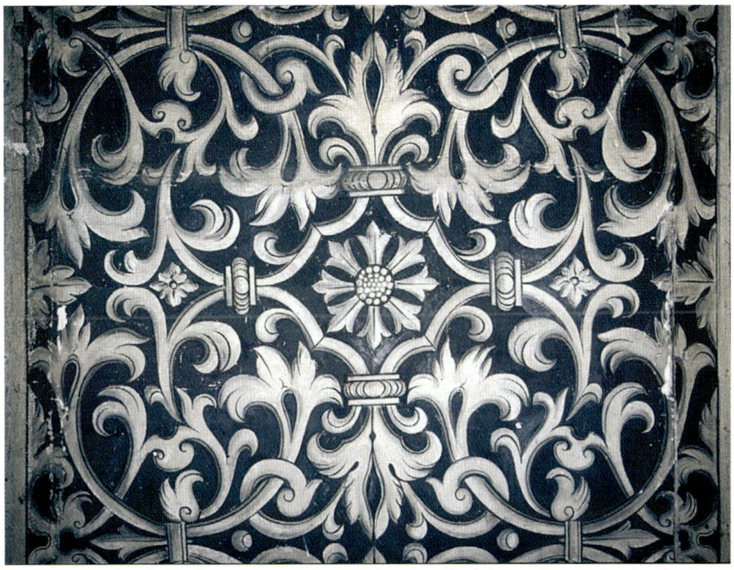

Figure 5 Whitehall, Shrewsbury, Shropshire: detail of the wall painting in the first-floor anteroom. *(© K. Davies)*

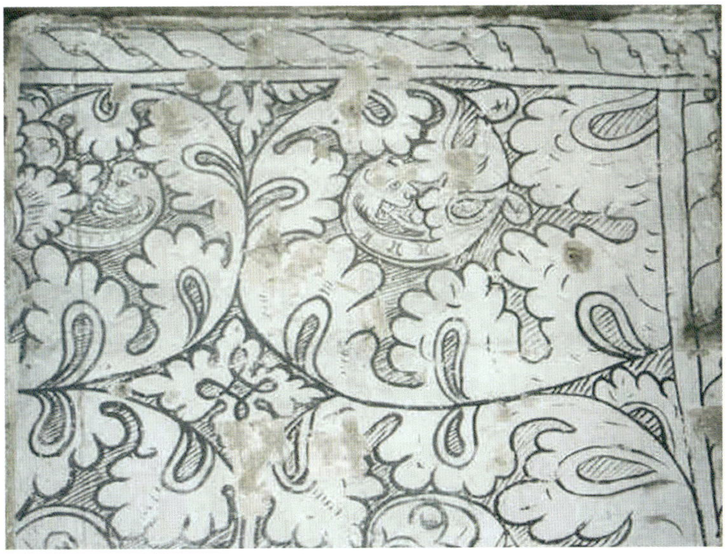

Figure 6 Petsey, near Wem, Shropshire: detail of the wall painting in the ground-floor parlour of a timber-framed, minor gentry house. *(© K. Davies)*

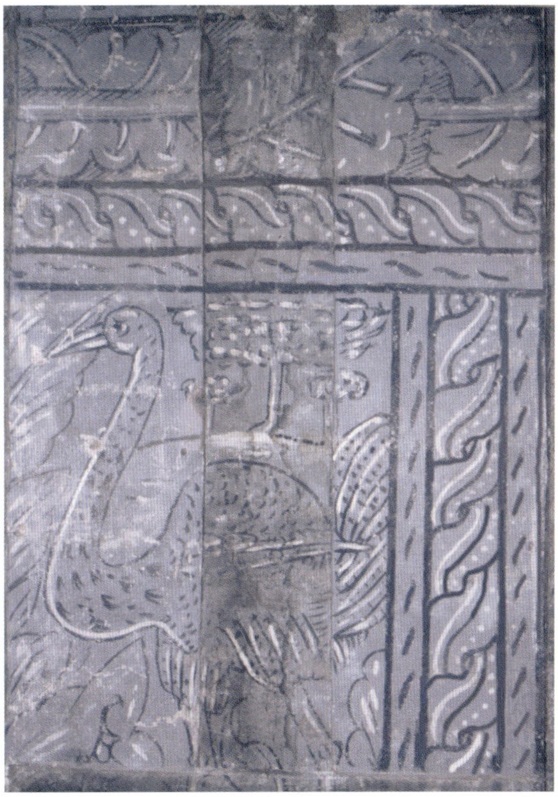

Figure 7 Cotton's House, Market Drayton, Shropshire: detail of the painting in the first-floor chamber. *(© K. Davies)*

Wall painting types

To make some sense of the range of wall paintings it is helpful to group them according to type. This can also assist in interpreting the New Hall paintings, which incorporate various features that belong to different types.

First, there are a significant number of figurative paintings. Some of these are vernacular portrait paintings, such as those that were in a first-floor chamber at Dowles Manor, Worcestershire, now demolished (see Fig. 18), the portrait (probably of Jane Andrew) at Coalknap Farm in Barry (Fig. 8), and Richard Ellis and his wife painted at Althrey Hall, Bangor-on-Dee in Flintshire (Fig. 9). Others figures feature in narrative paintings including those at New Hall and also Beale's Corner, Bewdley, in Worcestershire (see Fig. 17).

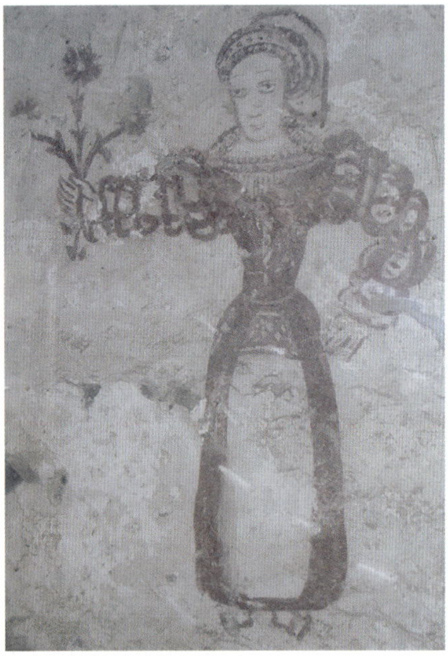

Figure 8 Coalknap Farm, Barry, Glamorgan: portrait in the ground-floor hall at the foot of the stairs. *(© K. Davies)*

Purely decorative schemes are by far the most common, with many variations in style and type. Floral and foliate design make up the majority of these, the most distinctive of which is the scroll design found almost exclusively in Shropshire (see Fig. 6). The decorative elements in the New Hall scheme relate most closely to antiquework schemes. Antiquework, or grotesque work, is the name given to the form of decoration which emerged in the Renaissance based on designs copied from the remains of Nero's Golden Palace, discovered in Rome in the late 15th century. This distinctive style of ornament consisted of fantastic flowing shapes and representations based on vegetation and animal forms reminiscent of mythological characters such as satyrs and centaurs. Other Renaissance decorations became incorporated, such as cartouches, classical vases, terms and caryatids (Fig. 11).[2] The decorative designs display varying degrees of skill – some are very crude, while others are much more accomplished. The quality of the painting does not appear related to the status of the house.

Architectural motifs were commonly used as a basis for design, sometimes framing other elements of the painting but most often found in fictive panelling. Friezes are usually based on decorative designs, although many incorporate texts with moralising or religious messages (see Fig. 3). Heraldic paintings are less common, and can depict personal or royal arms, such as those found at 53 Broad Street, Ludlow. There is also a wide range of miscellaneous designs such as guilloches and zigzags, used either on their own or as friezes or borders, and some, such as that found at Whittington Inn, Whittington, Staffordshire, and at Dowles Manor, Worcestershire (see Figs 10 and 18) appear to have been based on common sources.

Sources

There has been much research into possible sources for wall paintings, as exemplified by the papers by Wells-Cole and Bath

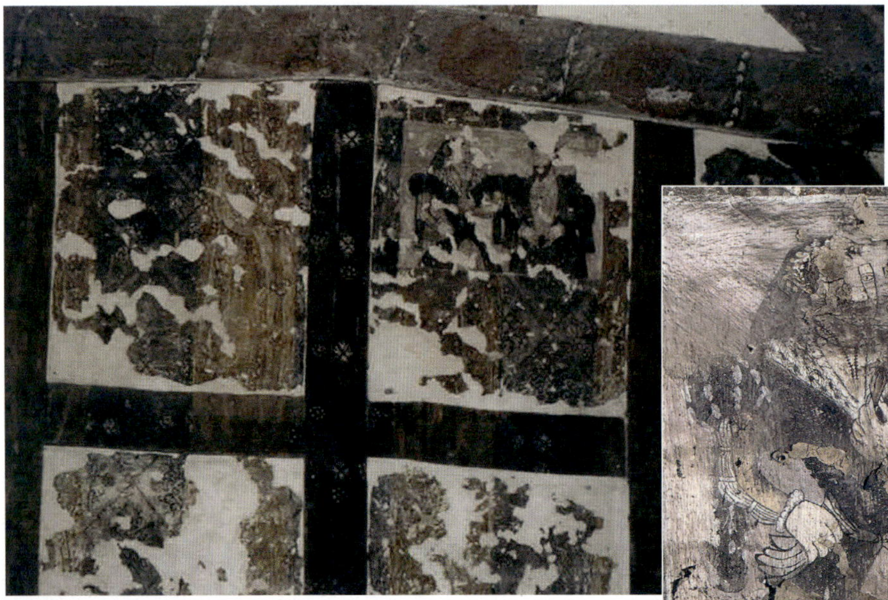

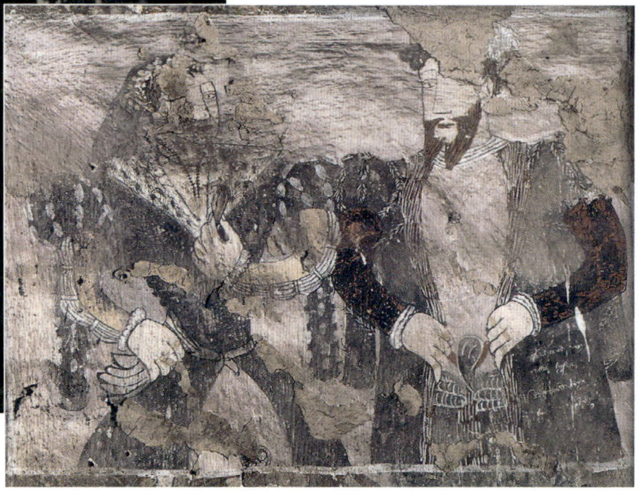

Figure 9 Althrey Hall, Bangor-on-Dee, Flintshire: general view of the wall paintings in the first-floor chamber, which include a portrait (approximate size 60 × 75cm). *(© K. Davies)*

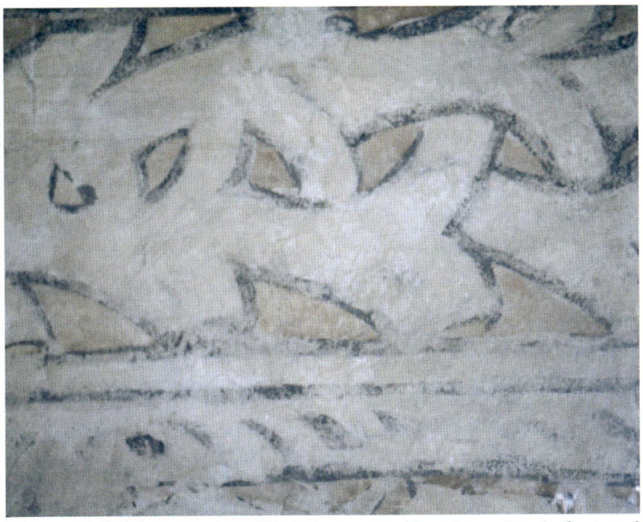

Figure 10 Whittington Inn, Whittington, Staffordshire: detail of painted frieze, the pattern of which is remarkably similar to that found at Dowles Manor, Worcestershire, shown in Figure 18. *(© K. Davies)*

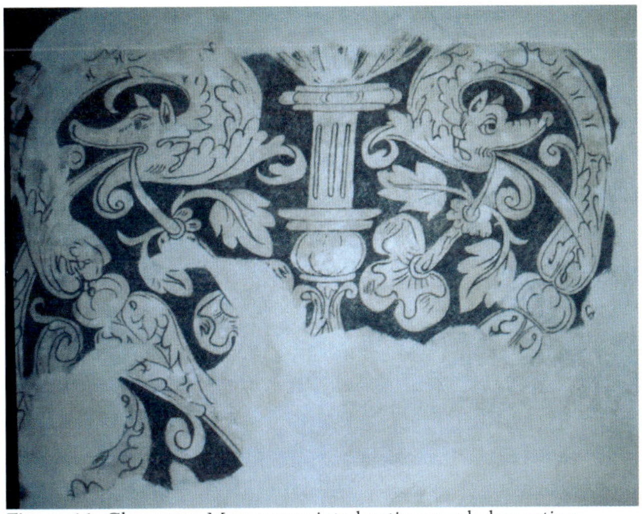

Figure 11 Gloucester Museum: painted antiquework decoration. *(© K. Davies)*

in this volume (pp. 3–9 and 11–21). In attempting to assess that research, it is important to ask the following question: if wall paintings were fashionable (using the term in the qualified sense), how do we know which, if any, designs were the *more* fashionable? Moreover, if people chose wall paintings to decorate their homes to transmit a message to the viewer, then there must have been some common cultural reference points embodied within the paintings to which viewers could relate – just as today the ways in which we decorate our homes says something about us to others. So what were these common cultural reference points? A search through various sources of design can reveal some interesting contenders.

Prints were one source which has been extensively researched and, not surprisingly, print sources have been identified for some of the paintings found in the Marches. A commonly found subject in interior decorative schemes is *The Sacrifice of Isaac*, and a print identified by Wells-Cole appears to be the source of the painting of this subject at The Batch, Sidbury, in Shropshire (Figs 12 and 13). The painting found at Castellymynach, Pentyrch, Glamorgan, which is dated 1602, is certainly derived from the top compartment of a title page that was used both for John Shute's *First and Chief Groundes of Architecture* and for the Welsh prayer book, both dating from the 1560s – either of these could have been the source. Other similar source material includes, for example, Walter Gedde's *A Booke of Sundry Draughtes*[3] which features instructions on how to draw strapwork of the kind found in 19 Watergate Street in Whitchurch, Shropshire (Figs 14 and 15). A very similar design is found at Maynards in Tenterden, Kent, a long way from Whitchurch, suggesting a readily accessible common source. Other examples of distinctive but similar designs can be found in paintings in locations quite distant from each other.

Given the expense of woven and richly embroidered textiles, it is not surprising that paintings based on their design were used to create an impression of luxury and wealth. At Althrey Hall, the walls have imitation paned textiles featuring a pomegranate motif and a diamond pattern with a rose motif. Interestingly, a very similar scheme can be found at Halstead

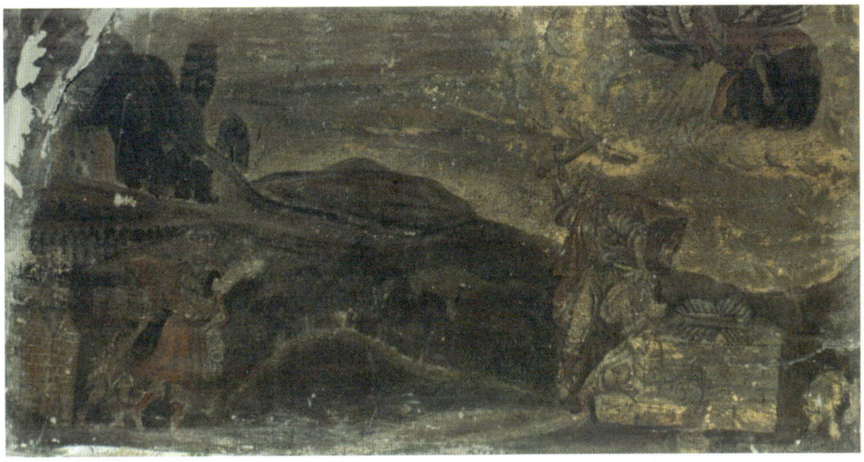

Figure 12 The Batch, Sidbury, Shropshire: a painting of *The Sacrifice of Isaac* that sadly no longer survives. *(©: M. Moran)*

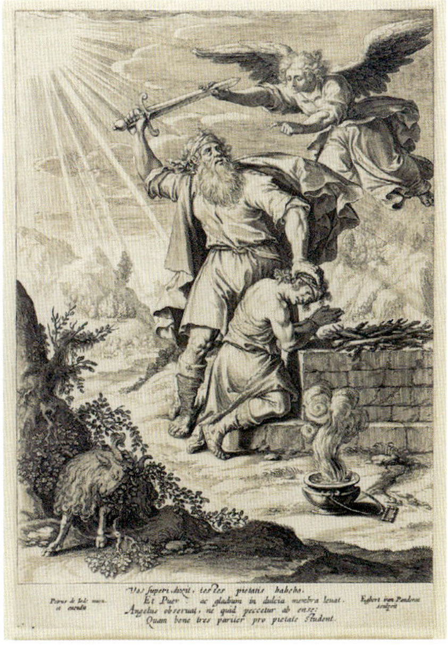

Figure 13 Egbert van Panderen after Pieter de Lode, *The Sacrifice of Isaac* c.1600. *(© Rijksmuseum, Amsterdam)*

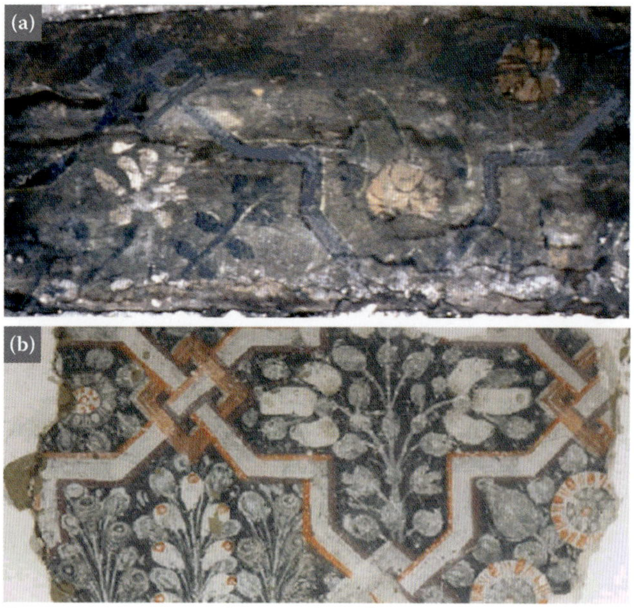

Figure 14 A comparison between the wall paintings at 17–19 Watergate Street, Whitchurch, Shropshire (a), and Maynard's in Tenterden, Kent (b). *(© K. Davies)*

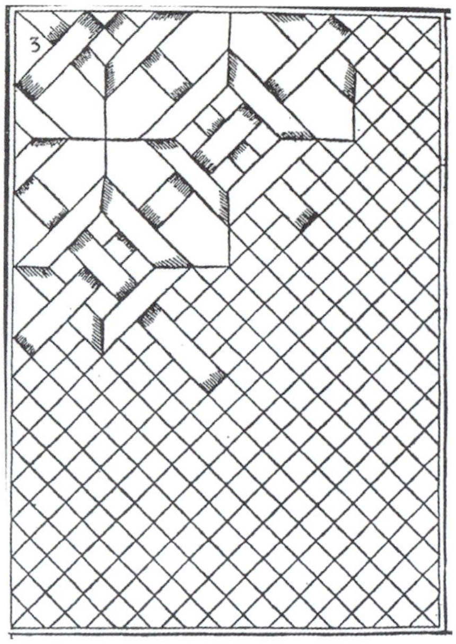

Figure 15 A strapwork design from Walter Gedde's *A Booke of Sundry Draughtes* (London 1615).

in Essex, again a long way away and, though the paintings are certainly not by the same hand, surely they are derived from a common source.

Emblem books have been identified as sources for painted decoration, particularly in higher status houses.[4] Not many of these have been found in vernacular houses in the Marches, though one interesting instance can be seen at Beale's Corner, Bewdley (see Fig. 17). This depicts Aesop's fable *The Fox and the Grapes* as illustrated in Geffrey Witney's *Choice of Emblems*, first published in 1586.[5]

In this brief look at some of the wall paintings found in the Marches, there is enough evidence to suggest that they did contain cultural reference points which had common meaning for both the patron and the viewer.

The meanings in vernacular wall paintings

The next and most important challenge is to try to understand what such meaning might be. While some schemes have a direct identifiable source, with a clearly associated meaning, many appear to be made up of elements from different sources, put together to make up a very personal statement. Other factors, such as location, contribute in a subtle way to significance. Maurice Howard has pointed out the importance of context in relation to portraits, and this was equally important for vernacular wall paintings.[6] If the owner intended the painting to convey a message to the viewer, then the question of who would see the painting is crucial. A painting in the hall of a house would have a different group of viewers from one located in a more private chamber. All members of the household, including servants and visitors, would have used the hall, but only close family members and favoured guests would have access to parlours and chambers.

With this in mind, certain meanings can be suggested for the different types of wall paintings surveyed. While inevitably these meanings must remain conjectural, they are based on information relating to the social and cultural environment of those likely to have commissioned the paintings, and often incorporate known details about the lives of some of the patrons.

Antiquework

Antiquework signified the exotic – it was certainly not indigenous decoration. More importantly perhaps, antiquework decoration signified status and was much in favour among the aristocracy as an expression of Renaissance learning. Thus an antiquework scheme might be chosen for a number of reasons. It could have been an attempt by the owner to convey to guests how fashionable and modern he was, but it could also allude to a knowledge of the classics, a mark of some form of higher education, which distinguished the gentry from their social inferiors (in their own eyes at least). For a social aspirant who had not quite achieved gentry status but wished to display the signs associated with it, a classically inspired wall painting might enhance his standing among his neighbours. Even if neither the patron nor his neighbours fully understood the motifs, a passing reference might be all that was required: an example of this must surely be that found at 26–28 Hereford Street in Presteigne, Radnorshire (Fig. 16). At Barnaby House in Ludlow, Shropshire, the antiquework decoration incorporates roundels which appear to have once contained heraldic devices. In this scheme the patron, Richard Barnaby, managed to display two key features of gentry standing: education and lineage.

Looking at their context, only two paintings with Renaissance detailing were found in halls – the rest were located in the more private chambers or parlours. This may be an accident of survival or it might be seen as reserving the exclusivity of erudition for those of higher rank.

Emblems

Another badge of the gentry was the use of emblems (symbolic illustrations with a written explanation in verse and headed with a motto or proverb), which were published in books from the mid-16th century onwards. Emblems became popular in Elizabethan England partly because they were entertaining and indicative of some education, requiring as they did the use of reasoning to understand the intellectual content of the symbolism. The devising of emblems was considered to be one of the accomplishments of a gentleman, although they were also a normal tool for the poet, and emblems abound in contemporary literature. As such, they formed part of the popular culture of the age and emblematic allusions would have been widely traded. While illustration and text were complementary and interdependent, it was expected that reference to one or the other would be understood. Deciphering allegories was a popular pastime, and they could be very complicated and difficult to understand.[7]

Stories

Closely related to emblems, because of their symbolism and allegorical potential, are the stories. The best preserved of the story paintings in the Marches is that found at Beale's

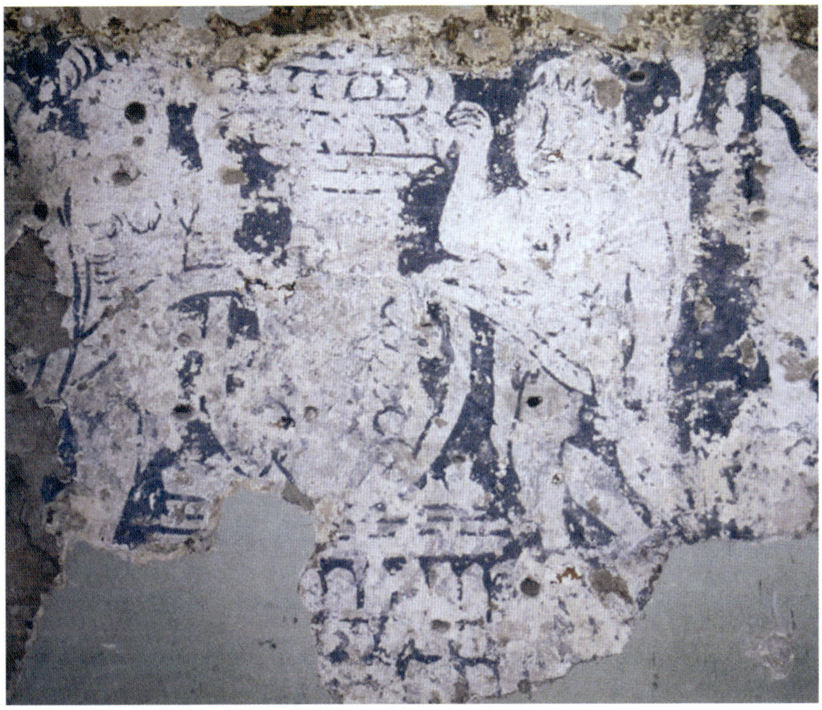

Figure 16 26–28 Hereford Road, Presteigne, Radnorshire: detail of antiquework. *(© K. Davies)*

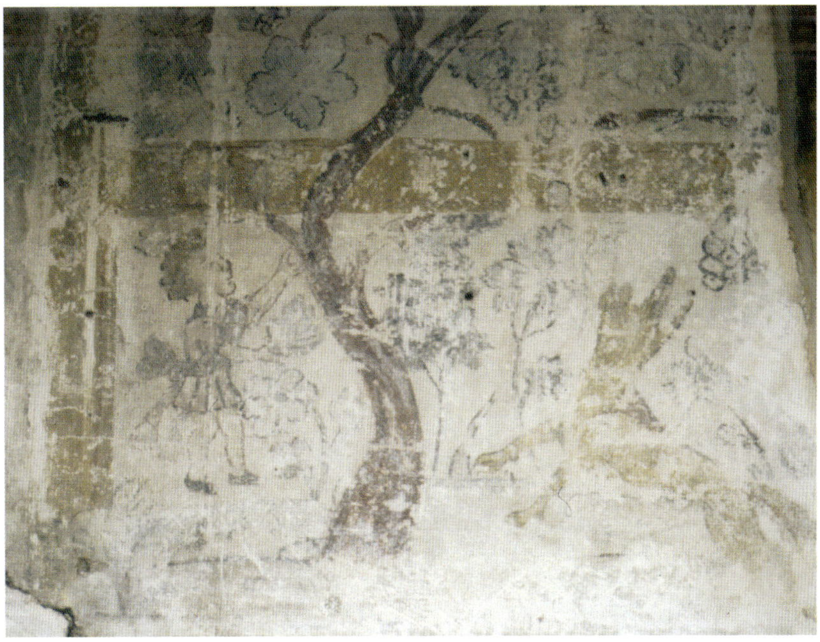

Figure 17 Beale's Corner, Bewdley, Worcestershire: showing a boy to the left and a fox leaping up at a bunch of grapes to the right. This is similar to an illustration in Geffrey Witney's *A Choice of Emblemes* first published in 1586. *(© K. Davies)*

Corner in Bewdley, which includes the *Fox and the Grapes* emblem (Fig. 17). The first-floor chamber at Beale's Corner is decorated with a narrative featuring a vineyard with figures – men, women and a child – carrying out seasonal tasks such as pruning and harvesting. The paintings also feature flowers and birds, a fox and a coiled snake. None of the other images have been definitely identified as being from a known source, and the meanings these had for the owner are therefore uncertain. In the 16th and 17th centuries Bewdley was a significant port, and the riverfront location of Beale's Corner suggests it was the house of a merchant. The painted first-floor chamber overlooks the river, and although it might have been a private chamber for the family, it may also have been a room for conducting business, where the merchant could entertain a client and at the same time keep an eye on the commercial comings and goings relating to his business. In this context an entertaining story depicted on the walls might impress the client, and the somewhat unusual contents may have alluded to something flattering to both parties, although the meaning is now obscure. The large snake is certainly not part of the normal wildlife of Bewdley, and so must have had some symbolic meaning which eludes the modern viewer. Not all aspects may be allegorical: although one might not think of vineyards as common in England, at this period there was one just downstream of Bewdley, at Ribbesford. Viticulture was an occupation pursued principally by the gentry, and one might speculate that the merchant was in some way involved, perhaps as an owner or marketer of the produce. In this case the wall painting could proclaim to clients the status of his business.

As suggested earlier, nothing at this period had a single meaning, and everything was imbued with allusion and allegory, so it is difficult to unravel the meanings embodied in paintings like those at Beale's Corner. Whatever its original intent, it is reasonable to assume that the painting had some significance for the owner over and above any purely decorative function. It is bold and striking in its design, creating an attractive, rich, entertaining decoration that would involve the viewer's intellect in its allegorical references. Perhaps it was intended to be seen by people who, understanding the messages, would assign certain favourable characteristics to the owner (or to his business). In turn, by communicating in this more sophisticated language of symbolism, the viewers themselves may have been flattered.

Portraits

Among the Tudor elite, portraits represented an opportunity to proclaim one's standing to the world, or at least to that part of the world invited to view the portrait. Surviving portrait paintings on canvas or panel are mostly of royalty and courtiers, yet those of lower rank also recorded the major events in their lives through portraits which they used to decorate the walls of their houses. There are significant differences, however, between the portraits of the two different groups. Unlike the more formal composition evident in those courtiers' paintings which have survived, portraits at the vernacular level mostly depict male and female figures together in companionable poses: noteworthy in such a patriarchal society (Fig. 18). These images could signify the harmony of a good household presided over by man and wife in an amicable relationship. Order and unity, godliness and charity were all laudable attributes embodied in the good household. Portraits such as these not only offered the opportunity to be recorded in fashionable clothes, but they also suggested the virtues of the well-run household.

The double portrait at Althrey Hall is almost certainly that of Jane Hanmer and her husband Richard Ellis, a gentleman who could trace his ancestry back for many generations (see Fig. 9). It is located in a first-floor chamber where all the walls are decorated with imitation paned textile hanging. The overall effect is richly decorative. The room was again a private chamber, possibly used for receiving guests. The painting can be dated to around the mid-1550s, and particularly interesting is the ermine collar worn by Jane Hanmer: a sign of wealth and high social standing. Richard Ellis is depicted in the latest fashion: with a forked beard and wearing a fur-trimmed gown. As with many of the Tudor portraits of courtiers, this wall painting has dynastic connotations. The woman holds a crocus, which could be read as a symbol of fertility, and this in turn tallies with fact that the man is holding his codpiece, decorated with a red ribbon – Jane Hanmer and Richard Ellis

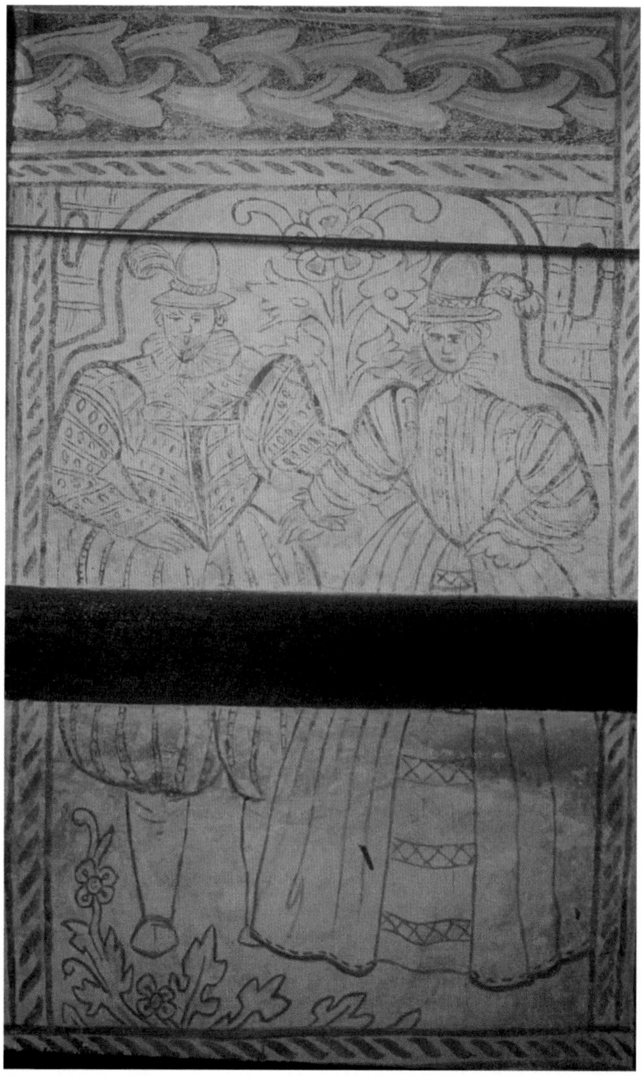

Figure 18 Dowles Manor, Worcestershire: a wall painting in the first-floor chamber, which incorporates a portrait. *(Photo: M. Moran)*

had nine sons and four daughters. Painted towards the end of Ellis' life, this picture could be interpreted as a record of his achievements as head of a large family of ancient lineage, producing children to secure its future.

The portrait at Coalknap Farm, Barry, which is probably of Jane Andrew, could well have been painted to mark her marriage in 1584 to Alexander Grant (see Fig. 8). She is holding out invitingly a bunch of three gillyflowers, a symbol of betrothal. The painting is located at the bottom of the spiral stairs leading from the ground-floor hall to a first-floor chamber. Her exaggeratedly narrow waist, the inviting pose with symbolic flowers, and the painting's location at the foot of the stairs all suggest the painting was deliberately placed on the way to the sleeping chamber. One can only speculate on quite what message this conveyed, and who was intended to view the painting.

The paintings at New Hall

On the basis of such examples, is it now possible to put forward some explanation for the significance of the paintings at New Hall? Although an interpretation of these paintings can only be speculative, it is worth attempting to explore what meanings might be ascribed to them, and consequently what they may have signified to their patron.

First, the scheme is located in the parlour, so must have been intended for select viewing only and not for general consumption. The figures are all expensively attired, announcing the gentry rank of the occupants. The playing of musical instruments was an accomplishment of the gentry, so again rank is signified. The main figures could be the owner and his wife, in which case this could be seen as a form of portrait, but there appears to be more to it than that. The figure holding the flowers is surely assigning some attribute to the main female by holding over her head the gillyflower, a symbol of betrothal. The musicians suggest a celebration of some sort, though the significance of the eagle and ape/devil is obscure (Fig. 19). The eagle was an ancient symbol of power and victory; allegorically, it signified pride. On account of its sharp vision, it was also used in the Renaissance as an attribute of *Sight*, one of the Five Senses. Another, *Taste*, was sometimes depicted as an ape, in which case the musicians could signify *Hearing*. The hare, located within the dado decoration, usually symbolised lust and fecundity.

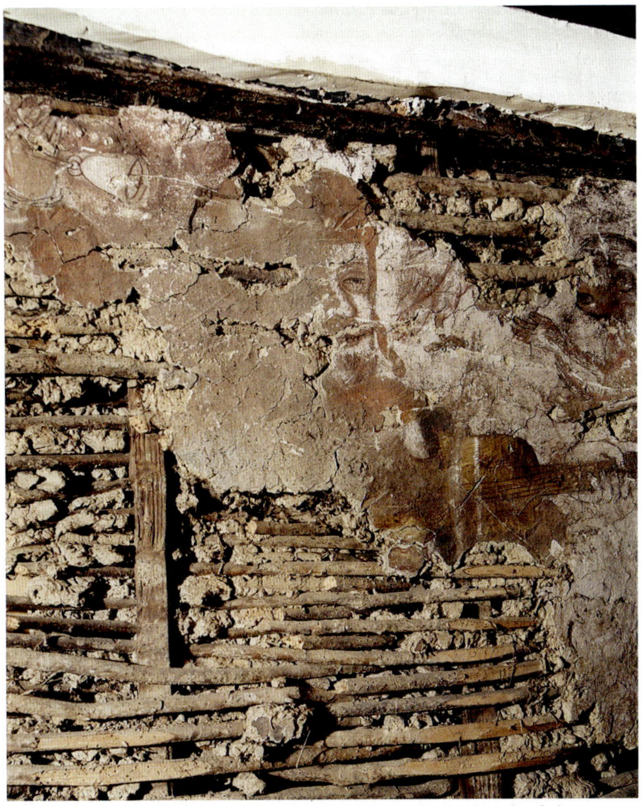

Figure 19 New Hall, near Ticklerton, Shropshire: detail of the upper section of panel 3 showing an ape and what may be an eagle. *(© English Heritage. NMR)*

It is plausible that the painting represents George Jenkes and his wife shortly after Jenkes entered the ranks of armigers. He had acquired New Hall via his marriage, which could explain the gillyflower (and possibly the hare, signifying their offspring). With this explanation, the musicians are celebrating his new fortunes and his wife is displaying that she has the accomplishments appropriate to their new rank by playing the lute. The eagle would signify his pride in his new position, and also his sharpness. Of course, there could be more than one story depicted here, and the scenes could be loosely based on the Five Senses, displaying the sophistication of the owner, reinforcing his armigerous status, and signifying his capacity to communicate in the same language as his new peers.

Alternatively, the ape could be a demon figure, in which case the painting could be read as Jenkes vanquishing evil of some kind. One of the figures at the left-most panel looks very much as though he has a tonsure and could therefore be a monk. He is shown in profile, as is the ape/demon – the common medieval means of representing evil figures. If these images are introduced into the discussion, a whole new set of meanings could be derived.

Whatever the exact iconography, a number of interpretations could be made, all of which are more or less guesswork to the modern mind. In the 16th century this ambiguity of interpretation was perhaps part of the 'game'. Ambiguous images, with multiple layered meanings, would exactly accord with the Elizabethan way of thinking. What is certain is that the decoration was of considerable significance to the owner. It is likely that Jenkes wished it to be viewed by a select group of people, and intended that they should assign certain laudable attributes to him as a result.

Conclusions

Wall paintings are an important element in vernacular buildings, offering a valuable source of information into the social and cultural aspects of the lives of ordinary people. The intangible qualities of the mindset of those commissioning the paintings may be glimpsed at through the subjects they chose to have painted in their houses. The show of expense through richly coloured, boldly textured designs; the knowledge of wider cultural horizons hinted at with classical allusions; the communication in the sophisticated language of emblems and allegory; the emulation of courtiers and greater gentry in portrait painting – all these betray the social and cultural values not evident in other records at the vernacular level and provide an invaluable insight into the social sensibilities of people in the late 16th and early 17th century.

Editors' note

The buildings mentioned in the text are private buildings *not* open to the public.

Notes

1. Baird 2002.
2. Harpham 1982.
3. Gedde 1615.
4. Bath 2003.
5. Witney 1989.
6. Howard 1995.
7. Freeman 1966.

References

Baird K. 2002, *Secular Wall Painting in the Sixteenth and Seventeenth Centuries*, unpublished D.Phil thesis, University of Oxford

Baird K. 2003, 'An overview of secular wall paintings in the sixteenth and seventeenth centuries in the Welsh Marches', in *Vernacular Architecture*, vol. 34, Maney Publications, London

Bath M. 2003, *Renaissance Decorative Painting in Scotland*, National Museums of Scotland Publishing, Edinburgh

Freeman R. 1966, *English Emblem Books*, Chatto and Windus, London

Gedde W. 1615, *A Booke of Sundry Draughtes*, Leadenhall Press, London

Harpham G. 1982, *On the Grotesque: Strategies of Contradiction in Art and Literature*, Princeton University Press, Princeton NJ

Howard M. 1995, *The Tudor Image*, Tate Gallery, London

McKerrow R.B. and Ferguson F.S. 1932, *Title Page Borders Used in England and Scotland 1485–1640*, Bibliographical Society, London

Wells-Cole A. 1997, *Art and Decoration in Elizabethan and Jacobean England: The Influence of Continental Prints, 1558–1625*, Yale University Press, New Haven and London

Witney, G. 1989, *A Choice of Emblemes*, facsimile edition, Scolar Press, Aldershot

The author

Kathryn Davies (formerly Baird) completed her doctoral research on secular wall painting in the Welsh Marches in 2002 and subsequently published an article in *Vernacular Architecture* on the principal findings of the research (Baird 2003). She has worked in building conservation for many years and is currently a Historic Buildings Inspector for English Heritage. She is particularly interested in what wall paintings can reveal about vernacular life in the early modern period.

Pattern and colour in late 16th- and 17th-century secular wall and panel paintings in Suffolk: an overview

Andrea Kirkham

Introduction

In Suffolk, over 400 secular wall paintings from the period around 1500 to 1700 have so far been identified.[1] This paper will focus on late 16th- to late 17th-century schemes in those vernacular buildings which were the typical houses of the lesser gentry, of merchants and of yeomen. It was a period that saw significant changes in fashion and taste, particularly a shift from richly patterned interiors popular from c.1575 to c.1610/20 (termed 'Phase 1' schemes) to a new aesthetic for simpler 'Plain schemes', which dominated practice from c.1610/20 to the late 17th century ('Phase 2').[2]

Nevertheless during Phase 2 a market remained for richly patterned and polychrome interiors, employing fashionable motifs such as imitation panelling. These more ostentatious styles were preferred by a smaller social group, typically urban-based in the south and south-east of the county, around the regional centre Ipswich.

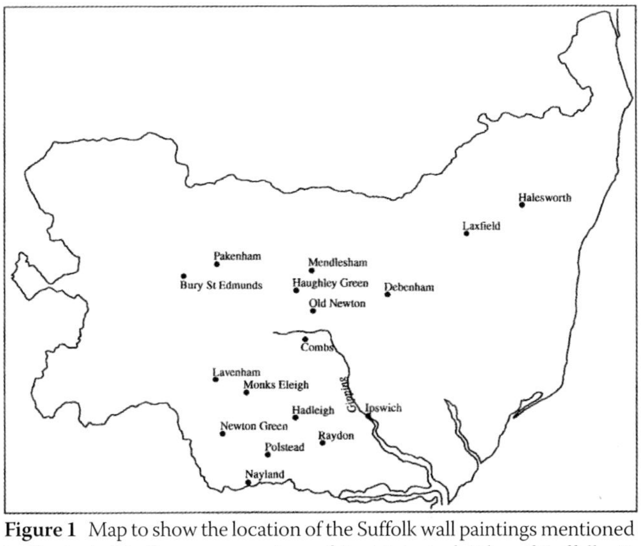

Figure 1 Map to show the location of the Suffolk wall paintings mentioned in the text. *(Outline map courtesy of* An Historical Atlas of Suffolk, *D. Dymond and E. Martin (eds), Suffolk County Council Archaeological Service, 1999)*

The majority of Suffolk schemes in Phase 1 are urban, or found in the higher status rural sites in south Suffolk, whereas wall painting at vernacular level in rural north Suffolk seems to have been virtually non-existent.[3] The numbers of rural sites with painted schemes, however, increases dramatically in the 17th century, as Plain schemes become a popular form of decoration not only in the towns and south Suffolk but also in the 'yeoman' houses of rural north Suffolk.

Although an extensive literature covers the styles and pattern sources of this period, surprisingly little information is found on the role played by colour within the vernacular interior. Availability and cost of the pigments were important considerations, but the cultural and ideological backgrounds of the patron and the patron's peer group also had a strong impact on the way colour was used. Blue, for instance, becomes more popular in Phase 2, and is clearly associated with conspicuous display. The appearance of blue verditer in the palette is an important element in the taste for lavish architectural schemes and imitation panelling in Phase 2.

Social, economic and cultural context

The county of Suffolk is defined by its eastern coastline, which stretches from the Orwell Haven in the south up to Lowestoft. The Little Ouse and Waveney rivers in the north, and the Stour in the south, mark its inland boundaries. Suffolk was a prosperous and advanced county in the 16th and 17th centuries, with a relatively high standard of living. Agriculture was the means of livelihood for the majority of the population, and the period was one of economic expansion that brought wealth to the rural gentry and yeomen farmers. In the early 17th century, Robert Reyce described the yeomen of Suffolk: 'their continual under living, saving, and the immunities from the costly charge of these unfaithfull times, do make them so to grow with the wealth of this world'.[4] Greater prosperity led to building, particularly in north Suffolk where many houses were first rebuilt in the 16th and then altered in the early 17th century. In the south-west of the county, buildings tended to be converted rather than rebuilt.

The cloth industry provided the greatest opportunity for families (such as the Springs of Lavenham, and the Martins of Long Melford) to dramatically increase their wealth. The years 1450–1530 saw a boom in the woollen cloth industry, especially in the broadcloth areas encompassed by Clare, Bury St Edmunds and East Bergholt.[5] Later, however, the cloth trade was hit by a series of recessions. Those towns producing broadcloth – Bury, Lavenham and East Bergholt – were particularly affected because they were unable to adapt to the new draperies introduced by immigrants from the Low Countries in the 16th century.[6]

Bury St Edmunds and Ipswich

The two principal towns of the county were Bury St Edmunds and Ipswich. Until the early 16th century, the Abbey Church of St Edmund dominated Bury. After the Dissolution, the town was left without a clear structure of authority, and did not receive its charter of incorporation until 1606.[7] Post-Reformation Bury was noted for its advanced Protestantism and town-appointed preachers. It was an important industrial town during the 16th and 17th centuries, with a brief spell of increased prosperity from c.1680 to 1700 which is reflected in internal room decorations characterised by a proliferation of bolection mouldings, barley-sugar twist balusters and overmantel paintings, exemplified by those at Cupola House, Bury St Edmunds, built 1693.[8]

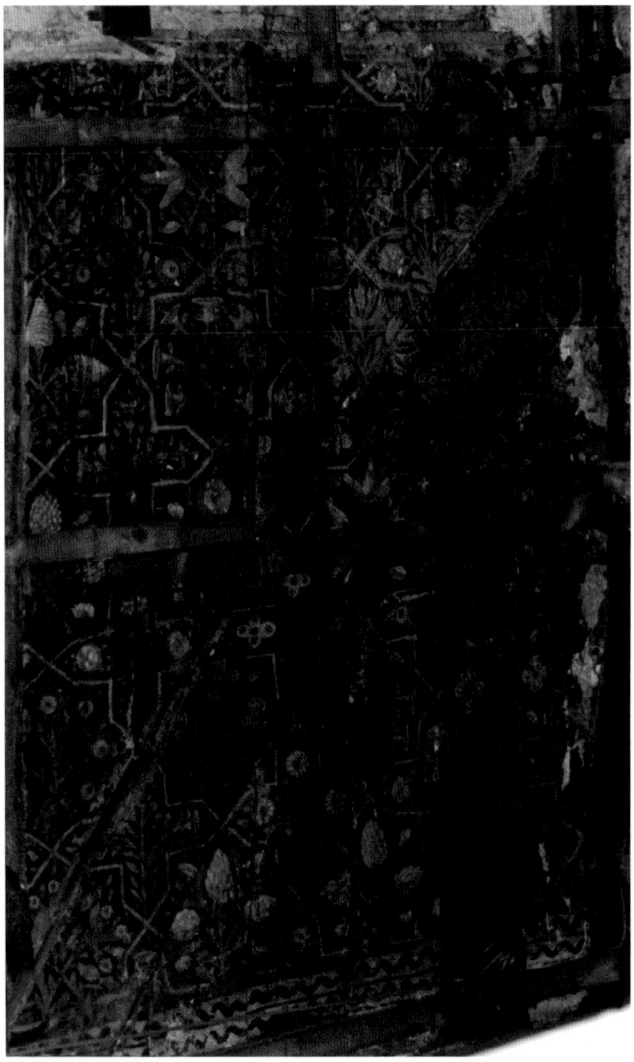

Figure 2 Bury St Edmunds, Suffolk: imitation textile decoration. *(© A. Kirkham)*

By the 18th century Bury St Edmunds had evolved into a key social centre. Buildings were given new facades, concealing earlier timber framing, and the town drew praise from contemporaries. Daniel Defoe commented that 'the beauty of this town consists in the number of gentry who dwell in and near it, the polite conversation among them, the affluence and plenty they live in',[9] echoing comments from a mid-17th-century antiquary who remarked 'many of the Gentry buy or hire houses in Bury because of the pleasantness of the place'.[10]

By contrast Ipswich was a chartered borough, with a more coherent town structure and established oligarchy.[11] An important commercial centre and a major port, Ipswich was described by William Smith in 1588 as 'the greatest Towne in Suffolk and one of the most famous Townes in England at this present, for trafike and other Respects'.[12] The late 1600s saw Ipswich in economic decline, but by the mid-18th century recovery was underway, and the town finally emerged as a key centre for the corn trade.[13]

The numerous wall paintings surviving in Bury St Edmunds enable a degree of interpretation not possible in Ipswich, where the vicissitudes of time and planning policies have destroyed many historic buildings. Nevertheless, enough wall paintings survive in both towns to illustrate the very different tastes and attitudes of their residents, embodied in the way colour and pattern were used.

Phase 1: c.1575 to c.1610/20

The majority of Phase 1 schemes are found in urban centres or (more rarely) in rural sites south of the Gipping valley, often in close proximity to a town. Phase 1 is characterised by schemes based on textiles not only in their format – with decorative borders infilled with painting – but also in terms of their function within the interior. The first impression on entering a room with Phase 1 decoration would be, typically, of expensive textile hangings imitating the way real textiles were used in grander houses. These schemes usually depend on a combination of surface pattern and colour to create rich effects, employing designs such as antiquework, grotesques, Moresque motifs and foliate patterns. Black backgrounds were particularly fashionable in urban interiors (Fig. 2) and red backgrounds can also be found (see Fig. 5).

Another fashionable form of decoration was black-and-white schemes. These are some of the most sophisticated paintings of the period, and can be seen for example in a gentry house at Polstead (Fig. 3) and in towns such as Bury St Edmunds, Debenham and Ipswich. More unusual are grotesque schemes with coloured backgrounds, which in Suffolk often make extensive use of organic pigments. This type is exemplified by a painting in Lavenham that imitates a textile hanging and uses candelabra grotesques against a red and green counter-colour background (Fig. 4). Here the green is indigo/woad mixed with organic yellow, charcoal black and yellow ochre, and the vertical red backgrounds are a red lake,[14] a rich purplish-red that contrasts with the red lead of the frieze.

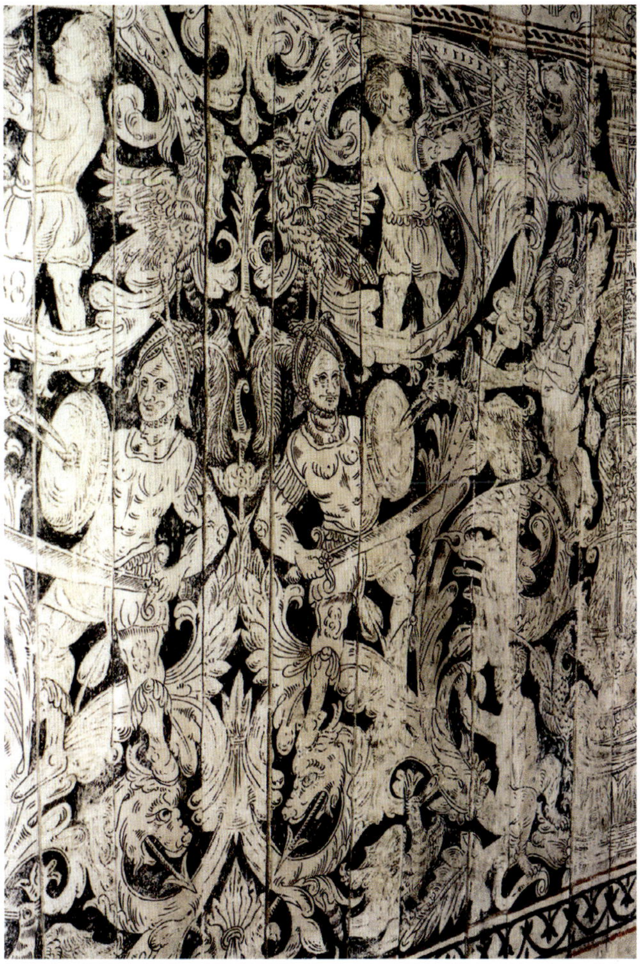

Figure 3 Polstead, Suffolk: antiquework decoration. *(© A. Kirkham)*

The use of a fugitive pigment such as brazilwood was not seen as problematic. Wall paintings were ephemeral, to be covered over as dictated by fashion, or by redecorations celebrating family occasions such as marriages or by changes of ownership. The brazilwood survives unfaded in Lavenham because, soon after painting, it was covered over by an early 17th-century scheme on lath and plaster.

Pigments

Availability and cost undoubtedly affected the choice of certain pigments for some schemes, and technical considerations may have restricted the use of others. The complexity of the design was also a component of the expense. The black and white pigments used in antiquework and grotesque schemes were cheap, but the labour costs were relatively high.[15] The cultural and ideological backgrounds of the patron and his peer group were also factors in the selection of pattern and pigment. It is arguable that the rejection by some patrons of certain styles and rich colours indicates tastes and attitudes in direct opposition to those of patrons who chose to have highly decorated, ostentatious rooms. In Bury St Edmunds in Phase 2, patrons seem to have been deliberately choosing simpler, plainer schemes with a restricted palette and a more limited range of motifs.

A wide range of pigments has been identified in Suffolk secular wall paintings, including natural and manufactured mineral pigments, and organic pigments derived from dyestuffs. Although earth pigments were used in Phase 1 schemes in the urban and rural south, bright mid-priced pigments such as green verditer, orpiment, organic reds and yellows seem to have been preferred. More unusual is a blackish organic pigment (now faded) which was probably derived from oak galls; this is the first identification of the use of this particular pigment in English wall painting.[16] Vermilion, typically, is used sparingly at vernacular level, often in pigment mixtures to make pinks. Comparing this range of pigments to those

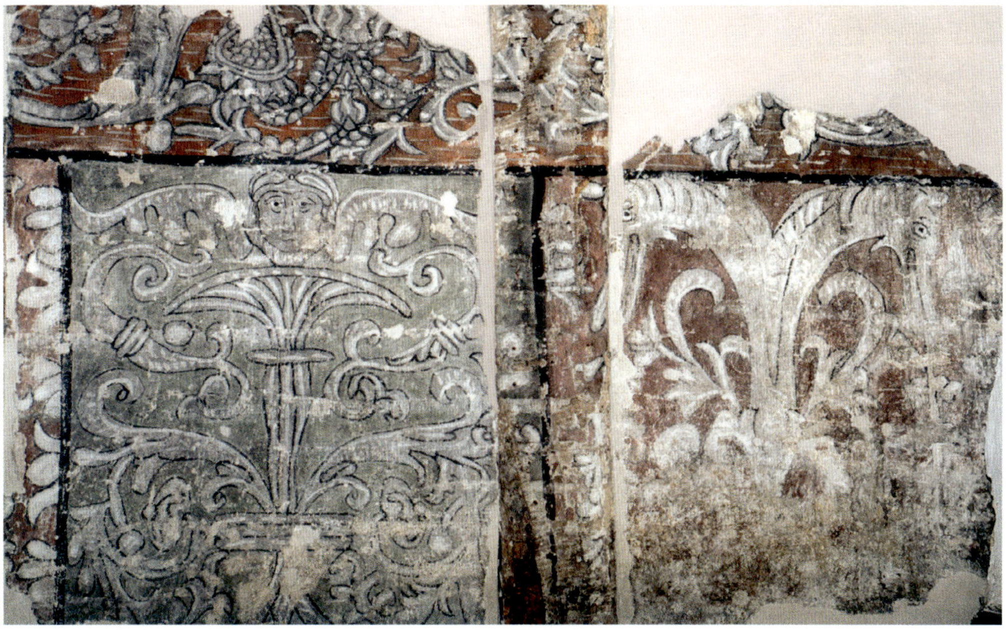

Figure 4 Lavenham, Suffolk: grotesque decoration. This scheme makes extensive use of organic pigments. *(© A. Kirkham)*

identified in schemes of similar status and date in Norfolk suggests a significant difference in taste and attitude to colour. In Norfolk earth pigments were often used in a sophisticated way to create a wide range of yellows and reds. There were, however, some important and specific uses for the earth pigments found in painted decoration in East Anglia and elsewhere. Red ochre, for example, was ubiquitous throughout the whole period for imitation brickwork, and yellow ochre was used for imitation oak panelling.

Of the other pigments identified in Suffolk decorative painting, lead-tin yellow was rarely employed (to date it has only been found in the internal decoration of one gentry site and one external scheme). Although azurite, an expensive blue pigment, is found in opulent high status interiors, it does not seem to occur in Suffolk in vernacular buildings. In fact, blue of any kind is rare in Phase 1. Where indigo/woad, the most common blue, is identified, it is usually in pigment mixtures to make green.[17] Blue verditer and smalt, both manufactured mineral blue pigments have only been found in Phase 2 patterned schemes.

Phase 2: c.1610/20 to late 17th century

Plain schemes

The change in fashion from the patterns and colours of Phase 1 to simpler, plainer decoration is illustrated by the first-floor 'best chamber' in Gracechurch Street, Debenham (Fig. 5). In the 17th century, an imitation textile scheme was painted over with green columns on a white background, the principal ceiling timbers being painted green to complete the ensemble. At Mendlesham, where both the parlour chamber and the hall chamber were decorated with imitation textiles in the late 16th century, the parlour was left unpainted until the 17th century, when it was decorated with a Plain scheme.[18] Elsewhere in the county, and particularly in rural north Suffolk, new 17th-century schemes were also applied to previously unpainted interiors (Old Newton and Pakenham are examples).

Plain schemes: style and colour

Although the detailed designs of Plain schemes vary, all make use of the existing timber frame while typically ignoring structural braces. Where infill panels are wide, or the support is lath and plaster, imitation studs may be painted in. Plain schemes can imitate textiles of the type described by Thornton as 'paned', loom-widths of material being 'impaned' with another (Fig. 6).[19] Sometimes the painted studs are turned into classical columns (see Fig. 5).

Alternatively, imitation textiles might be embellished with tasselled valences, a type common in Bury St Edmunds. Arcading, often with drop pendants, was an alternative particularly popular in urban and higher status rural sites (Fig. 7). These parallel the drop pendants common in contemporary carved woodwork, used for example on the pulpits at St Mary's Church, Yaxley, 1635, and St Mary's Church, Dennington (dated 1625, converted in 1628).[20]

Plain schemes usually had a single colour applied to the timbers, whether red, grey, black, yellow, green or blue, and the infill panels were left unpainted or painted white. The disposition of colour between rooms could reflect their relative hierarchy and importance, with green and blue usually reserved for the 'best' chamber.[21] Green, for instance, is used in the first-floor 'best' chamber in Debenham, but grey is used for the circulation areas. At East Street, Colchester, the two ground-floor rooms and one first-floor chamber are painted red, and another first-floor chamber is painted blue. Blue and green Plain schemes are typically found in urban houses; green, for example, proliferates in Bury St Edmunds. Those green schemes found in rural sites seem to be in houses where the occupiers had some degree of social pretension.[22] The

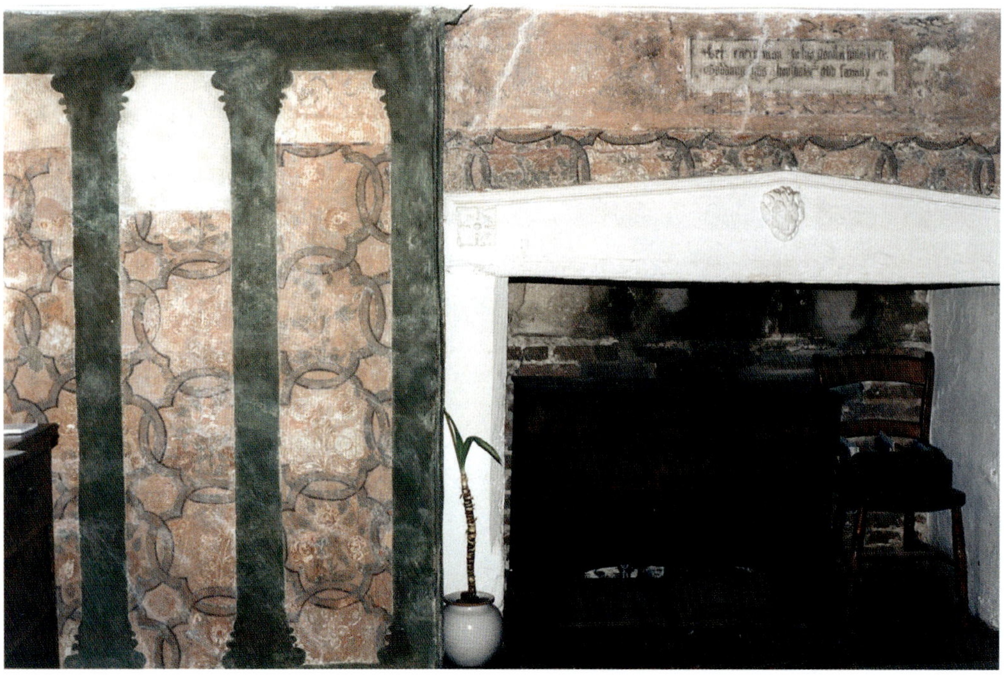

Figure 5 Debenham, Suffolk: the Phase 1 scheme was obliterated by a 17th-century Plain scheme of green columns on a white background. *(© A. Kirkham)*

Gardiners, for instance, at Manor Farmhouse, Monks Eleigh, were yeomen aspiring to be gentlemen in the first half of the 17th century (see Fig. 7).[23]

Pigments used for green schemes might be verdigris, or pigment mixtures with either yellow ochre or orpiment and indigo/woad as typical components. Blue verditer has never been identified in the blue variants, which employ indigo/woad or are optical blues (black mixed with white to form a bluish paint). The red, yellow, black and grey schemes use red and yellow earths, carbon black and chalk, not the bright mid-priced pigments seen in the patterned schemes of either Phase 1 or Phase 2. The Plain schemes represent a general change in attitude towards decoration, reflecting the fashion for plainer schemes seen at the court of James I. For 'godly' patrons, Plain schemes were an acceptable form of decoration within an ideological context. Numerous Plain schemes are found in Bury St Edmunds, a town known for its Puritanism.

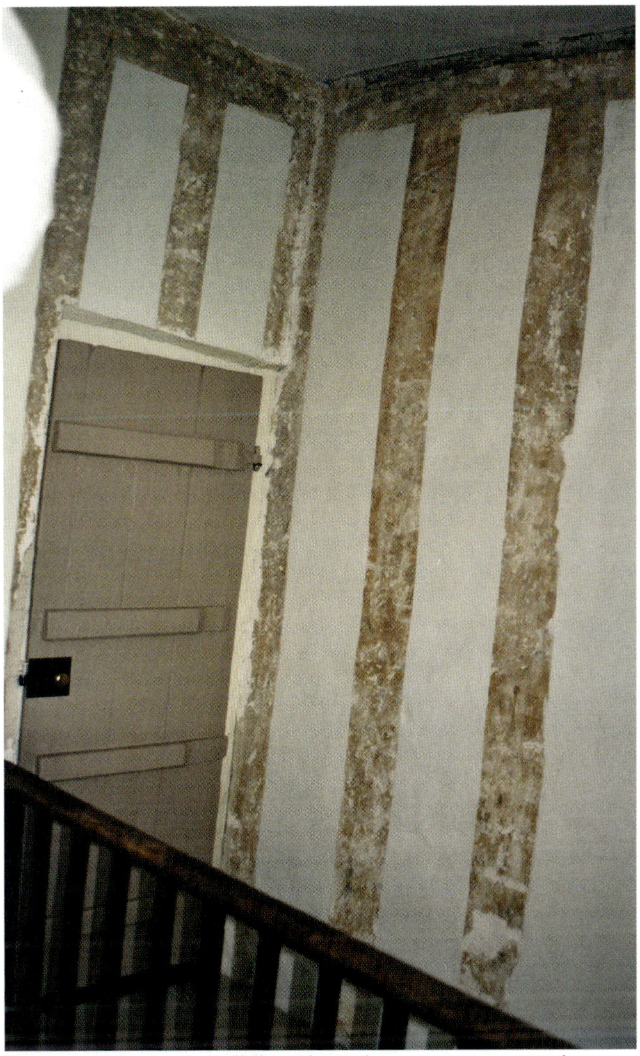

Figure 6 Halesworth, Suffolk: a Plain scheme imitating a textile. *(© A. Kirkham)*

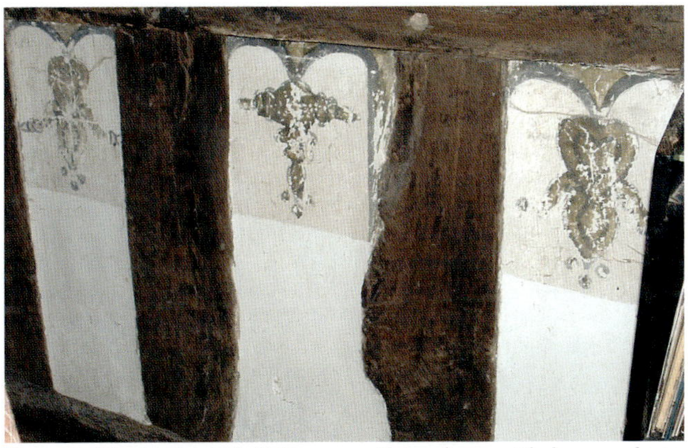

Figure 7 Monks Eleigh, Suffolk: a green Plain scheme with drop pendants. *(© A. Kirkham)*

Single colour schemes before the 17th century

Data from documents and a limited number of extant sites provide evidence for the use of a single colour applied to internal timbers before the 17th century, typically employing red or yellow earth pigments.[24] Simon Rabos for instance, was paid 73s 4d, 'for the pargetting and whitening of the whole of the great hall, together with the ochreing of the posts and beams, using his own supplies of chalk, size and okkere' at the Tower of London in 1337.[25] Accounts for painting timbers yellow appear with some regularity in the Kings Works associated with Henry VIII, such as the timber work of a chamber on the east side of a gallery at Bridewell Palace, London which was coloured with 'sprusse yellow oker' in 1534.[26] Extant examples of single colour painted timbers in medieval and early 16th-century contexts include the red beneath sooted timbers in the hall at Church Farm, Fressingfield, Suffolk, thought to date from the late 14th century. Red timbers can be seen beneath layers of limewash and the early 16th-century saints and scrolling foliage in the Canon's Cloister, the College of St George, Windsor Castle, and early 16th-century yellow timbers survive in the base court at Hampton Court Palace.

Sometimes the single colour schemes were meant to imitate the type of textiles that have equidistant counter-colour vertical panes. This can be seen in Bromley Hall, 43 Gillender Street, London, a high status non-domestic building (c.1490s), where the painted scheme makes use of close studding. Yellow ochre was applied to the timbers, alternating with white on the infill panels. Thus, the colour both emphasises the timbers and creates an impression of striped textiles.[27] At Bromley, these imitation textiles would have been seen at the same time as actual textiles in the adjacent room. An alternative arrangement can be seen at Sutton House, Hackney, where yellow was used in the late 16th or early 17th century to create a framework for the south wall of the low parlour, reflecting real timber-framing elsewhere in the room.[28] The spaces between were filled with fixed textiles; thus an apparently simple decoration was originally more elaborate than first appears.

Date, range and distribution of Plain schemes

To date, the surviving evidence suggests that Plain schemes appear in Suffolk early in the 17th century, with the majority found in the middle two quarters of that century. External painted examples are known, and variants of this form of decoration have been identified in the American east coast states. The emergence of Plain schemes at the vernacular level in the early 17th century appears to be a restart, rather than a continuation, of the single colour decoration seen earlier. The imitation skirtings found in vernacular buildings from the late 17th century, however, represent another shift in fashion.[29] Typically, the timber-frame structure is still visible, but unified by a layer of white with the imitation skirting along the bottom edge. This distinction needs to be made because the treatment of the wall surface is quite different to that used by the Plain schemes, which not only make use of the existing structure, but serve to enhance it. It can be argued, therefore, that in the late 17th century there is a transitional period when it was still acceptable to see the timber and infill panel structure, albeit disguised by a layer of white paint, even in important rooms. Later, the unevenness of the structure is visually unacceptable (except, perhaps, in low status rooms or circulation areas) and it is levelled with lath and plaster, or a wall covering such as panelling or wallpaper.

It is, however, clear that the Plain schemes were a form of decoration employed by a broader section of society than the patterned types, and with a wider geographical spread. That many of the rural examples in Suffolk are north of the Gipping valley is an accident of survival. The problem is that owners and conservation professionals do not recognise them, and timbers tend to be scrubbed bare without appropriate investigation. The grey schemes, for instance, are particularly difficult to identify because they resemble dirt. A greater problem, however, is one of attitude – they are simply not considered important because they are not 'artistic'. The result is the loss and destruction of a type of decoration which was once, it seems, common to many houses in the 17th century, certainly in Suffolk and south Norfolk. The evidence for Plain schemes is more scattered in other counties, but this may prove to be a problem of recognition and survival, rather than reflecting a pattern of use.[30]

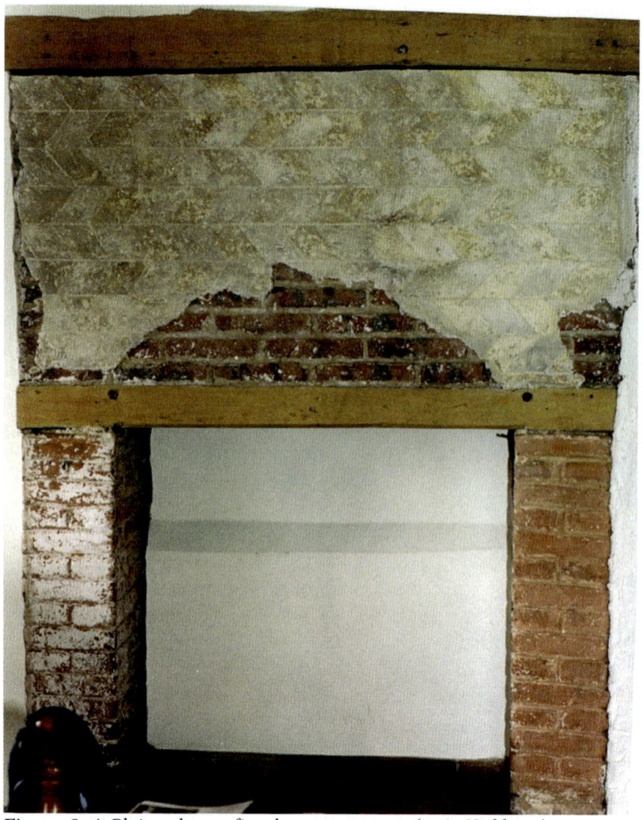

Figure 8 A Plain scheme fireplace treatment. *(© A. Kirkham)*

Plain schemes as part of a decorative ensemble

Where the evidence survives, it can be seen that Plain schemes were intended as part of a decorative ensemble, with the treatment of ceilings and fireplaces being important elements. Ceilings were variously treated; they might be lath and plaster with the principal timbers coloured to match the walls, or only the soffits of joists coloured to match the walls and lath and plaster on the boards. Alternatively soffits and sides of the joists were painted, abutting the lath and plaster. Where the ceiling timbers were painted, they were always painted to match the wall timbers. Treatment of the fireplace varied; the chimneybreasts might be plain or decorated with, for example, simple geometric patterns marked out with incised lines (Fig. 8).

The evidence suggests that the form and degree of decoration on the ceilings and fireplaces not only indicated the level of disposable income, but also the status and hierarchy of the rooms. The decorations of two houses in rural north Suffolk, Haughley Green and Laxfield, illustrate some of these points.[31] Neither building seems to have been painted when first built, but instead both were decorated during 17th-century refurbishments. In both cases the overall colour theme is grey, but the manner in which the paint is disposed in the various rooms, the degree and quality of detailing – particularly the treatment of the fireplaces and ceilings – is quite different.

Laxfield is a three-cell house, in which the parlour was clearly seen as the most important. This was panelled with an overmantel and an internal porch. Grey timbers now visible by the door to the right of the fireplace were originally interpreted as being part of the lobby decoration leading into the parlour (Fig. 9). The early 17th-century plaster ceiling has a moulded cornice of a type quite often seen in the area. By contrast, a two-cell house at Haughley Green has the timbers in the parlour painted grey, with a plain fireplace. The ceiling is lath and plaster with a crude plaster moulding for the cornice (Fig. 10). The parlour chambers show a similar contrast between the houses. In both the degree and quality of embellishment in the parlour chamber is significantly less than in the parlour itself.

Whether or not a room has been left unpainted can also be important: it can imply room function or that a wall covering (for example panelling) was used instead of a wall painting. The hall chamber at Haughley was unpainted because it was used for storage, and the parlour at Laxfield unpainted because it was panelled. Comparing the decorative schemes at Laxfield and Haughley allows us to draw certain conclusions about the relative status and income of their occupiers. Both were relatively prosperous, but with different levels of disposable income.[32]

Patterned schemes

This group of paintings includes a small number of richly patterned textile schemes, imitation panelling, three schemes derived from emblems and three subject paintings at Newton Green, Hadleigh and Combs near Stowmarket. The subject paintings include scenes from the *Life of Samson* and the *Martyrdom of St Stephen* at Newton Green, dated 1623; two scenes of the *Life of Joseph* in Hadleigh which must post-date the 1612 publication of the *Liber Genesis* by Crispijn de Passe

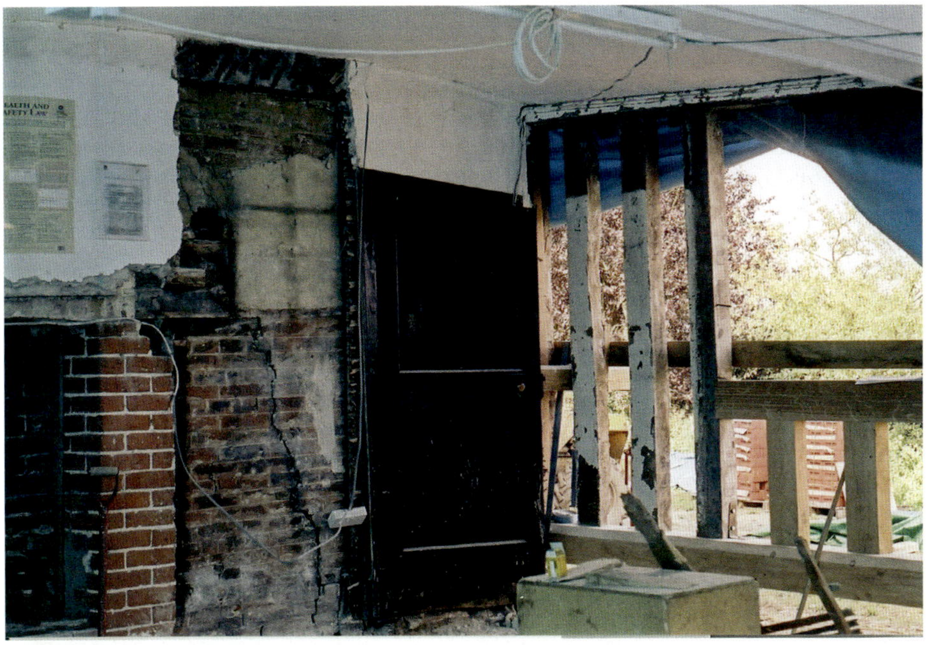

Figure 9 Laxfield, Suffolk: the parlour. *(© A. Kirkham)*

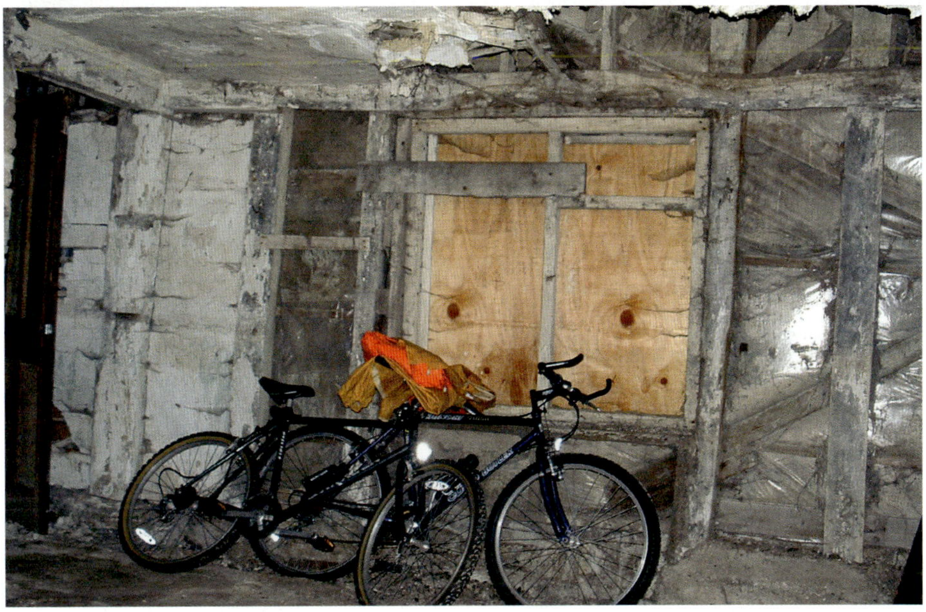

Figure 10 Haughley Green, Suffolk: the parlour. *(© A. Kirkham)*

(the source for the paintings); and the *Sacrifice of Isaac* at Combs, which probably dates from c.1630 on building evidence but is copied from a 1538 woodcut by Hans Holbein.[33] The Phase 2 patterned schemes and the subject paintings are found south of the Gipping valley and, to date, have not been found in the rural north of the county.

Characteristic of this phase are the designs based on imitation stile and rail panelling (Fig. 11), sometimes with elaborate strapwork cartouches, a form of decoration particularly popular in Ipswich and its hinterland, such as the gentry house at Raydon.

These schemes reflect an important change in the way the lavish vernacular interior was decorated: from the textile-influenced designs popular in the late 16th and early 17th century to architectural decoration and/or imitation panelling. Blue becomes more common; in the Suffolk examples, this is usually good quality blue verditer, a relatively cheap pigment that resembles the much more expensive azurite (an impression of affluence at a fraction of the cost).

To date there has been no decoration of this type – or for that matter any use of blue verditer – identified in any rural north Suffolk site. Neither have such schemes been found in Bury St Edmunds, a town known for its Puritanism, where texts and Plain schemes, more ideologically acceptable, seem to have prevailed.[34]

Plain schemes, panelling and imitation panelling

Plain schemes and imitation panelling have been discussed separately, but were they ever used within the same building at the same time? A major problem is that our view of the 17th-century vernacular interior is distorted because so much has been lost during restoration. Even though present-day owners might retain the patterned schemes, they have often not been aware of – or have chosen not to keep – Plain schemes. Despite the fragmentary nature of the remaining material, bringing together the scattered pieces of evidence suggests that in some of the higher-status rural houses and in some urban locations the imitation textile-type Plain schemes were used in the less important living rooms and in the circulation areas leading to the more elaborately decorated 'best' room, perhaps displaying real or fictive panelling.

Sufficient archaeological evidence survives at Laxfield to show that the 'best' room (in this case the parlour) had real panelling, while the other rooms were decorated with Plain schemes imitating textiles. Thus Laxfield sets a principle. It is possible that the yellow scheme in a small chamber at Halesworth (see Fig. 6) was contemporary with c.1640 real panelling and a richly carved mantelpiece in the parlour. Other possible examples of this layout can be found at Bury St Edmunds, Colchester and Hemel Hempstead, suggesting that this combination of imitation textiles with panelling or fictive panelling in the 'best' room may have been more common in the vernacular interior than at first appears.

Blue rooms

Historically blue is associated with status and expense; the lavish 17th-century schemes using blue (typically alongside other bright mid-priced pigments) were clearly associated with conspicuous display. The decoration at Birch Street, Nayland is an example. Until recently the parlour had a polychrome ceiling and is recorded as having had a landscape on the chimney-breast. All that survives now are fragments of sumptuous wall decoration, but these used both blue verditer and indigo/woad (Fig. 12). A first-floor chamber in East Street, Colchester has a blue Plain scheme, imitating a textile hanging, with a matching ceiling of the c.1640s (Fig. 13).

The schemes at Nayland and Colchester are probably versions of the 'blue room', a fashion emanating from aristocratic Parisian interiors of the early 17th century. The Marquise de Rambouillet's c.1620 Chambre Bleue, in the Hotel Rambouillet in Paris, was painted blue, the walls were hung with blue textiles, and other fabrics were blue embellished with gold and silver.[35] This influenced Parisian interiors from 1625 onwards.[36] It is possible that Queen Henrietta Maria, who arrived in England in 1625, knew of this or similar rooms, which may have influenced the use of blue paint in the Queen's Cabinet or Drawing Room at Greenwich.[37] William Murray may also have been aware of the fashion when he commissioned Matthew Gooderick to paint the Great Dining Room at Ham House in 1638 with the most lavish and expensive decoration, in contrast to the graining and green used elsewhere.[38] Clearly, the Colchester scheme reflects a very different taste to the

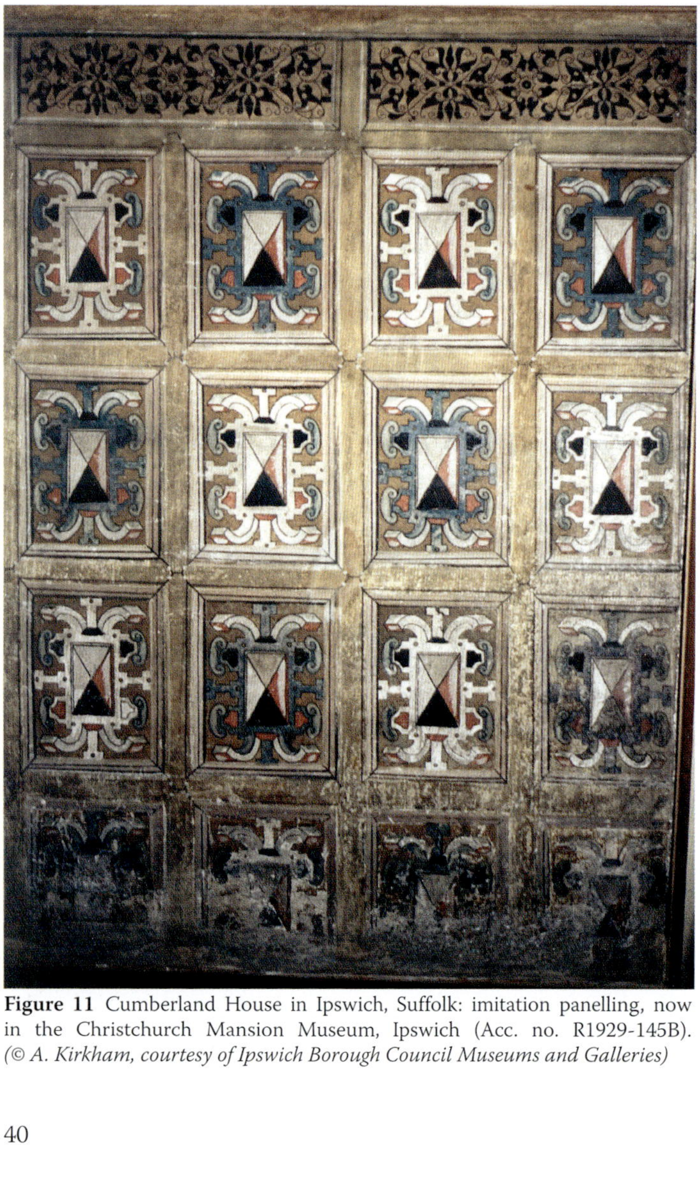

Figure 11 Cumberland House in Ipswich, Suffolk: imitation panelling, now in the Christchurch Mansion Museum, Ipswich (Acc. no. R1929-145B). *(© A. Kirkham, courtesy of Ipswich Borough Council Museums and Galleries)*

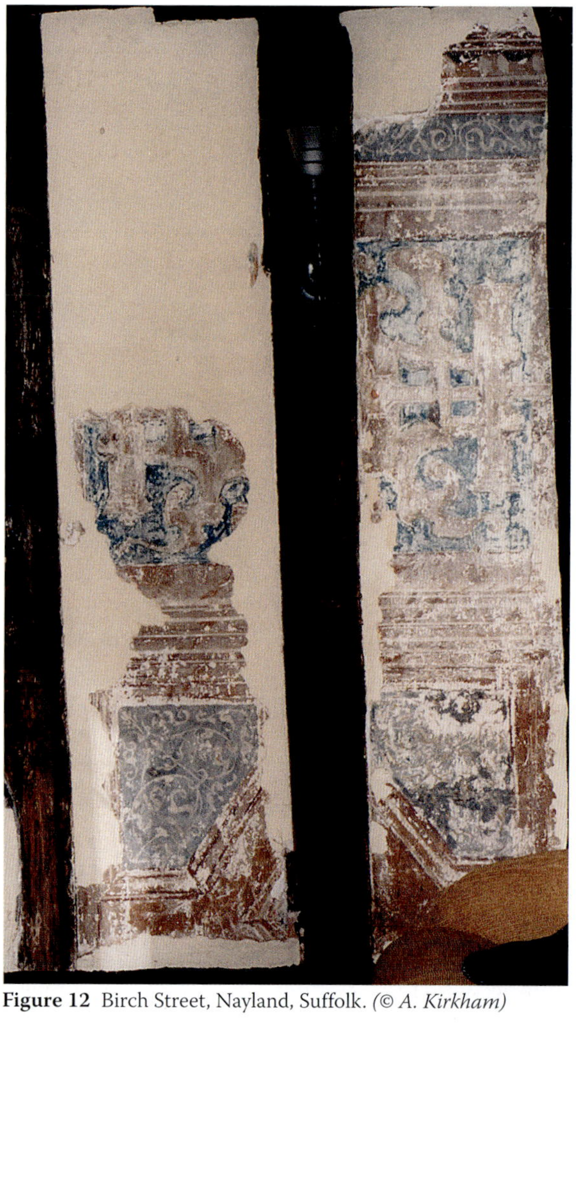

Figure 12 Birch Street, Nayland, Suffolk. *(© A. Kirkham)*

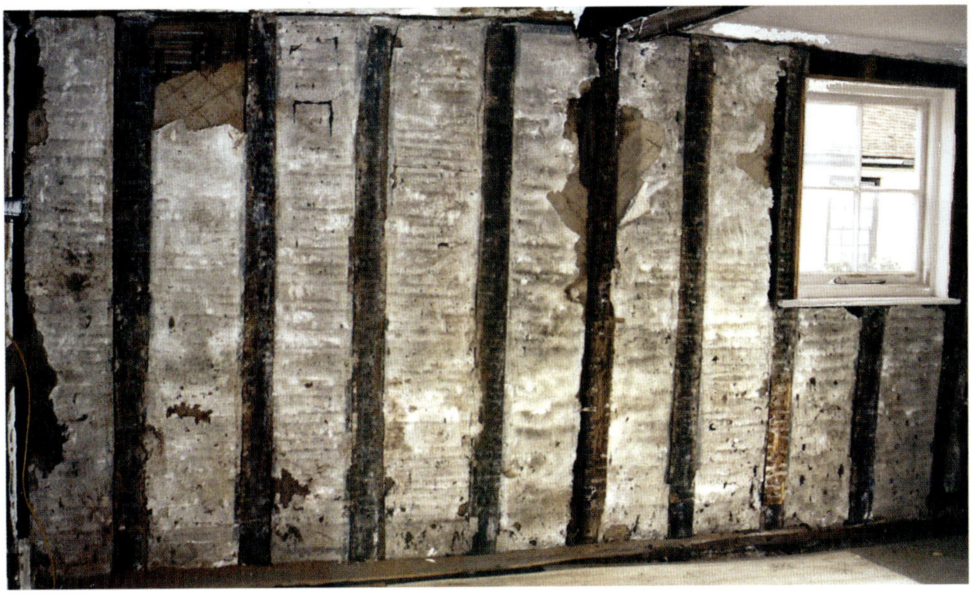

Figure 13 East Street, Colchester, Essex. *(© A. Kirkham)*

near-contemporary decoration at Nayland, but both schemes may be seen as the vernacular response to the fashion for blue rooms first seen at the aristocratic level.

Conclusions

Late 16th- and early 17th-century secular wall paintings are known for their surface pattern and rich, often jewel-like colours. As this paper argues, however, the form and quality that decoration takes may be influenced (to a greater or lesser degree) by a number of factors including status, cultural and ideological contexts, and the function of the room. The pattern of patronage seen in Phase 1, which was typically urban-based, widens in Phase 2 to encompass a broader cross-section of society. Certain types of schemes can be associated with specific social groups or geographical areas; blue rooms, for example, seem to have been the taste of urban patrons. In others, pattern and colour have been deliberately rejected, possibly for ideological or for cultural reasons. This can be seen in the two principal towns, Bury St Edmunds and Ipswich. Both towns have Phase 1 schemes, albeit with variations in the choice of motifs, yet in Phase 2 very different attitudes to decoration develop in Bury and in Ipswich.

Grotesques and imitation textile hangings are familiar images, but the 17th-century Plain schemes are less well understood, and unfortunately seldom recognised by either homeowners or conservation professionals. The Plain schemes are perhaps more vulnerable to loss than any other type of decoration. There needs to be a change in attitudes towards Plain schemes; we need to appreciate that these are an important and valuable part of the history of vernacular decoration.

Acknowledgements

I would like to thank Philip Aitkens and Leigh Alston for generous advice and discussions on the buildings and their dates. The outline map of the county of Suffolk (Fig. 1) is taken from *An Historical Atlas of Suffolk*, E. Martin and D. Dymond (eds), 1999 edition and used by permission.

Notes

1. The greatest cluster of secular wall and panel paintings is found in the central two-thirds of the county. Most of the vernacular sites in rural north Suffolk are 17th-century Plain schemes. There are a small number of pre-Reformation paintings, as well as some decorative painting in high-status buildings such as Hengrave Hall. Although these decorative schemes are not discussed in this paper, they do form an important part of the research of which this forms a part (Kirkham forthcoming). Sites outside the county are used to illustrate specific points.
2. Timothy Easton was one of the first to note these simpler, plainer schemes when restoring his house, Bedfield Hall in Suffolk.
3. Based on the evidence available to date. Interiors were not necessarily decorated with wall paintings. Some patrons preferred other wall coverings such as panelling and textiles. The relative lack of Plain schemes in south Suffolk is a problem of survival: many buildings were stripped back in the 1980s.
4. Hervey 1902, p. 58.
5. Dymond and Northeast 1995, p. 52.
6. The 'Old Draperies' were the broadcloths and kerseys. The 'New Draperies' were lighter bays and says, introduced by immigrants from the Low Countries in the 16th century. Other towns and villages such as Sudbury, Haverhill and Glemsford survived because their clothmakers had adapted to these new draperies (Dymond and Northeast 1995, p. 67).
7. Meeres 2002, p. 71.
8. Philip Aitkens, pers. comm.
9. Quoted in Dymond and Northeast 1995, p. 95.
10. BL Add. 15520, fol. 70r, quoted in MacCulloch 1977, p. 111.
11. See MacCulloch 1977 for a more detailed discussion of the social, economic and political structure of Ipswich and Bury St Edmunds.
12. BL Sloane MS 2596, quoted in MacCulloch 1977, p. 185.
13. Dymond and Northeast 1995, p. 95.
14. Identified as brazilwood by Jo Kirby at the National Gallery, London.
15. See chapter 9, 'Cost of Painted Decoration', in Baird 2002. A detailed discussion of the availability and cost of pigments and the use of colour in East Anglian secular wall paintings will be found in Kirkham forthcoming.
16. Identified by Jo Kirby at the National Gallery, London.

17. The term 'indigo/woad' is used throughout this paper because the plant source for this organic blue might be either woad (*Isatis tinctoria* L.) or indigo (*Indigofera tinctoria*), or a mixture of the two (Howard 2003, p. 58).
18. Michel and Park (1986) describe the schemes at Elms Farm, Mendlesham. They suggest that the paintings are contemporary – that is, late 16th century – and note the incongruity of the elaborate first-floor schemes with the simpler scheme in the parlour. The explanation is that Elms Farm has two periods of decoration, with the first-floor paintings being earlier than the painting in the parlour.
19. Thornton 1984, p. 36 and pl. 32.
20. Pevsner and Radcliffe 1975, p. 188.
21. The relative importance of a colour can depend on the colour combination used throughout the building. Thus red is a secondary colour when green is present, but red can be a focal colour when grey is used elsewhere in the building.
22. As research progresses, the number of green schemes identified in rural sites may increase.
23. Weller 2004. Green has a long history of use in chambers, for example in the 13th-century royal palaces, and 'green chambers' appear in the probate inventories of higher-status individuals (usually because of the colour of the soft furnishings).
24. The problem with the documentary evidence is one of interpretation. It is not always clear how these apparently simple schemes functioned within the interior.
25. Salzman 1952, p. 159.
26. Colvin *et al.* 1982, p. 55.
27. Tent design sometimes uses this format of a single colour alternating with white: see for example, a 1520 design for a royal tent, probably for the Field of the Cloth of Gold (British Library Cott. Aug.III.ii f19). An imitation textile with black and white panes can be seen in the room 'over' the chapel at The Vyne, Hampshire (Howard and Wilson 2003, p. 86).
28. Belcher *et al.* 2004, pp. 99–101.
29. Imitation skirtings can be seen in Bury St Edmunds (the range of buildings incorporating sections of the the west front of the abbey) and at Denham, near Eye.
30. Examples can be found in timber-framed buildings in other eastern region counties, in Oxfordshire and in the Welsh Marches. External examples are also known.
31. As first identified by Philip Aitkens; I am extremely grateful to him for drawing these buildings and their interiors to my attention.
32. On rare occasions the use of a Plain scheme can be associated with the decline in a building's status.
33. Access to Rogers, at Newton Green in Suffolk, has been denied, so information on the paintings is derived from an article by Benton (1941). See also the discussion on the paintings in Hamling 2002, pp. 93–5, and Wells-Cole (in this volume, pp. 3–9) for a discussion of the print sources at Stowmarket and Hadleigh.
34. Black or yellow Plain schemes are occasionally found in rural north Suffolk, but grey and red predominate.
35. Thornton 1984, pp. 14–15.
36. Thornton 1978, p. 8.
37. Bristow 1996, p. 19.
38. Bristow 1983, pp. 537–9.

References

Baird K. 2002, *Secular Wall Painting in the Sixteenth and Seventeenth Centuries*, unpublished D.Phil thesis, University of Oxford

Belcher V., Bond R., Gray M. and Wittrick A. 2004, *Sutton House: A Tudor Courtier's House in Hackney*, English Heritage, London

Benton G.M. 1941, 'Domestic wall-paintings, dated 1623, at Newton, Suffolk', *Antiquaries Journal* xxi, pp. 68–73

Bristow I.C. 1983, *Interior House-Painting from the Restoration to the Regency*, unpublished PhD thesis, University of York

Bristow I.C. 1996, *Architectural Colour in British Interiors 1615–1840*, 2 vols, Yale University Press for the Paul Mellon Center for Studies in British Art, New Haven and London

Colvin H.M., Summerson J., Biddle M., Hale J.R. and Merriman M. 1982, *The History of the Kings Works* IV (1485–1660), part 2, The Stationery Office Books, London

Dymond D. and Martin E. (eds) 1999, *An Historical Atlas of Suffolk*, 3rd edn, Suffolk County Council Archaeological Service

Dymond D. and Northeast P. 1995, *A History of Suffolk*, Darwen County History Series, Phillimore, Chichester

Hamling T. 2002, *Narrative and Figurative Imagery in the English Domestic Interior c.1558–c.1640*, unpublished PhD thesis, University of Sussex

Hervey F. 1902, *Suffolk in the XVIIth Century: The Breviary of Suffolk by Robert Reyce*, J. Murray, London

Howard H. 2003, *Pigments of English Medieval Wall Painting*, Archetype, London

Howard M. and Wilson E. 2003, *The Vyne: A Tudor House Revealed*, The National Trust, London

Kirby J. 2003, 'HPLC analysis of dyestuffs', unpublished report for Andrea Kirkham, 16 October 2003, National Gallery, London

Kirkham A. forthcoming, *Sixteenth- and Seventeenth-Century Secular Wall Paintings in East Anglia*, unpublished PhD thesis, University of East Anglia

MacCulloch D. 1977, *Power, Privilege and the County Community*, unpublished PhD thesis, University of Cambridge

Meeres F. 2002, *A History of Bury St Edmunds*, Phillimore, Chichester

Michel J. and Park D. 1986, 'Wall paintings at Elms Farm, Mendlesham', *Proceedings of the Suffolk Institute of Archaeology and History* XXXVI, pp. 221–3

Pevsner N. and Radcliffe E. (eds) 1975, *Suffolk* (The Buildings of England Series), Penguin, Harmondsworth

Salzman L.F. 1952, *Building in England down to 1540: A Documentary History*, Oxford University Press, Oxford

Thornton P. 1978, *Seventeenth-Century Interior Decoration in England, France and Holland*, Yale University Press, New Haven and London

Thornton P. 1984, *Authentic Decor: The Domestic Interior 1620–1920*, Weidenfeld and Nicolson, London

Weller J. 2004, 'Manor Farm and Farmhouse at Monks Eleigh, Part 2', *Eavesdropper: The Newsletter of the Suffolk Historic Buildings Group* 26, pp. 4–10

The author

Since 1984, Andrea Kirkham has trained and worked within the field of wall painting conservation on a wide variety of projects. She is an accredited wall painting conservator. Andrea completed an MA in 2002 on the *Sixteenth and Seventeenth Century Domestic Wall Paintings in Suffolk* (University of East Anglia). This research has been extended to include Norfolk as a part-time doctorate on the 16th- and 17th-century secular wall paintings in East Anglia (University of East Anglia).

Changing rooms: changes in use and their impact on wall painting conservation

Tom Organ

Introduction

Wall paintings are an integral part of the building that they occupy and cannot easily be removed or transferred to another location. While in some cases this has meant that they have survived intact for many centuries, it has also meant that they have been susceptible to damage linked to changes in the use or structure of the building, but most particularly to changes in taste. This paper looks at four examples of Renaissance wall paintings from various parts of the country, all of which have had conservation issues that are specifically linked to changes of use of the buildings in which they are located. We will also see one example – the wall paintings at Cullacott farmhouse in Cornwall – where a change in the use of the building was also responsible for the survival of a unique house and its rare decorative schemes.

The paintings

In private homes throughout the latter part of the 16th century, and during the 17th century, there was a move towards greater personal comfort and privacy. With the expansion of international trade, and the growth of our towns and cities, came an expanding class of wealthy businessmen. As new dwellings were built or as existing houses developed over time, greater emphasis was placed on improving levels of comfort and adding richer schemes of decoration. One of the characteristics of many of these wall painting schemes is the use of a fictive tapestry as a means of decoration. These schemes were clearly done in imitation of the expensive tapestries that were to be found adorning the walls of the homes of the very rich during the 15th and 16th centuries. Although these origins are not always immediately clear, on close inspection we find the use of imitation painted loops along a top edge or, in later examples where these loops disappear, the painted upper border remains, as might be found on a hanging tapestry. These are interesting details as they demonstrate the aspirational nature of the schemes that were being executed.

Many of the examples of wall paintings included here were covered over by subsequent generations of owners, as tastes and fashions changed. Sometimes the murals were painted out with limewash or plastered over; in other cases they might be simply concealed, for example by wainscoting or partition walls. The examples here are intended to illustrate the breadth of subject matter, which ranges from paintings of a dragon discovered in a former barn at Cullacott in Cornwall, through a dog in a kitchen in Sussex to fantastic Renaissance grotesques in an architect's office in Bagshot, Surrey.

Cullacott Farmhouse, Cornwall

The ancient farmhouse of Cullacott, near Launceston in Cornwall, is dated c.1525 and contains decoration that gives us our starting point at the end of the late medieval period.

During renovation works to an almost derelict set of farm buildings, it was realised that an important medieval cobb building had survived with many of its original features intact, and an almost total absence of modern 'improvements'.[1] Cullacott farmhouse is now Grade I listed: of outstanding regional and national importance. It is one of the county's best vernacular buildings, still with medieval and Renaissance wall paintings and a three-bay hall open to the underside of the roof. The original cobb- and stone-built house has an open three-bay hall, the third bay having a screen and an internal jetty with room above.

Conservation work, carried out in 1997 in collaboration with John Burbidge and English Heritage, involved the uncovering of a series of wall paintings in the hall, which included an imitation wall hanging with a religious theme (c.1485–1525), a later Tudor coat of arms, and an unusual rendering of St George and the Dragon (Figs 1–4). The reason for including Cullacott here is that it demonstrates on the one hand the continuation of a tradition in the use of painted imitation tapestries (as we shall see later), and on the other hand the artistic changes that accompanied the changing political climate. Cullacott was originally part of the huge swathes of land owned by Tavistock Abbey, Devon, and the earliest subject matter is clearly religious. Although very fragmentary and difficult to decipher, it seems that the wall painting probably depicted the owner and his wife praying to the central figure of the Virgin against the backdrop of an imitation tapestry, with Gothic text written diagonally across it. This subject matter was intended to demonstrate publicly the close connection between the owner and his religion, the Catholic faith. The location of the wall painting at the dais end of the hall is significant as it is a bold statement to all who entered for an audience with the owner.

After the Dissolution of the Monasteries in 1539, along with other properties Cullacott was given to John Russell, who became the Duke of Bedford. It seems highly likely that the Tudor arms, which now occupy the centre of the dais-end wall, were painted over the earlier wall painting in response. It is evident that the change of decoration here is intended to reflect the transfer of power and wealth from the Church of Rome to the Church of England, and the new owner's allegiance to the king.

In time the paintings were limewashed over and forgotten, and when a new house was constructed just up the hill in the 19th century, the family abandoned the old building. Over the next century Cullacott was left to the slow processes of neglect and decay, eventually being used as a stables and agricultural storage area.

Once traces of wall paintings were found, the significance of the central open hall became evident, and the paintings were eventually fully uncovered and conserved between 1994 and 1996. With the generous support of English Heritage, the property was carefully and sensitively restored, re-establishing the importance of the central hall and providing accommodation in two self-catering holiday lets, one at the old parlour end and the other at the kitchen end of the old hall-house.

Flushing Inn, Rye

A slightly later example of fictive tapestry survives at the Flushing Inn restaurant at Rye in Sussex. This remarkable wall painting was discovered in the autumn of 1905 during the temporary removal for repair of late 16th- or early 17th-

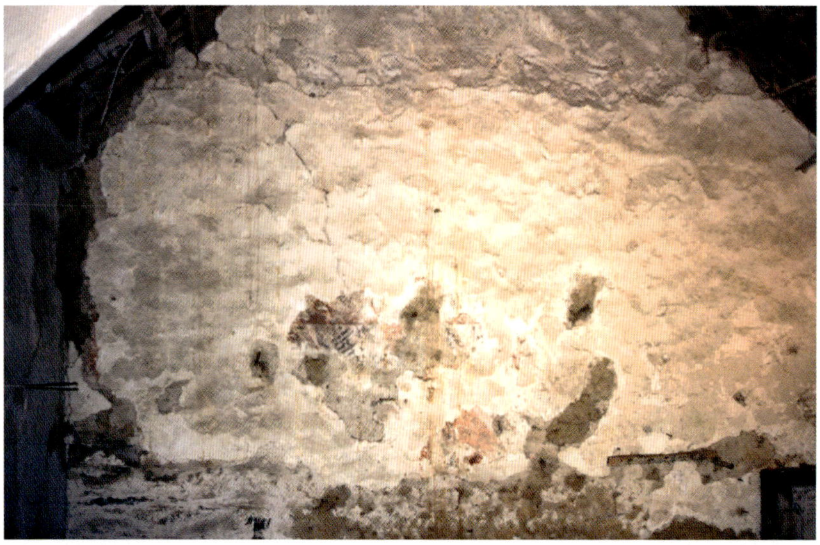

Figure 1 Cullacott Farmhouse, near Launceston, Cornwall: the north wall of the Great Hall before uncovering and conservation. *(© T. Organ)*

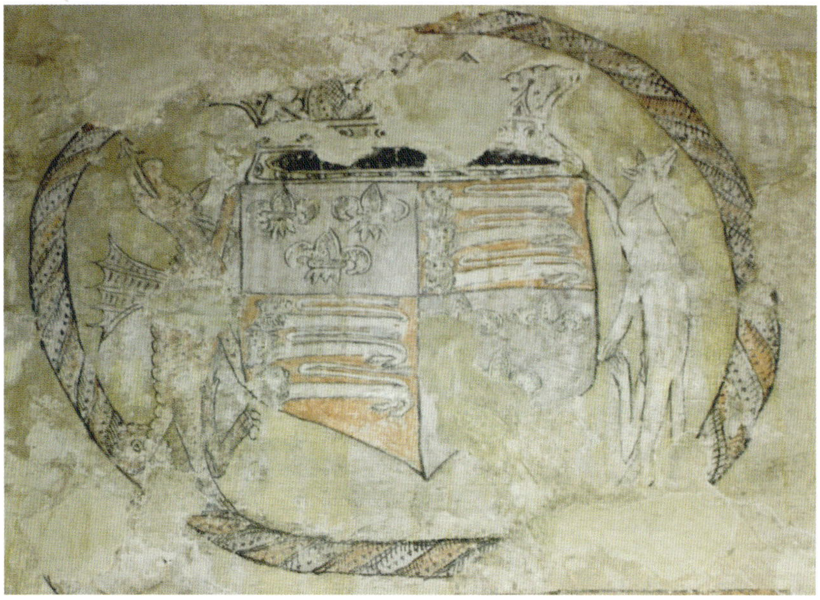

Figure 2 Cullacott Farmhouse, near Launceston, Cornwall: a detail of the north wall of the Great Hall after uncovering and conservation. *(© J. Davey)*

century panelling at the dais end of the late 15th- or early 16th-century hall. Like the late medieval decoration at Cullacott, this painting consists of fictive tapestry of a type popular during the 16th century, executed in a typically naive style. An upper frieze some 18 inches deep contains three cartouches, each supported on either side by single putti, and alternating with royal arms and badges (Fig. 5). The cartouches enclose the *Magnificat* in English, in a version close to that in Tynedale's Bible of 1525, and painted in Gothic Black Letter script.

The heraldry has been identified as the royal arms of King Edward VI (reigned 1547–53) and of his mother Queen Jane Seymour (d.1537), her lozenge-shaped shield depicted on a black field to indicate that she was deceased at the time that the painting was executed. It has been argued that it is unlikely that the arms of Jane Seymour would have been painted during Henry VIII's lifetime, which suggests that it was executed during Edward VI's reign. The royal badge – the *Rose en Soleil* first adopted by Edward IV – shows the white rose within the red. The main area of painting consists of a rich foliate tapestry with three diagonal bands each containing the text *SOLI DEO HONOR ET [GLORIA]*. The mural must have been commissioned by a supporter of the young king, and the motto may have belonged to the family of the house at the time.

The lettering has been described as 'a sort of mixed Lombardic and Roman, fashionable in this early Renaissance period'.[2] The letter *S* is reversed and the initial letter of each word is differentiated by being painted in red and embellished with white lines and dots. The Rye painting thus includes a range of lettering types, mixing Gothic Black Letter (commonly found on wall paintings of the first half of the 16th century) with Lombardic and Roman. This would indicate a transitional period during the early Renaissance, around the middle of the 16th century. The main field of the painting consists of extraordinary foliate scrollwork containing Tudor roses, pomegranates, pineapples, fantastic creatures and birds (Figs 6 and 7). The strangely painted animals include a doe, a stag, a lion (or heraldic leopard), a dog or fox and an Elephant and Castle, among others. The birds are harder to identify, although one can imagine a stork, an ostrich, a peacock and a swan. The mix of animals and foliate work is an early and unusually colourful example, and we shall see how this later develops into the black and white 'antiquework' which appears later in the century.

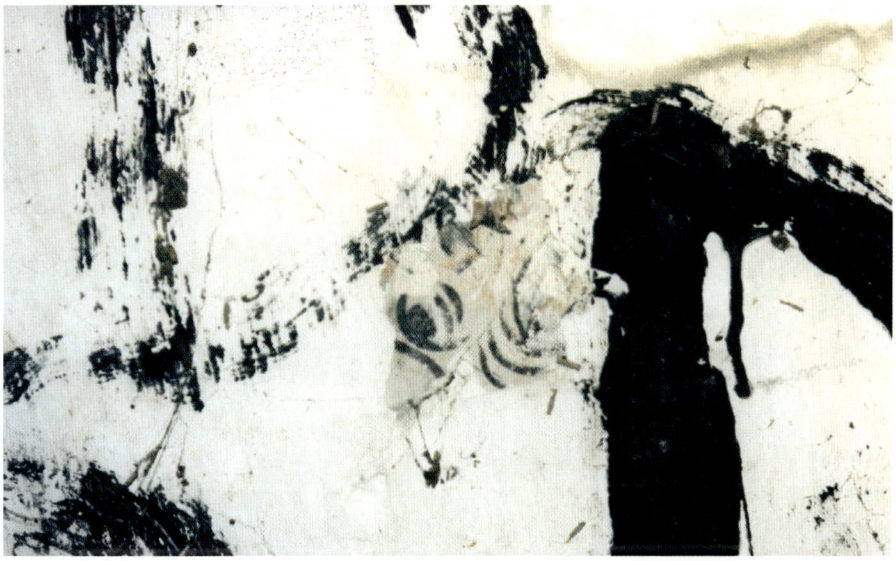

Figure 3 Cullacott Farmhouse, near Launceston, Cornwall: *St George and the Dragon* on the south wall of the Great Hall. (a) Detail of the dragon's eye before uncovering; (b) St George and the Dragon during uncovering and conservation. *(© T. Organ)*

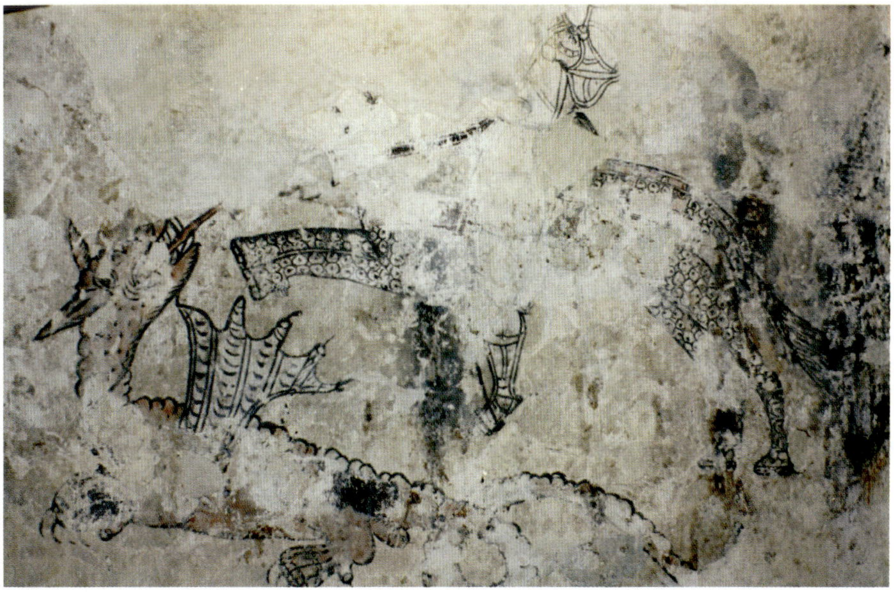

Figure 4 Cullacott Farmhouse, near Launceston, Cornwall: *St George and the Dragon* during uncovering and conservation. *(© J. Davey)*

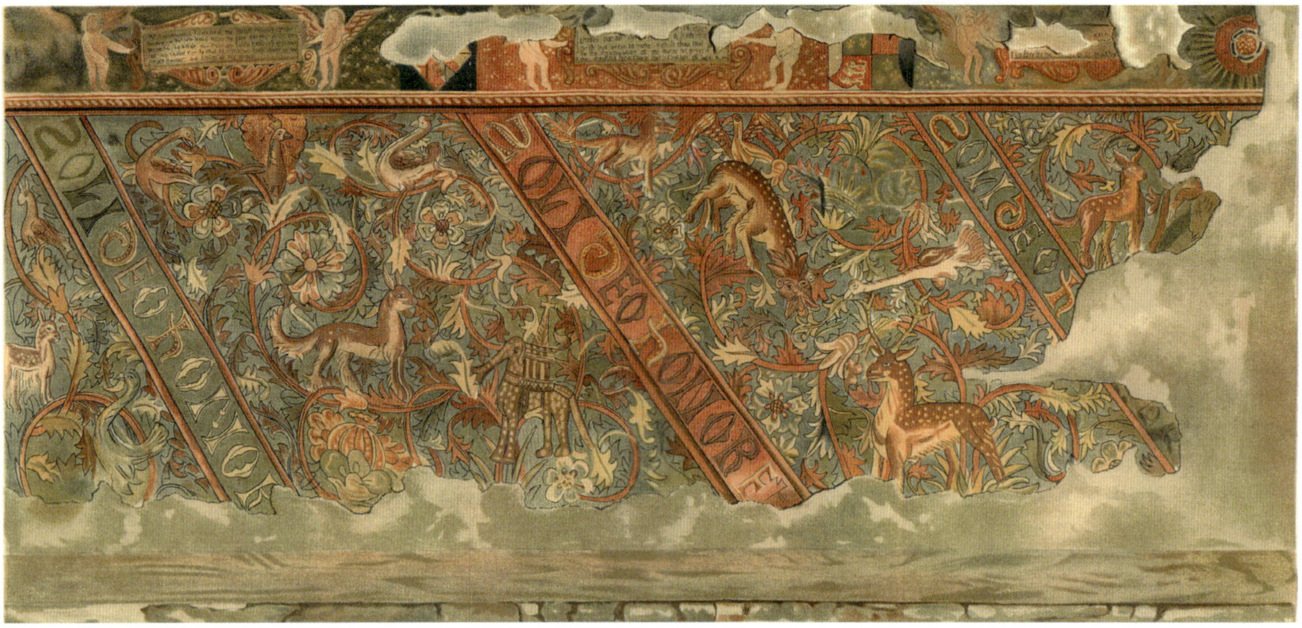

Figure 5 Flushing Inn, Rye, East Sussex: watercolour of the wall painting made by Elizabeth Drake at the time of its discovery in January 1906.

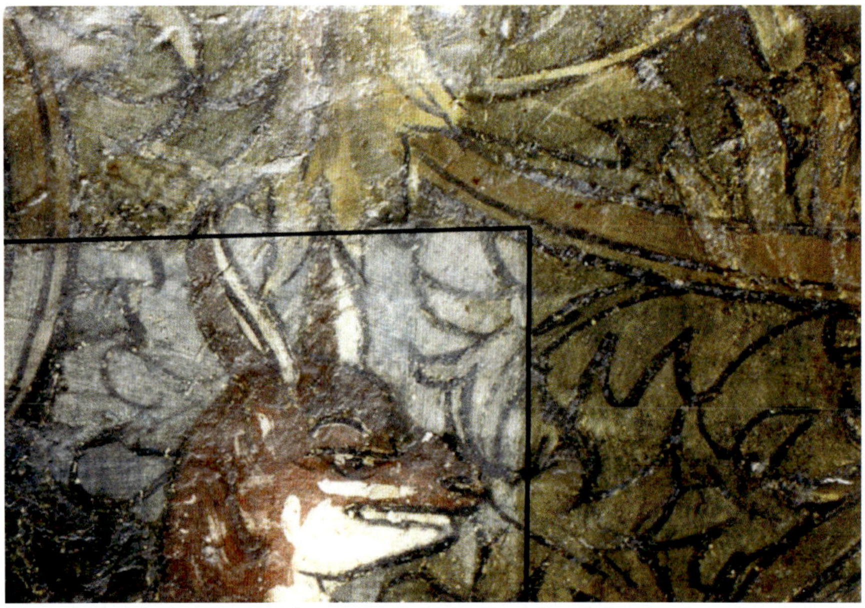

Figure 6 Flushing Inn, Rye, East Sussex: detail of the wall painting during cleaning and conservation work carried out to stabilise loose plaster and remove a heavily discoloured and darkened varnish. *(© T. Organ)*

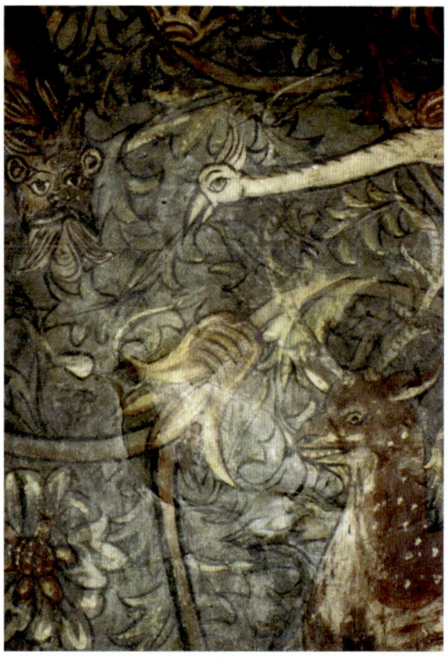

Figure 7 Flushing Inn, Rye, East Sussex: various details of the animal heads after removal of the darkened varnish. *(© T. Organ)*

For many years the Flushing Inn was a family restaurant and the painting has suffered ongoing deterioration, due mainly to the darkening and deterioration of the thick layers of varnish which were applied when the painting was first discovered, and again in 1961. By the late 1980s the painting had become almost indecipherable. A poor lighting system added to the problem, casting a raking light across the uneven plaster surface, creating shadows in some places and reflecting off the glossy varnish in others.

Apart from the visual aspects there were also more serious concerns over areas of apparently active deterioration. In several places, sections of plaster were detaching due to past structural movement and localised flaking paint was also evident. A programme of cleaning and conservation was carried out in early 1996, removing not only the varnish layers but also the splash marks from the odd glass of spilt wine (Fig. 8).

The Olde Tea Shoppe, Midhurst

Animals were a popular theme for domestic wall paintings, and other odd examples have come to light here and there, often in unusual locations. The Olde Tea Shoppe in Midhurst, West Sussex, contains several areas of Renaissance wall painting discovered by accident during building works. The paintings were first inspected in 1995, following alterations and refurbishment work carried out at the Tuck Shop tearooms in Midhurst during the early 1990s. The build-

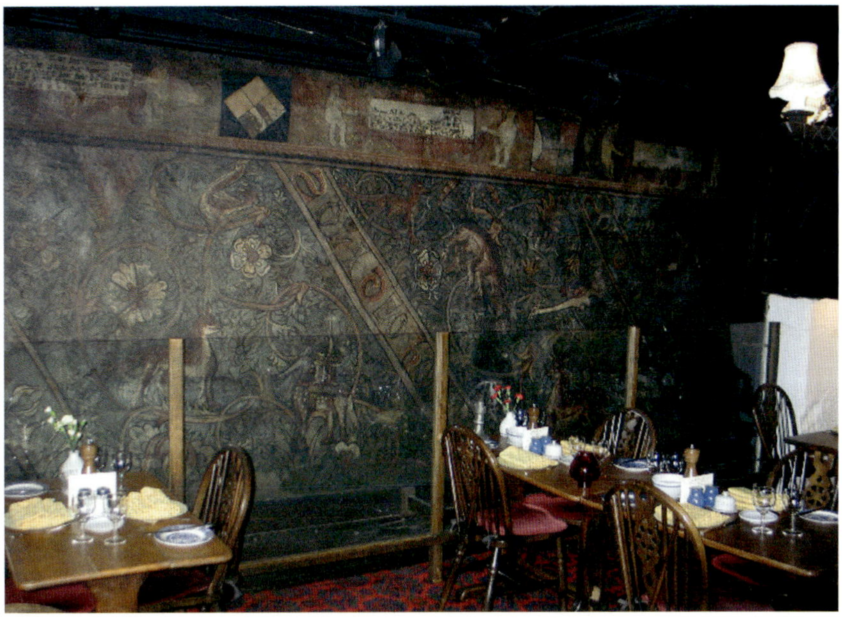

Figure 8 Flushing Inn, Rye, East Sussex: photograph taken by the owner showing how the wall painting currently forms a backdrop to one of the dining areas in the restaurant. *(© J. Flynn)*

ing had recently been subdivided; the wall paintings were now located in Ye Olde Tea Shoppe tearooms, adjacent to the Tuck Shop. Two small areas of mid-16th-century wall paintings were revealed from beneath later plasters and overpaints, one in the ground-floor tearoom and another in the first-floor kitchen. From what can be seen at present it appears that the two areas of decoration are coeval, showing similarities in technique, the paint palette used and the stratigraphic evidence.

The discovery of complete mural paintings is a rare event and here it was of particular importance in view of their quality and exceptional state of preservation. The painting on the ground floor is unique and has been identified as belonging to the Old Testament story of Naboth the Jezreelite, murdered

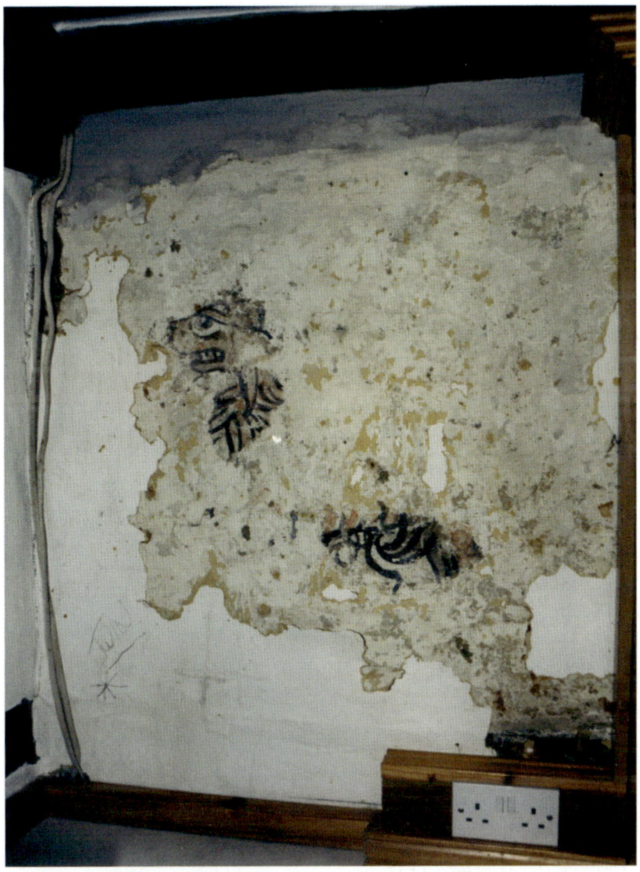

Figure 9 Midhurst, West Sussex: a 16th-century wall painting depicting a dog, discovered during renovation of the first-floor room above Ye Olde Tea Shoppe in the High Street. The room is now the kitchen of the family home. *(© T. Organ)*

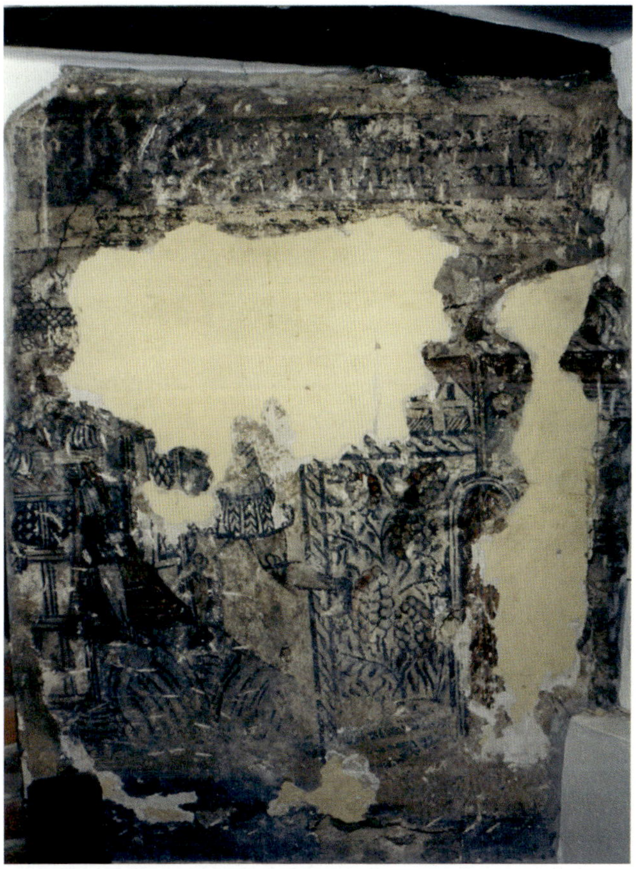

Figure 10 Midhurst, West Sussex: a 16th-century wall painting depicting Naboth's Vineyard. *(© T. Organ)*

on the orders of Jezebel (wife of King Ahab) for refusing to sell his vineyard to the king (I Kings: 21).[3] The wall painting consists of a figurative scene with a guilloche-bordered frieze above containing a two-line inscription illustrating the scene below:

King Ahab desyred To have the ?... vineyard of Naboth; but ...?

On the left of the scene sits the enthroned, crowned figure of a king, presumably Ahab, his left arm extended towards a second figure. Only the lower half of the second figure is currently visible, but it is presumed to be Naboth stepping forward towards the king. Behind Naboth is a stylised representation of the vineyard with large bunches of white and red grapes growing among luxuriant foliage. The vineyard is surrounded by guilloche or cable pattern borders. Along its upper edge are two 2-storey gable-ended Elizabethan buildings with red roofs. To the right of these is a curious dome-shaped structure, possibly a canopy covering a barely discernible group of small figures. The wall paintings can be dated to around the third quarter of the 16th century, c.1570, on stylistic grounds.

These paintings, which once formed the decoration in the principal rooms of a private house, are now at risk due to changes in the use of the building. In one of the first-floor rooms a large dog-like animal was painted on the wall next to one of the original doorways (Fig. 9). When inspected in 1995 the painting was just above the work surface in the new family kitchen, next to the kettle, toaster and deep-fat fryer. The painting was only partially exposed, the removal of superimposed limewash layers and wallpapers revealing part of the head and hindquarters of the animal.

The presence of these important paintings within the working environments of a tearoom and kitchen is obviously of concern, and any long-term conservation plan will have to take account of the use of the building and the likely future environmental factors. In its current location the painting of Naboth's Vineyard is probably relatively stable, but it is at risk of accidental damage and will be subjected to constantly changing environmental conditions (Fig. 10). The painting on the first floor is clearly at much greater risk of damage from the harsher environmental conditions of a kitchen.

These are some of the lucky examples that have come to light during alteration or repair to historic buildings and have been carefully preserved, as opposed to obliterated or deliberately destroyed. There are countless tales of paintings that have been discovered but subsequently disappeared because the then owners were worried about outside interference and the likelihood of costly repair bills.

No. 44, High Street Bagshot

No. 44, High Street, Bagshot, Surrey, is a medieval three-bay, timber-framed structure, now brick-clad, with modern extensions at the rear. The building contains extensive remains of post-Reformation wall paintings on the walls of the main ground-floor rooms. Originally probably a galleried coaching inn of late 15th- or early 16th-century date, with evidence of earlier 14th-century origins, the building is now used as offices.

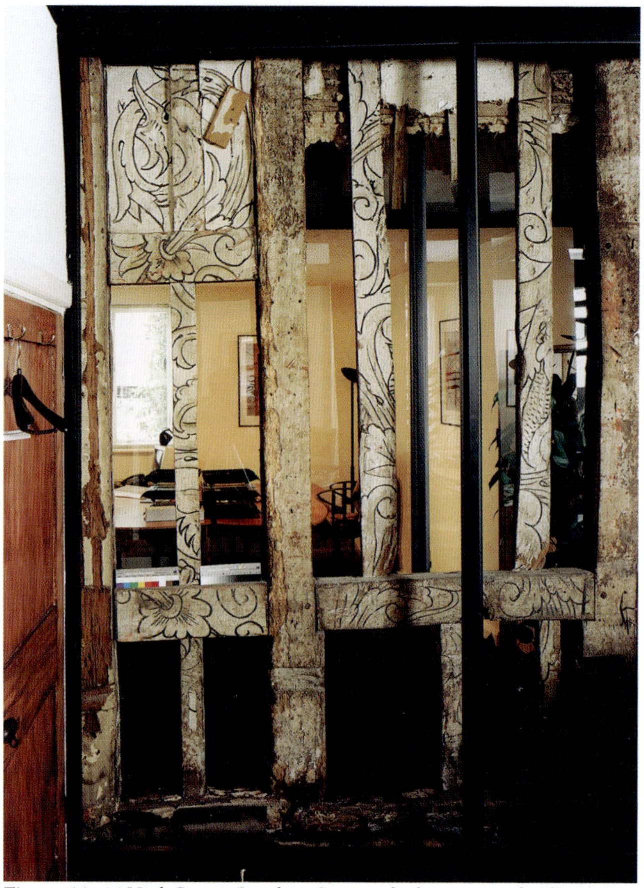

Figure 11 44 High Street, Bagshot, Surrey: the large area of wall painting was partially destroyed during renovation works to the building. Several sizeable sections were salvaged by the owner and remain in storage. *(© English Heritage Photo Library)*

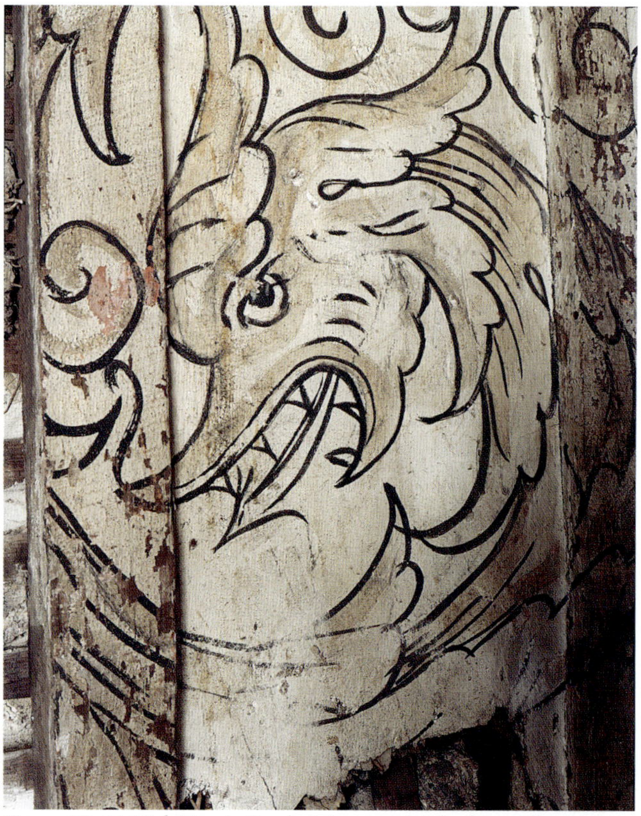

Figure 12 44 High Street, Bagshot, Surrey: detail of a small grotesque dog's head. *(© English Heritage Photo Library)*

At least three periods of wall painting are discernible, the main scheme (the last) consisting of ornate arabesque or antiquework, with traces of two earlier schemes (Fig. 11). The main scheme comprises a bold scrollwork design in black on a white background, extending across the timber, plaster and brick structures, with traces of royal arms bearing the Prince of Wales feathers in a 'sunburst' above the fireplace. Below this scheme is a similar antiquework design, in white on black, and areas of an earlier plain scheme of painting in red. Although the three periods of painting are not precisely dated, they appear to fall within a relatively short period of time between 1485 and 1553.[4]

The first antiquework scheme at Bagshot was covered with a thin layer of lime-hair plaster and a second, stylistically similar scheme of antiquework was executed on this. This second scheme of grotesques comprises large, boldly executed floral scrollwork in black outline against a white background, the stems terminating in stylised dragon or dog heads (Fig. 12). There are localised areas of tinting on the stems in a thin reddish-yellow colour.

The second scheme is particularly interesting because it includes a rare clue to its dating: a sunburst enclosing the feathers of the Prince of Wales, placed centrally over the fireplace. The sunburst device was found, together with the feathers of the Prince of Wales, on the arms of Prince Edward (1537–53). One could speculate that the painting was painted to commemorate his accession to the throne in 1547. The similar, but more colourful, foliate scheme linked to Prince Edward's accession to the throne at the Flushing Inn in Rye has already been mentioned. The discovery of a second wall painting displaying the arms of Prince Edward, again in the setting of an inn, is therefore clearly of some cultural and art-historical significance. Unfortunately, at Bagshot the central elements of the royal arms have been lost. It appears that they were deliberately defaced at a later date, probably during a period when the royal family were less popular, again indicating changes in the political and cultural climate.

Stylistically, these forms of decoration cover a rather wide period from the mid-16th to the early 17th century. They appear in England during the Renaissance, when artists rediscovered and copied sources from classical antiquity. Many of the subjects were first found in the ancient grottoes of Rome, and were copied and disseminated through books and engravings.[5] The supposed origins of these forms, as decorations for ancient grottoes, gave rise to the terms 'grotesque' and 'antiquework'. Other fine examples of decoration stylistically similar to the Bagshot paintings – grotesques painted using distemper with figures in white against a black background – exist at Polstead Hall in Suffolk (dated c.1550) and the Golden Cross, Oxford (dated 'before 1605').

Since decorative schemes of this general type cover such a wide period, in many cases dating has been a relatively imprecise process, often based on rather tenuous comparisons with other examples. The survival of painted details such as those at Bagshot and Rye that can help with more accurate dating is therefore of significance to our understanding of this type of decoration. The wall paintings at Bagshot were revealed during building works carried out in December 1997. Unfortunately, several sections of painted plaster were deliberately knocked off the timber frame by the building contractors; the fragments that could be salvaged are currently stored in the roof space of the building. Both the surviving *in-situ* wall paintings and the detached fragments are in a fragile and vulnerable condition. This example most vividly demonstrates the dangers faced by many wall paintings in domestic environments; it is only through a combination of luck and the timely intervention of the new owner that the paintings were not completely destroyed by the builder.

The Ancient House, Ipswich

One of the finest examples of its type in the country can be seen at the Ancient House, Ipswich (Fig. 13). Acquired by Ipswich Borough Council in 1979, the building is currently an outlet for the household goods company Lakeland Limited and the wall paintings are located in a room on the first floor. The paintings were discovered during renovation works in 1984 and subsequently conserved by Julie Crick. Dated c.1600, the paintings needed treatment in 1998 following accidental damage caused by an overflow from pipework in the roof space above.

Records show that the site of the Ancient House hosted knights or wealthy businessmen since the 14th century. In its present form, the house has six successive phases of building dating from 1460 to 1670. The wall paintings were originally painted as the fashionable wall covering of the period, in what was then the private quarters of a wealthy new owner of the building, William Sparrowe. He acquired the house after the death of the previous owner in 1591, although he did not take full possession until 1601.

The painting is again in the style known as antiquework based on the classical forms that re-emerged during the Renaissance, and is beautifully executed in sweeping freehand directly onto the limewashed plaster and woodwork with few signs of any preparatory work. Here the decoration is painted in black on white against a light red background and consists of a fantastic repeating pattern of ornate candelabra flanked by winged male and female figures wearing laurel wreaths. The background is filled with fantastical grotesques – foliage intertwined with bizarre creatures including winged dogs, cat heads, fish or dolphin heads, birds and human figures blowing trumpets.

The two surviving areas of wall painting are normally covered by protective polycarbonate sheeting, and while the company has helped to keep them safe by using the room as a small museum space where they display various finds made during the restoration of the building, another change of use could put the paintings at risk. As part of the conversion works carried out during the transformation of the property into a retail outlet, the new owners installed staff quarters within the roof space including a toilet. In late 1998 the soil pipe for the toilet burst directly above and dirty water seeped through the plaster and down across the face of the painting.

Although the paintings have been cleaned and conserved, they continue to be at risk of damage that can be directly linked to the daily use of the building. The movement of numerous members of the public through the timber-framed building causes vibration and, when associated with daily heating patterns, leads to fluctuations in temperature and humidity,

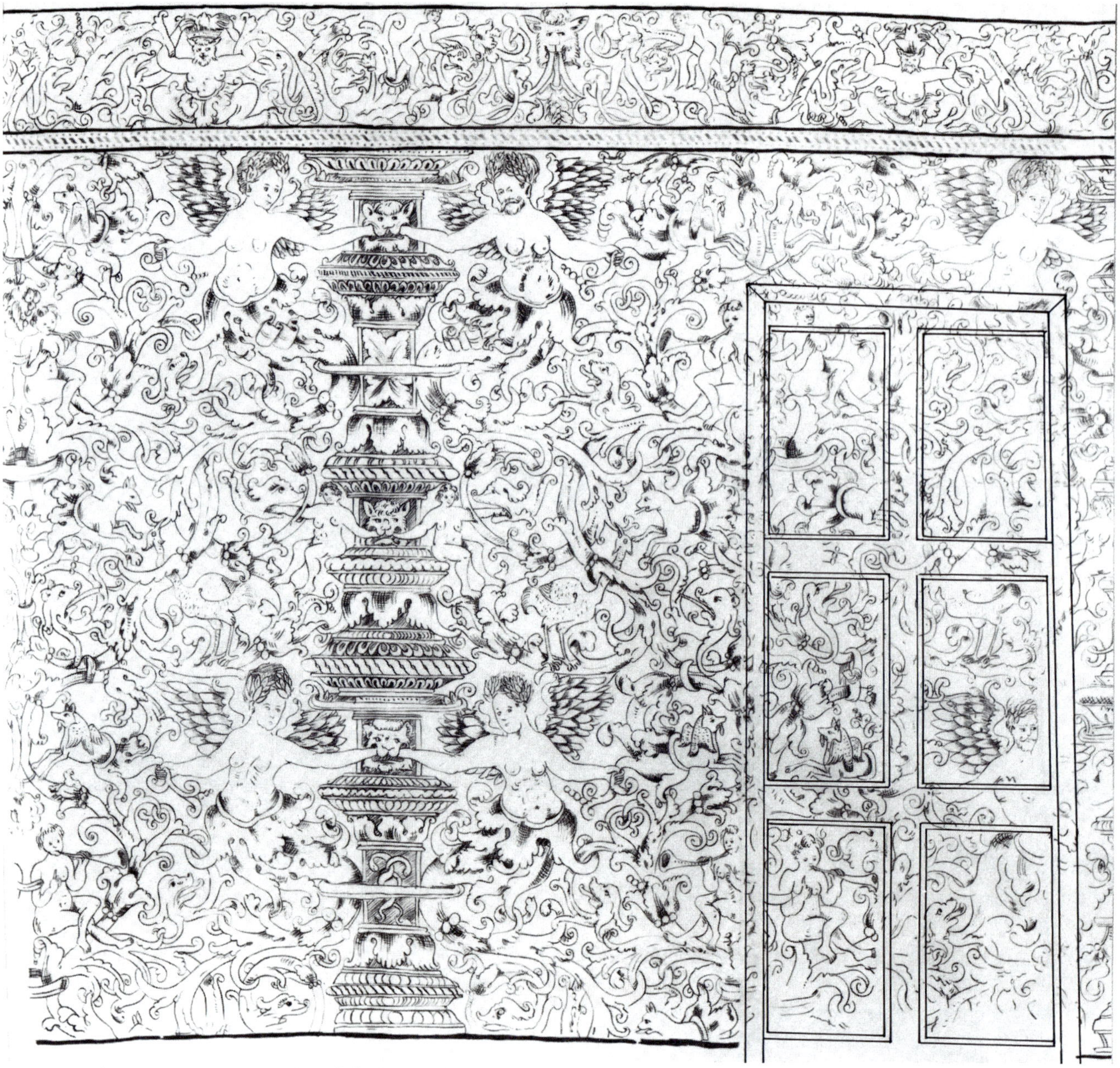

Figure 13 The Ancient House, Ipswich, Suffolk: drawing showing the ornate grotesque scheme in one of the first-floor rooms. *(© T. Organ)*

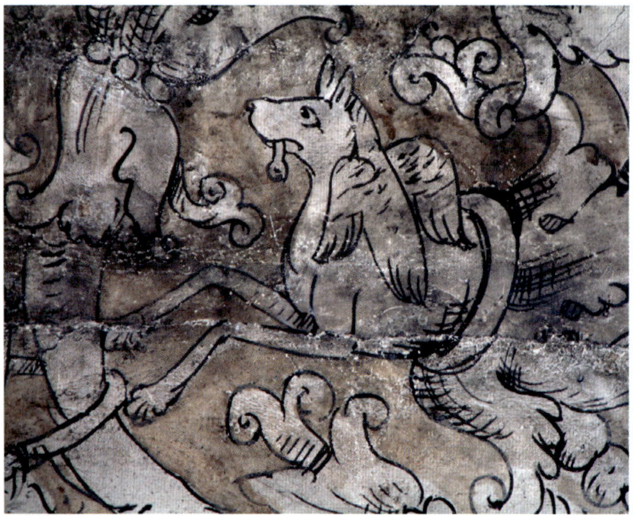

Figure 14 The Ancient House, Ipswich, Suffolk: a detail of the first-floor decoration. *(© T. Organ)*

both of which can adversely affect the fragile plaster and paint layers. On a more positive note it could be argued that the commercial redevelopment of the building has been an important and significant factor in the rediscovery and subsequent care and conservation of a fascinating scheme of wall painting.

Conclusions

In brief conclusion I would like to go back to the paintings at Cullacott. The interesting thing in this case is that while the building was left to decay for decades, it is arguable that it is just that very lack of intervention and modernisation that has resulted in the survival of the paintings. Had the central hall been floored over to provide more rooms at first-floor level, as many such halls were during the 16th century, and the house given a 'makeover' on a regular basis, it is unlikely that we would have much to look at now. This emphasises just how much we have lost over the years due to the actions of the followers of fashion.

Notes

1. Cobb is an unfired (i.e. used as dug) clay-earth material containing stones and added straw, which was traditionally used for making the walls of vernacular buildings in some parts of the country. These structures required the walls to be built up in courses of substantial width to provide not only strength but also insulation. The external surfaces rely on a protective coating of limewash as protection against the elements.
2. Johnston 1907.
3. The inscription at the top of the painting has been partially deciphered by David Coke, Pallant House Gallery and John Magilton, Chichester District Archaeological Unit.
4. Dendrochronological dating was carried out by Dr Martin Bridge and tree-ring analysis of one of the samples, taken from the SW post, provided a date of AD 1485–1517 (unpublished report no. 59/2001, English Heritage Centre for Archaeology).
5. These painted caves or grottoes were often simply the decorated rooms of ancient palaces, such as the Domus Aurea (Rome), which had been filled in with earth and subsequently buried under later structures. When these ancient structures were rediscovered during the Italian Renaissance, the discoveries were often made by digging down through the ceilings into earth-filled rooms, which were then interpreted as grottoes.

Reference

Johnston P.M. 1907, 'Wall painting in a house at Rye formerly known as "The Old Flushing Inn"', *Sussex Archaeological Society Journal* 50(1), p. 122

The author

The Wall Paintings Workshop was originally set up in 1979 by the Dean and Chapter of Canterbury to conserve the mural paintings at the cathedral. Since joining the workshop in 1981, Tom Organ has been involved with numerous prestigious conservation projects, both at Canterbury Cathedral and in other historic buildings around the country. He became the Director of the Wall Paintings Workshop in 1991 and since April 1992 it has been run as an independent team of conservators specialising in the treatment of painted and applied decoration on plaster, stone, wood and canvas, as well as mosaics. Tom currently works as a freelance conservation consultant and wall paintings conservator working extensively with English Heritage, the National Trust, cathedrals, churches, museums and public and private owners of historic buildings both in the UK and abroad.

Painted kings and painted gods (continental copy or English inspiration? The painted Baroque interior)

Giles Worsley

One of the glories of late 17th- and early 18th-century English architecture is the painted interior. Think of the Painted Hall at Greenwich, the staircase at Petworth in Sussex or the saloon at Blenheim in Oxfordshire. Monarchs preen, gods disport themselves, complex allegorical stories are played out in large-scale figurative schemes against elaborate architectural backdrops. Such rooms are classically Baroque. Or are they?

In fact, the English painted interior had remarkably little to do with the continental Baroque. It is true that the English did pick up on the iconographically rich, illusionistic painted ceiling that was so popular in 17th-century Rome. There is no lack of the putti, floating drapery and grandiloquent gestures that are such a feature of the Baroque. However, what set the English apart from their continental contemporaries was their passion for decorating whole rooms with figurative scenes set against a rich architectural background.

The Heaven Room at Burghley House in Stamford, painted by Antonio Verrio (1639–1707) in about 1696, is a particularly sumptuous example, its framework of Corinthian columns giving the illusion that the visitor is sitting within a Roman temple watching the gods themselves (Fig. 1). The staircase Gerard Lanscroon painted before 1700 at Burley-on-the-Hill in Rutland – with its *trompe l'oeil* columns and niches framing the story of Perseus – is even more characteristic because the English had a particular passion for the painted staircase (Fig. 2) (see also paper by J. Davies in this volume, pp. 59–67).

It is true that such rooms (although apparently not staircases) can be found in Italy, but not in the late 17th century. One of the finest examples is Baldassare Peruzzi's Villa Farnesina in Rome of 1516 to 1517, where the Sala delle Prospettive gives the impression – like the Heaven Room at Burghley – of being ringed by an open colonnade giving views out over the city. Many similar rooms can be found throughout the 16th century, but they come largely to an end in the 1630s. By the 1680s, when the English picked up the habit, such rooms would have seemed old-fashioned. The Romans preferred more complex interiors, with painted ceilings broken into panels and walls ornamented with stucco or carved wooden decoration. This fashion was equally popular in France, as in the Gallerie d'Apollon in the Louvre, created by Louis le Vau and Charles le Brun from 1661 to 1663.

So, if covering walls with large-scale illusionistic paintings and architectural settings had fallen out of fashion in Italy in the 1630s, why did the English revive the tradition half a century later? Were they so backward that they thought such interiors were still fashionable? This seems unlikely. The court of Charles II was keenly aware of contemporary French and Italian fashion. The answer is, or was, to be found at the building that set the precedent for the English painted interior – Windsor Castle.

Windsor was the project for the grand palace that Charles II had been forced to abandon at Greenwich in 1669. Rebuilt by Hugh May between 1675 and 1684, at the enormous cost of £127,729, it was Charles II's riposte to Louis XIV's contemporary creation of the château of Versailles, begun in 1668 and effectively completed with the creation of the Galerie des Glaces by Jules Hardouin Mansart in 1678 to 1684. Unlike Louis XIV, Charles II did not create a grandly classical palace but deliberately emphasised the historic elements of a building that had epitomised the English monarchy for centuries. May's medievalising exteriors are well known, but what is less appreciated is that he was equally insistent on emphasising tradition within the building. This is clear from the way that he refused to create a fashionable enfilade of state rooms – an easy and obvious change – but retained the complex layout of the medieval royal apartments almost unchanged.

It is within this context that the two most dramatic interiors created by Verrio, the Royal Chapel and St George's Hall (1680–84 and 1682–84 respectively) need to be understood. Tragically, both have been destroyed, but we gain a good impression of what they were like in the watercolours by Charles Wild, published in Pyne's *The History of the Royal Residences* (1817–20) (Fig. 3).

Here we see the rich, gaudy interior of the Royal Chapel, complete with barley-sugar columns flanking the altar. In the ceiling, Christ ascends dramatically to heaven; the long wall shows him healing the sick against a framework of columns. St George's Hall, a paean to the Order of the Garter, must have

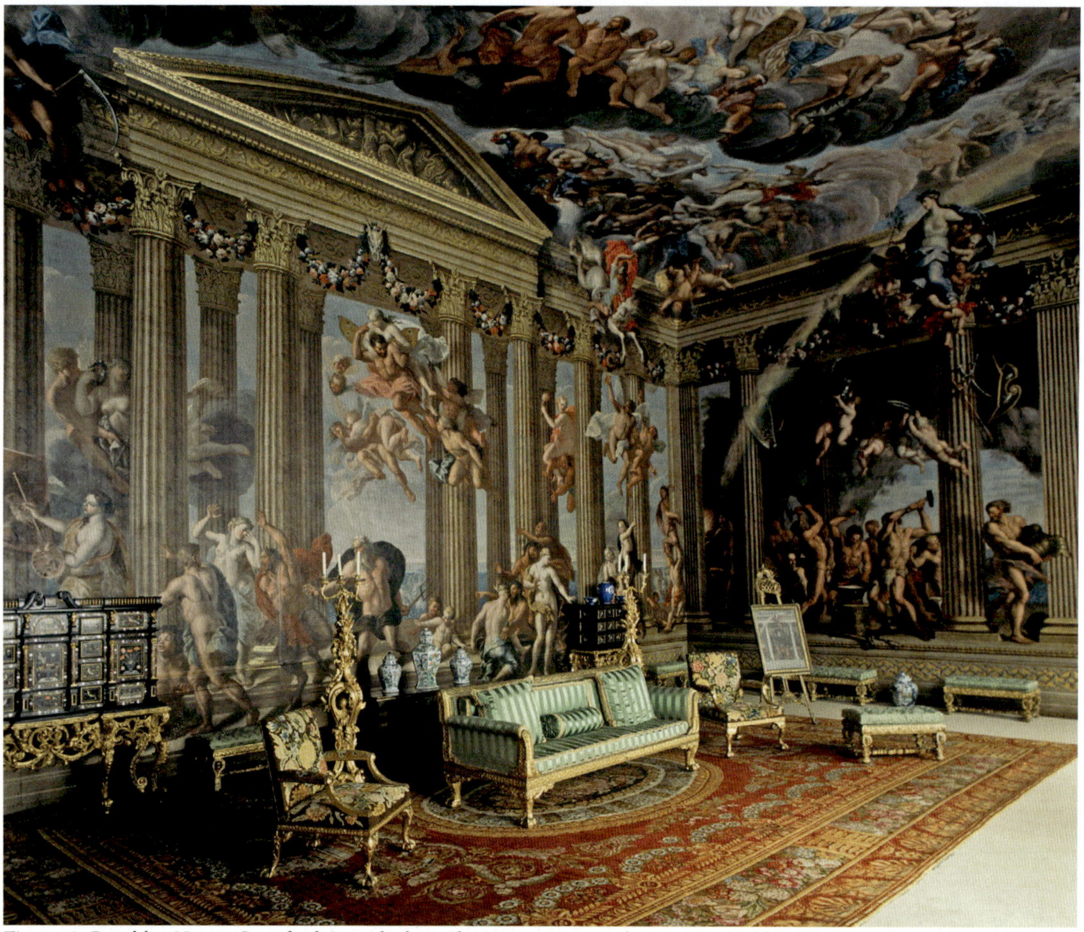

Figure 1 Burghley House, Stamford, Lincolnshire: the Heaven Room. *(© Martyn Goddard/Country Life Picture Library)*

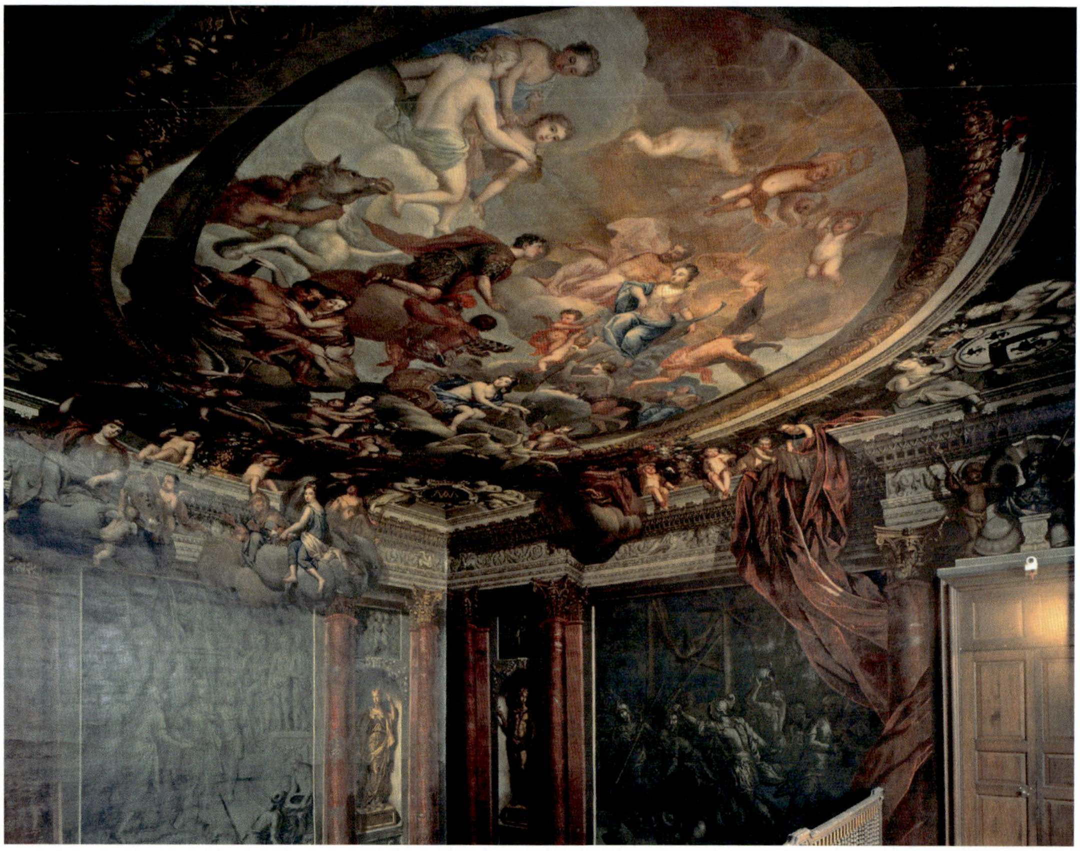

Figure 2 Burley-on-the-Hill, Rutland: Gerard Lanscroon's staircase hall has trompe l'oeil columns and niches framing the story of Perseus. *(© Mark Fiennes/Country Life Picture Library)*

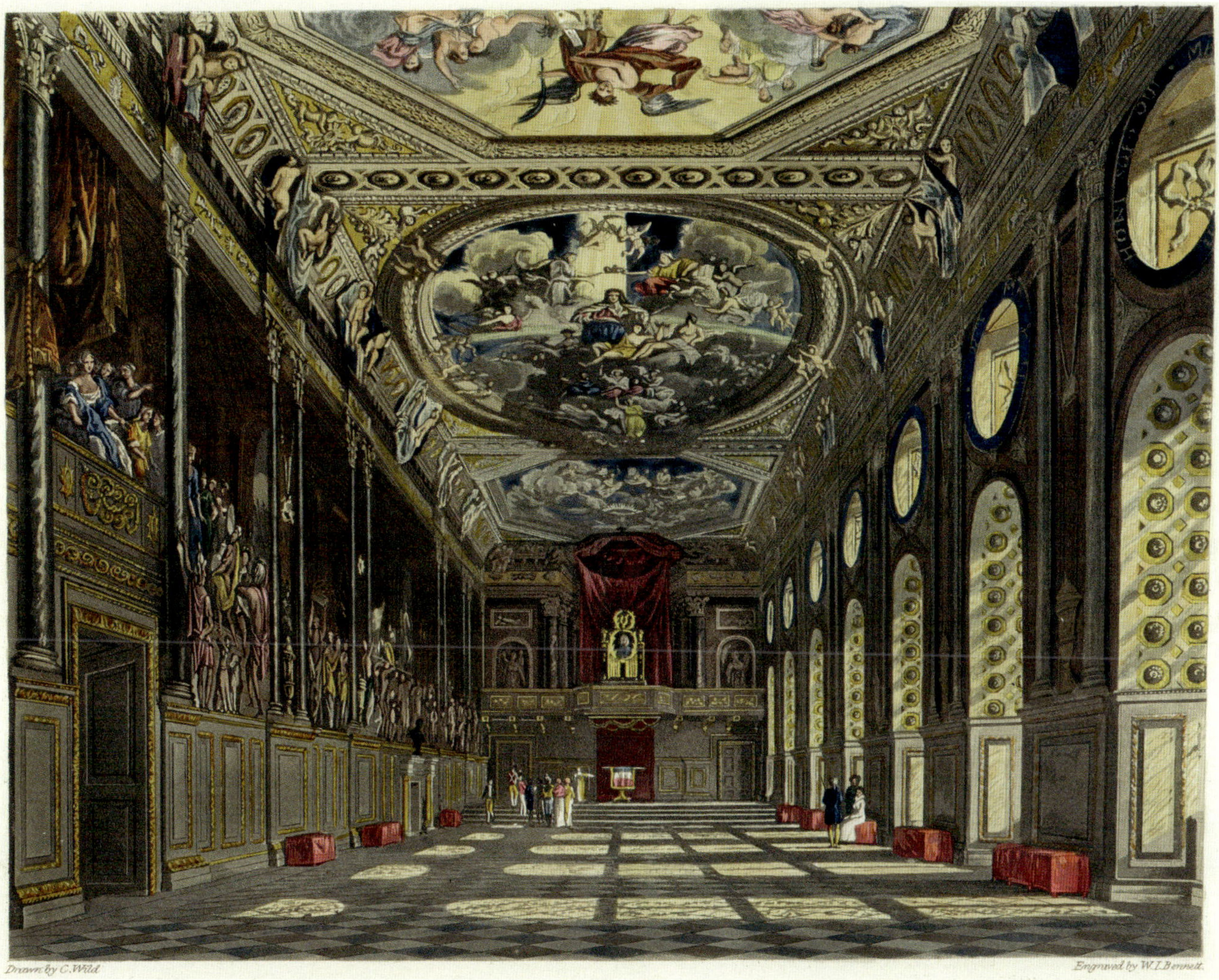

Figure 3 St George's Hall, Windsor Castle, Berkshire: watercolour showing the grandeur of Antonio Verrio's painted interior (1682–4). From Royal Residences, engraved by W.J. Bennett, published by William Henry Pyne (1769–1843) after Charles Wild (1781–1835). *(Private collection/Stapleton Collection/Bridgeman Art Library)*

been even more impressive (Fig. 3). In the ceiling, Charles II appears in his Garter robes, enthroned in glory and attended by allegorical figures. The star and collar of the Garter surrounded by allegorical figures were placed in subsidiary ovals. The cove was decorated with putti supporting Garter mantles, the round windows were encircled by large-scale versions of the Garter itself, and a *trompe l'oeil* tapestry with St George and the dragon was placed on the west wall. But the dominant feature of the room ran along the north wall, where the Black Prince, set within a framework of Corinthian columns, was seen being received in triumph by Edward III, the founder of the Order of the Garter.

The model for the decoration of both rooms is not contemporary Rome or Versailles, but the two great masterpieces of early 16th-century Italian art in English hands. The scene of *The Black Prince being Received in Triumph by Edward III* is a close reworking of Andrea Mantegna's *Triumphs of Caesar*, painted in about 1500 and among the great catches of Charles I's art collection displayed at Hampton Court. In Verrio's scene, we see the Black Prince borne on high in the midst of a procession of triumphant soldiers, like Caesar in Mantegna's *Triumphs*. In the Royal Chapel, Verrio's scene of *Christ Healing the Sick* is closely based on *Healing the Blind*, one of the Raphael cartoons commissioned by Leo X in 1515 and purchased by Charles I. These were also displayed at Hampton Court. The source for the imagery and the style of these two rooms thus predates the Baroque.

For all their ambition, these rooms were less innovative than we might think. Large-scale figurative wall decoration, usually achieved with tapestries, was an established tradition in the grand reception rooms of England's royal palaces. This had even been the case with Inigo Jones's Banqueting House, but was particularly true of Henry VIII's Hampton Court.

The painted decoration of the walls of St George's Hall and the Chapel is best understood as a continuation of this traditional way of decorating English royal residences with the addition of Baroque illusionistic ceiling painting. It needs to be read as part of the same thinking that led to the deliberate retention of the medieval ground plan and the attention paid to the medieval silhouette and elevations. The subject of the major decorative scheme, *The Black Prince being Received in Triumph by Edward III*, makes this point clear.

So why was St George's Hall decorated with wall paintings and not tapestries? The reason is probably cost. Tapestry was considerably more expensive than painting and Charles II's finances were always straitened. It is said

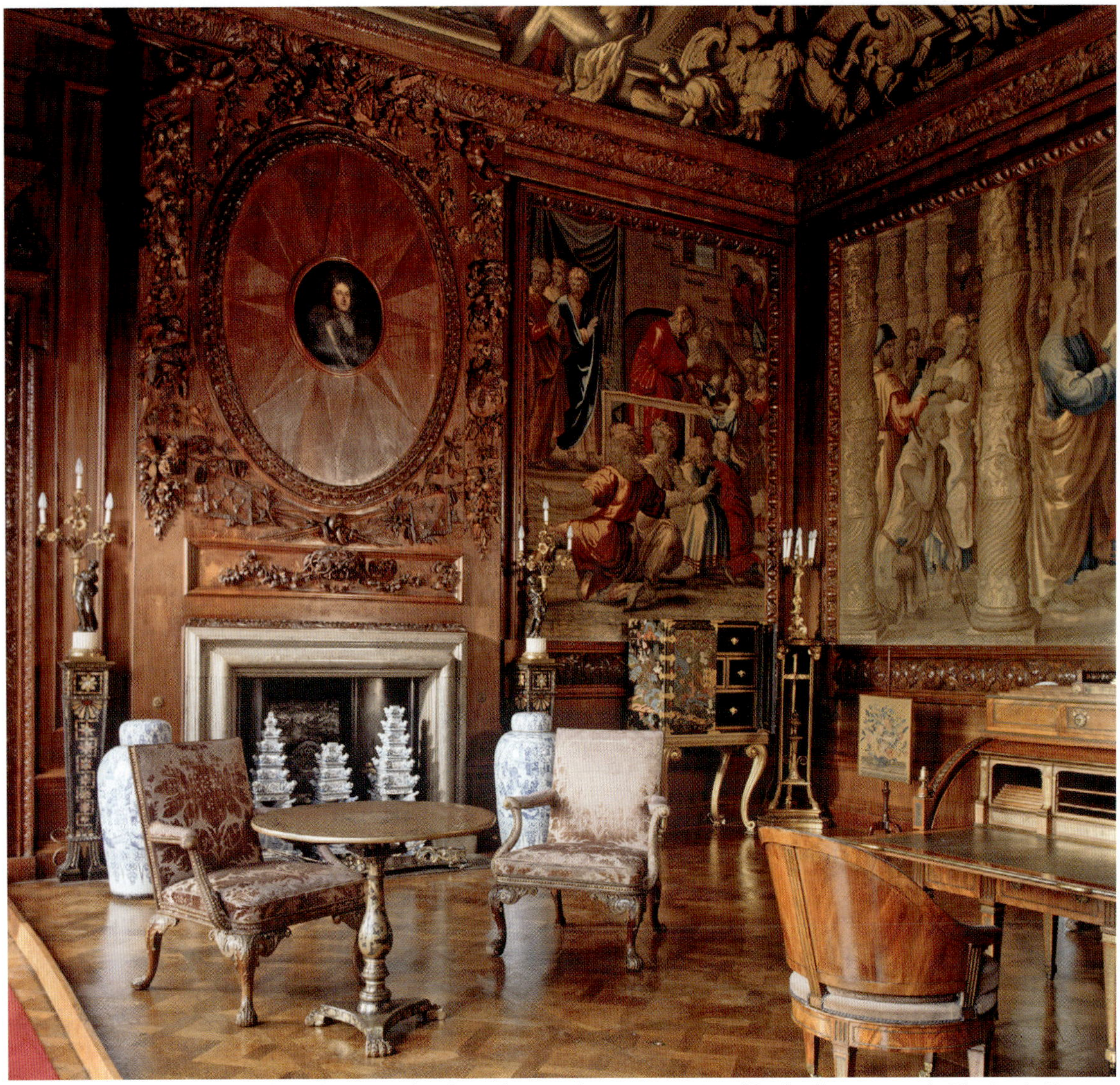

Figure 4 Chatsworth, Derbyshire: the Great Chamber is hung with tapestry copies of Raphael's cartoons. *(© Tim Imrie/Country Life Picture Library)*

that initially the suggestion was made that Verrio should work for the tapestry workshop at Mortlake. Perhaps the intention was that he should create cartoons for new tapestries for Windsor Castle, as Raphael had created cartoons for the Vatican tapestries, only for this approach to be abandoned as too expensive.

Some sense of what these rooms must have been like – although on a much smaller scale – can be found in William Talman's Great Chamber at Chatsworth of 1687–93 (Fig. 4). With a ceiling painted by Verrio and the walls hung with tapestry copies of the Raphael cartoons, including *The Healing of the Blind Man*, the Great Chamber was one of the most fash-

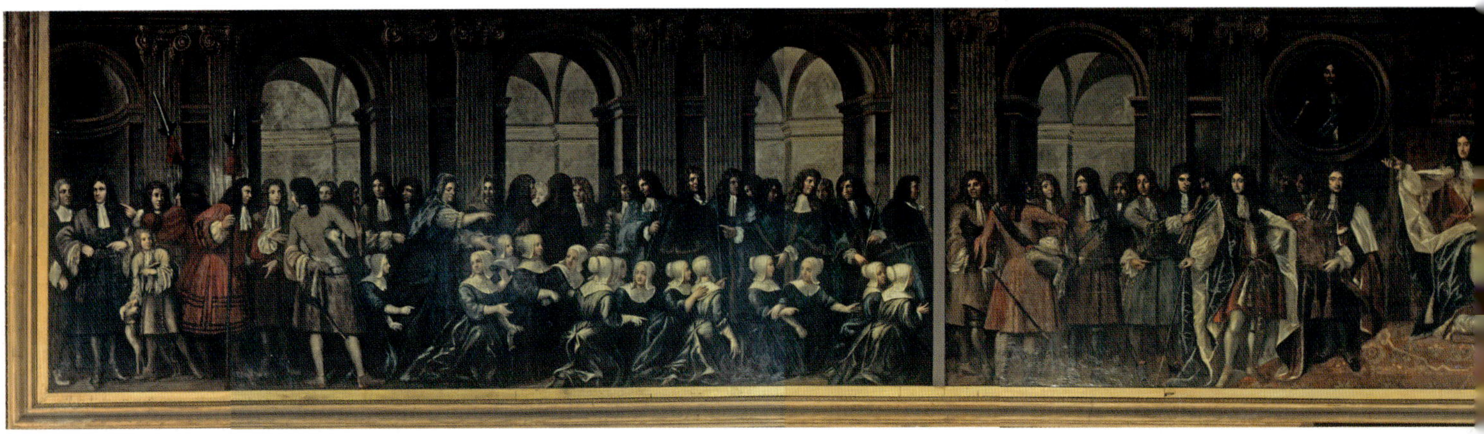

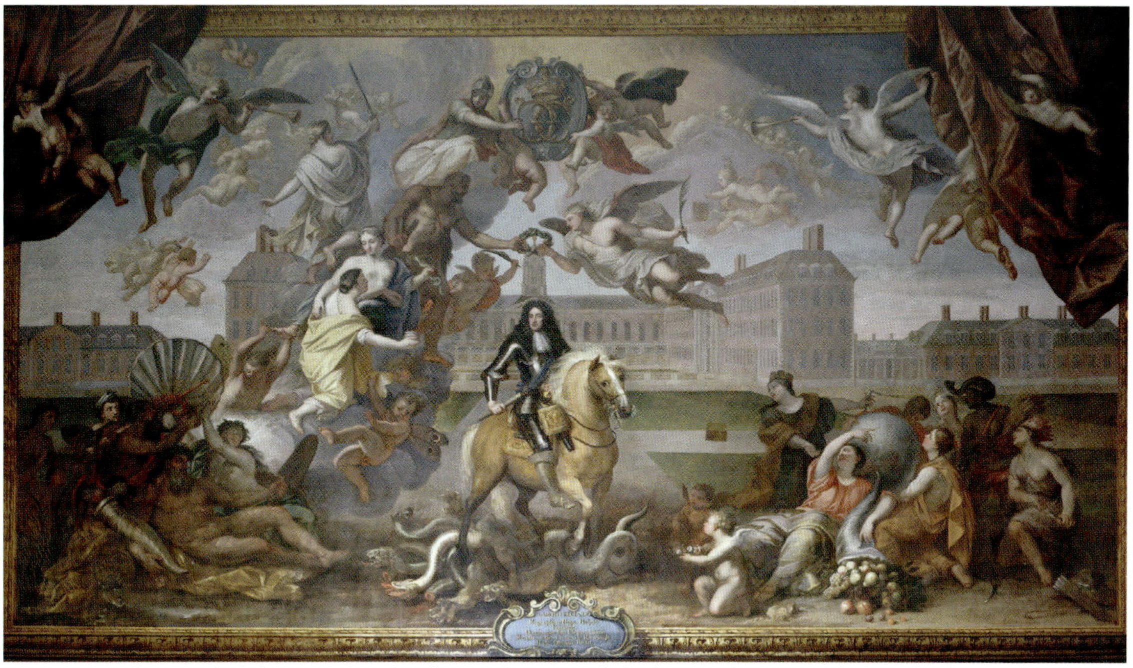

Figure 5 Royal Hospital Chelsea, London: the allegorical portrait of Charles II in the Great Hall. *(© Crown copyright. NMR)*

ionable interiors of its day and proof that tapestries remained the ideal for wall decoration.

The prestige of the monarchy and the person of Verrio meant that the decorative language of illusionistic painted walls spread swiftly from Windsor. The royal connotations of Windsor's decorations were soon forgotten, as Verrio and his imitators took the tradition to country house, townhouse and public building. For the better part of four decades, painted interiors were an essential part of any fashionable interior and there seems no reason to doubt that the driving force behind this new fashion was Windsor.

The staircases in the royal apartments seem to have been particularly influential. Although they do not survive and no views of them are known, descriptions indicate they were elaborately decorated with *trompe l'oeil* architecture and scenes, a new fashion for England. The Queen's Great Staircase of 1679–80 was the most elaborate. Here the dome was painted with Apollo granting Phaeton permission to drive the chariot of the gods. The cove was painted with signs of the zodiac. The walls were decorated with figures of the arts, painted in umber and heightened with gold to appear like brass statues, standing in niches and flanked by pilasters, together with two square niches containing Phaeton's sisters changed into trees and Cygnus turned into a swan. The inspiration for the Burley-on-the-Hill staircase is clear.

If final confirmation is needed of the fact that the English painted interior is part of an essentially traditional, native movement, not an innovatively Baroque creation, it is worth visiting two of the least known and most remarkable creations of the 1680s. In the Great Hall of the Royal Hospital Chelsea, the pensioners dine beneath a vast and complex allegorical portrait of Charles II, painted by Verrio and Henry Cooke in 1687–90 (Fig. 5) (see also the paper by Babington and Pelter in this volume, pp. 133–42). In the portrait, Charles II appears

Figure 6 Christ's Hospital, West Sussex: monumental mural depicting James II giving audience to the governors, masters and pupils of the Hospital. *(© June Buck/Country Life Picture Library, reproduced by kind permission of Christ's Hospital)*

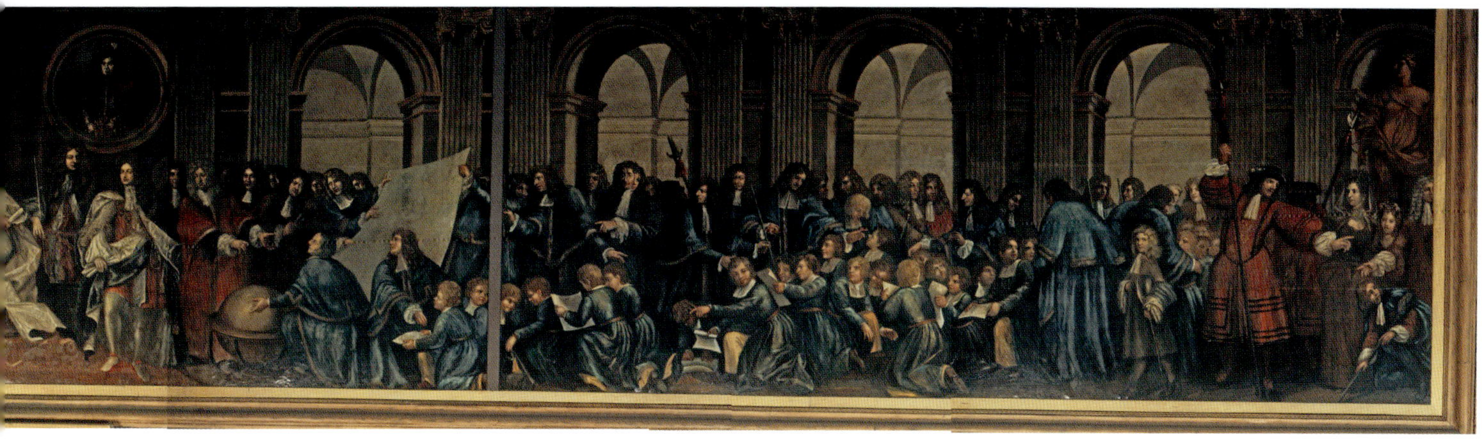

on horseback in front of the Royal Hospital, clad in armour, trampling serpents and receiving the grateful thanks of gods and people.

The vast portrait group commemorating the foundation of the Royal Mathematical School at Christ's Hospital, painted in 1684–8, is even more remarkable (Fig. 6). This frieze-like creation, which was originally in Christ's Hospital in London but moved with the school to Horsham, shows James II giving audience to the governors, masters, boys and girls of the hospital. Yeomen of the Guard keep order, boys kneel under the watchful eyes of their masters, noblemen and courtiers strut self-importantly, and above them all rises the hierarchic figure of the monarch, icon-like in his majesty. Technically adept it may be, but there is nothing modern about this painting.

Stylistically the whole creation is again rooted in 16th-century Italy, but the image of the monarch is the lineal descendant of a powerful tradition of royal portraiture, most famously Hans Holbein's imposing 1537 wall painting of Henry VIII, which dominated the Privy Chamber of Whitehall Palace. Sophisticated and Francophile though the late Stuart courts might have been, the fashion for painted interiors that are such a feature of their time remind us of an essential conservatism at the heart of English culture.

Editors' note

Dr Giles Worsley, who died in January 2006, battled illness to finish the manuscript of his seminal work on the English Baroque. The above article, which first appeared in the 21 April 2005 issue of *Country Life*, covers the same subject matter as the talk he gave to the *Illusions of Grandeur* conference. We are grateful to the editors of *Country Life* for their permission to reprint it here.

The author

Until his untimely death, Dr Giles Worsley was a Senior Research Fellow at the Institute of Historical Research and architecture critic of the *Daily Telegraph*. He had formerly been Architectural Editor of *Country Life* and Editor of *Perspectives on Architecture*, as well as the founding Editor of the *Georgian Group Journal*. His books include *Classical Architecture in Britain: The Heroic Age* (Yale University Press 1995) and *England's Lost Houses* (Aurum 2002) and he also edited *The Life and Work of John Carr* by Brian Wragg (Oblong 2000). *The British Stable* was published by Yale University Press in 2004, and shortly before his death he completed a monograph on Inigo Jones and a study of English Baroque architecture, both of which will be published by Yale University Press.

'The negligence of men' – restoration techniques and the altered appearance of Baroque wall paintings

Jane Davies

Introduction

> Some fine paintings by the hands of Signor Verrio, which are much damaged, and some in a manner quite spoiled by the dampness of the air, and the ravages of time or, which is at least equal to both, the negligence of men (Lord Oxford in 1725, describing the ceiling of the chapel at Snape Castle, Yorkshire).[1]

Despite their huge scale, lavish constituents and grand pretensions, English Baroque murals are in reality very fragile and vulnerable. In common with all wall paintings, their intimate relationship with the building in which they are housed makes them highly susceptible to physical damage. That they are found as part of high-status interiors has also proved problematic, as this has sometimes resulted in their extensive alteration, or even replacement, to reflect changes in fashionable taste. Where they have survived within luxury apartments their general condition and appearance has been kept under close scrutiny, which has often led to extensive restoration campaigns aimed at keeping them looking suitably 'smart'. Changes in ownership of the property, and the consequent influx of money, also tend to create occasions for restoration.

The essence of Baroque mural painting is its extravagance and flamboyance, characterised by the use of *trompe l'oeil* architecture, illusionistic spatial recession, implied dynamic movement, vivid colour, steep perspectives and complexity of form and ornament (see paper by Worsley, pp. 53–8). Their dependence upon illusion and spatial deceit mean that the fragile pictorial balance is easily spoiled by damage or by crude retouching.[2] The vibrant palette of the best paintings — luscious organic glazes, ultramarine blue skies, colourful drapery, extensive gilding — is quickly obliterated by the repeated application of varnishes that deteriorate, and overlying retouchings that discolour. In this visual sense Baroque murals are also particularly vulnerable (Fig. 1).

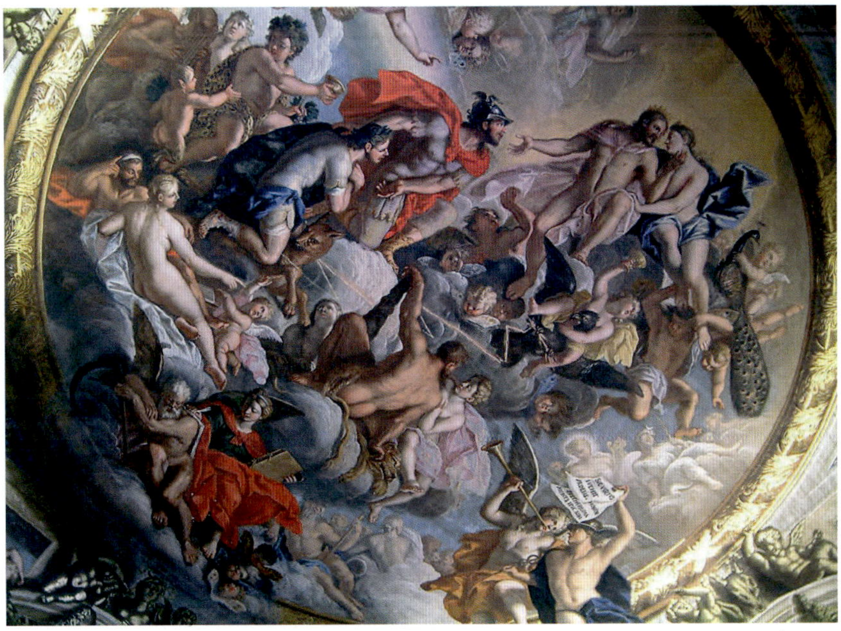

Figure 1 Burghley House, Stamford, Lincolnshire: second George Room ceiling, painted by Antonio Verrio between 1694 and 1696. *(© Burghley House)*

Unfortunately the huge scale of the typical Baroque wall painting tends to limit the attention that can be paid to individual areas. It can be difficult to treat these massive paintings with the same minute focus as is accorded to easel paintings of similar type and date. Since historic restoration has frequently involved 'broad brush' applications of natural resin varnishes – which darken over time – and more or less extensive overpainting of losses and damage, often using materials which will also deteriorate, the appearance of the post-restoration painting rapidly declines. This encourages further invasive treatments in cycles of ever-increasing frequency.

Rapid-onset deterioration

As the quotation above suggests, some Baroque murals began to deteriorate quite rapidly after painting. Snape Castle is provincial, but this was also true of more prestigious examples. When the north range of Windsor Castle was extensively remodelled for Charles II by the architect Hugh May, the premier Baroque muralist Antonio Verrio (1639–1707) was commissioned to decorate several of the new rooms. St George's Hall contained the most expensive of these schemes, illustrating the Black Prince and his entourage being received in triumph by Edward III, a fictive tapestry showing *St George and the Dragon*, and Charles II in Garter robes, all with elaborate subsidiary decoration. Completed between 1682 and 1684, the paintings cost £1,250. As early as 1724–6 Daniel Defoe writes 'the Salts in the Lime in the Wall, having worked out ... spoiled a great piece of Paint',[3] and reports that the entire decoration of the west wall has been repainted, with alterations to the design. He explains that he has been some 'years out of the Nation', and that since his last visit the representation of 'Prince Edward's Triumph in imitation of Caesar's glorious entry into Rome', which had been shown marching from north to south had been 'wholly inverted' with the 'march turned just the other way'. Defoe says Verrio himself returned to Windsor after 12 years at Burghley House and repainted the scene 'with greater Mastership of hand, than he had done the first'.

The repainting specified may have been the result of William III's dissatisfaction with the work's artistic standard, as is hinted by Defoe, who continues: 'the ceilings ... remain, being finished by the same hand in the most exquisite Manner at first'.[4] The subsequent history of the paintings at Windsor and Defoe's own note on salt damage, however, imply that deterioration may also have been a contributory cause for repainting. Interestingly, the scheme was also altered and 'modernised' by Sir Godfrey Kneller, who painted William III enthroned on the west wall over Verrio's *St George and the Dragon*.[5]

Archive documentation confirms the rapid onset of restoration cycles at Windsor Castle. The Royal Treasury Books and Papers record that William Kent was employed frequently by the Crown between 1730 and 1747 to repair and restore Verrio's work.[6] For example, in 1746 Kent undertook the repainting onto canvas and lath of the entire window side of the Hall, for which he was paid £260. Kent died in 1748 and the restoration programme continued in 1750–1 with William Oram and Stephen Wright, who were paid £590 for restoration of the 'King's staircase'. The painting again required attention in 1778, when Cipriani is recorded as receiving £75 for 'repairing and new painting a great number of figures in the Queen's Back stairs and in St George's Hall'. At the same date, £179 was paid to a John Richards – an 'Architect Painter' – for 'repairing painting in St George's Hall and finishing the Queen's Back Stairs, expenses included'.[7]

The majority of the St George's Hall scheme was obliterated in 1824 when Sir Jeffrey Wyatville undertook extensive rebuilding and redecoration of the castle interior for George IV. Various portrait heads were cut out at this time, and are now presented as easel paintings in frames.[8] The fire of 1992, which gutted the Hall, revealed fragments of figurative murals still surviving below the lath and plaster of the severely damaged Wyatville scheme (Fig. 2).[9]

While the documentary evidence of extensive interventions to the paintings at Windsor Castle is clear, the underlying cause of the extremely rapid and catastrophic deterioration

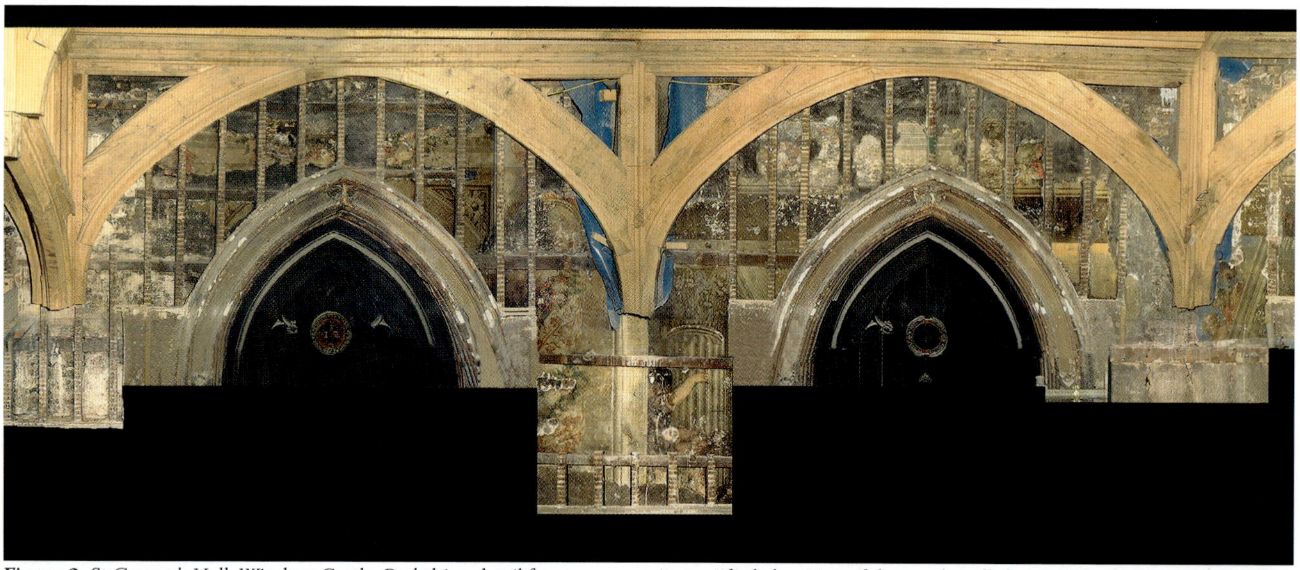

Figure 2 St George's Hall, Windsor Castle, Berkshire: detail from a composite rectified elevation of the south wall showing the fragmentary remains of wall paintings by Verrio that were exposed following the 1992 fire. *(© English Heritage Metric Survey Team)*

of Baroque wall paintings such as these remains less certain. I would argue that it is commonly related to dampness in the building structure, either from faults within the building or possibly from large quantities of new building materials (such as the underlying plaster). Perhaps it also relates to whether the support is lath and plaster, or whether the painting plaster was applied directly on the building fabric.

Surviving Baroque murals do not generally appear to have been dramatically affected by dampness. Rather, their poor appearance seems to reflect the 'negligence of men'. The causes of restoration in these paintings are not always those often associated with wall paintings – such as substrate cracking, dampness, or uncontrolled environment – but arise from a combination of the inherent deterioration of the constituent materials, failures associated with the original technique, and last but by no means least, historic restoration. The following two case studies illustrate these points.

Case studies

Burghley House

As with the archival evidence, technical examination frequently shows that Baroque wall paintings have been extensively restored. This is not always the case, however, and at Burghley House in Stamford, there survives in apparently almost pristine condition a remarkable sequence of rooms painted by Verrio and his assistants.

The majority of the existing house was built during the mid-16th century for William Cecil (Lord Burghley), with the Elizabethan structure being given slight external alterations during the late 17th century by William Talman for the 5th Earl of Exeter. During the 1690s, Verrio was working extensively for the 5th Earl, and between 1694 and 1696 he decorated the magnificent Heaven Room at Burghley with images

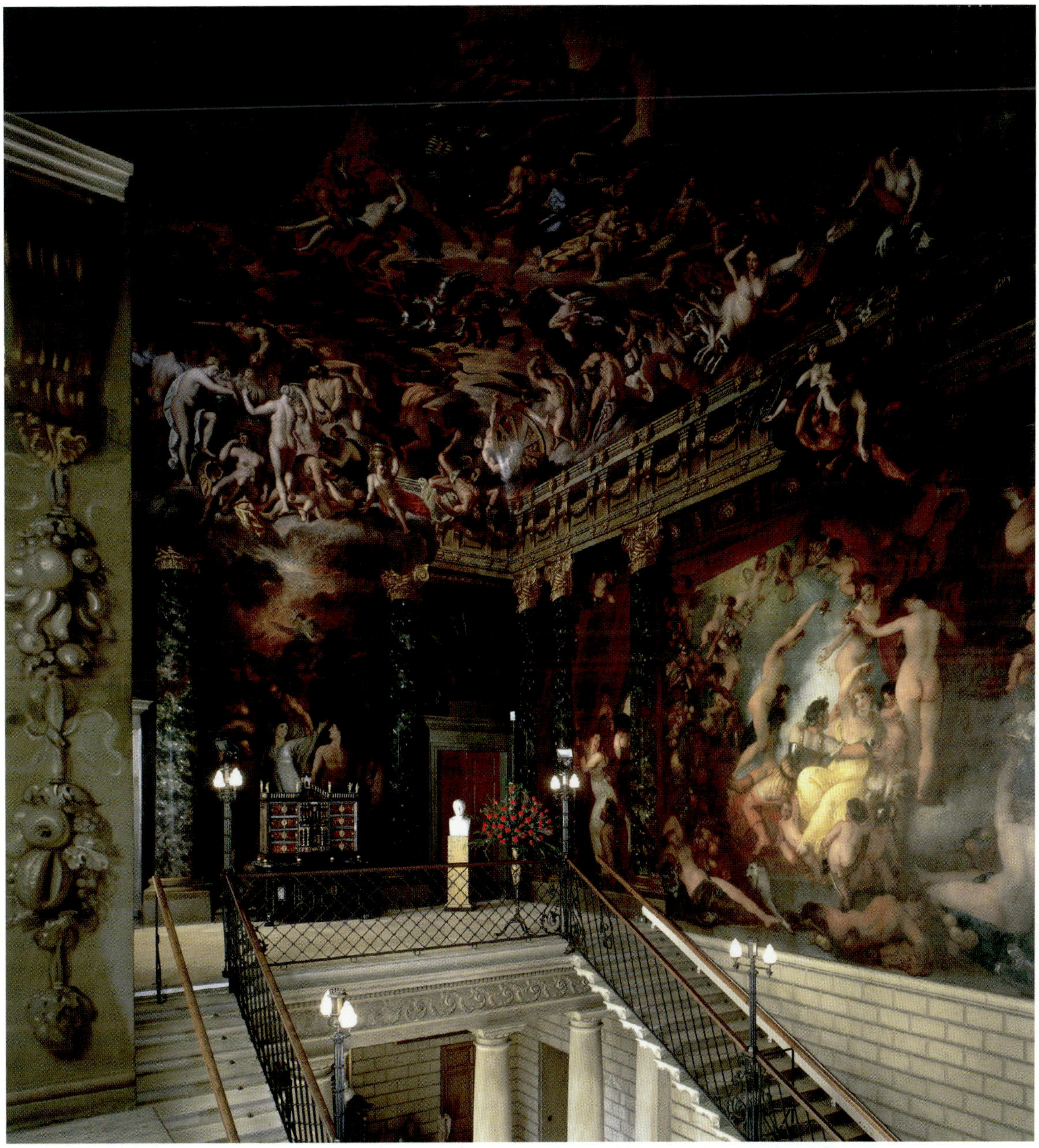

Figure 3 Burghley House, Stamford, Lincolnshire: the Hell Staircase, painted by Verrio between 1694 and 1696. *(© Burghley House)*

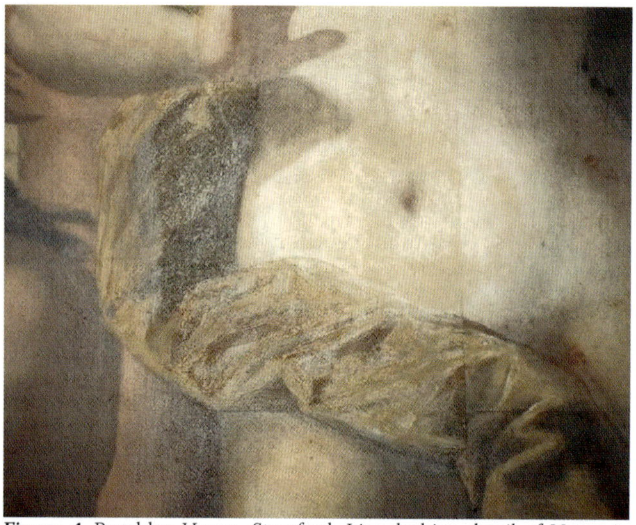

Figure 4 Burghley House, Stamford, Lincolnshire: detail of Venus in the Heaven Room showing horizontal and vertical pentimenti from underlying architectural elements, together with disfiguring delamination and cupping of specific areas of painted drapery overlying the architectural elements. *(© J. Davies)*

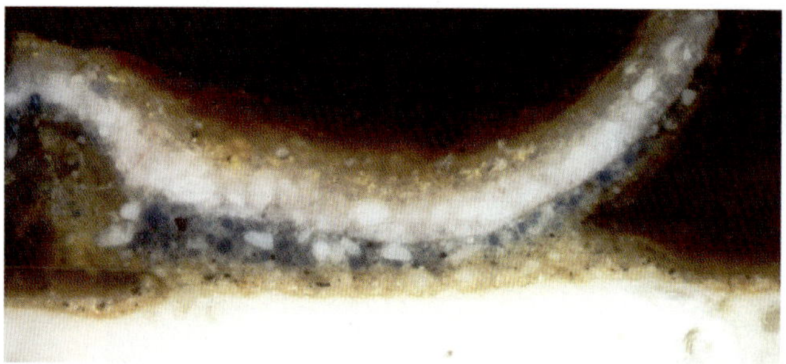

Figure 5 Burghley House, Stamford, Lincolnshire: photomicrograph showing a sample from the cracked drapery in cross-section. Photographed in dark-field reflected light at 200× magnification (printed magnification not calculated). The sample illustrates the separation of the upper from the lower paint layers. Thomas Stothard's varnish can be seen both on the surface and surrounding the edges of the paint flake. *(© J. Davies)*

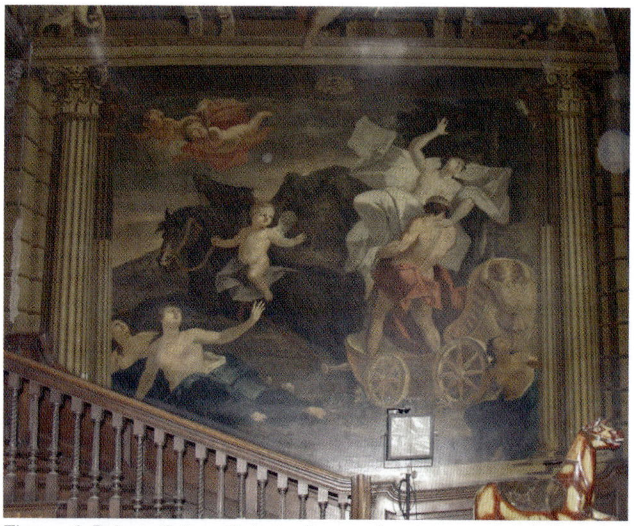

Figure 6 Reigate Priory, Reigate, Surrey: the staircase, painted around the end of the 17th or beginning of the 18th century. View of the south wall showing the *Rape of Proserpina* with overlying restoration layers. *(© Paine and Stewart)*

of Neptune and his court, an *Assembly of the Gods*, Venus caught in Vulcan's net, and a Cyclop's forge which includes a self-portrait (Figs 3, 4 and 5 and Fig. 1, p. 54).[10] The work is well documented and records survive not only of materials purchased by Verrio, but also of some of the assistants who helped him to produce these enormous paintings. As at Windsor Castle, several assistants were employed, some for colour grinding and others for more specialised tasks such as flower painting and gilding.[11] The splendid Heaven Room paintings have remained in very reasonable condition: there is only one recorded historic intervention – some restoration carried out in 1801 by the painter Thomas Stothard. A recent conservation programme included removal of 19th-century overpaint, and of a thin degraded varnish that had been applied to the walls but not the ceiling.[12]

Reigate Priory

Reigate Priory in Surrey, a Grade I-listed building set in 65 acres of parkland, was originally founded before 1200. In June 1541 Henry VIII granted the manor and priory of Reigate to Lord William Howard, uncle of Katherine Howard (Henry's fifth wife), and Reigate Priory became the Howard family seat, with the old monastic buildings being converted into a comfortable Tudor mansion. In 1681 Sir John Parsons, a wealthy brewer, purchased the manor and lands as a family home. He commissioned a fine timber staircase, ornamented with parquetry, which was constructed in the Great Hall between 1681 and 1685. The walls and ceiling of this staircase are decorated with paintings depicting *The Choice of Hercules*, *The Rape of Prosperina*, *The Liberal Arts* and an *Assembly of the Gods* (Fig. 6).

Edward Croft-Murray describes the paintings in his seminal book *Decorative Painting in England 1537–1837* (1962) and suggests that they were 'painted probably for Sir John Parsons, M.P. for Reigate, 1685–1714, and Lord Mayor of London, 1703...[their] approximate date given by a copy of Dr John Goodman's *A Winter-Evening Conference between neighbours*, first edition, which forms part of a pile of books introduced into the composition of the *Choice of Hercules*'.[13] Croft-Murray refers to the paintings as being by Verrio, but no documentary evidence relating to their painting survives.

After Sir John's death, the Priory passed to his son Humphrey, but in 1766 the property was sold to Richard Ireland. He made numerous alterations to the structure, giving it its current 18th-century appearance. The property was left to Ireland's niece Ann Jones, whose son and grandson then lived in the house. In 1801 the estate was purchased from them by George Mowbray, who in turn sold it in 1808 to John Somers Cocks, later 1st Earl Somers. The house was sold again in 1821 to Countess Beatty. The final private owner to occupy the house was Admiral Earl Beatty, whose son Peter sold the property to Reigate Corporation in 1942.[14] The house is now home to Reigate Priory School and Reigate Priory Museum.

In contrast to the relatively pristine condition of Burghley's Heaven Room, the staircase paintings at Reigate Priory are coated with up to five sequential varnish layers – each of which is associated with some level of restoration – overpaint, and incidental surface accretions (Figs 7 and 8). The scheme has

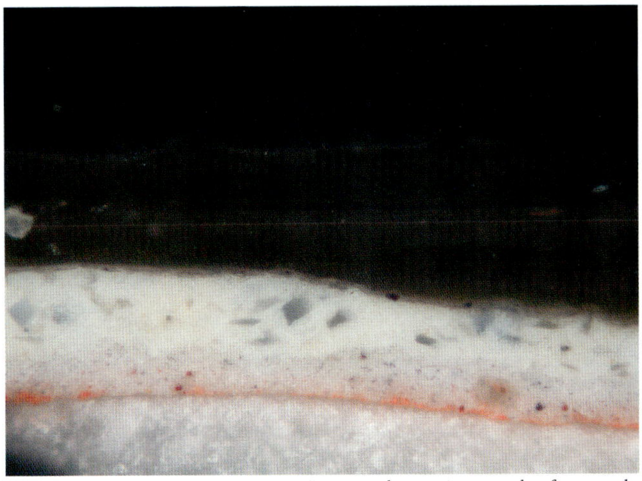

Figure 7 Reigate Priory, Reigate, Surrey: photomicrograph of a sample from the trompe l'oeil architecture of the *Rape of Proserpina* in cross-section. Photographed in dark-field reflected light at 200× magnification (printed magnification not calculated). The sample shows the plaster substrate, red sealant, double grey ground and blue-grey architecture containing smalt pigment, together with overlying varnish layers. *(© J. Davies)*

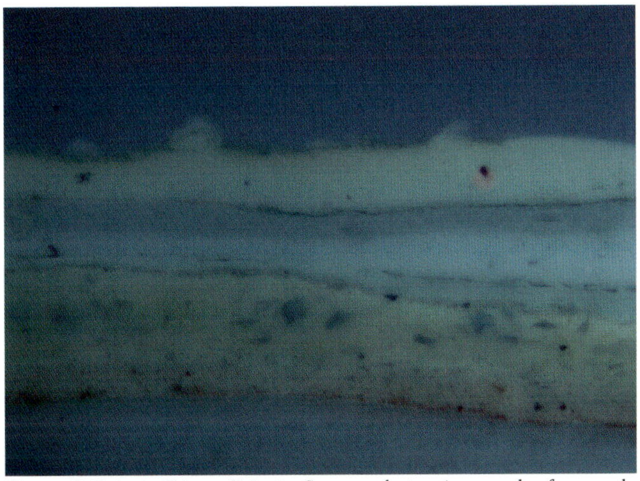

Figure 8 Reigate Priory, Reigate, Surrey: photomicrograph of a sample from the trompe l'oeil architecture of the *Rape of Proserpina* in cross-section. Photographed under ultraviolet illumination, with Leica filter cube A at 200× magnification (printed magnification not calculated). The sample shows the differential fluorescence of four varnish layers present on the sample surface. *(© J. Davies)*

suffered some cracking of the plaster substrate (apparently due to movement of the building) which would have occasioned treatment, but it seems likely that the number of times the Priory changed hands has influenced the frequency of restorations of the painting.

Original techniques and inherent deterioration

The typical materials and techniques of English Baroque wall painting can be summarised quite simply: several layers of oil paint were applied over one or more oil-bound ground layers, in turn applied over an oil-rich, sparsely pigmented 'sealant' brushed onto the plaster surface. The plaster rendering is composed of several coats, the finest surface layer or skim being applied over one or more coarser plaster layers. The plaster skim will normally contain a low percentage of small-sized aggregate, but fine skims have been identified with little or no aggregate, sometimes modified with organic fluids including oils and/or resins and proteins. The plaster layers are fixed either directly onto the building fabric (brick or stone) or onto a wooden lath system fixed to the building structure.[15]

While the techniques employed seem generally robust, the use of certain materials may predispose English Baroque wall paintings to failure. The use of impervious drying oils to coat the porous plaster is problematic if high levels of moisture occur. The presence of proteins (glues) at the interface of oil paint and plaster poses two potential threats: the delamination of the paint in response to changes in relative humidity or moisture ingress, and the potential for microbiological growth.

The use of unstable pigments such as realgar and orpiment has been noted in several works. These pigments can discolour to whitish-brown arsenic trioxide, and evidence of this deterioration can be seen at Burghley House. During the Baroque period, artists commonly used organic pigments for producing beautiful glazes; these pigments fade upon exposure to light. A defect that appears on many Baroque murals is a distracting 'alligator' craquelure. This has an appearance generally associated with poor drying of an oil medium, where the upper paint surface has contracted to form a series of scales. In the paintings studied, however, the alligatoring appears to be associated as much with the number of underlying layers of ground and painting as with any inherent fault in the paint mixtures.

The completion of the painted architecture prior to inserting the figures is believed to have been common practice, as the raised outlines of pillars, pavements and so forth are frequently visible in raking light beneath overlying painting, and are occasionally apparent as *pentimenti*. The raised outlines of the painted architecture probably result from the use of straight edges and templates, presumably utilised in conjunction with plumb lines and compasses. Observations by Dudley Ryder, who visited Sir James Thornhill in 1716 when he was working on the dome of St Paul's Cathedral, corroborates visual evidence. Ryder noted that the *trompe l'oeil* architecture was finished, the gilding partially done, but that none of the 'history part' had yet been painted.[16]

Examination of samples from the alligatored areas reveals the cleavage of the upper paint layers from the layer associated with the underlying *trompe l'oeil* architecture. Figures 9 and 10 show a detail of the head of Bacchus on the north wall at Burghley; the disfiguring craquelure exists only where underlying 'architectural' paint layers are present.

Restorations

The causes of restoration deserve consideration. Two factors are critical: deterioration (whether innate or associated with previous restoration) and location. The position of these paintings within high-status properties means they are subject to close scrutiny, and where the householders were wealthy the paintings may have been altered or obliterated to accord with fashionable taste. Burghley House and Reigate Priory illustrate

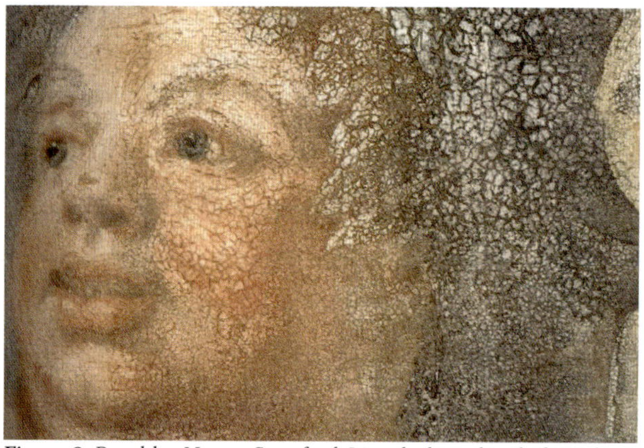

Figure 9 Burghley House, Stamford, Lincolnshire: detail of Bacchus's head in the Heaven Room showing the disfiguring 'alligator' craquelure that appears on many Baroque murals. This appears to be associated with aspects of original technique, in particular the sequential application of numerous paint layers representing *trompe l'oeil* architecture. The left side (as seen) of Bacchus is sound, while the right is damaged. Dark areas have noticeably more severe craquelure, and it is probable that more than one phenomenon is affecting the paint in this area. *(© J. Davies)*

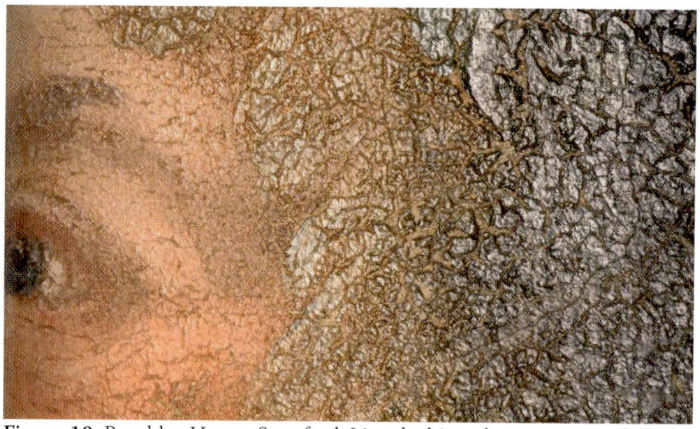

Figure 10 Burghley House, Stamford, Lincolnshire: photomacrograph detail of Bacchus's head in the Heaven Room showing the disfiguring 'alligator' craquelure that appears on many Baroque murals and seems to be associated with aspects of original technique. *(© J. Davies)*

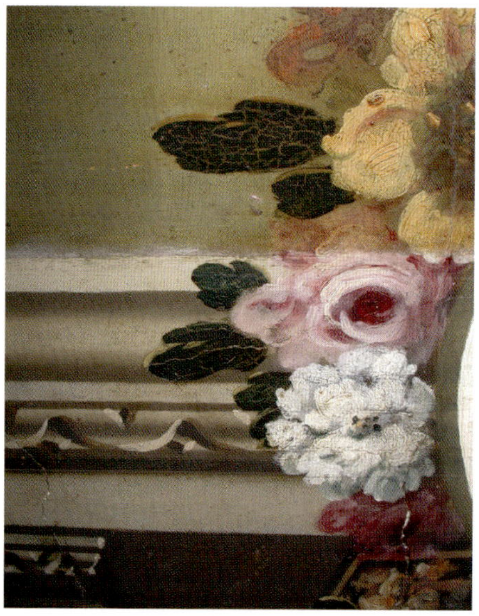

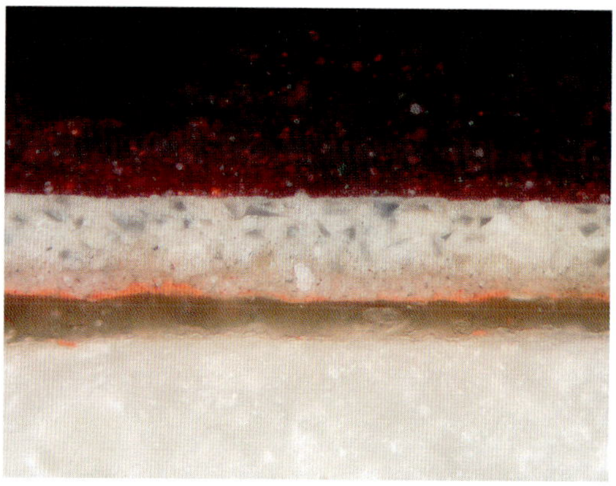

Figure 12 Reigate Priory, Reigate, Surrey: photomicrograph of a sample from the glaze on the pink roses on the ceiling, shown in cross-section. Photographed in dark-field reflected light at 200× magnification (printed magnification not calculated). The sample shows the plaster substrate, a gap in the sample where slight delamination has occurred during sampling, red sealant, double grey ground and pale blue paint, thickly glazed with red lake pigment. *(© J. Davies)*

Figure 11 Reigate Priory, Reigate, Surrey: detail of the ceiling during conservatioln showing the different appearance of the flowers and foliage before and after varnish removal. *(© J. Davies)*

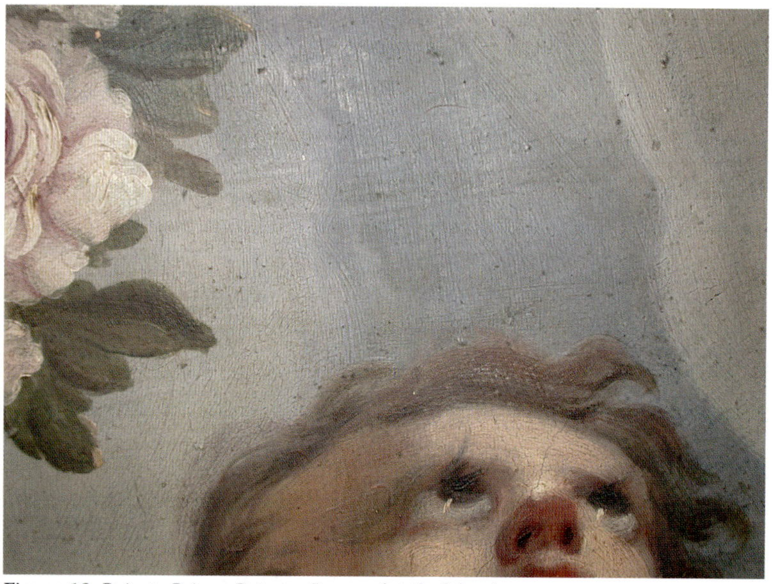

Figure 13 Reigate Priory, Reigate, Surrey: detail of the sky on the ceiling after varnish removal. *(© J. Davies)*

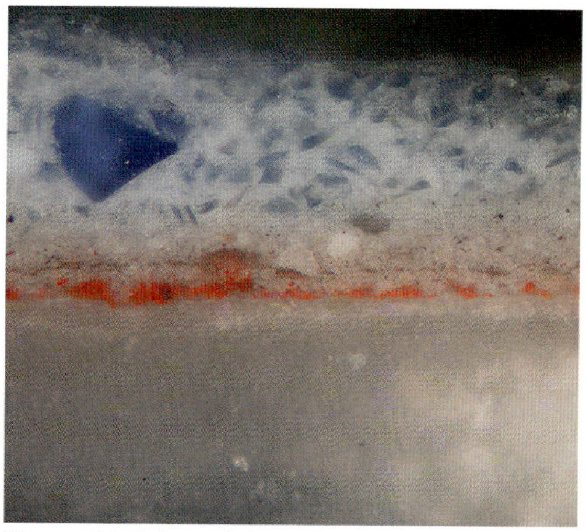

Figure 14 Reigate Priory, Reigate, Surrey: photomicrograph of a sample from the blue sky on the ceiling, shown in cross-section. Photographed in dark-field reflected light at 200× magnification (printed magnification not calculated). The sample shows the plaster substrate, red sealant, double grey ground and blue sky containing a significantly large smalt pigment particle. *(© J. Davies)*

how wealth and changes of ownership seem to have a direct relationship on the number of interventions that have occurred. At Burghley House, which has remained within the Cecil family, very little treatment has been carried out to the paintings. At Reigate Priory, where the house has periodically been sold, a significant number of restorations have taken place.

The problems associated with restoration of Baroque wall paintings are many. The huge scale of these schemes will tend to limit the amount of time that can be given to specific areas. Financial considerations may have limited treatments to broad-brush campaigns, such as may be seen at Reigate, where the new varnishes were simply applied directly over the old with only the most cursory surface cleaning. While 'wetting out' the surface of the underlying varnish may temporarily freshen the appearance, eventually it inevitably obscures the painting as the new varnish too begins to age and discolour. The surface sheen of the paintings can also be dramatically altered by the application of varnish. Gloss finishes tend to highlight any unevenness of the surface and can cause reflections preventing the viewer from reading the illusionistic effects of the paintings (Figs 11–14).

More difficult to quantify are the effects restoration treatments may have had on the original materials. For example, it may be possible that applications of spirit-based, relatively fast-drying varnish exacerbate the alligatoring discussed above. The visual impacts of deterioration and restoration can be classified into distinct categories. Those caused by deterioration include fading or discoloration of original materials (for example organic glazes and unstable pigments), disruption of the original surface from cracks (either within the plaster substrate or as paint craquelure), and paint delamination and flaking. Restoration can have a visual impact from poorly executed repairs, inadequately matched or discoloured overpaint, and applications of inappropriate varnishes.

Conclusions

The purpose of this paper is to illuminate Baroque wall paintings by providing information on the materials and techniques used in their production, and some of the range of restoration treatments and alterations to which they have been subject. A debate is overdue on the significance of these important paintings today, as is a considered discussion of the passive and active conservation programmes that may be safely applied to them. Such information is essential for conservator and art historian alike if we are to reach a fuller understanding of these majestic works.

A discussion of conservation best practice raises many complex issues. Each painting, with its unique physical history, will have to be approached in a slightly different way. Some must be accepted as 18th- or 19th-century restorations of earlier paintings – the extent to which they have been treated and the irreversibility of the materials used may mean that in some cases it will be more damaging to attempt to remove later additions than to leave well alone. All paintings will benefit from a watching brief, whereby their condition is surveyed at regular intervals and any deterioration monitored. Where deterioration is observed, it is important to identify and understand its causes so that an effective conservation strategy can be planned.

For some paintings there is justification for considered intervention. It may sound controversial to suggest cosmetic treatment, but if certain paintings are to be read in the way the artists intended, then significant treatment will be necessary. Removal of varnishes and overpaint is common practice in easel painting conservation, and in terms of surface materials and finish, English baroque murals can be very like huge easel paintings. Removal of later materials introduced by restoration cannot be dismissed as a treatment option. Where

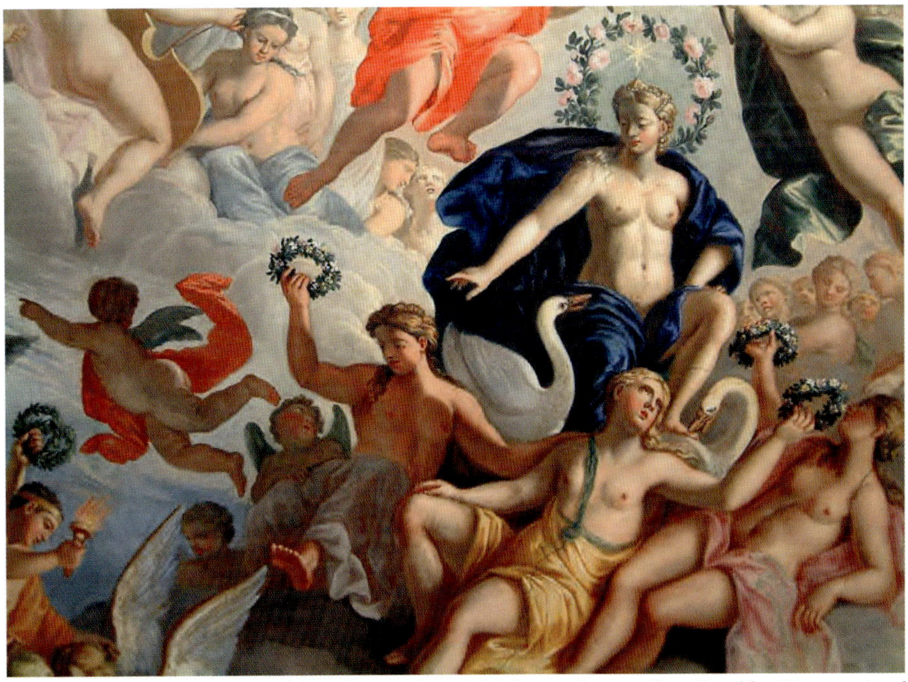

Figure 15 Burghley House, Stamford, Lincolnshire: third George Room ceiling, Burghley House, painted by Verrio between 1694 and 1696. *(© Burghley House)*

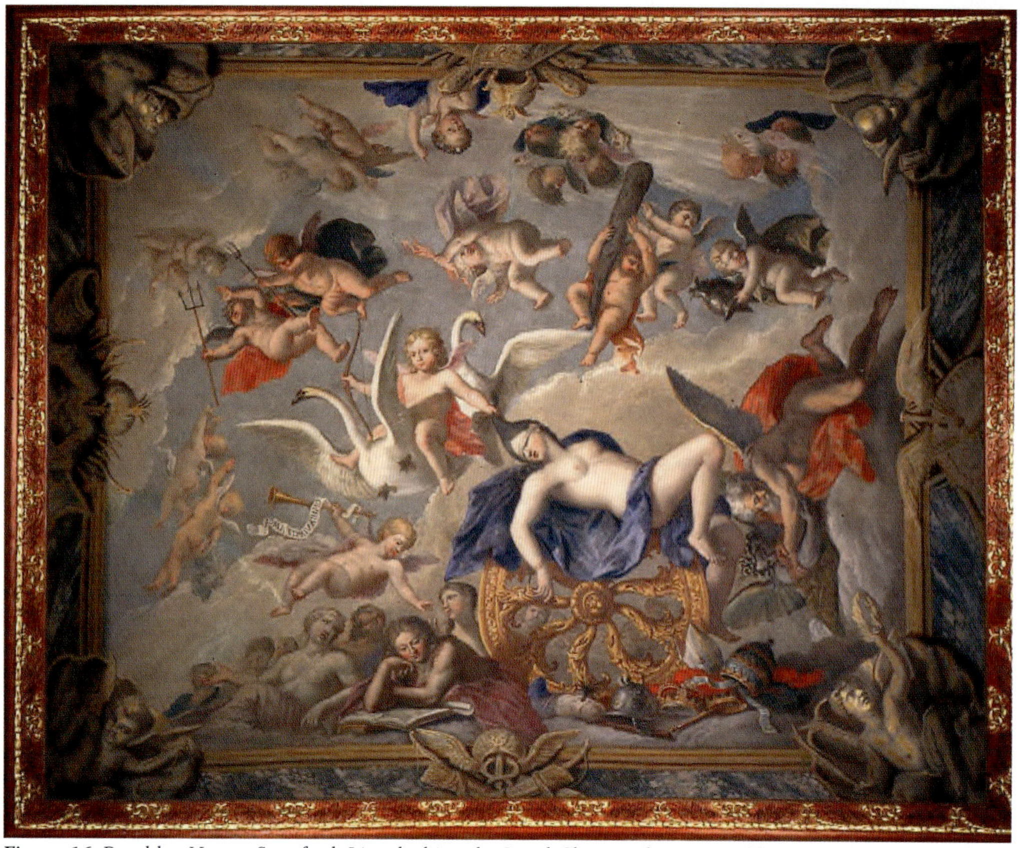

Figure 16 Burghley House, Stamford, Lincolnshire: the Jewel Closet ceiling painted by Verrio between 1694 and 1696. *(© Burghley House)*

these paintings differ from easel paintings is in their situation, and in their physical relationship with the building in which they are found; they cannot be separated physically or visually from the space for which they were designed. These factors can limit or alter treatments which may otherwise be deemed suitable (Fig. 15).

Contemporary accounts such as John Evelyn's *Diary* illustrate the high esteem in which artists such as Verrio were held in fashionable 17th-century society: 'Signor Verrio's fresco Paintings ... I think ... comparable certainly to the greatest of old Masters, or what they so celebrate at Rome.'[17] Today, English Baroque murals are usually seen merely as one decorative element of the opulent interiors of stately homes. They have been derided in art-historical studies: Waterhouse (1953) for example, describes Verrio as 'one of the worst' painters in Britain (Fig. 16).[18]

This assessment may in part be accounted for by the poor condition of the paintings. Often they have suffered considerable deterioration: fine glazes have faded, varnishes have darkened, images have disappeared in the reflective sheen of glossy coatings, detail has been hidden by crude overpaint, and images disfigured by cracks. In these circumstances it is hard to appreciate the impact these lavish works would have had when freshly painted. Jewel-bright with ultramarine skies, luscious with lake glazes and glittering with gilding, these paintings embodied the social superiority, taste and education of their aristocratic patrons.

Notes

1. The ceiling of the chapel at Snape Castle in Yorkshire was painted by Verrio, probably during the 1690s, with an illustration of the *Wonder and War in Heaven* from Revelation XII. Lord Oxford visited Snape Castle during his tour of the north-east of England in 1725 (Croft-Murray 1962, p. 240).
2. The diarist John Evelyn commented 'Virio the Painter's Invention is likewise admirable, his Ord'nance full and flowing, antique and heroical, his figures move; and if the walls hold ... the work will preserve his name to ages' (Evelyn 1955, p. 317).
3. Defoe 1968, p. 308.
4. *Ibid.*
5. Croft-Murray 1962, p. 241.
6. Colvin *et al.* 1976, pp. 182 and 336–7.
7. *Ibid.*, p. 341.
8. Janice Sacher, Royal Collection, pers. comm. The Royal Collection holds three pictures from Verrio's murals at Windsor: two portraits of Charles II and a fragment of a warrior's head from St George's Hall and from the ceiling of the King's Presence Chamber. There is also a portrait of Charles II at Packwood House that originates from the ceiling of the King's Drawing Room.
9. Adrian Buckley (at the time Head of Easel Painting Conservation, English Heritage, now retired), pers. comm.
10. Croft-Murray 1962, p. 236.
11. *Ibid.*, pp. 55 and 243–62.
12. Mike Cowell, Burghley House Conservation Officer, pers. comm. Mike Cowell undertook conservation over a 5-year period from October 1998 to February 2003, working during five winter seasons while the house was closed and during two summer seasons. Small areas were treated individually, with access provided from tower scaffolding. Stothard's restoration materials were removed except for a few discreet sections where they were preserved as evidence of the physical history of the painting. The cleaned paintings were varnished using matt Paraloid B72, and

retouching of localised damage was carried out using pigments bound in Paraloid B72.
13. Croft-Murray 1962, pp. 239–40.
14. Paine and Stewart 2002.
15. For a fuller discussion of original materials and techniques, see Davies 1994, 1996 (pp. 15–27), 1997 and Friedrichs 1995–2000.
16. Croft-Murray 1962, p. 73.
17. Evelyn 1955, p. 344.
18. Waterhouse 1953, p. 87.

References

Colvin H.M., Mordaunt Crook J., Downes K. and Newman J. 1976, *The History of the King's Works*, Vol. 5: *1660–1782*, HMSO, London

Croft-Murray E. 1962, *Decorative Painting in England 1537–1837*, vol. 1, *Country Life*, London

Davies J. 1994, *On Gilded Clouds ... A Study of the Materials and Techniques of Oil on Plaster Murals of the Late Seventeenth and Eighteenth Centuries in England*, unpublished M.Phil thesis, Royal College of Art/Victoria and Albert Museum Conservation Course

Davies J. 1996, 'On painted ceilings ... the techniques of Baroque murals in England', *The Conservator* 20, pp. 15–27

Davies J. 1997, 'Five Baroque wall paintings: an analytical investigation', *The Analysis of Pigments and Plasters: Its Relevance to Current Wall Painting and Stone Conservation Practice*, Postprints of the Wall Paintings Section Conference, February 1997, UKIC, London

Defoe, D 1968, *A Tour thro' the whole Island of Great Britain 1724–6, with an introduction by G.D.H. Cole* [originally published London, 1927], 2nd impression, 2 vols, Cass & Co., London

Evelyn J. 1955, *Diary 1640–1706*, E.S. Beer (ed.), vol. 4, Clarendon Press, Oxford

Friedrichs A. 1995–2000, *Baroque Wall Paintings in National Trust Properties*, unpublished thesis for the Training Programme for Research and Conservation of Painted Objects and Historic Interiors, The National Trust

Paine and Stewart 2002, *Reigate Priory: Condition Survey of the Painted Decoration in the Staircase*, unpublished report produced for Surrey County Council

Waterhouse E. 1953, *Painting in Britain 1530 to 1790*, Penguin, London

The author

After graduating in 1989, Jane Davies worked for a conservation company specialising in the conservation of architectural surface finishes, paint and wall paintings. Her M.Phil with the Victoria and Albert Museum/Royal College of Art Conservation course examined the materials and techniques of English Baroque wall paintings, and she then worked at the English Heritage Conservation Studio, first as a member of the Wall Painting Conservation Section and later with the Architectural Paint Research team. Jane set up as an independent consultant in 1996, undertaking detailed examination of decorative architectural plasters and paints and the technical investigation of wall paintings for a broad range of clients.

Mural paintings within the Historic Royal Palaces: our approach to their continuous care

Kate Frame and Sophie Julien-Lees

Introduction

Historic Royal Palaces (HRP) is the latest in a continuous line of bodies to have custodial responsibility for royal wall paintings: a line that stretches back to at least the 17th century and that has included various royal painters of the day, the pre-1900s Office of Works, the Ministry of Works, the Department of the Environment, the Property Services Agency and English Heritage. Historic Royal Palaces was created in 1989 to conserve and manage five royal palaces, all heritage sites of international significance: HM Tower of London, Hampton Court Palace, Kensington Palace State Apartments, the Banqueting House Whitehall, and Kew Palace (including Queen Charlotte's Cottage).

Under this mantle it assumed responsibility for the conservation of 26 large-scale and richly decorative wall paintings. Sixteen of these are Baroque or Italian-inspired, and they represent the work of four important artists: Antonio Verrio (1639–1707), James Thornhill (1675–1734), William Kent (1685–1748), and Peter Paul Rubens (1577–1640) (Figs 1–4). All these spectacular schemes came into being as a result of royal commissions to highlight the significance of important rooms, usually as part of major rebuilding.

Each past custodial body has been active in its care of the paintings, cleaning and restoring them in ways consistent with restoration practices and aesthetic standards of the day and the condition of the works. Past conservation philosophies may perhaps have been less observant of the historic and original aesthetic qualities of a work than those of today, and less likely to have based interventions on scientific principles. As a consequence, the Baroque wall paintings throughout the palaces have been extensively altered: repeatedly cleaned (in some cases over-cleaned), heavily overpainted and retouched, and coated many times. Even structures have been modified, most notably affecting the paintings of Rubens at the Banqueting House, Whitehall, much of Kent's 1725 King's Staircase scheme at Kensington Palace, and Kent's 1734 Queen's Staircase at Hampton Court Palace. Originally canvas paintings on timber stretchers, these paintings were adhered directly onto plywood supports during major treatment campaigns in the 1930s, 1940s and 1950s (Fig. 5).

Extensive retouching continued as common practice as late as the 1960s. Some enhancements could even be viewed as amusing: on Verrio's painted schemes at Hampton Court Palace, eyelashes have been painted on a female figure on the King's Staircase (Fig. 6), and a wristwatch is prominent on a satyr within a grisaille panel in the Queen's Drawing Room. Nevertheless it is worth remembering that this legacy of work also served the collection well, saving it from the damaging effects of past accidents typically due to water leaks and building movement. Wherever a palace building has survived, so too have its wall paintings, however altered. In part their survival might be due to the fact that none of these palaces remained the principal royal residence for long after the decorative commissions were completed and so, by and large, interiors were simply maintained rather than redecorated. Perhaps one exception to this is the loss of the William Kent scheme in the former King's State Bedchamber at Kensington Palace, subsequently converted to apartments for the young Princess Victoria and her mother the Duchess of Kent.

The legacy of this highly interventive approach, along with HRP's likely temporary status (as with the custodians before us), has led us to adopt a conservative programme for the continued preservation of the wall paintings. In many respects we are continuing with the conservation-focused approach to preserving the works started by English Heritage. Thus, at present, our primary interest is twofold: first to do the minimum treatment necessary to ensure retention of a collection of stable paintings, and secondly to create a permanent archive of information that will enable us and future conservators to be both technically and art historically informed when approaching their conservation needs. This also takes account of limited resources. It is more effective to target wall paintings in a programme of continuous care, which prevents the build-up of large treatment backlogs, than to embark on large-scale treatment programmes with no conservation priority.

In 1999 an increase in conservation staff and new budgets for regular conservation allowed HRP to set up a roll-

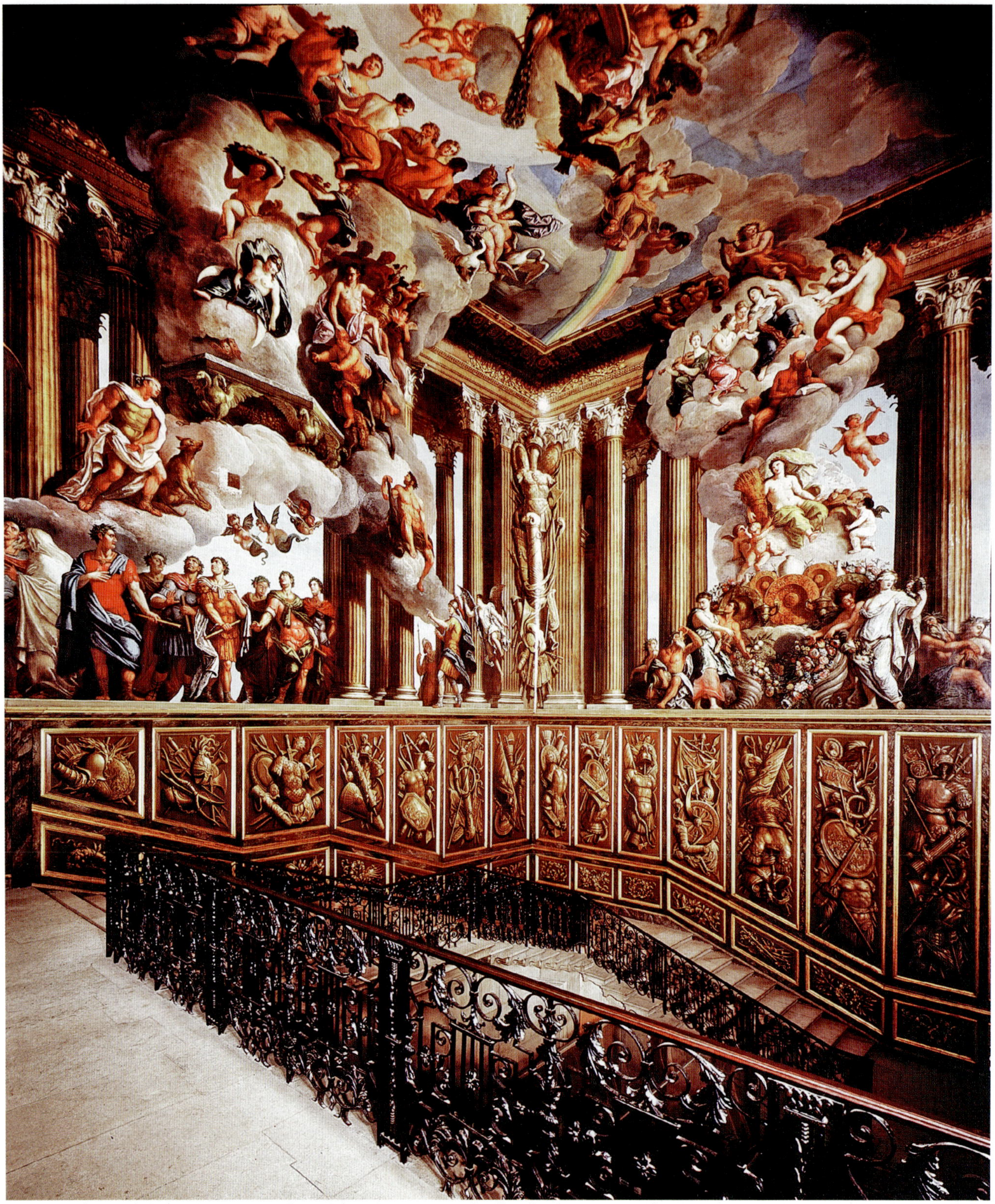

Figure 1 The King's Staircase, Hampton Court Palace, Surrey: view of wall and ceiling paintings by Antonio Verrio. *(© Crown copyright: Historic Royal Palaces)*

ing programme of conservation care for its wall paintings, integrated with a programme for the moveable collections. The goal is to comprehensively cover all preventive and treatment needs to ensure a stable collection. The programme is designed and managed by general objects conservators, with advice from specialist painting-conservator contractors. Its aim is to first address the basic conservation needs of the collection overall, before embarking on investigations that are perhaps more specialist in focus. The programme is also intended to develop as resources allow, however, expanding to include technical and art-historical investigations to increase the information available on Baroque wall paintings, for which to date very little has been published.

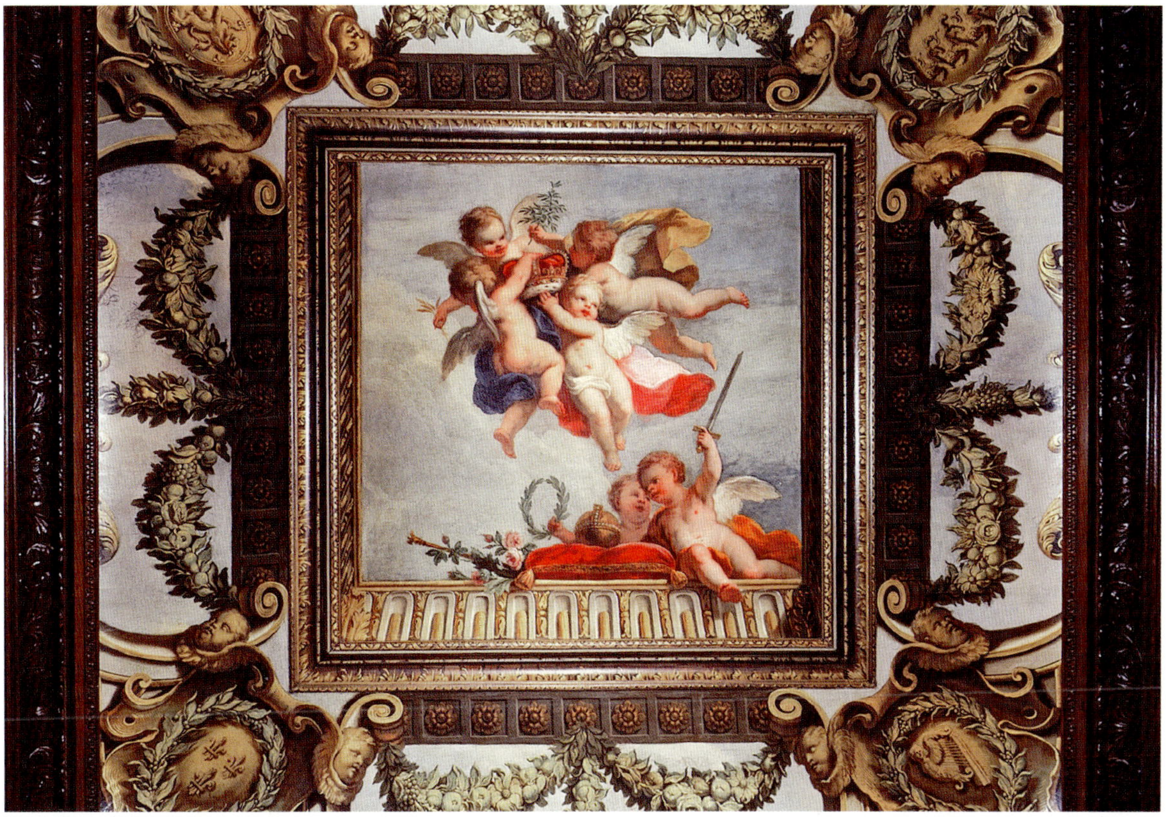

Figure 2 The Royal Pew, Hampton Court Palace, Surrey: detail of the painted ceiling by Sir James Thornhill.
(© Crown copyright: Historic Royal Palaces)

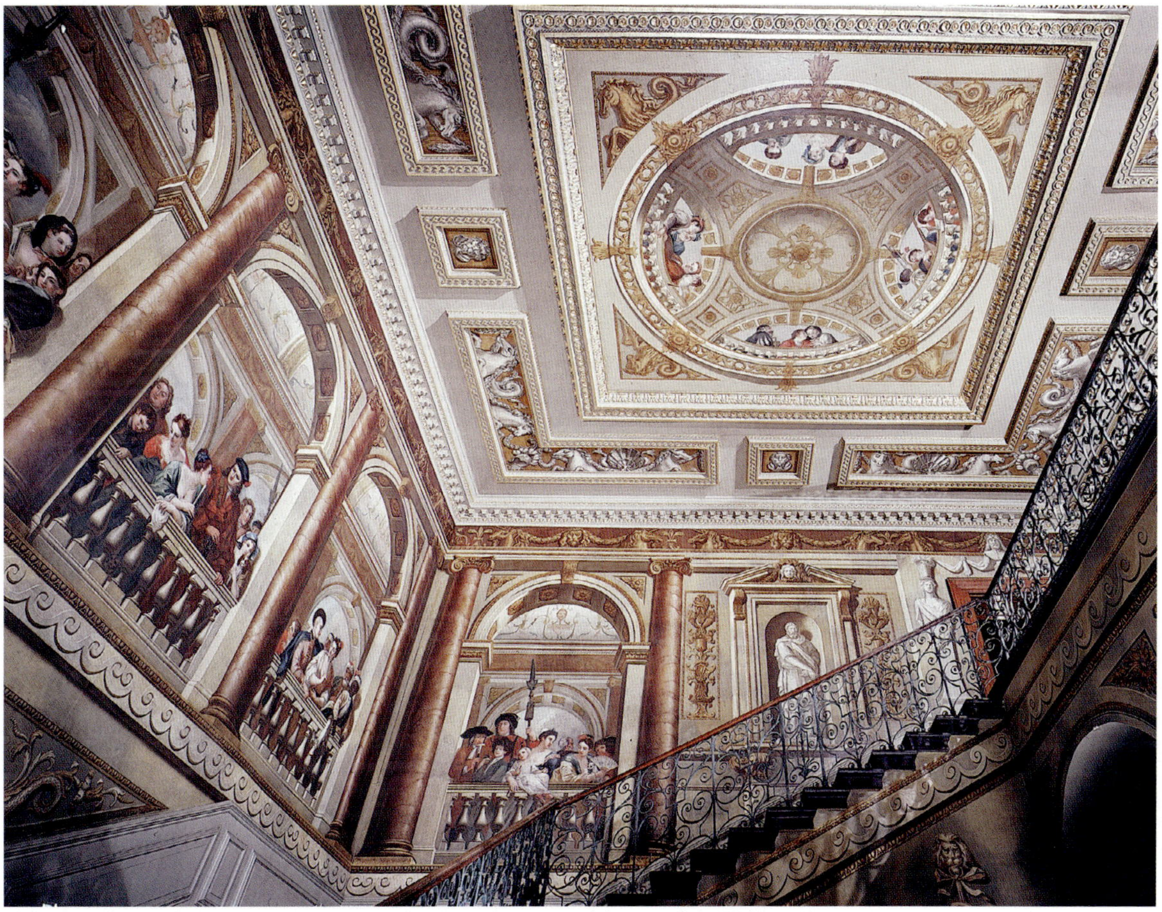

Figure 3 The King's Staircase, Kensington Palace, London: view of the murals by William Kent.
(© Crown copyright: Historic Royal Palaces)

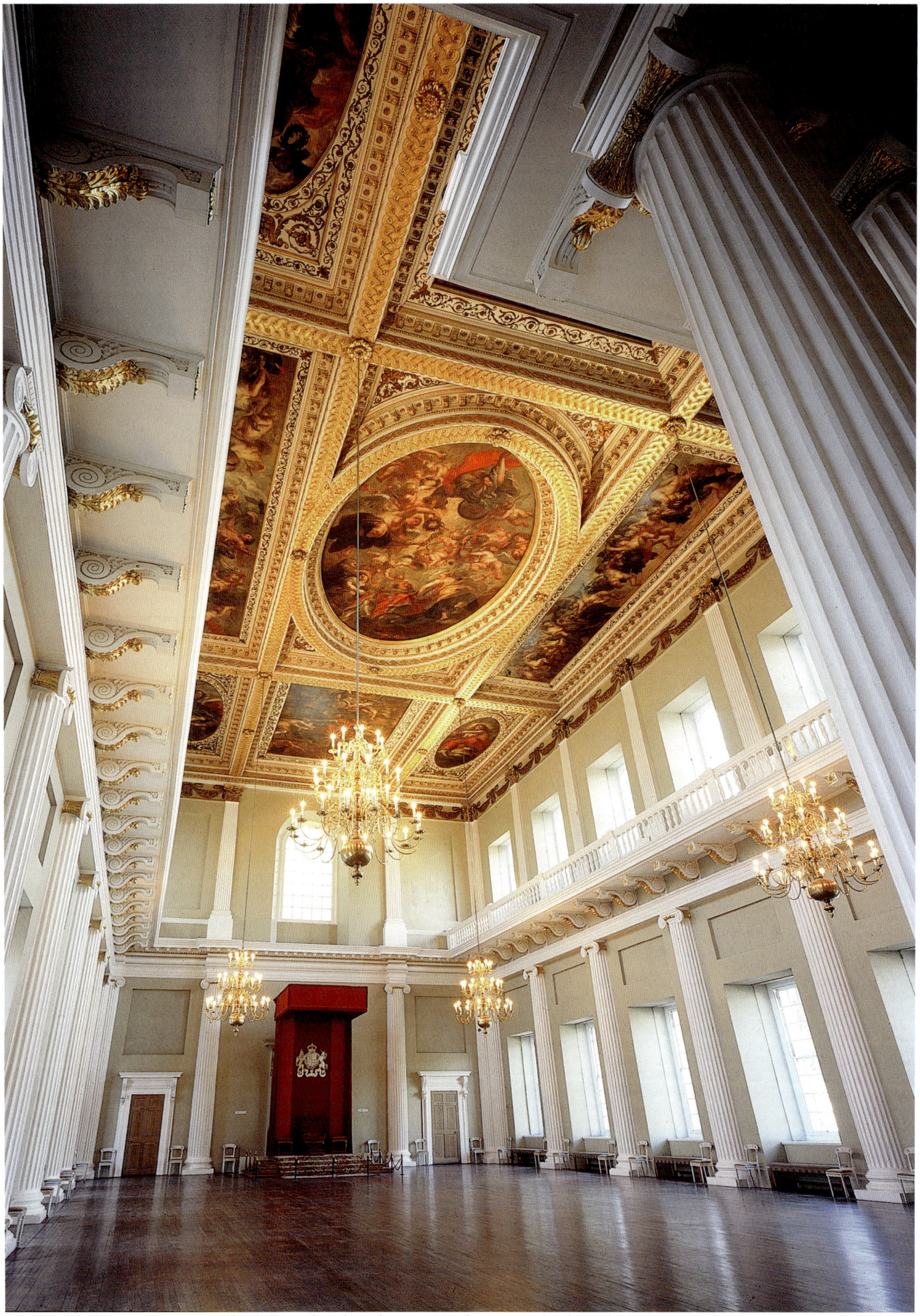

Figure 4 The Banqueting House, Whitehall, London: the ceiling paintings by Peter Paul Rubens. *(© Crown copyright: Historic Royal Palaces)*

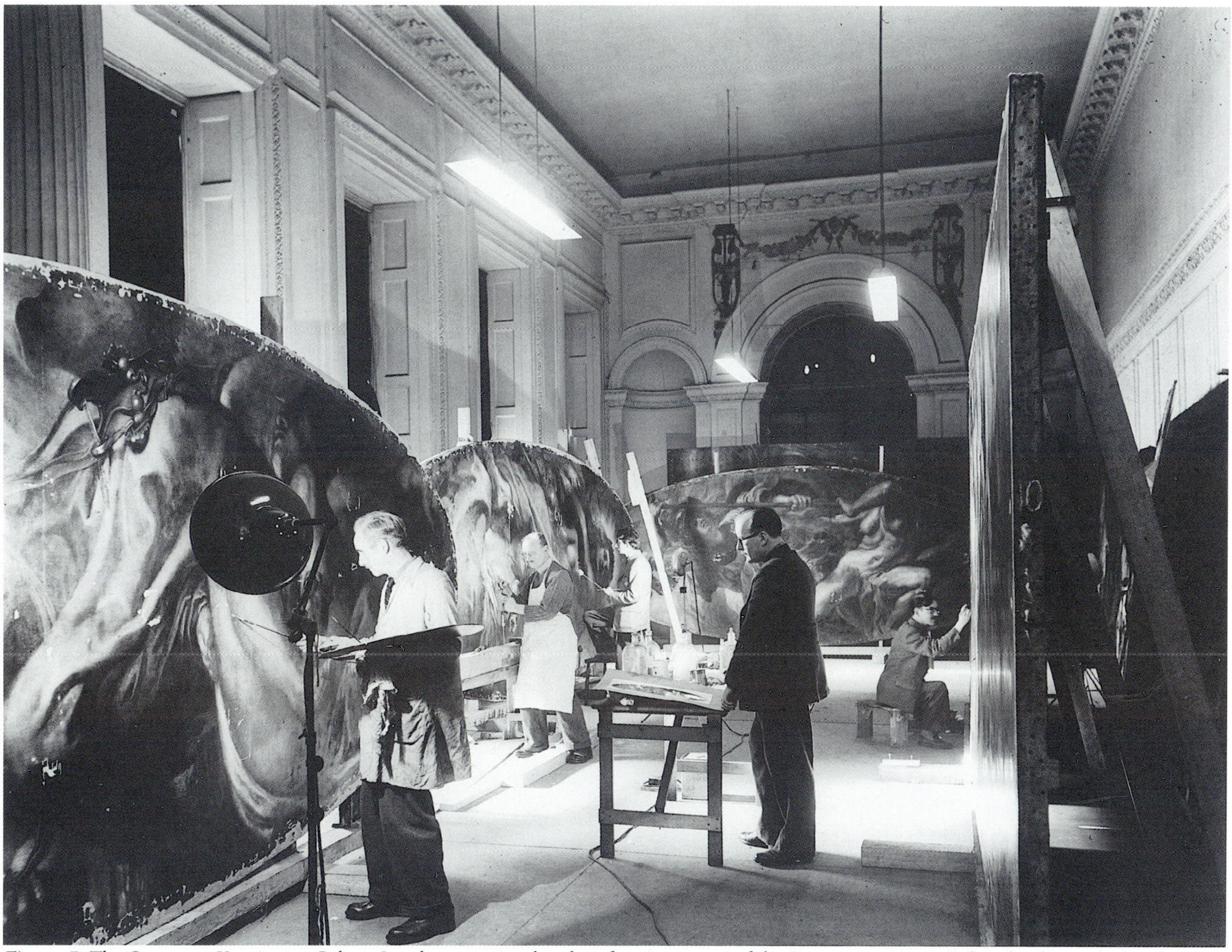

Figure 5 The Orangery, Kensington Palace, London: structural and surface treatment of the Banqueting House Rubens' ceiling paintings in 1949. *(© Crown copyright: Historic Royal Palaces)*

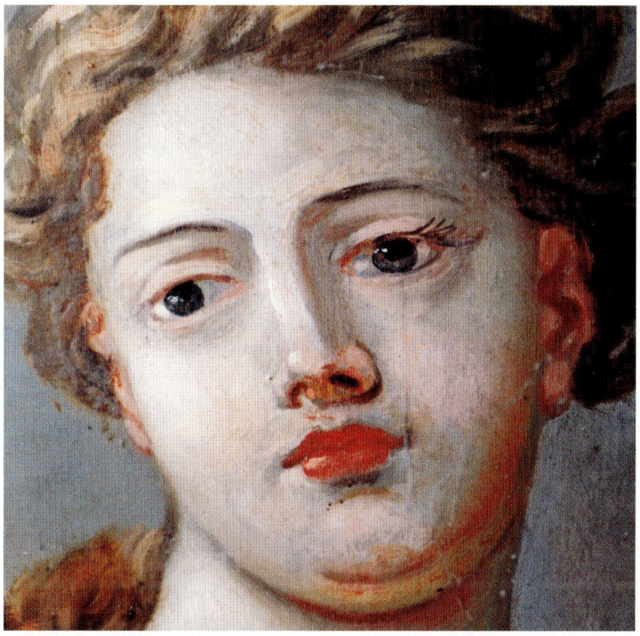

Figure 6 The King's Staircase, Hampton Court Palace, Surrey: detail of a heavily repainted female head from the top of the north wall. *(© J. Burbidge)*

This paper will describe some aspects of the developing approach to conservation of HRP's Baroque wall paintings, focusing on our work to build up an archive of information, on our programme of preventive care, and finally on our approach to conservation treatment.

Archive of information

The accepted first steps to setting up a conservation programme for any historic collection are to survey the collection and the records of past treatment. Establishing a documentation archive of the HRP wall paintings became a primary focus in 1999, when we discovered that records of past work were not at hand but were scattered in various archives including the Public Record Office and English Heritage. We decided to create a basic base record archive from scratch to quickly familiarise ourselves with the collection, to identify the scope of work (ensuring a stable collection before problems advanced), and to use this as a basic management tool to begin tracking condition changes. At the same time, this exercise has enabled us to gather more detailed information on the past interventions, condition history and technique of each scheme. Newly commissioned information is added whenever

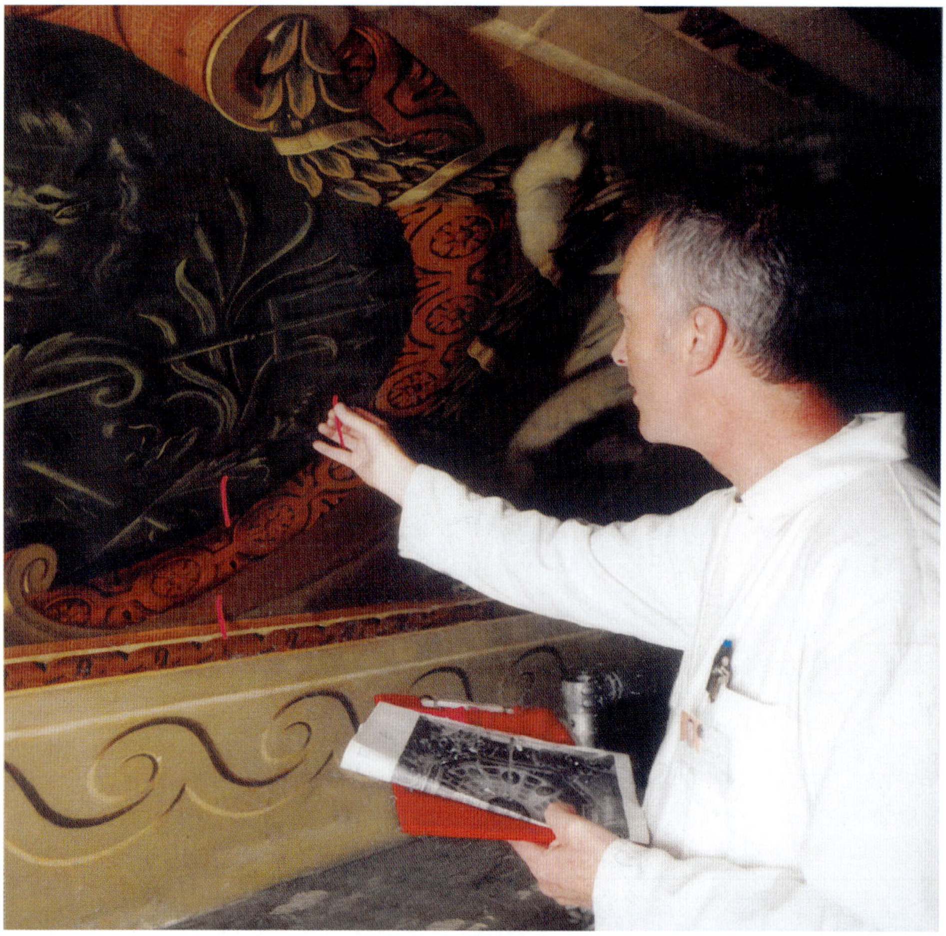

Figure 7 The Queen's Staircase, Hampton Court Palace, Surrey: documenting the condition of the Kent painting. *(© Crown copyright: Historic Royal Palaces)*

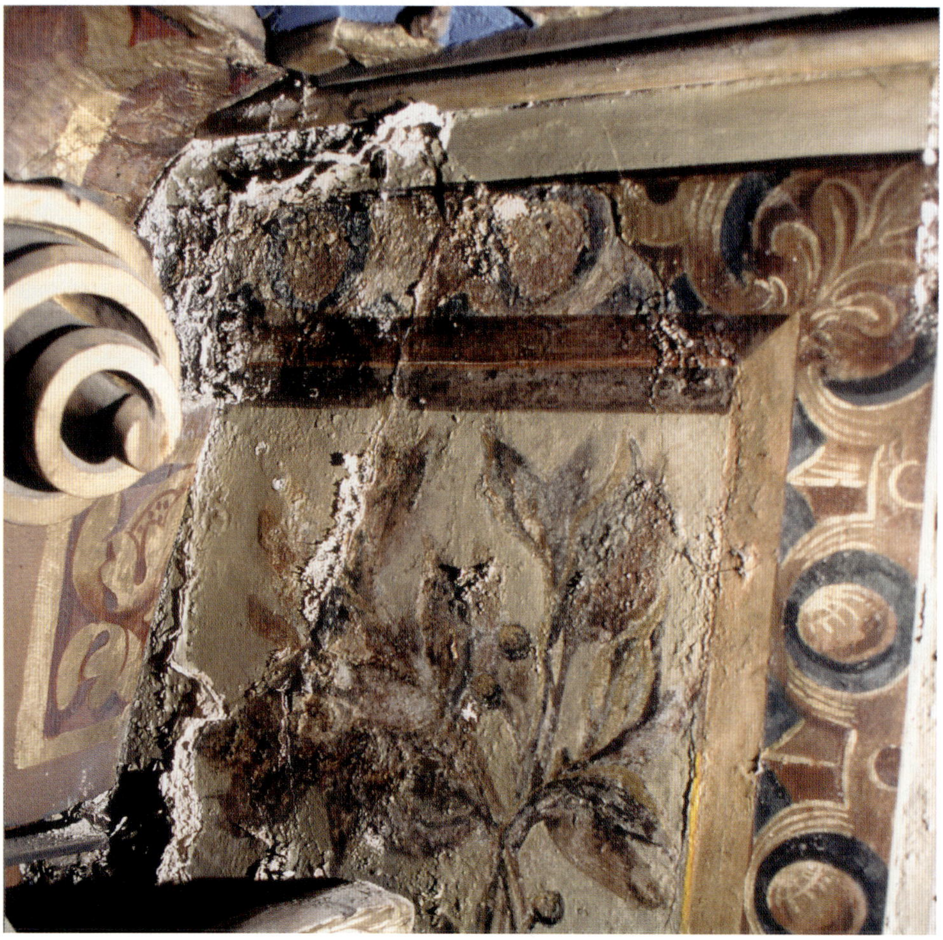

Figure 8 The Chapel Royal, Hampton Court Palace, Surrey: detail of salt damage to a pilaster in Thornhill's decorative painted scheme. *(© J. Burbidge)*

research is critically needed to understand and resolve a particular problem of deterioration, or as resources for research permit. Postgraduate students of painting conservation have been employed on two occasions for such research, one being for the Rubens ceiling in the Banqueting House.

Using specialist painting conservators, HRP began commissioning illustrated reports for each painted scheme to describe it specifically, and to cover:

- original technique (using visual examination with enhanced lighting and magnification);
- alterations due to restoration (using visual examination with enhanced lighting and magnification);
- condition;
- the main treatment steps recommended to address any problems, prioritised by degrees of urgency; and
- recommendations for any scientific investigative work necessary to understand and resolve any specific instability discovered.

The standard of documentation and its permanency was a major consideration, particularly since HRP was just starting to expand its IT infrastructure across the palaces. A basic requirement was for a paper-based archive of written reports illustrated with colour slides and prints and annotated graphics to represent condition information. This would enable us to quickly understand the wall paintings' treatment needs as well as to explain them, involving all conservation staff in tracking condition changes. We are confident of the known permanency of a paper-based system and can guarantee handover of the information to future conservators. Nevertheless we have also benefited from advances in photographic and imaging technology, such as rectified photography, digital cameras and PC-based image manipulation software. These have been used over the past few years to develop and improve HRP documentation, although we have found that a simple system of Mylar overlays on large-scale photographic prints still serves us well (Fig. 7). Our next challenge is to ensure that the same standards of recording are used whenever HRP commissions studies from private practitioners.[1]

Currently there are opportunities for advancing our archive technologically and organisationally, and by so doing increase the level and accuracy of information. In one department, for example, object conservators have now joined the HRP building conservation surveyors, and are able to make use of their advanced graphic recording and tracking system. Of particular interest to us is the surveyor's software-based building management system Atrium that allows tracking and managing changes to the historic fabric of the buildings. Given the susceptibility of wall paintings to damage by movement and damp, Atrium has the potential to serve as a backup system, tracking changes in the wall paintings against real and potential decay of the building fabric. It could also act as an early warning system.

Historic Royal Palaces is also keen to develop a database of images and information to illustrate ongoing and historic deterioration. This would allow us to call up, print off, review and update as needed. The IT structure is not yet in place for this and indeed increasing the level of graphic detail of our records is not our first priority. Most of the works are in sound condition, and the removal of past restorations (which would otherwise warrant the highest level of visual recording) is not part of our current policy. Instead we have decided to focus resources on building up the archive of information about what has taken place historically, original techniques and the effect of past interventions.

Preventive care

As our main aim must be to hand over a stable collection of wall paintings to future custodial bodies, we have an active two-part programme of conservation with prevention as its basis. Prevention perhaps best reflects HRP's approach as custodians of 'our time and place'. The wall paintings receive continuous care as part of the overall preventive programme, which also introduces measures of environmental and physical protection.

Since 1999 there has been a planned programme of stabilisation treatments. Our recent specialist surveys indicate that, although extensively altered by past cleaning and restoration work, with only a few exceptions the wall painting collection is generally in sound and stable condition. Five of the wall paintings were found to be suffering minor instability: localised flaking of paint from their plaster or timber substrate. Three of these have been successfully conserved, including most recently the lower stairwell areas of painted timber and plaster on William Kent's King's Staircase at Kensington Palace.

Of the two still needing treatment, one is Sir James Thornhill's decorative scheme in the Chapel Royal at Hampton Court. A faulty drainpipe directly outside has left a painted pilaster on the north wall severely water- and salt-damaged; efflorescence had caused the plaster substrate to expand, and the overlying oil-paint layer has split and deformed (Fig. 8).

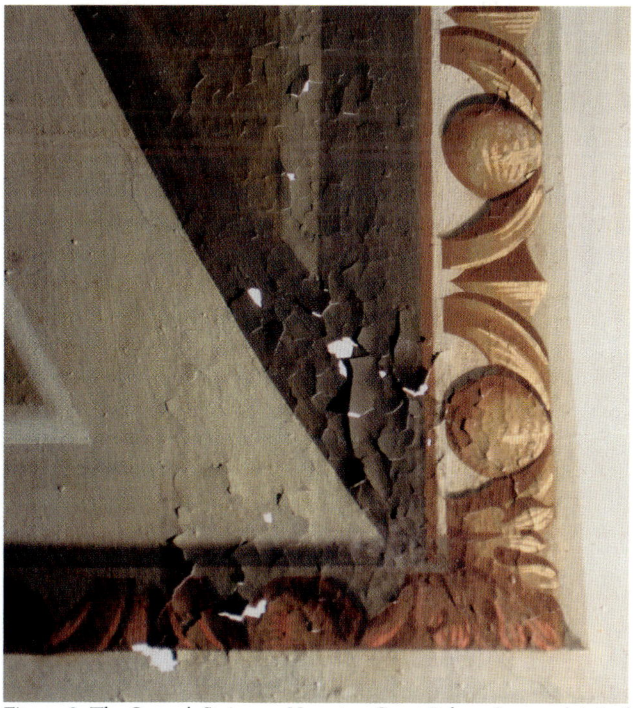

Figure 9 The Queen's Staircase, Hampton Court Palace, Surrey: detail of extensive flaking on Kent's ceiling painting. *(© J. Burbidge)*

The downpipe is now repaired and a programme of monitored slow drying of the plaster substrate is in place. Once the plaster is dry, treatment will follow to repair both plaster and paint. The second problematic painting is the Queen's Staircase at Hampton Court Palace. Here extensive flaking continues to affect Kent's painted ceiling, despite thorough consolidation. The problems have necessitated detailed environmental and technical analysis to determine the cause and to find the most appropriate solution (Fig. 9).

Preventive programme

With the majority of works being in generally sound condition, the palaces' conservation funds are not required for major treatment campaigns and can be spread across HRP's two-part preventive programme. There are perhaps two aspects of the programme that are of special benefit for the preservation of the wall paintings. The first is that the palaces have 12 full-time object conservators who have sufficient training to recognise and track deterioration on a wide range of materials, including wall paintings. They work regularly within touching distance of many of the wall paintings in the course of carrying out collections monitoring and hands-on care regimes (Fig. 10). Thus the palaces have a built-in, fast-reacting system able to call in when necessary a specialist to document and address wall painting problems before they have a chance to advance. The conservators also work closely with the palaces' full-time maintenance staff and building surveyors, who also react quickly to stop problems such as water leaks before they can cause extensive damage. Huge campaigns of remedial work are therefore avoided.

It is worth noting, however, that where access is exceptionally difficult – so that preventive routines are infrequent or impossible – problems can progress undetected (as with the painted scheme by Thornhill in the Chapel Royal, discussed above). This situation we now hope to avoid by working closely with our palace building surveyors and maintenance staff to proactively track changes to the building and its mechanical systems, and to react promptly to repair faults that could affect the palaces' interior decorative painted schemes.

The second important aspect of the preventive programme for wall paintings is the way in which they benefit from the palaces' risk management framework. This serves to identify and minimise risks through prioritised preventive actions implemented collectively by all stakeholders. Large- and small-scale mitigating strategies are worked out in the palaces' recently established Environmental Management Strategy Steering Group, with design input and approval from conservators, curators, operations, warding and maintenance staff, building surveyors and key directors. This steering group is firmly resolved on continuous improvement and has identified and prioritised the most pressing problems.

One of these problems is William Kent's Queen's Staircase scheme, discussed above, where the post-consolidation paint continues to cleave away from its plaster substrate. The steering group is currently facilitating a specialist scientific study of the paint layer stratigraphy and of the underlying substrate and the

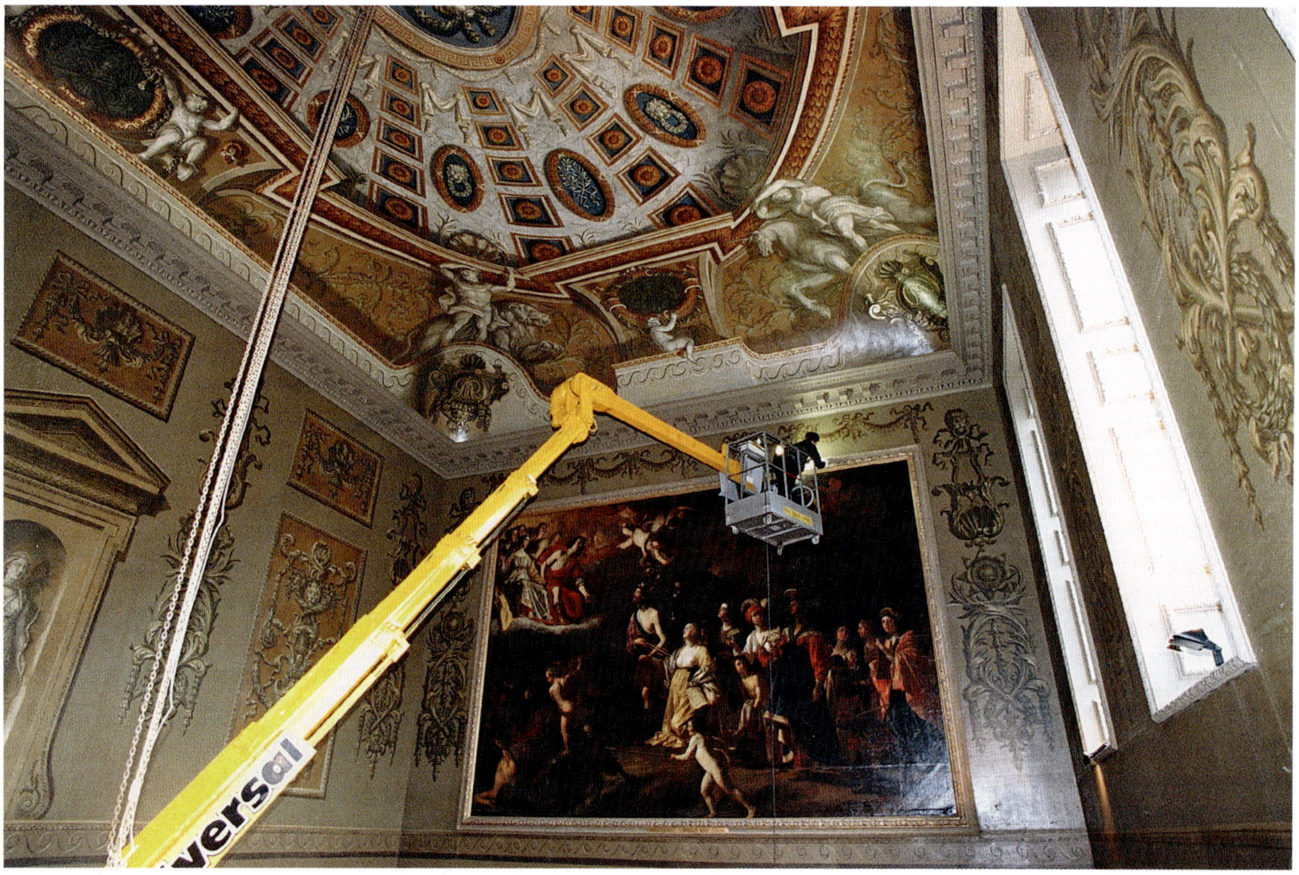

Figure 10 The Queen's Staircase painting, Hampton Court Palace, Surrey: a palace conservator carrying out the condition monitoring and preventive care regime. *(© Crown copyright: Historic Royal Palaces)*

environment. Pertinent trial testing is being made of mitigating treatment and environmental measures intended to halt paint loss. The steering group tracks both actions taken and their success, ensuring that problems are fully resolved. It also considers potential problems, typically those arising from a change of use. For example, the reopening of the King's Staircase at Kensington Palace, with its huge all-surrounding wall painting by Kent, must depend upon balancing the use of this royal route with preservation of the painting. To ensure this balance is achievable, the area is being monitored for the effect of vibrations (using people counters, tell-tale tags on cracks, time-lapse photography, possibly vibration testing, and so forth) and of environmental changes (humidity and light, dust levels etc.). Reports on the new visitor use impact will be presented to the group at regular intervals, and it will make decisions about mitigating measures and revised usage as necessary to achieve the desired balance of use and preservation.

Finally, in common with all preventive programmes, environmental conditions at the palaces are recorded both continuously and using spot measurements. Relative humidity, temperature and light data are available to support analysis of potential sources of problems and of the effectiveness of mitigating solutions. Additionally, the wall paintings are well protected at all times from the activities of building and maintenance works, filming, functions and other events. Conservators are thoroughly integrated into the process of planning protection specifications for these contracts, and they oversee the associated work of the contractors on site. This minimises the chance of accidental damage (such as gouging of a wall painting with a scaffold pole). Conservators are also involved in high-level decisions regarding the planned use of a room or area, and can ensure that the wall paintings are not inadvertently put at undue risk. Further benefit derives from the preventive programme's cyclical condition assessments of the wall paintings, scheduled within the overall collection's audit programme and carried out every two or five years depending on need and on ease of access.

Conservation treatment

Regarding conservation treatment, HRP's approach is conservative by intention, and generally targeted to doing the minimum necessary to stabilise the wall paintings. Typically this includes cleaning to remove surface dust and dirt, localised consolidation to prevent paint loss and, at maximum, filling and inpainting cracks that are particularly distracting to the viewers' appreciation of the decorative schemes. Since 1999 this treatment programme has been conservator-led.

At present we are for the most part avoiding conservation treatments that improve the presentation of the work and involve in-depth cleaning, removal of retouchings, overpaint and darkened varnish or revarnishing for two main reasons. First, from a practical viewpoint, presentation treatments are very costly, especially as the wall paintings are exceptionally large and much altered. Secondly, as yet we are not sufficiently informed about the palaces' wall paintings – or indeed English Baroque wall paintings in general – to embark with confidence upon interventive treatments that go beyond stabilisation. In-depth scientific and art-historical investigative work is first required to gain a fuller understanding of each of the wall paintings. Specifically we need to understand the artist's painting technique, his aesthetic intentions and his royal patron, the extent of remaining original work, and the technical feasibility of removing restoration additions safely without disturbing underlying original layers of paint and possibly varnish. We must also determine the significance of retaining restoration schemes at the palaces, as their royal provenance may give them unique historical value. For example, academic curatorial consideration is needed to decide whether or not to save the 1781 restoration scheme of Antonio Verrio's mural on the King's Staircase at Hampton Court Palace, as this is thought to have been commissioned directly by George III.[2]

In addition, HRP is still in the process of articulating its conservation philosophy. This is needed, for instance, to help decide aesthetic goals regarding the appearance of the wall paintings. Should we continue with an approach to conservation that is fully archaeological or move towards one that addresses the need of the art connoisseur too, perhaps recapturing the vibrant colours of the original Baroque palette through removal of darkened varnishes and overpaint? Finally, the varying success of past interventions suggests the prudence of a generally cautious approach when extending treatment beyond stabilisation.

Conservation treatments are carried out through competitive commissioning. The brief for each project specifies the need to comply with standard health and safety measures, to provide a high level of skill and experience (specifically in the conservation of English wall paintings in general and increasingly, as expertise develops in this area, in English Baroque wall paintings in particular), and the highest standard of treatment consistent with accredited practices of professional conservators today. Historic Royal Palaces' conservation standards must also be met, doing the minimum to clean and stabilise a wall painting, and recording findings and the work carried out according to our prescribed standards for enhanced documentation.

Increasingly, as the information becomes available, contract conservators are provided with detailed descriptions of past interventions. This is essential to understand the wall paintings fully and to sensitively design the most appropriate intervention. Continuity of care is starting to be built into treatment contracts, with follow-up inspections scheduled to assess the effectiveness of work carried out and the preventive recommendations implemented. Treatment contracts are managed directly by senior palace conservators thereby enabling the contractor and client to have meaningful dialogue, conservator-to-conservator, through all stages of the treatment project (including post-treatment) so that they can design the most suitable solution for individual wall paintings. This becomes necessarily intense during the course of cleaning, for example, when decisions about appropriate visual balance must be made jointly.

Conservation work on the palaces' wall paintings is carried out under the public eye and contract conservators are expected to act as ambassadors for their work, from providing written text for visitor panels to participating in information events for the media or public. A primary goal of this is to educate and increase visitors' interest in – and thus gain support for – conserving the wall paintings in HRP's care.

Looking towards the future

Once the basic conservation programme is fully in place, the stability and protection of the wall paintings as a minimum will be assured, and each work will be supported by a full written record. Palace conservators will then be in a position to develop the wall painting conservation programme further, increasing our knowledge of the artists' technique and the histories of changes made to the paintings, and perhaps where sensible to do so conserving the works beyond the strict parameters of stabilisation to reveal some of their original bright colours and fine detail. Some development on this front is already occurring as an outcome of having to extend analyses to include original pigment and binding media, the stratigraphy of later paint and coating layers, and so on, in order to determine the cause of recurring condition problems (as with the paint loss on Kent's Queen's Staircase painting at Hampton Court Palace, for example).

We foresee greater developments being made possible through curators and interpreters showing an increased interest in highlighting areas of the collection in scholarly and public programmes. This would be likely to include the palaces' wall paintings, both medieval and Baroque. For example, a potential interpretative programme on the theme 'Art at the Palaces' is currently being discussed, and this would be expected to give rise to a scientific study of how the wall paintings were made and a forensic look at changes over time, including an exploration of just what remains of the original. This would probably be backed up by curatorial research on such subject areas as royal commissions for creating and for 'refreshing' the works. The result would be an information base for the visitor and academic programmes, in addition to which it would give a greater scholarly understanding of English Baroque wall paintings. In turn, this should encourage public interest in this part of our artistic heritage. Finally, such a programme might encourage further treatment to conserve key works to their once-spectacular former selves, wherever investigations reveal that sufficient original material survives. Indeed it may make such treatment both technically and financially viable.

Eventually HRP's general wall painting conservation programme may be able to be tuned more specifically to the specialist needs of the now-historic techniques and aspirations of Antonio Verrio, James Thornhill, William Kent and their royal patrons.

Conclusions

By continuing to develop its programme, HRP hopes to achieve its aim of continuous care, establishing a stable collection of wall paintings, a growing body of useful technical and historical information about the paintings, a permanent record of their condition today (from which changes can be tracked accurately), and an understanding of risks to the collection and planned response for their mitigation. We hope that we have designed a programme that is able to grow to suit the requirements of future conservation strategies as well as our needs and those of subsequent custodial bodies in charge of this important and challenging artistic endowment.

Acknowledgements

Our thanks to Sebastian Edwards (HRP Curator) and John Burbidge (Granville and Burbidge) for ideas, comments and feedback on the text of this paper, and to John Burbidge (Granville and Burbidge), Caroline Babington and Richard Pelter (IFACS) for permission to use images from their specialist reports.

Notes

1. Heritage and Gowing 2002.
2. Thurley 2003.

References

Apollo 1994, 'The King's Apartments, Hampton Court Palace', *Apollo* Special Issue CXL 390 August 1994

Heritage A. and Gowing R. 2002, *Practical Information Leaflet 1: The Production of Wall Painting Conservation Documents*, English Heritage, London

Historic Royal Palaces 1996, *Hampton Court Palace: The Official Guide Book*, Historic Royal Palaces, London

Historic Royal Palaces 1997, *The Banqueting House, Whitehall Palace*, Historic Royal Palaces, London

Historic Royal Palaces 2001, *Kensington Palace: The Official Guidebook*, Historic Royal Palaces, London

Impey E. 2003, *Kensington Palace: The Official Illustrated History*, Merrel, London

Thurley S. 2003, *Hampton Court: A Social and Architectural History*, Yale University Press, New Haven and London

The authors

- Kate Frame has worked on various contracts for the British School of Rome, the Ontario Ministry of Culture and Tourism, Canada, and the Canadian Conservation Institute in Ottawa. She became the first Head of Conservation for Heritage Toronto in Canada in 1986, and managed the conservation of public art and monuments and the City of Toronto's artefact collections. Kate took up the post as Head of Conservation Housekeeping, Historic Royal Palaces in 1998, in 2003 becoming Head of Conservation and Collection Care, responsible for the conservation of the interior fabrics and contents of the five palaces managed by Historic Royal Palaces.
- Following her graduation, Sophie Julien-Lees worked as an objects conservator for major institutions including the Museum of London, the Horniman Museum and the Victoria and Albert Museum before undertaking a two-year environmental monitoring and control internship at the National Trust. Sophie joined Historic Royal Palaces in 2001 as a Senior Preventive Conservator and currently coordinates the commissioned conservation treatment and environmental management programmes at the five palaces.

The art of the house painter: vernacular mural decoration c.1650–1841

James Ayres

In considering the use of paints and distempers, it is clearly important to contemplate their practical uses before reviewing any aspect of their aesthetic effect. Paint – by which I mean oil paint – could be used by joiners as an informal glue and by glaziers as a means of maintaining the flexibility of putty. The repertoire of possibilities for distempers and limewashes is even wider. For example, the limewashing and distempering of such structures as the Tower of London (which indeed gave the White Tower its name), and the polychromatic embellishment of the west fronts of cathedrals such as Wells, did much to preserve the stonework – both masonry and sculpture – into modern times, and the recent use of lime shelter coats is, in many ways, an extension of such means of protection, albeit without the pigments. Distemper was also used to consolidate mud floors and applied externally to thatch as a fire retardant.[1] Doubtless there were many other practical uses for these 'mucilaginous substances'.[2] The most widespread application of limewash was as a disinfectant – in the dairy, the cow byre and the home. This was an annual or even twice-yearly purification; Celia Fiennes, writing in 1698, noted that each year on Holy Thursday the citizens of Norwich 'new washe and plaister their houses within and without'.[3] It is little wonder that many layers of limewash are often found on old buildings. Although the white 'wash' may sometimes have been tinted with pigments, its natural colour would have produced the effect of cleanliness seen in the domestic scenes by Dutch painters such as Vermeer and de Hooch.

This tradition for physical and visual cleanliness persisted into the 18th century and beyond. Indeed, in the early 20th century the medical officer for health for the Great Western Railway issued distemper brushes to employees living in Brunel's railway village at Swindon (Fig. 1). Interiors with polychromatic decoration were predicated on glazed windows that tended to be larger than unglazed openings, making rooms more visible. Furthermore, chimneys established a better level of cleanliness than was possible with open central hearths.[4] With these two features of buildings in place, mural decoration would be visible and therefore worth doing.

In view of the differing functions being met by paints, distempers and limewashes, it is scarcely surprising that the tradesmen involved in applying them were drawn from a similarly diverse range of trades. Of these, the first that spring to mind are London's Painter-Stainers. Even in a city as large as London, some of the more recondite trades sought the protection offered by incorporation into one of the larger guilds, which was doubtless why in 1502 the Stainers merged with the Painters. Their company also included the Gilders and, by 1619, the Gold Beaters.[5]

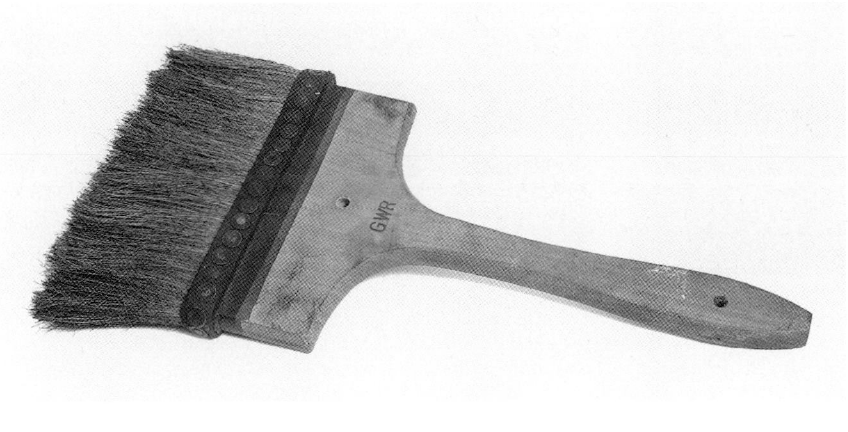

Figure 1 Limewash brush, early 20th century: issued by the medical officer for health for the Great Western Railway. This grass brush has a leather ferrule held in place by copper rivets. Overall length 15½ inches (39.4cm). *(© Railway Museum, Swindon)*

The Stainers, in contrast to the Painters, used pigments and dyes suspended in a size-based medium used to embellish coarse unbleached linen or hempen canvases, known as *hurds* or *hards*. These were used as hangings to decorate the home, a cheap (or cheaper) alternative to the expensive (dyed-in-the-wool) woven tapestries (Fig. 2). Stained hangings had been important since the Middle Ages, but from the 16th century they had an extraordinarily wide social distribution. With the rise of panelling in the course of the 17th century their popularity declined, although they persisted as mural decoration into the opening decades of the 18th century.[6] Today stained cloths are very seldom found *in situ*. Sometimes a surviving row of tenter hooks along a wall near the ceiling is the only evidence left to suggest where stained cloths once hung.[7] Even the well-known examples of c.1700–20 at Owlpen Manor in Gloucestershire no longer inhabit the room in which they first hung. Among the late 17th- or early 18th-century examples of stained hangings that may be seen out of context are those at Gainsborough Old Hall, Lincolnshire, and at Sherborne Museum, Dorset.

Eastlake[8] cites a medieval English method of staining hangings, and a comparable method is offered by John Abbott of Devon (1639/40–1727). Abbott's recipe describes a medium of 'glew' dissolved 'in hot water and with it some what claimmy [clammy] which you may try between your fingers'.[9] Robert Dossie, writing in 1764, first lumps together all kinds of 'painting in distemper', and then promptly dismisses such work as 'being for scenes; canvas hangings and other coarser work, less expensive colours and simpler means'.[10]

In some ways, transparent blinds (and transparencies in general), stained onto Scotch cambric rather than coarse canvas, perpetuated the craft into the first half of the 19th century (Fig. 3). An early example of this revised tradition was the series of transparencies illuminated by 'lampions' and exhibited in London's Hyde Park in 1748, in conjunction with fireworks and music by Handel, to celebrate the Treaty of Aix la Chapelle.[11] By 1774–5 Thomas Gainsborough was painting transparent window blinds or shades for a concert room in Hanover Square, London.[12] By 1807, when Edward Orme published his *Essay on Transparencies...*, this type of work was nearly always confined to windows. In general, such blinds were intended to be pulled down during daylight hours to minimise sun bleaching of textiles and furniture. For this reason they were sometimes made to resemble stained glass windows; designs of this kind are illustrated as exemplars by Whittock in his manual of 1827.

In contradistinction to the Stainers, with their size-based media, the Painters specialised in oil paints. In medieval London, the Painters had been a branch of the saddle-making trade, which presumably explains why, when painting emerged as a distinct trade, it was oils – the permanent means of decorating a saddle – that became their most significant media.[13] This inevitably meant that, although Painters did gilding using an oil-based mordant, they did not water-gild – water-gilding

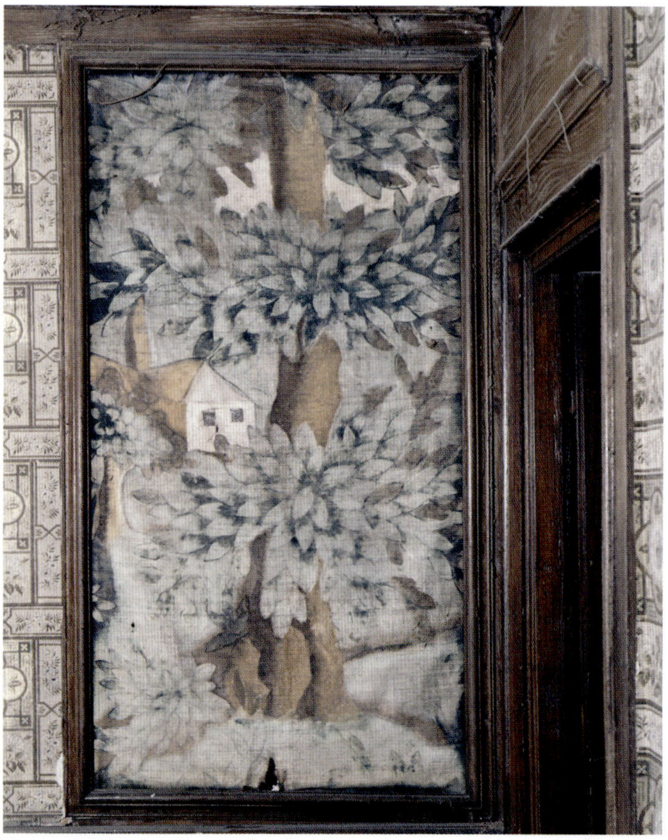

Figure 2 Munslow Farm, Munslow, Shropshire: stained hangings, late 17th or early 18th century. These were removed by the owner of the house and their present whereabouts (or even their survival) is unknown. Very few such hangings remain in the context for which they were first intended. *(© Crown copyright. NMR)*

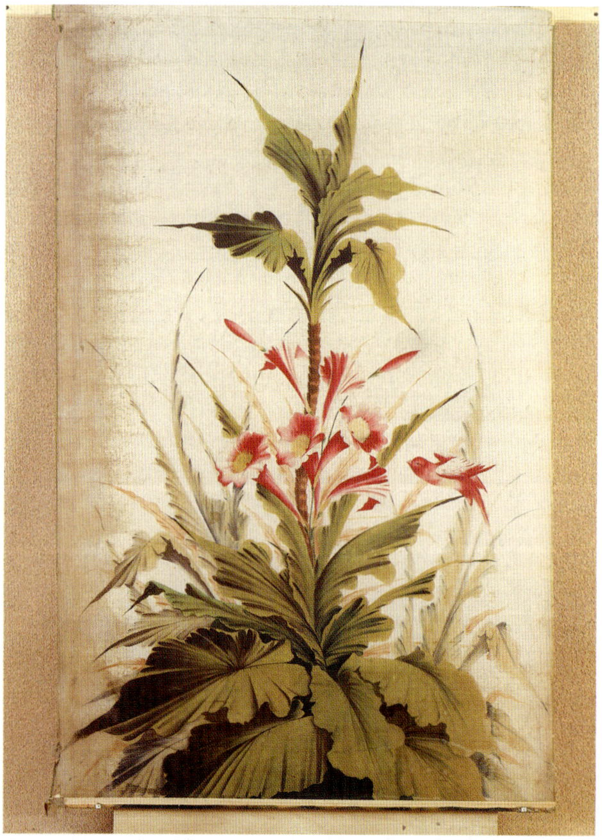

Figure 3 Window blind, Scotch cambric, decorated c.1835–40 as a 'transparency' with pigments bound in isinglass. This blind is of a scale and proportion suitable for a large sash window. *(©: Judkyn/Pratt Collection)*

remained a separate and distinct craft. In some ways this use of oil size for gilding resembles the use of a similar preparation for the application of powdered smalt in which the oil mordant may be seen as a prospective media.[14]

Despite their 1502 merger, the Painters and the Stainers of London maintained their separate identities within the one guild, at least until stained hangings went out of favour in the late 17th century. Nevertheless, demarcation disputes with the Heralds persisted as late as 1738, not least because successive earls marshall had the ear of the court and parliament. The greatest threat to the *trade* of painting, however, was to come from those who had been educated in the *art* of painting. Many of these often continental 'artists' were employed by the Crown, so there was little that the members of the guild could do to protect their 'art and mystery'. Under these circumstances, the Painter-Stainers of London succumbed to the inevitable. As early as the late 16th century, they had come to terms with these 'picture makers' and with their strange habit of painting 'to the life'.[15] By 1784, Joshua Reynolds had been admitted to the Freedom of the Company. He was the first in a long line of academicians to be so honoured; other recipients included Frederick Leighton in 1889 and John Everett Millais in 1896.[16]

Since Painters were primarily concerned with the application of oil paints to various supports, and Stainers used a size-based medium on fabric, the Plasterers considered limewash and distemper as but an extension of their own materials, of their 'art and mystery'. Very evidently this was not a view shared by the Painter-Stainers who, for much of the 17th century, engaged in litigation with the Plasterers. As early as 1606, the Painter-Stainers had succeeded in getting an Act of Parliament passed (4 Jac.1.c20) which limited the pigments and media available for use by Plasterers to 'Whiting, Blacking, Redlead, Redoker, Yellow Oker and Russet mingled with size only'.[17] Although these regulations were, of course, officially confined to the city and its suburbs, London clearly set the pace as far as trade regulation was concerned, though it did so mainly in those regions with a large population base. Specialisation was a matter of demography.

What, then, was the connection between plastering and the application of distempers? In my view it began with the natural association between lime plaster and limewash – so that much the same material was applied by the same artisans. A drawing of 1803 by W.H. Pyne[18] shows plasterers applying limewash or distemper using the characteristic brush for the purpose (see Fig. 1). This makes sense of numerous building account books for plasterers' work, which include 'washing and stopping'. Naturally the application of all-over white and colour washes was one thing – polychromatic mural decoration quite another. In this context the decorative *sgraffito* work (for example for fireplace linings) carried out by plasterers using two layers of different coloured plasters may have been a way of sidestepping the problem of demarcation (Figs 4–6). Another sidelight on this dispute is the word 'daub', which, although it may be used in a neutral sense (wattle and daub), was deployed as early as 1630 as a term of abuse for inadequate easel painting.[19]

Another trade with which the Painter-Stainers regularly battled was that of the Plumbers, who also used oil paint (Fig. 7). What was the common ground between these two ostensibly unrelated trades? It was partly the production of lead-based paints and dryers. It is my belief, however, that the most significant explanation is based on a situation of the type that I understand is known to economists as 'backward linkage'.

The Plumbers, by means of a 'plumbers' vice', extruded the lead cames that held in place the glass quarrels of windows. By extension, glazing became part of their trade. With the introduction of timber sash windows, the Plumbers

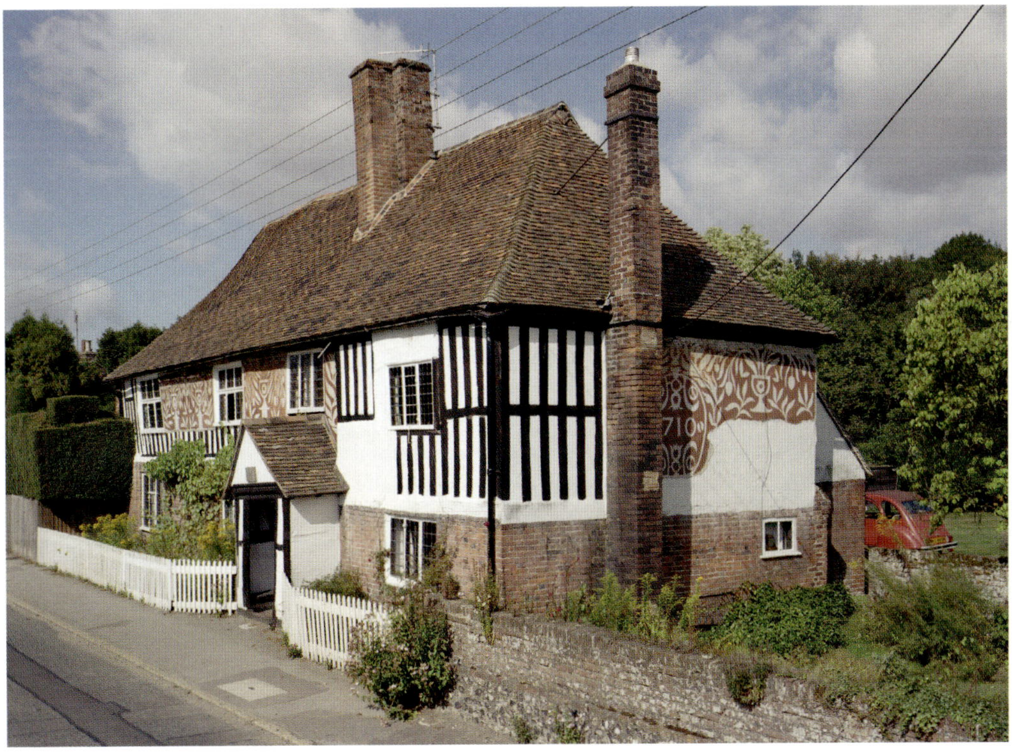

Figure 4 Calico House, Newnham, Kent: sgraffito decoration, dated 1710 and carried out in two coats of plaster (brick red over white). The red matches the bricks of the underbuilt jetty. Sadly, the decoration has been somewhat mutilated by 'restoration'. The sgraffito technique was used both internally and, as here, externally. *(© Crown copyright. NMR)*

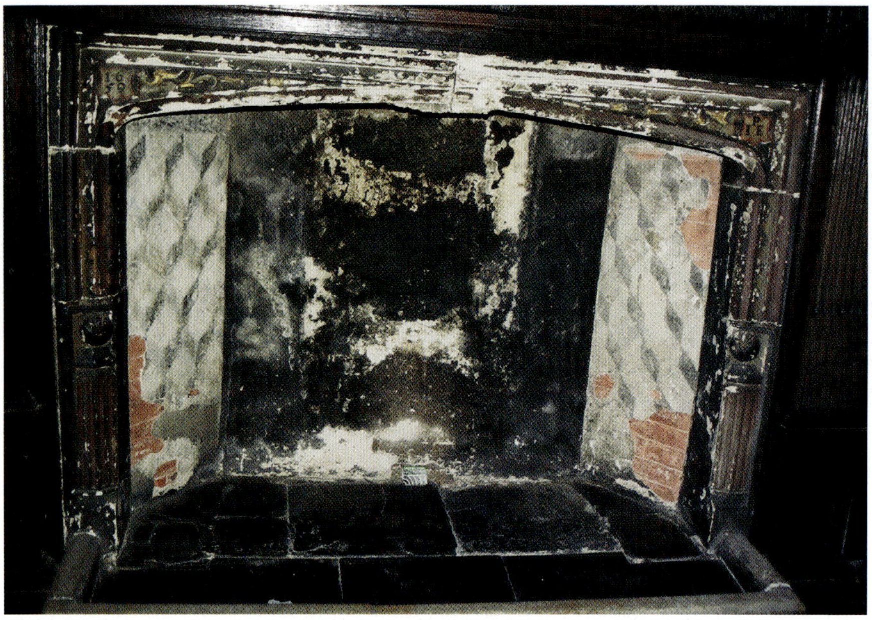

Figure 5 Stranger's Hall, Norwich: decorated fireplace lining, executed in lime plaster or thick limewash. The 'tumbling blocks' design overlays an earlier (c.1620–30) scheme in roddel (red lead) and white lines, intended to resemble tuck-pointed brickwork. The later scheme carries the initials J.&E. P. (Joseph & Emma Payne) and the date 1659. In such a location, work of this kind was redone every generation (Norfolk Museums & Archaeology Service: Strangers' Hall Museum). *(© A. Kirkham)*

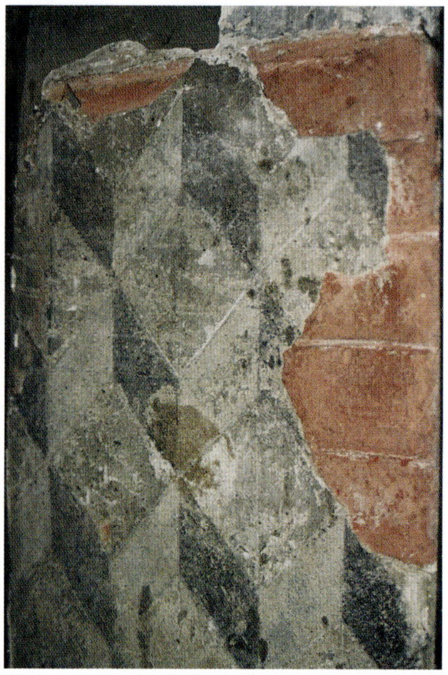

Figure 6 Detail of Figure 5: as can be seen here, the design of tumbling blocks, like the earlier fictive brickwork, has been scribed. In earlier phases of this kind of work a sgraffito technique was used while later examples exhibit the use of a brush with more fluid designs. In this case the diagonally set dark diamond shapes alternate with pale blue. Although the present distribution maps for decorated fireplace linings in England, New England and Scotland are somewhat patchy, ephemeral decoration such as this was probably quite widespread in the mid-to-late 17th century (Norfolk Museums & Archaeology Service: Strangers' Hall Museum). *(© A. Kirkham)*

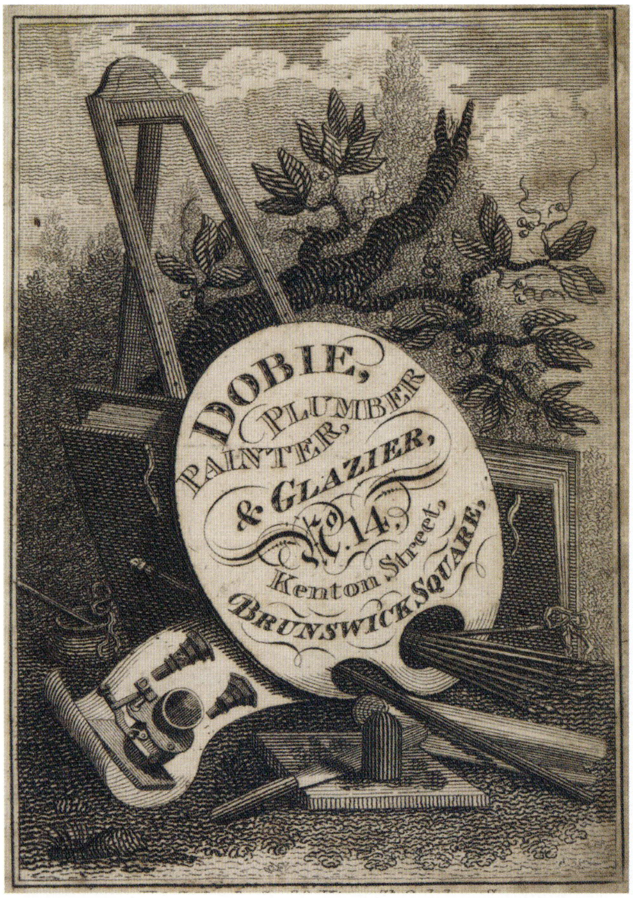

Figure 7 Trade card, for a 'Plumber, Painter & Glazier', early 19th century. The accoutrements of the 'artist' (easel, palette and portfolio) are not merely decorative devices but tools of this trade. *(© British Museum, Department of Prints and Drawings)*

maintained their role as Glaziers, but with wooden glazing bars the window panes were now held in place with sprigs and putty. To avoid the window panes snapping, should the joinery of the window warp, the putty (made with linseed oil and whitening) needed to remain flexible, and the only way of doing this was to seal it with oil paint.[20] Consequently the introduction of sash windows, in the late 17th century, occasioned a dramatic increase in the activities of plumbers as painters, a feature characterised in numerous trade labels and trade directories of the 18th and 19th centuries. Indeed Whittock's 1827 manual, cited above, acknowledges as much in its title: *The Decorative Painters' and Glaziers' Guide.* It is this association that explains John Constable's friendship with the plumber-glazier John Dunthorne – they shared a common craft language of materials and tools.[21] By the 1870s this sort of shared understanding was a thing of the past. In these changed circumstances the American artist, William Morris Hunt, could make in his lectures the provocative assertion that artists had much to learn from the 'trade' – 'People who paint for a living, house painters, etc., always get flat surfaces. They don't stop to niggle.'[22]

With plasterers and plumbers actively involved in both the art and the trade of painting, we must confront some important questions regarding the authorship of certain mural schemes. That is why I tentatively suggest that the Merchant's House murals (c.1656–70) are by the plasterer William Brunson (Figs 8 and 9).[23]

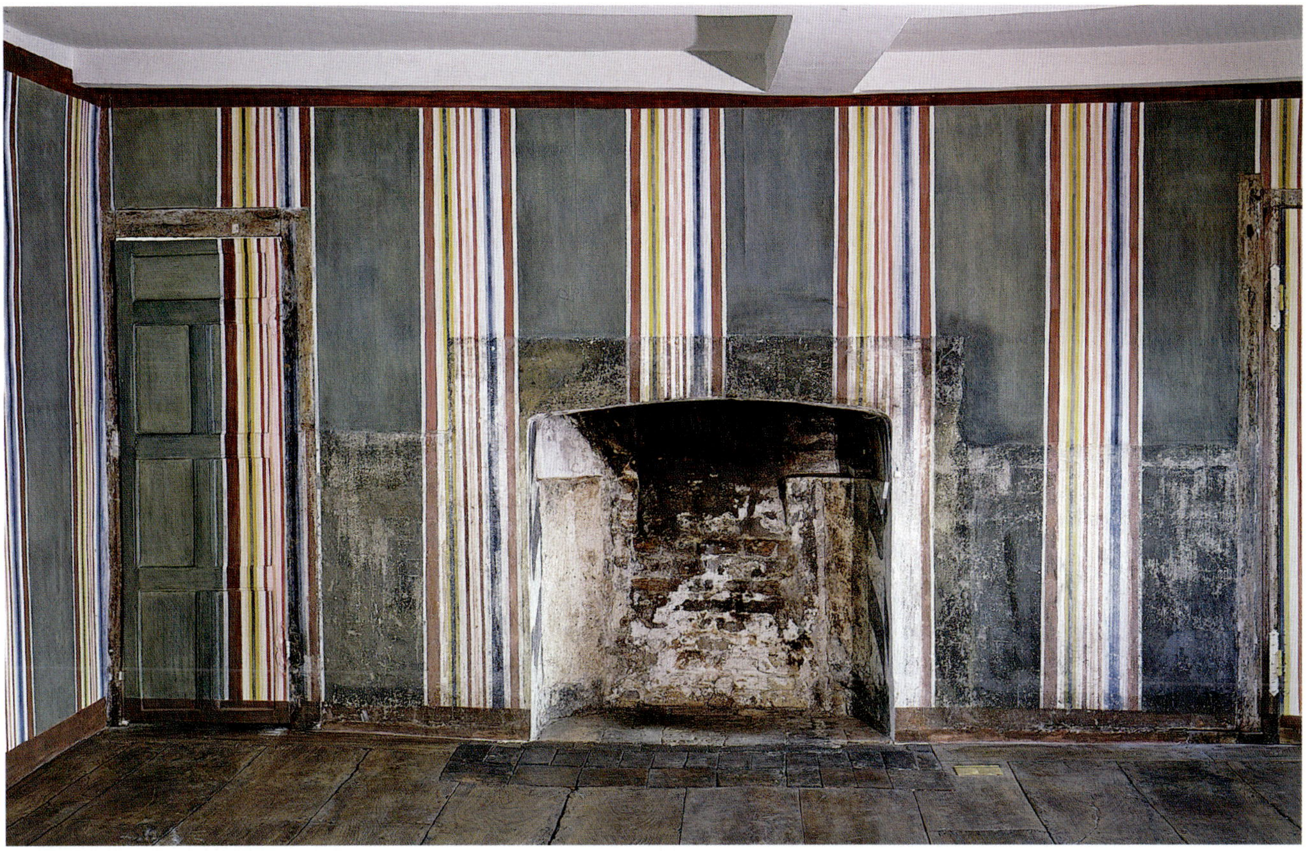

Figure 8 The Merchant's House, Marlborough, Wiltshire: restored mural scheme in the 'Dineing Roome', c.1656–60. Despite its apparent complexity, this colour scheme uses just three pigments: indigo, red and yellow on a white ground (plus combinations of these). Note the fragmentary black and white decoration on the left-hand jamb of the fireplace. *(Photo: D. Parker)*

The application of all-over colour – scumbled or otherwise – to walls was probably the 'bread and butter' in the livelihoods of most house painters. Nevertheless many must have extended their range to encompass patterned work based on graining, marbling and (at least in Colonial North America) spotting.[24] Most of these forms of decoration had been common since the 16th century, if not earlier. With the decline of panelling in the 18th century, patterned wallpaper became fashionable, but it was expensive (largely due to the excise duty on printed paper). Consequently, most households from c.1790 to 1840 relied on stencilled decoration as a relatively cheaper substitute (Fig. 10). With the abolition of the excise duty in 1836, labour-intensive stencilling could revert to the fashionable position it had enjoyed from the Middle Ages to the 17th century.[25] The decline of stencilling at the vernacular level is chronicled in 1847 by the Hull-born shipwright turned house painter Christopher Thomson in his *Autobiography of an Artisan*.[26]

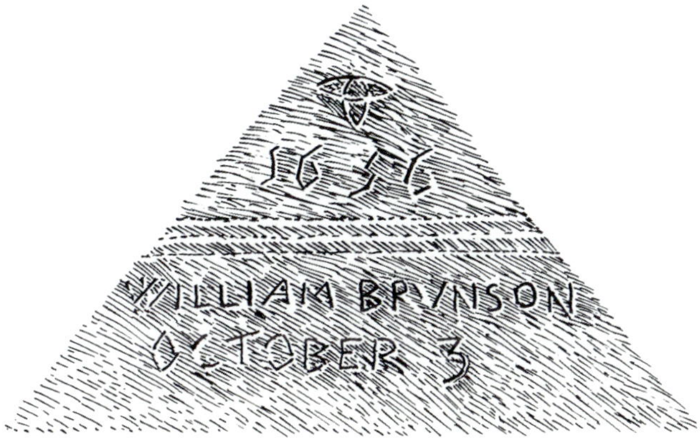

Figure 9 The Merchant's House, Marlborough, Wiltshire: signature of William Brunson dated 1656 with his logo scratched in the plaster inside the east gable. In addition to his work as a plasterer it is very likely that Brunson was responsible for the distemper decoration in the house (see Fig. 8). *(Drawing: J. Ayres)*

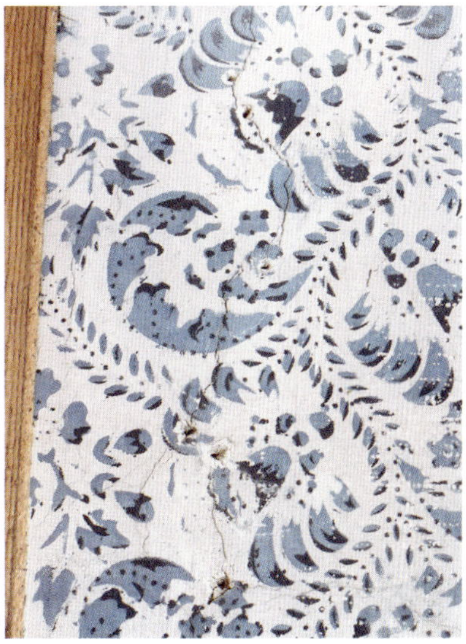

Figure 10 No. 4 Highfield, Lymington, Hampshire: stencilled decoration c.1830. The tax on printed paper (between 1712 and 1836) made wallpaper too expensive for most householders. *(© J. Close-Brooks)*

For all these surface embellishments, a megilp was an important constituent of the medium. Many such 'tricks of the trade' are to be found in the late 18th- and early 19th-century instruction manuals. In contrast, earlier generations had shown greater discretion in preserving craft secrets. For example, John Elsum, in his *The Art of Painting after the Italian Manner* (1704) expresses the hope that his book would not cause 'offence to the Masters of the Mystery'.[27]

Although Whittock's manual is largely concerned with practical issues, it is extensively illustrated and he does include a number of pictorial schemes as exemplars (e.g. for transparent blinds and inn signs) and argues that, with practice, many house painters should be capable of painting murals. The implication is that it was part of a long-standing tradition for such artisans to produce quite elaborate mural schemes. Certainly, in the second decade of the 18th century, Daniel Defoe describes the medieval murals then surviving in the choir of Salisbury Cathedral as 'mean', resembling more a 'common drawing room or tavern painting than that of a church'.[28] He probably had in mind the sort of work that survives in the George Inn at Chesham, Buckinghamshire, of c.1714 (Fig. 11). In many ways the George Inn mural, despite its 'modern dress', harks back to an earlier tradition, being innocent of the Dutch idiom for 'landskip'. This fashion, characterised by an earlier overmantel mural (of c.1689) at Wardrobe Place in the City of London, took root in Britain and generated a wide range of overmantel, over-door and whole wall schemes, painted either on plaster or forming part of a scheme of panelling (Fig. 12). Such work is to be found in 18th- and early 19th-century interiors in Britain and in North America. An

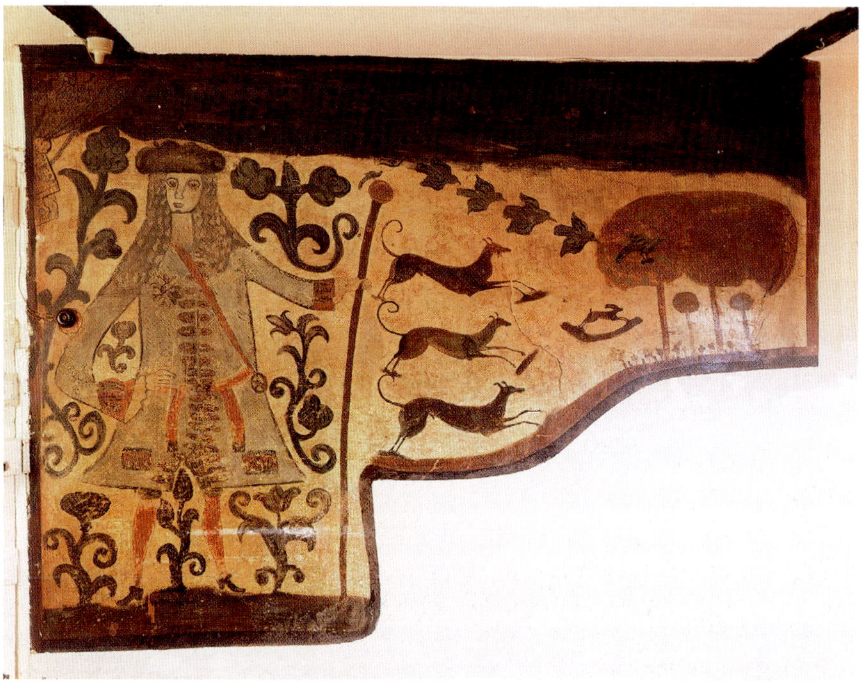

Figure 11 The George Inn, Chesham, Buckinghamshire: mural c.1714 in an upper chamber – possibly painted to celebrate the coronation of George I. The overall dimensions of this distemper-on-plaster painting are 228.6cm wide by 183cm high. *(© J. Ayres)*

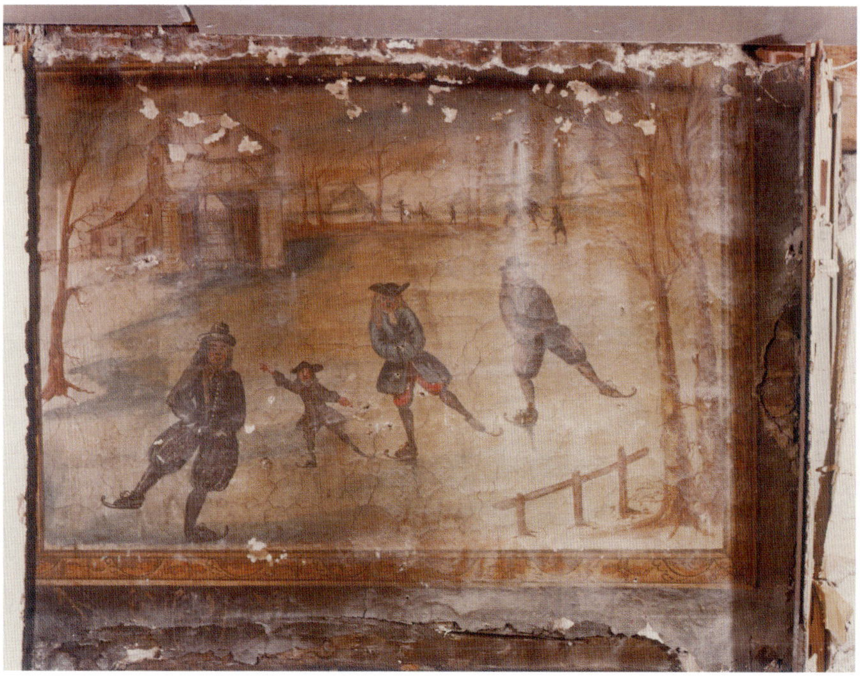

Figure 12 No. 2 Wardrobe Place in the City of London: overmantel mural on plaster with a trompe l'oeil frame, c.1680. This distemper-on-plaster decoration has a distinct Anglo-Dutch character. Photographed as found in 1983. *(©: City of London, London Metropolitan Archives)*

example of the genre at Sundial House, Corton, Wiltshire, datable to 1775, is painted on plaster over a fireplace, and may even be a rare example of a true fresco.[29] If so, this work (by an unknown artist) is more accomplished than Thomas Barker's (1769–1847) large *fresco buono* of *The Massacre of the Sciotes* of 1824 in the Doric House, Bath.[30]

By the early 19th century, many of the trade disputes of the past were less impassioned, a sure sign of the declining importance of the guilds to their respective trades. A publication such as Nathaniel Whittock's 1827 manual acknowledges, in its title, the involvement of more than one trade, but also underlines the extraordinary range of work undertaken by these tradesmen. Not for nothing were they to become known as 'Painters and Decorators'. The diversification implicit in such a term not only reflected the presence of no less than four trades in these activities (painters, stainers, plumbers and plasterers), but was to be compounded by industrialisation. Although many painters did continue to make their paints by reducing lump colour in a pestle and mortar and grinding the pigments with the chosen medium (a volatile oil or water) on a ledger with a muller, others bought in powder colours or even ready-made paints (Figs 13 and 14). Accordingly many trade painters were deprived of one element in their employment. This lies behind the sort of adaptation illustrated on the reverse of the early 19th-century trade label of Meggitt & Son of Hull, which (in addition to graining, marbling and gilding) lists the firm's products such as 'Papier Mache Decorations' and services including 'Room Floors Chalked for Balls, &'.[31]

The first of these paint manufacturers seems to have been the Emerton dynasty of London who, throughout much of the first half of the 18th century, produced paint by means of horse mills. Indeed Campbell, writing in 1747, explicitly blames the Emertons for the poor state of the painters' trade in London. He argued that no parent should be 'so mad as to bind his child Apprentice for seven years, to a branch that may be learned ... in as many hours, in which he cannot earn a subsistence [and] runs the risk of breaking his neck every day, and in the end turns out a mere blackguard'.[32] The final indignity to be suffered by painters, whether 'polite' or 'mechanical', was the production of oil paint in collapsible metal tubes in place of the difficult-to-use bladder colours. This innovation was devised by the American portrait painter John G. Rand (1801–73) while resident in London. Rand took out his patent in 1841, hence the closing date of this paper.[33]

All these developments in the production of paints were to have far-reaching effects, as were many other aspects of industrialisation. Even in large cities, artisan painters undertook an astonishing range of activities. A house painter like Michael Edkins of Bristol (active 1763–85) did house, carriage, boat and furniture painting. He also decorated tinware, applied resists to gun barrels for blueing, and painted stage scenery, signs and funeral hatchments.[34] This extensive repertoire demonstrates that mural painting would have been well within the capabilities of such a 'trade painter'. This was certainly the case with Thomas Walters (active c.1820–40), another Bristol-based 'decorative painter'. Not only did he stencil walls and produce easel paintings, he also painted murals in imitation of the more expensive landscape wallpapers produced by such firms as Zuber of Rixheim (from c.1804) and Dufour of Paris (from c.1815) (Fig. 15).[35] These wallpapers were not widely

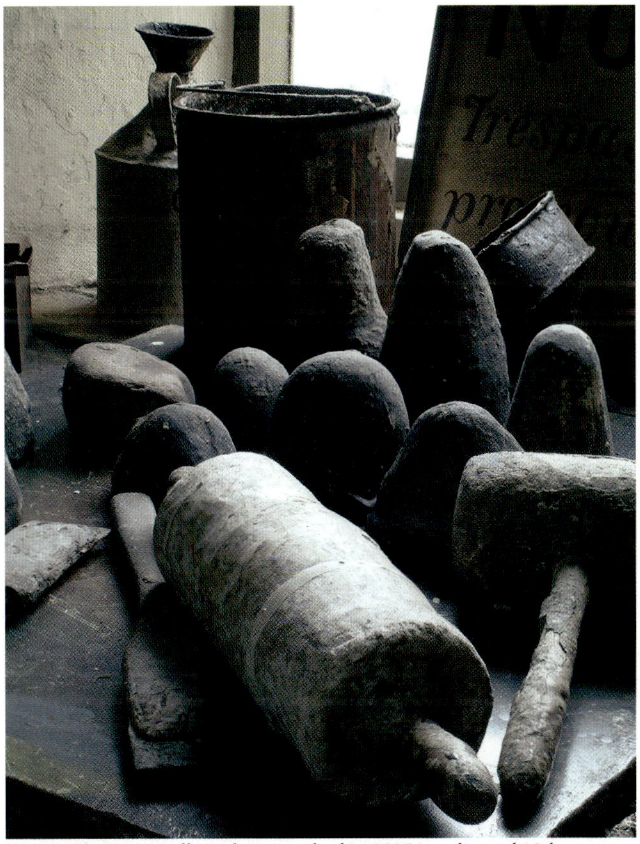

Figure 13 Paint mullers photographed in 2005 in a disused 19th-century paint shop in Yorkshire. *(© Justin Battong/Beamish, The North of England Open Air Museum)*

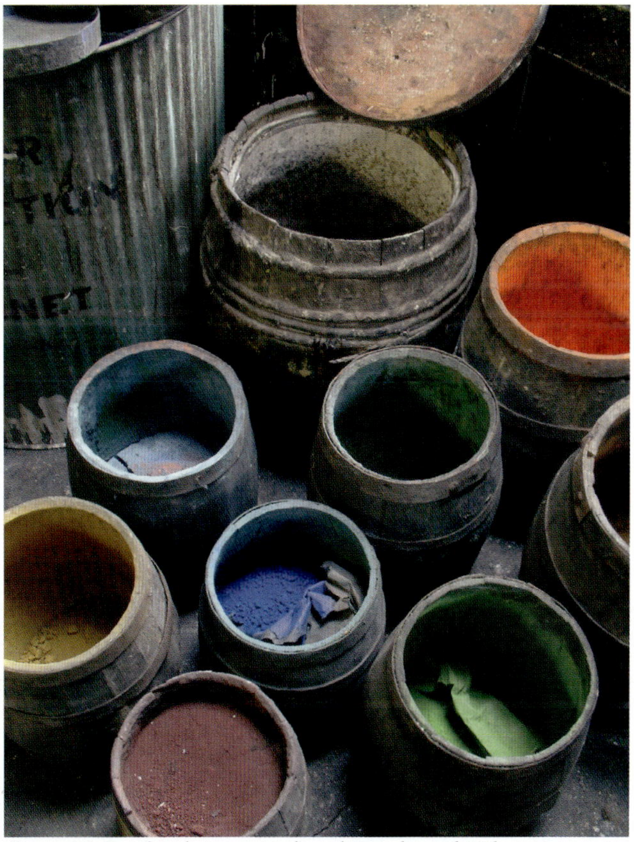

Figure 14 Powdered pigment in barrels in a disused 19th-century paint shop in Yorkshire. *(© Justin Battong/Beamish, The North of England Open Air Museum)*

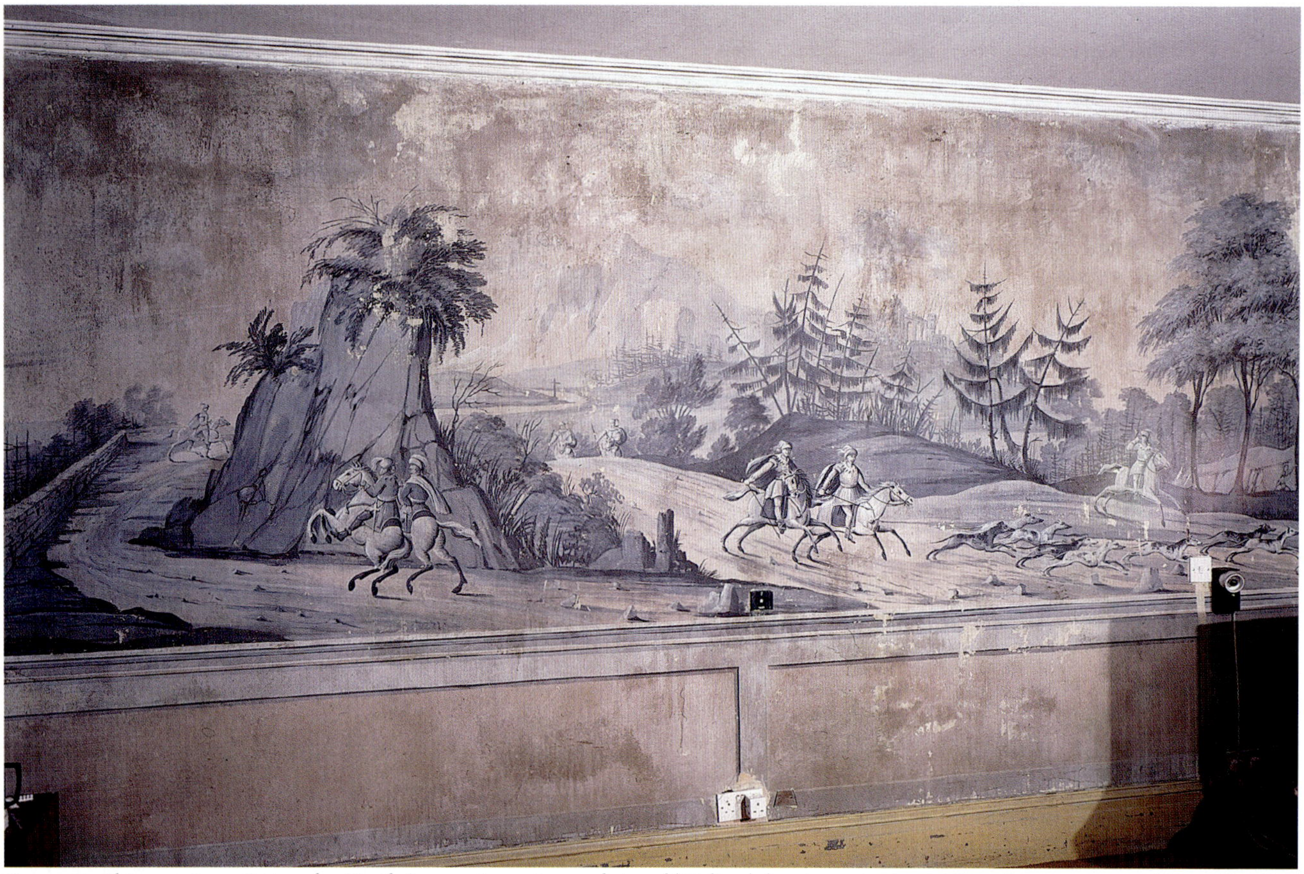

Figure 15 Phippens Farm, Butcombe, North Somerset: scenic mural signed 'Walters' showing a stag hunt. This scheme runs round the walls of the principal bedroom. It is painted in distemper on plaster although highlights appear to be rendered in oil paint. This, together with a simpler mural in the dining room and stencilled decoration elsewhere in the house, is almost certainly the work of Thomas Walters who is listed in an 1830 trade directory as a 'decorative painter' living at Upper Maudlin Street, Bristol. *(© J. Ayres)*

used in Britain, probably because of the Napoleonic Wars and difficulties with France thereafter. They were however widely used in early Federal America, where they were also imitated by house painters. Of these the most significant – indeed the most remarkable house painter of all time – was Rufus Porter (1792–1884). In addition to painting furniture, murals, and portraits, Porter devised an airship, invented the revolver (selling his designs to Samuel Colt), founded the *Scientific American* in 1845 and became its first editor.[36]

Postscript

By the second half of the 19th century, the academic artist was less likely to see himself as a 'brother brush'[37] of the tradesman painter. John Constable's friendship with the plumber-painter John Dunthorn was probably based on shared experience of materials and tools, but industrialisation and its products intervened, and easel painters retreated into an academic world that was only in part of their own creation. This emerging 'them and us' situation was probably at its worst in the late 19th and early 20th century. As a result Robert Noonan (alias Robert Tressell), in his semi-autobiographical *Ragged Trousered Philanthropists* (1914), has more to tell us about labour relations than about the art of the painter's craft. The 'hero' in the novel certainly worked on decorative mural schemes, but the bad-tempered tenor of the book may owe more to Noonan's inadequacies as a painter[38] than to the iniquities faced by 'Tressell' as an employee.

Noonan lived from 1868 to 1911; a tradesman painter of his generation was placed in a totally different artistic and social situation to that experienced by the best artisan artists of Georgian Britain – whatever Campbell may have had to say on the subject. Indeed, a number of the founder members of the Royal Academy of Arts came from a trade background. In Hanoverian Britain, men like Dunthorne of East Anglia, Edkins of Bristol and Thomson of Hull could, in a well-worn 18th-century phrase, be described as 'artists in their trades'.[39]

Notes

1. For the use of distemper or limewash as a means of consolidating mud floors, see Hughes and North 1979, p. 65. Animal blood was also used for this purpose. For whitewash used as a fire retardant see Innocent 1971, p. 212.
2. Gwilt 1876, p. 693.
3. Morris 1982, p. 137.
4. Harrison 1877, re: glazed windows, when 'glasse is come to be so plentifull' (p. 236) and 'the multitude of chimnies latelie erected' (pp. 239–40).
5. For Gold Beaters etc., see Englefield 1936, p. 26.
6. Mander 1997, pp. 119–148. See also Watt 1991, especially chapter 5 'Stories for Walls'.
7. Ayres 2003, fig. 97.
8. Eastlake 1960, pp. 95–7. Eastlake is here citing a manuscript of 1410 which is now in Bologna.

9. Abbott n.d.
10. Dossie 1764, p. 177.
11. An engraving of these transparencies and fireworks is in the British Library, Map Room, K.top XXVI, 7. p. 1.
12. Sloman 2002, p. 164.
13. For painted saddles, see Ayres 1985, p. 20, fig. 17.
14. Harley 1982: smalt is discussed on pp. 53–6.
15. Englefield 1936, pp. 101–23 and 138–63.
16. *Ibid.*, pp. 181 and 212.
17. *Ibid.*, p. 75.
18. Reproduced as plate 28 in Myers 1996.
19. *Shorter Oxford English Dictionary.*
20. Ayres 1998, pp. 194–6.
21. Ayres 1985, p. 51; figure 65 illustrates the large wooden model of a windmill that Dunthorne made for his friend John Constable as a studio prop.
22. Movalli 1976, p. 17. See also p. 124, where Hunt argues that artists should 'get sash tools from the paint shop ... If you want to know what brush to use, watch the painters at work on windows and doors.'
23. Ayres 2003, pp. 146–9 and figs 172, 183, 210 and 212.
24. A good example of Colonial North American 'spotting' is illustrated in figs 265 and 266 of Cummings 1979, p. 196. The 'restored' spotting in the Peter Wentz house in Pennsylvania is less than convincing.
25. Ayres 1998, pp. 220–22, and Ayres 2003, pp. 159–63.
26. Thomson 1847, p. 271. This incident is quoted in full in Ayres 1998, pp. 221–2.
27. Elsum 1704, Introduction.
28. Furbank and Owens 1991, p. 78.
29. Illustrated in Ayres 2003, fig. 216.
30. Bishop 1986. This illustrates Thomas Barker's fresco of 1824.
31. Illustrated in Ayres 1998, figs 317 and 318.
32. Campbell 1747, pp. 103–4.
33. For John G. Rand (1801–1873), see Ayres 1985, p. 132.
34. Manuscript Ledger of Michael Edkins. For extracts from this ledger, see Ayres 1998, pp. 225–8.
35. Entwisle 1970 – see chapter 5 and plates 46 and 47. See also Nylander *et al.* 1986, plate 14.
36. Lipman 1980.
37. The term 'brother brush' was used by Michael Edkins in his ledger (see note 34 above) when explaining a discount for a fellow painter.
38. If the manuscript title page for his book may be used to judge his artistry. This is reproduced in the Robert Tressell Workshop 1982, p. 18.
39. 'Artists in their trades' – there are many possible examples, but a notably early one (1660) is cited by Cummings 1979, p. 40.

References

Abbott J. (n.d.) Manuscript notebook and sketch book, Devon Record Office, Exeter (404 M/B1 B2)

Ayres J. 1985, *The Artist's Craft*, Phaidon, Oxford

Ayres J. 1998, *Building the Georgian City*, Yale University Press, New Haven and London

Ayres J. 2003, *Domestic Interiors: The British Tradition 1500–1850*, Yale University Press, New Haven & London

Bishop P. 1986, *The Barkers of Bath*, exhibition catalogue, Bath Museums Service

Campbell R. 1747, *The London Tradesman*, T. Gardner, London

Cummings A.L. 1979, *The Framed Houses of Massachusetts Bay 1625-1725*, Belknap Press of Harvard University Press, Cambridge, Mass. and London

Dossie R. 1764, *The Handmaid to the Arts*, London

Eastlake C.L. 1960, *Materials for a History of Oil Painting* [originally published in 1847, reprinted as *Methods & Materials of Painting etc.*], Dover, New York

Elsum J. 1704, *The Art of Painting After The Italian Manner*, D. Brown, C. King and S. Clark, London

Englefield W.A.D. 1936, *The History of the Painter-Stainers of London* [originally published in 1923], reprinted Chapman & Dodd, London

Entwisle E.A. 1970, *The Book of Wallpaper* [originally published in 1954], reprinted Kingsmead Reprints, Bath

Furbank P.N. and Owens W.R. (eds) 1991, *Daniel Defoe: A Tour Through the Whole Island of Great Britain* (1724), reprinted Yale University Press, New Haven and London

Gwilt J. 1876, *Encyclopaedia of Architecture* [originally published in 1842], reprinted Longmans, London

Harley R.D. 1982, *Artists Pigments c.1600–1835* [originally published in 1970], reprinted Butterworth Scientific, London

Harrison W. 1877, *Description of England* [originally published in 1577], reprinted F.J. Furnival (ed.). London

Hughes H. and North H.L. 1979, *The Old Cottages of Snowdonia* [originally published in 1908], reprinted Snowdonia National Park

Innocent C.F. 1971, *The Development of English Building Construction* [originally published in 1916], reprinted David & Charles, Newton Abbot

Lipman J. 1980, *Rufus Porter Rediscovered: Artist, Inventor, Journalist 1792–1884* [originally published in 1968], reprinted Clarkson N. Potter, New York

Mander N. 1997, 'Painted cloths: history, craftsmen and techniques', *Textile History* 28(2), pp. 119–48

Manuscript Ledger of Michael Edkins, Bristol Central Library (B 20196)

Morris C. (ed.) 1982, *The Journeys of Celia Fiennes 1685–c.1712*, MacDonald/London and Webb & Bower/Exeter

Movalli C. (ed.) 1976, *William Morris Hunt on Painting and Drawing*, Dover, New York

Myers H. 1996, *William Henry Pyne and his Microcosm*, Sutton, Stroud

Nylander R.C., Redmond E. and Sander P.J. 1986, *Wallpaper in New England*, Society for the Preservation of New England Antiquities (SPNEA), Boston, Mass.

Robert Tressell Workshop 1982, *The Robert Tressell Papers*, Workers Educational Association (WEA), Rochester, Kent

Sloman S. 2002, *Gainsborough in Bath*, Yale University Press, New Haven and London

Thomson C. 1847, *The Autobiography of An Artisan*, Athenaeum Reference 1034 (August 17, 1847), 887

Tressell R. 1993, *The Ragged Trousered Philanthropists* [originally published in 1914], Flamingo/Harper Collins, London

Watt T. 1996, *Cheap Print and Popular Piety 1550–1640* [originally published in 1991], reprinted Cambridge University Press, Cambridge

Whittock N. 1827, *The Decorative Painters' and Glaziers' Guide*, London

The author

James Ayres is a freelance writer and consultant. He is author of some seven books on art and architecture, including *Building the Georgian City* (Yale 1998) and most recently *Domestic Interiors: The British Tradition 1500–1850* (Yale 2003). Founder of the Building of Bath Museum, former director of the John Judkyn Memorial (American Museum) in Bath, Ayres has enjoyed a distinguished career as curator and historian and is a Fellow of the British Society of Antiquaries of London.

Image and identity in mural painting in British public buildings, 1840–1940

Clare A.P. Willsdon

The venue of the *Modern Traditions* conference, Skinners' Hall in London, houses one of the jewels in the crown of British mural painting – the scheme by Sir Frank Brangwyn on the history of the Skinners' Livery Company, begun in 1902 (Fig. 1). When Brangwyn wrote in 1912 to thank the Master of the Skinners 'for having given me an opportunity that has seldom if ever fallen to the lot of a British artist in this country'[1] however, this was an oversimplification. By 1912, the 'modern tradition' of British public mural painting, launched by Prince Albert at the new Palace of Westminster in the 1840s, had already seen some notable highlights, and many more would follow, in locations ranging from town halls to schools, hospitals, hotels, and even ocean-going liners.[2]

This paper considers the nature and process of invention of this 'modern tradition', with reference to some of its key works from 1840–1940. As a discussion of secular and public murals, it necessarily excludes the significant revival both of church mural painting – some of high quality, some frankly bad – and of private house decoration, which developed from 1840.[3] It nonetheless deals both with beliefs (often strongly held) and with the role of individuals, for public murals in Britain were frequently didactic or commemorative or both. In the absence of a system of state or centralised patronage – as found, for example, in France – they typically depended on what the polymath Sir Patrick Geddes, speaking in Edinburgh in 1889, called 'individual efforts of voluntary associations'. Geddes argued that such efforts 'in turn should rise to civic, and hence also national completeness',[4] and was himself responsible both for sponsoring murals in the city and for goading the Glasgow city fathers into sending a delegation to report on the new murals in French buildings such as the Panthéon and Hôtel de Ville in Paris. This led to the Glasgow City Chambers murals, completed in 1901 by local Francophile artists, which included Sir John Lavery's *Modern Ship-Building on the Clyde* – a clear reflection of the contemporary preference for decorating Parisian *mairies* (town halls) with modern-life subjects.[5]

Although themes from history were the norm for public secular murals in Britain, the lead taken by individual or voluntary initiative meant they expressed many different identities, whether corporate, personal, national or local. The Palace of Westminster is a case in point. While Prince Albert's personal initiative, as chairman of the Royal Fine Arts Commission, was the driving force, his ideals came into conflict with those of the Whigs – men such as the historian Macaulay who were drafted onto the Commission after the fall of the Tory government in 1846. Albert had envisaged an apotheosis of Queen Victoria for the Royal Gallery murals, and wanted another monarch, Alfred, at the head of the historical scheme planned for St Stephen's Hall, the site of the first House of Commons and therefore of democracy. The Whigs preferred to emphasise the role of Britain's common people.[6] Both E.M. Ward's 1850s murals of Stuart history for the Commons Corridor, and Charles Cope's 1853–67 Stuart and Cromwellian murals for the Peers' Corridor, give prominence to everyday citizens and domestic detail, and bear vivid witness to this change in policy.[7]

So too, where Albert had favoured fresco for its grandeur – its 'large and simple forms', as its great 19th-century German practitioner Peter Cornelius had called them[8] – which articulated his vision of the monarchy's role in national government, technical problems forced him to accept alternatives such as waterglass. Pioneered in Germany, this was adopted from the late 1850s at Westminster by Maclise. Waterglass enabled an even more Macaulayan delight in the incidentals of history: the soldiers' buttons, ships' rigging, or the 'identity badge' of Jack Tar's tattoo; details that seize the attention in *The Meeting of Wellington and Blücher at Waterloo* and *The Death of Nelson* (Fig. 2). These, the largest of the Westminster murals, were completed for the Royal Gallery in 1862 and 1865. Maclise's realistic details are combined, however, with a bold reinvention of religious *topoi* (Nelson's death recalls a *Pietà*) which effectively creates an alternative grandeur for a hero regarded as the saviour of national identity.[9]

The identity celebrated by the work at Westminster, was, in short, a complex mixture of the individual and political with the national, just as the selection of technique – so vital to the role of murals as an artform intended to last – was as much symbolic as pragmatic. In murals for the new town halls which sprang up in the wake of the Municipal Corporations

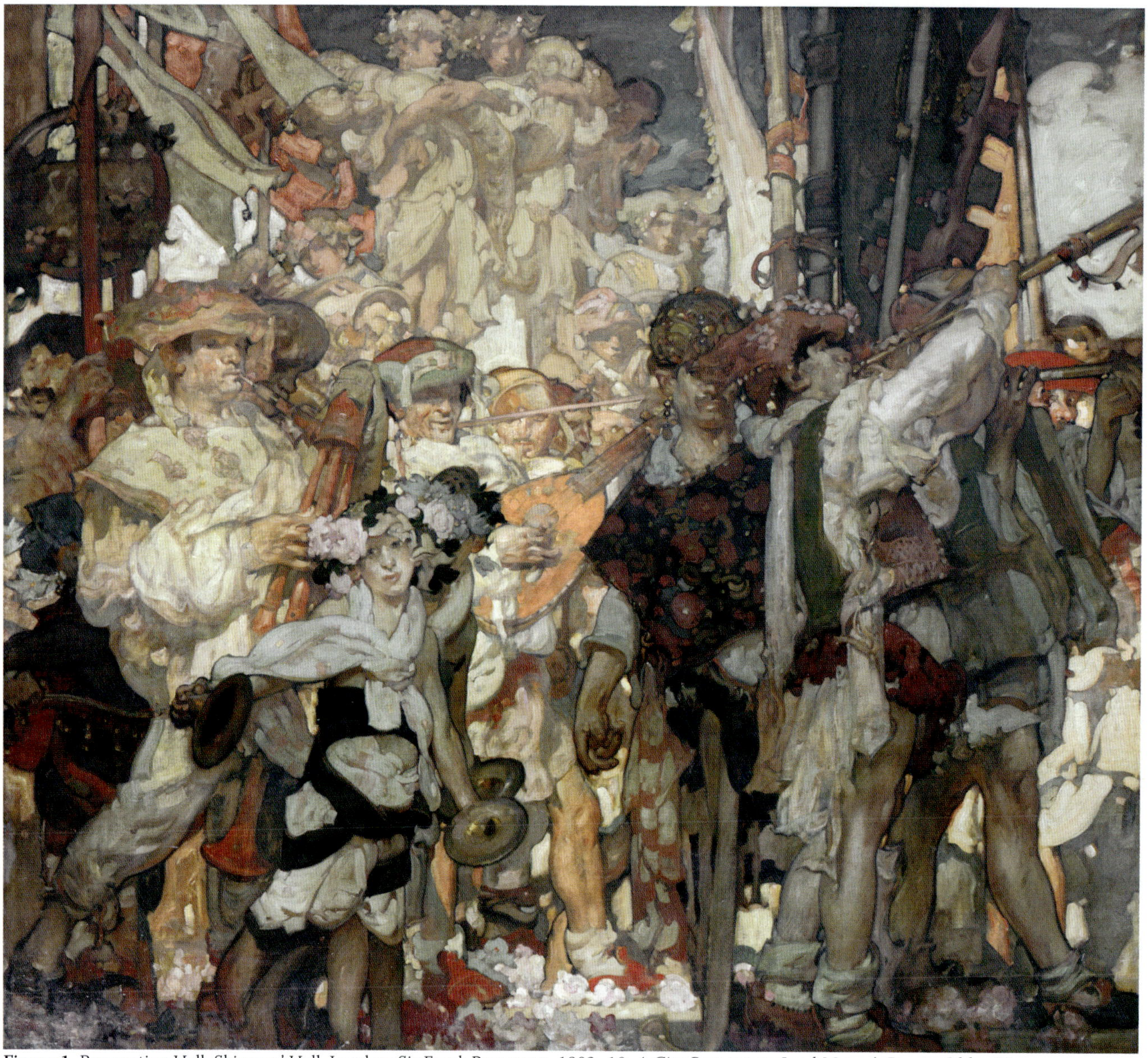

Figure 1 Banqueting Hall, Skinners' Hall, London: Sir Frank Brangwyn, 1902–10, *A City Pageant on Lord Mayor's Day in Olden Times.* *(© Crown copyright. NMR)*

Act of 1835, it was local identity which came to the fore, as at Glasgow, but in practice this too involved wider motives. In the northern English town halls the very medium of mural art, with its venerable medieval and Renaissance lineage, became a means to lend authority to the Radical politics favoured by their councils.[10] Such legitimising of the new by reference to the old constitutes what the modern historian David Cannadine has called 'invention of tradition'[11] and it recurs repeatedly in British public murals, with their predilection for historical motifs.

At both Rochdale and Manchester town halls, for example, politics overlaid their architects' view of murals as integral to Gothic style. In Rochdale, where W.H. Crossland's great hall has a hammer beam roof tellingly modelled on that of Westminster Hall, there are images of Victoria and Albert adorning the end walls, but Cromwell – the Chartists' hero – is significantly prominent among the monarchs in the stained glass windows, who literally illuminate the users of the hall. Meanwhile a large, richly coloured mural of *Magna Carta*, the incident believed to mark the origins of Britain's government 'by the people for the people', adorns the wall above the dais, its frieze arrangement of barons suggestively guiding the eye to Cromwell in the adjacent glass. Completed by Henry Holiday in 1871, this scheme is complemented by the stencils and murals of local trades and of the tools of Rochdale's industrial prosperity (including wool- and cotton-weaving machines drawn from designs in the Patent Office), which were painted in other parts of the building by the commercial decorating company Heaton, Butler and Bayne.[12] In its day, the ensemble would have offered a highly potent 'invention of tradition', in which sanction was given to the ideals of Free Trade and universal suffrage espoused by Rochdale's Chartist heroes Richard Cobden and John Bright.

In turn, in Manchester in 1876, outrage greeted the architect Alfred Waterhouse's suggestion that artists from Belgium should decorate his new town hall: Ford Madox Brown was employed instead to paint subjects from local history.[13] Where Holiday's Rochdale *Magna Carta* had employed a traditional

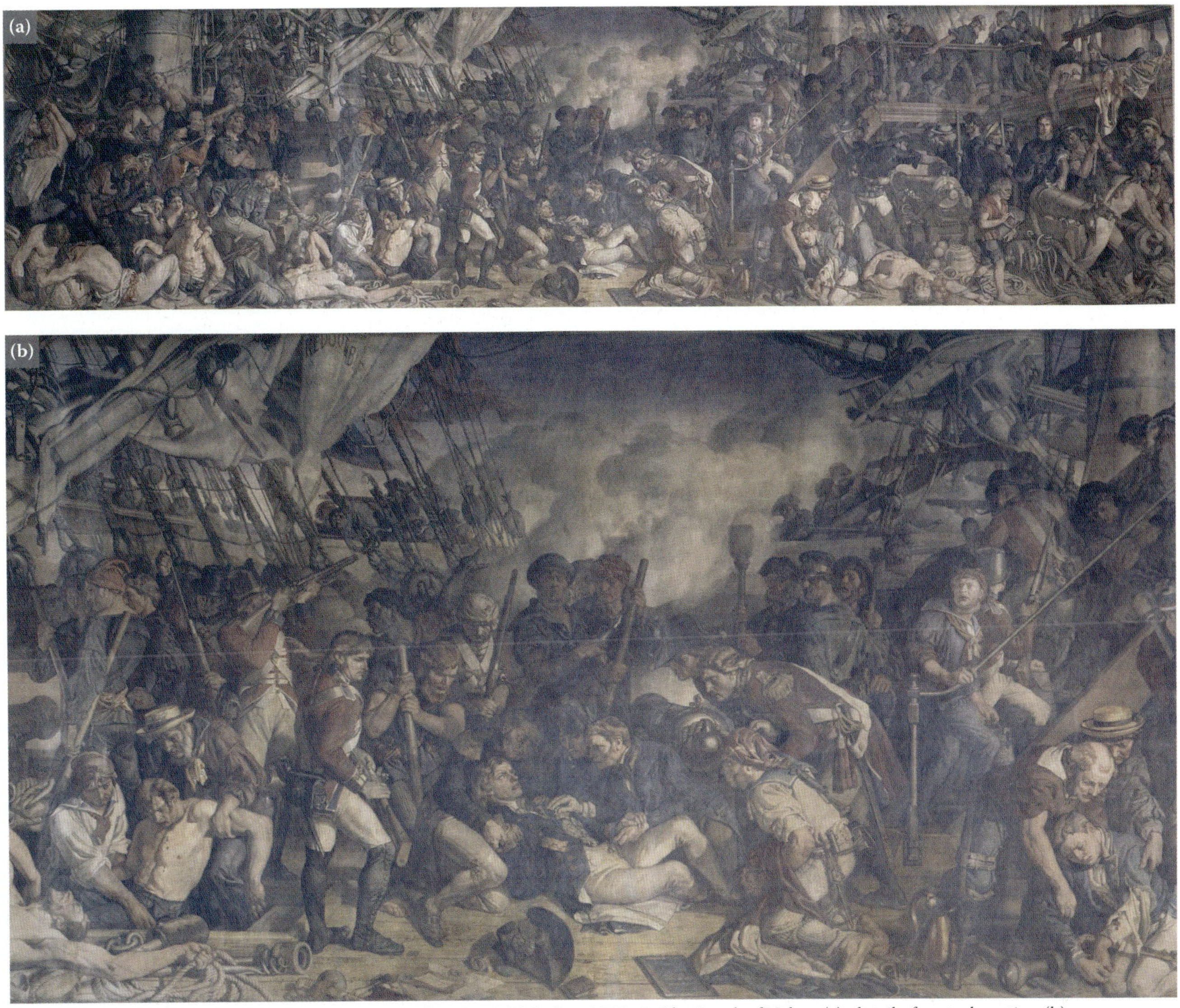

Figure 2 Royal Gallery, Palace of Westminster, London: Daniel Maclise, 1863–5, *The Death of Nelson* (a); detail of central portion (b).
(© Palace of Westminster)

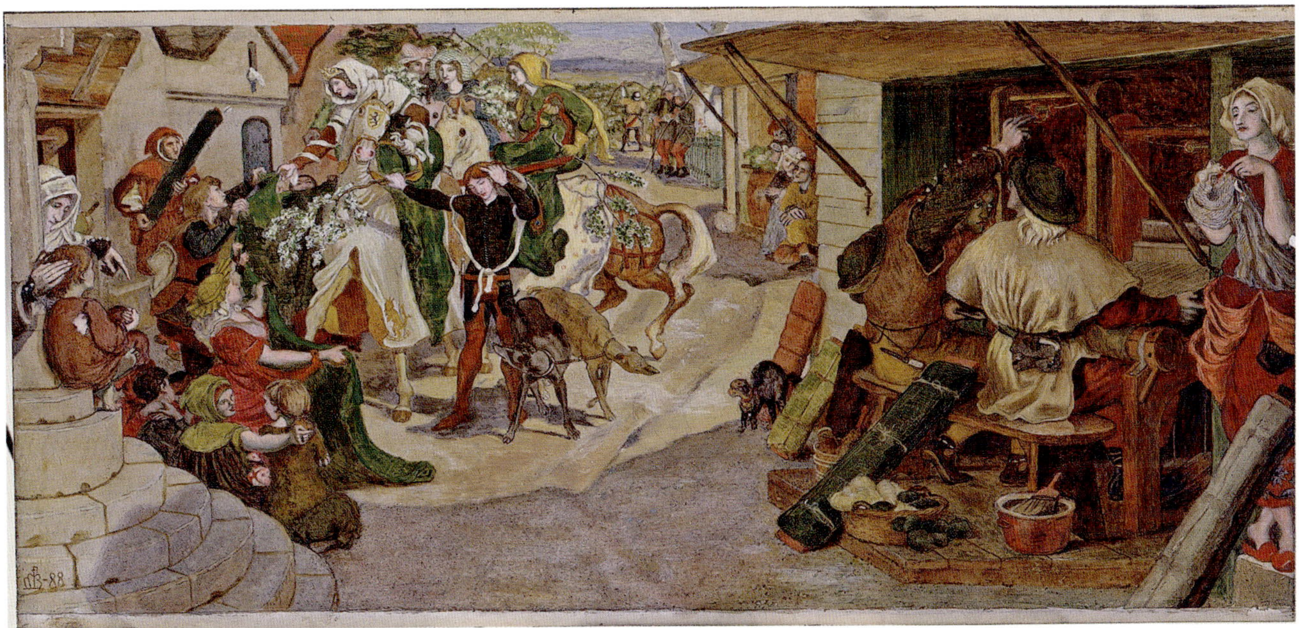

Figure 3 Manchester Town Hall, Manchester: Ford Madox Brown, 1881–2, *The Establishment of Flemish Weavers in Manchester AD 1363.*
(© Manchester City Art Galleries)

frieze format, however, Brown engaged the viewer's attention in new, dynamic ways that took the art of the public mural – a large-scale image for mass consumption – into an almost psychological realm, laying important foundations for the tactics used by Brangwyn and other later muralists. It is the selectivity of human vision, which so often seizes on the trivial detail before the main event, that the artist exploited here. For example, in *The Establishment of Flemish Weavers in Manchester AD 1363* (Fig. 3), an illustration of free trade in olden times, Queen Philippa of Hainault can be seen inspecting bales of cloth produced by the Flemish weavers she introduced into Britain, but it is the foreground subplots – children playing games and an apprentice weaver distracted by the master's daughter dallying with a kitten – that first catch the eye. These launch an exchange between real and painted worlds, and between past and present, as the viewer is 'drawn' into the weavers' space. A luminous arc of blue shadow in turn sweeps back from the viewer's feet, guiding the eye to the sunlit queen in the background, so that the whole composition unrolls beneath the viewer's gaze, just as bales of cloth are unrolled before the queen. Thomas Carlyle, who Brown much admired, had defined time itself as 'Systole' and 'Diastole', a cycle in which 'vernal growth' follows on from 'winter dissolution'.[14] The queen has just returned from gathering May blossoms, which are being carried by her entourage.[15]

The theme of identity is clearly multilayered here, embracing our own identity as well as that of the common Flemish and Mancunian people of medieval times and of the queen. Brown's manipulation of the way the eye reads pictures can be set specifically in the wider context of emergent appreciation of the power of sight as distinctive of human identity itself: by the late 19th century, followers of Darwin would regard human vision as a prime 'biological survival mechanism'.[16]

Already, in the wake of the publication of Darwin's *Origin of Species* in 1859, Ruskin had actually called a halt to the painting of murals of geological formations that he was supervising at the new Oxford Museum, evidently fearing that what he called art's 'exciting address to the observant faculties'[17] might here be mistaken for praise for the theory of evolution rather than of God. Only two of the murals, painted by the Reverend Tyrwhitt, were actually completed, one showing the 'Mer de Glace' and the other of 'The Lava Streams of Vesuvius'.[18] It was of course on fossil evidence taken from geological sites that Darwin based some of his theories.

'Exciting address to the observant faculties' was however exactly what began to be powerfully deployed in a number of other public murals, notably G.F. Watts' 1859 *School of Lawgivers* for Lincoln's Inn in London. In an age of film and television, it is easy to underestimate the visual impact that this vast, 45-foot-wide fresco must originally have made. It was intended to imbue successive generations of future lawyers and judges with respect for Truth, Justice and Mercy, and if the composition is unashamedly modelled on Raphael's great Renaissance *School at Athens*, many of the figures have the features of Watts's contemporaries (Tennyson is King Minos, Holman Hunt the Saxon King Ina, and so on).[19] At the apex is a detail that wickedly subverts tradition, and was rediscovered only when the mural was conserved in the 1950s: the personification of Truth, flanked by Justice and Mercy, winks at the viewer![20] Here is a theatricality that reminds us of Shakespeare's 'All the world's a stage ...', in which, indeed, Justice 'plays his part'.

Meanwhile, Rossetti, in his contribution to murals illustrating Malory's *Morte d'Arthur* at the Oxford Union,[21] used the very mechanics of looking to make his viewers 'become' the medieval knight Sir Launcelot. Sunk upon the ground, Launcelot's body frames one of the roundel windows of the Union Library, so that the viewer is dazzled by real light – just as Launcelot, on entering the Chapel of the Holy Grail, experienced a fiery 'breethe' which 'smote him so sore ... that him thought hit brente hys vysage'.[22] We are made involuntarily to enter that pre-industrial world of Arthurian legend, so yearned for by Rossetti and his pre-Raphaelite colleagues, and in so doing that marker of human identity itself, the power of sight, is again placed centre stage.

Lincoln's Inn and the Oxford Union are just two of the numerous educational or welfare institutions which, like town and county halls, turned to mural decoration in the wake of Westminster as a means of vouchsafing the values and beliefs of the present to future generations.[23] At the South Kensington Museum in the 1870s, Lord Leighton – a vigorous advocate of mural art – actually portrayed the boatman ferrying pottery at the left of his *Arts of Industry Applied to Peace*, steering straight from his painted, classical world into the real space occupied by the viewer (see Fig. 16, p. 194). The boatman's open mouth, by implication, utters a rallying call to modern mankind to reinvent the beauty of antiquity, just as Leighton's South Kensington murals were intended as a visual manifesto for the new technique of 'spirit fresco'.[24]

In Edinburgh by the 1890s, in the first of the murals commissioned from John Duncan by Sir Patrick Geddes for the Common Room of his pioneer student hall of residence in Ramsay Garden, the Celtic hero Cuchullin gives what has surely now become a piercing shout as he awakes to fight fresh battles (Fig. 4). Geddes, an admirer both of Watts and Ruskin, was the leader of the 'Celtic Revival', which aimed to renew modern Scotland by reference to the ancient Celtic past. Above the mural of Cuchullin, St Columba's prophecy is inscribed, 'As it hath been, so it shall be'. But the French Symbolist vision of mural painting as a psychologically affective and even synaesthetic medium is also brought to mind by Duncan's appeal to the ear via sight. Duncan, like Geddes's other young Scots artists, had first-hand experience of French Nabi art, and employed marouflage, a technique of oil painting on canvases fixed to the wall that was in widespread use on the Continent.[25]

By the late 19th century, public murals were in fact rarely true wall paintings. At the Royal Exchange (1895–1927), spirit fresco or oil was painted onto canvas marouflaged to panels of slate, to provide the necessary ventilation, and marouflage was also used at Drapers' Hall in London in 1901. At Skinners' Hall, the murals were simply painted on stretched canvas and then let into the panelling. When Joseph Southall painted a true fresco of 'modern life' at Birmingham City Art Gallery, his revivalist medium was actually his message: his mural, painted in 1915–16 as youth was being slaughtered in the First World War, shows a child symbolically reaching for a flower-seller's nosegays in Birmingham's Corporation Street. Southall was a pacifist, and the painting's Renaissance technique pleads for a 'renaissance' of life.[26]

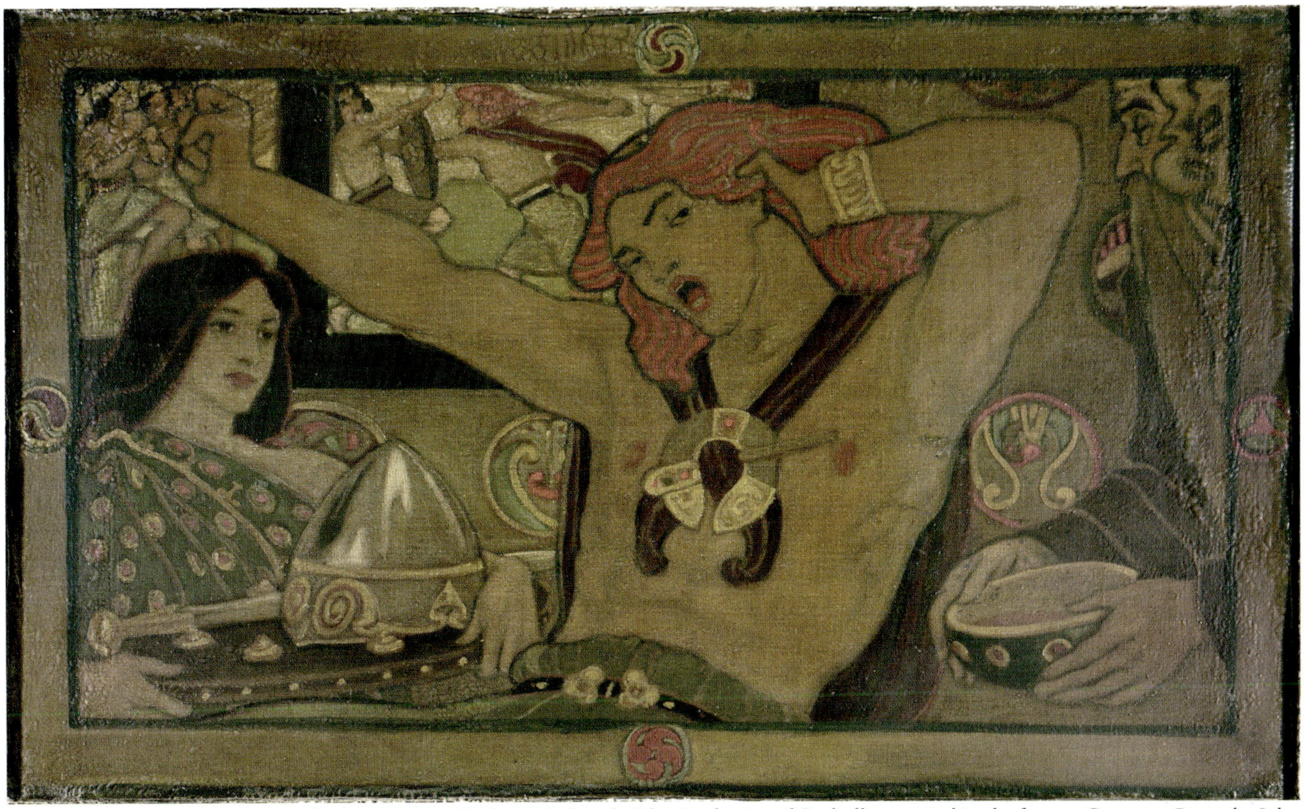

Figure 4 University Hall, Ramsay Lodge, Ramsay Garden, Edinburgh: *The Awakening of Cuchullin*, painted in the former Common Room by John Duncan, 1895–8. *(Courtesy of the Royal Commission on the Ancient and Historical Monuments of Scotland)*

Before turning to later 20th-century examples, it is instructive to consider both the Royal Exchange and Skinners' Hall murals and those of 1908–10 in the East Corridor at Westminster. These are works whose assertion of identity for posterity had a particular urgency. The Exchange and Skinners' murals came into being in the context of the so-called 'struggle for London', as the London County Council, newly established in 1889, sought to take the rights and powers in the regulation of markets, control of river traffic, provision of welfare and building and so on, that for centuries had lain with the livery companies and/or the City of London Corporation.[27] It was their historic claims to these rights and powers that were asserted through mural art by the Companies and Company members who donated the Exchange panels, and by the Skinners' Company at Skinners' Hall. The Exchange murals were born of Lord Leighton's recommendation that fine artists (rather then commercial artists) should decorate the building:[28] the images of Company and City history inscribed on the walls for posterity were clearly intended to have an almost ritual power, as emblems both of institutional and of personal identity. Similar purposes are apparent in the Skinners' iconography.

Ernest Crofts' *Opening of the First Exchange by Queen Elizabeth, 23 January 1570–71* (Fig. 5), unveiled at the Exchange in 1899, shows Sir Thomas Gresham, the building's founder, proudly welcoming his monarch. This mural was donated by the Mercers' Company, which, along with the Corporation, controlled the Exchange. But the eye is drawn first to the servant in the foreground, who strews rushes right across the viewer's 'path'. We become as active participants in the events re-enacted in the mural – and many of the Exchange artists also in fact designed sets for the innovative *verismo* performances of Shakespeare mounted by Sir Henry Irving and Sir Herbert Beerbohm Tree.[29] So, too, as we look at *The Great Fire of London, 1666*, by Stanhope Forbes (donated to the Exchange in 1899 by the Sun Fire Office), by implication we are made to sit in the rescue boats into which children, chattels, and (tellingly) a portrait of an ancestor are being loaded for the journey to safety along the river Thames; as mentioned, the Thames was a key target for control for the London County Council. Forbes's spiral of descending figures is based on Tintoretto's *Presentation of the Virgin* – an 'invention of tradition' that associates the merchants of modern London with the might of the great merchant princes who had patronised art in Renaissance Italy. But the realism of the flickering, threatening flames derives from Forbes's first-hand studies of the forge at Newlyn. Past, present and the future – symbolised by the children – are graphically fused.

Although Leighton had regarded Brangwyn as untried,[30] in 1901 the Skinner Sir Thomas Lane Devitt chose him to paint *Modern Commerce*, the panel Devitt donated to the Exchange, and then recommended him for the Skinners' own murals. The sequence of Company history in these paintings begins with *Pelts and Furs at City Mart before the Charter*, in which early Skinners ply their trade at a market in Walbrook (City markets were another of the areas the London County Council wished to control), and ends with the famous 17th-century banquet mounted by Lord Mayor Pilkington (a Skinner) for William and Mary. William and Mary had restored the ancient rights that Cromwell had taken away from the Skinners during the Commonwealth – and which the London County Council was threatening again to remove in the early 20th century. Brangwyn responded with imaginative sympathy to

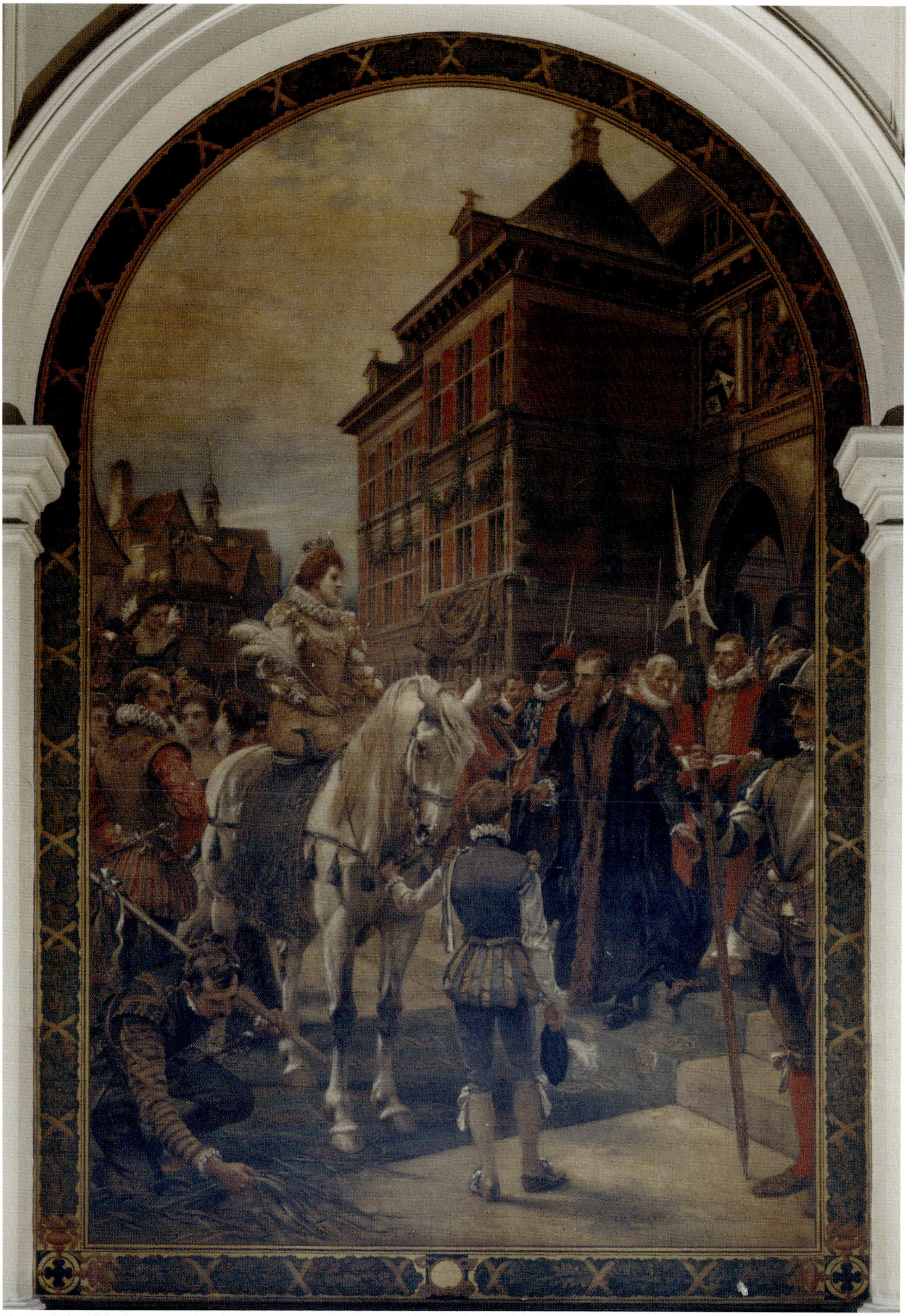

Figure 5 Royal Exchange, London: Ernest Crofts, *The Opening of the First Royal Exchange by Queen Elizabeth, 23 January 1570–71*. Presented by the Mercers' Company, 1899. *(© The Mercers' Company and the Joint Grand Gresham Committee)*

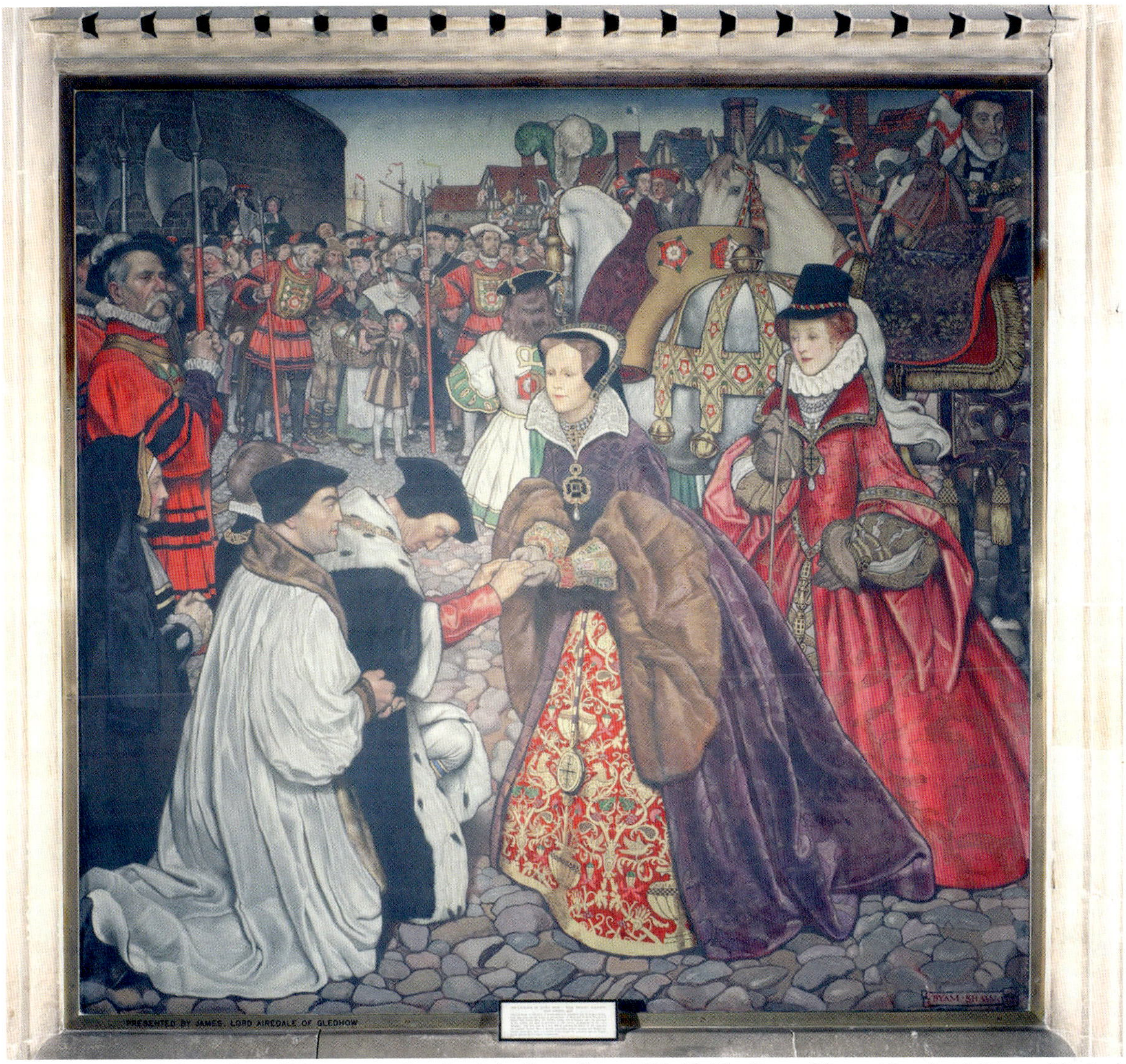

Figure 6 East Corridor, Palace of Westminster, London: John Byam Shaw, 1908–10, *The Entry of Queen Mary I with Princess Elizabeth into London 1553*. Presented by Lord Airedale. *(© Palace of Westminster)*

his patrons' concerns. Where, for example, he shows the primitive Skinners at Walbrook eating green apples, it is basketfuls of golden fruits that he places in the foreground of *Lord Mayor Pilkington entertaining King and Queen, 1689* – emblems of the wealth, achievement and munificence of the Skinners whose rights William and Mary restored. In turn, he makes the floral-garlanded crown in *A City Pageant on Lord Mayor's Day in Olden Times* (see Fig. 1) a leitmotif of the Skinners' identity, featuring the crown throughout the scheme even though it was traditionally worn only at the Corpus Christi Day election of the Master and wardens of the Company.[31] It even appears on the head of the young boy who represents the promise of the future in *The Founding of Tonbridge School by Sir Andrew Judd*.

Brangwyn's supporter Devitt's personal identity is reflected in the prominence of ships, barges and river in the two main murals, *The Departure of Sir James Lancaster for the East Indies, AD 1594* and *River Procession of the City's and Companies' Barges to Westminster AD 1453*. Devitt was President of the Shipping Federation that controlled the Thames. But just as Brangwyn gave prominence in these murals to the common labourers of Elizabethan society, reflecting his personal belief in the 'brotherhood of man', so he also wrote himself into the Skinners' history. The primitive *Skinner in Pelts and Furs* – whose hunched posture brings to mind Rodin's *Burghers of Calais*, representatives of civic freedom – is a self-portrait.[32] It is as though Brangwyn here equates the Skinners' labour with their knives to that of an artist with his brush – a symmetry of craft and art that betrays his admiration for William Morris.[33] With their almost kinaesthetic rhythms, Brangwyn's murals join his own ideals together with those of the Skinners' Company and Devitt in a powerful visual unity. His symbolic motifs, like the floral crown, are progenitors of what we today associate with corporate branding, or even, perhaps, subliminal advertising.

In the East Corridor at Westminster we find a very different style, but once again, the expression of identity which (as in Brangwyn's murals) was in its time a form of propaganda. Each mural here was donated either by a newly created Liberal peer or by a peer sympathetic to the new Liberal government's desire to reform the House of Lords, at that time blocking the passage of its radical social legislation.[34] The subjects are episodes from the English Reformation, but these can be recognised as allusions to the Liberals' programme of modern 'reform'. Educational reform, for example, is suggested through the topic of Erasmus and Sir Thomas More – ambassadors of 'the New Learning' of the Renaissance – visiting the children of Henry VII at Greenwich. This mural, by Frank Cadogan Cowper, reflects the late 19th-century historian J.A. Froude's belief that the origin of modern England could best be seen 'through the eyes of Erasmus',[35] and in conjunction with the adjacent panel by Frank Salisbury portraying Henry VIII's divorce from Catherine of Aragon – the catalyst for the Reformation itself – creates an almost zoom-lens effect, as if the viewer were watching a film. Time is telescoped, 'little' Henry turning into 'big' Henry. It comes as no surprise to find that the child in the foreground of the final mural, showing Princess Elizabeth welcoming the young Queen Mary into London, by Byam Shaw (Fig. 6), is a portrait of the artist's young son (James Byam Shaw, the late art historian).[36] Past and present were now literally made as one. The murals were effectively a trial run for the telling of history through appeal to the eye that would be developed by George Macaulay Trevelyan (great-nephew of Macaulay) in his famous *Illustrated English Social History* books; the young Trevelyan advised on the choice of subjects at Westminster.[37] At the same time, the murals' intensely realistic idiom, partly inspired by Holbein, is combined with a decorative, almost bejewelled effect that underlines their inherently symbolic purpose.[38]

When the next Westminster murals were created, at St Stephen's Hall in 1924–7, the austere British School at Rome style was deemed appropriate for what, in the wake of the First World War, was intended to be a symbolically sober, even understated evocation of "The Building of Britain'.[39] Sir George Clausen's *The English People ... Gathering Secretly to Read Aloud Wycliffe's English Bible*, for example, is a calm pastoral idyll. This stands in implicit contrast to the overtly imperialistic mood of Sigismund Goetze's Foreign Office murals, begun just before the First World War, which show Britain 'teaching her sons the arts of war' and 'the arts of peace', and so on.[40] By the early 1920s there had been much diplomatic wrangling over Goetze's final panel, a symbolic League of Nations, as changing international relations overtook its iconography. Lord Curzon, then Foreign Secretary, did his best to have the scheme rejected, but failed.

The public mural as such now faced a crisis of its own identity as the approaching Depression brought a mood of austerity, and grand mural projects were felt to be anachronistic. Plain 'facts' were preferred, for example, for the murals at the Bank of England in the early 1930s (again by members of the British School at Rome).[41] A variant of the British School's spare reinterpretation of early Italian models was also employed at Essex County Hall in Chelmsford by A.K. Lawrence, a St Stephen's Hall artist.[42]

In contrast, Rex Whistler's 1927 *The Pursuit of Rare Meats* for the Tate Gallery restaurant seems positively escapist. Its depiction of a fanciful journey through a Rococo-style landscape was surely a witty skit on the St Stephen's Hall murals – exactly contemporary – for its travellers include Ugpin, an anagram of Pugin, and Crown Prince Etienne, whose name, of course, is French for Stephen.[43] But it is Król Duziarz the artist (a self-portrait of Whistler) who has the most up-to-date form of transport in the mural, leading the travellers on his bicycle as if to project Whistler's delight, as a Slade-trained artist, in poking fun at his British School at Rome colleagues at Westminster. Brangwyn, meanwhile, was at work on what would have been the peers' First World War Memorial, had they accepted it, in the Royal Gallery of the Palace of Westminster. Sponsored by Lord Iveagh, this is a prime example of the role of private initiative in British public murals. What the Royal Fine Art Commission called its 'insistent motifs' – images of the peoples of the Empire enjoying the products of their native lands – were, in the event, felt by the Lords to be unsuited to their Gothic Revival surroundings.[44] Yet the real reason for their disquiet was surely again political. Brangwyn's imagery would, by the date of the murals' completion in 1933, have been embarrassingly in conflict with the government's moves to stem colonial claims to independence. Today, the paintings may be seen in Swansea Guildhall; their rejection by the Lords marked the end of the tradition of Westminster murals launched in the 1840s by Prince Albert.

It was, perhaps, some of the schemes that dealt with local or group identity, rather than national identity, which proved the most successful 'inventions of tradition' in 20th-century Britain. These include Delmar Banner's colourful scenes of historical trades and crafts at the Regent Street Polytechnic (1922); C.R. Napier's whimsical, slightly Cubist murals of local legends at the Children's Library in Huddersfield (begun 1939), and E.I. Halliday's 1929 murals of the legend of Athena at the Liverpool Athenaeum Club (a social forum for the city's businessmen). In the final, dramatic panel of Halliday's scheme, Athena strikes Arachne with her shuttle (Fig. 7); Arachne's fate, being turned into a spider, is foretold by the spider-shaped shadow on the wall and the web-like pattern mapped by the sightlines. Halliday suggestively portrayed himself as an Athenian cloth-dyer, and his wife as Athena.[45]

Several local schemes remembered the sacrifice of war. Neville Lytton's 1924 series of wall paintings at Balcombe Village Hall in Sussex is one of the starkest: a recollection of the hand-to-hand combat he had witnessed as a war correspondent. The chalky colours of Lytton's *buon fresco* technique give a chilling overtone, as does Cayley Robinson's simulation of fresco tonalities in his First World War memorial at the Middlesex Hospital in London (1915–20). Technique remained as symbolic as it had been at Westminster in the 1840s, or at Birmingham in 1915–16.

At Woodgreen Village Hall, Hampshire, the murals of village life that Robert Baker painted in 1931–8 with Edward Payne (son of one of the 1906–10 East Corridor artists at Westminster) incorporate over 50 portraits of local residents (Fig. 8). The continuity of rural life amidst the rapidly changing social order, politics, inventions and ideals which emerged in the wake of the First World War is here celebrated with an almost Stanley Spencer-like sense of the ritual within the quotidian. The vital and enduring link between image and identity is perhaps most vividly encapsulated at Brighton, Hove and Sussex Grammar School, however, whose murals on local history project the theme of human identity itself – that theme which Darwin's theories had first thrust into focus some 80 years before.[46] Begun in 1913 by Louis Ginnett, a former pupil of the school, they were completed only in 1939 with *The Excavation of Hollingbury Camp* (Fig. 9), an illustration of the discovery of Piltdown Man that includes T.E. Lawrence dropping by on his motorbike. The rhythmic linear progressions

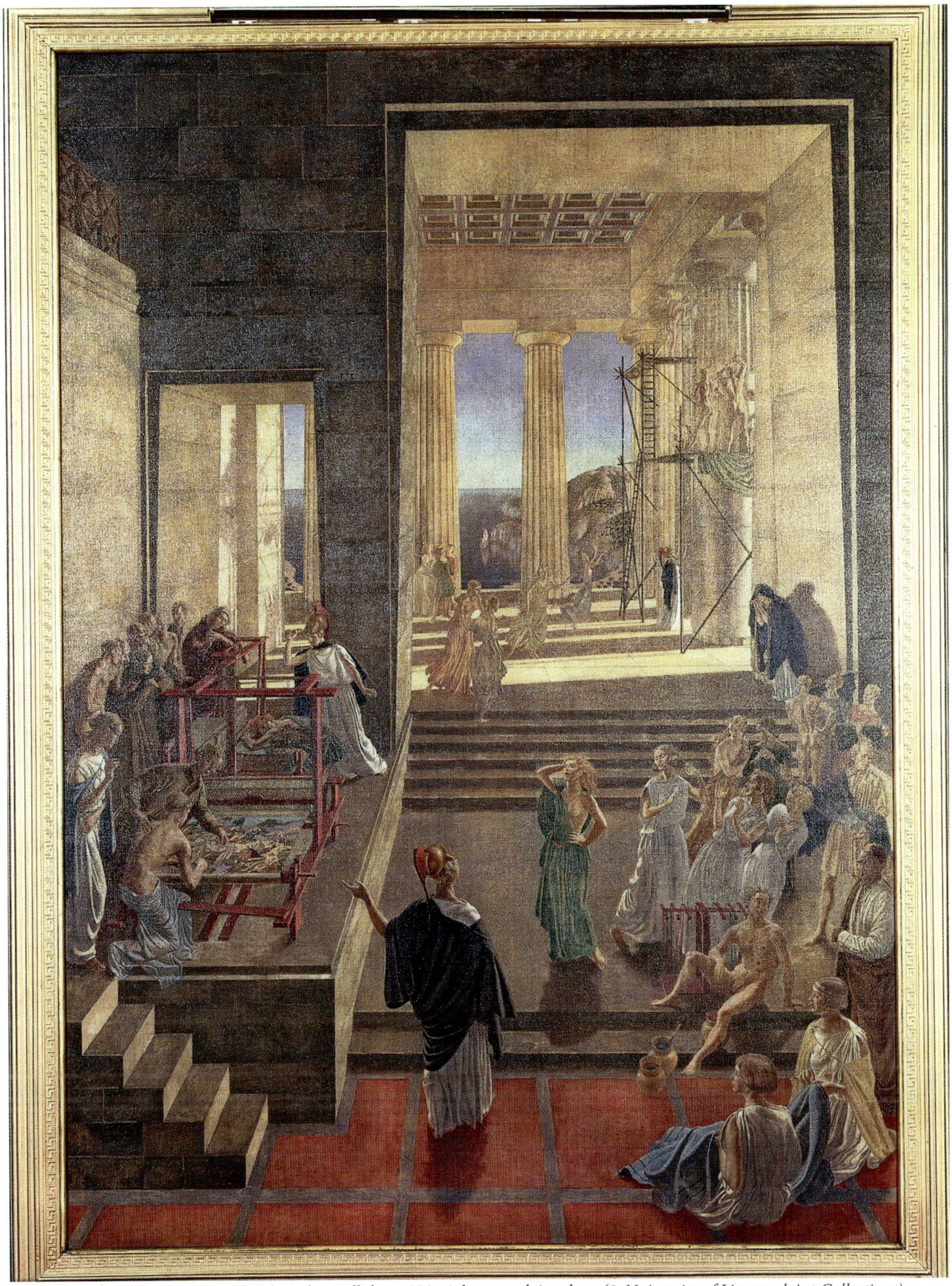

Figure 7 Athenaeum, Liverpool: Edward I. Halliday, 1929, *Athena and Arachne. (© University of Liverpool Art Collections)*

of the composition directly link the Piltdown bones – then believed to be genuine – to 1930s man and woman, and are subtly echoed in turn in the rolling contours of the distant Sussex weald.

Space does not allow consideration of other examples of the remarkable heritage of British public murals from 1840–1940. But the varied schemes discussed above show how an inherently conservative artform, which consciously 'invented tradition' and may initially seem conventional in style or subject, could nonetheless embody radical messages and political, social, symbolic or richly personal meanings. As with much public mural art elsewhere, British figurative murals were characterised by a concern to demonstrate personal or institutional philosophies, achievements or aspirations; a concern reflected also in choices of technique. At the same time, the British were drawing upon European models and traditions of

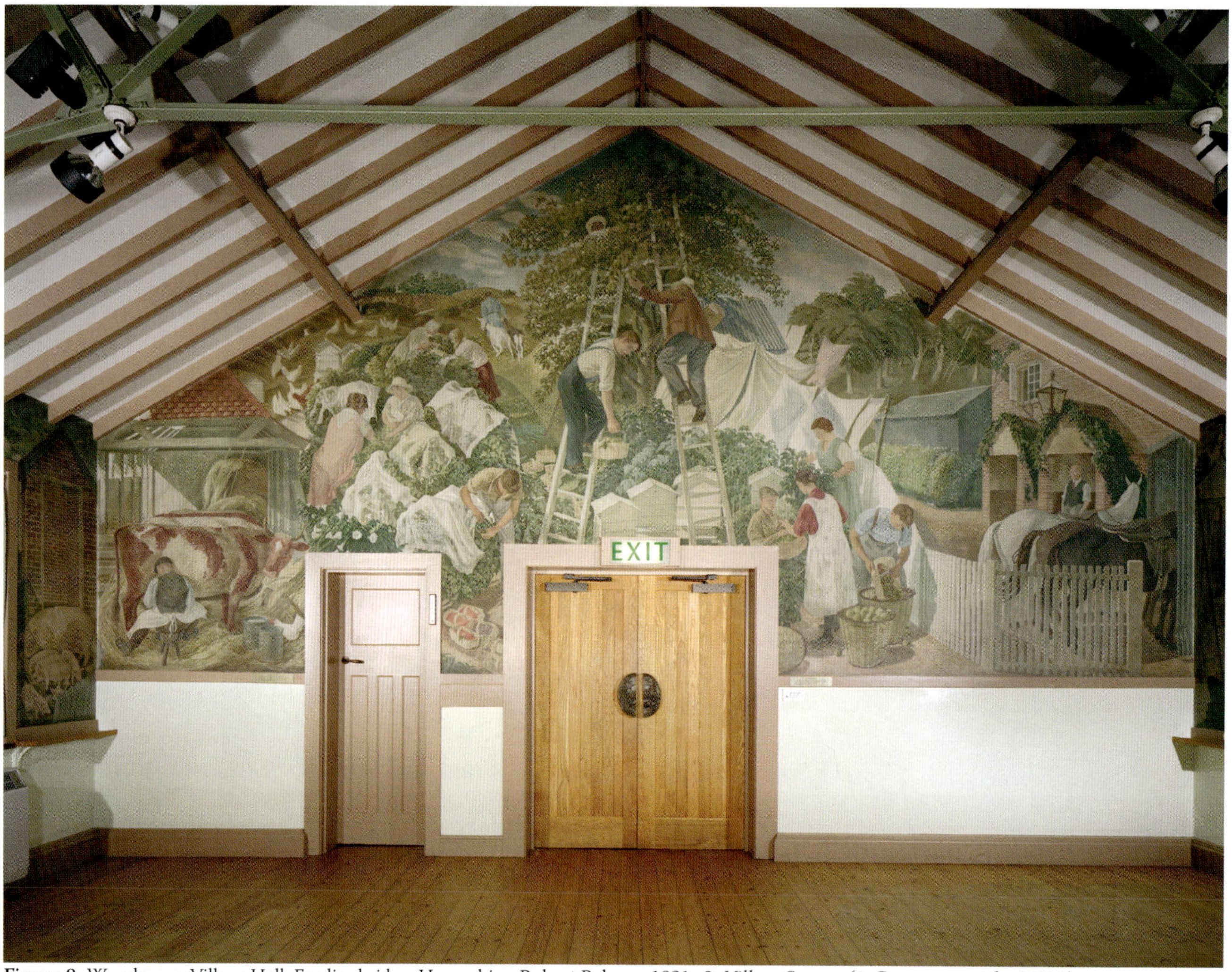

Figure 8 Woodgreen Village Hall, Fordingbridge, Hampshire: Robert Baker, c.1931–8, *Village Scenes*. *(© Crown copyright. NMR)*

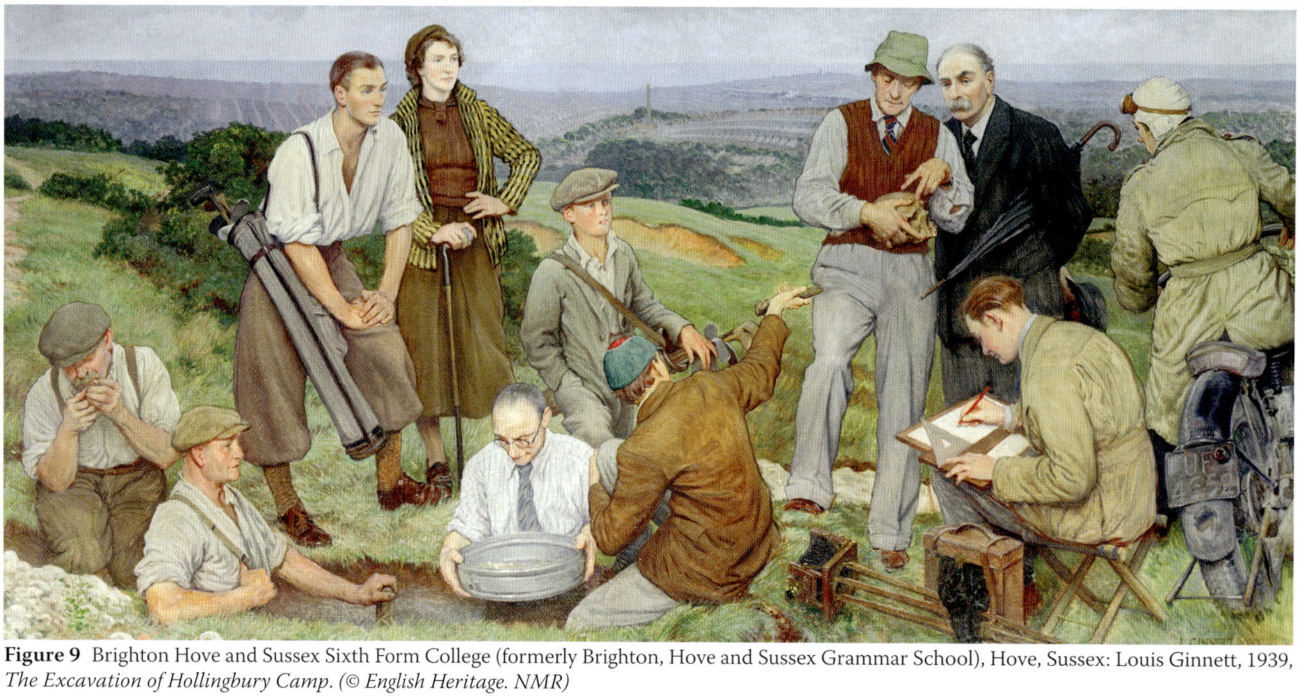

Figure 9 Brighton Hove and Sussex Sixth Form College (formerly Brighton, Hove and Sussex Grammar School), Hove, Sussex: Louis Ginnett, 1939, *The Excavation of Hollingbury Camp*. *(© English Heritage. NMR)*

symbolic expression. Public murals in Britain were an art with something to say, and if we are to understand them we must not only take aesthetic or technical factors into account, but must also try to reconstruct – by reference to their wider and international contexts – the fascinating ways in which they so often fused identity with image.

Acknowledgements

I am grateful to UKIC (now Icon) and English Heritage for being given the opportunity to contribute this paper to the *Modern Traditions* conference in March 2005. For kind permission to illustrate the work by Sir Frank Brangwyn at Skinners' Hall, I would like to thank Rodney Brangwyn and the Worshipful Company of Skinners. I am similarly grateful to Mrs Bunty Martin, and Michael Shea (CVO, DL), and DACS for their permission to illustrate work by John Duncan at Ramsay Garden, Edinburgh. For valuable help in relation to my research, or for providing illustration or copyright permission, thanks are also due to the following: The Athenaeum, Liverpool; the late Robert Baker; Christopher Thomson, Brighton Hove and Sussex Sixth Form College; Christina Byam Shaw and the late John Byam Shaw; Charlotte and Stephen Halliday; the late Sir John Stuart Knill; Ann Compton, University of Liverpool Art Collections; Anne Sutton and Ursula Carlyle, Mercers' Company; Malcolm Hay and Phyllis Rogers, Palace of Westminster; the late Edward Payne; Lady de Bellaigue, Royal Archives; K.S. Sales, Woodgreen, Hants; Myles Glover, former Clerk of the Worshipful Company of Skinners; and Richard Jefferies, Watts Gallery, Compton.

Notes

1. Letter from Brangwyn to the Clerk of the Skinners' Company, 28 April 1912, Skinners' Company Archives. Quoted in Willsdon 2000, p. 82.
2. Willsdon 2000.
3. *Ibid.*, chapters 8 and 10.
4. Geddes 1889, p. 7; in this paper Geddes also praised the recent patronage of murals by the City of Paris.
5. The Council's delegation followed Geddes's advocacy of murals for the new Glasgow City Chambers at a meeting of the Glasgow Ruskin Society: see Willsdon 2000, p. 184 and Willsdon 1986, pp. 36–8. For the use of modern-life subjects in the Paris *mairies*, see Burollet *et al.* 1987 (especially pp. 67–8).
6. For Albert's subject preferences for the Royal Gallery and St Stephen's Hall, see his Memorandum to Sir Robert Peel (c.1844) (F30/32 in the Royal Archives, Windsor), quoted in Willsdon 2000, pp. 31–3. For the history of the 19th- and 20th-century murals at Westminster, see *ibid.*, chapters 4–6; Boase 1954; Bond 1980; Hay *et al.* 1996; Riding and Riding 2000; and the entries on individual Westminster murals in Walker 1959–77 and 1965–76.
7. For Ward's and Cope's Corridor schemes, see Willsdon 2000, pp. 35, 53 and 56–7. Hay *et al.* 1996, pp. 86–9, note that Ward's emphasis on the common people of the past reflects his friendship with the Whig historian and Royal Fine Arts Commission member Thomas Babington Macaulay. For Cope's scheme, see Bond 1980, pp. 92–3.
8. Cornelius' words were quoted by Thomas Wyse in evidence to the Select Committee on the Fine Arts (1841) (see Select Committee 1841, p. vii). Cornelius himself provided the Committee with a lengthy report on fresco technique in 1841; for this and Cornelius' related visit to Britain, see Büttner 1999, pp. 269–73 and 480–83.
9. For Maclise's Royal Gallery work, see Willsdon 2000, pp. 40–45, 46, 56–7 and 59; Bond 1980, pp. 60–65; and entries in Walker 1959–77 and 1965–76.
10. For the Radical political sympathies of, for example, Rochdale in the 19th century, see Garrard 1983, pp. 35 and 101ff.
11. See Cannadine 1982, p. 108; the concept of 'invention of tradition' is amplified in Hobsbawm and Ranger 1983.
12. Holiday had gained a reputation as a decorative painter through mural commissions for some of William Burges's houses; he also designed stained glass for Heaton, Butler and Bayne. See Willsdon 2000, pp. 175–6 and Cormack 1989. Holiday's *Magna Carta* mural, almost 36ft long by 12ft high, was 'thoroughly renovated' by the artist in 1893 (Maxim 1959, p. 35).
13. Waterhouse, accompanied by a deputation from Manchester City Council, visited Belgium to view recent murals in buildings including the Courtrai town hall and interviewed Egide Guffens (one of the Courtrai artists) with a view to his receiving a commission at Manchester; see Waterhouse 1876; Treuherz 1985, pp. 169–71; and Willsdon 2000 p. 177. Protests against the use of foreign artists were mounted by, *inter alia*, the artist Frederic Shields, who helped Brown secure the commission.
14. See Carlyle 2000, p. 87.
15. See Brown's text on this mural in Manchester City Council 1969.
16. Crary 2001, p. 351 and see also pp. 40–41.
17. Letter from Ruskin to H.W. Acland (Acland 1860, p. 53).
18. Acland in *ibid.*, p. 8.
19. As identified in Draper 1906, p. 9. According to Speed (1928, p. 406), Edward I (at the bottom-left foreground of the fresco) is a portrait of Watts himself. For further information on the mural, see Watts 1912, p. 151.
20. Information from anonymous newspaper cutting from the *Daily Telegraph*, c.1955, in the collection of the Watts Gallery, Compton.
21. This scheme, on which Ruskin advised, was carried out in 1857 and consists of murals by Rossetti, Burne-Jones, Arthur Hughes, William Morris and others associated with the Pre-Raphaelite Brotherhood. The tempera medium was applied direct to the brick walls, and by 1858 was already beginning to perish. For the murals' history, see Renton 1983.
22. Thomas Malory, *La Morte d'Arthur*, book XVII, chapter 15, quoted in Renton 1987.
23. For further examples of such schemes, see Willsdon 2000, chapter 9.
24. For Leighton's two lunettes for the South Court of the South Kensington Museum, *The Arts of Industry Applied to War* (1871–80), and *The Arts of Industry Applied to Peace* (1873–85), see *ibid.*, pp. 268–73; Ormond 1975; Barringer 1999; and the paper by Gowing in this volume, pp. 181–95. Leighton's promotion of spirit fresco through these murals is discussed in Farr 1993, pp. 50–52.
25. For relationships between aspects of French Symbolism and the murals commissioned by Geddes for Ramsay Garden, see Willsdon 2004.
26. For Southall's pacifism, see Farr *et al.* 1980, pp. 101–3, which also (pp. 90–91) details the history of his mural, entitled *Corporation Street, Birmingham, in March 1914*.
27. The London County Council was created by the Local Government Act of 1888; its supporters regarded the City as 'a sort of obsolete appendix at the centre' of London (a Liberal journalist, quoted in Briggs 1963, p. 345). In 1893 a Royal Commission added fuel to such claims by recommending that the City's administration should be subsumed in a larger London administration. See Willsdon 1996 (pp. 314–18) and 2000 (p. 185).
28. Leighton recommended 'well-known artists of proven ability' (letter to Gresham Committee, 13 July 1892, quoted in Willsdon 1996, p. 313).
29. The artists Edwin A. Abbey (*The Reconciliation of the Skinners' and Merchant Taylors' Companies by Lord Mayor Billesden, 1484*), John Seymour Lucas (*William the Conqueror Granting a Charter to the Citizens of London*), and Frank Salisbury (*Alfred the Great Repairing the Walls of the City of London*) were all designers for historical pageants and for the Shakespeare productions of Irving or of Tree.

30. Leighton, who painted and donated the first mural, *Ancient Commerce* (unveiled in 1895), was responsible for artistic coordination of the Royal Exchange scheme until his death in 1896. For his 1894 rejection of Brangwyn as too inexperienced to paint a Royal Exchange mural, see the Gresham Committee Minutes for 8 June 1894 (Mercers' Company Archives, London).
31. It is the cap of the 'cocks and caps' ceremony, as described in an anonymous booklet of c.1909 on the murals (Skinners' Company Archive, London).
32. A sketch of this figure, in possession of the Fine Art Society London in c.1981, is even more clearly a self-portrait.
33. Of Anglo-Welsh parentage, Brangwyn was brought up in Bruges but worked as a copyist in Morris's Oxford Street workshop in the 1880s before gaining a reputation on the Continent in the 1890s (see Willsdon 2000, p. 82).
34. The murals were the result of a Select Committee recommendation in 1907 that the decoration of the Palace of Westminster be resumed, and the project was taken up with enthusiasm by the Liberal government which had come to power in 1906. For its evolution, see Willsdon 2000, pp. 94–105.
35. Froude 1894, p. 431.
36. I am grateful to the late James Byam Shaw, CBE, for this information.
37. Trevelyan was a Liberal sympathiser and the great-nephew of Thomas Babington Macaulay.
38. Because of the disunity of style felt by many to mar the Exchange scheme, the East Corridor work was placed under the artistic coordination of Edwin A. Abbey; its artists were all so-called 'Neo-Pre-Raphaelites'.
39. See the booklet of this title describing the scheme, written by the poet Henry Newbolt and published in c.1927 to accompany the murals' unveiling.
40. The St Stephen's Hall and the Foreign Office murals are discussed in Willsdon 2000, pp. 130–42 and 109–21. The latter decorate the Ambassadors' Staircase.
41. Sir D.Y. Cameron, appointed artistic coordinator for the Bank scheme, described its subjects as 'dry and ugly facts' in comparison to the 'imaginings' at St Stephen's Hall (where he had also been coordinator) (letter to the Bank architect Sir Herbert Baker, 4 January 1936, in Bank of England Archives; quoted in Willsdon 2000, p. 354).
42. This scheme, showing local history, was completed by 1939; see Council Chamber of the Essex County Council 1939.
43. See Olivier n.d., p. 10.
44. Select Committee on the House of Lords Offices 1929–30; see also Willsdon 2000, pp. 143–64.
45. For this scheme, see Halliday n.d., Compton 1997 and Willsdon 2000, pp. 370–73.
46. The school is now Brighton Hove and Sussex Sixth Form College. For its murals, see Willsdon 2000, p. 291.

References

Acland H.W. 1860, *The Oxford Museum: Remarks Addressed to a Meeting of Architectural Societies*, 2nd edn, Oxford

Barringer T. 1999, 'Leighton in Albertopolis: monumental art and objects of desire', in T.J. Barringer and E. Prettejohn (eds) *Frederic Leighton: Antiquity, Renaissance, Modernity*, Yale University Press, New Haven and London

Boase T.S.R. 1954, 'The decoration of the New Palace of Westminster 1841–1863', *Journal of the Warburg and Courtauld Institutes* 17, pp. 319–58

Bond M. (ed.) 1980, *Works of Art in the House of Lords*, HMSO, London

Briggs A. 1963, *Victorian Cities*, Odham's Press, London

Burollet T. *et al.* 1987, *Le triomphe des mairies. Grands décors républicains à Paris 1870–1914*, exhibition catalogue, Musée du Petit Palais, Paris

Büttner F. 1999, *Peter Cornelius Fresken und Freskenprojekte*, 2, Franz Steiner Verlag, Stuttgart

Cannadine D. 1982, 'The transformation of civic ritual in modern Britain: the Colchester Oyster Feast', *Past and Present* 94, pp. 107–30

Carlyle T. 2000, *Sartor Resartus* (introduction by R.L. Tarr), University of California Press, Berkeley, Los Angeles and London

Compton A. 1997, *Edward Halliday Art for Life 1925–1939*, exhibition catalogue, University of Liverpool Art Gallery, Liverpool

Cormack P. 1989, *Henry Holiday*, exhibition catalogue, William Morris Gallery, Walthamstow

Crary J. 2001, *Suspensions of Perception: Attention, Spectacle and Modern Culture*, MIT Press, Cambridge, Mass. and London

Draper W.H. 1906, 'The Watts fresco', *Burlington Magazine* **9**, pp. 8–15

Essex County Council 1939. *An Account of the Decorations [...]*, Essex County Council, Colchester

Farr D. (ed.) 1993, *Thomas Gambier Parry 1816-1888 as Artist and Collector*, exhibition catalogue, Courtauld Institute Galleries, London

Farr D. *et al.* 1980, *Joseph Southall 1861–1944: Artist-Craftsman*, exhibition catalogue, Birmingham Museums and Art Gallery, Birmingham

Froude J.A. 1894, *Life and Letters of Erasmus: Lectures delivered at Oxford 1893–4*, Longmans Green and Co., London

Garrard J. 1983, *Leadership and Power in Victorian Industrial Towns 1830–80*, Manchester University Press, Manchester

Geddes P. 1889, 'On national and municipal encouragement of art upon the Continent', paper to Edinburgh Art Congress 1889 (in Strathclyde University Archives)

Halliday E.I. n.d., *The Athena Panels in the Library of the Athenaeum Liverpool*, Liverpool

Hay M. *et al.* 1996, *Art in Parliament: The Permanent Collection of the House of Commons*, The Palace of Westminster/London and Jarrold Publishing/Norwich

Hobsbawm E. and Ranger T. (eds) 1983, *The Invention of Tradition*, Cambridge University Press, Cambridge

Manchester City Council 1969, *Mural Paintings in the Large Hall Town Hall Manchester*, Manchester City Council, Manchester (contains texts by Madox Brown)

Maxim J.L. 1959, *Rochdale Town Hall*, G. and A.N. Scott, Rochdale

Olivier E. n.d. *In Pursuit of Rare Meats*, London, Tate Gallery, London (post-1928)

Ormond R. 1975, *Leighton's Frescoes in the Victoria and Albert Museum*, Victoria and Albert Museum, London

Renton J.D. 1983, *The Oxford Union Murals*, J.D. Denton, Oxford

Renton J.D. 1987, *Notes and Quotations Related to the Oxford Union Murals*, pamphlet, Oxford Union, Oxford

Riding C. and Riding J. (eds) 2000, *The Houses of Parliament: History, Art and Architecture*, Merrell, London

Select Committee on Fine Arts 1841, Committee's Report, 18 June 1841, in *Parliamentary Papers* VI

Select Committee on the House of Lords Offices 1929–30, *Fourth Report of the Select Committee on the House of Lords Offices*, Command Paper HL84, HMSO, London

Speed H. 1928, 'Watts's "Law Givers"', *The Studio* 95, pp. 405–6

Treuherz J. 1985, 'Ford Madox Brown and the Manchester murals', in J.H.G. Archer (ed.) *Art and Architecture in Victorian Manchester*, Manchester University Press, Manchester, pp. 162–85

Walker R.J.B. 1959–77 and 1965–76, *Catalogue of Paintings, Drawings, Sculpture and Engravings in the Palace of Westminster*, 7 vols with 10 vol. Supplement, 1965–76 (unpublished text held in the House of Lords Record Office, London)

Waterhouse A. 1876, *Report to the New Town Hall Sub-Committee*, 21 June 1876 (M79/35, Manchester Town Hall Archives, Local Studies Unit, Manchester Central Library)

Watts M.S. 1912, *G.F. Watts, The Annals of an Artist's Life, 1*, Macmillan, London

Willsdon C.A.P. (ed.) 1986, *Town and Country: The Social Scene in Scotland 1850–1900*, exhibition catalogue, Hunterian Art Gallery, University of Glasgow, Glasgow.

Willsdon C.A.P. 1996, 'The mural decoration at the Royal Exchange', in A. Saunders (ed.) *The Royal Exchange*, London Topographical Society, London, pp. 311–35

Willsdon C.A.P. 2000, *Mural Painting in Britain 1840–1940: Image and Meaning*, Oxford University Press, Oxford

Willsdon C.A.P. 2004, 'The Ramsay Garden murals and their links with French mural painting', *Journal of the Scottish Society for Art History* 9, pp. 69–78

The author

Clare A.P. Willsdon is a graduate of Cambridge University, where she took her doctorate in History of Art. She is a Reader in History of Art at the University of Glasgow, and Fellow of the Royal Historical Society and Royal Society of Arts. A specialist in 19th- and early 20th-century European art and culture, she is the author of *Mural Painting in Britain 1840–1940: Image and Meaning* (OUP 2000), which won the 2002–3 Historians of British Art international book prize (post-1800 category) and of *In the Gardens of Impressionism* (Thames and Hudson 2004), which was nominated for the National Library of Scotland/Saltire Society 2005 'Research Book of the Year', and 2006 'Sir Banister Fletcher' awards. She has published extensively on the subject of mural painting and has given invited lectures at institutions including the National Gallery, London, the National Gallery of Scotland, and the Fondation de l'Hermitage, Lausanne. Dr Willsdon has also contributed to arts broadcasts by BBC Radio 4 and Radio Scotland, and BBC Television.

Contemporary mural painting: trends and traditions

Ernestine McKay

Introduction

To appreciate the full breadth of modern wall painting, we should begin by considering the driving forces behind trends in contemporary painting, and how these changes are likely to affect the most ancient of art techniques – mural painting. We begin to understand the reality behind the publicity by looking at the motivation and ambitions of those who commission and create this kind of work.

The greatest contemporary murals are those that truly reflect the times in which we live. They draw on modern subject themes to illustrate the spirit and energy of communities across the world. Compelling paintings are created by a fortunate fusion of highly creative artists and visionary patrons. This transformation combines with the influence of local cultures and fashions to create shifts in style that evolve into tomorrow's traditions. When looking at contemporary wall painting, it helps to make a clear distinction between the different styles of murals that have emerged in recent years. For simplicity, I have defined these in three principal categories, each characterised by their own individual patronage:

1. Public murals: these paintings are often external and are funded largely by the public sector. Commissions are usually characterised by a strong local community focus – sometimes mainstream, sometimes more cutting edge, depending on the socio-political and cultural context.
2. Private murals: private individuals and corporate institutions traditionally sponsor murals for interior locations, usually found within stylish domestic, retail, leisure and entertainment environments, or as a key element in major interior design projects. A range of pigments and techniques is available today to decorate internal walls. Fresco painting remains the most enduring and high quality technique in use, and is applied both for commissions of new work and the restoration of historical murals within large-scale conservation projects.
3. Architectural murals: property developers or architectural designers generally commission these paintings as a crucial component of sophisticated construction plans. In the early 1900s, the Prairie School architects, a group of US designers, were the first to make extensive use of what became known as architectural painting. These commissions are primarily functional, intended to visually integrate an external wall or structure with a particular location or environment. More recently, architectural paintings have been commissioned to help reduce the ugliness of aesthetic flaws or temporary obstructions in modern urban landscapes.

Patronage since the 1970s: recent trends

Patrons will occasionally sponsor work across a range of sites. Murals tend to be planned and executed by specialist artists with unique rationales and personal styles, however, which they apply to the needs of specific locations and architectural settings. As a result, we see distinct traditions emerging between public sector and privately commissioned murals. Significant historic, civic and personal milestones inspire a modern generation of mural artists and patrons to make creative public statements through bold and dramatic mural designs.

It is fascinating to observe how similar trends arise in different areas of the world. As patrons increasingly operate on a global scale, the resulting trends in each category have also become global. Public murals, in particular, are influenced by themes that resonate with large social groups across the world's urban communities. Common interests include environmental protection, healthcare, cultural heritage, education, crime prevention, sports victories, pride in local landscapes and history. Muralists are finding inspiration from these shared concerns and social issues. Internet communications raise awareness and build support for artistic concepts and visions worldwide in much shorter timescales than ever before.

When we look back at how far the art of mural painting developed during the 20th century, we can only dream of what is possible in this century. The powerful combination of radical social upheaval and new media will bring with it exceptional possibilities in terms of large-scale mural art.

Public murals

Overview

The most significant development in mural painting during the 20th century was its association with major social and political change, and how art was used to promote radical political ideals. There are several examples. Murals were used to communicate the ambitions of the Russian Revolution in 1917, and to help promote the new political and cultural direction in China following the 1919 May Fourth Movement. Muralists in the United States united in their efforts to create socially conscious public art within the Works Progress Administration (WPA) cultural programme of the 1930s. The Mexican social-realist painters Diego Rivera, David Alfaro Siquerios and José Clemente Orozco achieved global recognition for frescoes expressing their distinct vision of social justice in the 1920s and 30s. The tradition they created of public, socially responsible mural painting continues to the present day.

Public art, and murals in particular, became a means of reaching a wide audience, many of whom would not necessarily choose to enter a traditional art gallery. Unlike private and architectural muralists, public mural painters are less likely to become known as global brand names. It is the collective work that becomes renowned, more than the name of any individual artist. The medium – and, more importantly, the cause behind the painting – becomes the brand. In many cases of what is often referred to as 'community art' or even 'group graffiti', mural artists will come together to create influential social movements (such as the Social and Public Art Resource Center in Los Angeles and the Public Art Squad in Sydney).

Cultural awareness in the community

The Social and Public Art Resource Center (SPARC)

Mural painting in Los Angeles and southern California shows the potential of public art to play an important part in our cultural heritage. Although in this area murals had been painted since the early 1900s, a mural painting revival emerged from the national civil rights struggles of the Hispanic community in the 1960s. Murals became an important tool for social and political expression, and a symbol of Los Angeles' social and ethnic change and diversity. In the 1970s young artists in Los Angeles, including Kent Twitchell, Judy F. Baca and Alonzo Davis, built on the legacy left by the Mexican painters of the 1930s. Soon a new generation of West Coast US muralists was creating work that represented contemporary ideologies.

Founded in 1976 by Baca, painter Christina Schlesinger and filmmaker Donna Deitch, SPARC is an arts centre that produces and preserves community-based public artwork, as well as running educational programmes. *The Great Wall*, SPARC's signature piece – thought to be the world's longest mural – portrays the history of ethnic Californians. Started in 1976 and completed in 1984, involving the collaboration of 700 painters including 400 underprivileged teenagers, it stands 13ft high and 2470ft long, and runs for half a mile along the Tujunga canal in north Hollywood (Fig. 1). The Center is renowned for producing and promoting work, which, like *The Great Wall*, reflects the lives and concerns of America's ethnically and economically diverse communities. Key to SPARC is the deeply held belief that cultural expression is a basic human right and that people can participate in the creation of art. It

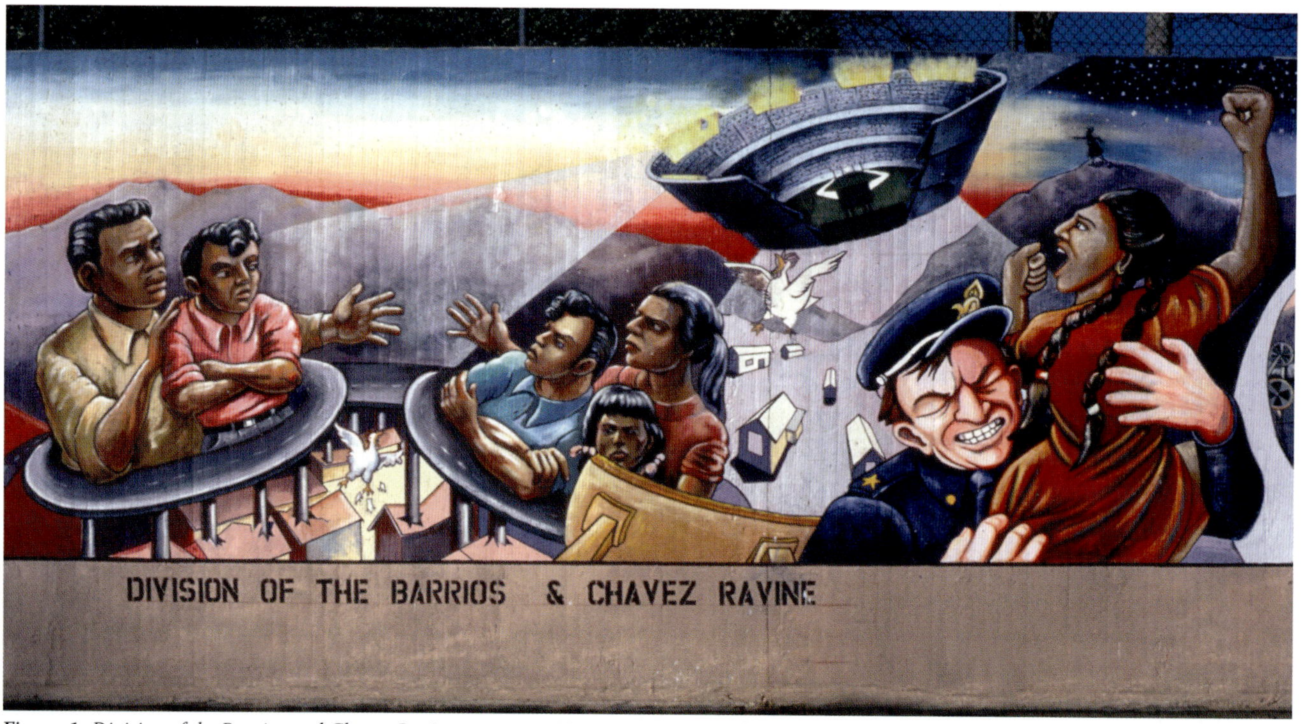

Figure 1 *Division of the Barrios and Chavez Ravine*, summer 1983: 1950s segment of the Great Wall of Los Angeles, USA. Artist: Judith F. Baca. *(© SPARC/www.sparcmurals.org)*

has created murals and other forms of public art in neighbourhoods throughout Los Angeles, and more recently in national and international locations.

In 1988 SPARC created and implemented a mural programme Great Walls Unlimited: Neighborhood Pride. This has since employed over 90 established and emerging muralists, trained hundreds of youth apprentices, and collaborated with countless community-based organisations. As the first programme of its kind in the US, Neighborhood Pride has set a standard for other cities across the States. The Center has perfected its community-based art process, pioneering the use of different materials and developing new techniques in wall painting and conservation. It has helped open up entire communities to the benefits and pleasure of mural painting and will undoubtedly continue to inspire further evolution of public art in the 21st century.

In November 1997, at the first International Public Art and Muralism Congress (Jornada de Arte Publico y Muralismo, held in Tlaxcalo, Mexico), the following 'Mural Manifesto' was declared by Baca, artistic director and founder of SPARC, and Irene Herner of Tepozitlan, Mexico:

1. That cultural expression is a basic human right from which we learn from others and express ourselves.
2. That the legacy which remains of great civilizations is its monuments and cultural products which provide insight into our common human condition.
3. That a common denominator in the history of public art is the process of inclusion in which artists and audience interact to create a vision of shared dreams, aspirations and struggles. Public art is an unending public process of communication which is instrumental to the creation of a civil society.
4. It is people who make nations. The context of the individual is fundamental to personal and national identity. Every person and their community must have the opportunity to develop and tell their stories which represent them to others. This self-expression is innately public because it is the basis of language, humankind's anonymous creation from which visual language emanates and is continually reinvented. This reinvention can only flourish with guaranteed freedom of expression.
5. That governments should not be the makers of culture but the facilitators by establishing truly 'public space' and supporting public dialogue while providing resources for artistic expression. That government officials should not engage in any type of censorship or undue obstruction of artistic process.

Political awareness in the community

The Berlin wall

During the summer of 1990, shortly after the collapse of the East German regime, artists covered a kilometre-long stretch of the Berlin wall on Mühlenstrasse with colourful murals retelling German history and bearing slogans of peace. Thus the East Side Gallery was born. Some of these murals became famous in their own right, such as Dmitri Vrubel's *Bruderkuss*, which portrays former Soviet leader Leonid Brezhnev and East German Prime Minister Eric Honecker (Fig 2).

Despite the efforts of artists to maintain their condition, the East Side Gallery murals are now flaking and disintegrating, seriously endangering their future. In 2000, the artists themselves organised a partial restoration, but more investment is required to prevent the work suffering the fate of so many

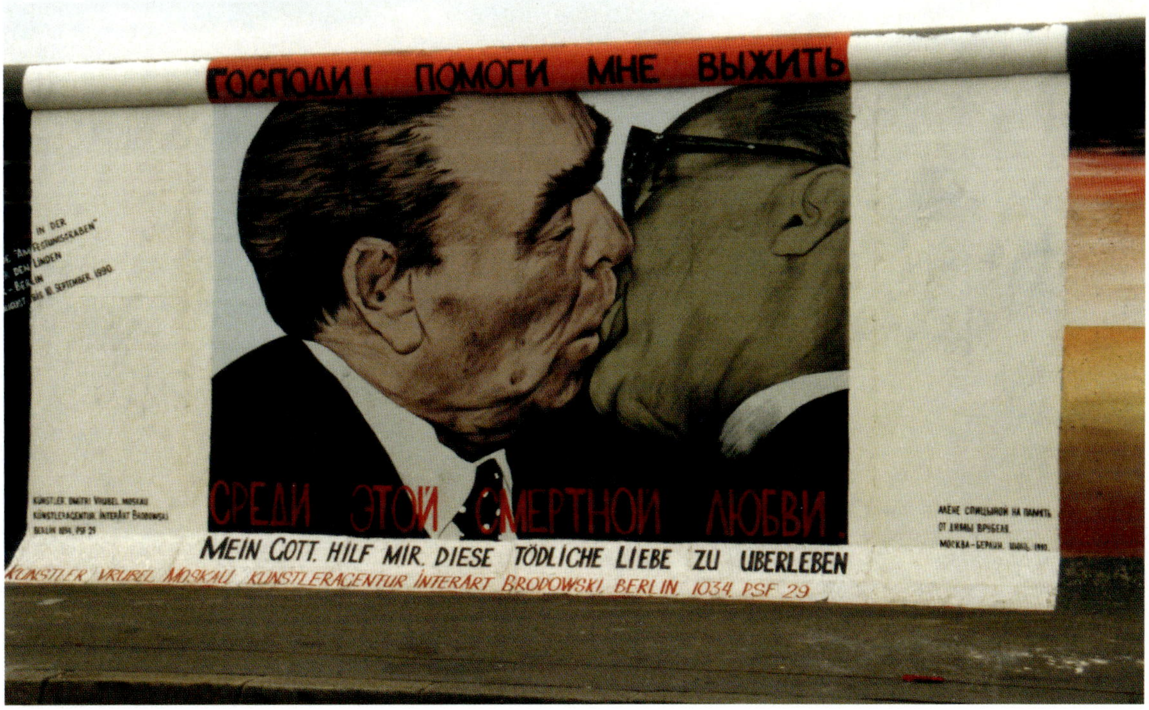

Figure 2 The East Side Gallery of the Berlin Wall, Germany: *Bruderkuss* by Dmitri Vrubel 1990, depicting former Soviet leader Leonid Brezhnev and East German Prime Minister Eric Honecker embracing. *(© C. Leverentz)*

earlier mural paintings, lost to future generations because of a lack of timely care and conservation.

History in the community

The Katikati murals

Situated along the Pacific Coast Highway in the Bay of Plenty region on New Zealand's North Island, the quaint township of Katikati has become known as the Mural Town of New Zealand. The murals of Katikati are an interpretation of the town's history – of its pioneers and of their vanished way of life. From the three murals originally painted in 1991, the town has come to feature over 20 magnificent paintings on the outside walls of its commercial buildings, demonstrating its great pride in its past and inspiring optimism for its future (Fig. 3).

Sport in the community

The Pembroke Heritage Murals

Downtown Pembroke in Ottawa is home to one of Canada's largest public mural galleries. Since the first five murals were painted in 1990, Pembroke Heritage Murals has commissioned 28 full-scale paintings from local and national artists for the walls of its public buildings. The murals vividly depict the rich history of Pembroke and its local neighbourhood, from the first settlers through the logging era, up to the first newborn child of 2000.

The Mackay Street Arena 1905–1951 is a commemorative mural paying tribute to the era and the townspeople of the first half of the 20th century. The Pembroke Scouts hockey team was owned for decades by William Bogart (1879–1971) and his son Art (1912–1995). This painting celebrates the numerous championship teams and superb hockey players Pembroke produced over the years including the legends Frank Nighbor, Hugh Lehman and Harry Cameron (who played there before going on to the National Hockey League) (Fig. 4).

The environment in the community

The Wyland Foundation

The American artist Steve Wyland is one of the world's most celebrated and recognised marine painters, widely known for his towering murals. He established the Wyland Foundation to produce a range of mural projects that help reshape attitudes about marine life and environmental conservation. The *Whaling Wall* murals in particular have been raising awareness about the undersea world for over 20 years. Each year these monumental life-size paintings of migrating grey whales, breaching humpbacks, blue whales and other marine life attract an estimated audience of 1 billion (Fig. 5). They have become valued landmarks in over 70 cities across four continents: in the United States, Europe, Australia, New Zealand, Mexico and Japan. All of the *Whaling Wall* murals are painted life-size to help people understand and appreciate the true scale of these magnificent creatures. Wyland's declared goal is to save the whales, and he intends to have painted 100 murals by the year 2008. Among the locations that prominently display these murals is the *Long Beach* wall in California, which covers three acres and required 7000 gallons of paint. Not only is he creating impressive works of art, but he is also inspiring people to preserve and protect endangered marine animals.

Education in the community

The Public Art Squad

Australian artist Rodney Monk believes public art should reflect the aspirations and values of the community in which it

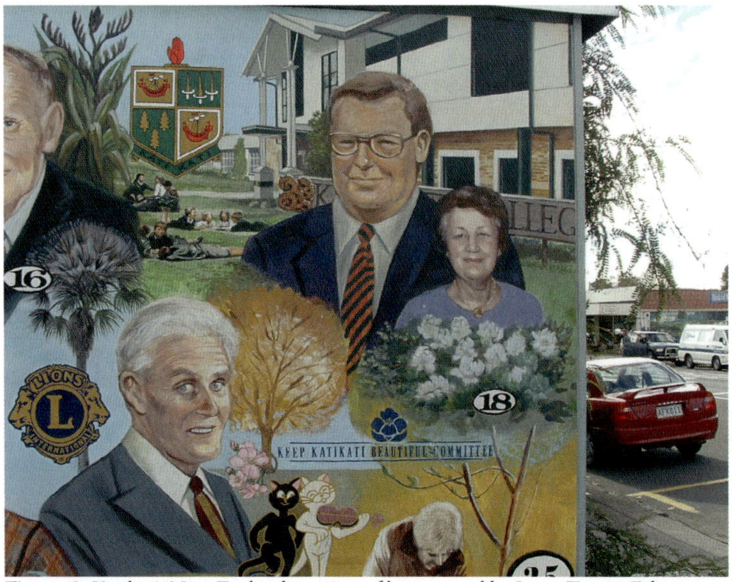

Figure 3 Katikati, New Zealand: section of large mural by Irene Tuscia-Falconer *(© Katikati Open Air Art)*

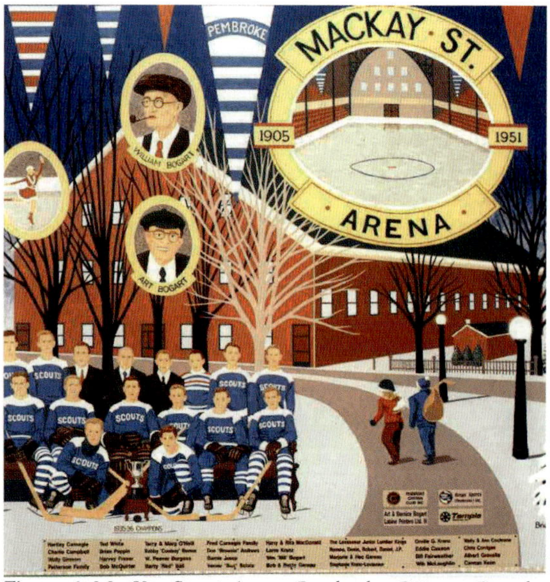

Figure 4 MacKay Street Arena, Pembroke, Ottawa, Canada: *Pembroke Scouts Hockey Team*, one of the paintings in the Pembroke Heritage mural cycle started in 1989–90. *(© Pembroke Heritage Murals).*

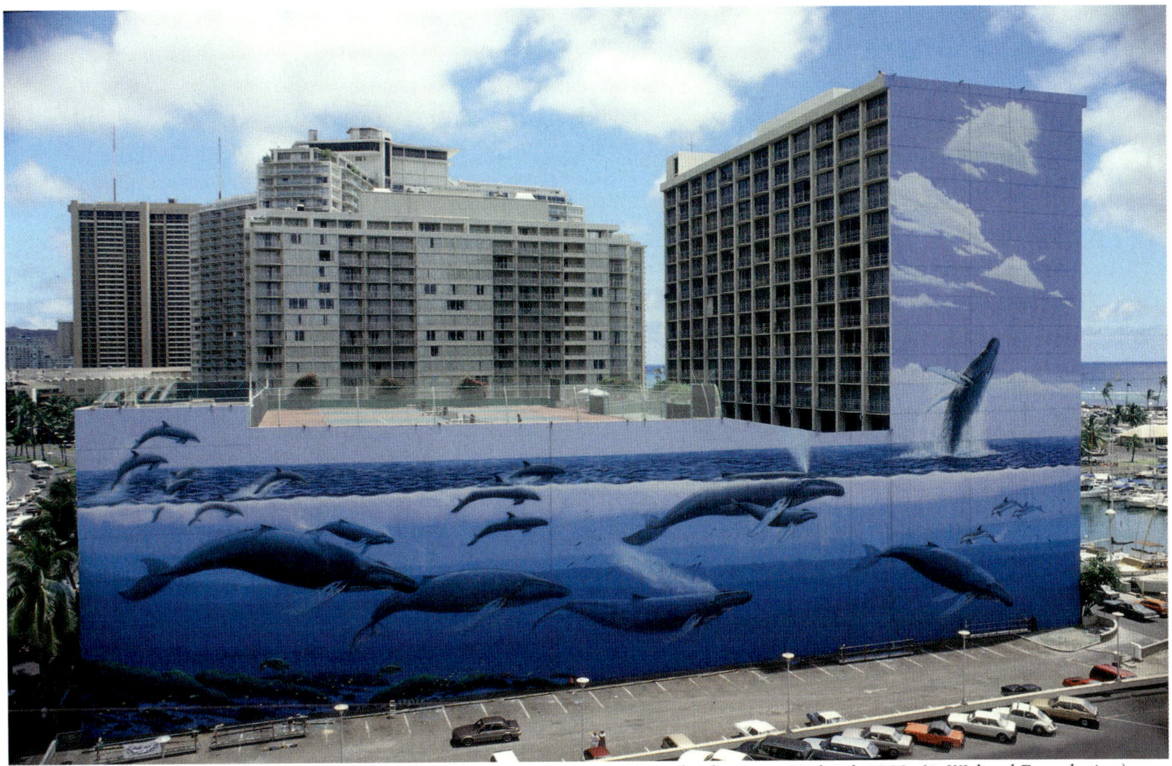

Figure 5 Pacifica Airport Center, Honolulu, Hawaii, USA: *Hawaiian Humpbacks*, Steve Wyland, 1999. *(© Wyland Foundation)*

is placed. He is inspired by the diversity of the natural and built landscape and its people. His creative and vibrant images identify places and entertain audiences making his work sought after for public spaces, hospitals, schools and commercial developments. He produced the decorative art components – murals, terrazzo carpets, mosaics and banners – for many of Sydney's major retail precincts such as Harbourside at Darling Harbour, and the modern retail centre Skygarden. He often collaborates on large glass art, light and terrazzo commissions with partner Giselle Courtney.

Monk's work inspires and creates community identity. In 2004 he was invited to Tegucigalpa, Honduras by the United Nations Volunteers to paint *Healthy Children for a Peaceful World*, a 22m-high mural on the city's Hospital Escuela. He has designed and painted more than 200 murals throughout Australia and overseas, ranging from spirited community art projects on streets and in schools to paintings on the walls of private homes. Monk co-authored *The Mural Manual* (1981) with David Humphries, and for 13 years they developed the Public Art Squad as a leader of the Australian mural and community art resurgence. In 1985, the street mural *Think Globally, Act Locally* won the major Sulman Prize from the Art Gallery of New South Wales. Mural painting became recognised as a multimedia art form for view in public places – streets, neighbourhoods and shopping centres. The audience was the open community and the clients, co-workers, and source of inspiration were all drawn from local residents. The *Machismo* mural was part of a project run by the education department in New South Wales to inspire and involve children in art projects (Fig. 6).

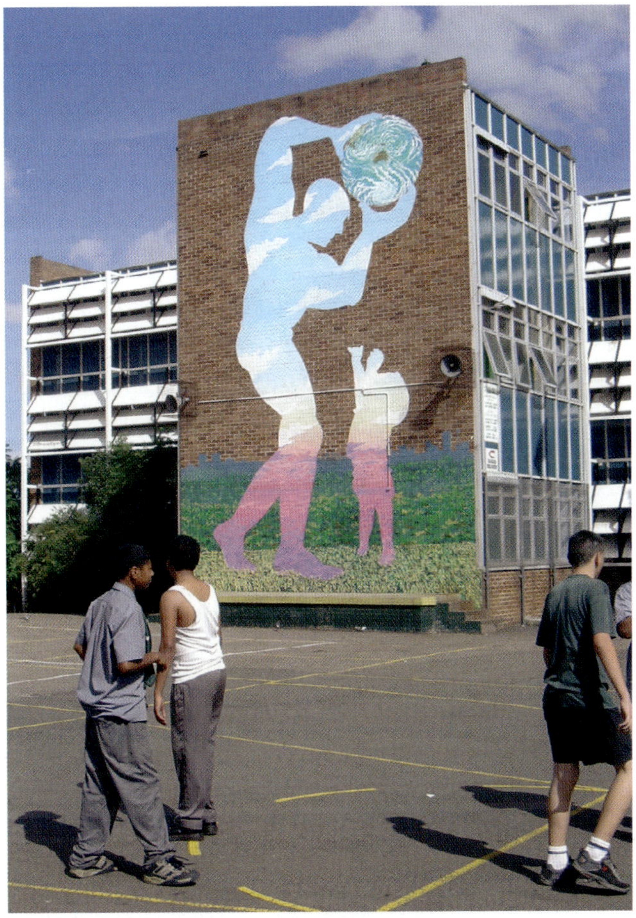

Figure 6 Granville Boys' High School, Sydney, NSW, Australia: Machismo by Rodney Monk, Courtney + Monk Studios Pty Ltd 2001 (approx 11 × 7m), to a design developed with students. Acrylic on masonry. *(© Rodney Monk, Courtney + Monk Studios Pty Ltd)*

Healthcare in the community

For many years national movements worldwide have aimed at incorporating the arts into healthcare environments as a healing tool for the sick. Children's hospitals in particular have long understood that integration of the arts with healthcare is essential, particularly for long-term patients and their carers.

In the 1930s the WPA cultural programme sponsored mural projects in hospitals throughout the US. In the 1950s, New York City launched the United Hospital Fund, which placed thousands of paintings in hospitals. More recently, in the 1980s, groups of US hospital arts administrators convened to set up a support and service organisation for the arts in healthcare. There are now a number of private and public charities throughout the US who provide and commission such paintings. In the UK, the national charity Paintings in Hospitals was founded in 1959 when Sheridan Russell, a social worker, decided to improve his consulting rooms in a London hospital by borrowing pictures for his walls. He soon noticed the positive effects, and by the following year had secured funding to establish a permanent collection for hospitals. The charity has since accumulated over 4000 works of art, including a prized collection of mural paintings.

Private murals

Overview

If public murals tend to be inclusive, driven by local communities and acting as an overt branding tool to identify local people or a particular cause, private murals are by their nature more exclusive and commercially driven. Their purpose is often to create a particular atmosphere in a building, rather than communicate any strong socio-political message.

Private murals have over the centuries been subject to the whims of fashion. In a European context, wall paintings commissioned primarily for functional purposes were greatly in demand in classical Greece and Rome, decorating flat surfaces with simple landscapes and gardens to create illusions of light in dark rooms. During the late Renaissance and 16th-century Mannerism, artists combined the newly determined rules of linear perspective drawing with the luminous colour palette of fresco painting to create sophisticated illusions of space, light and depth inside dark interiors. Patrons would hire the most famous artists of their period to produce scenes of great theatricality and grandeur, reflecting the patron's wealth and status.

For centuries since, we have seen a steady decline in the historic tradition of decorating private homes and public building interiors with large-scale murals and frescoes. There are now signs of a revival of interest, however, certainly in historic painting techniques. Luxury wall coatings mixed from primitive pigments are being used to create stunning, colourful interiors in private and commercial settings. Where the request for high quality materials and bright, textured colours combines with a desire for contemporary subject themes, an entirely new fashion in mural painting is created. Reflecting the highly individualistic approach now taken to modern interiors, patrons are looking for the simplicity of decorative schemes that reflect their lifestyles and carry some personal resonance. The desire for calm, spiritual self-expression within the home or place of rest in contrast to the chaos of the urban working environment translates into more personalised decoration. Wall painting is perfectly poised to take advantage of this growing aspiration. Mural artists have an essential role to play in bringing realistic and personal subject themes to life to equal the great illusionary wall paintings of previous generations.

Trompe l'oeil

Massimo De Carolis is an Italian mural and fresco painter based in the town of Modena. He is widely known for his delicate interior decorations, which combine functionality and style to create brightly coloured, playful interior spaces in both residential and commercial locations. De Carolis, who also restores wall paintings, is able to work in true fresco, to which he sometimes adds high quality contemporary wall finishes and coatings.

De Carolis continues to develop his individual style through other techniques including *trompe l'oeil* paintings on canvas, wood and walls to create a sense of light and space in a wide selection of venues from residential villas, public offices, hotels and country chapels to a number of restaurants in the region of Emilia Romagna. His work is deeply rooted in the history and traditional artistic craftsmanship that is so typical of his native region (Figs 7 and 8).

Architectural murals

Overview

More than any other art technique, mural painting has the potential to have a direct impact on the mood and atmosphere

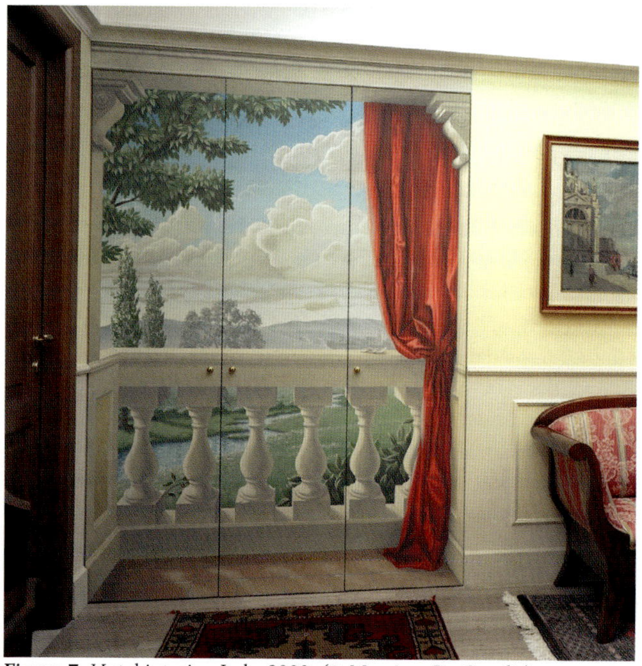

Figure 7 Hotel interior, Italy, 2000. *(© Massimo De Carolis)*

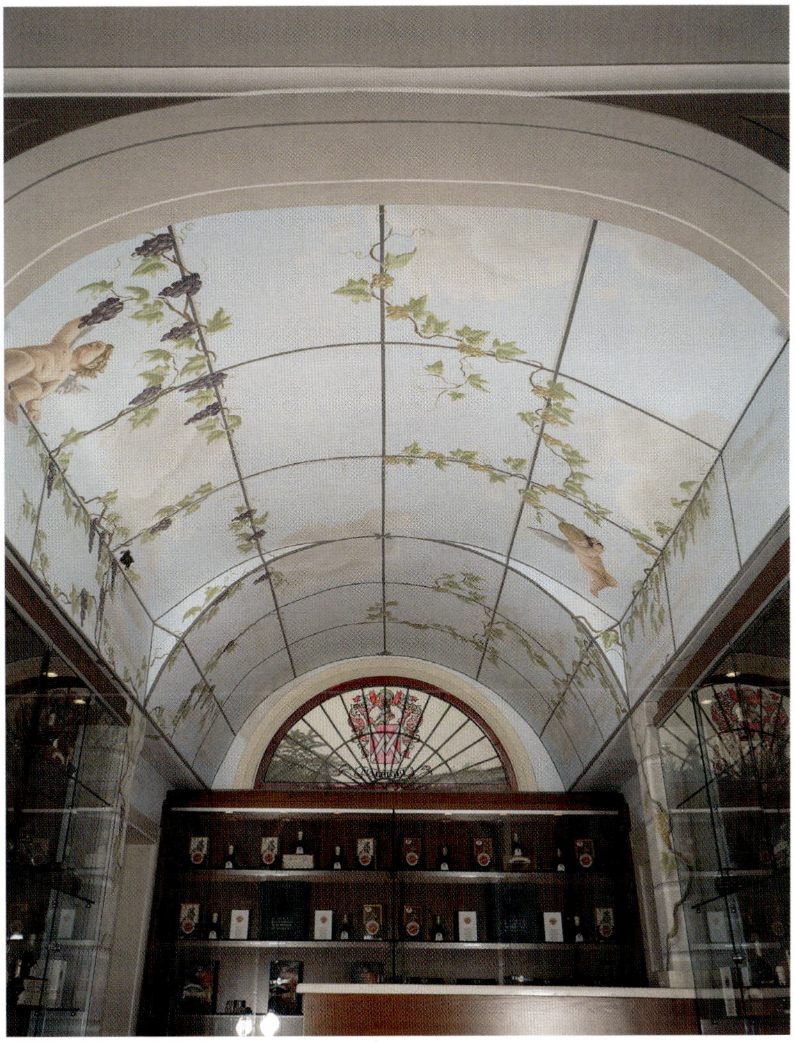

Figure 8 Ceiling of retail reception, Italy, 2001. *(© Massimo De Carolis).*

of the buildings that we inhabit in our daily lives. Clever optical illusions created with wall paint can achieve an extraordinary visual impact, transforming a neglected façade or a deserted location. A new industry of architectural painting grew up in the US around the turn of the 20th century. Prairie School architects such as George Washington Maher and Frank Lloyd Wright commissioned designs for the exteriors of their buildings to complement the decorations of the interior, incorporating scenes from the surrounding landscapes. As part of the WPA cultural programme in the 1930s and 40s, hundreds of schools, libraries, post offices and other governmental buildings were decorated in this style, but as tastes changed the murals were often removed and destroyed.

Although the original practice ended decades ago, the concepts behind architectural painting have not ceased to develop: large-scale architectural painting is a trend that continues to transform the urban landscape in the US. John Wehrle is an American mural artist, based in California, specialising in site-specific public paintings for interior and exterior walls in complex architectural spaces. In the 1980s Wehrle's work heralded a new breed of mural painter who carries out significant historical research to tailor each mural to its own particular context. His more elaborate work combines text, paintings and relief sculpture to create a unique sense of time and place. He adds metaphor, history and local portraits to make bold, contemporary visual statements that help create a unique atmosphere in each of his venues. He has completed murals for a variety of locations including libraries, banks, architectural exteriors and freeway walls that have since become established local landmarks.

The colourful interior of the Ocean View Library comes to life with the images and language of the books that are housed within its walls (Fig. 9 a and b). Wehrle creates a joyful and intriguing game where the visitor tries to capture the words flying across the walls in an attempt to piece them together as part of a magical puzzle, eventually revealing their true meaning. The words appear against a backdrop of sky blue landscapes and white and pastel interiors that seem to remove the confines of the walls and lead the viewer into the realms of the imagination hidden within the pages of each book (Fig. 10).

New York-based Richard Haas is renowned throughout the US and worldwide for his murals on the exteriors of major public buildings. Born in Spring Green, Wisconsin, Haas' interest in art and architecture was nurtured by a fortunate acquaintance with the architect Frank Lloyd Wright who he befriended in his formative years. Haas later visited southern Germany and Liguria, Italy, where he was particularly fascinated by the early technique of illusionist decoration known as *quadratura*. Haas subsequently brought this European style of architectural paint-

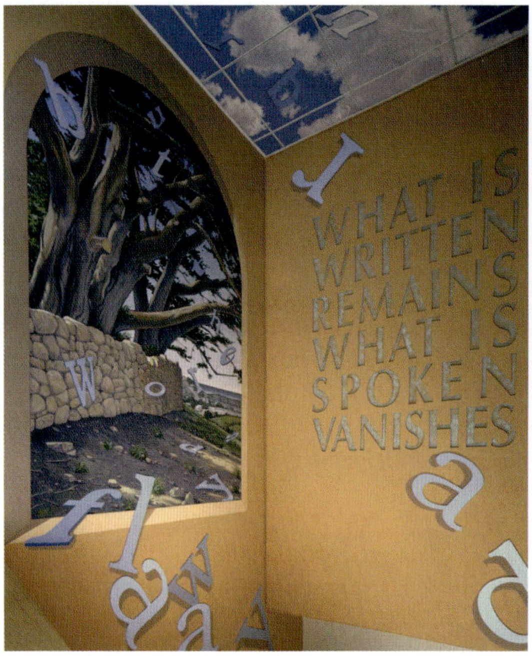

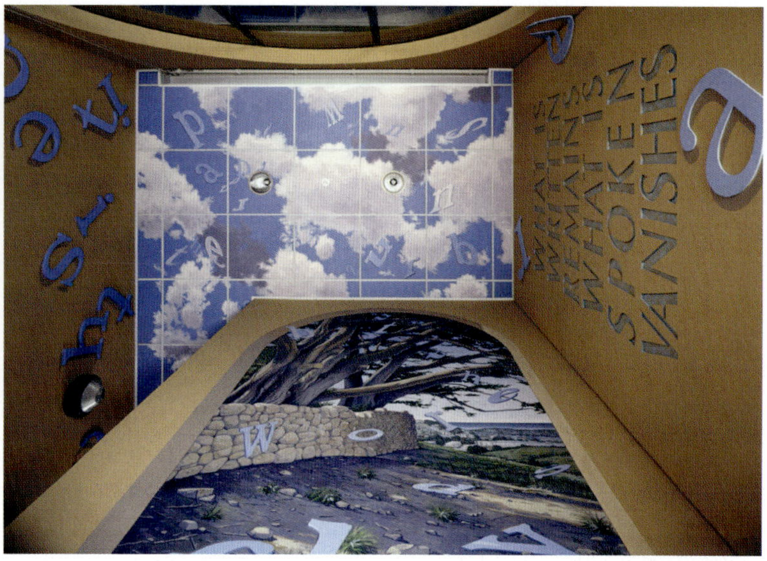

Figure 9 Ocean View Library, San Francisco, USA: two views of the decorative murals by John Wehrle in the downstairs area, depicting quotes about reading and literature in different languages. *(Courtesy of J. Wehrle © S. Nuseibeh)*

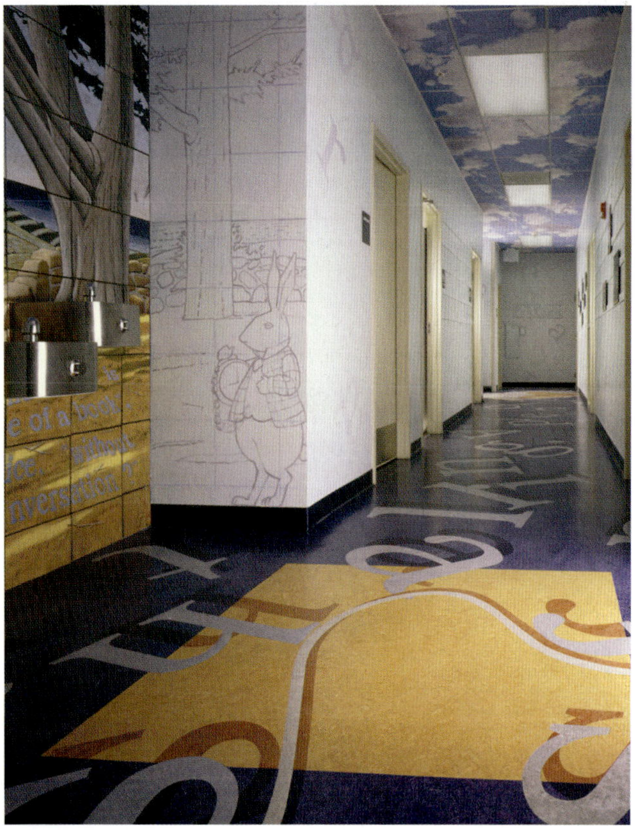

Figure 10 Ocean View Library, San Francisco, USA: view of the hallway looking west. *(Courtesy of J. Wehrle © S. Nuseibeh)*

ing to the US, where he developed it on an unprecedented scale, painting illusionist decorations that appear to be an extension of the real architecture (Fig. 11a and b).

He was one of the first painters to understand how gaps left by the eradication of the established grid pattern in American cities could be replaced by large-scale architectural illusions, thus transforming the face of the American urban landscape (Fig. 12 a and b). Haas created his unique style largely in response to what he sees as the need to mend the aesthetic 'wounds' in our modern cities. His colourful, large-scale mural paintings are carefully designed to reflect the heritage of their locations and many remain on permanent display to large numbers of the appreciative public.

Patronage in 2000: emerging trends

Often great political and social beliefs inspire new movements in painting. Where those beliefs are given free expression, new trends will emerge in mural painting to take their place in modern traditions. By way of summary, it is helpful to list the key driving forces behind recent trends in contemporary mural painting.

Public murals – the visualisation of local ideals and causes, by the people for the people

- Making socio-political statements
  - To educate and inspire as well as to build a sense of identity and pride in local culture and communities where there has been mass immigration into an established culture.
  - To help heal political wounds or announce a new political order (the East Side Gallery of the Berlin Wall is an excellent example).
- Commemorating history
  - To commemorate local history (for example, the Katikati murals).
  - To recognise local and national sports legacies (the Pembroke Heritage Murals).
- Supporting education
  - To educate the public on environmental protection issues (the Wyland Foundation marine life murals).

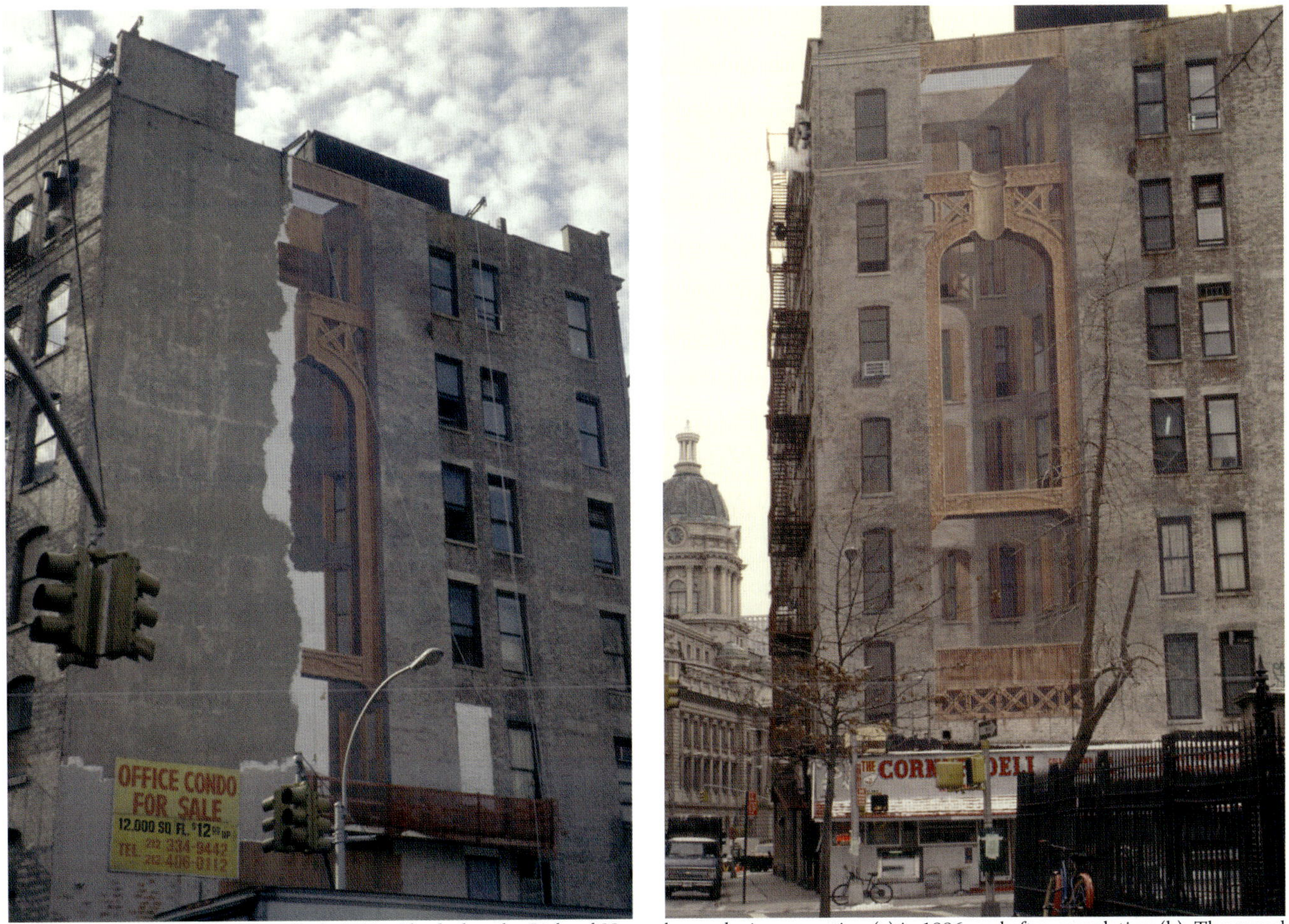

Figure 11 New York City, New York, USA: *Absoluthass* by Richard Haas, shown during execution (a) in 1996, and after completion (b). The mural was later removed in 1998. *((a) © R. Haas, (b) © P. Mauss)*

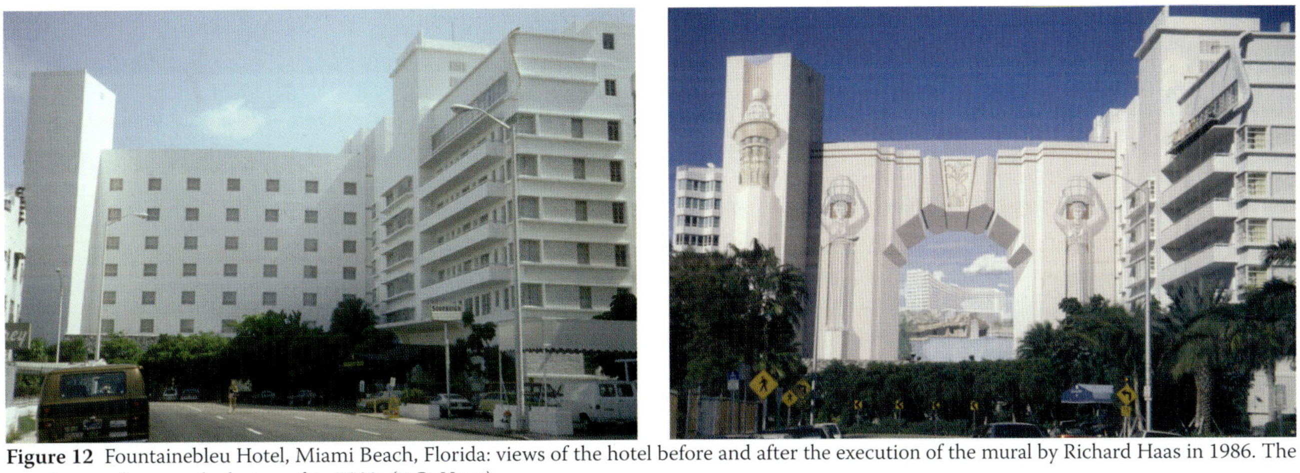

Figure 12 Fountainebleu Hotel, Miami Beach, Florida: views of the hotel before and after the execution of the mural by Richard Haas in 1986. The mural was subsequently destroyed in 2002. *(© R. Haas)*

  - To inspire social change in deprived inner city areas (Rodney Monk, the Public Art Squad).
- Improving healthcare
  - To promote positive art therapy in hospitals and day-care centres, and to integrate art within the healthcare process. This type of mural painting is supported by dedicated charities and commercial artists such as Art Heals (USA), Splashes of Hope (USA), Paintings in Hospitals (UK).

Private murals – higher lifestyle aspirations

- Using high quality pigments and rich textures
  - To decorate walls with quality pigments, free of damaging chemicals. The use of true fresco sits well with the contemporary shift towards an organic lifestyle.
- Introducing bright colour palettes
  - To stimulate or relax depending on the purpose of

the location. An upbeat or relaxing mood can be created with appropriate colours that transform the mood of an interior.

- Articulating contemporary subject themes
  - To fill blank walls and corridors with atmosphere created by suitable contemporary themes: particularly sought after in corporate and public locations.
- Creating illusions of light
  - To decorate large, flat surfaces and create immediate illusions of light in dark spaces.
- Building brands
  - To add character and personality to more anonymous large-scale constructions.

Architectural murals – extending architecture and adding balance to exterior structures

- Creating illusions of space within the urban environment
  - To create illusions of light and help break down the oppression of tall, imposing skyscrapers in inner city environments.
- Enhancing exteriors with painted design
  - Where the exterior is aesthetically flawed or not in proportion with its surroundings, to compensate and balance the structure with functional decoration.

Setting the context for contemporary murals

One conclusion is clear above all others: mural painting, perhaps more than any other art technique, has an increasingly important social role to play in the development and improvement of the world's urban environments and communities.

In public mural painting, the community and architectural categories may begin to collaborate, partly because of the widespread increase in corporate social responsibility programmes. Large corporate institutions are beginning to see public relations value in sponsoring community art through large-scale mural projects. There is enormous potential for further growth and experimentation in this important area.

In private mural painting, changes will be influenced primarily by fashions in interior design. If current trends continue, the revival of luxury wall finishes and coatings – including true fresco – will become more desirable. Until now fresco commissions have been restricted to private patronage because of a lack of awareness that this earliest of techniques is still being enjoyed and developed today in exciting, contemporary settings by modern artists and patrons.

The author

Ernestine McKay is the founding director of Frescoes Forever, a London-based art consultancy that specialises in the promotion and commission of modern fresco paintings by European artists. She qualified in the conservation and restoration of works of art at the leading conservation university, Università Internazionale dell'Arte (UIA), in Florence, Italy where she was taught by the distinguished art historian Carlo L Ragghianti and renowned Professors Umberto Baldini and Antonio Paolucci, who restored the Cimabue and Giotto crucifixes respectively. Ernestine specialised in fresco restoration under the direction of Professor Ornella Casazza, who restored the magnificent Brancacci Chapel frescoes. Originally a watercolour painter, Ernestine has exhibited her paintings and drawings across Europe. Frescoes Forever was established in 2004 primarily to create opportunities for modern fresco commissions inspired by exciting new subjects and socio-political themes.

Part 2

Conservation and research case studies

The Catherine Room, Windsor Castle

Ann Ballantyne

Introduction

This paper covers the conservation history, treatment and consequential reassessment of the dating of a series of wall paintings discovered when the coved ceiling of a first-floor room was removed in No. 2 The Cloisters, Windsor Castle, in 1965. The painting survives on three walls and depicts Saints Anthony, Catherine, John the Baptist, part of (what appears to be) George and the Prince of Wales Feathers, all set against an elaborate foliate background.

The room

The south wall of the room is part of the stone and rubble south wall of Henry III's 'new' residence of c.1240, gutted by fire in 1295–6, against which the south range of the timber-framed cloister buildings was constructed 1354–61[1] using timbers with dendrochronological dates of spring 1351 and summer 1352. On the timber-framed east wall the painting is, in places, carried over as many as 17 layers of limewash on a straw-rich daub and oak studs. There is no plaster layer.[2] The

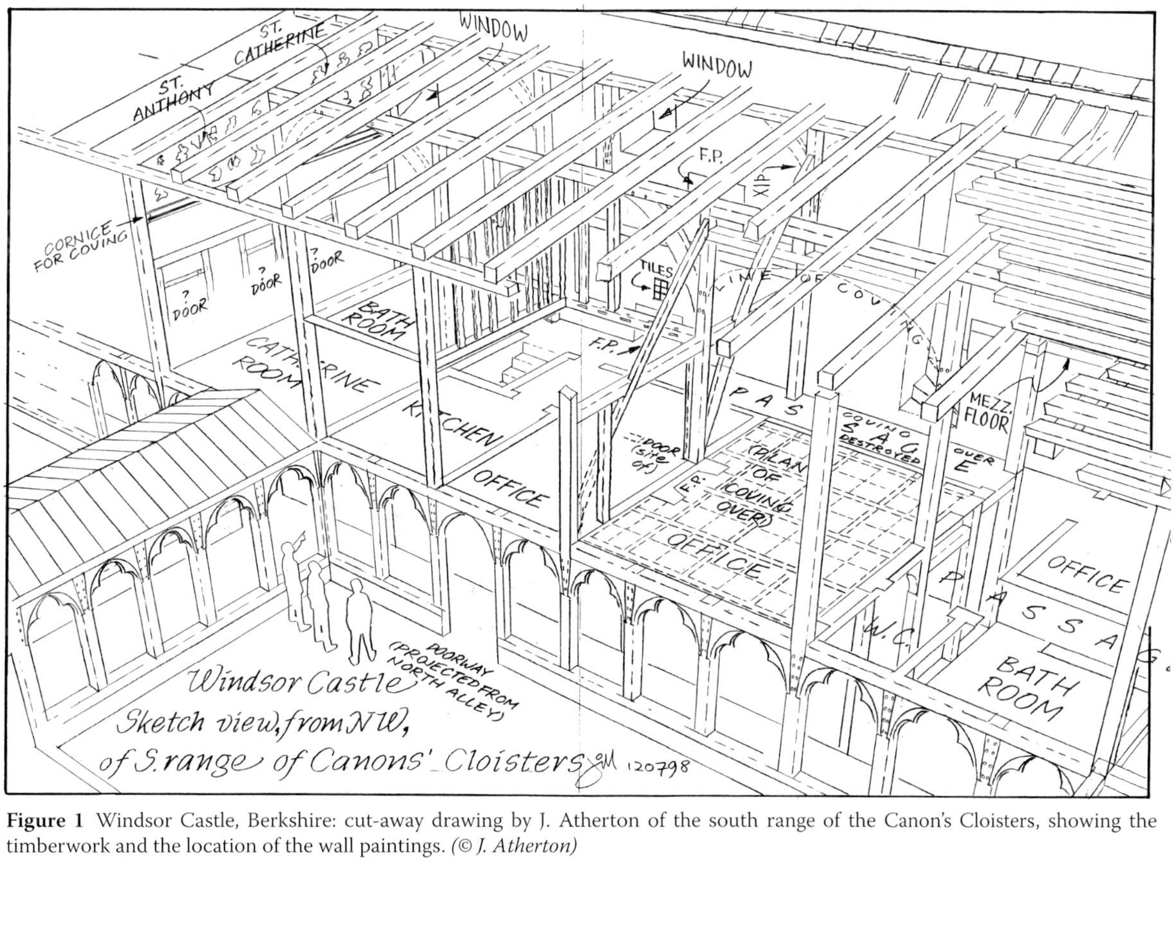

Figure 1 Windsor Castle, Berkshire: cut-away drawing by J. Atherton of the south range of the Canon's Cloisters, showing the timberwork and the location of the wall paintings. *(© J. Atherton)*

west wall appears to be a later insertion in which the daub was taken over the studs. This was covered by a thin layer of lime plaster and a single layer of limewash (as a ground for the painting). The insertion of this west wall created a tall and narrow room in which the wall paintings form a frieze approximately 3m above floor level. It looks as though the present room is the eastern end of what was once a much larger room.

If the room once extended to encompass the adjoining bay of the timber framing (see Fig. 1), then instead of the awkward position currently occupied by the Prince of Wales Feathers at the west end of the south wall, they would have been central to the design, with a further branch of foliage and another figure to the west.

The painting

During conservation work in 2003, it soon became obvious both from a stylistic[3] and a technical point of view, that the painting on the south wall is of an earlier date than those on the east and west walls. The painting on this south wall is stiffer and less sophisticated than those on the other walls. The leaves of the foliate background are not only smaller and flatter, but lack the elegance of those on the east and west walls, where the leaves are large and more naturalistic and the figures are more elegantly painted. The pigment on the south wall is powdery and far less well bound than that on the east and west walls. Pigment analysis[4] showed that yellow ochre, orpiment, indigo (applied over a grey of charcoal black and chalk), red lead applied over red iron oxide, an organic red and charcoal black had been used. St John the Baptist's halo (on the south wall) was painted using just yellow ochre, whereas St Anthony's halo on the east wall had orpiment applied over a mixture of yellow ochre and charcoal black, which would have created a greater illusion of gold.

There is, unfortunately, a scarcity of surviving documentation relating to works carried out in The Cloisters during the relevant years. The dating of the two phases of painting is therefore a matter of conjecture.

South wall

Although the painting on the south wall is obviously the earlier, it could not have been painted before the marriage of Henry VII to Elizabeth of York in 1486, as it shows red and white roses on either side of a trailing branch, eventually uniting 'as dimidiation or impalement (half of each rose joined together vertically)' (Fig. 2).[5] This is one of the early versions of the Tudor rose, which symbolised the union of the houses of York and Lancaster. According to an account of the Arms and Badges of the Kings of England prepared by Sir William Segar (died 1633 as Garter of Arms), Henry VII 'first impaled the two long separated Badges of eyther howse and afterwards incorporated them one within another as his sonne KH8 bore it' (Coll Arm L14 fol. 382v).[6] The presence of the Prince of Wales Feathers would seem to indicate a date of c.1486 (the date of Arthur's birth) or 1490 (the investment of the young prince as the Prince of Wales).

East and west walls

The design on the east and west walls appears to have consisted of single figures of saints, set against a background of richly scrolling foliage, flowers and fruits. On the east wall, the saints are identified by their emblems, which are also displayed on accompanying shields: Anthony by a Tau cross, bell and pig; and Catherine by a wheel 'of iron, environed with sharp razors'[7] and sword of martyrdom (Fig. 3).

Imagery associated with Katherine of Aragon dominates the east wall (Fig. 4). Not only is her patron saint (Catherine of Alexandria) portrayed, but her pomegranate emblem is carried on both the vine of the foliate background and on the brocade under-robe worn by the saint (Fig. 5). The painting is unlikely to date from Katherine's arrival in England and marriage to Prince Arthur in 1501, as she does not appear to have visited Windsor on her journey from Plymouth to London and following the marriage they left London for Ludlow in Wales, where Arthur died in 1502. A more probable date would seem to be either June 1509 – which saw not only her marriage to Henry, but also their sumptuous coronation[8] – or 1511, when

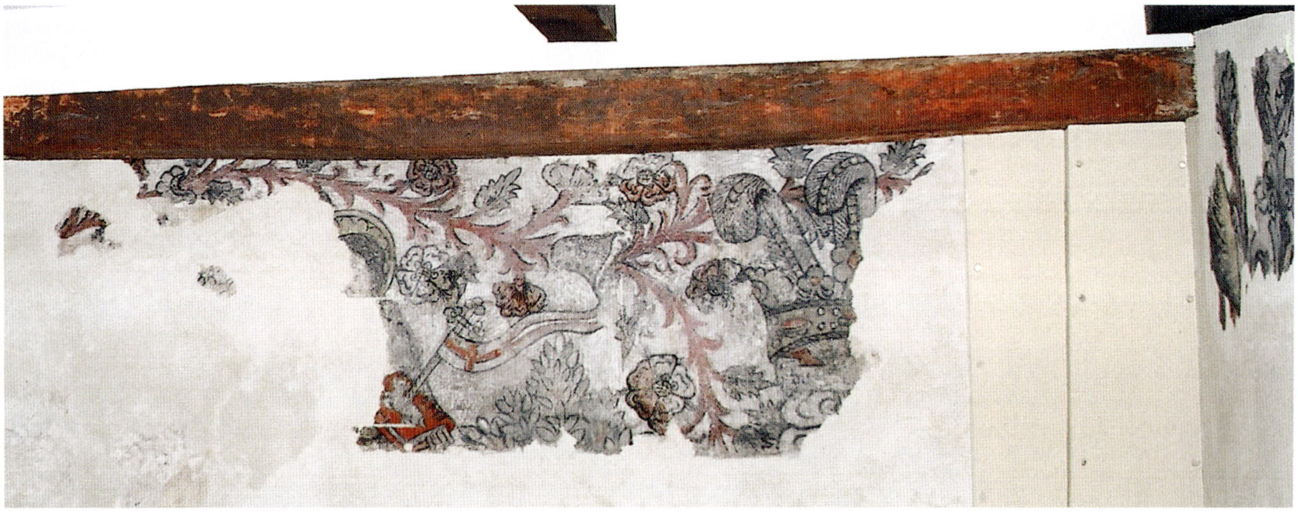

Figure 2 No. 2 The Cloisters, Windsor Castle, Berkshire: general view of the south wall. *(© A. Ballantyne)*

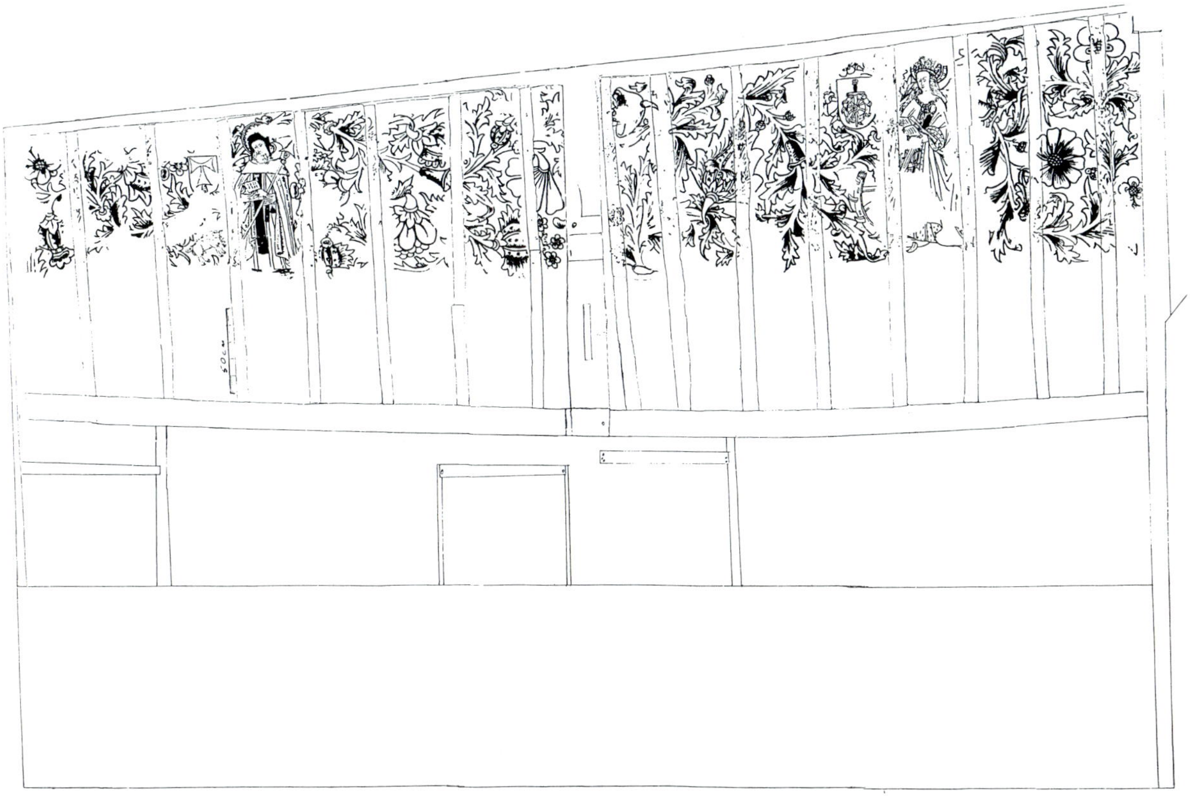

Figure 3 Tracing of the east wall of the first room showing the composition and survival of the wall paintings. The left side contains an image of St Anthony, the right side an image of St Catherine. *(© A. Ballantyne)*

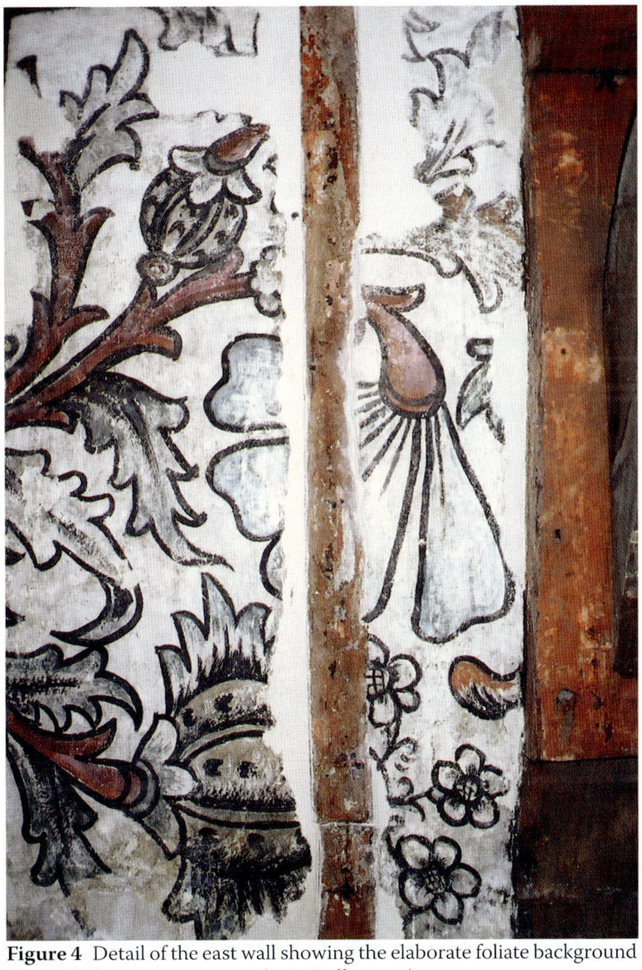

Figure 4 Detail of the east wall showing the elaborate foliate background that includes pomegranates. *(© A. Ballantyne)*

the birth of their son Henry on 1 January was followed by celebrations and an elaborate tournament.

Apparently, 'In the Westminster Tournament Roll, an illuminated manuscript belonging to the College of Arms and prepared soon after the birth of a son to Katharine of Aragon on New Years Day, a number of Royal Badges are depicted on horse trappings and elsewhere. King Henry VIII himself is represented on membrane 36 by a large rose per pale Gules and Argent slipped and leaved Vert, surmounted by a Royal crown gold and russet, set with jewels, all between the two letters H and K. On membrane 15 the bard (i.e. horse trappings) of a mounted Royal page is set with large roses-en-soleil per pale Gules and Argent. The conventional Tudor Badge of one rose superimposed on another does not appear in the roll.'[9] This could explain why, when the east and west walls were painted, it was not thought necessary to alter the roses on the earlier painting on the south wall.

Unfortunately, most of the painting on the west wall has been lost. However, enough of the figure of a haloed knight in armour with sword arm upraised, survives at the south end of the wall to suggest that this was St George (Fig. 6). It is more difficult to identify the saint portrayed at the north end of the west wall as all that remains are a few leaves, the head of a small bird eating a berry, and the corner of a shield carrying part of the head of another bird (Fig. 7). No birds are portrayed elsewhere in the room. The only other creatures are the pig with St Anthony and (presumably) the horse and dragon with St George. I would therefore venture to suggest that this painting might have been St Francis of Assisi.

Although St Francis is not one of the more commonly portrayed saints in England, the Observant Friars – the Franciscans

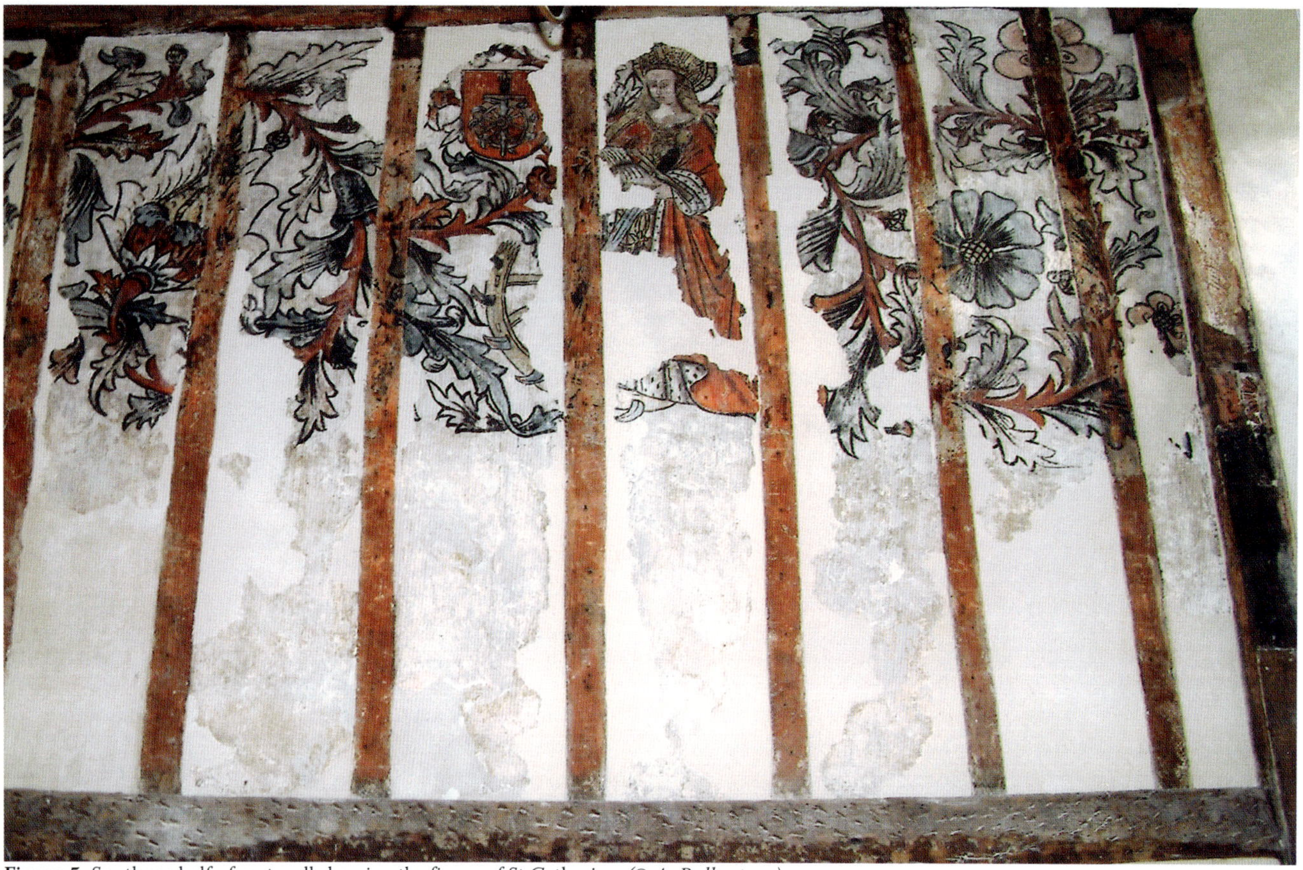

Figure 5 Southern half of east wall showing the figure of St Catherine. *(© A. Ballantyne)*

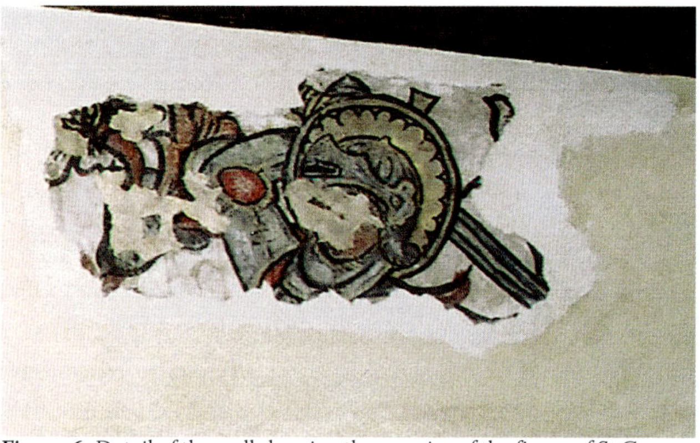

Figure 6 Detail of the wall showing the remains of the figure of St George. *(© A. Ballantyne)*

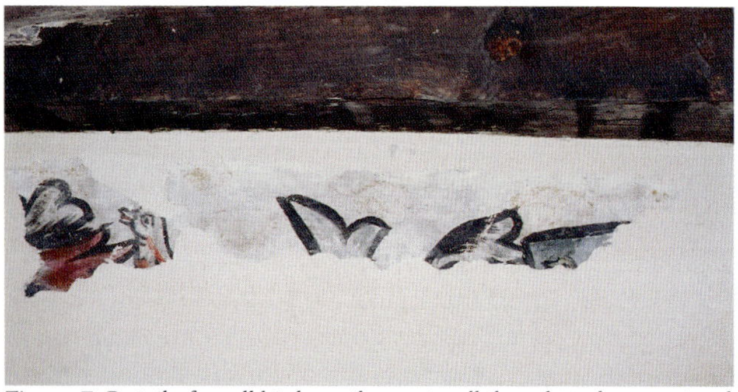

Figure 7 Detail of small birds on the west wall thought to be associated with a figure of St Francis (now lost). *(© A. Ballantyne)*

– were Katherine's favourite Order. The christening of Prince Henry, on Sunday, 5 January 1511, took place in the church of the Observant Friars at Richmond Palace.[10] On 12 January, Henry VIII left on a pilgrimage of thanksgiving for the safe delivery of a son, to the Shrine of Our Lady of Walsingham. The shrine at Walsingham was in the care of the Grey Friars, or friars of the Franciscan Order.

Why was a large room subdivided and then so richly painted? Could it be because of a sudden need for more accommodation to house the much enlarged household with the marriage and coronation of Henry VIII and Katherine – might this be the mysterious 'shift guest house, empty for many years' to which the archivist, Eileen Scarff[11] has found a 1627 reference? One of the explanations of the word 'shift' given by the *Shorter Oxford Dictionary* is 'an expedient, an ingenious device for effecting some purpose, 1530'. Perhaps it was originally subdivided to 'make shift' as a guest house? The resultant space, which would have looked rather tall and narrow, would have appeared less so once the lower part of the walls was covered by panelling and the upper parts decorated with paintings. What could be more fitting for housing one of the guests from Aragon than a wall painting that flattered Katherine by depicting her patron saint and incorporating pomegranates?

Conservation history

When discovered in 1965, it was recognised that the fragile condition of the wall paintings would necessitate an extensive

Table 1 Summary of inspections and condition assessments 1965–90.

Conservator	Date	Details
E. Clive Rouse	1965	described their condition as 'very bad' and compared them, iconographically, to those found in a cottage in Piccotts End (Hertfordshire)[12]
Max C. Delise	1971	recommended removing the paintings and mounting them on an artificial support
Maurice Keevil	January 1976	described them as fragile
Jan Keevil	June 1976	described them as fragile
Jan Keevil	February 1978	recommended that the canons approach Paul Foder, Eve Baker, Maurice Keevil, Pauline Plummer and Clive Rouse
Paul Foder	22 May 1978	recommended consolidation of paint with acrylic resin B72, re-laying detached layers with acrylic AC34 and filling holes with sand, lime and PVA
E. Clive Rouse	30 May 1978	thought that their condition was not much changed though he noted a number of flakes of the painting on top of the false ceiling
Eve Baker	20 June 1978	described the paintings as delaminating badly, some areas flapping and with a delicate powdering surface – needing to be taken down and attached to artificial support, as the wall was not strong enough to withstand her methods of reattaching detached paintings
The Perry Lithgow Partnership	early 1980s	reported that the surface was delaminating and recommended the removal and reattachment of the painting
M.M. Katkov and C. Oldenbourg	1983	described them as very unstable, detaching and flaking
Wolfgang Gartner	1990	proposed injecting lime casein for re-laying detached areas and applying a 'binder' to powdering paint

programme of consolidation. In order to avoid holding up the building work for an extended period, it was agreed that as an interim measure, a 'temporary' ceiling should be installed below the paintings.

Over the following 25 years, a number of different conservators inspected and reported on the condition of the paintings (see Table 1).

In 1991, 26 years after their discovery, the flat ceiling was removed and the paintings were secured by Wolfgang Gartner with two assistants. Attention was again drawn to the condition of these paintings in 2003, when a flake of paint was lost from the image of St Catherine. A close inspection of the paintings revealed that, although no problems were apparent when viewed from the ground, large areas were in fact in a very delicate condition, particularly on the east wall where multilayer delamination was occurring between the layers of limewash and considerable areas of painting were so loose that they moved when very lightly tapped (Fig. 8). The 1991 plaster repairs had been carried out using a very coarse lime mortar, applied in the Germanic style where the repair is 'set back' behind the surface of the original plaster. Both the coarse texture of the plaster and the projecting edges of the painted plaster had attracted dust and dirt.

The delamination and detachment was not necessarily an indication of a lack of thoroughness during previous conservation. It could well have occurred in the intervening years (radiators were installed in 1989). Fortunately, there is no sign of recent cracking or shrinkage between the timbers and the

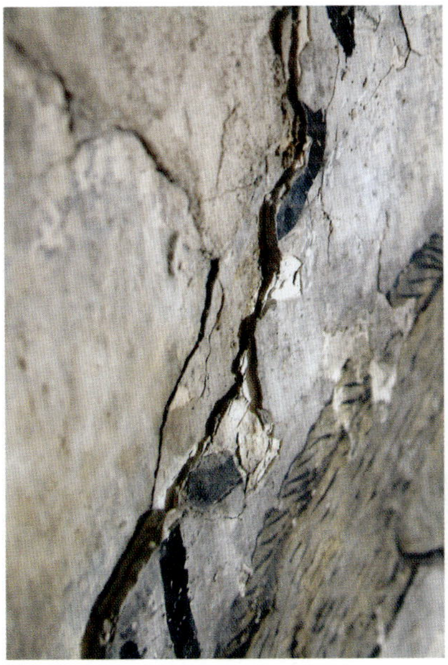

Figure 8 Detail of the east wall before conservation showing the extent of delamination in the area around the image of the pig next to St Anthony. *(© A. Ballantyne)*

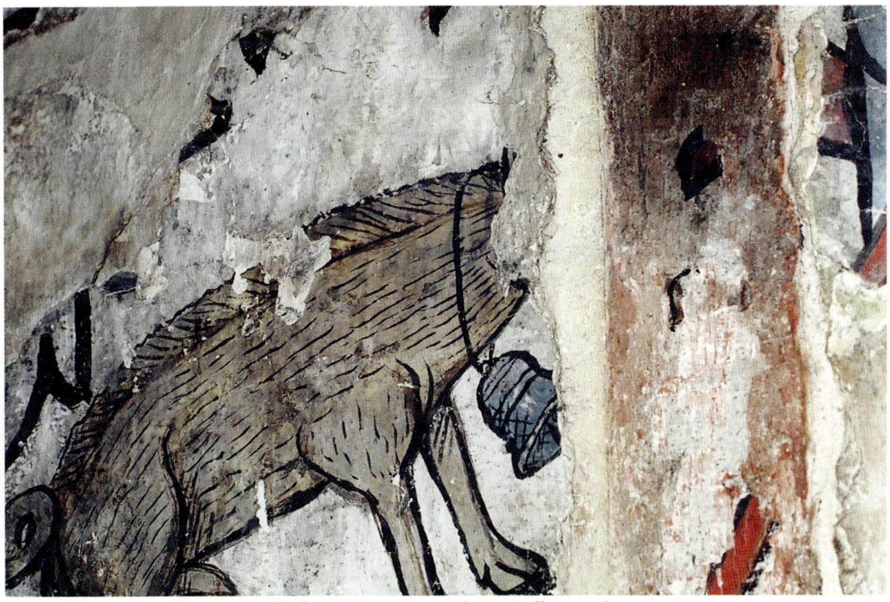

Figure 9 Detail of the east wall after conservation. *(© A. Ballantyne)*

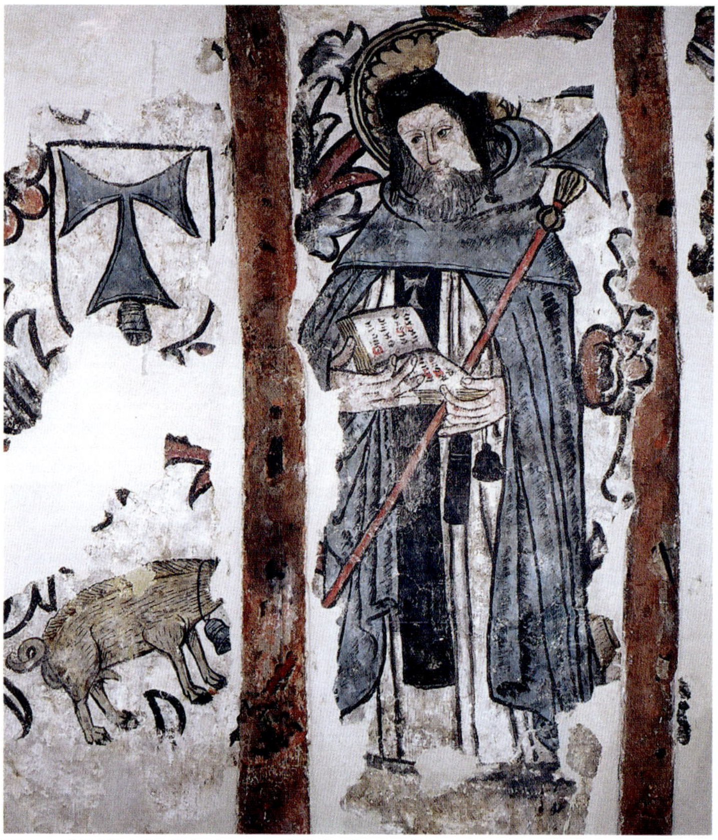

Figure 10 Detail of the image of St Anthony after conservation. *(© A. Ballantyne)*

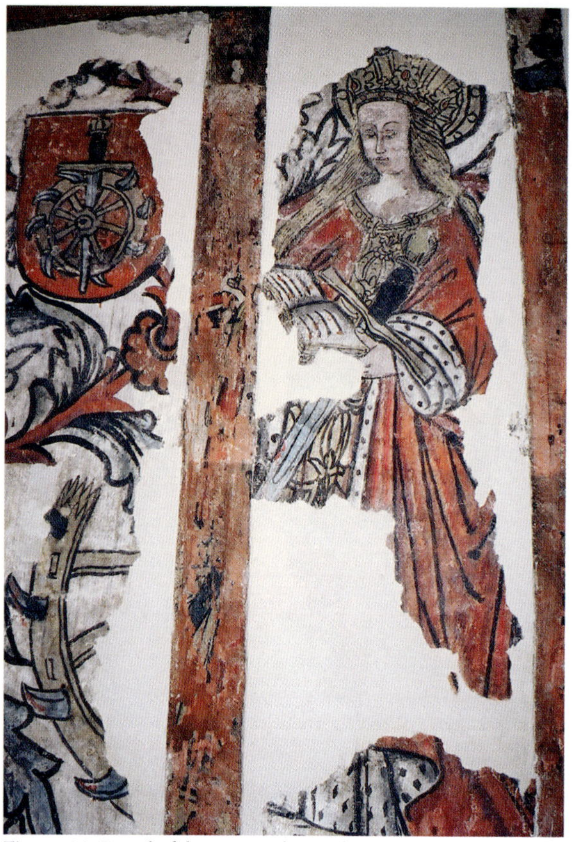

Figure 11 Detail of the image of St Catherine after conservation. *(© A. Ballantyne)*

plaster or within the timbers themselves. During conservation work in 2003, delaminating areas were reattached using injections of slaked lime. The discoloured surfaces of the 1991 repairs were cut back and plaster losses were filled using a lime mortar (slaked lime and sharp washed sand) (Figs 10 and 11). By taking the new plaster repairs to the same plane as the painting, previously exposed broken edges of the plaster (comprised of numerous layers of limewash) were secured.

Notes

1. Tatton-Brown 2001–02.
2. There appears to have been an earlier scheme of decoration which consisted of plain limewash and red ochre studs.
3. As first noted by Andrea Kirkham.
4. Pigment analysis by Catherine Hassall: Report no. W264, January 2004.
5. Letter to the author from Timothy Duke, Chester Herald, College of Arms, 16 April 2004.
6. *Ibid.*
7. de Voragine 1939, p. 23.
8. Fraser 1993, p. 50.
9. See note 5 above.
10. Starkey 2004, pp. 120–21.
11. Archivist to the College of Saint George, Windsor Castle.
12. Described by Dr E. Clive Rouse in Rouse 1965–66, pp. 275–81. This article also describes paintings discovered in No. 25 The Cloisters, Windsor.

References

Fraser A. 1993, *The Six Wives of Henry VIII*, Mandarin, London

Rouse E.C. 1965–66, 'The recently discovered wall paintings in the Lower Ward, Windsor Castle', *Report of the Society of the Friends of Saint George's and Descendants of the Knights of the Garter*, pp. 275–81

Starkey D. 2004, *Six Wives, the Queens of Henry VIII*, Vintage, London

Tatton-Brown T. 2001–02, 'The Canons' Houses and Cloisters at Windsor', *Report of the Society of the Friends of Saint George's and Descendants of the Knights of the Garter*, pp. 121–5

de Voragine J. 1939, *The Golden Legends 1270, Englished by William Caxton 1483, Vol. VII*, J.M. Dent and Sons, London

The author

Ann Ballantyne has been working on the conservation of medieval wall paintings since 1966, for the first 15 years as assistant to Dr E. Clive Rouse. A member of the Board of Studies for the Courtauld Institute of Art/Getty Conservation Institute Course in the Conservation of Wall Paintings from its inauguration in 1985 until 1991. Chairman of the Wall Paintings Section of UKIC 1988–91, Ann served on the Council for the Care of Churches 'Paintings' Conservation Committee from 1996 until 1999.

Sixteenth-century wall paintings at The Forge, Much Hadham, Hertfordshire

Jane Rutherfoord

A tiny dining room, a retired primary-school teacher, almost a lifetime of restraint and nearly ten years of dogged determination and enthusiasm and the result was the revelation of one of the most complete and exciting cycles of domestic wall painting in this country.

The paintings are located in a ground-floor, front room of a dwelling that was once a farmhouse and which now adjoins The Forge at Much Hadham in Hertfordshire. They include a *Judgement of Solomon*, a particularly fine royal arms of Elizabeth I and the arms of a member of the Newce family, owners of the property in the 1570s and probably amongst the most influential people in Much Hadham at that time.

The buildings at The Forge form a small complex, the core of which is a timber-framed 'H' hall-house (since the discovery of the paintings, listed Grade II*) (Figs 1 and 2). The part of the south cross-wing where they are located is considered to be late 15th century but most of the rest of the house dates from the early to mid-16th century. Since then there have been additions and alterations and the hall-house has been divided into three units.

In 1811 The Forge was taken over by the Pages and their business as blacksmiths continued there through four generations, until Charles Page retired at the age of eighty-seven. He died in 1983. His only child, Jean, continued to live in the family home until her death, in 1999. However, Jean had ensured the future of The Forge by a deed of gift which, in 1988, conveyed the entire property to the Hertfordshire Building Preservation Trust.

Jean Page was a popular and formidable character and a pillar of the community. Her home and heritage were central

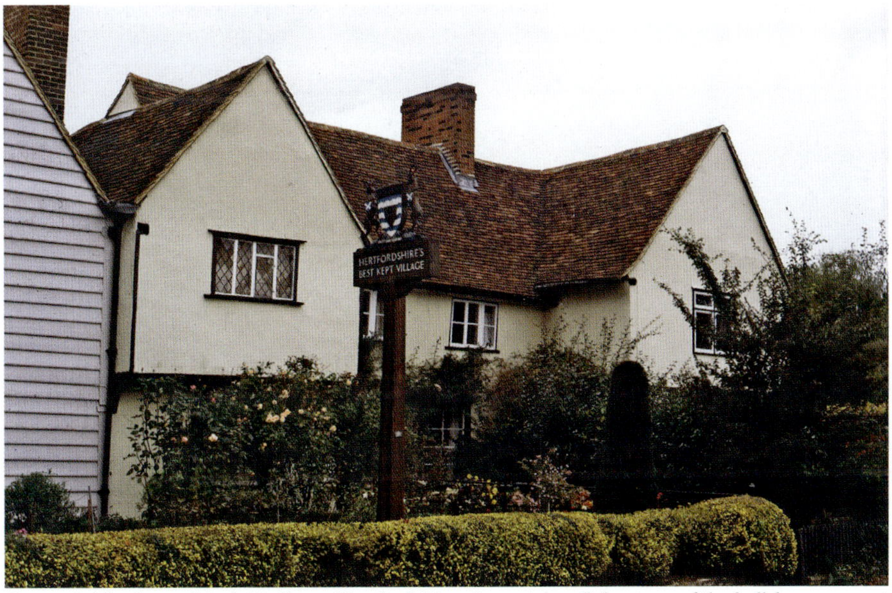

Figure 1 The Forge, Much Hadham, Hertfordshire: the east (road) frontage of the hall-house – part of the complex consisting of the The Forge House and associated cottages. *(© J. Rutherfoord)*

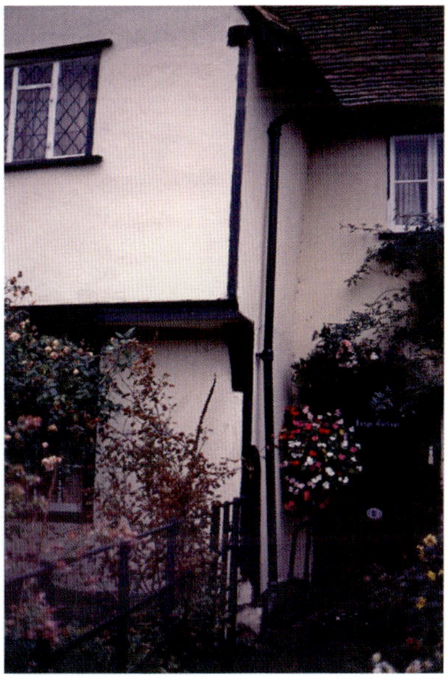

Figure 2 The north-east corner of the south cross-wing: the paintings are located on the ground floor. *(© J. Rutherfoord)*

to her life and in her agreement with the Trust she remained firmly in control of matters relating to the interior of the house. Having retired from teaching, Jean started to put a long-cherished plan into action: the discovery of what was on the walls of her dining room.

When I was first invited to visit The Forge, in 1988, the section of the building occupied by Jean (known as The Forge House) and the adjoining smithy were still in a time warp: apart from basic services, their furnishing and contents had remained unchanged for decades. Both then and on many subsequent occasions, Jean enjoyed describing the memory of a particular afternoon in the early 1940s. Her mother was taking tea to the decorator when she noticed some "curious stains and outlines". He had finished "removing old wallpaper" and was about to continue the preparatory scraping "before starting to paint ... and she stopped him there and then from going any further". The walls were to stay as they were, covered in various layers of distemper and house paint, for approximately half a century.

The retrieval of Jean's wall paintings was an intensely personal project and the following account sets out to show how the achievements were driven by the human story behind it. From the start, Jean was looking to employ one conservator rather than a team and there were good reasons for this, as will become clear. The essence of the original brief was to keep the proposed work private, simple and to tackle it in stages, a little at a time. Jean was determined to pay for the work from her own resources. She was vehemently protective of her privacy and her independence from any funding institution or public authority, to the extent that throughout all the years of working for her I was under an obligation not to disclose the identity of the property. While these stipulations remained entirely understandable, they nevertheless imposed intellectual and practical constraints that played a highly significant part in creating an unconventional modus operandi – at times a complete departure from standard practice. Consultation and exchange of information with specialists working in allied fields of research within certain institutions was often very difficult and sometimes impossible.

The engagement of a single conservator was not only compatible with Jean's personality and lifestyle but also with the flexibility she desired for the best management of her budget.

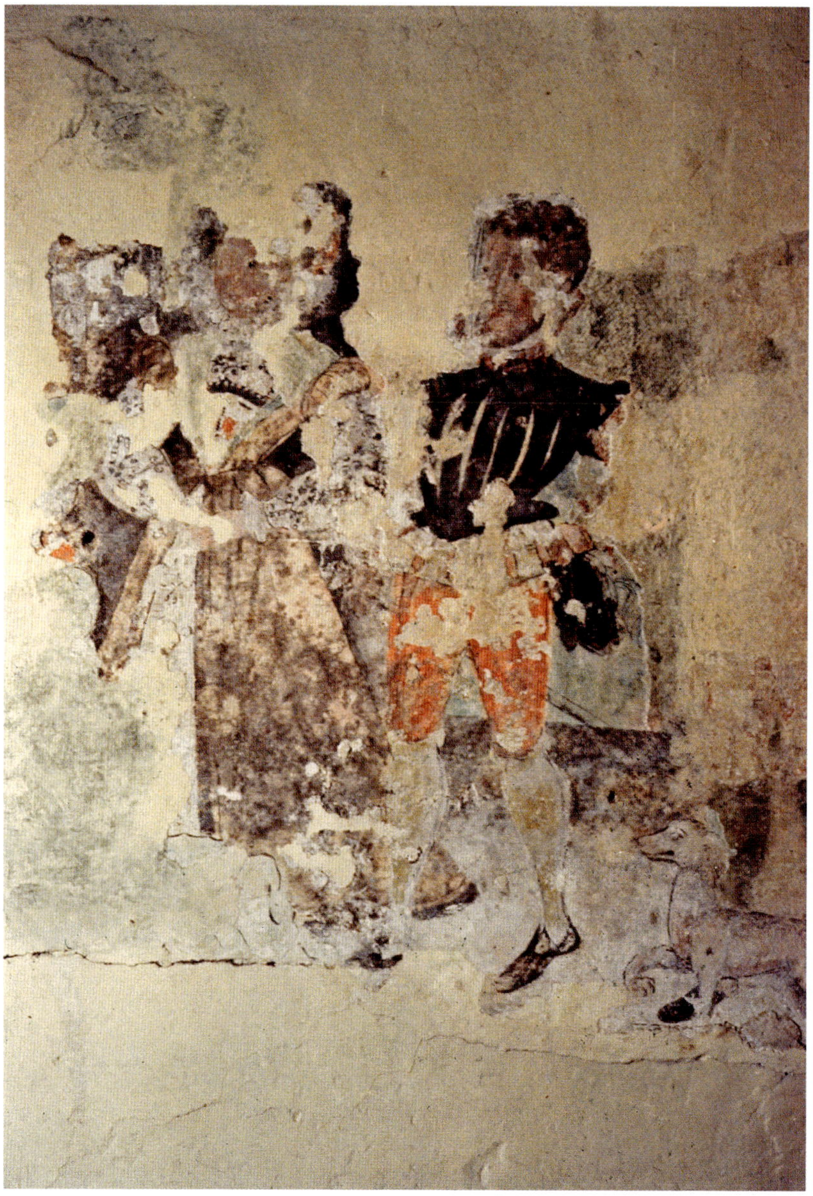

Figure 3 North wall (east end) at an early stage of uncovering: two figures in Elizabethan court dress; a dog is emerging at the feet of a third figure. *(© J. Rutherfoord)*

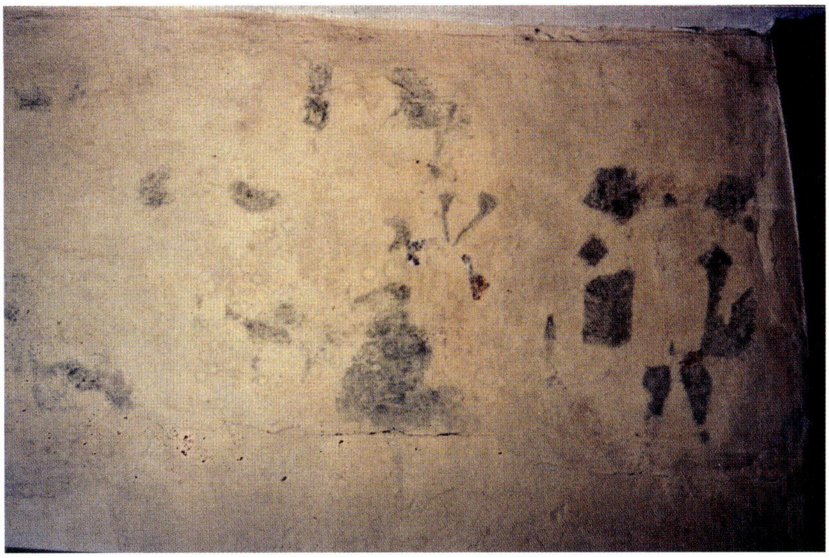

Figure 4 North wall (east end) as it was in 1989, before the start of uncovering. Copper-based pigment had stained through to the surface of the overlying layers of distemper and 20th-century house paint, creating images of some of the figures beneath. *(© J. Rutherfoord)*

Moreover, for much of the project, maximum efficiency was going to be achieved by one conservator working alone. The work-space was very limited and the extreme delicacy of the painting made it an unsuitable job on which to engage conservation students.

Until the structural interventions got underway in 1995, most of the room's furniture had to remain *in situ*. The floorspace was filled to bursting on some of the frequent occasions when Jean invited her friends and neighbours to see the latest discovery (Fig. 3). These conversations were an essential part of the project. Its continuation was dependent upon Jean's optimism and courage and her confidence in the result. Her frugality and the enthusiasm with which she invested her savings in her paintings won great respect. A number of her most supportive friends sponsored the uncovering of certain individual features, such as the lion, Solomon's shoes and a gentleman's ruff.

The technical demands of the project were, however, critically interwoven with navigating the challenges of personal and professional relationships. Winning a client's confidence at the beginning of a project should not be difficult but maintaining it through the vicissitudes of a protracted enterprise such as this is another matter. For Jean's part, it was a huge intrusion upon her privacy to have the conservator not just working in her house but also living there (in her second bedroom, above the dining room). While this arrangement was economical and practical and worked very well for much of the time, when the project intensified, in 1995, it became a strain. Jean had never shared her home with anyone other than her parents and, through middle age, just with her father.

Here were two strong-minded and independent women living and working under the same small roof, trying to arrive at the same goal but, for the most part, from a different angle of approach from that to which they were accustomed. Like most friendships formed in strange conditions, the friendship became deep but not without some bumpy rides along the way. Balancing the paintings' needs with the client's wishes and resources became the greatest challenge of all – for the client as well as for the conservator.

For as long as Jean could remember, evidence of the paintings' existence had been provided by copper-based pigment that had produced staining through to the surface of the overlying layers, creating images of some of the figures beneath (Fig. 4). The remains of these overlying layers consisted of at least five coats of white distemper followed by a thick layer of what appeared to be 20th-century house paint, probably oil-based. (As distemper is often washed off before a new covering layer is applied, there is no way of knowing precisely how many times the murals were painted over.)

There was nothing to suggest that, if left in place, the overlying layers would cause any further harm to the paintings, i.e. in addition to the damage already inflicted by their application. But, to leave the paintings covered up was not an option: Jean's ambition was to see them. By 1990 the uncovering was well underway and a limited amount was carried out each year until the project was accelerated in 1995.

The starting points were governed by Jean's curiosity. As the difficulties of the uncovering became apparent, first and foremost she wanted the subject matter to be revealed rather than having neatly defined areas completed before moving on to an adjacent section. The work was done with fine scalpels and under magnification – occasionally a microscope and otherwise with head magnifiers. To remove the overlying layers safely was an excruciatingly slow process (up to five hours per square centimetre and often longer), chiefly because the house paint had sunk so deeply into the surface (Fig. 5). This was excavation for its own sake and it is highly unlikely that this work would have qualified for a grant from any of the usual sources. But then Jean was so insistent upon retaining independent control and avoiding 'red tape' that she even declined the offer of funds from a well-known private foundation.

The room is barely eleven feet (3.35m) square and the paintings extend round all four walls, from dado to ceiling. They are on a lime-and-hair plaster applied over laths and studwork. The technical examination (by cross-section and EDX analysis) of a restricted number of samples[1] in the early stages of the project, focused upon the north wall. It confirmed that the supporting plaster was built up in three coats: a coarse layer containing grit and animal hair, followed by two layers of pure lime plaster.

(b)

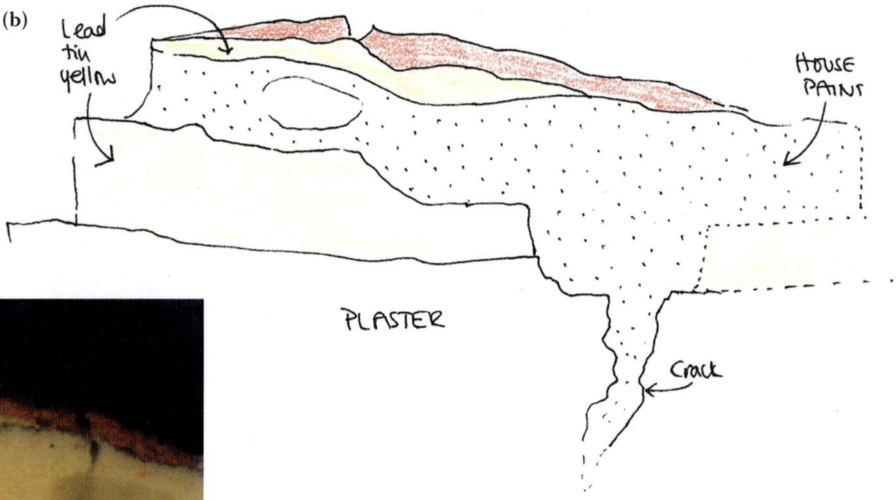

(a)

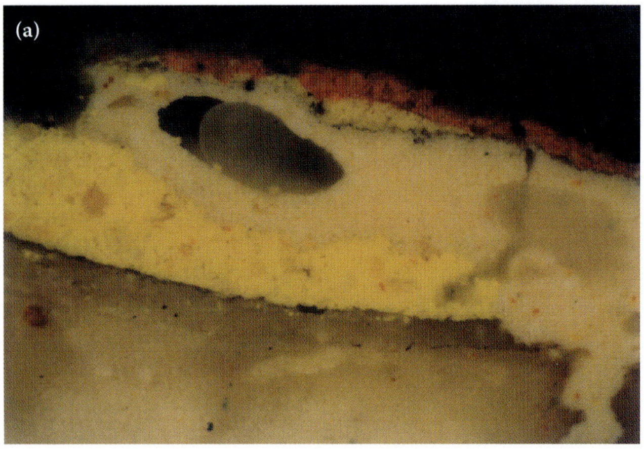

Figure 5 (a) North wall (centre background): cross-section of a sample taken from an architectural detail highlighted (or 'gilded') with lead-tin yellow and red lead. Overlying house paint has filtered into a crack, splitting apart the 16th-century paint layers. The carbon black drawing line is very clear and is overlaid by a very thick layer of lead-tin yellow. The red/orange is a mixture of red lead and lead-tin yellow. (b) Diagram of the cross-section showing how the modern paint has saturated the 16th-century paint layers. *(© UCL Painting Analysis Ltd)*

Uncovering began on the north wall, towards the east (right-hand) end, where the 'stains' and outlines were most obvious. The first figures to emerge were a standing woman and a gentleman, in Elizabethan court dress, and a dog (Fig. 6). The quality and detail of the painting caused great excitement and without the need for any persuasion Jean had a window blind installed and took pleasure in choosing curtains, made for her by a friend.

As work continued, it became clear that the subject was *The Judgement of Solomon*. Centre left, Solomon, dressed in black, is seated upon a chair of state beneath a gilded and draped baldachin, flanked by courtiers. In the description of Solomon's building of the house of Lebanon and of "his house where he dwelt ... he made a porch for the throne where he might judge, even the porch of judgment ..." (I Kings 7:7–8). Before Solomon, in the centre of the painting, stands an executioner dressed in scarlet, his sword raised and his left fist dangling a baby by the ankle. Opposite, centre right, the second woman is kneeling, pleading for the child's life. The dead infant lies on the floor in front of her (Fig. 7).

The paint has all the appearance of being aqueous – probably either gum or size. It has the air-pockets and uneven surface of a paint that evaporates to dryness and the analysis showed that it had been applied onto a clean, unsized plaster surface. (Only a water-mixed paint could be used successfully on unsized plaster.) The costumes are portrayed in elaborate detail with a beautiful and rarely surviving variety of colour. The palette contained both lead-based pigments and organic pigments, thereby providing a range of very strong, bright colours. The pigments identified to date include: lead-tin yellow, lead white, red lead, carbon black, smalt, red ochre, red lake and indigo. Both lead-tin yellow and carbon black were used extensively on their own, as pure colour – note the yellow used for the gilding of the floor tiles and elsewhere in the painting, as on the baldachin (Fig. 8). They are also used in combination

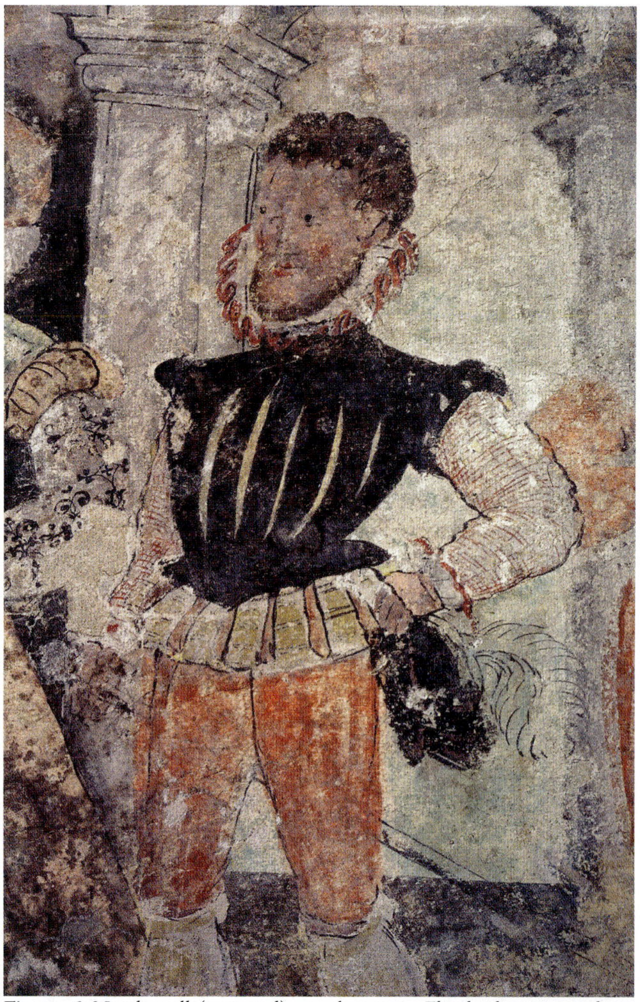

Figure 6 North wall (east end): gentleman in Elizabethan court dress – detail, after uncovering. *(© J. Rutherfoord)*

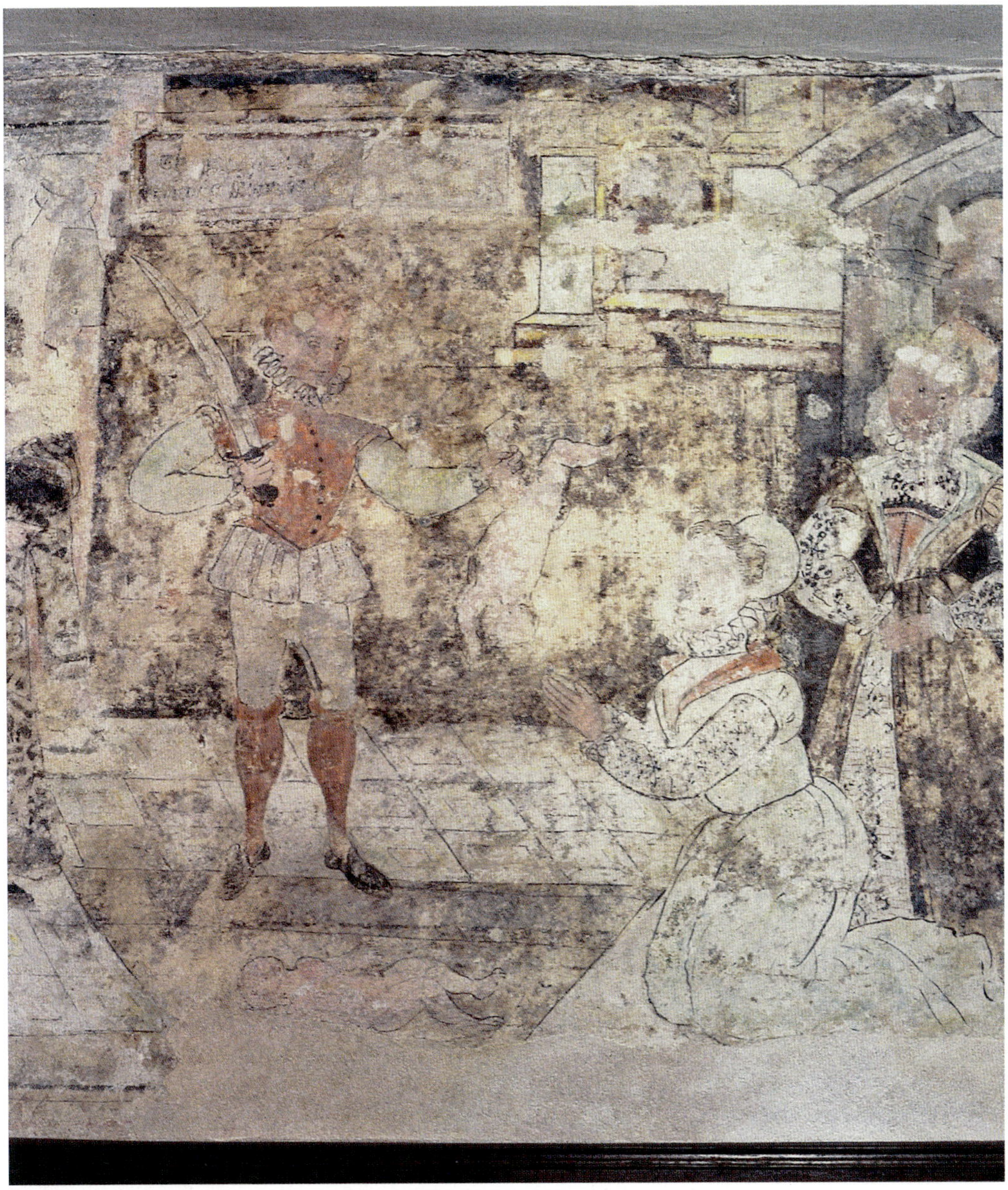

Figure 7 North wall (centre): an executioner, dressed in scarlet, dangles a baby by the ankle and raises his sword, while the kneeling woman pleads for the child's life and the dead infant lies on the floor. *(© J. Rutherfoord)*

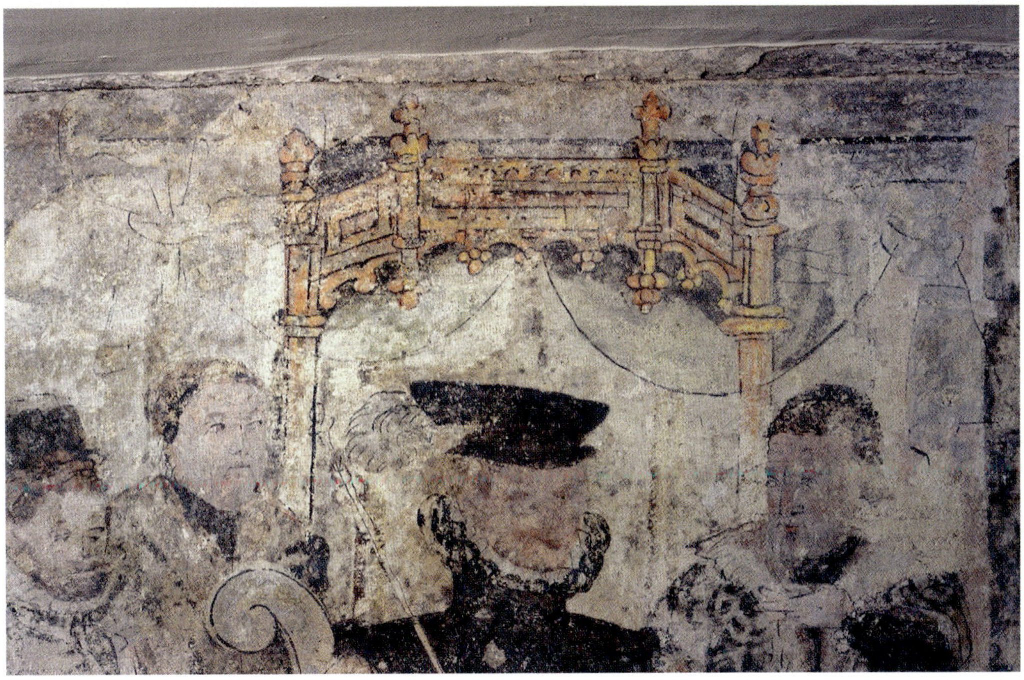

Figure 8 North wall (centre left): Solomon's "porch of judgement" – the baldachin 'gilded' with lead-tin yellow. *(© J. Rutherfoord)*

(a)

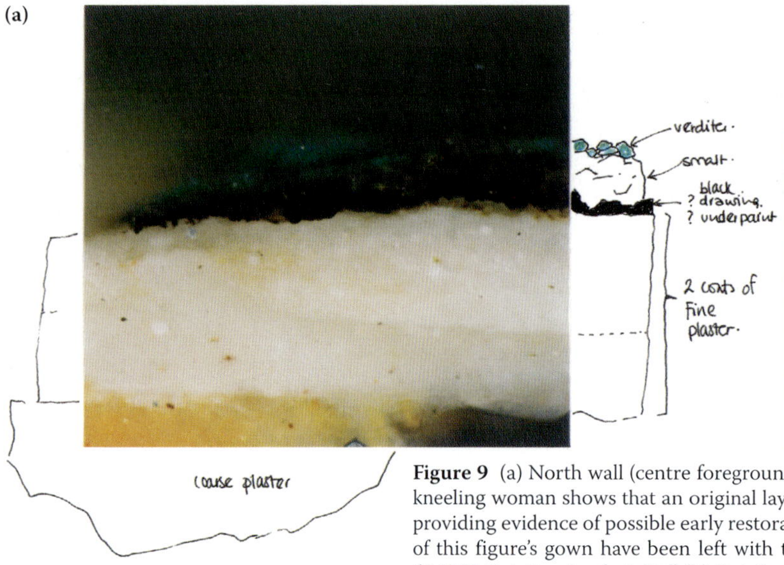

(b)

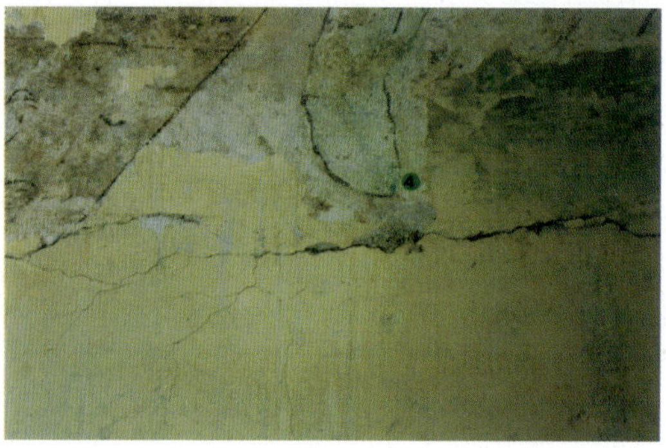

Figure 9 (a) North wall (centre foreground): a cross-section of a sample taken from the gown of the kneeling woman shows that an original layer of smalt has been overpainted with blue/green verditer, providing evidence of possible early restoration. Under the smalt is a thick layer of carbon black. Parts of this figure's gown have been left with the overlying layers untouched, pending further research. *(© UCL Painting Analysis Ltd)* (b) Detail of the knee area of the woman's gown, showing the location of the sample illustrated in Fig. 9 (a). *(© J. Rutherfoord)*

– for example, lead-tin yellow with a small addition of carbon black for the greyish pale green of Solomon's chair. The drawing lines are very clear and were carried out in carbon black. It is interesting to note, however, that the drawing in this painting actually lacks confidence and is quite naive.

In the figure of the courtier to Solomon's left, the purple behind the left sleeve was identified as a mixture of red lake and indigo blue. The red/orange in the central, lower section of the same courtier's gown is a mixture of red lead and lead-tin yellow. Elsewhere in the painting there are examples of a similar mixture of red lead and lead-tin yellow being used as a highlight over a base coat of red ochre. Evidence of possible early restoration was found in a blue-green sample taken from the gown of the kneeling woman. The cross-section is an original layer of smalt, overpainted with blue/green verditer (artificial copper carbonate) (Fig. 9). The smalt is painted over a thick layer of carbon black. This black may be part of the drawing or it may be an underpaint for the blue (a common way of making the best of expensive blue pigments). In its characteristically decayed state, the smalt looks whitish and is almost impossible to see with the naked eye. The later, verditer layer rests cleanly on top of the smalt, showing that the lower paint layer was dry before the second one was added. If the verditer was brushed on to give colour to an area that had become colourless, it was probably done in the 17th or early 18th century; after this period verditer is rarely found. Parts of this figure's gown have not yet been uncovered but left with the overlying layers untouched, pending further research.

The excavation of the paintings on the west and east walls was begun in 1992 and from thereon the uncovering work alternated irregularly between the north, west and east sides of the room. Work on the south wall did not start until 1994. The west wall is filled with the royal arms, flanked on either side by a large and striking figure of a guard carrying a halberd (Figs 10 and 11). The supporters (the lion and the dragon) are expertly drawn and painted in glorious colour, using the same materials and palette as were found on the north wall. The guards are painted in grisaille and bear a very rare example of the Tudor badge on the breast of their jerkins. On the east wall the Newce arms, also painted in grisaille, are repeated on both sides of the window (Fig. 12). The painting on the south wall is limited to what remains of a bold decoration in the area above and surrounding a small, internal window at the west end (the painting continues over the window frame) (Fig. 13). Here, too, it is in grisaille, similar to that on the east wall.

Notwithstanding the various structural alterations – consisting principally of the changes to the south wall but also, apparently, to the height of the ceiling (particularly noticeable where the top of the painting on the west wall is now either hidden or missing) – one of the most remarkable things about these paintings was their condition. On the whole, damage was limited to nail holes and localised abrasion – the evidence of preparation for new covering(s). Otherwise, the original paint was reasonably sound. In the few areas on the north and east walls where it was tending to crumble or flake it was consolidated and fixed with weak gelatine size.

The condition of the supporting plaster was very good indeed. Again, it had suffered relatively limited mechanical damage. In addition to a variety of large and small nail holes, there are only a couple of significant losses: one adjacent to the door in the west wall and the other at the east end of the north wall. The losses had been repaired on a number of occasions and the majority of these repairs have now been replaced with slaked lime putty and washed sand, plus hair where appropriate.

During April, 1995, the late Janet Arnold, author and leading authority on Elizabethan costume, visited The Forge to inspect the paintings while uncovering was still in progress. She dated the *Judgement of Solomon* to c.1576 and was determined to make another visit, after more detail had been revealed. Sadly, this was not possible because of illness, but she remained in communication until her death. Her passionate enthusiasm injected the project with a tremendous boost at a time when the grinding slowness of the work was taking its toll.

The Heraldry Society subsequently identified the family arms, granted in 1575. They are probably the arms of Clement Newce, described on his tomb as 'sometime citizen and mercer of London'. Upon being granted arms, their owner would

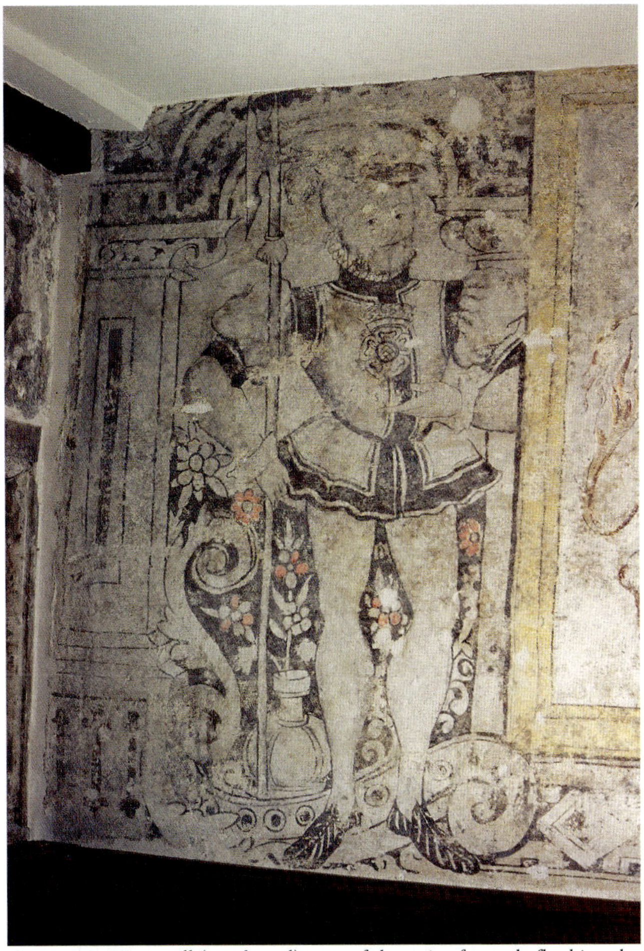

Figure 10 West wall (south end): one of the pair of guards flanking the royal arms – uncovering and treatment almost complete. *(© J. Rutherfoord)*

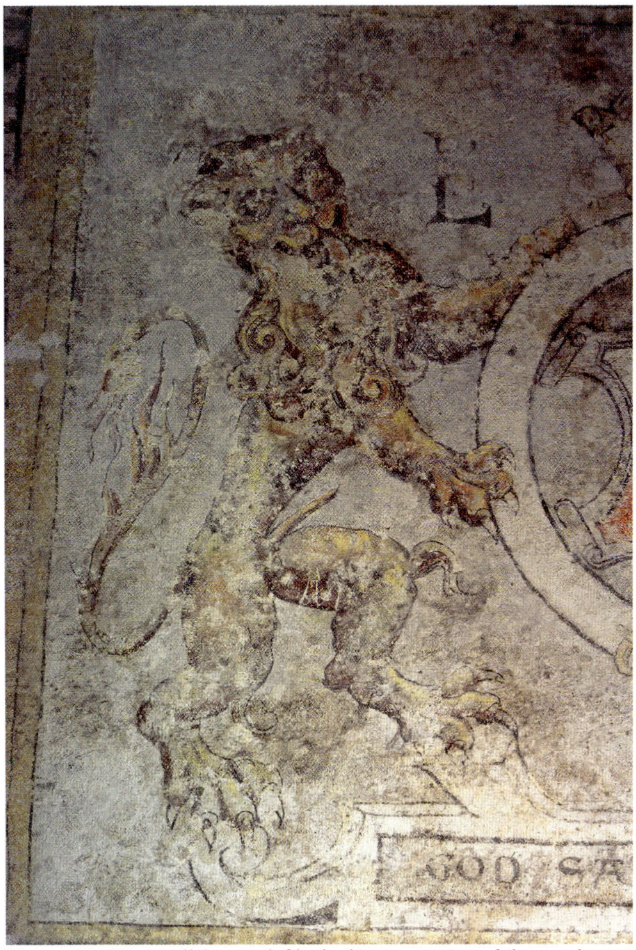

Figure 11 West wall (centre left): the lion supporter of the royal arms – uncovering almost complete. *(© J. Rutherfoord)*

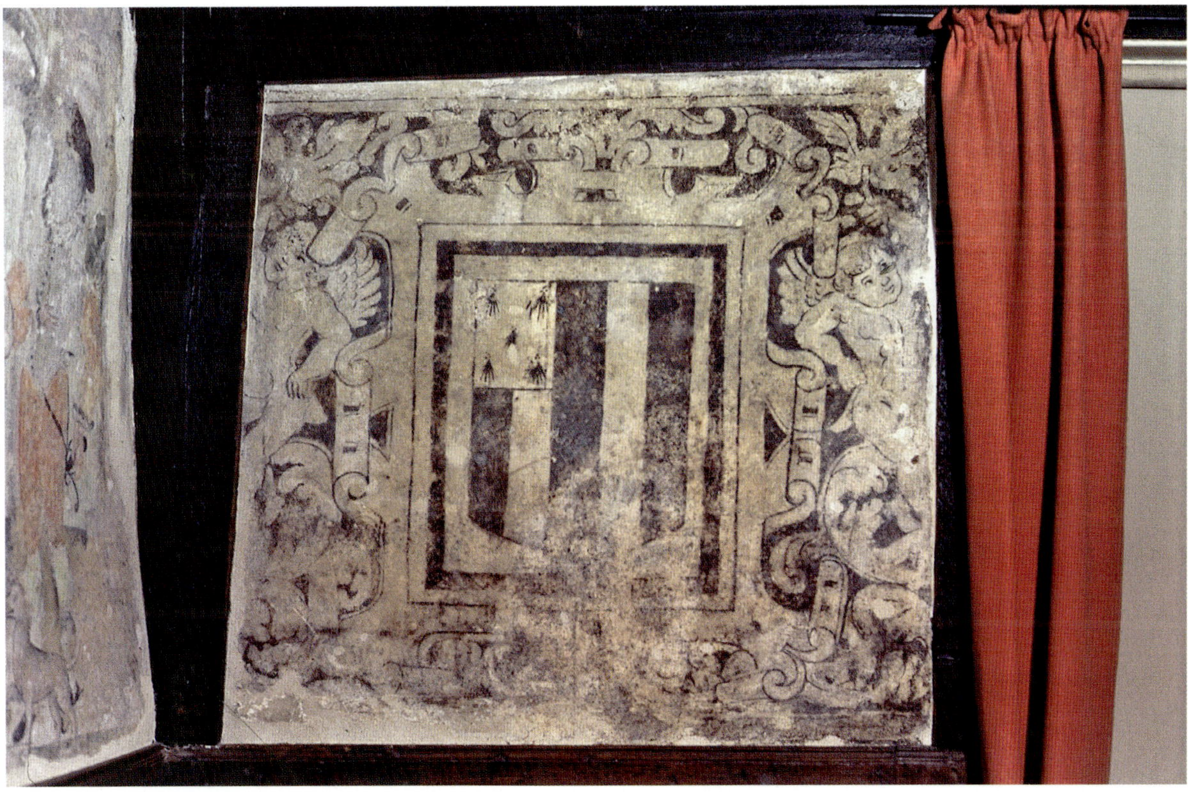

Figure 12 East wall (north end): the Newce arms abutting the painting of the Judgement of Solomon on the north wall. (The Newce arms are repeated, again in grisaille, on the south side of the window.) *(© J. Rutherfoord)*

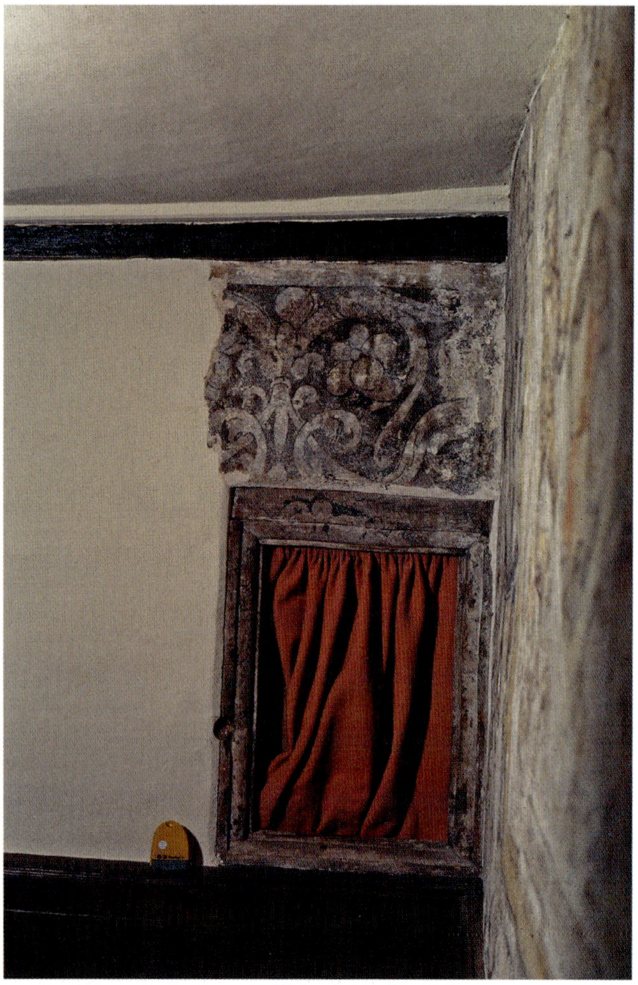

Figure 13 South wall (west end): remains of a bold decoration in grisaille above a small, internal window and continuing over the frame – uncovering almost complete. *(© J. Rutherfoord)*

have been quick to utilise opportunities for displaying them. The royal arms, on the opposite wall, are likely to have been painted at the same time and appear to be by the same hand. The *Judgement of Solomon* could have followed shortly afterwards, in readiness for the queen's visit to Hadham during her Progress of 1578. Despite its vivid colour and detail, it has the appearance of being by a less competent artist – as already mentioned, the draughtsmanship is crude compared with that of the royal arms (Figs 14 and 15).

The existence of paintings of this calibre and subject matter in this modest building was clearly connected to the ascending fortunes and local importance of the Newce family. By this period, they owned significant properties in and around Much Hadham and held official posts over several subsequent generations. (In 1572, Clement's son William built The Hall, a grand house only 92 metres (100 yards) or so north of The Forge, and in 1578, Clement's daughter Martha married Lawrence Washington, the Registrar of the High Court of Chancery.) When Clement Newce died, in 1579, in accordance with his instructions he was buried in the forenave of the parish church. A stone was to 'be laid upon the grave with a plate fixed thereon engraved with pictures of himself, his wife, and all his children'. The stone and brasses are still there.

Jean's project was a classic example of the interdependency of a private client's excitement, interest and pride, and the preservation of their paintings. The conservator's role in nurturing both is critical, especially on those occasions when they do not necessarily exactly coincide. Sometimes these situations can be provoked by an outsider, perhaps a 'helpful' party becoming too closely involved, and they can become quite undermining and difficult to handle. Indeed, there was more than one occasion when, in my absence, enthusiastic amateurs – friends who were "good with their hands" – were invited to 'have a go' at uncovering, with predictable results. In other situations, a satisfactory outcome, although perhaps

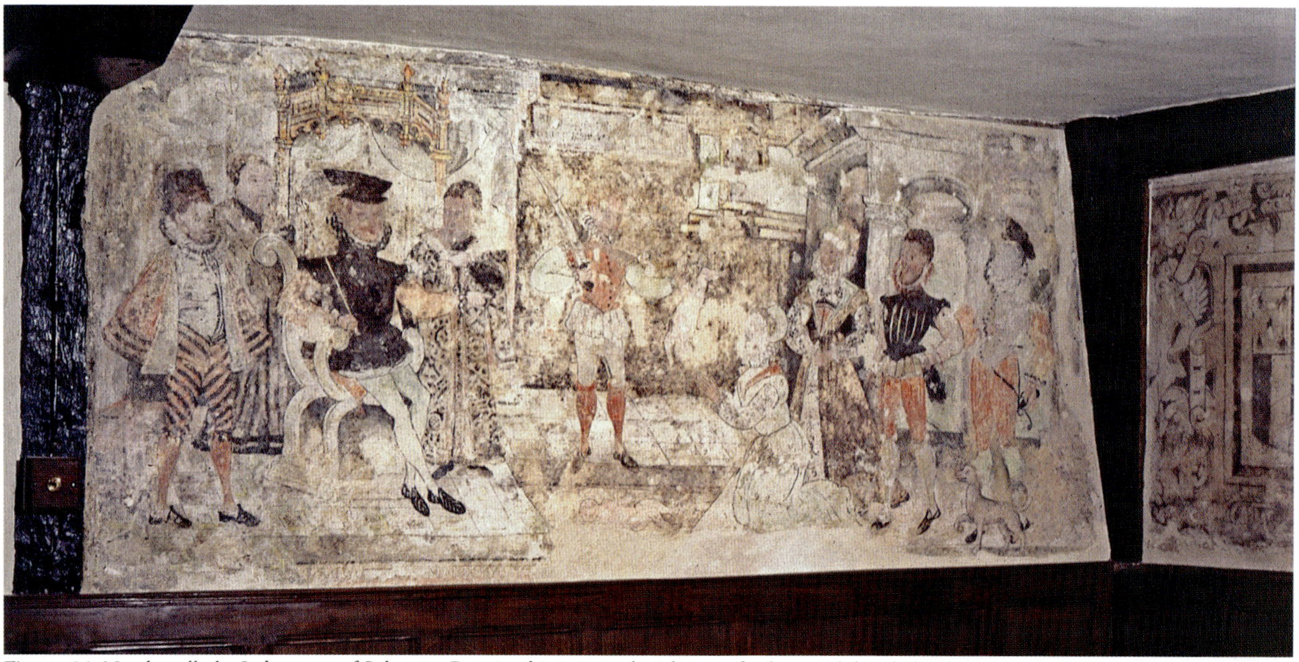

Figure 14 North wall: the Judgement of Solomon. Despite this painting's richness of colour and detail, the draughtsmanship is not as sophisticated as that of the painting on the west wall. *(© J. Rutherfoord)*

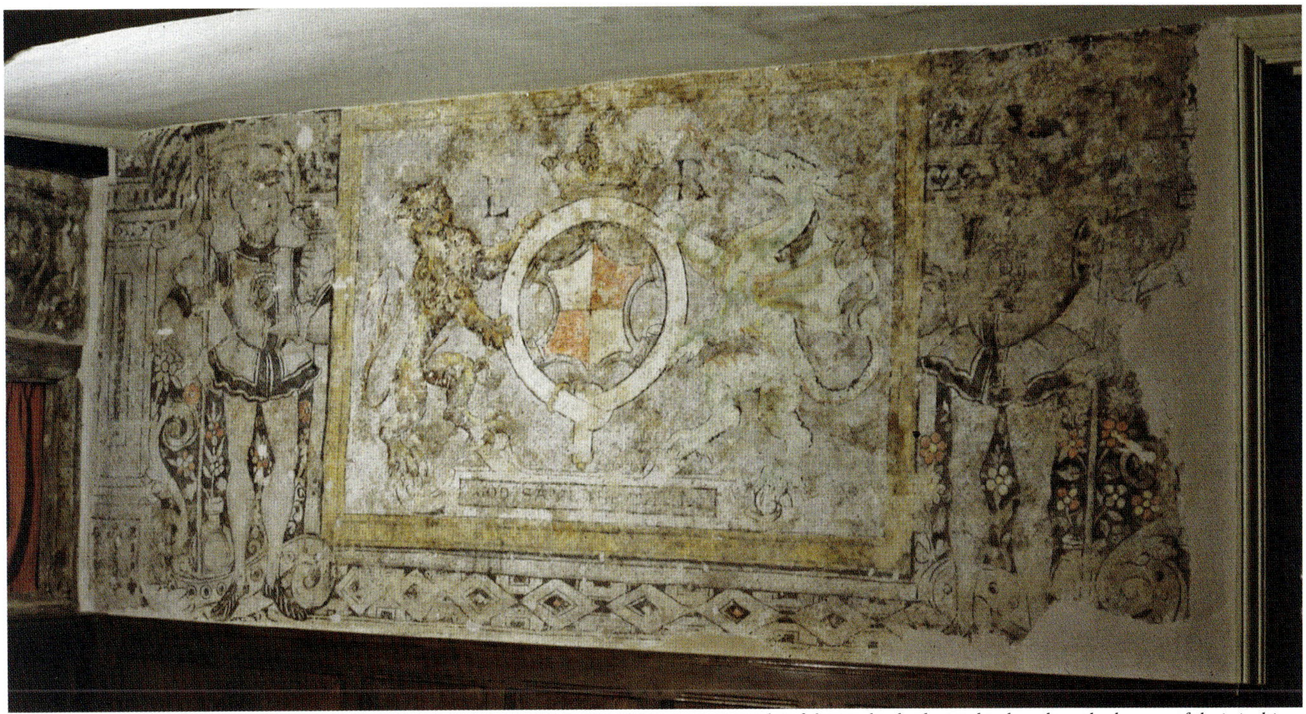

Figure 15 West wall: the royal arms flanked by guards carrying halberds. A rare example of the Tudor badge is displayed on the breast of their jerkins. Uncovering and treatment are not yet complete. *(© J. Rutherfoord)*

not perfect, can be achieved through compromise. Such a circumstance was presented by the evident structural instability of the internal side of the north wall.

Ideally, the structural interventions would have been undertaken in the early stages of the project, once the nature of the painting had been ascertained. However, these interventions were clearly going to create a big disruption and, quite understandably, Jean was not ready to take on the cost and stress of the upheaval before having more of the paintings revealed to justify the effort. As the uncovering of the *Judgement of Solomon* continued, the severe shocks that were being inflicted several times a day through the centre of the painting by the ill-fitting front door of the adjoining dwelling (the hall of the 'H') were a constant reminder that the structural problems would have to be addressed sooner or later. In January, 1995, it was agreed that a start should be made from the inside and that the external work should be tackled during the summer.

The involvement of the Hertfordshire Building Preservation Trust and the division of responsibility for external and internal work to the building presented additional complications for all parties. The Trust was in a difficult position between what Jean wanted to do within her lifetime and what it was able to do. It is the lot of the conservator and/or the architect (in this case both) to be the proverbial 'jam in the sandwich' and, with only a small budget available, Russ Craig (the architect acting on behalf of the Trust) gave his time free and organised an acceptable solution.

The year 1995 was to become the most significant year of the project for the most fundamental of reasons: Jean's health. As the months went by this was the cause of increasing concern and after a time breast cancer was diagnosed. Although, with treatment, her prognosis was apparently reasonably good, nothing of course was certain. But Jean was not inclined to discuss the matter: life was to continue as normal. Nevertheless, the pressure to draw the project to a conclusion was very much to the fore.

These problems had not yet manifested themselves when the pine dado boarding installed round the room by Jean's great-uncle in the early 20th century was removed from the north-east corner. The bottoms of the walls were found to be saturated and the bases of two of the studs in the north wall badly rotted. The back of 'modern' external render, applied over wire mesh, was visible and this render continued to the level of the dining room ceiling. The vibration this intervention would have caused had undoubtedly contributed to the instability of the wall. A large section of wattle and daub had dislodged and was pushing heavily against studs and laths at the east end of the north wall in the area where they were at their weakest (Fig. 16). In the middle of the *Judgement of Solomon*, at the top, there is a pronounced bulge in the plaster caused by an old repair: the filling had been pushed into the cavity with such enthusiasm that it had forced the laths and plaster apart and split the lath. With the combination of the detachment of the plaster from the laths, the detachment of the laths from the studs – particularly in the north-east corner – and the rotting of the studs at their base, it was not surprising the wall was unstable.

Repairs to stabilise the timber frame were governed by the need to avoid vibration. In certain areas, new oak was inserted but in others (such as the bases of the studs) resin bonding and stainless-steel dowels were used.[2] Facing tissue, foam sponge and board were used to protect the painting from the inside. The external render was then removed by the contractor, a rudimentary, external porch was constructed and – following repairs to the timber frame – the laths and plaster support were stabilised from the outside (Fig. 17). This work coincided with appalling summer weather conditions and the roof gutters above the porch overflowed in torrents.[3]

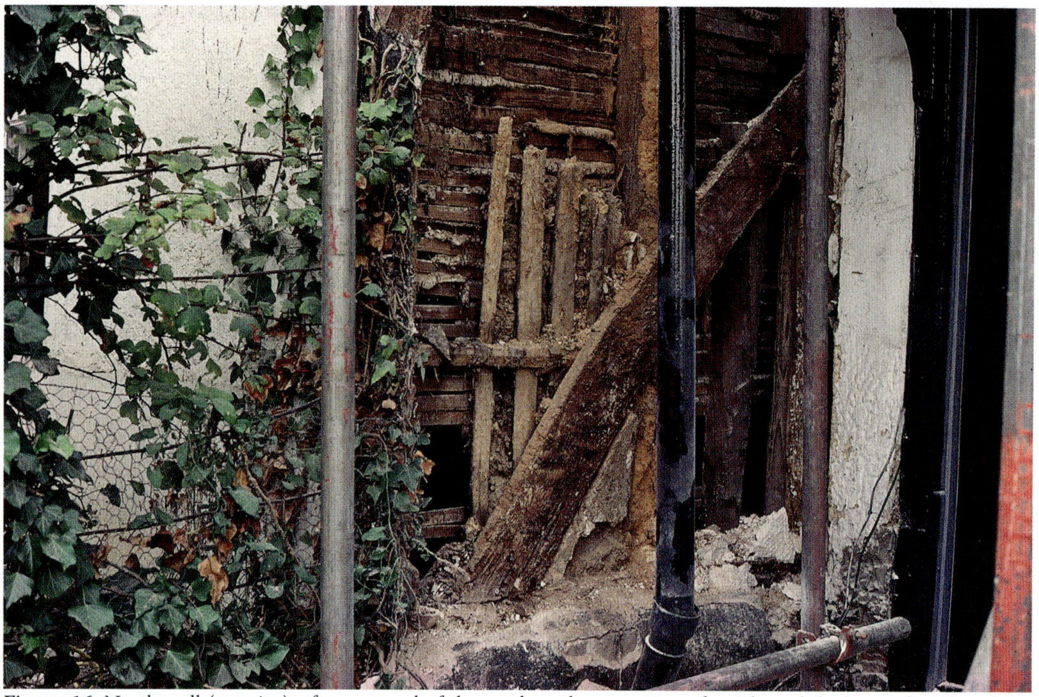

Figure 16 North wall (exterior): after removal of the render, a large section of wattle and daub was found pushing heavily against studs and laths in the area where they were at their weakest. *(© J. Rutherfoord)*

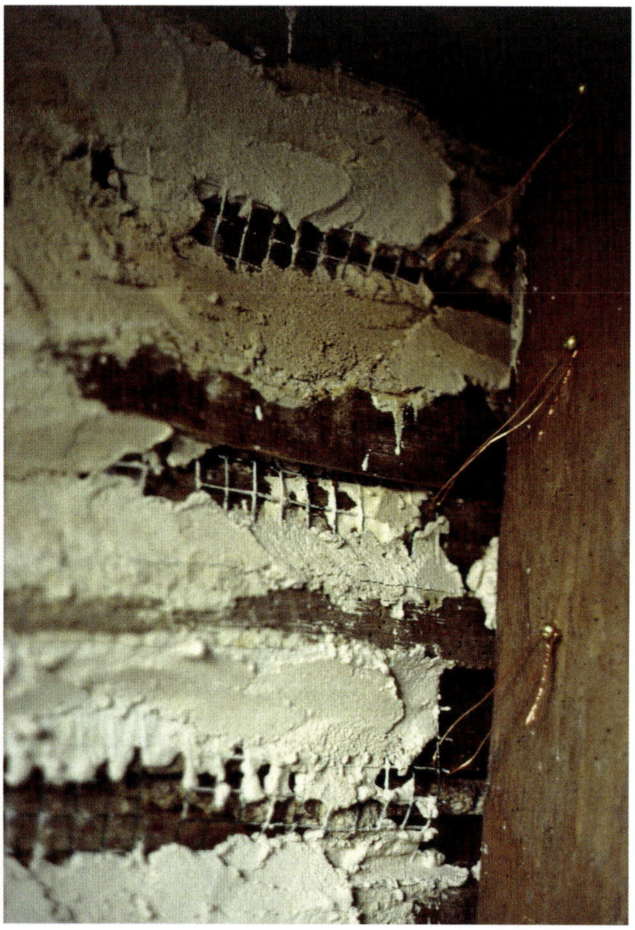

Figure 17 North wall, stabilised from the outside. Strips of plastic-coated wire mesh were woven through the gaps between the plaster and the laths. These were then grouted and bonded in with a thick slurry of slaked lime putty and fine, washed sand. Where laths had broken away from the studs, copper wire was looped round the lath (and through the wire mesh) and secured to the stud with a brass screw. *(© J. Rutherfoord)*

Strips of plastic-coated wire mesh were woven vertically through the gaps between the plaster and the laths. These were then grouted and bonded in with a thick slurry of slaked lime putty and fine, washed sand. Where the laths had broken away from the studs, a back-up mechanism was introduced: copper wire was looped round the lath and secured to the stud with a brass screw. The contractor was subsequently re-engaged to replace the external surface using breather paper, stainless-steel lath and lime mortar render.

Work continued indoors on the paintings until shortly before Christmas 1995. During the following year, while Jean was mastering her health problems, replica oak panelling matching the original pieces that have survived on the east wall was made and instated.[4] By the beginning of January, 1997, Jean was feeling well enough to have some further work carried out on the paintings. The minimum was done to achieve the maximum effect – a little more uncovering and some 'temporary' fillings and toning out – so that the work could be drawn to a conclusion for her and she could enjoy her paintings in peace (Fig. 18). Jean died nearly two years later, in December, 1999.

Since Jean's death, in addition to the various building repairs, an environmental assessment has been undertaken. During 2003, a climate-control system was installed and a policy was drawn up for the continued maintenance and care of the buildings and the paintings. The last stages of the 'hands-on' treatment of the paintings had to be curtailed but the Trust is making arrangements for this work to be completed, hopefully in the near future.

Jean would undoubtedly be thrilled by and very proud of what the Trust has already achieved with her legacy, largely as a result of the dedicated effort of Cristina Harrison, curator of The Forge Museum. The museum has set up a variety of educational initiatives and principal amongst these are the

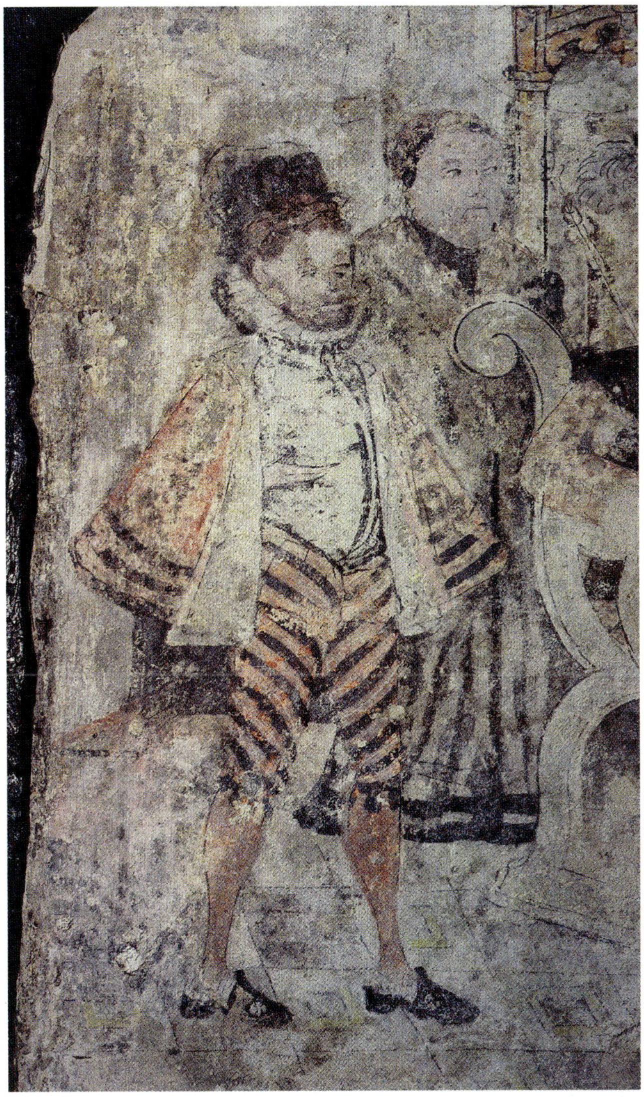

Figure 18 North wall (west end): two of Solomon's courtiers. The flamboyantly dressed gentleman in the foreground was Jean Page's favourite figure. *(© J. Rutherfoord)*

opportunities provided for children, especially of primary-school age. In partnership with the Hertfordshire Archives and Library Service, The Forge Museum now runs a project offering to schools a Tudor Day that is rapidly becoming very popular and in which the wall paintings play a key role. The Heritage Lottery Fund and East Hertfordshire Council have also funded a Learning Links project to develop Tudor activities, arts and crafts. An application to the Heritage Lottery Fund has recently been made to fund the development of the museum as a regional resource for the study of Tudor history and wall paintings.

To lighten the stresses and strains of a dim day in 1995, Jean and I composed a short rhyme together:

Where horses were shod
There's also a treasure
A painting's uncovered
To give the World pleasure.

When you contribute
You will pay tribute
To the care of the Pages
Who've preserved it for ages.

Acknowledgements

I should like to thank Ann Ballantyne for her continued interest and support and for her invaluable help on two special occasions during the last few months of work. I am grateful to Frances Rutherfoord for her suggestions and her assistance with proof-reading of this paper and to Stephanie Teeken for her help with the final documentation of photographs.

Notes

1. Carried out by UCL Painting Analysis Ltd.
2. This work was carried out by a specialist contractor.
3. Since 2000, the roof and rainwater goods have all been repaired, as has the drainage system beneath the house.
4. By Joe Dawes.

The author

Jane Rutherfoord completed three years' training in the conservation of easel paintings with Professor Gori in Florence. After returning to England in 1978 she worked as assistant to Anna Hulbert, Pauline Plummer and Dr Clive Rouse in the conservation of architectural polychromy and wall paintings. The most notable of these projects was the polychromed roof bosses of Exeter Cathedral. In 1980 she was given an internship to study polychromy and wall paintings at the Bayerisches Landesamt für Denkmalpflege, Munich, under Dr Karl Ludwig Dasser. Later that year she was awarded scholarships by the Crafts Council of Great Britain and the Austrian Ministry of Science and Research to study the conservation of wall paintings and polychromed sculpture in the care of the State Departments for Conservation in Vienna, under Dr Manfred Koller. Since 1982 Jane has run her own practice for the conservation of easel paintings and wall paintings and has worked on a wide variety of wall paintings and architectural polychromy in English and foreign churches and secular buildings. Clients include museums, charitable trusts, schools, colleges, churches, stately homes and private collections.

The public and private face of English Baroque wall painting: Milgate House, Kent and the Royal Hospital, Chelsea

Caroline Babington and Richard Pelter

Introduction

In the waning decades of the 17th century, Baroque wall paintings were the height of fashion. Charles II's passion for the artform led to the appointment of Antonio Verrio as his chief artist, and to murals being painted in all the grandest houses. A small group of continental painters dominated the field, of whom Verrio, Laguerre and Lanscroon are perhaps the best known. Perhaps reflecting the turbulent political climate, however, it did not take long for fashions to change. The early 18th-century paintings at Milgate House are one of the last examples of the British Baroque.

Sadly, relatively few wall paintings of this period survive in Britain, and even fewer are to be found in anything like their original condition (see paper by J. Davies, pp. 59–67). While in part this is due to the usual vulnerability of mural art, it is also because, once out of fashion, British Baroque wall paintings were entirely eclipsed, and no one hesitated to cover them over or to restore them crudely. The rarity of well-preserved Baroque wall paintings makes the Chelsea and Milgate examples particularly significant. Recent conservations of the two schemes, by the International Fine Art Conservation Studios (IFACS), have given an excellent opportunity to compare their iconographies, techniques and conditions. Apart from the obvious technical similarities and the rich use of symbolism typical of the Baroque period, the two schemes would at first appear to have little in common. The Chelsea painting is very public, dominating the west wall of Christopher Wren's Royal Hospital Dining Hall. Commissioned by Lord Ranelagh in the late 1680s to celebrate the Restoration, the painting is large – some 7.5m long by 4.5m high – and an unequivocal depiction of the supreme status of King Charles II. By contrast Milgate, near Maidstone in Kent, is a private house dating back to the late medieval period. It was refurbished in the early 18th century and the paintings are likely to be part of this modernisation. The scheme is painted over the walls and ceiling of the main staircase, and depicts scenes of classical mythology. Painted 20 or even 30 years apart, the schemes do however share one special feature: although previously attributed to prominent continental artists, they have both recently been shown to be substantially the work of English painters.

Relatively little research on this period has been published. Of the existing literature, perhaps the best examples are Croft-Murray's two volumes on decorative painting in England (1962 and 1970), and Whinney and Millar's book on English art of the 17th and early 18th centuries (1957). While both authors do refer to native artists, however, inevitably their focus is on the work of the continentals.

The Chelsea and Milgate schemes

The Royal Hospital, Chelsea

The Royal Hospital, Chelsea wall painting centres around an equestrian portrait of Charles II (Fig. 1; see also Fig. 5, p. 57). An inscription on an escutcheon at the foot of the painting reads:

Carolo Secundo
Regi Optimo Hujus Hofpitti
Fundatori
Dominique fuo Clementillimo
Ricardus Jones Comes de Ranelagh
Hanc Tabulum Pofuit

(Richard Jones Count of Ranelagh put up this painting to King Charles II, most merciful lord and founder of this hospital)

The symbolism is bold and theatrical. Billowing curtains are pulled back to reveal the mounted Charles in all his finery, surrounded by allegorical figures set against a backdrop of the hospital itself (Fig. 2). On the lower left is *Father Thames*, reclining on yellow draperies, with attendant figures and gigantic seashells (since the scallop shell is the symbol of St James, this may be a reference to Charles' son, the future James II).

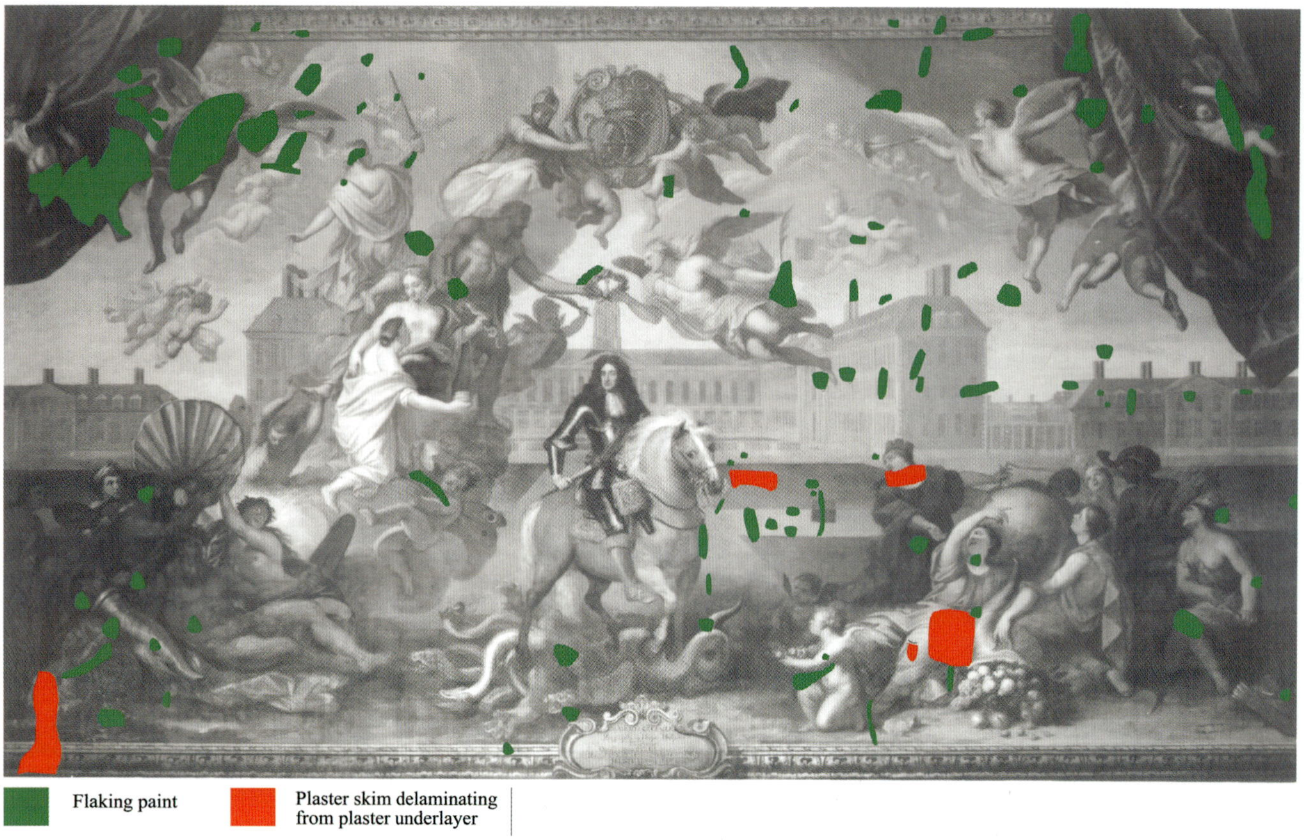

Figure 1 The Royal Hospital Chelsea, London: documentation of the wall painting of Charles II, showing aspects of condition before conservation, July 2002. *(© IFACS)*

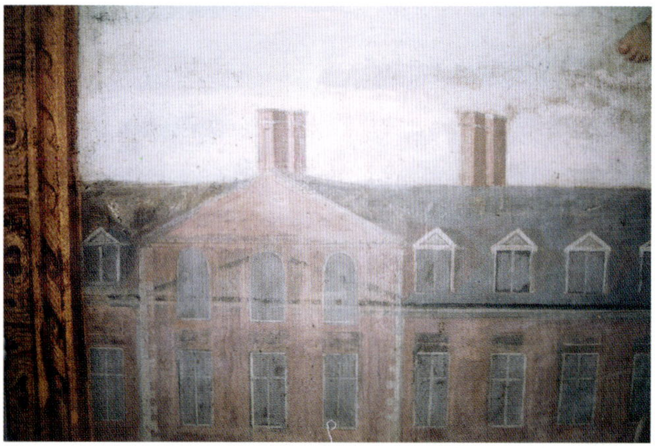

Figure 2 The Royal Hospital Chelsea, London: detail of architecture, left side of the painting of Charles II, showing the black underdrawing and subsequent changes to the building. *(© IFACS)*

Thames holds a spade: a rather unexpected implement that may refer to the relationship between the irrigation of the hospital grounds and the river. To the right, figures represent the four corners of the globe. Black-skinned *Africa* wears an elephant's trunk headdress, and *America* wears feathers and bears a bow. *Europe*, holding a cornucopia of fruit and flowers, points to her location on the globe. The fourth figure is harder to interpret – it is holding what appears to be a set square – but must represent Asia. Heavenly figures place a laurel wreath on the king's head, and the royal crown is painted above. The symbolism is clear: Charles II as divinely appointed ruler of land and sea.

To either side, the north and south walls are decorated with painted panels depicting symmetrical arrays of small arms (Fig. 3). These imitate the fashionable arrangements by 17th-century gunsmith John Harris, examples of which can be found at the Tower of London, Whitehall, Hampton Court and Windsor, among other important sites.[1] These side panels are probably not contemporary with the west wall painting: they are substantially overpainted and overlie replastered window recesses. An 1810 Rowlandson watercolour of the Dining Hall shows figurative scenes instead, and analysis of a sample taken from the painted curtains at the top left of the north wall reveals multiple layers of paint, including at least one repainting (Fig. 4). Croft-Murray notes that in such a context it would in fact be more usual to show classical trophies or statues in niches. The ground and priming do appear to match those of the main painting, so more detailed analysis could perhaps clarify the situation.

The Dining Hall paintings have traditionally been attributed to Antonio Verrio (1639–1707). Originally from Lecce in Italy, Verrio had an enormous impact on the English art scene; Alexander Pope even immortalised him in verse. Visiting France, he was inspired by Versailles, in particular the work of Le Brun. It was while Verrio was working at the French court in the 1670s that the English ambassador, Ralph Montagu, persuaded him to travel to Britain. With the Restoration there had been a rash of building work for the court and the aristocracy, and decoration was needed to match. Verrio's first commission – for a townhouse at St James' – immediately caught the eye of the king and Charles II became his greatest patron, commissioning vast schemes for the Windsor apartments redesigned by Hugh May. In 1684 Verrio succeeded Sir Peter Lely as the king's first and chief painter, with an annual salary of £200. He did not work exclusively for Charles: the great houses of Chatsworth and Burghley were also painted by him. He weathered the turbulent politics around him with aplomb, going on to paint at both Windsor and Hampton Court for three subsequent monarchs. His English patrons were entranced by the extravagance and flamboyance of his work, enjoying his use of mythology and symbols. The energy and theatricality of Verrio's style must have been very welcome after the bleak years of the Commonwealth.

How much of the Chelsea painting is actually by Verrio is debatable. Two payments are recorded: the first to Verrio for £210 15s in 1688, the second to Henry Cooke for £295 in 1690.[2] These figures suggest that Verrio was responsible for much less than half the work: the Windsor commission (admittedly for 14 rooms) earned him £2,430, an annual pension of £200 and various gifts,[3] and in 1684 he had been paid £1,050 for the King's Chapel and £1,250 for St George's Hall. The 1688 date equally suggests a limited input from Verrio, since from the late 1680s until 1700 he was working almost exclusively at Burghley. Significantly, Verrio did not sign the painting, whereas Cooke very visibly did: *H.cooke pinxit* can be found on a quiver in the lower right corner. During conservation work in September 2004, another signature was discovered that had not previously been noted. On a wing of a cherub to the right of the central crest, several metres from ground level and apparently deliberately inconspicuous, the signature

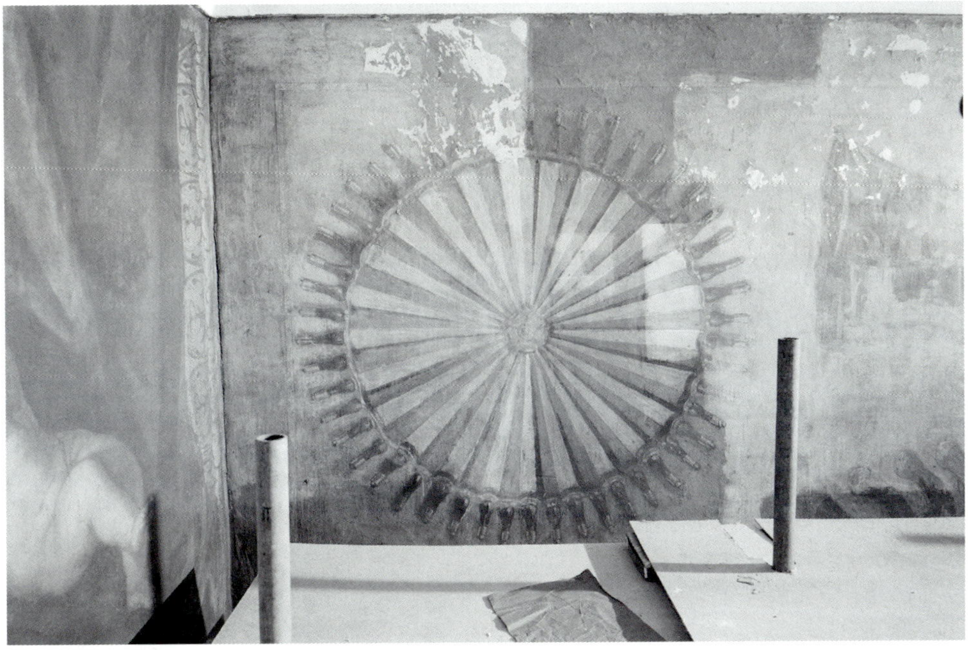

Figure 3 The Royal Hospital Chelsea, London: late 17th-century decorative panel on the north wall. *(© Crown copyright. NMR)*

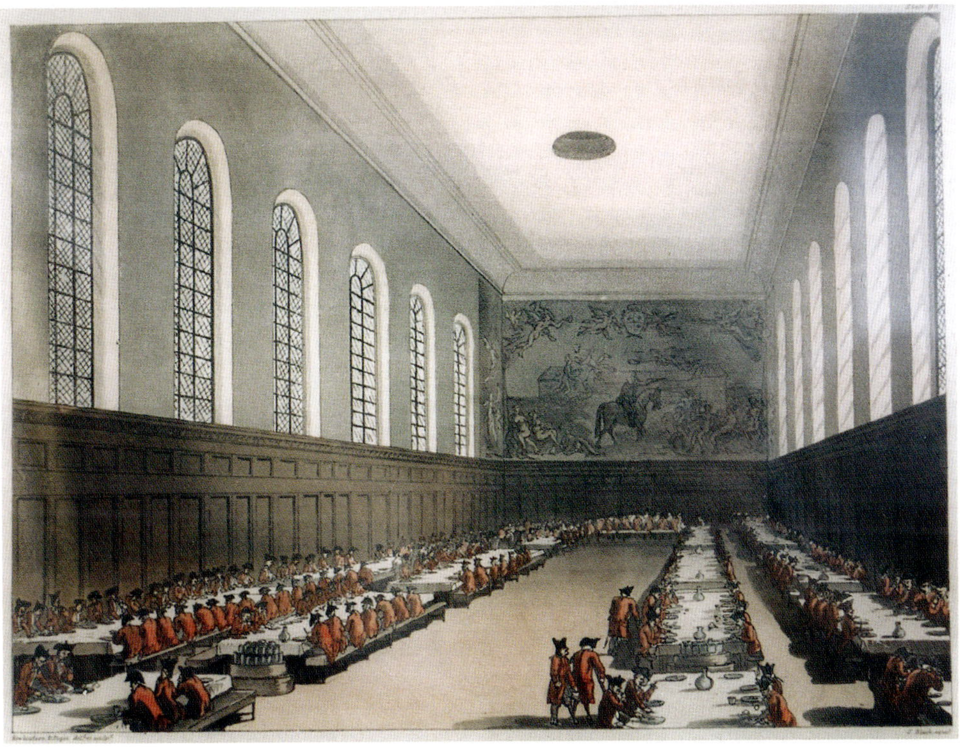

Figure 4 The Royal Hospital Chelsea, London: Rowlandson watercolour of the dining hall, 1810. *(© IFACS, reproduced by kind permission of the Royal Hospital Chelsea)*

appears to read *Lanscroon*. Lanscroon certainly worked as Verrio's assistant, and the dates fit perfectly. How much of the Chelsea painting is the work of Lanscroon rather than Verrio himself? As with so many Baroque wall paintings, later restoration and crude repainting make stylistic assessment difficult.

Why Verrio and his team failed to complete the Royal Hospital painting is not known. Henry Cooke (c.1642–1700), who took over, was a popular society figure and a rather colourful character. His early career may have been as a portrait painter. Buckeridge, his earliest biographer, records several easel paintings and portraits by him. Indicted for murder after a fight over the woman who was to become his wife, he spent more than 14 years in exile in Italy. Studying and working in Rome, he became a pupil of Salvator Rosa, and so ironically his exile provided the groundwork for his later success: on returning to England in 1688 he was commissioned by William III to repair Raphael's cartoons, which was an extraordinary leap in status. Cooke lived for around five years with Theodore Russel, the nephew of Cornelius Johnson and copyist of Van Dyck. He became famous as a mural painter, working mostly in London's better houses. Seven schemes are recorded as having been painted by Cooke, though other than Chelsea only one survives, and this has been transferred from its original location.

In contrast to Verrio, very little has been written on Cooke, and some of the available information conflicts. Few if any other homegrown mural painters are documented for this period, the vast majority of artists having been lured over from Holland, France and Italy by wealthy English patrons. Perhaps the dearth of artistic activity during the Commonwealth had so disrupted training and apprenticeship that the required skills were rare. Working as a mural painter certainly required high investment, since the artist needed a small army of assistants.

Milgate House, Bearsted, Kent

The scheme at Milgate House is also ambitious, covering the ceiling and walls of a substantial staircase with scenes from classical mythology. Prior to conservation by IFACS in 2002, substantial parts of the painting were not visible, so treatment gave the first opportunity for a serious study of the iconography.[4] Mythological subjects set within an architectural framework, with grisaille decoration at the base, are very typical of Baroque paintings. Here, however, there are some unusual elements, and it seems likely that the Milgate scheme was a very personal one, perhaps chosen to commemorate an important family event – in common with similar paintings at Bolsover Castle in Derbyshire, this was most probably a wedding.[5]

The ceiling painting

Until part of the modern ceiling was removed during the recent conservation, the ceiling painting had been thought to be an *Assembly of the Olympians*: Jupiter was present, identified by an eagle, alongside Juno (with peacock and crown), and Neptune (Fig. 5). In fact, the subject is a much more popular one: the discovery of Venus and Mars *in fragrante delicto*, as

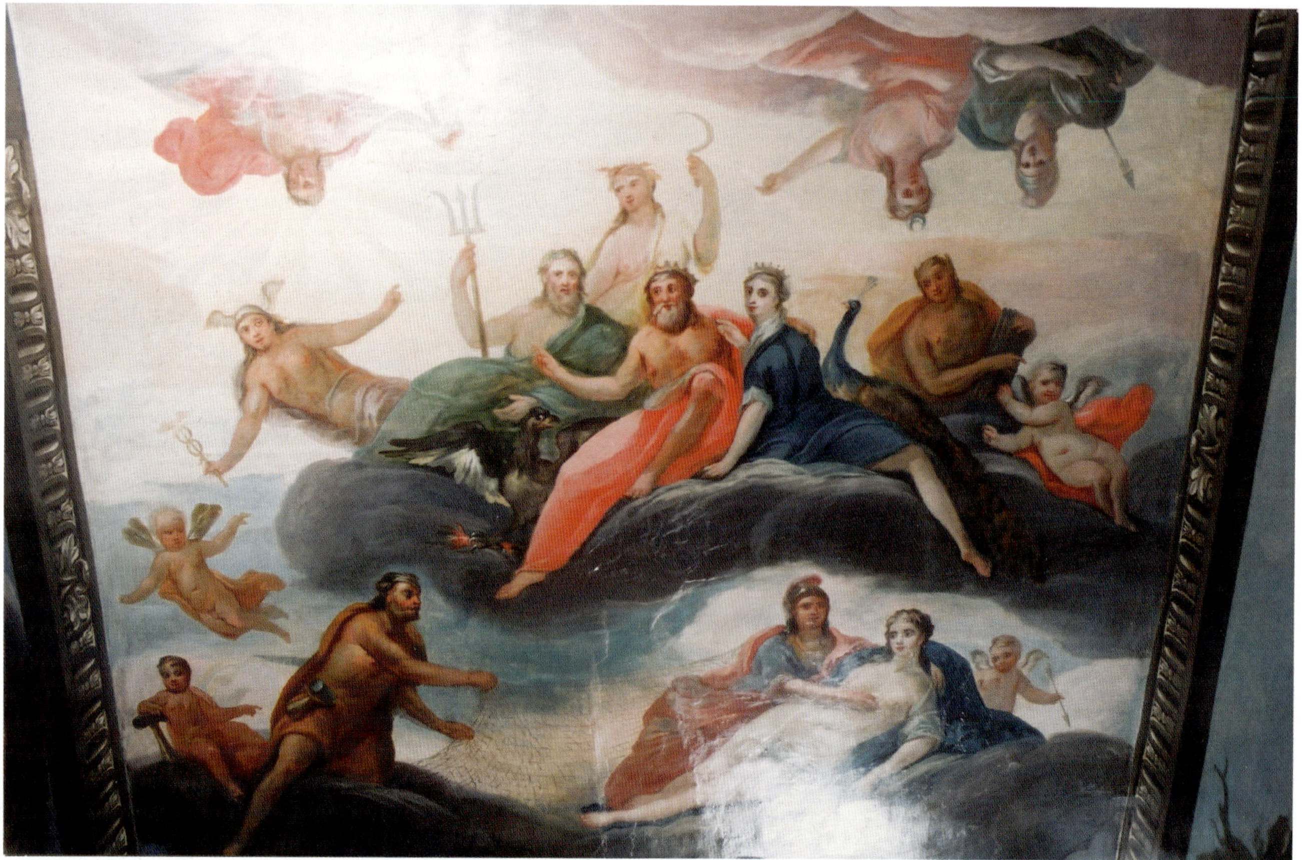

Figure 5 Milgate House, Bearsted, Kent: *The Assembly of the Gods* ceiling, viewed south to north (after conservation). *(© E. Schneider/IFACS, reproduced by kind permission of the Augustan Trust)*

described by Ovid in his *Metamorphoses* and *Ars Amatoria.* Verrio himself painted this story for the Heaven Room at Burghley House. Vulcan is throwing his net to capture the lovers and we can identify Ceres (crowned with a sheaf of corn, and holding a sickle), Apollo with his lyre and Mercury (with winged helmet and caduceus). The figure to Juno's right may be Pan with his pipes, or possibly Pluto. Minerva (helmeted, with shield and spear) sits beside Diana the moon goddess.

Staircase walls

The lower areas of the east, south and west walls were all uncovered during conservation. The grisaille decoration revealed is a feature typical of Baroque schemes. The west wall is covered with garlands; on the south wall we find Mercury and Minerva shown as statues in masonry niches. The east wall is rather more unusual. Two panels are set in fictive masonry, the first (as one climbs the stairs) containing a winged female figure with a palette and a mahl stick, a trumpet and a small relief sculpture of a man holding a club, perhaps Hercules, another Olympian. A cherub, holding what may be a quill, gazes left. The palette has been signed (the signature is discussed below), and the panel probably depicts the creative arts, though in an uncommon manner. The second panel is simpler, with an arrangement of weapons and a shield. Fragments of a dark grey paint have been found beneath pine panelling in the entrance hall, under the architrave of the present-day kitchen entrance. This suggests that the grisaille decoration might originally have extended into the hall.[6]

South wall

The arms of the Cage family, owners of Milgate House, are painted above the central window of the south wall. Figures on balconies to either side have not yet been identified: there are four female figures to the left and four male figures to the right (Fig. 6).

West wall

On the west wall, above the doorway on the left, is a small panel showing Apollo flaying Marsyas, hanging by his wrists from a tree. There is a female bust in the foreground but the significance of this is unclear. Prior to conservation, the female figures in the main scene had been variously identified: ideas included *Geometry* (holding a globe), *Pomona* (holding an apple), and *Industry* (seated next to a beehive). It is far more likely that the scene depicts *The Judgement of Paris,* a subject perfectly in keeping with the Ovidian ceiling. Paris, the Trojan prince, must award a golden apple inscribed 'to the fairest' to one of three goddesses, Venus, Minerva, or Juno (Fig. 7).[7]

East wall

The east wall scene – an armoured hero on a white horse with accompanying soldiers hurrying towards a group of women – was previously identified as the sacrifice of Iphigenia by Agamemnon. In the context of the new identifications of the ceiling and west wall paintings, this is probably an *Abduction of Helen* (Fig. 8).

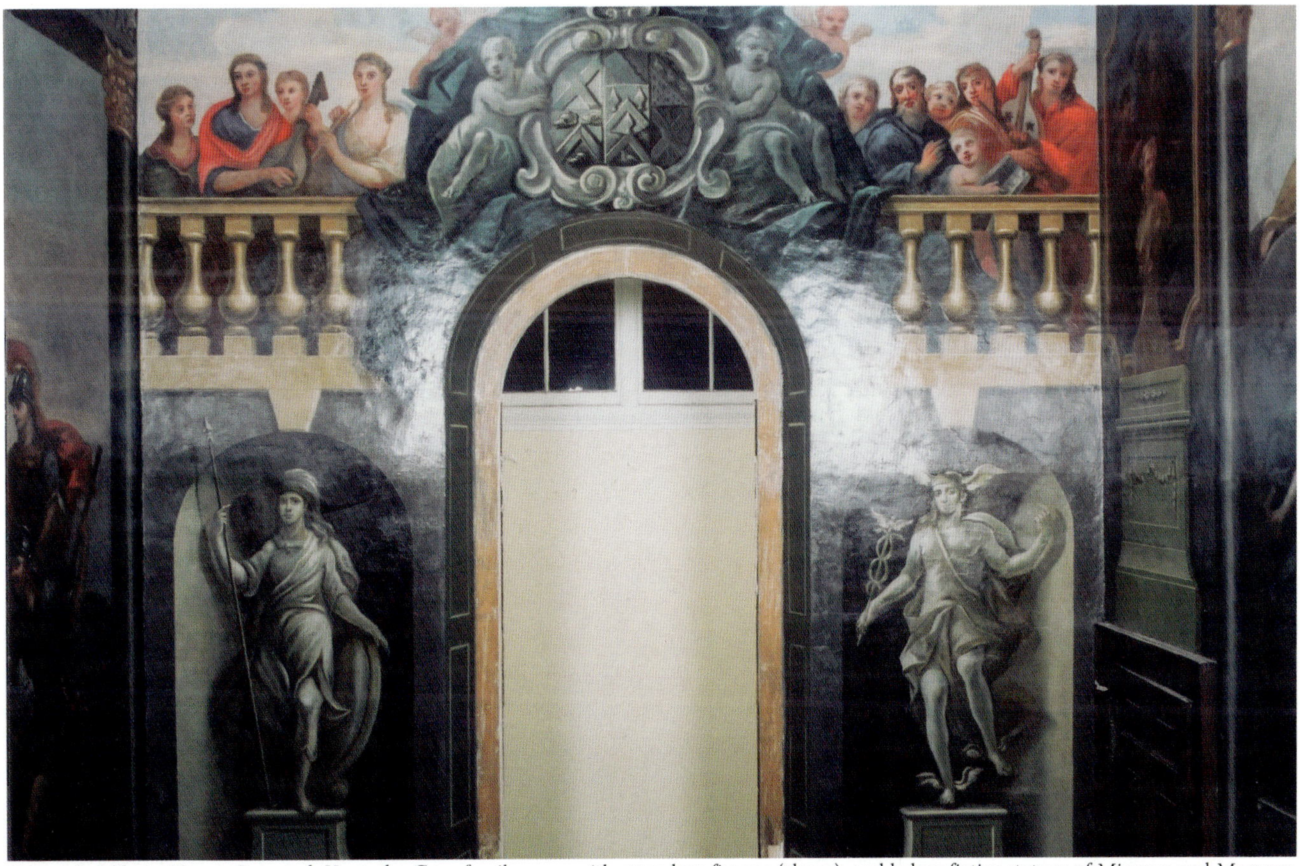

Figure 6 Milgate House, Bearsted, Kent: the Cage family arms with attendant figures (above), and below fictive statues of Minerva and Mercury. General view of the south wall after conservation. *(© E. Schneider/IFACS, reproduced by kind permission of the Augustan Trust)*

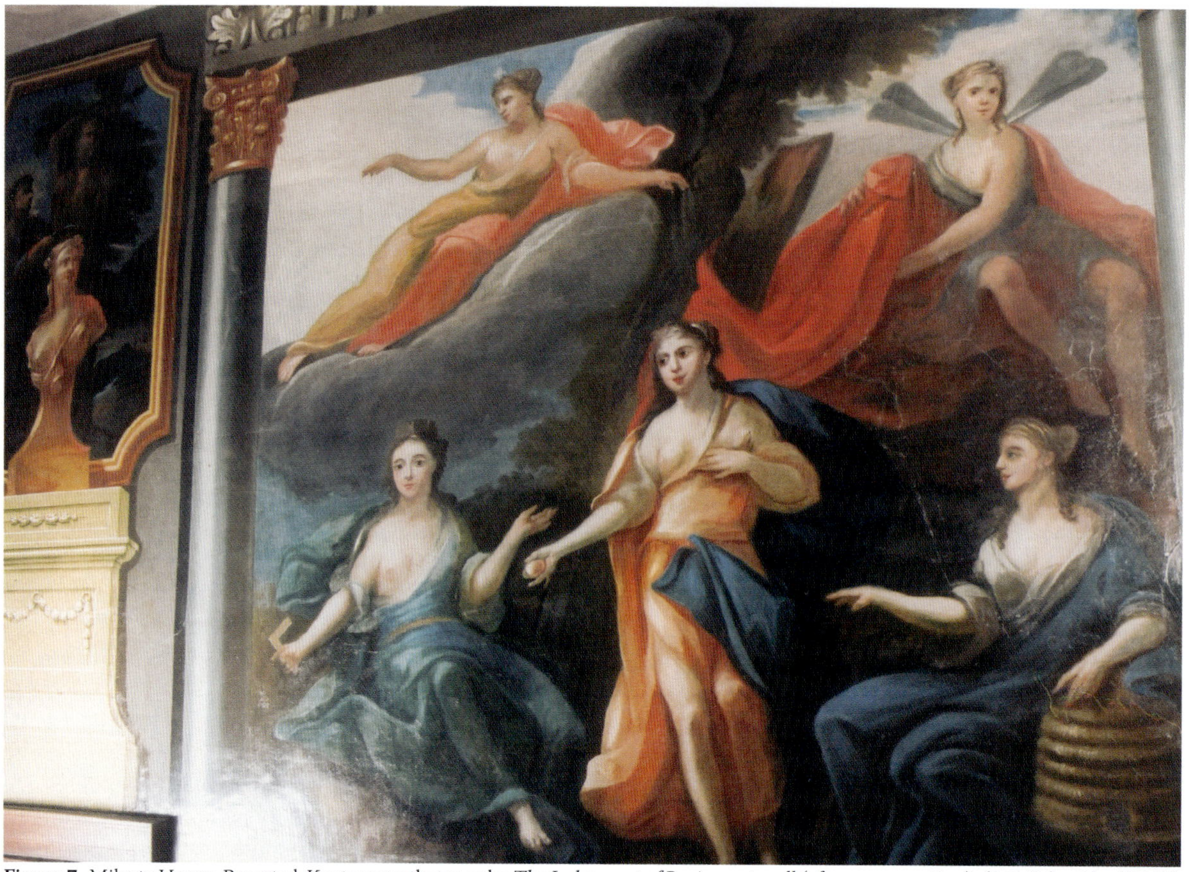

Figure 7 Milgate House, Bearsted, Kent: scene that may be *The Judgement of Paris*, west wall (after conservation). *(© E. Schneider/IFACS, reproduced by kind permission of the Augustan Trust)*

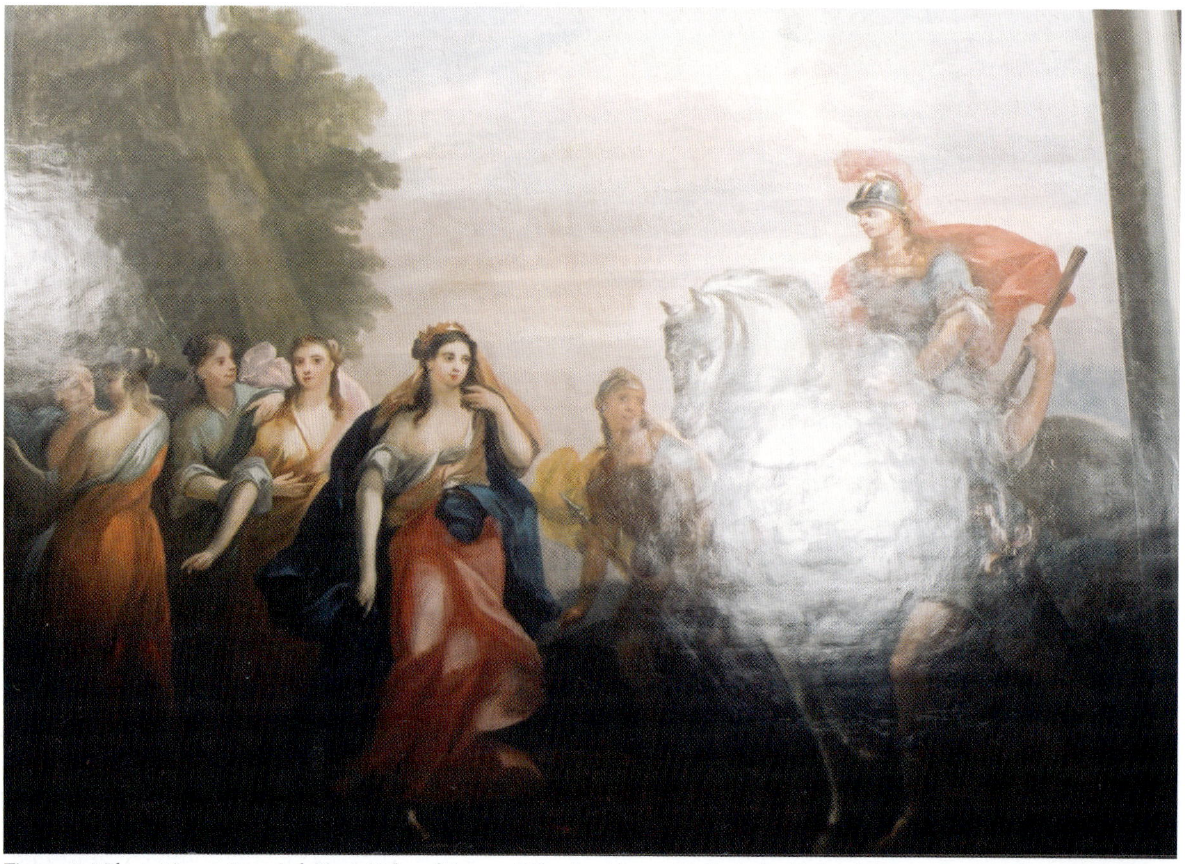

Figure 8 Milgate House, Bearsted, Kent: *Helen of Troy and Handmaidens, with Paris the Trojan Prince*, east wall (after conservation). The unfortunate glare is a result of the impact of previous varnishing of the painting, a problem common to many restored Baroque wall paintings (see paper by J. Davies, pp. 59–67) *(© E. Schneider/IFACS, reproduced by kind permission of the Augustan Trust)*

History of the Milgate paintings

A marriage has been suggested as the reason for the commissioning of the wall paintings at Milgate. The brief published references to the paintings date them variously to 1695 (Croft-Murray 1970) and 1710 (Newman 1969). The best evidence that Newman's dating is correct is provided by the architecture. The staircase scheme is clearly coeval with the early Georgian north front of the house, and both features date from the aforementioned refurbishment. John Watts' drawing of the north front, on the base of an estate map dating to 1707, shows the older Tudor building (Fig. 9). Unfortunately, the parish registers are very badly damaged for this period, so do not provide us with information on the family that might help confirm dates.

For many years the Milgate paintings were heavily obscured by thick discoloured varnish, dirt and poor quality overpaint. Croft-Murray observed they were 'not documented as by Lanscroon, but near enough in style to warrant attribution to him'.[8] Newman recorded Pauline Plummer's comments that they are 'à la Verrio or Laguerre, but disappointingly crude'.[9] Now that conservation has dramatically improved the appearance of the paintings (and incidentally revealed a signature), we can see an artist working in a very distinctive and personal style. Faces are characterised by powerful, rather deepset eyes, and if the figure modelling is occasionally weak, and the hands loosely drawn, still the overall impression is of a coherent, confidently painted scheme. It should also be stressed that some of the subtlety of the work has been destroyed by the crude early restorations.

The signature proved rather difficult to decipher, but an expert in early lettering confirmed that *Robert Hawker* or *Robert Harker* are the most likely readings (Fig. 10). Published lists of artists reveal no exact matches.[10] Since Robert Hawker/Harker was not recorded by Vertue or by Horace Walpole, we know he cannot have been at the forefront of the artistic world.[11] Nevertheless the Milgate artist was no amateur, and it seems unlikely that this was a one-off scheme. Expensive and requiring a good deal of technical knowledge, mural paintings by necessity demanded teams of specialist assistants. Verrio, for example, had a dozen or more people working for him, each a specialist in grinding pigments, applying priming layers or mapping out architectural elements. Possibly there was a family firm of artists named Hawker.

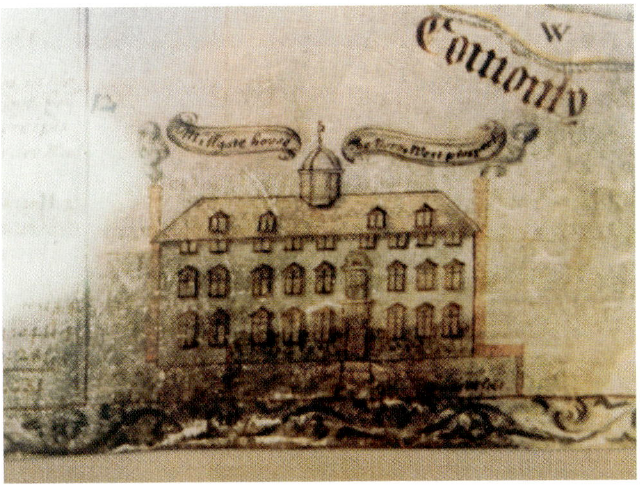

Figure 9 Milgate House, Bearsted, Kent: detail from the 1707 estate map for William Cage by John Watt of Thurnham showing Milgate House prior to its rebuilding in the early 18th century. *(© IFACS, reproduced by kind permission of the Augustan Trust)*

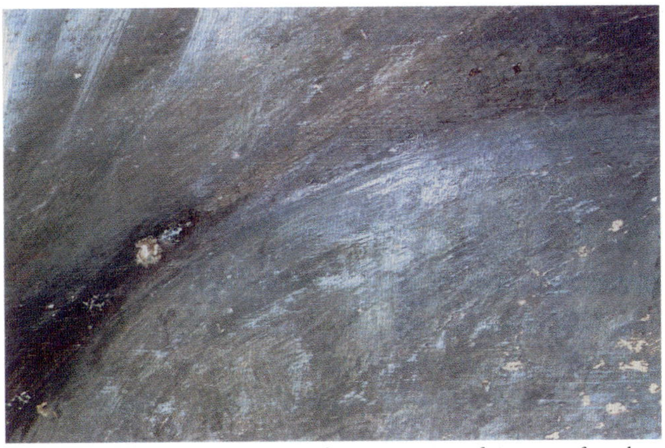

Figure 10 Milgate House, Bearsted, Kent: tracing of signature found on the painted palette on the east wall which may read 'Robert Hawker'. *(© IFACS, reproduced by kind permission of the Augustan Trust)*

Technique of the Milgate paintings

Although little has been published on the history of English Baroque wall painting, some excellent studies on technique have recently appeared.[12] Jane Davies describes the Baroque wall painters as a technically coherent group,[13] with schemes built up of layers of oil paint applied over oil-rich and sparsely pigmented 'sealant' layers brushed onto the plaster surface. Most now have in addition an overlying varnish. They are often characterised by areas of vivid colour, arising from the use of pigments such as orpiment, realgar, lead-tin yellow, vermilion and ultramarine. These were applied pure, in thick layers, with form being created through the layering of colours and glazes.

During the IFACS conservation programme, the technique of the Milgate House paintings was studied. They seem to fit with the working practice described by Davies, the layer structure having a sealant, a preparatory layer, then one or two paint layers. Pigments are simple, with no expensive blues: the blue is smalt, far cheaper than the ultramarine and azurite favoured by artists such as Verrio, Laguerre and Lanscroon. Other pigments include red and white lead, vermilion, copper green, green earth, ochre and black.

Conservation of the Chelsea and Milgate schemes

The conservation of the Chelsea and the Milgate schemes were both large undertakings, requiring teams of specialist conservators. The conservation at Chelsea was the more straightforward. The paintings had been restored twice in the past, the most recently in the 1970s by the Ministry of Works. The room is still used as a refectory for Chelsea pensioners, and the painting had become extremely dirty and discoloured. Following stabilisation and treatment, IFACS commissioned a study of the environmental conditions and as a result some measures have been taken to optimise conditions in the room. A simple

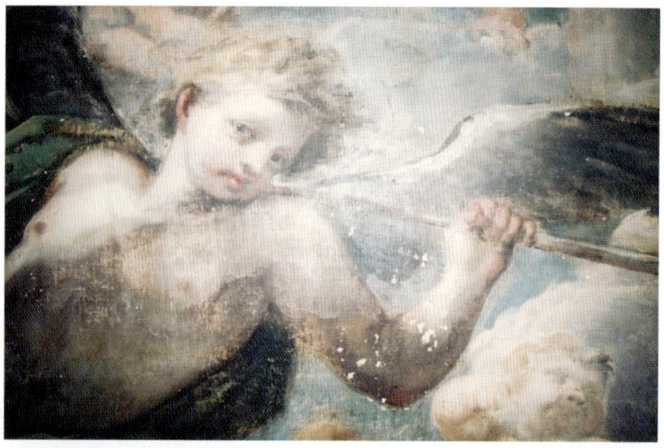

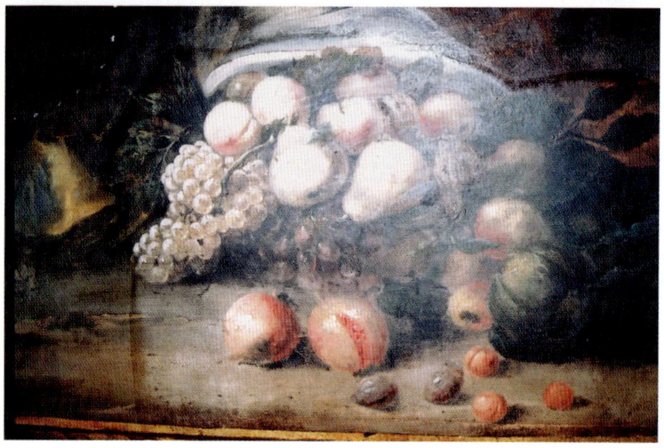

Figures 11 and 12 The Royal Hospital Chelsea, London: two details from the *Charles II* mural during conservation, showing losses and abrasion to the paint layer (above) and varnish removal (below). *(© IFACS)*

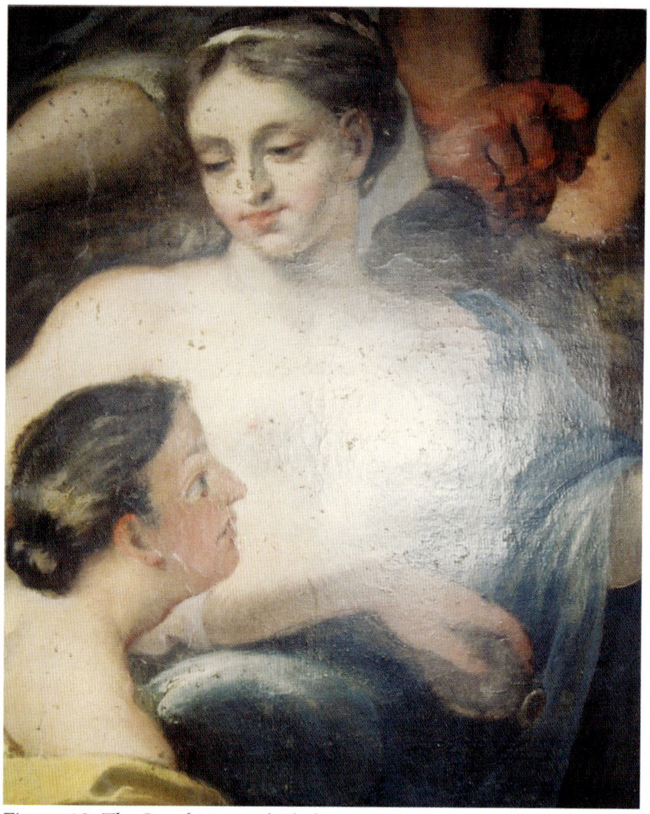

Figure 13 The Royal Hospital Chelsea, London: detail from the *Charles II* mural during conservation, showing dust on the paint layer prior to conservation. *(© IFACS)*

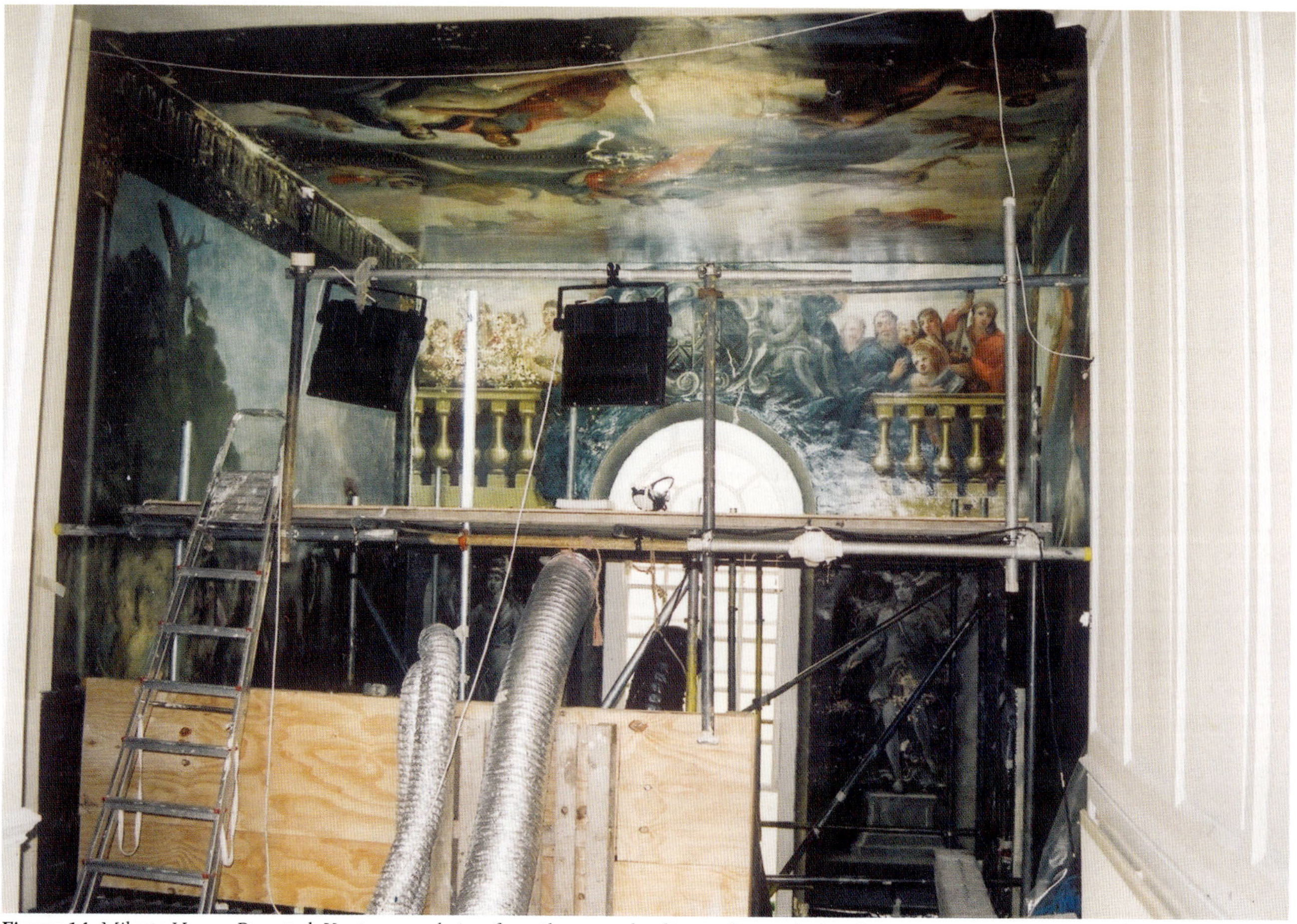

Figure 14 Milgate House, Bearsted, Kent: general view from the upper landing to the south showing conservation in progress. *(© IFACS)*

improvement was to stop the practice of frying the breakfast eggs on hotplates immediately beneath the painting! To avoid the rapid deterioration witnessed over the past few decades, IFACS has proposed an annual surface cleaning and condition assessment (Figs 11–13).

The technical challenges at Milgate were far greater. The modern timber cross-beams partly covering the ceiling were removed, and the ceiling plaster consolidated from above. Layers of wallpaper and paint needed to be painstakingly removed from the staircase walls. Cleaning followed to remove crude retouching and badly discoloured varnish, and substantial areas of paint loss and flaking were addressed. Finally the scheme was reintegrated (Figs 14–16).

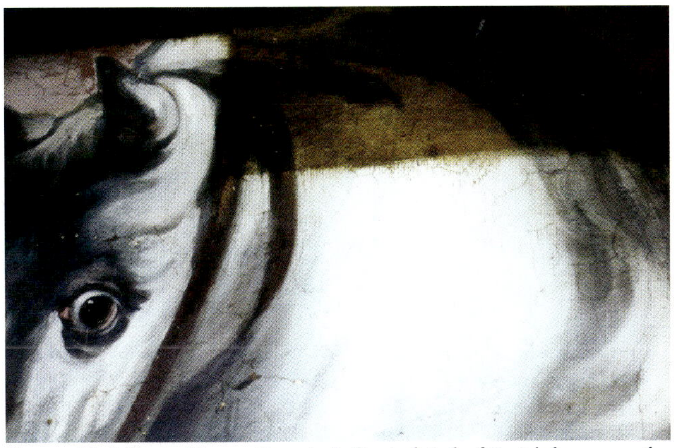

Figure 15 Milgate House, Bearsted, Kent: detail of Paris's horse on the east wall during conservation. The photo shows the discoloured varnish partially removed. *(© IFACS)*

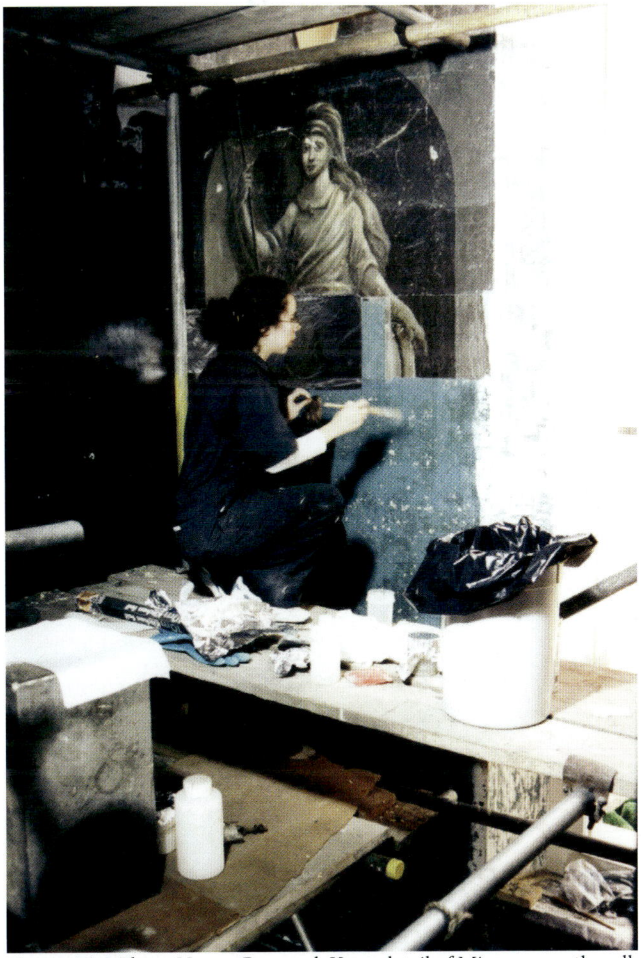

Figure 16 Milgate House, Bearsted, Kent: detail of Minerva, south wall, during conservation, showing removal of the blue overpaint. *(© IFACS)*

Conclusions

The results of the Milgate conservation have been very exciting: an artist rediscovered and a painting lost to view for centuries revealed and interpreted. With the paintings at Chelsea too, there has been a dramatic improvement in their appearance following conservation. Here again, assumptions as to the identities of the artists and for what they were responsible have been overturned. All this significantly adds to our knowledge of English Baroque wall painting. In addition, the idea of instigating a regular 'health check' of the paintings at Chelsea is a very positive move away from the practice of leaving paintings until they reach a serious state of deterioration, and should encourage a far more minimalist approach to treatment.

Acknowledgements

We wish to thank Katy Lithgow and Alistair Laing at the National Trust and Dr Robyn Pender at English Heritage for their help with the Milgate iconography, and John Burbidge and English Heritage's Robert Gowing for their observations. We also thank Liz Finn, research archivist at the Centre for Kentish Studies for her suggestions regarding Robert Hawker's signature. We are grateful to Robyn Pender for her advice on the environmental conditions of the Royal Hospital Dining Room, and to Ed Schneider for his excellent photography of Milgate. Thanks are also due, of course, to the conservation teams of both the Chelsea and the Milgate projects, and particularly to Tracy Manning, who painstakingly edited the reports for both.

Notes

1. Croft-Murray 1962, p. 66.
2. Croft-Murray 1970, p. 246.
3. Croft-Murray 1970, pp. 245–6.
4. In a letter of 9 August 2002, Katy Lithgow (National Trust) provided a detailed analysis of the iconography of the Milgate paintings, and also discussed the possible identity of the artist. Many of her observations are reproduced in this paper.
5. Robert Gowing of English Heritage suggested this parallel. The Bolsover paintings are currently being researched by Stephen Paine.
6. Burbidge 2001, p. 4.
7. The scene is described in book 4 of Ovid's *Metamorphosis*.
8. Croft-Murray 1970, p. 320.
9. Newman 1969, p. 145.
10. Standard reference works (such Cooke, and Benezit's dictionary of artists) were checked, as well as computerised sources including the Courtauld Institute's Witt Library, the National Portrait Gallery, the National Art Library databases, and the Access to Archives A2A archival database for England.
11. A *Stephen Harke* or *Hawke* appears in Croft-Murray 1962, but he is listed as active between 1644 and 1677, and he was noted for decorative finishes such as graining, rather than for mural painting. 'Edward or Thomas' Hawker (1640–1721), listed by

Waterhouse 1988 and included in the National Portrait Gallery database, was a well-established artist working as chief assistant to Peter Lely. One example of his work illustrated by Waterhouse – a portrait of the son of the Earl of Rochester – hints at a Kentish connection. The contemporary biographer George Vertue (1947) documents Edward and Thomas as two separate artists. Vertue describes Edward Hawker as a 'poor Knight of Windsor' and a painter, alive in 1721. Thomas, also described as a painter, is reported as living in Lely's house after his death, where he painted portraits of Henry 1st Duke of Grafton and Sir Dudley North, thought to have died in 1723.
12. Davies 1996 and Friedrichs 1999.
13. Davies 1996, p. 15.

References

Burbidge J. 2001, *Preliminary Survey of the Painted Scheme in the Staircase Hall, Milgate House, Bearsted, Kent*, unpublished report for English Heritage

Croft-Murray E. 1962, *Decorative Painting in England 1537–1837*, vol. 1, *Country Life*, London

Croft-Murray E. 1970, *Decorative Painting in England 1537–1837*, vol. 2, *Country Life*, London

Davies J. 1996, 'On painted ceilings ... the techniques of Baroque murals in England', *The Conservator* 20, pp. 15–27

Friedrichs A. 1995–2000, *Baroque Wall Paintings in National Trust Properties*, unpublished thesis for the Training Programme for Research and Conservation of Painted Objects and Historic Interiors, The National Trust

Hall J. 1974, *Dictionary of Subjects and Symbols in Art*, Westview Press, London

Newman J. 1969, *West Kent and the Weald*, N. Pevsner (ed.), The Buildings of England series, Penguin, Harmondsworth, p. 145

Room A. 1959, *Brewer's Dictionary of Phrase and Fable*, HarperCollins, New York

Vertue G. 1947, *Index to Vertue Notebooks, Vols 1–5, Walpole Society Journal* (1940–42) 29, p. 104

Walpole H. 1849, *Anecdotes of Painting in England with Some Account of Principal Artists*, Henry G. Bohn, London

Waterhouse E. 1988, *The Dictionary of 16th and 17th Century British Painters*, Antique Collectors' Club, Woodbridge, p. 117

Whinney M. and Millar O. 1957, *English Art 1625–1714*, Clarendon Press, Oxford

The authors

- Caroline Babington joined English Heritage as Wall Painting Conservator in 1988, becoming Head of Wall Painting Section in 1994 (a post later shared with Sophie Stewart). In 2003, Caroline became a Senior Wall Painting Conservator at International Fine Art Conservation Studios Ltd (IFACS). Most recently, she joined the Curatorial Department at the Palace of Westminster.
- Richard Pelter was an apprentice painting conservator at the Fine Art Trade Guild and Frost & Reed in Bristol (1963–68). He worked as a qualified conservator for Frost & Reed until 1969 before setting up his own practice West of England Studios, later becoming International Fine Art Studios Ltd. Specialising in large-scale conservation projects here and in America, Richard employs a large team of specialist conservators in easel and wall paintings, and has been the recipient of numerous awards including English Heritage Chairman's Award (1995) and City of New York Art Commission Award (1996).

Bedfordshire's Baroque masterpiece: the Thomas Archer Pavilion at Wrest Park

Stephen Paine and Sophie Stewart

Home to the Grey family from the 13th until the 20th century, Wrest Park is justly noted for its distinctive landscaped gardens, designed by three influential members of the family during the 18th and 19th centuries. Henry, Duke of Kent between 1706 and 1740, created the formal woodland gardens; Jemima, Marchioness Grey employed Lancelot 'Capability' Brown from 1758 to make various alterations, and finally Thomas, Earl de Grey (Jemima's grandson) built the present house in the 1830s and created a French formal garden in keeping with the style of the new building. The estate was sold after the First World War and a part of this was purchased for the nation in 1946. The principal house and grounds are currently owned and managed by English Heritage.

Visible from the main house in the far distance at the end of the Long Water (an artificial waterway), the Archer Pavilion – a domed rotunda designed by Thomas Archer in 1709–11– forms one of the key focal points of the magnificent formal grounds (Figs 1 and 2).[1] The pavilion is considered to be the first truly continentally inspired Baroque building in England. It is constructed of red and yellow brick with some stone detailing. The red bricks that make up quoins and other principal delineations articulating the overall design are of a very fine quality. The recessed panelling between the red brick elements are constructed in a much coarser yellow brick. It seems likely that these were not intended to be visible, and would probably have been coated in a toned limewash, producing a highly decorative finish to the building as a whole. These coatings have subsequently been largely lost through age and weathering (Fig. 3).

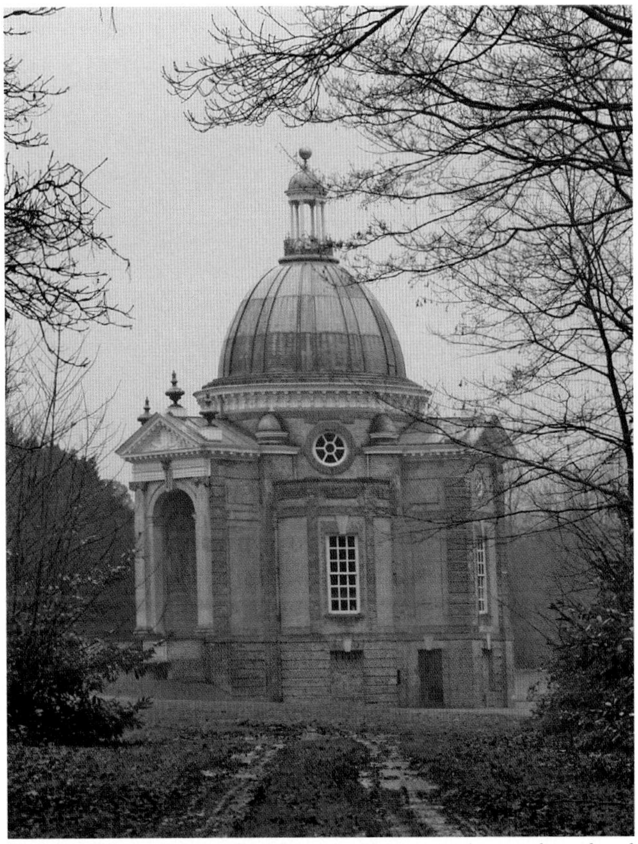

Figure 1 Wrest Park, Bedfordshire: the Thomas Archer pavilion played a crucial role in the orchestration of a series of planned vistas within the gardens of Wrest Park. *(© Paine and Stewart)*

The pavilion was designed as a place for genteel retreat and entertainment for the de Grey family. An inventory of 1740 offers a fascinating insight as to its likely use: after recording at least 22 chairs of various types and styles, the document goes on to mention that within each of the five alcove rooms there were a miscellany of stools, choice cupboards, teapot stands and other tea-making accoutrements. Elsewhere backgammon and other games boards are noted, as well as a telescope. The plan of the Archer Pavilion consists of a central circular space surmounted by a dome, from which radiate three pedimented two-storey chambers. These alternate with three apsidal single-storey side rooms, with the probable intention that every room should face a specific avenue of the garden and thus close a vista. The main entrance consists of a portico approached by a flight of steps, and the whole building stands on a basement that originally served as kitchens (Fig. 4). A plan of 1711 suggests that the small upper rooms were used as servants quarters while the rectangular ground-floor

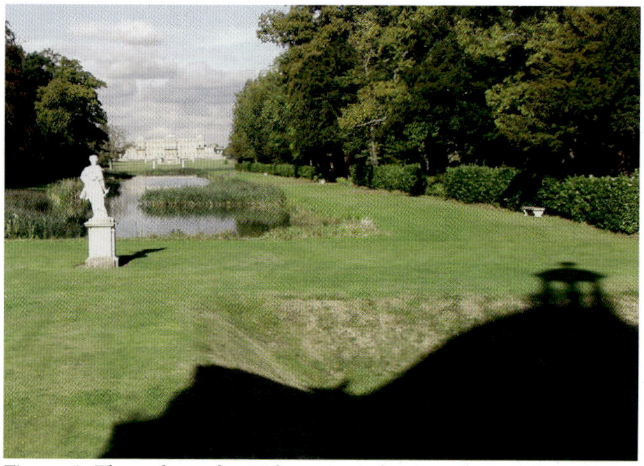

Figure 2 Throughout the 18th century, the incumbent dukes of Kent were enthusiastic landscape designers who, with the assistance of Archer and others, created one of the great English Baroque estate gardens. *(© Paine and Stewart)*

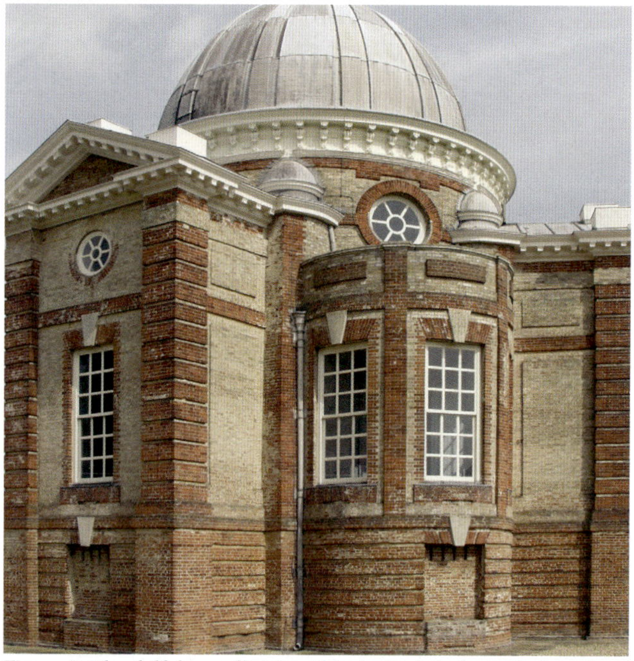

Figure 3 The skilful use of brick within Archer's design articulates form by overlying the core classical dimensions with contrasting textures and colour tones. The yellow brick insets may well have received additional coloured limewash to enhance tonal differences within the surface decoration. *(© Paine and Stewart)*

rooms were bedchambers, the Lady's Room containing a fireplace. This plan also indicates that there was a water closet with constantly flowing water.[2]

Thomas Archer (c.1668–1743) can best be described as a gentleman architect, who, having travelled extensively in Europe studying the great buildings of Italy, Germany and Austria, worked principally for other members of the English aristocracy.[3] An able designer, his importance lay in his direct experience of European Baroque, and his style contrasts with the more insular and specifically English designs of such contemporary architects as Vanbrugh and Hawksmoor.[4] Stylistically the Wrest Park pavilion is quintessentially Baroque, clearly reflecting Archer's keen interest in the revolutionary designs of Borromini and Bernini, for example. Nicola Smith writes that Archer's 'accomplished interweaving of contrasting geometrical forms also has much in common with designs by his Austrian contemporary Johann Bernhard Fischer von Erlach'.[5] A particularly close parallel for the plan of the Pavilion is to be found in the plan of an ancient Roman temple, however, which was published by the 16th-century architect Giovanni Battista Montano. Michelangelo's plan of *S.Giovanni di Fiorentino* in Rome may offer an even more convincing source of influence.[6]

Archer also designed another structure within the grounds of the park, which is now demolished. Hill House (c.1712–15) was, like the pavilion, strongly influenced by another architect's work: specifically Antoine Le Pautres' plan for a Maison de Campagne, published in the Fourth Discourse of his 1681 *Les Oeuvres d'Architecture*.[7]

The painted decoration

The decorative scheme within the pavilion is composed of fictive architectural detailing, with Corinthian columns articulating the main entrance and the doors to each of the five side-rooms (Fig. 5). Above each door are heraldic devices, flanked by putti. Between the columns above the internal doorways that lead to the upper rooms are roundels containing classical busts. The space between the lower doorways and the oculi above is divided by an entablature with modillions, upon which stand classical male herms and female figures flanking urns contained within niches (Figs 6 and 7). The domed ceiling displays fictive coffering, culminating in a lantern. The small doors that lead to the kitchens below, the servants quarters above in the south-west and south-east areas, the privy and the small fireplace, are all painted to blend into the overall decoration. The interior of the lantern is also painted with black-and-white garlands (Fig. 7). The scheme is signed and dated along the top edge of one of the service doors that face onto the central hall: *Hauduroy pinxit 1712*.[8] Further decoration also exists on the east and west walls of the portico, which contain niches with large standing figures set against a background of fictive rustication (Fig. 8).

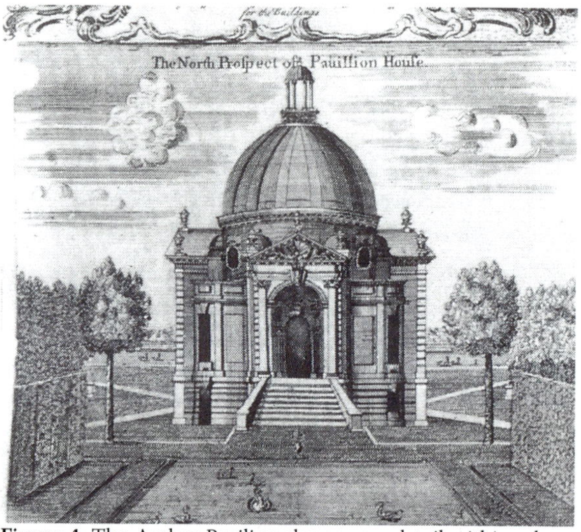

Figure 4 The Archer Pavilion shown as a detail within a large engraving of the grounds of Wrest Park in 1735 by John Rocque. *(© English Heritage)*

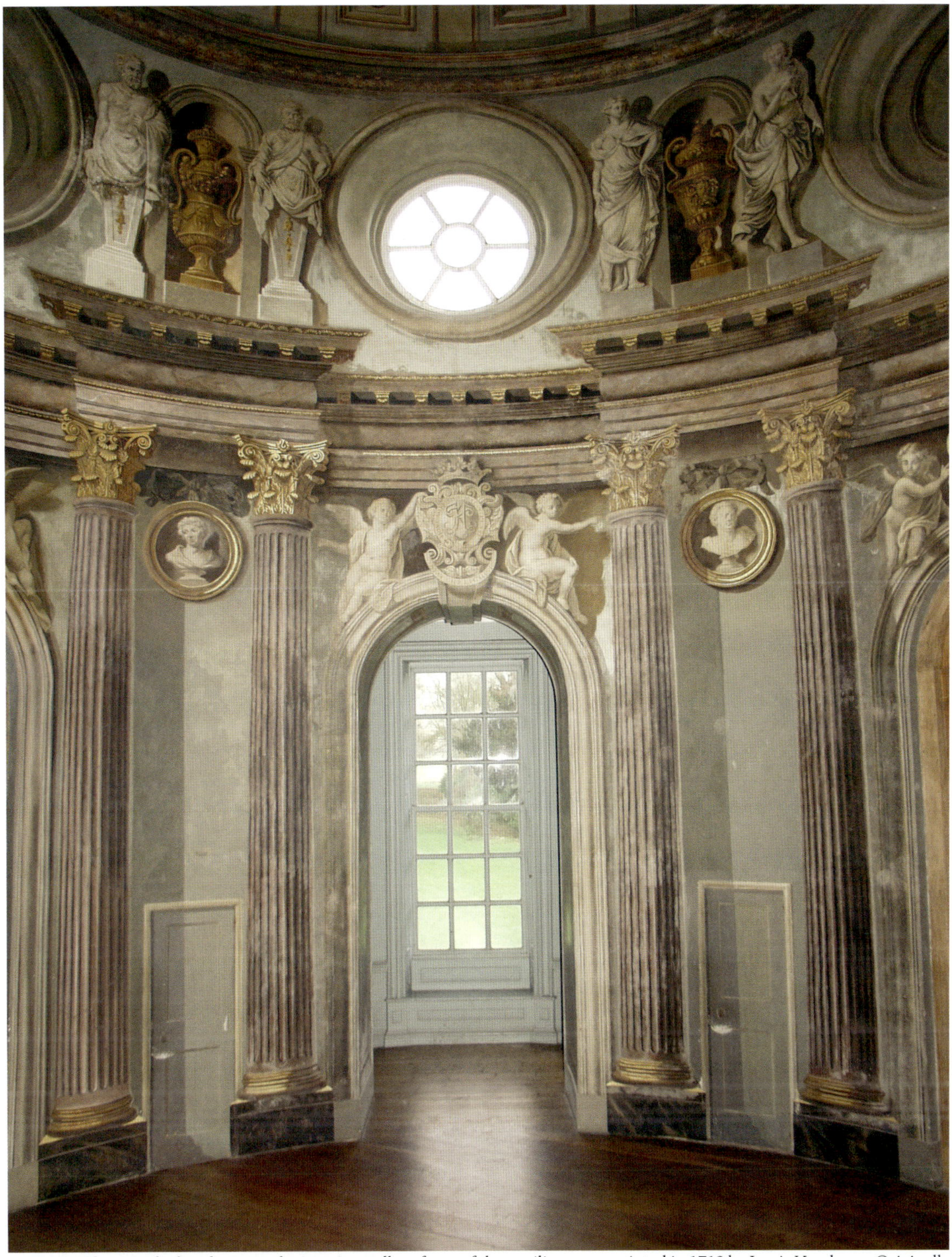

Figure 5 The murals that decorate the interior wall surfaces of the pavilion were painted in 1712 by Louis Hauduroy. Originally the design was more elaborate, but a restoration campaign of the 1840s saw a rationalisation of the background fields. *(© Paine and Stewart)*

The painter Louis Hauduroy was a French Huguenot, but like many of his compatriots by the end of the 17th century he had emigrated to avoid persecution. Two other members of his family joined him in England around the same time: Samuel Hauduroy, who was to practise as an architect, and Mark Anthony Hauduroy, a painter (he may have been Louis's son). Louis was subsequently to become part of the wave of foreign artists who dominated the early 18th-century market for decorating aristocratic English country and town residences. Schemes of wall painting that can specifically be attributed to Louis Hauduroy are however very rare. Those recorded reflect the typical artistic milieu of the early 18th century, which saw aristocratic patronage invested in some extraordinarily bold, lavish and stylistically innovative structures. Although not perhaps to be ranked alongside such contemporaries as Verrio, Laguerre or Thornhill in terms of the breadth of his commissions, Hauduroy did nonetheless contribute to a number of significant projects. His record suggests an artist with the ability

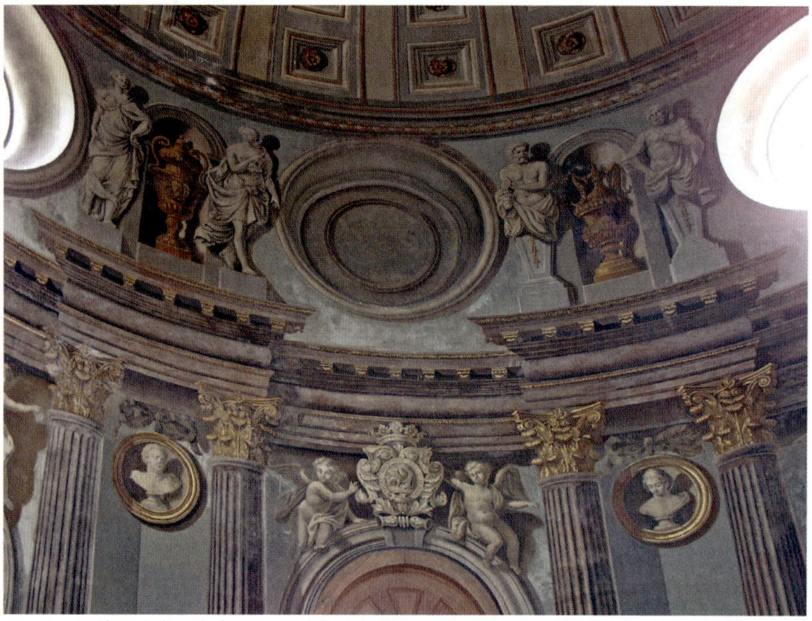

Figure 7 Classical male herms and female figures flank urns within niches to articulate the wall surfaces below the fictively coffered domed ceiling. *(© Paine and Stewart)*

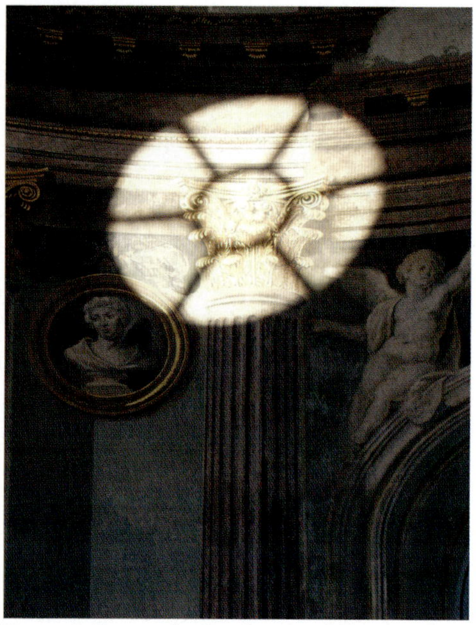

Figure 6 Trompe l'oeil architectural elements flank roundels with busts and putti. *(© Paine and Stewart)*

and talent to handle complex and sizeable spaces, as well as a skilled exponent of that particular Baroque style of secular design so revered by English patrons of the period.

Hauduroy's first recorded work was at Dyrham Park, Gloucestershire. Records mention a 'Monsieur Hauduroy' as having painted fictive marbling for the walls of the staircase, and fictive Ionic columns in the Balcony Room over the West Hall.[9] It is perhaps significant that between 1692 and 1696, Samuel Hauduroy had designed the first phase of building there for William Blathwayt. Before 1702 Hauduroy executed 56 decorative panels over doors and chimneypieces at Kiveton House in Yorkshire for Thomas Osborne, Duke of Leeds. The principal showcase areas at Kiveton House, which was demolished around 1812, were painted by Laguerre with scenes from the story of Cupid and Psyche.[10]

Perhaps one of Hauduroy's most significant works – the only other of his schemes that has survived apart from the Archer Pavilion, although it is currently concealed under overpainting – is the *Cupid and Psyche* cycle he executed for the staircase walls at Culverthorpe Hall in Lincolnshire in 1704–5 (see Fig. 9).[11] This substantial cycle coincided with a major programme of architectural modification to the north-facing staircase bay, commissioned by the then owner of the house Sir John Newton (who died in 1734). The contract between Hauduroy and Newton stated that the artist was 'obliged to paint the history of Psyche and on the ceiling to be the marriage of Psyche with all her lovers; on the other great side right against this, is to represent a sacrifice by Psyche's father to Apollo, where architecture is to be coloured marble; the capital and base of the columns and all the ornaments of the cornice are to painted with right gold; in one of the great sides under the great picture a bas-relief of Psyche with the goddess.'[12] While it is not known exactly how Culverthorpe's wall designs originally appeared, the ceiling painting remained extant until at least 1923, when a photograph of the stairwell shows all the walls overpainted, but reveals a small detail of the ceiling decoration.[13] Pevsner's 1963 account of Culverthorpe Hall describes the walls of the stairwell thus: 'only the Marriage remains, but now whitewashed over'.[14] It can be concluded that sometime between 1923 and 1963 the ceiling decoration was covered

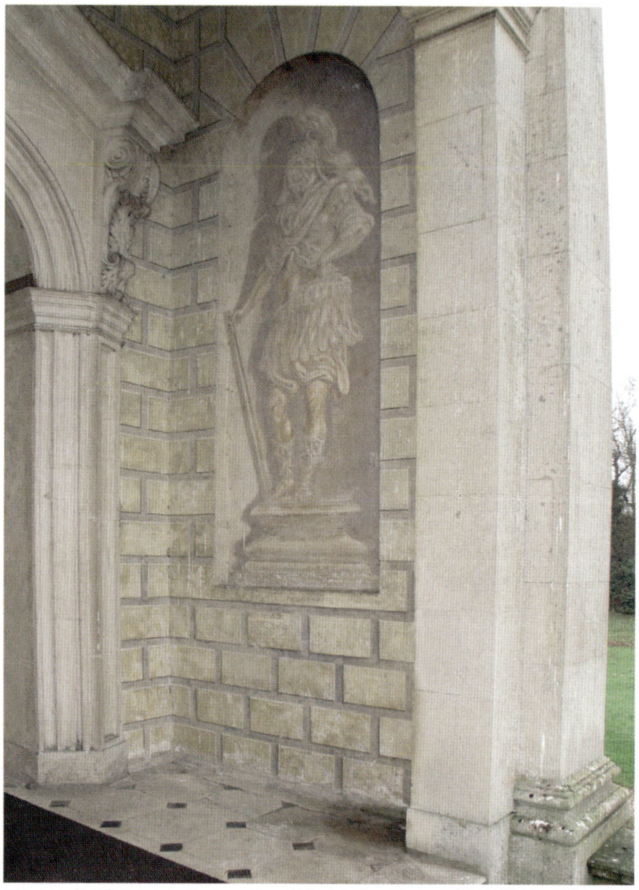

Figure 8 The opposing walls of the entrance portico display classical warriors within niches, painted in a grisaille style. *(© Paine and Stewart)*

over. For the overpainting of the wall surfaces, no record survives giving a likely date, although the nature of the earliest overpaint layer (determined by cross-sectional paint analysis) suggests a date within the late 18th century. The obliteration of the principal wall decoration was almost certainly the result of a change of fashion, since there is no apparent damage to the original plaster surface to suggest other reasons for disguising the walls. A close parallel to Culverthorpe's arrangement and general painting style can be found at Burley-on-the-Hill, nearby in Rutland. This scheme was commissioned (around 1710) by Daniel Finch, Earl of Nottingham from the painter Gerard Lanscroon. Nottingham was familiar with Hauduroy's work at Lord Russell's House in Lincoln's Inn Fields, London (c.1700, now destroyed), and this scheme is a possible source of influence. It is known that enquiries about the Lincoln's Inn paintings were made by Nottingham, specifically in relation to his intended scheme at Burley.[15]

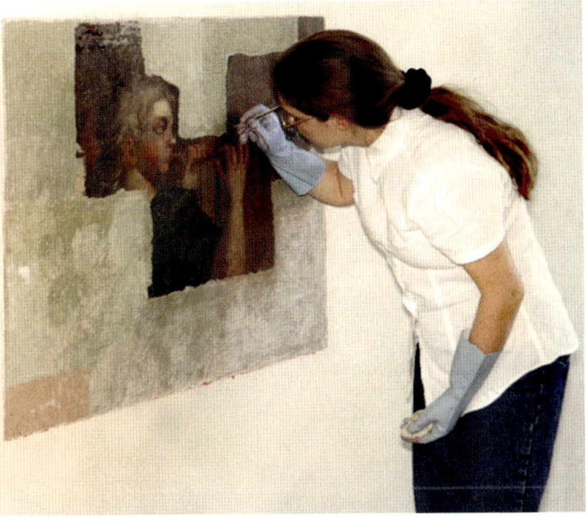

Figure 9 Culverthorpe Hall, Lincolnshire: the only other extant example of Hauduroy's work is to be found here, although it is entirely hidden by later overpainting. Uncovering trials carried out in 1996 by Jane Davies and Stephen Paine revealed high quality details from a scene of Cupid and Psyche, which had decorated the walls of the main stairwell. *(© Paine and Stewart)*

The association between Archer and Hauduroy is intriguing. On stylistic grounds it is thought that Archer may have been involved with the design of the projecting stair bay at Culverthorpe: there are similarities between this and certain architectural elements Archer utilised at Heythrop House (Oxfordshire, 1705–8). Through marriage Archer was associated to the Newton family who were Culverthorpe's owners. Hauduroy's decoration of the stairwell may well have brought him into contact with Archer, and thus their collaboration at Wrest Park seems logical. It is also interesting to surmise whether Hauduroy may have been called upon to decorate the interior of Archer's Hill House. Certainly a 1735 print of this shows external figures within niches, probably painted in the style of the grisaille figures seen to either side of the Archer Pavilion's entrance portico.

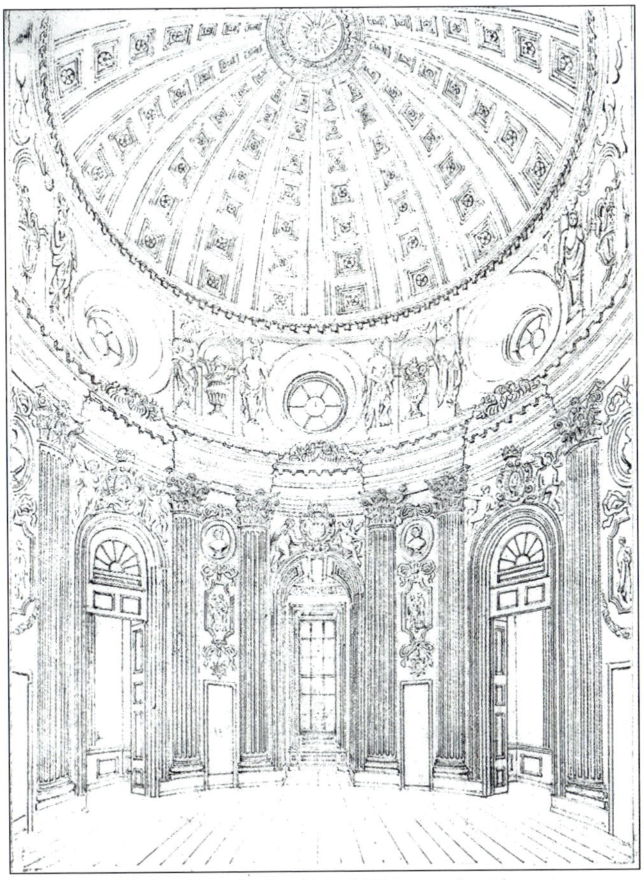

Figure 10 A drawing by John Buckler of 1831 records with great accuracy the extent of the decoration prior to the major rationalisation of the wall surfaces that took place in the restoration of 1845 (Buckler, John Chessill (drawings), MIC 100). *(© Bedfordshire and Luton Archives and Records Service)*

The conservation history of the paintings

The first early reference to the building is the inventory of 1740 recording: 'In the Great Room of the Pavilion House: twelve Chairs cover'd with Scarlet Morocco Leather, A handsom Stove Grate Iron Door.'[16] The next document is particularly important: a remarkably accurate interior drawing of the pavilion by J. Buckler dated to 1831 (Fig. 12). This shows that the scheme originally incorporated further elements that have subsequently been painted over, including cartouches containing figures on either side of the entrance to the south antechamber. There would also appear to be star motifs above the two southernmost fictive doors. Also, just visible, is the same decoration on the east and west above the doorways, but instead of a riband decoration below the cartouche there is some form of decorative festoon. There are also curvilinear motifs below each of the oculi, as well as further drapery above the terms and female figures. The decoration in the soffit of the south doorway is also just visible. Fictive fenestration is shown in one of the blind oculi.

Buckler's drawing indicates the nature of what would appear to be a major remodelling of the interior, and probably was the one recorded in the painted inscription *Bertrand Iterum Restaurit 1845*, applied to the top edge of a fictive doorway. Comparison between the 1831 drawing and photographs of the scheme taken in 1917 for *Country Life* suggests that the interventions undertaken in 1845 almost certainly included overpainting some areas in a blue-grey paint, as well as modifying of some of the doors. A further reference to an intervention of 1919 is recorded along the upper edge of one of the service doors leading onto the central hall.[17] How extensive this restoration phase was is not clear.

When the building came under the care of the Ministry of Works (later English Heritage) in the 1950s, a major campaign of work was begun that continued throughout the decade. There is scant written documentation relating to this work, though a number of photographs provide a crucial chronology of the various interventions undertaken (Fig. 12). Following this, no work was carried out on the scheme until 2002, when some significant structural repairs were undertaken to areas of the dome, and the first major condition audit of the wall paintings was undertaken.[18]

In summary, the scheme has undergone various interventions that have had dramatic consequences for its present appearance. First is the restoration of 1845, when various elements of the original painting were covered over probably as a consequence of poor condition (understandable after 133 years of exposure). This intervention may also have formed part of a major reordering of the entire estate begun when the present house was built by Earl de Grey between 1834 and 1839. The restored scheme would appear to have remained in good condition until the sale of the estate in 1919, when a further restoration was carried out, the nature of which is unknown. Subsequently the condition of the fabric declined, leading to devastating water damage. Finally, a long programme of restoration was undertaken during the 1950s, which appears to have consisted of a range of invasive interventions including removal of sections of original painting, cleaning, consolidation with wax, and retouching. Reconstruction was also undertaken, predominantly on the north wall, and it would appear that substantial areas of the dome were also overpainted when large sections of plaster were removed to repair the roof timbers.

Nature of the original scheme and the extent of later restorations

An important task of the 2002 survey, carried out by the present authors, was to try to establish just how much of the original Hauduroy scheme still survived, and how much of the scheme was in fact later restoration. Certainly until that time the commonly accepted view was that most of the interior was the result of later campaigns of restoration. This had had the effect of relegating the pavilion paintings towards the bottom of the 'league table' of important English Baroque schemes. To assess how significantly the original appearance of the interior had been compromised by the later restorations, the painted surface was systematically examined in normal, raking and ultraviolet (UV) light to ascertain the types and patterns of repainting.

The original paint layer

The original painted decoration was executed in a range of muted blues, greens, greys, browns, whites and yellows. It appears to have been executed in an oil medium, the paint layer having the characteristic appearance of an aged oil film, showing a slight surface craquelure (Fig. 11). There are also extensive areas of gilding under which the bright red bole

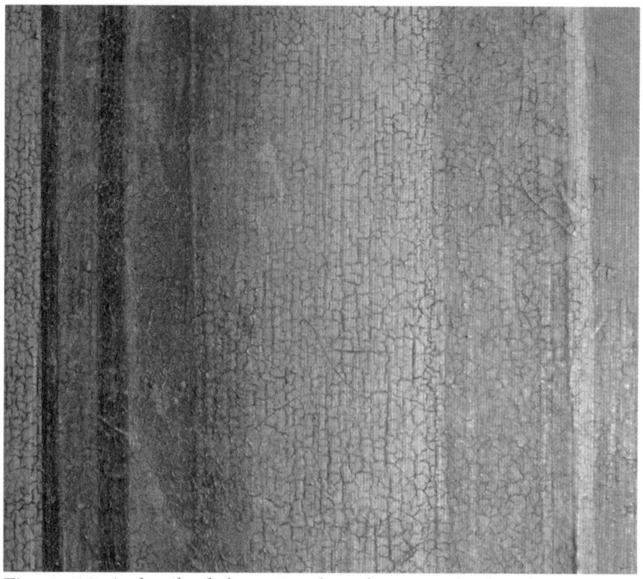

Figure 11 A detail of the painted surface reveals the characteristic craquelure usually associated with the drying or ageing of an oil medium. *(© Paine and Stewart)*

used as a preparatory base can be seen, although much of this appears to have been restored. While the original painting has obviously been compromised by some rather clumsy restoration, it was clearly executed in an assured manner, with the figures confidently modelled. Its overall layout and style reflect the early 18th-century taste for classically themed decorative designs.

The 1845 overpainting

The blue-grey paint found principally over the soffits of the three doorways to the square antechambers, in the wall space between the columns, and above the entablature below the roundels, was almost certainly applied during the restoration of 1845. Indeed, in raking light the topography of the original decoration (as visible in Buckler's print of 1831) can just be made out. As noted above, 1845 overpainting also appears to extend over some historic lateral repairs, the natures of which are unknown.

The 1919 restoration

The nature of this intervention is not clear, but it may have included the repainting of the blind oculi.

The 1950 retouching and repainting

Partially visible in UV light, the 1950s retouching is in fact fairly obvious in normal light, appearing smooth and matt in contrast to the more fragmentary and abraded original paint layer. It was rather crudely applied over the original, and generally used to broadly strengthen or define elements. In the dome almost all the background has been retouched, the frames of the coffers have been strengthened, and the central rosette motif overpainted. Comparison with the 1950s photographs

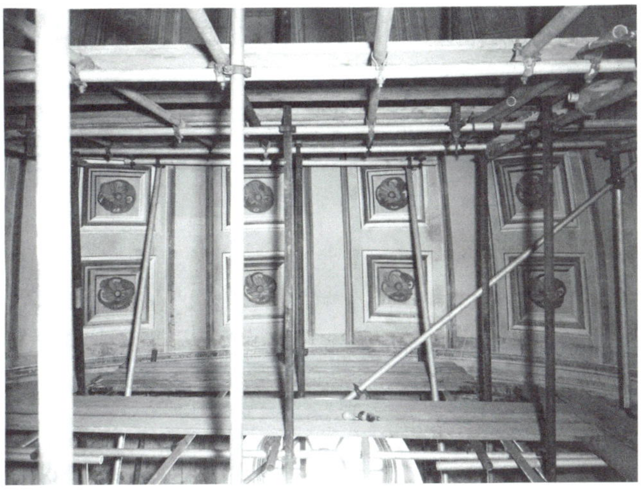

Figure 12 Photograph taken in the 1950s when the then Ministry of Works carried out various campaigns at Wrest Park to deal with the decay of the structure of the pavilion. (© Crown copyright. NMR)

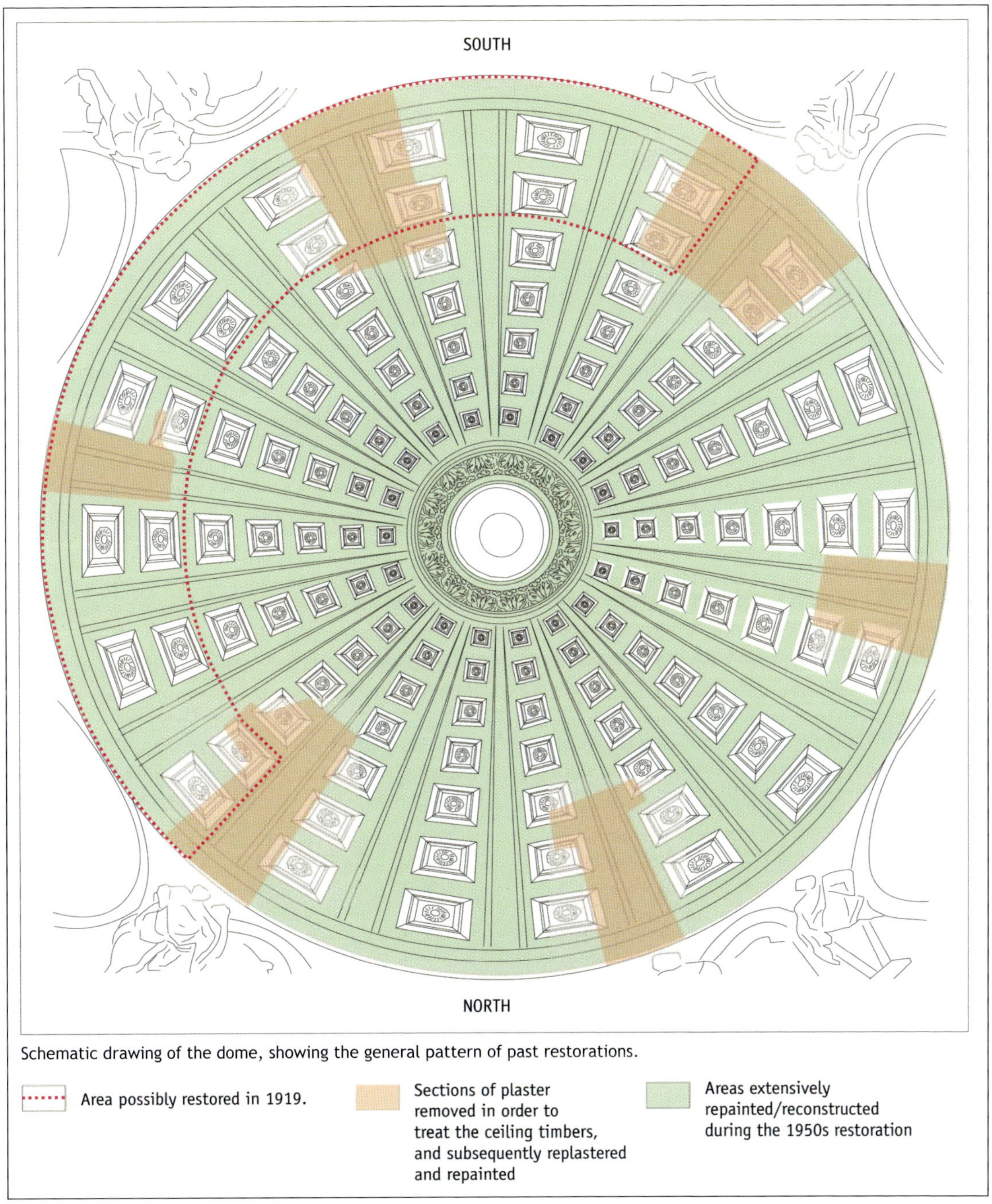

Figure 13 Documentation showing past conservation of the Hauduroy dome scheme, recorded as part of the 2002 survey. *(© Paine and Stewart)*

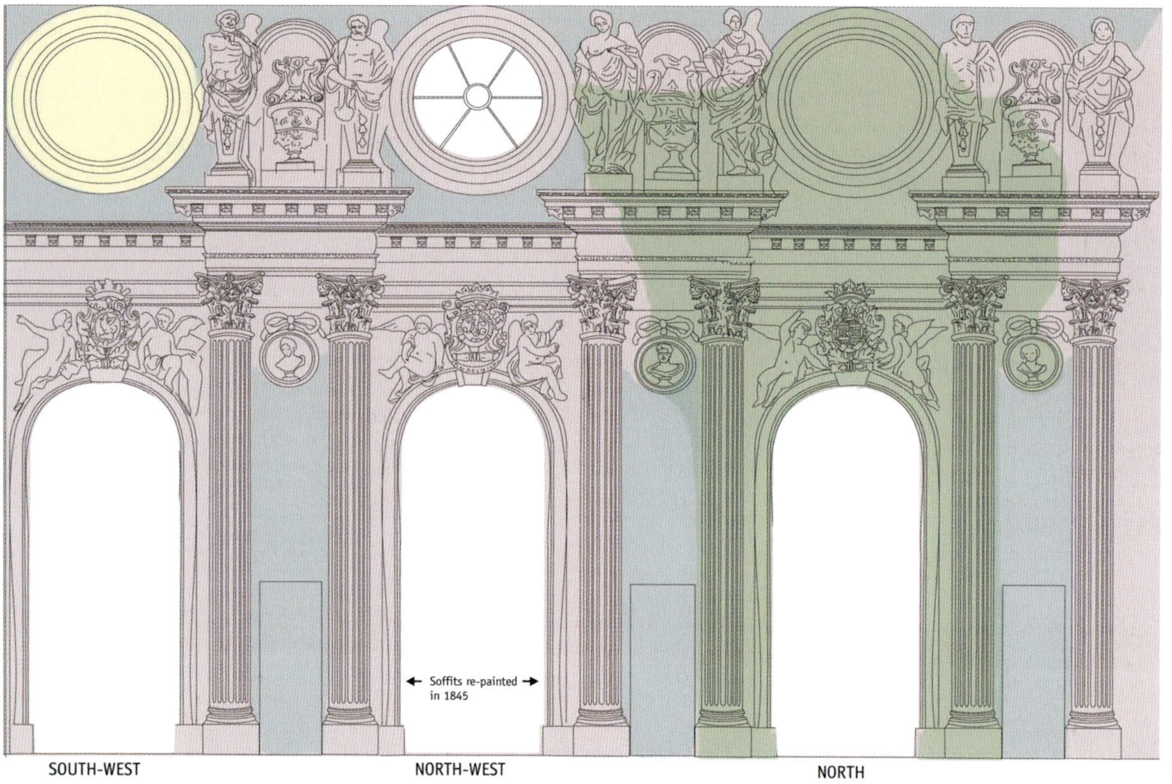

Schematic drawing of the walls from the south-west to the north side, showing the general pattern of restorations.

Figure 14 The recent examination has allowed a reassessment of the extent of the surviving original decoration. The notion that most of the visible scheme was in fact restoration from the 1950s can now be seen to be wrong: a significant majority of extant painting is in fact by Louis Hauduroy. *(© Paine and Stewart)*

also shows the consequent loss of detail: some of the figures and coffers appear quite crude and are not in keeping with Hauduroy's more elegant and confident original technique. The brown paint used to redecorate the skirting panel also dates to this period. Much of the decoration in the lantern would also appear to have been restored, and certainly the upper section has been replaced.

A further issue is the rather confusing phenomenon evident in the area between the entablature and the roundels, where the repainting is rather haphazardly applied in places, in a mixture of light and dark tones. It may be that the intention was to try to replicate the somewhat blanched appearance of the blue-grey paint applied in 1845 to cover these areas.

Conclusions

From the 2002 survey, it is clear that probably as much as 75% of Hauduroy's original 18th-century paint layer does survive (Fig. 14). In places this has been heavily retouched and reconstructed in areas of total loss. Overpaint covers a significant proportion of the original paint layer, although some of these areas (such as the 1845 intervention) can now be considered historically significant. The current painted scheme in the pavilion is therefore a complex palimpsest of original and later paint layers, with perhaps 25% of the surface composed of restorations and other additions. In the dome there has been a greater level of restoration, probably to reintegrate the surface after repair of large sections of replaced plaster. Nevertheless, enough survives of the original to make this – the only extant painting by Hauduroy surviving in England today – a very significant addition to Archer's Baroque masterpiece.

Notes

1. The distance between the original house (demolished c.1834) and the pavilion was originally less, as the present building was constructed further to the north.
2. Unpublished guide, Silsoe Research Institute, 1991.
3. His secure financial status is probably due to the fact that in 1705 'he obtained the court post of Groom Porter, which gave him control of gaming tables in the royal palaces, and was reputed to be worth £1000 a year' (Colvin 1995, p.76).
4. Colvin 1995, p. 77.
5. Smith 1995, p. 23.

6. Whiffen 1950, pp. 26–7.
7. *Ibid.*
8. It should be noted that there is a further inscription on the south-west door, too badly damaged to decipher, which falls between the 1712 signature and the inscription relating to the 1845 restoration (see below). It is not clear whether this relates to an aspect of the construction and decoration of the interior, or to a later restoration or other intervention.
9. See Beard 1981, p. 263: 'To Monsieur Hauduroy in part for painting of ye house. August 22 1694. £10 Painted rooms, staircases, veining in imitation of marble etc. Received in all £229.4s.7d.' In Croft-Murray 1970 (p. 218), the work at Dyrham Park is accredited to Mark Anthony Hauduroy. This attribution is incorrect, however, since Mark Anthony was only active some 30 years later (c.1735–7).
10. Beard 1981, p. 143.
11. See the unpublished report by Stephen Paine Conservation and Jane Davies Conservation, *Culverthorpe Hall, Lincolnshire: A Report on the Wall Paintings of Louis Hauduroy*, July 1996.
12. *Newton Miscellany, CXCVI, No. 286* and *Country Life* 15 September 1923, p. 355, as quoted in Croft-Murray 1970, p. 248.
13. *Ibid., Country Life*, fig. 8, p. 354.
14. Pevsner and Harris 1963, pp. 244–5.
15. *Ibid.* Croft-Murray 1970, p. 248: 'The painting upon cloth in the staircase at my Lord James Russell's in Lincoln's Inn Fields contains 150 and 160 yds. Was painted by Messrs. Hoddery for £100 and found cloth was at My Lords charges.' The reference to 'Messrs. Hoddery' may suggest Mark Anthony was working with his father on this project. The relatively low fee for a substantial area of painting suggests that the scheme was probably largely decorative, with reduced figurative work (*cf* Hauduroy's fee of £180 for his figurative scheme at Culverthorpe, or Louis Laguerre' fees of £357.15s for his *Cupid and Psyche* at Kiveton House).
16. Collett-White 1995, p. 271.
17. The inscription is located along the top edge of one of the doors. It reads: *H.W..R(?)CEY IT..UM - RESTAURAUIT 1919.*
18. The 2002 condition survey of the wall paintings was undertaken by the authors in association with a wider fabric survey, commissioned by English Heritage (which is responsible for the pavilion and surrounding gardens), and led by Helen Axworthy of the RH Partnership (architects).

References

Beard G. 1981, *Craftsmen and Interior Decoration in England 1660–1820*, Holmes and Meier, New York (1986, Bloomsbury, London)

Bristow I.C. 1996a, *Architectural Colour in British Interiors 1615–1840*, 2 vols, Yale University Press for the Paul Mellon Center for Studies in British Art, New Haven and London

Bristow I. C. 1996b, *Interior House-painting Colours and technology 1615–1840*, Yale University Press for the Paul Mellon Center for Studies in British Art, New Haven and London

Collett-White J. (ed.) 1995, *Inventories of Bedfordshire Country Houses 1714–1830*, Bedfordshire Historical Record Society, Bedford

Colvin H. 1995, *A Biographical Dictionary of British Architects 1600–1840*, 3rd edn, Yale University Press, New Haven and London

Country Life 4 August 1917, pp. 112–14

Croft-Murray E. 1970, *Decorative Painting in England 1537–1837*, vol. 2, *Country Life*, London

Pevsner N. and Harris J. 1963, *Lincolnshire*, N. Pevsner (ed.), The Buildings of England series, Penguin, Harmondsworth

Smith N. 1995, *Wrest Park*, English Heritage, London

Whiffen M. 1950, *Thomas Archer*, Art and Technics Ltd, London

The authors

- Stephen Paine completed a Getty Conservation Institute post-diploma internship leading to the award of the Courtauld Institute of Art Certificate of Advanced Practical Training in the Conservation of Wall Paintings in 1992. He has since been working as a private conservator in the UK, working on many significant wall paintings of all periods for a wide variety of clients.
- Sophie Stewart also completed a Getty Conservation Institute post-diploma internship leading to the award of the Courtauld Institute of Art Certificate of Advanced Practical Training in the Conservation of Wall Paintings. In 1992, she joined English Heritage as Wall Painting Conservator, becoming joint Head of Section in 1998. Since leaving English Heritage in 1999 she has worked in private practice in partnership with Stephen Paine.

The rediscovery of the lost ceiling decorations in the Saloon at Burlington House

Pauline Plummer and Peter Schmitt

A brief history of the architecture of Burlington House (by Peter Schmitt)

If, to paraphrase Sir Philip Dowson, past President of the Royal Academy of Arts, architecture is the clothing of society, then undressing Burlington House in London reveals a series of marked changes in architectural fashion. The outer garment of Portland stone is neo-Palladian classicism of the Enlightenment, beneath which is Restoration brickwork of the original double-pile house. At the core is a model so strong that architects through three centuries have responded coherently in the same rational neo-Classical style, imported from Renaissance Italy, which has served as the catwalk for the parade of London Society.

In *The Englishness of English Art*, Pevsner pointed out that 'England was the first country to break the unity of interior and exterior and wrap buildings up in clothes not made for them but for buildings of other ages and purposes.'[1] The effect is evocative, not strictly aesthetic, encapsulating a cache of meaning and memory; in this case, from classical antiquity, in particular, the ruins of ancient Rome as witnessed on the obligatory Grand Tour, and as studied in the published reconstructions by Palladio. His *Quattro libri dell'architettura* (1570) was the focal point for 'right models of perfection ... independent of fancy (décor)', to quote the Whig arbiter of virtuosi taste, Lord Shaftesbury (1711).[2] While the libertine excesses of the Baroque were eschewed in theory, the forbidden fruit of Catholic Italy was directly studied, imported and imitated by a handful of fashion-setters. The re-clothing of Burlington House *al gusto Italiano*, restrained outside and lavish inside, is tied to the political and cultural history of London and of the monarchy; an architectural transvestite, imitating a classical past, while legitimising the present in each reincarnation.

A post-Restoration town palace of Puritan tailoring

Burlington House is the only great house to survive of the four built along the north side of 'Pickadilly' in the 1660s (known then as Portugal Street in deference to the queen consort, Catherine of Braganza) (Fig. 1). Sir John Denham's appointment as Charles II's Surveyor General of the King's Works came with 3.5 acres of open land north of Piccadilly, owned by Charles's mother, Queen Henrietta Maria. He 'designed' a two-storey mansion for himself, although it may have been that craftsmen within the Works supplied the design, since no building designed by Denham is known.[3] It was built of fashionable red brick, dressed simply with stone quoins and capped

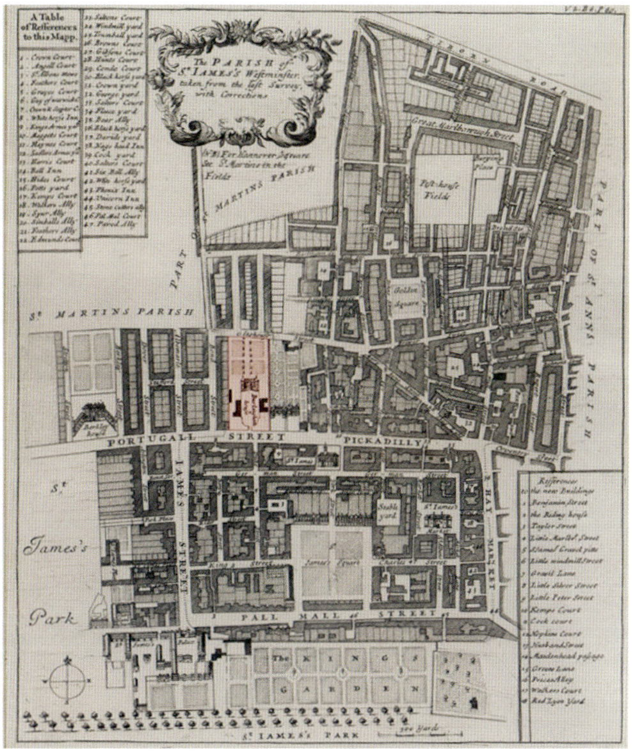

Figure 1 Map of the parish of St James's Westminster as surveyed by Richard Blome about 1689, published (without Blome's name and with a key to new buildings) in Strype's Stow, 1720. Of all the great houses depicted, only Burlington House still survives. *(Reproduced in F. Barker and P. Jackson,* The History of London in Maps, *Barrie & Jenkins, 1990)*

by a hipped slate roof with a row of dormers for the garret. The compact plan was in the shape of the letter 'H', favoured by Elizabethan and Jacobean great houses. The side wings were single pile and the central cross-bar double-pile. The design had a uniform structural width of 20ft (6m), dictated by the size of Scandinavian trees, which were pit-sawn for floor beams spanning between outside walls or onto the spine wall.

Best known to Restoration society for his 1642 topographical poem *Cooper's Hill*, which is still included in anthologies, 'celebrated poet and an eminent Royalist' Sir John Denham was the ideal symbolic Surveyor-figure for the decade when the heroic couplet and Puritan minimalism became established as the national norms of poetry and of architecture.[4] The two emerged together. The heroic couplet – prosaic and unvaried – was a register that dominated English verse-writing until the end of the 18th century. The utilitarian, frugal style of Puritan minimalism, supported by cost-conscious merchant gentry, was a watered-down developer's classicism of simple brick units with regular fenestration.

Denham sold his shell of a house hurriedly in 1668, and it was completed by Denham's deputy within the Office of Works, Hugh May, for its new owners the first Earl and Countess of Burlington.[5] The marked contrast between the balance of the exterior and the haphazard asymmetry of the interior planning suggests it was laid out to suit their special needs. The house was a grand one: in the 1690s it paid the highest residential rates in London.[6]

Knyff-Kip's engraving of 1698–9 shows the original concept, based on a Serlian axial layout (Fig. 2). The prototype was Parisian: the aristocratic town palace, or *hôtel particulier*, which had crystallised by the 1640s into a symmetrical disposition of elements around a spacious *cour d'honneur*. The earliest example is the 1639 Hôtel Tambonneau by Louis le Vau, which would have been familiar to Charles II and his companions-in-exile in Paris.[7] The ancillary wings on both sides were designed to the same height with the same window treatment, and walled off from the street. The larger scale of the gate in the middle announced its status: the only link between the teeming, noisy urban populace and the private dwelling. The courtyard served as service yard as well as a ceremonial transition space before the hospitality of the house raised on its slight podium, creating a linear movement from public realm, to forecourt, to private enclosure, to tranquillity in a parterre garden at the back.

Cross-dressing in 18th-century neo-Palladianism

By the early 18th century, fashion had swung away from both Baroque excess and the bland minimalism of Denham's (or May's) facades. A tension and discipline was favoured, exhibiting the Classical orders according to the classical principles that had lost their way since the buildings of Inigo Jones in the 17th century. In 1714, the 2nd Countess, Lady Juliana,

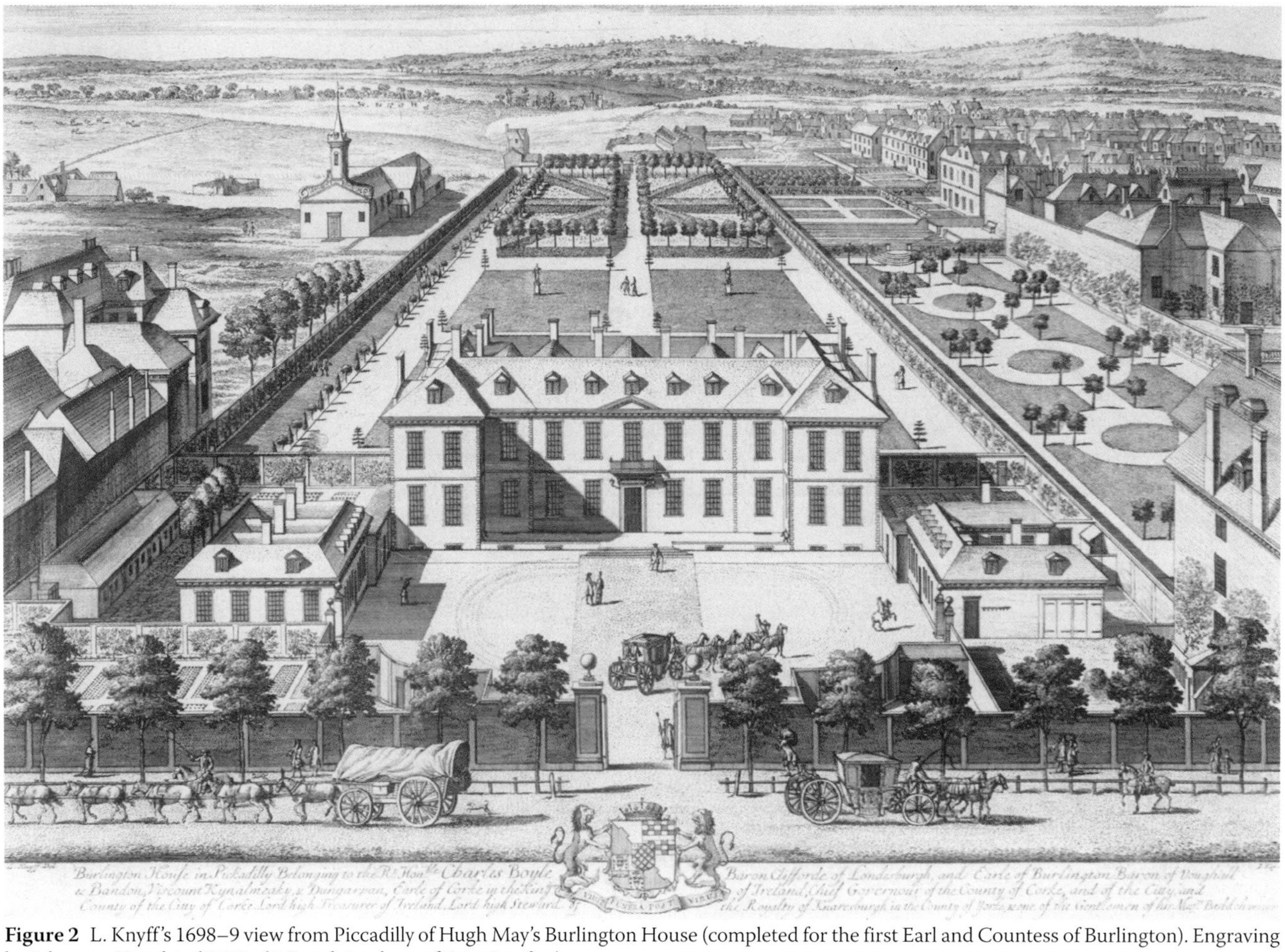

Figure 2 L. Knyff's 1698–9 view from Piccadilly of Hugh May's Burlington House (completed for the first Earl and Countess of Burlington). Engraving by Johannes Kip, dated 1707. *(© Royal Academy of Arts, London)*

commissioned Sir James Gibbs, who had studied in Rome under the Baroque architect Carlo Fontana and was the first British architect to be professionally trained, to improve and aggrandise the forecourt and to enlarge and embellish Hugh May's staircase. Between 1708 and 1715, Dowager Countess Juliana commissioned two Venetian painters: Giovanni Pellegrini to provide large-scale decorative canvases for the entrance hall (these are now at Narford Hall in Norfolk), and Sebastiano Ricci to decorate the stair compartment being designed by Gibbs.

Lady Juliana's son, the 3rd Earl of Burlington, formed his taste in architecture on two Grand Tours to Italy: in 1714, for one year, and in 1719 to Venice and Vicenza, specifically to study at first hand the buildings of Andrea Palladio and to find an Italian-trained architect/painter/decorator.[8] He returned home with a copy of *I Quattro libri dell' architettura* (1570) and an astonishing corpus of Palladio's drawings. This was later augmented by purchasing John Talman's collection in 1720 and 1721, which also included works by Inigo Jones, the 'English Palladio'. Burlington and his 'Augustan' literary circle saw themselves as the new Romans: Roman architecture, as described by Vitruvius and reconstructed by Palladio, appealed to Whig liberals. Burlington was now committed to making the rather plain old house into a manifesto for this new style.

Between 1715 and 1717, Gibbs designed an elegant colonnade to enfold the courtyard, a miniature version of Bernini's colonnade at St Peter's (Fig. 6). The two quadrants (recorded in pen and ink watercolour by George Meredith of 1782, and a watercolour of c.1806–8 (Fig. 3)) were set out on the footprint of Denham's (or more likely Hugh May's) quadrants (on a radius of 68ft), in Renaissance Doric – near to Palladio – with plain shafts 2ft in diameter, and an entablature of triglyphs interspaced with metopes in the correct manner.[9] The oft-quoted words of the fastidious critic, Horace Walpole, testify to the power of the result:

> As we have few samples of architecture more antique and imposing than that colonnade, I cannot help mentioning the effect it had on myself. I had not only never seen it, but had never heard of it, at least with any attention, when soon after my return from Italy, I was invited to a ball at Burlington-house. As I passed under the gate by night, it could not strike me. At day-break looking out of the window to see the sun rise, I was surprised with the vision of the colonnade that fronted me. It seemed one of those edifices in fairy-tales that are raised by genii in a night's time.[10]

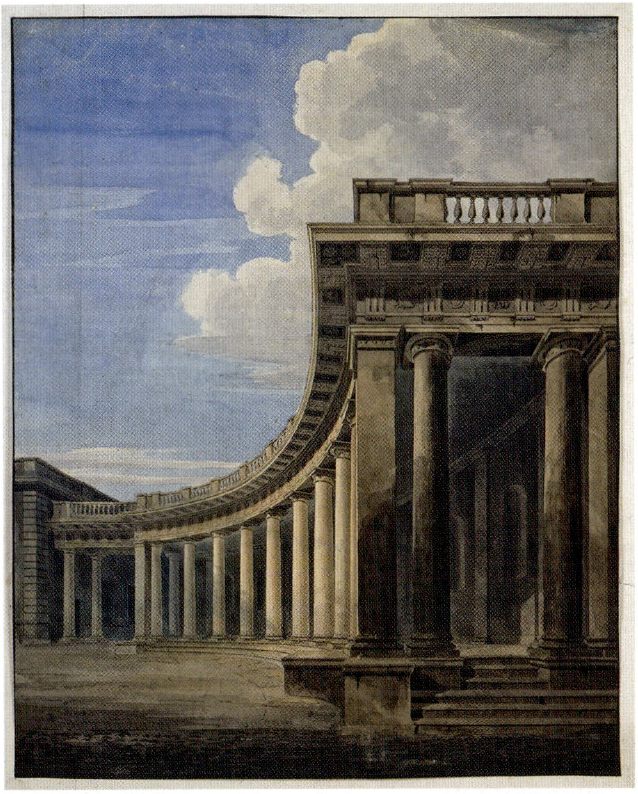

Figure 3 Watercolour (c.1806–8) by an unidentified artist of the east quadrant of Sir James Gibbs's colonnade (looking towards the stable block). Horace Walpole remarked, '... we have few samples of architecture more antique and imposing that that colonnade'. *(© Royal Academy of Arts, London)*

After 1717 Burlington transferred his patronage from Gibbs (who was tainted by Baroque leanings) to the Scottish Whig Colen Campbell. Campbell, who hated Gibbs, adorned Gibbs's colonnade with a Roman triumphal arch as an axial gateway from Piccadilly, using the same Roman Doric and to the same dimensions, but raising the arch on pedestals (Fig. 4). It was a version of the York Water Gate of 1626–7 on Victoria Embankment. He also built a kitchen block on the west side of the forecourt to match Gibbs's stables on the east.

The general plan of Burlington House appeared in Campbell's third volume of *Vitruvius Britannicus* (1725), where it had been absorbed into his own design. Campbell's most important innovation in the architectural dress code of the forecourt was to breathe 'truth' and discipline (*ordinatio*) into the south front of the house, transforming it from red Restoration brick to chaste, quite white, Palladian stone, applied as a veneer (Fig. 7). The façade is loosely based on Palladio's Palazzo Porto (*Issepo dei Porti*) in Vicenza, and closely resembles Campbell's unused 'New design for the Earl of Islay' published as plate 54 in his first volume of *Vitruvius Britannicus* (1715) to inject a note of 'Antique Simplicity' and catch the imagination of the aristocracy. Lady Juliana was a subscriber. The design of Burlington House acknowledges Inigo Jones as a model, and derives its rustic ground storey (Mannerist in precedent, to express a solid base, and adopted by canonical Palladianism) from his Queen's House in Greenwich. It applies the Ionic colonnade of the *piano nobile* from the first storey of his Whitehall Banqueting House, with framed windows of alternating triangular and segmental pediments. Like Gibbs's colonnade, Campbell's three-quarter engaged Ionic columns were 2ft in diameter, and human in scale. In correct Ionic on the *piano nobile*, they were a homage to Palladio, and having no pedestals, Vitruvian in their handling. The sterility of the front, like the Villa Savoye (1929–31) by the purist Le Corbusier, is partly due to the lack of central emphasis, except for the subtle balustraded aprons under the central three windows. The side wings were each dressed like pavilions with a Serliana window, for which no precedent is found in Palladio.

The effect upon entering the courtyard from Piccadilly was theatrical. The disposition of elements with the curved regiment of columns by Gibbs as *cavea*, facing Campbell's

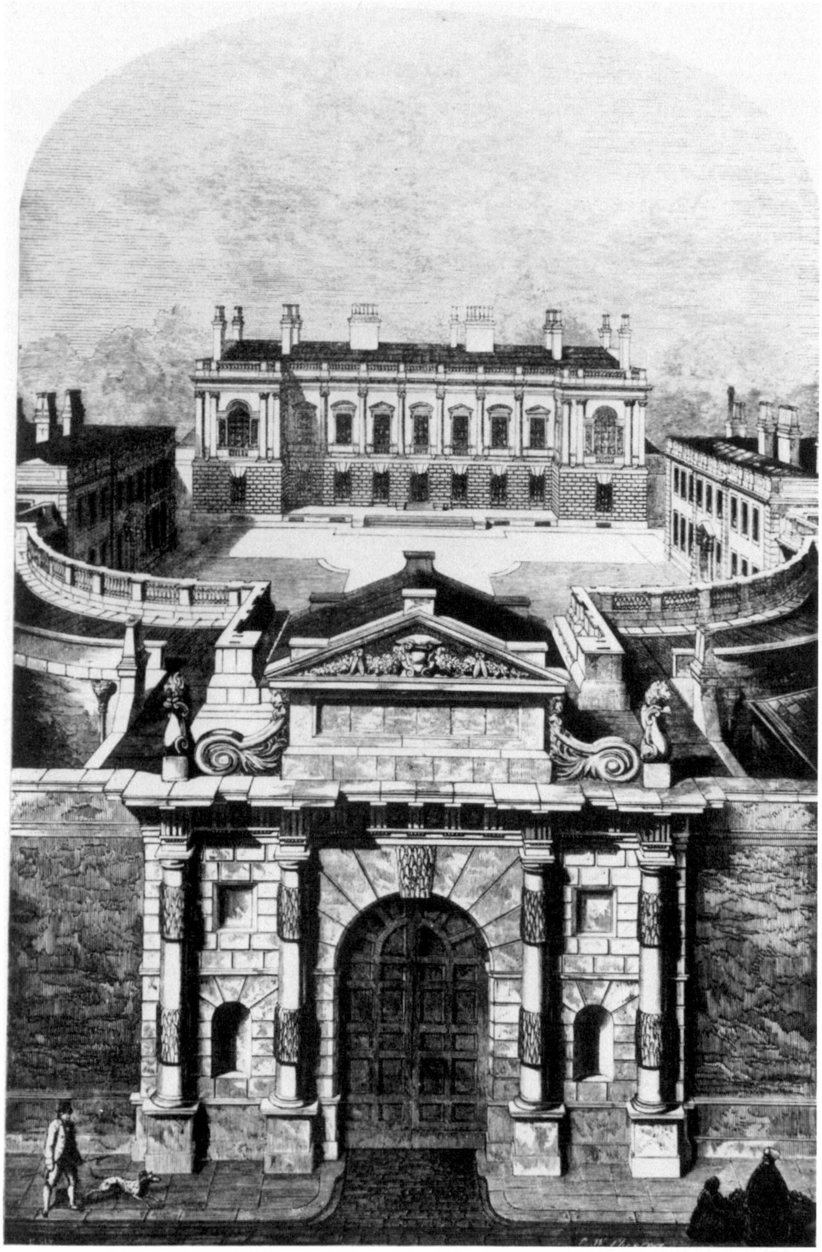

Figure 4 Elevated view of Burlington House presenting Colen Campbell's 1719 façade as *frons scaena* and the inward-looking courtyard as *cavea*, and highlighting his 1717 'great gate' on Piccadilly. The balustrade of Gibbs's colonnade is also visible. From the *Illustrated London News*, 15 September 1866. *(© Royal Academy of Arts, London)*

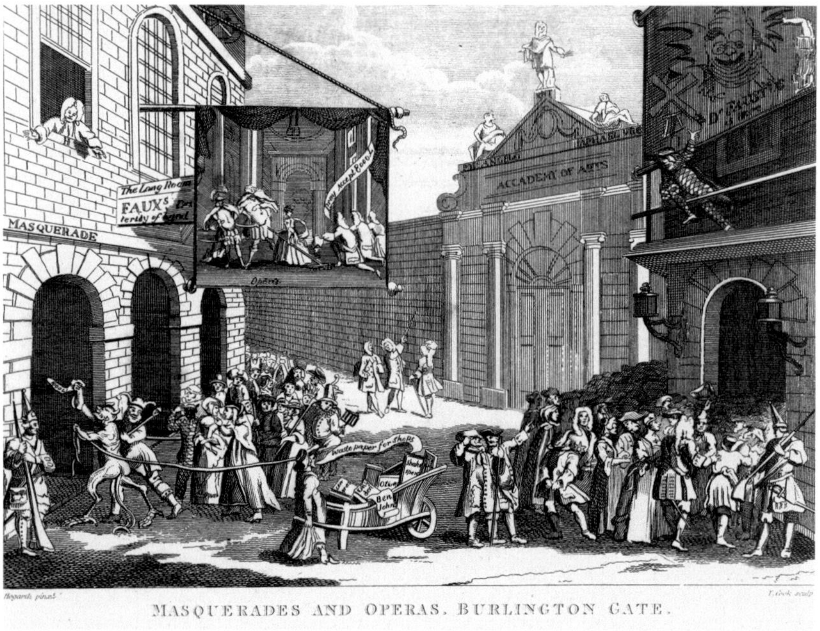

Figure 5 Royal Academy of Arts engraving after William Hogarth's *Masquerades and Operas*: Burlington Gate, 1724. Compare with Campbell's 'great gate' in Figure 4. Hogarth's use of the Ionic order is a solecism, or was it irony? The central of three figures in front of the gate is Burlington himself, who is addressing Campbell on his right. *(© Royal Academy of Arts, London)*

colonnaded façade (Figs 4 and 6) as *frons scaena*, is directly related to Roman theatres (as delineated in Vitruvius), and not unlike the key parts in Palladio's Teatro Olimpico at Vicenza, or Aleoti's Teatro Farnese at Parma. It was a forecourt as well as an 'approach', an enclosed space as well as a processional space, clothed in the Classical orders for the purpose of containing and displaying the entrances and exits of the Burlington circle, whose lifestyle was centred on friendship, hospitality and good conversation and who were tolerant of satire and opposition, unique for any ruling class. By using orders of the same size and superimposing them, the scale was not overblown but human and civilised, and wittingly fashioned in its fabric the literary attitude of Burlington's friends, Alexander Pope and John Gay, whose *Beggar's Opera* (1728), from which we inherit musical comedy, satirised the pomposity of Italian opera. Not to be gainsaid, Handel, who lived at Burlington House from 1712 to 1715, enjoyed the irony of composing the opening aria in *Xerxes* to a tree. William Hogarth, irked by Burlington's imported talent, published a scathing engraving, *Masquerades and Operas* (1724), which poked fun at Handel as well as Burlington and his artist-designer protégé, William Kent (Fig. 5).[11] Hogarth (who touted work for his father-in-law, Thornhill, an expensive painter) inscribed on Campbell's 'great gate' in the background 'Accademy of Arts' and placed on the pediment the figure of Kent (spelt KNT, Georgian slang for kunt or cunt), with Michelangelo and Raphael reclining on either side.

William Kent's Baroque interior undressed

Searching to establish a coherent neo-Palladian architecture, Lord Burlington needed a model for an authentic Palladian interior. This he found in the designs of Inigo Jones, who saw no contradiction between restrained Palladian classicism on the exterior, which Campbell's manifesto had dubbed with a British character – a stiff-upper lip – and lavish decoration within. Jones's double-cube room at Wilton House proved the point.[12]

The opulent upgrading of the principal first-floor rooms began before Burlington came of age in 1715. His mother, Dowager Countess Juliana, played a role in her son's interest in music, and was a patron of Handel during his first visit to London in 1710–11. Lady Burlington would have been the moving spirit behind the commission to substitute May's stair for a double-height stair compartment, lavishly designed by the mildly Baroque Sir James Gibbs to display a mythological cycle painted by Ricci, who was brought over from Italy in 1712 and stayed until 1716. Occupying two bays just east of the present Saloon, Gibbs designed a halpace stair with an old-fashioned closed string, plinth-like newels and bottle-shaped balusters of oak (Fig. 10). The upper part was reserved for the Ricci murals. As part of Samuel Ware's alterations of 1815–18, the Ricci canvases were redistributed around the house, except for the two small paintings that had been positioned over the landing doors and which travelled to Chiswick House. *The Triumph of Bacchus*, once on the north wall, is displayed (without half the sky) on the ceiling of what is now the General Assembly Room. The other two major scenes, *The Triumph of Galatea* and *Diana and her Nymphs*, can now be seen on the walls of the main staircase, relocated by Ware to the centre of the house, leading to the Main Galleries. The only original element surviving *in situ* is the ceiling painting of Olympus, in what is now called the Council Room.

At the time of his completion of the house in 1668, Hugh May planned the Saloon (after the Italian *salone*) on the first floor as a dining room, a fashionable idea that lasted into the 1730s. Situated remote from the kitchen, it would have been impractical for everyday use. The basic form of the Saloon is Campbell's and dates from 1717–19. The cubic dimension of Gibbs's stair compartment meant Campbell had to shunt the new Saloon into the central three bays of the house, where he was able to vault the ceiling as befitted the room's importance. The Saloon is also odd in that it never had a chimneypiece, which must have limited its use in winter. Without a clear precedent from Vitruvius – or for that matter Palladio – Campbell produced a strongly architectural space, equivalent to an open-air loggia in a Palladian villa, possibly with the Queen's House in mind. The pedimented doorcases are external in detail and resemble the façade treatment of Palladio's Palazzo Porto, where pairs of putti recline on pedimented window architraves. Here the four pairs of plaster cherubs on the doorcase pediments were probably sculpted by Giovanni Battista Guelphi, whom Lord Burlington had brought to England in 1719 along with William Kent as his new architect/painter/designer in residence specifically to replace Campbell and to introduce the *gusto Italiano*. Campbell had been forced to retire in disgrace as Deputy Surveyor General of the King's Works.[13] Kent's arrival was greeted with a series of affectionate nicknames, summed up by Thomas Coke's epithet, 'Signor Cazzo Vestito', which John Harris freely translates as 'a prick in a suit'.[14] The lavish gilding of the architectural elements, which stand out as crowded but isolated incidents, can only be Kent's.[15]

Although Campbell may have been responsible for the Saloon's Corinthian entablature, its central tabernacle door surround and even the pedimented pier glasses between the windows, John Cornforth attributes without hesitation to Kent the four swagged Italianate frames with ornate cartouches that stand on projecting pedestal dados (Fig. 14).[16] There is no documentary evidence that Lord Burlington ever actually acquired a set of four large pictures to fill these frames.[17] Cinzia Maria Sicca argues that Kent, the son of a humble joiner, was fully trained in post-Raphaelesque classicism under Giuseppe Chiari after spending ten years in Rome, and that his treatment of walls destined as a backdrop for paintings concentrated on the cornices, doorcases and ceilings.[18] He strove to recreate an antique *tablinum*, the main room in a Roman classical house. All of the relieving colour in the Saloon is on the ceiling, where Kent executed an oil-on-canvas painting depicting the wedding feast of Cupid and Psyche (Fig. 11), circumscribed by an oil-on-plaster cove, illustrating events from that mythology, which have only just come to light as a result of Pauline Plummer's efforts.

To the west of the Saloon, Campbell amalgamated May's dressing room into a two-bay bedroom – now known as the Lee and James C. Slaughter Room – to balance Gibbs's staircase. For this, Kent created a flat, ceiling painting on plaster, set within a carved-and-gilded guilloche frame of wood (Fig. 12).[19] There was attic space above to house Burlington's armoury (*sic*) within the queen-post trusses that supported the flat lead roof. (This has now been converted into a plant room.)

Axial vistas were a favourite concept of the Baroque period, and the life of a nobleman such as Burlington was played out with the kind of theatricality we now associate with London fashion week. For this, Campbell redesigned the suite of first-floor rooms and linked them together, every door in perfect alignment; the west bedroom would have been a through route to Burlington's bedroom in the west wing (now the General Assembly Room). This enfilade was intended not only to impress by its length and diminishing perspective, but to form an ideal setting for the formal processions that would have preceded Burlington's *lever* in the morning, his dinner in the afternoon, and his *coucher* at night.

The authorship of Burlington's chapel is a puzzle. Following Restoration precedent in H-plan houses like Belton (1685–8),[20] there had been a chapel in the east wing from the time of Denham, but it occupied the basement and ground floor with bedrooms above (designed by Hugh May and accessible from his stair). No drawings or descriptions have come to light. Campbell's plan in the 1725 volume of *Vitruvius Britannicus* clearly labels a chapel in the same location, but at ground-floor level, and entered directly from Gibbs's stair compartment (Fig. 6). There is no corresponding plan of the *piano nobile* to confirm its volume. John Carr's alterations for the Duke of Portland in the 1770s show a ballroom at first-floor level, but no access from Gibbs's stair compartment: just his false door on the landing for symmetry, which would indicate the presence at one time of an inaccessible double-height space beyond. Giles Worsley argues convincingly that the Venetian window is a sign of divine and earthly kingship. Burlington and Campbell would only have so used one, aware of its symbolic import.[21] One can speculate that the treatment of the chapel may have been similar to Inigo Jones's nearby 1632–4 Queen's Chapel. Logically it would have needed a segmental vault or raised ceiling to expose the Serliana, for which there was space under the new lead roof (Burlington's armoury was inserted in an attic void in the west wing, as noted above), and it would have had an altar and reredos in front of the small ground-floor window.

Regency finery: Samuel Ware's Revival of Kent from 1815–18

In 1811–12, Burlington House was bought by Lord George Cavendish, a relation of the Duke of Devonshire. He rationalised the 3.5-acre site by hiving off a narrow strip of land on the western boundary, and employing Samuel Ware to design Burlington Arcade as a commercial venture. His immense wealth enabled him to sweep away the changes that had been made in the 1770s by John Carr of York, for the Duke of Portland, to reorganise the house to achieve a symmetrical layout on the *piano nobile*, and to face the brick garden frontage in stucco, mirroring Campbell's Palladian courtyard facade (Fig. 7) but without columns.

Cavendish's architect, Samuel Ware, was an ardent admirer of Kent. He floored over Gibbs's stair compartment (now the Council Room) to create an uninterrupted east–west enfilade, which linked together all of the rooms along the entire south front of the house (as captured so well in J.W. Archer's watercolour of 1855 of the view from the GA Room). The logic of Ware's plan realised an axial symmetry that Burlington – his attention diverted to Chiswick from 1724 – had failed to achieve.

A ballroom with a heavily gilded, coved and compartmented ceiling, based on a drawing of Kent's, was designed to colonise the whole of the east wing, and this was balanced by a State Dining Room in the west wing. The main stair was relocated on the central north–south axis. Ware redistributed Ricci's stair compartment murals (1712–15) to line the flanking walls of the new staircase, although he had to cut off half the sky to make Ricci's *Bacchus and Ariadne* fit the coved and gilded ceiling of his new State Dining Room. During the Regency period Lord Cavendish's suite of rooms was restyled in Kent Revival for entertaining on a grand scale.[22]

The Emperor's new clothes: lease to the Royal Academy of Arts, 1867

Burlington House was purchased by the government in 1854, which in 1867 granted the Royal Academy (RA) a 999-year lease on condition that it financed the construction of a block of exhibition galleries in the adjoining half of the garden, built studios in the undercroft for its art schools, and superimposed on the original house an attic storey to serve as Diploma Galleries. A house for the Keeper was built on the east side.[23] Designed by the RA's treasurer, Sydney Smirke, all of these additions were completed by 1876. Norman Shaw filled vacant space to the east and west with further galleries in 1885, destroying in the process the west end of Ware's garden facade to insert a staircase from the new Refreshment Room underneath. The result, based on the French modular planning of Durand (*Précis et leçons d'architecture* 1802–5) and Boullée, is home to some of Europe's most exceptional top-lit axial art galleries.

The flanking forecourt structures and Gibbs's colonnade were dismantled and supplanted by Banks and Barry's classical range of buildings, designed to house six learned societies. With architectural good manners, Campbell's rusticated base and Ionic colonnade were wrapped around the other three sides of the forecourt, but in a more ornate Italian Renaissance style, and with an attic storey for libraries. Smirke responded with a lofty, high-Victorian second storey in Corinthian for the Diploma Galleries (1872–3) above Campbell's Ionic, and softened the now cliff-like face of Burlington House with a portico arcade with a glass roof (Fig. 8). The government of the day had recast the forecourt as a quadrangle of institutional buildings to act as a powerhouse of learning and art (Hogarth's 'Academy of Arts' reborn) to rival Albertropolis in South Kensington.

The presidency of Lord Leighton (1878–96) put Burlington House back on the London social calendar. The interconnected sequence of 'private' rooms, as realised under Lord Cavendish in 1818, was now fragmented by the RA into discrete Victorian statements. The dining room was sealed off by Shaw as the General Assembly Room. The ballroom was dressed up as the Library until 1927, when it became the Reynolds Room. The two ante rooms were re-designated for the Secretary (now the Slaughter Room) and Council. Lady

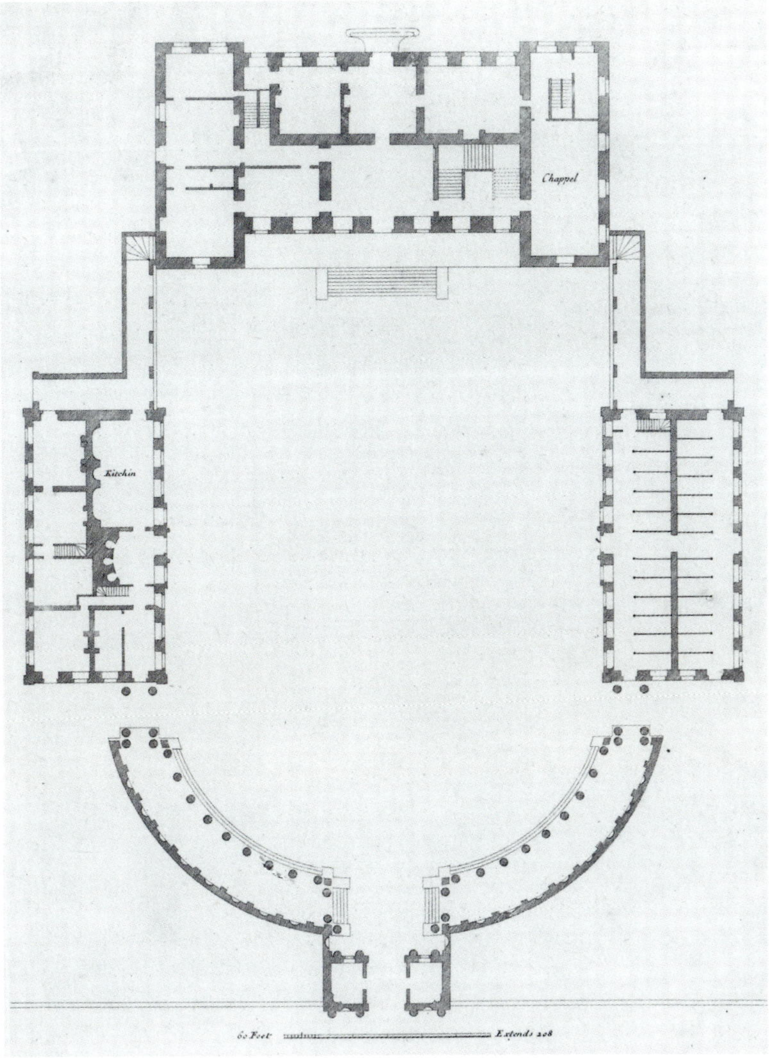

Figure 6 Plan of the ground floor of Burlington House and forecourt showing the stables on the east side and the kitchen block on the west side, with Gibbs's semicircular colonnade to the south, published in *Vitruvius Britannicus* (vol. III, 1725, p. 22). Note Gibbs's stair compartment showing access to an adjacent 'chappel' in the east wing. *(© Royal Academy of Arts, London)*

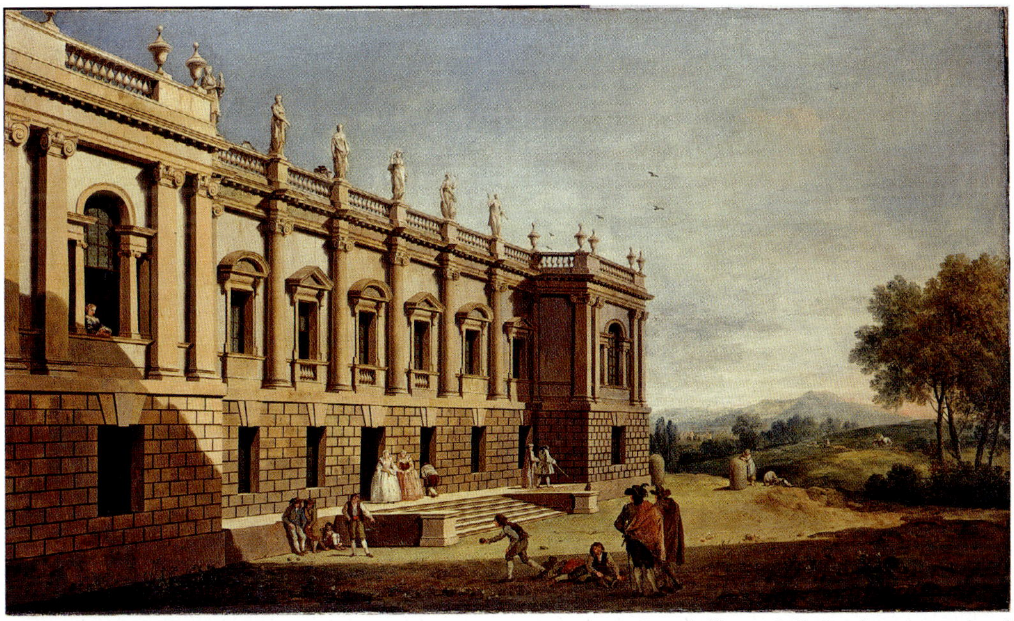

Figure 7 Francesco Zuccarelli's view of Burlington House in 1746. Here Campbell's neo-Palladian front is translated into an idealised landscape which was Kent's contribution to garden design and formed part of the process that shaped the British constitution and the English way of life. The country house in France is seen as symbol of oppression. It was Burlington's banker, Henry Hoare I, who also engaged Campbell and succeeded in creating Elysium in England. The famous circuit walk around the lake at Stourhead is an allegory of Virgil's *Aeneid* and the founding of Rome – like Kent's garden at Rousham. Burlington's circle saw themselves as important and as grand as Roman senators. *(The Royal Collection © Her Majesty Queen Elizabeth II)*

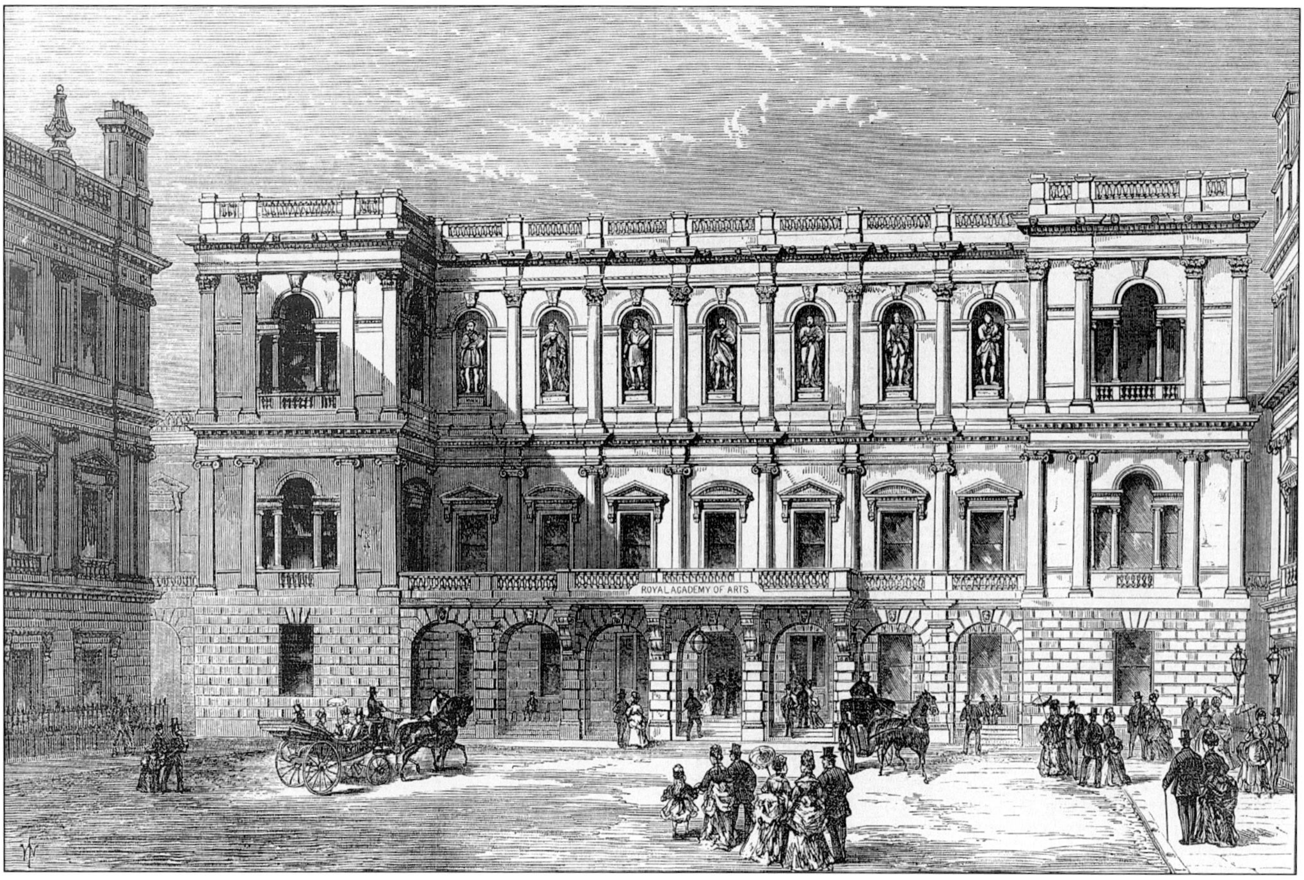

Figure 8 Burlington House from the south in the late 19th century showing Sydney Smirke's 1872–4 superimposed second storey and 1774 front portico arcade, added to which was Norman Shaw's 1885 projecting cornice hood. Shaw's hood was removed in 2001 as part of the re-paving of the Courtyard. Banks and Barry's 1869–73 buildings for the Learned Societies can be seen framing the courtyard, now quadrangle, giving it greater scale and inherited today as a robust, urban open space. Engraving after 1885 from the *Illustrated London News*. *(© Royal Academy of Arts, London)*

Cavendish's drawing room was partitioned into a Members' lavatory and a lift and stair to Smirke's Diploma Galleries. The purest element, the Saloon, was re-clothed by J.D. Crace in 1891 with an iconographic programme on the ceiling for the RA as an institution, much as walls in an Oxbridge college dining hall would be dressed with portraits of masters and provosts. Here a series of decorative relieving arches was animated by cameo portraits on canvas of the institution's past presidents, founding patron, patron in 1891 and plaques painted with names of its illustrious artists (Figs 16 and 18). This was an RA pantheon in response to statues of worthy artists, both ancient and modern, that graced the façade niches of Smirke's second-storey (Diploma Galleries) extension on Burlington House (Fig. 8), and to eight busts of Italian and English artists looking down from the clerestory of the Central Hall of Smirke's Main Galleries. Crace's Victorian scheme was dark and overly delicate (Fig. 18). It survived no more than a few decades and was painted out by 1920.

Ware's axial staircase had to be widened in 1876 to cope with the crowds visiting the Summer Exhibition and a columned screen added. The entrance hall was extended to its present size in 1900. Ultimately, in 1991, Lord Foster inserted glass stairs and a lift in the gap between Burlington House and the Main Galleries as vertical access to the Diploma Galleries, which he remodelled as the Sackler Wing of Galleries: an object lesson in how to stitch contemporary design suiting modern needs sensitively into old, historically significant fabric.

Alfred Drury's statue of Sir Joshua Reynolds was erected in 1932 on the axes of the courtyard, which reached its present form as a quadrangle in 1873 and was paved in granite sets and flagstones in 2000 to a scheme by Sir Michael Hopkins. Fountain jets were laid out to reflect the star pattern at the birth of Reynolds on 16 July 1723 (Fig. 9).

The iconography of the Cupid-and-Psyche mythology: Ricci and Kent

The exceptional quality of Ricci's scheme for Gibbs's halpace stair has long been recognised (Fig. 10). It must have been one of the most glorious demonstrations of Venetian painting in England. It was a rich setting designed to impress Burlington's bewigged circle of friends, who would have been steeped in the Roman literature of Horace, Virgil and Pliny as well as Vitruvius.[24] George Knox's article in *The Burlington Magazine* in 1985 convincingly decoded Ricci's mythology as illustrating the *Fortunes of Love*:[25] soft pornographic art to suit the tastes of 18th-century gentlemen, as captured in Alexander Pope's *Epistle to Burlington*:

> But treat the Goddess like a modest fair,
> Nor over-dress, nor leave her wholly bare;
> Let not each beauty ev'ry where be spy'd,
> Where half the skill is decently to hide.
>
> (51-4, Dec. 1731)

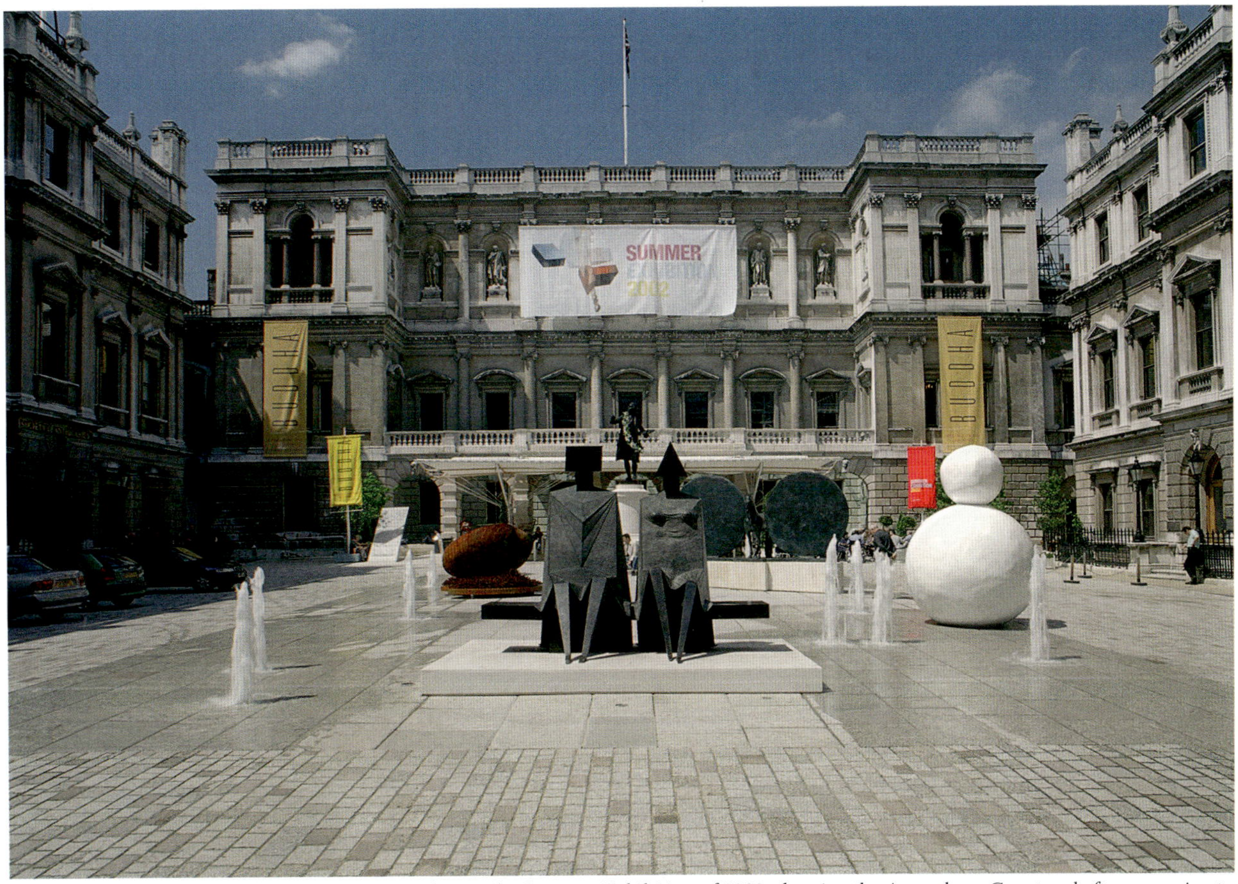

Figure 9 The appearance of Burlington House during the Summer Exhibition of 2002, showing the Annenberg Courtyard after re-paving to Michael Hopkins's scheme, with fountains laid out to the star pattern at the birth of Sir Joshua Reynolds, as designed by Phillip King PPRA, Ian Ritchie RA and Peter Schmitt, Surveyor to the Fabric. *(© F. Ware)*

The original scheme can now be visualised in a reconstruction (Fig. 10).[26] After entering the staircase directly from Pellegrini's hall, you looked up towards the oculus and Ricci's Mount Olympus. Venus fixed your gaze and extended her hand to show the apple awarded to her by Paris, the gods' choice of an impartial judge of divine beauty. The giant stone herms carrying urns or baskets in the corners of the paintings act to define the limits between real architectural space and the fictive landscape of the narrative scenes depicted on canvas.

Ascending, you moved from the real world into the classical world of the Elysian Fields. On the first flight you encountered the *Marriage of Bacchus and Ariadne*, both a reunion and a Triumph of Marital Fidelity. Turning to the right to climb the second flight, you rose with Galatea's sea-horses out of the foamy depths to bear witness to the Triumph of Faithful Love. Mounting the final flight, your attention was drawn to the overdoor *Venus and Cupid* (the painting now at Chiswick House), which, as you turned, led your gaze back up to Olympus and to Venus, whose eyes always followed your progress. Cupid (Eros) is approaching Jupiter on his throne, either to be brought to book, or possibly to ask for the hand of Psyche (signifying Betrothal). From the landing you engaged on a level footing in the action of *Diana and her Nymphs Bathing*. In the centre of the woodland scene, Diana glances down to a nymph on the left, who points to Pan on the right (transformed into one of the corner caryatids). No misbehaviour here, while one contemplated the Triumph of Chastity. The Saloon, on the left in the perspective reconstruction, was entered under the painting of *Diana and Endymion* (again, now at Chiswick House) where, as Burlington's guest, you were invited to enjoy the 'fruits of the hunt'.

Like Laguerre's grand painted staircase at Petworth House of the same date,[27] or the later parallel at Buckingham House (where the Saloon was also approached via a lavish painted staircase), Ricci's scheme was conceived as a theatrical approach to the dining room, an Ascent to Olympus, suggesting to Burlington and his literary circle of guests that they were leaving the world of mere mortals below, defined by Gibbs's staircase, to sup with the gods above. Great buffet tables would have lined the walls of the Saloon itself, presenting the spectacle of the family silver, and one long trestle table would have been put up in the centre and covered in the best white linen damask.

Kent's first task, after arriving with Burlington from Italy in December 1719, was to paint on canvas an Olympian feast on Campbell's newly vaulted Saloon ceiling, directly above Burlington's own groaning table. Il Kentino, to use Burlington's nickname, depicted the gods' table with grey-bearded Jupiter at the head, celebrating the *Wedding Feast of Cupid and Psyche* (Fig. 11). The banquet table and layout, suspended on heavenly clouds, is taken directly from Raphael's *Banquet of the Gods*, frescoed in 1517 by Giulio Romano on the ceiling of the Loggia di Psiche in the Villa Farnesina, perhaps copied by Kent himself while at the studio of Chiari. In the background he created the illusion of architectural depth with a *trompe l'oeil* Venetian-motif archway almost identical to the one painted by Andrea Pozzo for

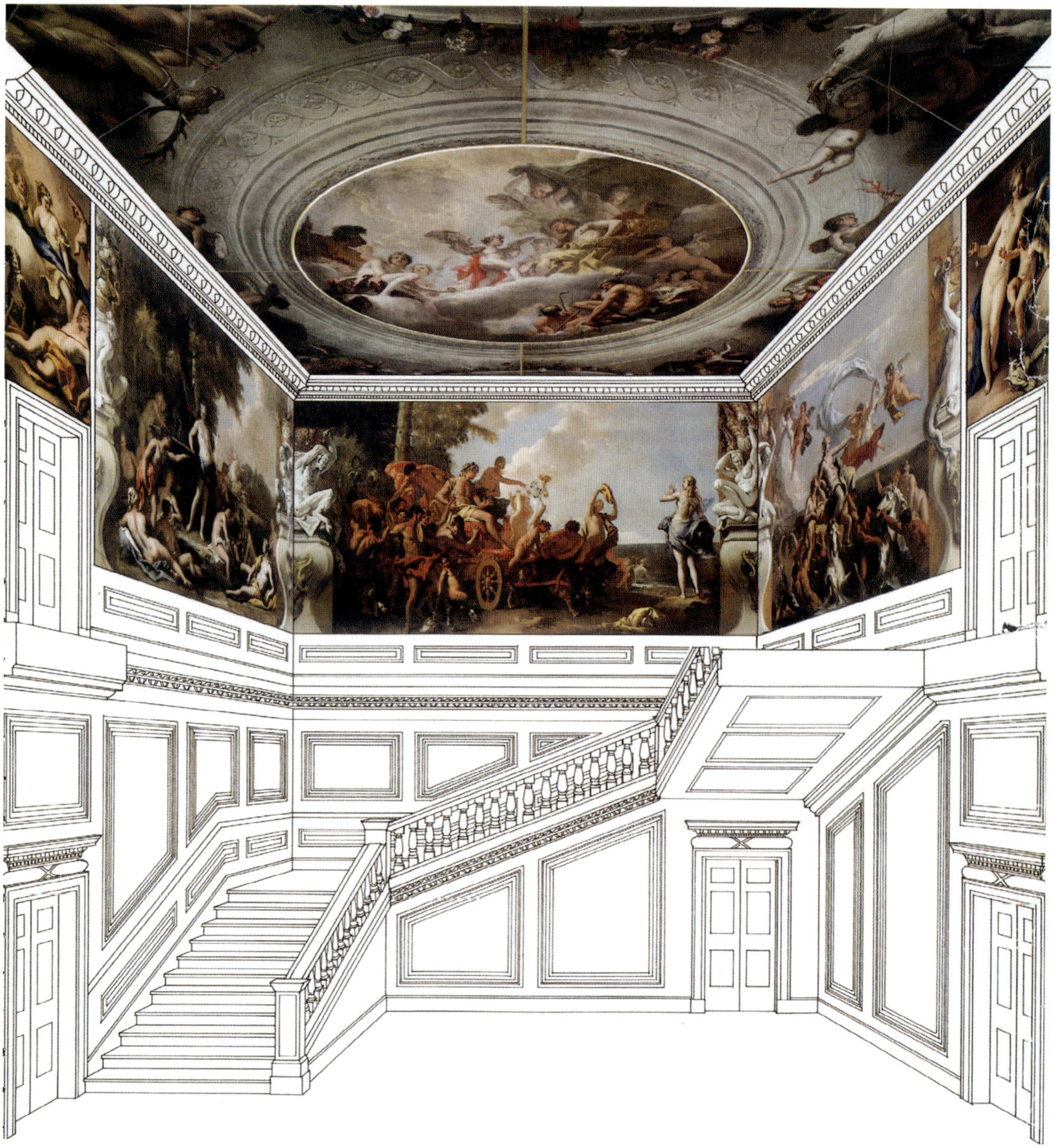

Figure 10 Reconstruction by Peter Schmitt and Phil Crewdson of the original oak staircase compartment designed by Sir James Gibbs in 1715 and decorated with Sebastiano Ricci's mural canvases (cleaned by Bush and Berry in 2002–4). Based on Ware's record drawing of 1812 (before he demolished Gibbs's stair), Ian Bristow's paint investigations and Peter Schmitt's survey of the Ricci paintings. First published in *Country Life*, 1 April 2004. *(© P. Schmitt)*

his Baroque ceiling in San Ignatio in Rome (*St Ignatius Loyola Curing Victims of the Plague*), which he must also have known.

Kent's ceiling in the adjacent bedroom (now the Lee and James C. Slaughter room) derives its square, carved-and-gilded guilloche frame from Ricci's painted oculus. The scene Kent painted here, in oil on the flat, plaster-and-lath ceiling, has been dubbed *Jupiter's Consent to the Nuptials of Cupid and Psyche* by the Survey of London (1963), and is so accepted by Tim Knox in his *Decorative History of the Private Rooms of Burlington House* (May 1998 for the Royal Academy), although it has alternatively been called *Assembly of the Gods* (Fig. 12).[28] Surely the former title describes the theme of the Ricci ceiling. Jupiter and Juno also inhabit Kent's clouds on Olympus to balance Ricci's canvas of Olympus, which crowned Gibbs's halpace stair, and was of the same two-bay size, square and on the same ceiling plane (again, not vaulted). But Ricci's iconography should be decoded thus: 'Cupid, as swift as lightning penetrating the heights of heaven, presented himself before Jupiter with his supplication (Psyche's hand in marriage). Jupiter lent a favouring ear, and pleaded the cause of the lovers so earnestly with Venus that he

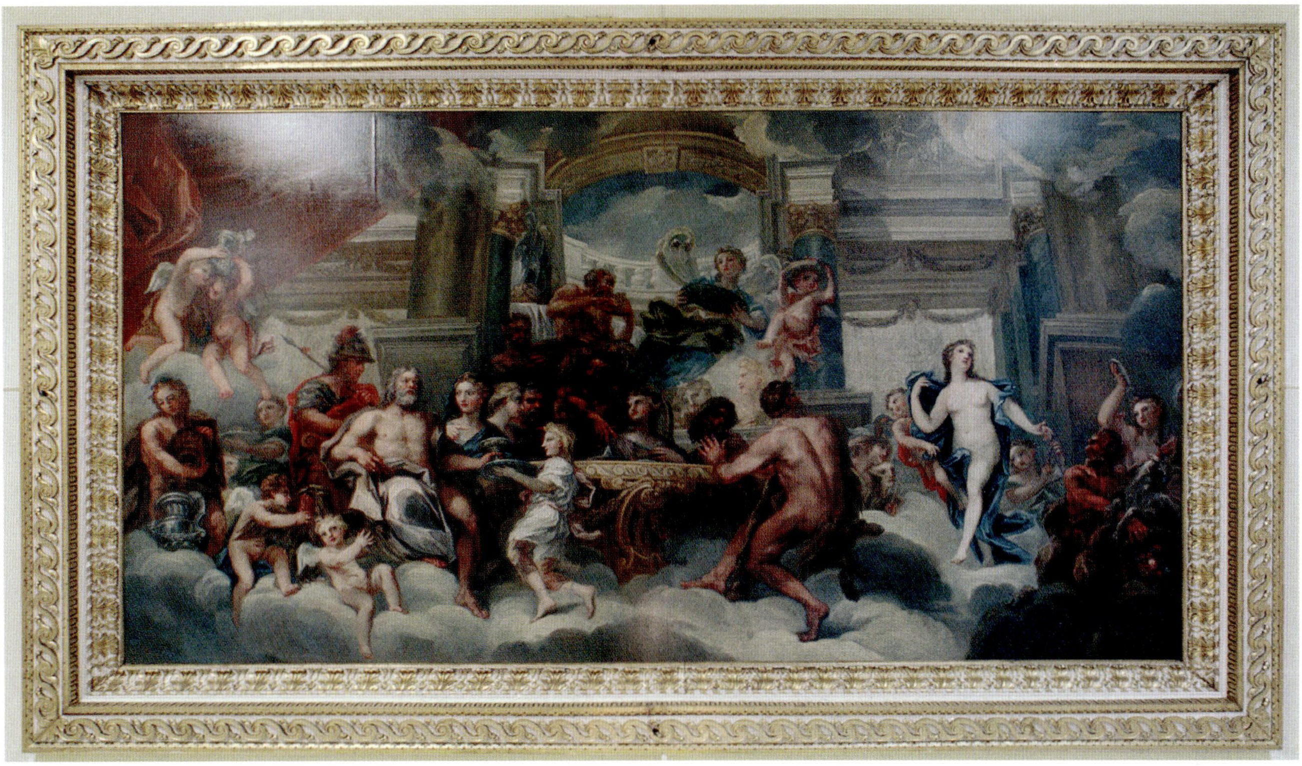

Figure 11 Royal Academy, London: *The Wedding Feast of Cupid and Psyche*, painted by William Kent on canvas and set within a gilded wooden frame on the vaulted Saloon ceiling in 1720. The painting is oriented to be seen from south (or window) side, with the viewer entering from Gibbs's staircase. Eyes at one end of the table are focused on bearded Jupiter, who sits and stares towards the other end, where lovely Psyche does a striptease. *(© F. Ware)*

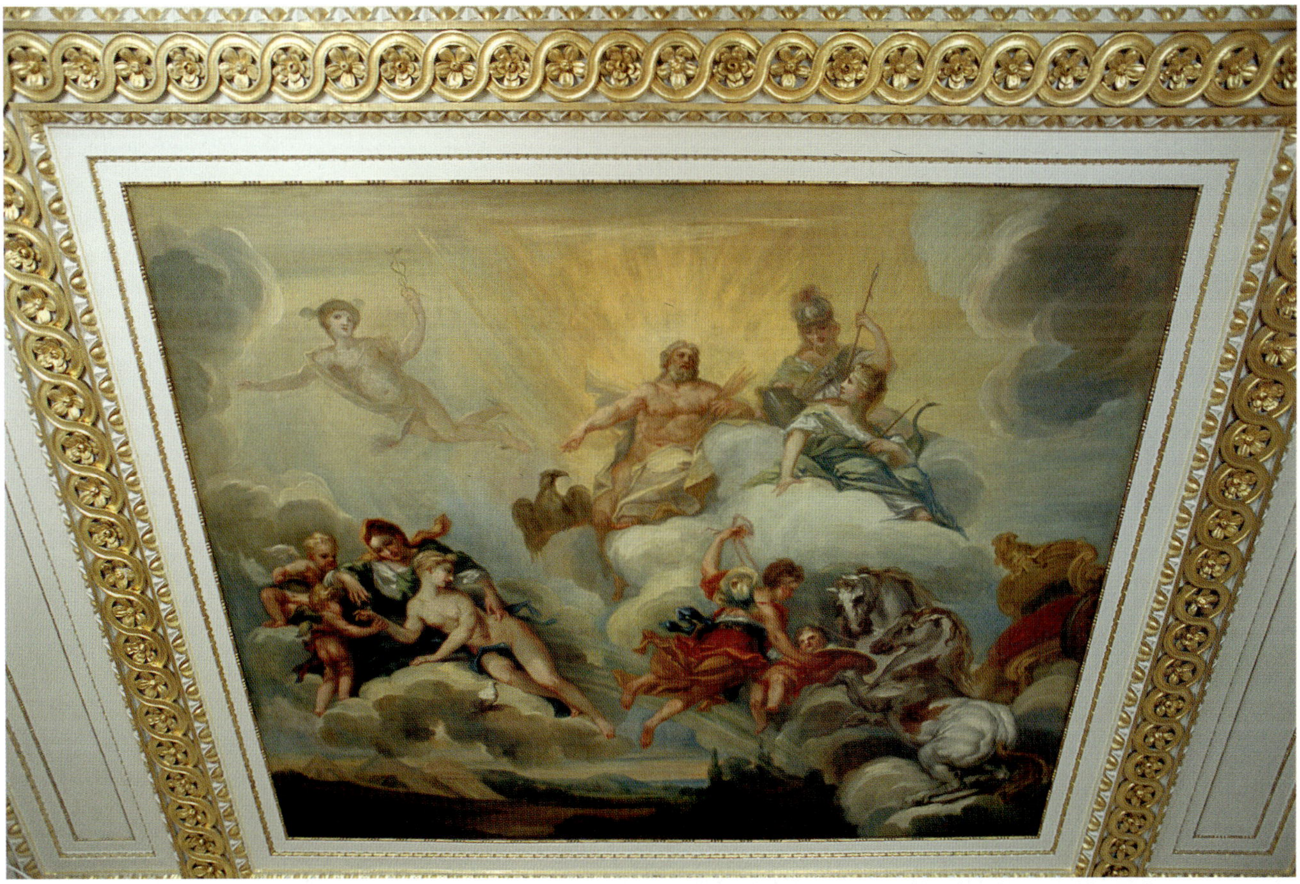

Figure 12 Royal Academy, London: *Psyche Created Immortal (on her Nuptial Night) Before an Assembly of Gods*, painted by William Kent on the ceiling of what is now the Lee and James C. Slaughter Room. The horses are copied in every detail from Ricci's muscular equine beasts propelling Galatea out of the sea. *(© F. Ware)*

won her consent.'[29] Venus, no longer jealous of Psyche's beauty, extends in her hand the apple from Paris, as proof that her beauty surpasses all others.

To undress Kent's bedroom tableau (Fig. 12): winged Mercury can be spotted, beckoning Psyche, who has descended from a one-seater chariot parked where it had whisked her away from the wedding feast next door in the Saloon. Kent copied his snorting horses from Ricci. The same cupids, with red ribbons from the feast, offer trays of wine. She is 'wholly bare', holding a cup, which is being filled, while Jupiter gestures with outstretched arm, and Juno and Mars serve as witnesses: 'On this he (Jupiter) sent Mercury to bring Psyche up to the heavenly assembly, and when she arrived, handing her a cup of ambrosia, he said, "Drink this Psyche, and be immortal, nor shall Cupid ever break away from the knot in which he is tied, but these nuptials shall be perpetual".'[30] Kent's ceiling painting should be re-titled, while the sun sets in the distance, *Psyche Created Immortal (on her Nuptial Night) Before an Assembly of Gods*. The result of their union was a daughter, Pleasure.

The two ceilings, therefore, circumscribe like bookends the vaulted three-bay Saloon in the middle, where Kent painted the wedding banquet and where Burlington entertained his friends to dinner. Unlike Raphael's composition, however, Kent's window onto the mythological feasting on Olympus floated unsatisfactorily within a gilded rectangular frame, which had no visible anchor in the rich architecture of the Saloon. This absence of decoration on the plaster cove became the focus of investigation during the redecoration of the room in 2001.

The discovery and conservation of two painted schemes (by Pauline Plummer)

In autumn 2001 Peter Schmitt, as architect in charge of the conservation of the Fine Rooms, asked me to examine the coving in the Saloon to see if I could find any trace of a design contemporary with the earliest decoration of the room. The Saloon, unlike other parts of the RA, has retained its original William Kent scheme, including the large, painted, ceiling canvas representing the marriage feast of Cupid and Psyche described above (Figs 11 and 13). While the walls present a richly gilded arrangement of architectural and foliate details, on my first visit to the room, the coving was white, and, disturbingly, the rather dark ceiling painting appeared to hang unsupported.

There are no known records – neither drawings nor written descriptions – of the original treatment of the coving in this room. Schemes painted by Kent in several other grand houses used *trompe l'oeil* coffering in this position, but some early Kent drawings do exist for two schemes that were never executed (Houghton and at Kensington Palace) (Fig. 15).[31] These are much the same date as the Saloon scheme, and both show lunettes and spandrels, the lunettes containing crowded groups of overlapping figures, visible from the shins upward, sitting or standing behind a decorative parapet. In the spandrels, figures support the frames of the lunettes and there are swags of foliage. The reason for the obliteration of the Kent scheme was not known. One possibility was that continual seepage of rainwater through a leaking roof might have caused

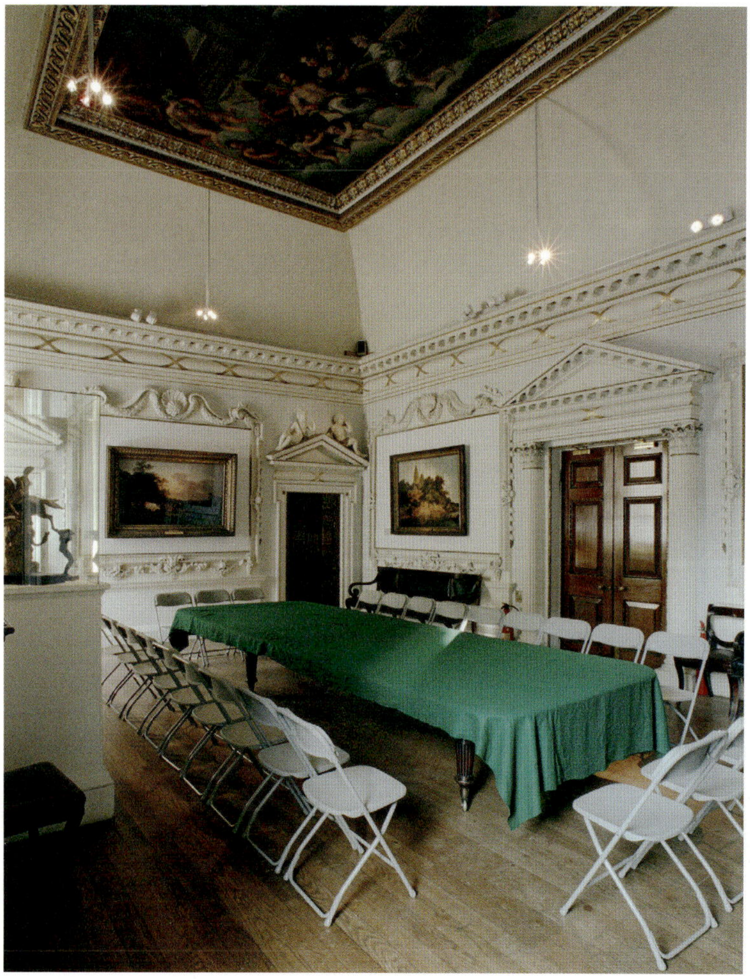

Figure 13 Royal Academy, London: the Saloon in 2000, before its restoration, with Kent's ceiling canvas *The Nuptial Feast of Cupid and Psyche* (1720) in place. The decorations on the plaster cove had long since been covered over: Kent's scheme in the 1770s and Crace's by 1924. The gilding of the crossed ribbons on the pulvinated frieze is Crace's. (© F. Ware)

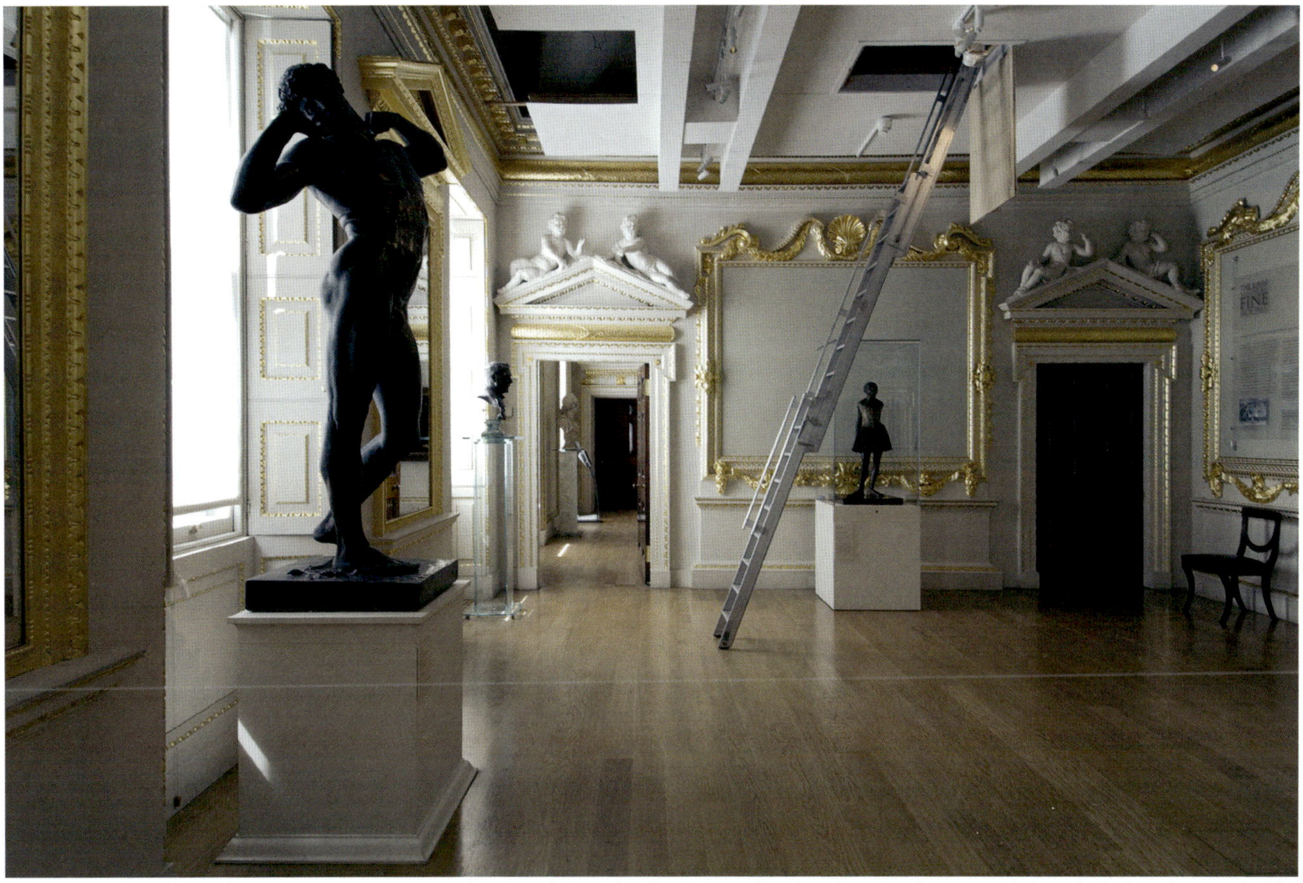

Figure 14 The Saloon after restoration as reopened in March 2004 by the Prince of Wales, showing the suspended crash deck and access ladder still in place. Based on Ian Bristow's paint analysis, Ware's enfilade was re-established along the entire length of the front, and Kent's lavish gilding recreated in 24-carat gold leaf. *(© F. Ware)*

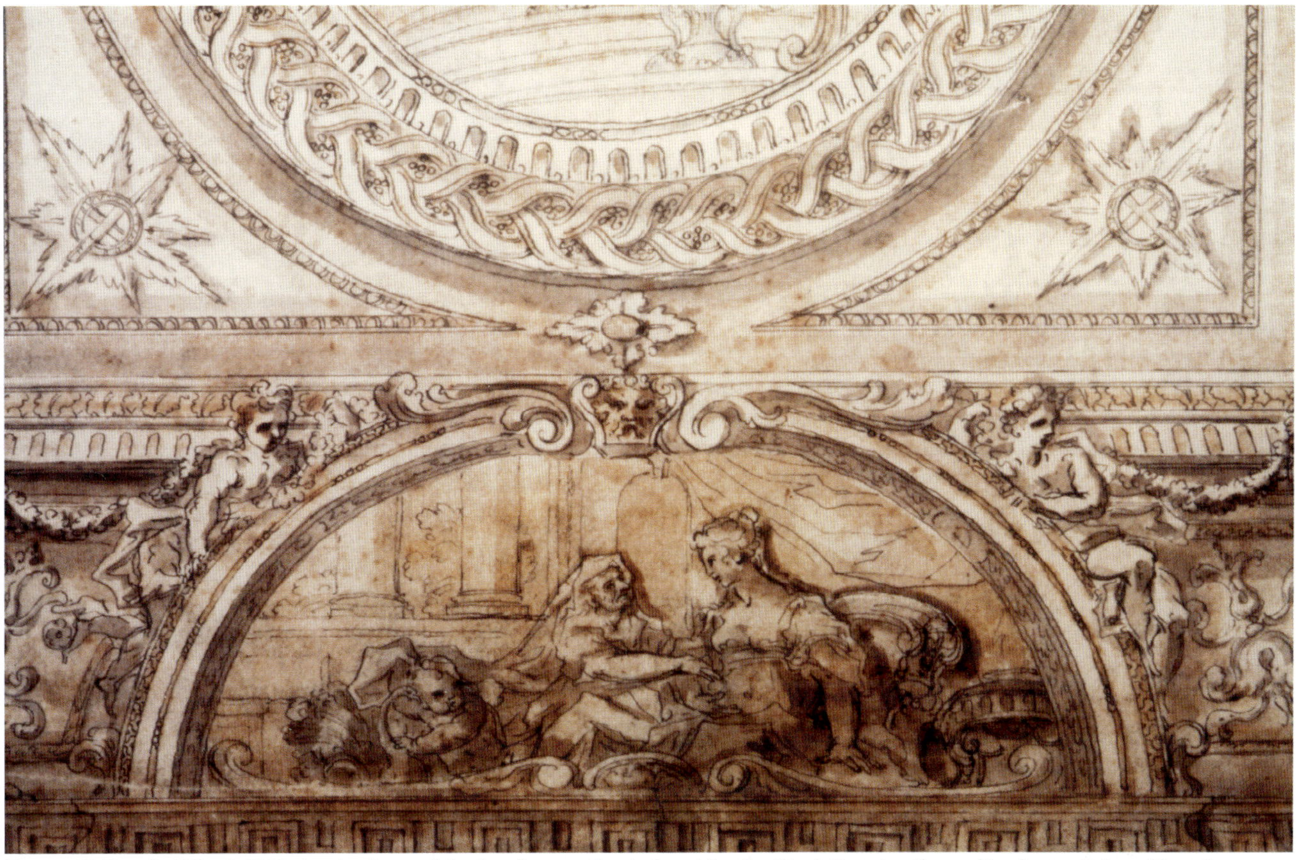

Figure 15 Detail of Kent's 1723 sketch of one of the four lunettes he designed for the King's Drawing Room, Kensington Palace. The scheme was never executed. *(Photo courtesy of John Harris)*

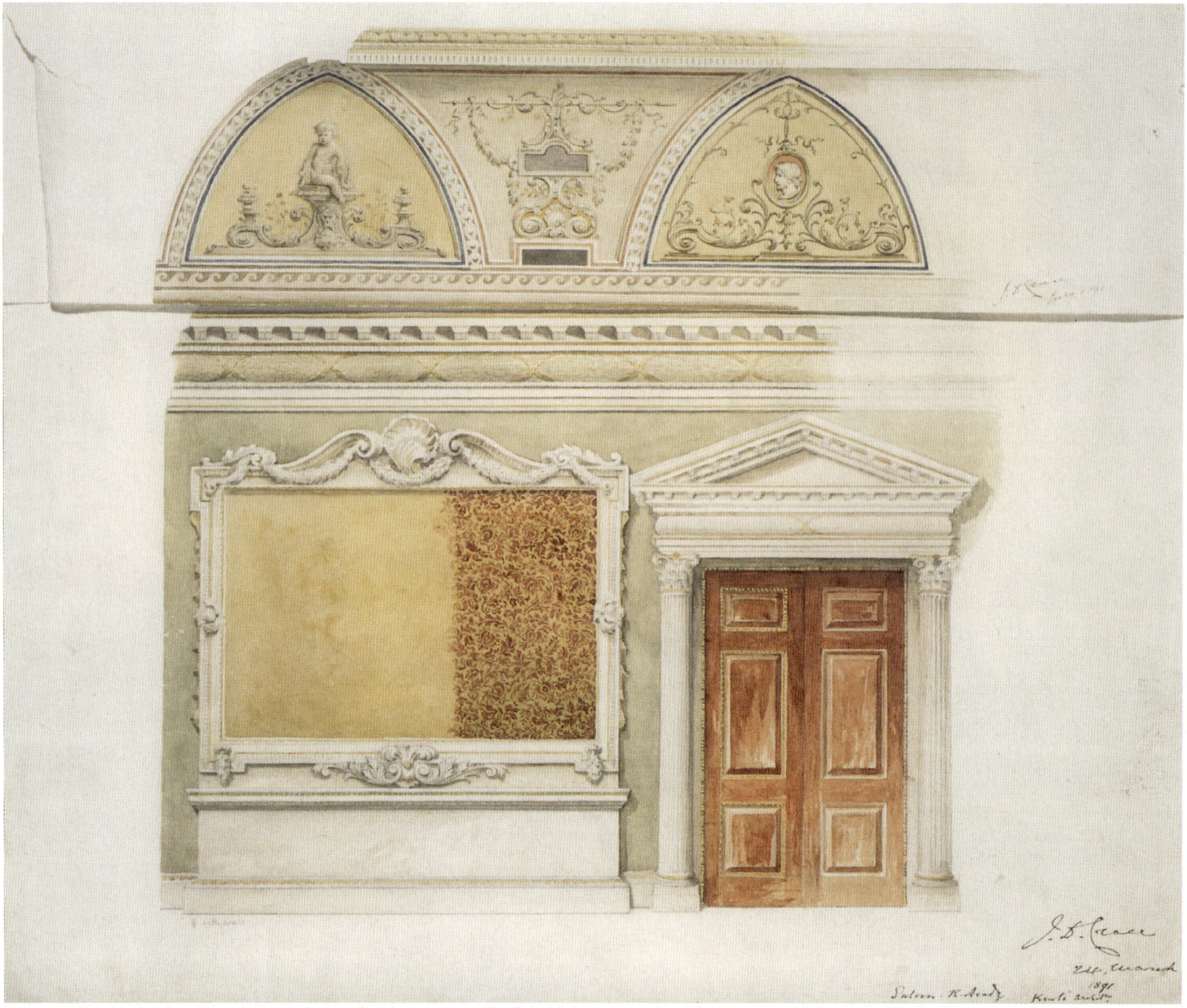

Figure 16 John Diblee Crace's 1891 design for the north wall of the Saloon showing Kent's swagged frame infilled with mottled fabric, and one of the three schemes proposed for the cove. Between two alternative designs for the lunettes (one with a cameo portrait) are decorated plaques similar to those eventually executed. *(© The Board of Trustees of the Victoria and Albert Museum)*

considerable damage, and after retouching flaking paint for a few decades, the owners might have decided to paint over the whole scheme.

The story was complicated by the fact that the coving was also known to have been painted in 1891 by the Crace firm of interior decorators to a design by John Diblee Crace, the fifth and last of the Crace dynasty (Fig. 16).[32] Crace's preliminary watercolours survive in the V&A Museum, with optional variations shown in his design. Dim photographs of the 1890s proved that the Crace scheme had certainly been executed, although it was not known which version had been chosen. This Victorian scheme had in its turn disappeared beneath several layers of plain paint, applied from about 1920 onwards. Most of the overlying layers were plain coats of oil-bound house paint, all in pale tones of blue, green, cream or grey.

The plan of redecoration for the Saloon focused attention on the coving, and raised a number of questions. Was there a 1720 design for the coving, and, if so, what was it? Was it executed, did it still exist, and if so in what condition? Finally, if the scheme still existed, could it be uncovered?

Preliminary investigations

The coving had already been sampled but only a nondescript dark colour as the lowest layer had been found.[33] Above this were some 14 layers of oil-based overpaint, making 17 layers altogether from plaster to surface. Some areas had also been scraped back to the level of the speculative Kent painting, with the same dull green/brown being found as in the cross-sections. Neither the Kent nor Crace schemes could be detected by infrared reflectography (IRR).[34] The main lines of the Crace scheme were, however, clear in raking light. It could be seen that a series of pointed lunettes and spandrels ran round the room, while the cameos, indicated in the watercolours, had been painted on canvas, presumably in the studio, and subsequently stuck in place.

Peter Schmitt wished to have a section of the Crace scheme uncovered: since it was a repetitive design, theoretically one section, uncovered and retouched, would be sufficient for recording the whole. It was also possible that the canvas cameos could be removed and stored.

Uncovering

Faced with a 6ft-deep coving (in a room about 20 × 30ft), completely white apart from Hassall's small test scrapes, initial investigations were unhelpful, until at last a tiny patch of crimson pink was found, only a centimetre further on from the test scrapes. It could have been a flower petal, or drapery, or part of a hand, but whatever it was, it proved that the Kent scheme existed, had not been completely scraped off, or rubbed down, and was not merely an overall green/brown. With such a colour in that position, the design was very unlikely to be a totally architectural design (such as a *trompe l'oeil* coffering). It was decided that we should concentrate on the 30ft southern section of the coving. A complete crash deck was constructed with a telescopic ladder and trap door, so that all could be shut away when the room was used for evening events. There were usually seven or eight conservators working on the project at any one time. In due course, air conditioning was installed, and with a good level of lighting, very satisfactory working conditions were achieved.

Method of uncovering

After exhaustive experimentation with different combinations of chemicals, and variations in their use with pastes and gels, heated scalpels and hot-air jets, an ultrasonic vibrating scalpel, and even consideration of laser cleaning, as the weeks went past the simplest and most successful methods were evolved. To uncover the Crace scheme, the upper four layers of overpaint were removed with a repeated sequence using an application of Nitromors green-label paint stripper, followed by acetone and cellosolve, and careful scraping.

To uncover the Kent painting the most effective method was found to be a combination of white spirit and scraping until a natural point of separation was reached, just below the priming of the Crace scheme. From there work continued with very sharp scalpels alone until only the slightest haze of overpaint was left. Saliva and further scalpel work at that stage resulted in a perfect clearance, and the colours were revealed in all their depth of tone and colour. Most of the paint proved firmly bound, but where it showed a tendency to chip, it was treated with Paraloid B72 and ironed (Fig. 17).

All around the room, and on the east wall in particular, were areas where the plaster skim coat and all the subsequent paint layers had separated from the main plaster. These areas were fixed by injecting lime slurry.[35] We found it necessary to remove the top few layers of modern overpaint first to allow the remaining layers to relax, so they could be eased back into position.

Sequence of uncovering

At first work concentrated on the Crace scheme. Along three walls we marked in the outlines of the lunettes and spandrels where these could be seen in raking light (the east wall was flaking rather badly so we avoided touching it until it could be stabilised). We gradually uncovered and plotted the outlines of the Crace motifs at the west end of the south wall, comparing them with the watercolours in case there were discrepancies, until it was possible to establish the areas of the background colour, a plain yellow ochre. These areas were marked onto the overpaint. The same shapes were then traced and redrawn in the identical positions on the adjacent two lunettes and on the spandrels of the south coving. We knew that, if we cut through those areas, we should only be destroying the plain background of the Crace scheme and not the finely painted architectural and floral details.

When we had enough information, and it seemed safe to risk cutting through to the Kent layer, a test was made in the centre of one of the lunettes. At once a head was found, which naturally aroused tremendous excitement. It was soon realised, however, that the surface of the Kent painting had been abraded before being overpainted. The level of damage varies from place to place, but is scarcely noticeable a few feet back from the wall.

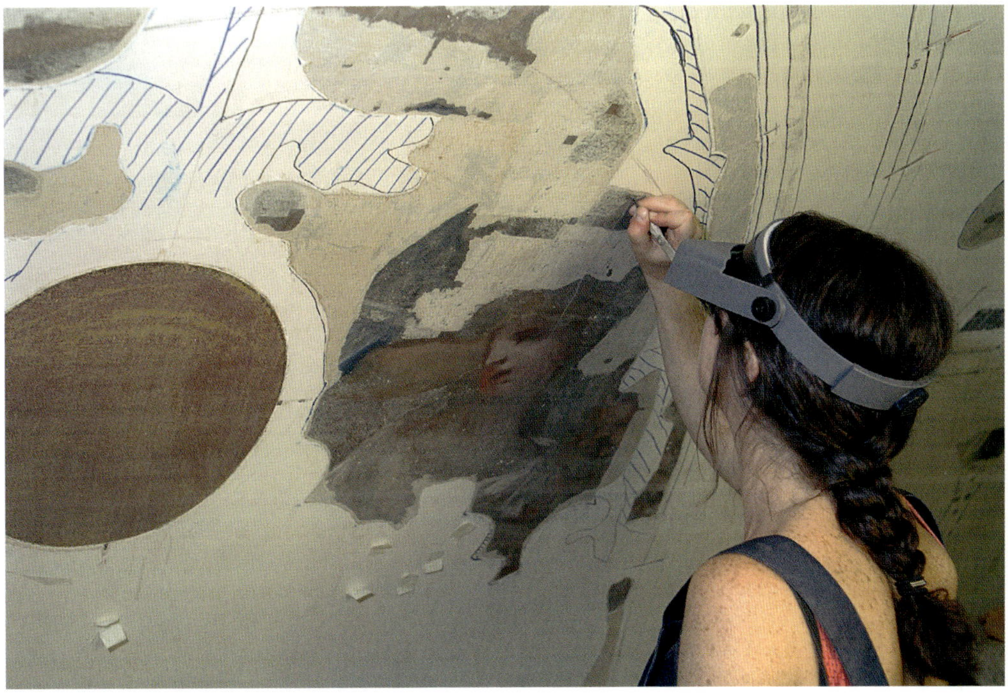

Figure 17 Uncovering of the Kent scheme in the eastern lunette of the south cove by Adeline Wartner. Revealed is the face of Psyche and beside her head the arm of Cupid. Removed from the oval to the left was Crace's portrait on canvas of Sir Thomas Lawrence (PRA 1820–30), now in the RA picture store. *(© F. Ware)*

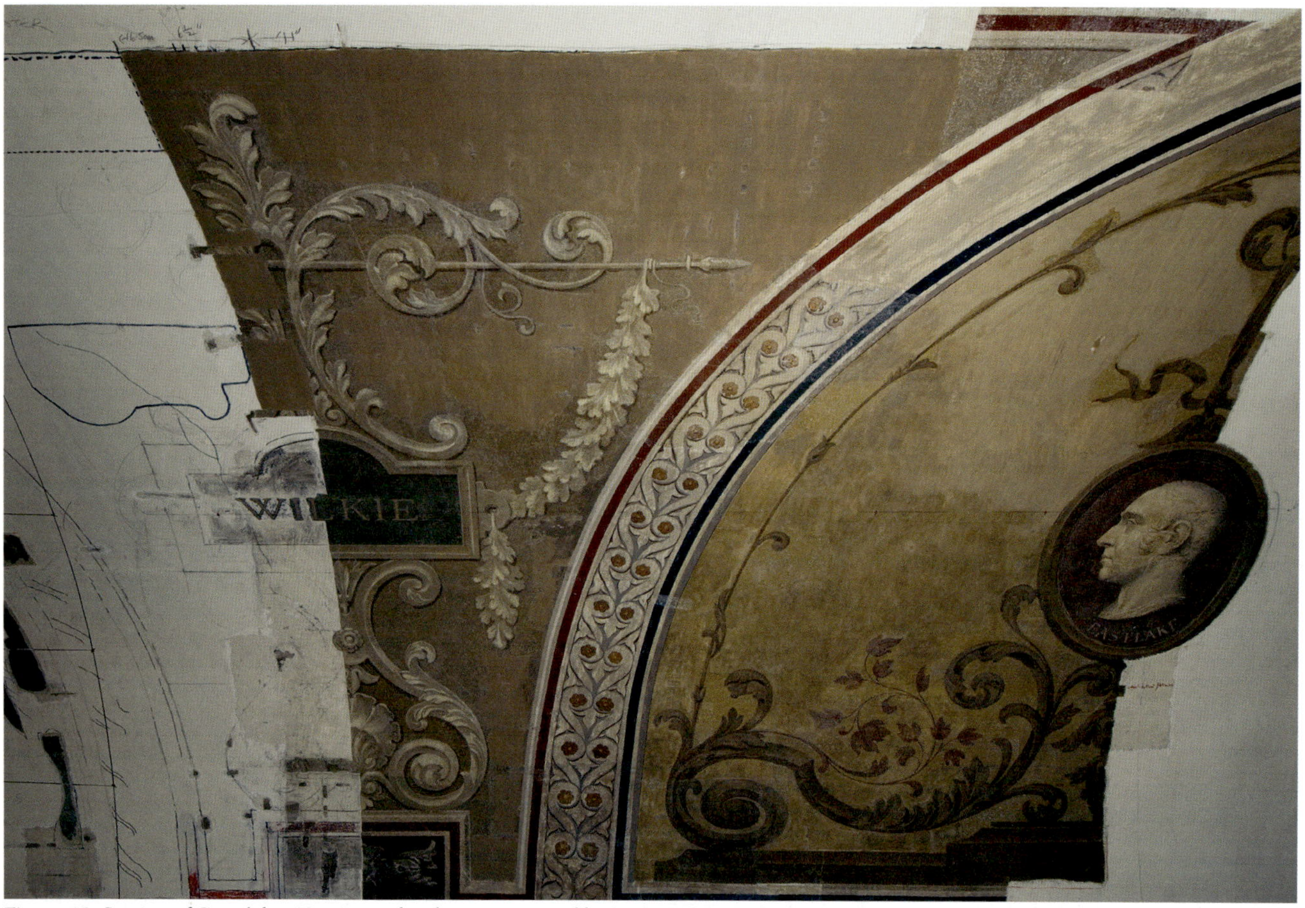

Figure 18 Section of Crace's late Kentian-style scheme uncovered by Pauline Plummer's team. A cameo portrait of Sir Charles Eastlake, President of the Royal Academy from 1850 to 1865, is painted on canvas set on a background of yellow ochre in the lunette. Sir David Wilkie RA has been named on the plaque in the triangular spandrel. *(© F. Ware)*

Uncovering was very slow and the areas uncovered were dictated by the Crace design, and not by the apparent composition of the Kent. The scheme appeared almost imperceptibly, although over the weeks and months the conservators honed their skills, until a nicety of judgement and a remarkable speed was reached in uncovering. The more that the painting was exposed, the more closely it appeared to correspond with the early Kent drawings: semicircular lunettes with architectural framework enclosing compact groups of figures, and grisaille painting in the spandrels.

Work continued on both schemes simultaneously. As the months passed the Crace was gradually uncovered (Fig. 18). This work was restricted to half a lunette[36] for the purposes of making a careful record, in case the Crace scheme should eventually be destroyed to uncover the earlier painting. To save time and expense, after various sections had been uncovered the remainder of the repetitive parts (such as the framing border along the top and round the lunettes, and the Vitruvian scroll at the base) were reconstructed sufficiently for recording. Original paint was then varnished with matt Paraloid B72, and overpainting and reconstructions were executed with acrylic paints.

Removal of some of the attached cameos allowed us to increase the area of the Kent that could be uncovered without destroying more of the Crace paint layer. It was decided to remove two of the cameos from the south coving (portraits of *Lawrence* and *Archer Shee*), together with a cameo of the RA monogram from the north wall. The adhesive proved to be animal glue, not (as feared) white-lead paste. We found that after facing up with tissue and Paraloid B72, and then with muslin, it was possible to ease the canvases off the wall with a hot-air pen and a heated scalpel. At the time of writing, only these three canvases have been taken down and currently reside in the RA's picture store.

To investigate the Kent paintings further, after consultations with English Heritage it was agreed that we should cut through in the central scene in wide vertical and horizontal bands to establish the shape of the framework round the figures (Fig. 19). This was a difficult decision to make, since the Crace is of high quality and was in good condition. Although beautifully painted, however, the style is too delicate to go with the bold, Baroque style of Kent's work, as exemplified in ceiling painting and wall decorations.

The Crace scheme

The colour scheme is practically monochrome carried out in tones of yellow ochre, browns and buffs, with red and blue outlines to the arches and small yellow flowers on the framework. The cameos on canvas proved to be portraits of seven presidents of the RA, from Reynolds to Leighton (president at the date of the painting).[37]

On the north wall, over the entrance door from the landing, the central canvas bore the RA monogram and the foundation date 1768, while on the right is George III, patron at the time of

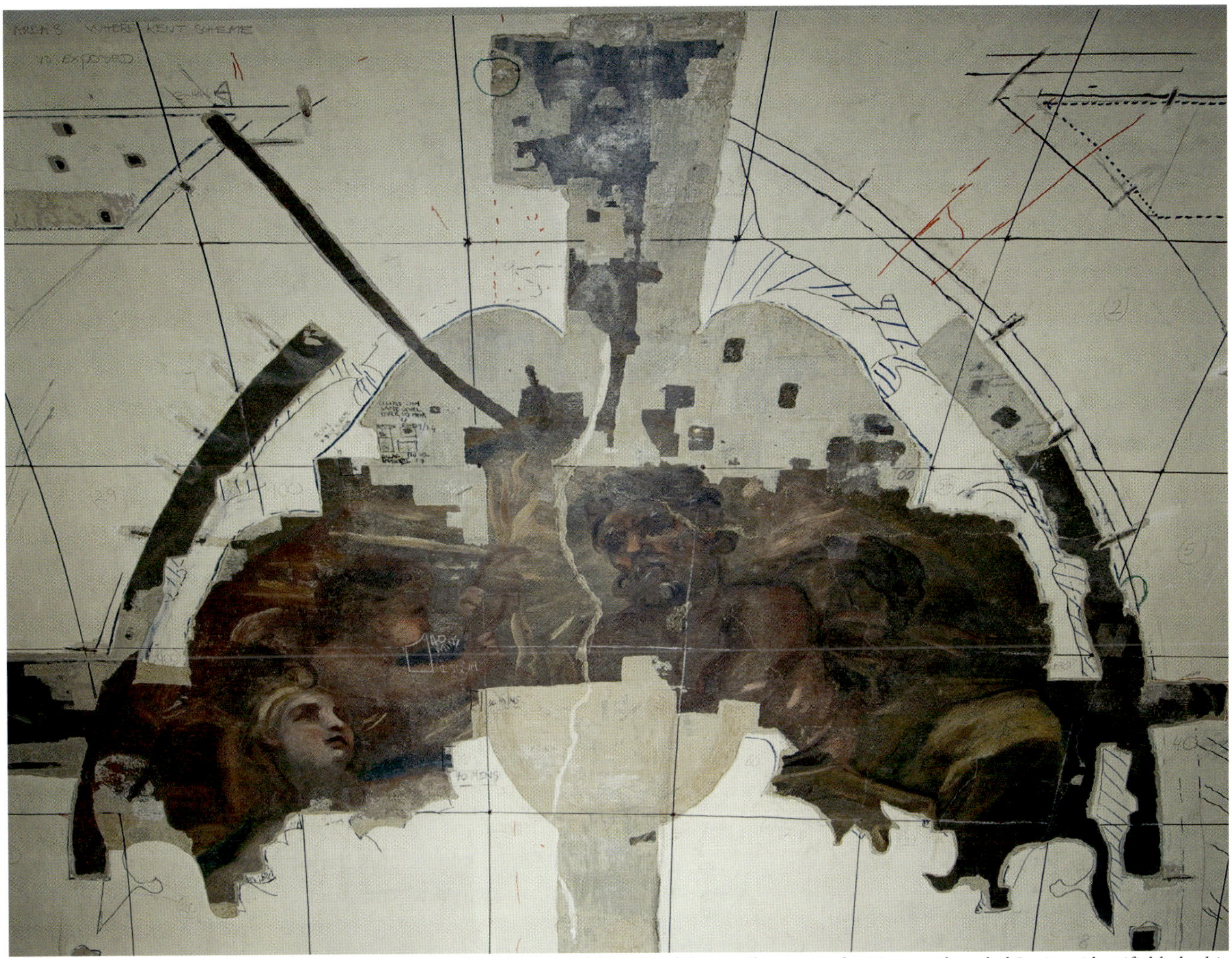

Figure 19 A section of Kent's 1720 scheme uncovered in the central lunette of the south cove. It depicts grey-bearded Jupiter, identifiable by his thunderbolt, and presumably jealous Venus to the left wearing a diadem and flaming heart, one of her attributes. Above Jupiter's head is a grisaille mask, the keystone of the arch. On the arch (partially uncovered to the left beyond the photograph) recline grisaille figures, as in Kent's drawing for Kensington Palace (Fig. 15). *(© F. Ware)*

the RA's foundation, and on the left Queen Victoria, monarch at the time of the Crace commission. These portraits are all in similar colours to the decorative work: greys, buffs and ochres against a deep-red background. Between the canvas portraits are the names of some of the most prominent academicians, painted directly on the wall on fictive tablets in the centre of the spandrels. Sufficient was uncovered of each name to identify them as Chambers, Gainsborough, Flaxman, Wilkie, Turner and Landseer, celebrating outstanding representatives of architecture, painting and sculpture in the eighteenth and nineteenth centuries.

The Kent scheme

By the time we brought the first stage to a halt at the end of August 2003 (after some 5000 hours of work), we had established that the Kent decoration was a compressed version of his slightly later Kensington Palace design. Of the three lunettes on the south wall, two have been partially explored. They are coloured, the scheme being predominantly warm – browns, reds, pinks and flesh colour with occasional blues over a green-grey ground. The design consists of tightly grouped figures, their heads roughly at the mid-point of the coving, and the lower part of their bodies hidden behind a decorative parapet. They are placed within concentric arches and there is a grisaille mask as keystone.

The spandrels, painted in tones of grey, appear to include caryatids, or figures supporting the framework, and there is also foliage. One assumes that they, too, are similar to those in the drawing. Peter Schmitt discusses their iconography and their relationship to the Kent scheme as a whole below.

Conclusions

It would seem that the paintings were covered over after only a couple of generations. There was a change of occupancy in the 1770s and the very different style of decoration fashionable at the time might account for their obliteration. I have seen little to bear out my initial theory of water damage. The east wall might have suffered at some time. Since it was delaminating quite badly, we did not investigate it, waiting until it had been consolidated and was safe to touch. Several cracks had been filled, very carefully and evenly, before the Crace scheme was begun. Naturally, once the overpaint was removed down to the surface of the Kent paint, those fills were proud. There were also some 20th-century repairs on the west and north walls, possibly dealing with war damage, but the extent of these was not investigated.

For the future, it is hoped to continue the uncovering of the south coving, to carry out any necessary repairs and to retouch sufficiently to present a uniform appearance from ground level. Even with a large team, this one wall would be likely to take several years to uncover. In 2004 trial samples were made using gel mixtures with lipase.[38] One of the mixtures was extremely promising and removed the last paint layer, including the milky haze, revealing Kent's brushwork with amazing clarity. It has the potential of halving the estimated time to restore the Kent cove to its original quality. Test areas on the remaining three sides of the coving would be recorded, and then the coving might be coloured to harmonise with the exposed paintings on the southern section. The rhythm of lunettes and spandrels might be recreated, but the painting would be of the simplest kind, and it would always remain possible to continue to uncover the remaining walls at any time in the future.

The project is, of course, subject to ethical considerations, and particularly to financial constraints. It is hoped, however, that it can be resumed before too long.

William Kent's painted scheme in the Saloon revealed (by Peter Schmitt)

When Pauline Plummer and her team rediscovered Kent's elaborate figurative scheme for the Saloon coving of 1720, lost for 250 years, it became possible to make sense of the painted mythology of the Saloon, and of how it related to the decoration of the adjoining spaces. The iconographical programme for the ceilings in the Saloon and in the adjoining bedroom[39] took their inspiration from the events on Olympus depicted in Sebastiano Ricci's ceiling canvas, involving Cupid and his mother Venus. From this only Psyche, Cupid's future wife, was absent.

The story Kent was illustrating, told in the *Metamorphoses* by the Roman writer Apuleius (usually known as *The Golden Ass*), would have been well known to the Burlington circle.[40] Episodes from the legend were depicted in Raphael's decorative scheme for the ceiling of the Loggia di Psiche in the Villa Farnesina in Rome (executed in 1517–18 by Giulio Romano from a Raphael cartoon). Ten years later Giulio Romano created an orgy of bare flesh in fresco for Federico Gonzaga in the Sala di Amore e Psiche (room of Cupid and Psyche) in Palazzo Te in Mantua (completed by five assistants in 1528). He engulfed the space with episodes from Apuleius (as well as stories of heroes and gods derived from *Hypnerotomachia Poliphili*, which Ricci had also borrowed for his stair murals). Kent visited Palazzo Te in 1714.[41] The story is an allegory of the soul in search of love, which can be interpreted as the soul's ascent through suffering to purification in the celestial realm. Apuleius recounts Psyche's trials at the hands of Venus, Cupid's jealous mother, and of her living happily ever after when finally rescued and wedded by Cupid. It is recognisably retold in fairytales such as *Snow White and the Seven Dwarfs*, *Beauty and the Beast* and *Cinderella*.[42]

No drawings by Kent appear to have survived for the Saloon decoration. As John Harris suggested,[43] however, Kent's unexecuted design of 1723 for the ceiling of the King's Drawing Room in Kensington Palace (which was his next project and obtained through Burlington's introduction) might be used as a guide. In both, the lunette scenes along the cove are contained within a series of grisaille arches, which also feature caryatids and keystone masks (see Fig. 19), and which structurally support the gilded frame that opens a window onto heaven (Fig. 11). The motif was derived from Ricci's *trompe l'oeil* arches on the ceiling of the balancing staircase, which hold aloft a massive oculus. Unfortunately Ricci's arches are mere vestiges today, having been drastically cut down in 1815–18, when Samuel Ware inserted a plaster cove and raised the canvas to its present position.

So far, two scenes from Kent's *Cupid and Psyche* have been partially revealed on the Saloon cove (see Figs 17 and 19). The central scene shows Jupiter brandishing a thunderbolt, his arm held in restraint by a putto (too youthful to be Cupid himself), to prevent him unleashing it on envious and vengeful Venus, whose face, we believe, can be seen just below his arm. The other episode shows Psyche, who had unwittingly opened a casket (thinking its contents would make her more beautiful) and had fallen into deathly sleep, being roused by an arm, presumably Cupid's, when he, 'gathering up the sleep from her body, closed it again in the box, and waked Psyche with a light touch of one of his arrows'.[44] Kent's paintbrush is alive with Ricci's eyes and faces.

The denouement of the mythology was concluded by Kent on his central ceiling canvas in the Saloon, depicting the nude and semi-nude heavenly crowd at the wedding banquet (Fig. 11). In the nuptial bedroom next door, Psyche lives happily ever after on the ceiling, holding a cup of ambrosia, which dubs her immortal and her marriage to Cupid 'perpetual'. During the Crace interlude of 1891 the Saloon ceiling cove was redecorated with Victorian iconography, tailored to the Royal Academy as an institution and illustrating the pedigree of its patrons and artist-Members (Fig. 18). It was short-lived and covered over in white paint by 1920.

The Saloon, whose proportions conform to Palladio's ideal ratio of 1:1.414 (square root of 2), is the purest element in the sequence of spaces on the *piano nobile*. It is the *gusto Italiano* that Kent was brought over to create. It is a strongly architectural space of classical purity, ornately gilded, with the relieving colour up on the ceiling. All is balanced and symmetrical. Kent's swagged-and-gilded picture frames, however, stand empty, in anticipation of *trompe l'oeil* landscapes, which were never painted. It is a belvedere waiting to happen. In the adjacent staircase compartment, Ricci's woodland setting for *Diana and her Nymphs Bathing* (1712–15) might be pornography's justification as art. However it must have inspired an appetite for a new type of garden, a landscape garden, later realised by Kent at Stowe and Rousham, but preached in 1712 by Shaftesbury, when he wrote from Naples, 'The Wilderness pleases. We seem to live alone with Nature. We view her in her inmost recesses, and contemplate her with more Delight in these original Wilds, than in the artificial labyrinths and feign'd Wildernesses of the Palace.'[45]

Between 2000 and 2004, the RA removed more than a century of accretions and at a cost of £6m restored and air conditioned Lord Cavendish's enfilade suite of principal rooms, whose imprint of white and gold is Kentian and Kent Revival, but whose critical rearrangement was the work of Samuel Ware between 1815 and 1818. They are now open to the public as the John Madejski Fine Rooms to display the RA's Permanent Collection. The idea of the Royal Academy was the outcome of the 18th century's concern for cultural superiority at the forefront of which were Burlington and his mother and which resulted in the foundation in 1768 of a body of professional artists and schools for their training. The Royal Academy of Arts still embodies English 'liberty', independent creativity, unshackled by state obligations or patronage.

A crash deck is still suspended in the Saloon (Fig. 14), awaiting a benefactor so Kent's Cupid-and-Psyche cycle on the cove can be revealed and the finest neo-Palladian interior in England experienced in all its lavish splendour. The result of Burlington's 10-year programme of decorations had provided Burlington House with some of the most sumptuous interiors in London. John Gay wrote in his *Trivia* (Bk II, 11.23–8, 1715):

Yet Burlington's fair palace still remains;
Beauty within, without proportion reigns,
Beneath his eye declining art revives,
The wall with animated picture lives;
There Handel strikes the strings, the melting strain
Transports the soul and thrills through every vein,
There oft I enter (but with cleaner shoes)
For Burlington's belov'd by Ev'ry Muse.

Acknowledgements

We would like to thank the following: John Harris for finding the Kent drawings for the Kensington Palace ceiling design believed to be dated 1723 and Kent's 1725 design for the saloon at Houghton; Cinzia Maria Sicca for information about Kent's training in Rome, where Burlington recruited him, for her judgement that Kent's figurative painting on the Saloon cove is of quality and for her information on Roman decorative schemes; and Megan Aldrich for her advice on the Crace decorations; and intrepid Francis Ware for photographing every stage of the restoration over five years. Ian Bristow has been stalwart in his support throughout the restoration work, in examining more than 800 paint samples to identify the paintwork and gilding on all of the mouldings in all of the rooms at all periods and for producing a definitive *Report on an Investigation of Paint Samples from the Fine Rooms of Lord Burlington's House* (March 2005). The late John Cornforth's advice and encouragement proved invaluable to the project.

Notes

1. Pevsner 1993, p. 48.
2. See Anthony Ashley Cooper, 3rd Earl of Shaftesbury, *Characteristicks of Men, Manners, Opinions, Times*, 3 vols, 1732, vol. 3, p. 398. This is the 5th corrected edition, which contains the 'Letter concerning Design'.
3. Bradley and Pevsner 2003, p. 488.
4. Mowl and Earnshaw 1999, p. 3.
5. Hewlings 1995.
6. Bradley and Pevsner, p. 487.
7. Worsley 1995, p. 42.
8. Survey of London 1963, Parish of St James's, vol. XXXII, chapter XXIII, Burlington House: Stone Conduit Close, pp. 396 and 400.
9. *Ibid.*, p. 398.
10. *Ibid.*, p. 405.
11. Redmond 1994, p. 41.
12. Worsley 1995, p. 229.
13. Mowl 2006, p. 89.
14. See review by Dan Cruickshank, 'The gardens of Kent', in *Building Design* (27 November 1998) of 'William Kent 1685–1748: A Poet on Paper', exhibition at the Sir John Soane Museum, curated by John Harris.
15. See unpublished report by Ian Bristow for the Royal Academy, *Report on an Investigation of Paint Samples from the Fine Rooms of Lord Burlington's House*, March 2005, pp. 27–50 and figs I–XV. Also Cornforth 2004b, p. 76.
16. Cornforth 2004a, p. 140.
17. Cornforth 2004b, p. 78.
18. Sicca 1986, p. 142.
19. This ceiling was restored by Bush and Berry in 2002.
20. Jackson-Stops 1990, p. 59.
21. Worsley personal communication 2005.
22. Restored between 2000 and 2004 at a cost of £6m, these have been opened to the public as the John Madejski Fine Rooms.
23. Sir Walter R.M. Lamb 1951, *The Royal Academy: A Short History of its Foundation and Development*, G. Bell & Sons, Ltd., London; Sidney C. Hutchison 1986, *The History of the Royal Academy: 1768–1986*, Robert Royce Ltd., London; James Fenton 2006, *School of Genius: A History of the Royal Academy of Arts*, Salamander Press Ltd., London.
24. Ackerman 1990, p. 140.
25. Knox 1985.
26. Using a drawing by Phil Crewdson, and computer-manipulating photographs of the restored paintings taken by *Country Life*.
27. Jackson-Stops 1990, p. 75.
28. Croft-Murray 1969, p. 17.
29. Bulfinch 1855.
30. *Ibid.*
31. Photocopies of these were kindly supplied by John Harris.
32. J.D. Crace retired in 1899, finding that his style of highly detailed, historical schemes was going out of fashion. His son did not wish to succeed him, and he decided to close the business and devote his time to lecturing and writing about the history of decorative design (Aldrich 1990).
33. Sampling was carried out by Catherine Hassall.
34. Testing carried out by Nicholas Easthaugh.
35. This work was kindly carried out by Ann Ballantyne.
36. This lunette contained a portrait on canvas of Charles Eastlake PRA, and half a spandrel with a painted tablet bearing the name David Wilkie RA.
37. Reading clockwise from the east wall, the portraits are of Reynolds, West, Lawrence, Archer Shee, Eastlake, Grant and Leighton.
38. Samples prepared by Raymond White at the National Gallery, London.
39. After restoration in 2003 this was renamed the Lee and James C. Slaughter Room. From 1885 until then it had been the RA's Secretary's Room, when bell pulls were installed.
40. Warner 1994, p. 277.
41. Mowl 2006, p. 53.
42. Warner 1994, p. 224.
43. J. Harris, pers. comm. 2003.
44. Bulfinch 1855.
45. Anthony Ashley Cooper, 3rd Earl of Shaftesbury 1732, *Characteristicks of Men, Manners, Opinions, Times*, vol. 2, p. 388.

References

Ackerman J. 1990, *The Villa: Form and Ideology of Country Houses*, Thames and Hudson, London

Aldrich M. (ed.) 1990, *The Craces: Royal Decorators 1768–1899*, John Murray Publishers and the Royal Pavilion Art Gallery and Museum, Brighton

Bradley S. and Pevsner N. 2003, *London 6: Westminster*, N. Pevsner (ed.), The Buildings of England series, Yale University Press, New Haven and London

Bulfinch T. 1855, *The Age of Fable*, Sanborn, Carter and Bazin, Boston (later enlarged and revised as *The Golden Age of Myth and Legend*, Harrap, London)

Cornforth J. 2004a, *Early Georgian Interiors*, Yale University Press, New Haven and London

Cornforth J. 2004b, 'A pantheon in Piccadilly', *Country Life*, 1 April 2004

Croft-Murray E. 1969, 'Decorative paintings for Lord Burlington and the Royal Academy', *Apollo*, January 1969

Hewlings R. 1995, *Burlington House*, unpublished paper for English Heritage

Jackson-Stops G. 1990, *The Country House in Perspective*, Pavilion Books, London

Knox, G. 1985. 'Sebastiano Ricci at Burlington House: a Venetian decoration *alla Romana*', *Burlington Magazine*, September 1985, pp. 601–9

Mowl T. 2006, *William Kent: Architect, Designer, Opportunist*, Jonathan Cape, London

Mowl T. and Earnshaw B. 1999, *Architecture without Kings: The Rise of Puritan Classicism under Cromwell*, Manchester University Press, Manchester

Pevsner N. 1993, *The Englishness of English Art*, Penguin Books, Harmondsworth (first pub. 1956 by Architectural Press)

Redmond, J. 1994 'The "useful" moral stage: pro and contra Burlington', in D. Arnold (ed.), *Belov'd by Ev'ry Muse: Richard Boyle, 3rd Earl of Burlington and 4th Earl of Cork (1694–1753)*, The Georgian Group, London

Sicca C-M. 1986, 'On William Kent's Roman sources', *Architectural History: Journal of the Society of Architectural Historians of Great Britain* vol. 29

Survey of London 1963, Parish of St. James's, vol. XXXII, chapter XXIII

Warner, M. 1994, *From the Beast to the Blonde: On Fairy Tales and their Tellers*, Chatto and Windus, London

Worsley G. 1995, *Classical Architecture in Britain: The Heroic* Age, Yale University Press, New Haven and London

Suppliers

- Nitromors, methylene dichloride in a gel form, produced by Henkel Consumer Adhesives, Road 5, Winsford Industrial Estate, Winsford, Cheshire, CW7 3QY, available generally.
- Paraloid B72, ethyl methacrylate copolymer, available from Conservation Resources, Unit 2, Ashville Way, off Watlington Road, Cowley, Oxford, OX4 6TU.

The authors

- Pauline Plummer studied painting conservation at the Courtauld Institute of Art, funded by the Pilgrim Trust on behalf of the Council for the Care of Churches. Further student experience was gained in Denmark and Germany, and she also worked at the V&A Museum and the Tate Gallery. Since then Pauline has conserved a large and varied range of painted works, mainly *in situ*, on behalf of clients ecclesiastical and secular, institutional and private.
- Peter Schmitt received his BA from Georgetown University in philosophy and his Master of Architecture from Yale. He was then awarded the Rome Prize in architecture in 1970 and spent two years as a Fellow of the American Academy in Rome. As the Royal Academy's Surveyor to the Fabric, he has been responsible for the restoration, lighting and air conditioning of the John Madejski Fine Rooms (2000–04). He also restored Sydney Smirke's Main Galleries (1994–2000), winning a Millennium Products Award for his revolutionary lighting system. Before joining the Royal Academy he worked in private practice with the firm of architects Howell Killick Partridge and Amis, winning awards in England and abroad and taught architecture at the University of Brighton.

The treatment of the Entrance Hall at the Fitzwilliam Museum, Cambridge: changing approaches to the conservation of 19th-century polychromy

Tobit Curteis

Introduction

Why is it that simple 17th-century decorative architectural painting (such as the scheme of marbling at 121 High Street, Marlborough) has long been regarded as of historical and archaeological interest while 19th-century architectural polychromy has often been viewed as a replaceable decorative surface – impressive visually, but of little historical worth (Fig. 1)? The reason appears simply to be their relative ages, for in artistic terms they are often of similar merit. Nineteenth- and 20th-century decorative polychromy is still routinely overpainted, either because it is not in tune with contemporary taste or because repainting to 'freshen it up' is seen as a more cost-effective solution than conservation.

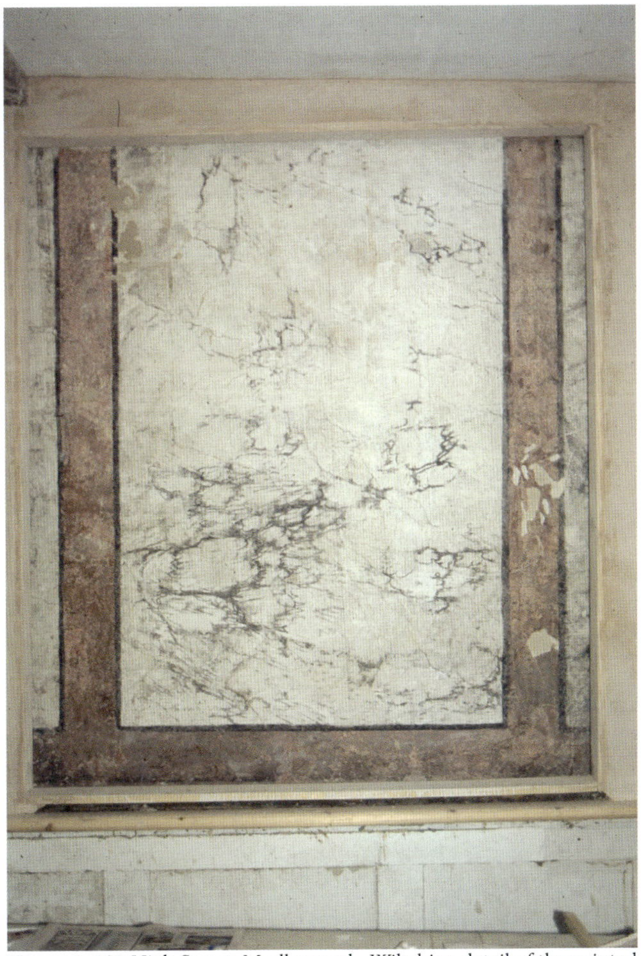

Figure 1 121 High Street, Marlborough, Wiltshire: detail of the painted marble panels. *(© T. Curteis)*

Fitzwilliam Museum

The Entrance Hall at the Fitzwilliam Museum in Cambridge provides an interesting case study for this debate (Fig. 2). From the outset of the programme, the conservator and museum authorities agreed that the elaborate polychrome decoration should be treated with the same conservation criteria as was applied to objects displayed in the museum. Preliminary tests demonstrated that this approach was technically feasible with acceptable aesthetic results, therefore between 1998 and 2001, a full-scale programme of research, documentation and conservation was undertaken.[1] One interesting aspect of dealing with 19th–20th-century paintings is that many of the original design records survive. Because it is part of the University of Cambridge, the construction of the Fitzwilliam is particularly well documented and many of the original drawings are stored in the museum, allowing direct comparison with the surviving fabric. This allowed an unusually thorough study of the original design and painting technique.

Construction history

In 1834, a competition held to design the Fitzwilliam Museum building and its internal decoration was won by the architect George Basevi. Building began in 1837 and by 1842 the main structure was nearing completion. In the following year, Basevi prepared a number of preliminary designs for the internal dec-

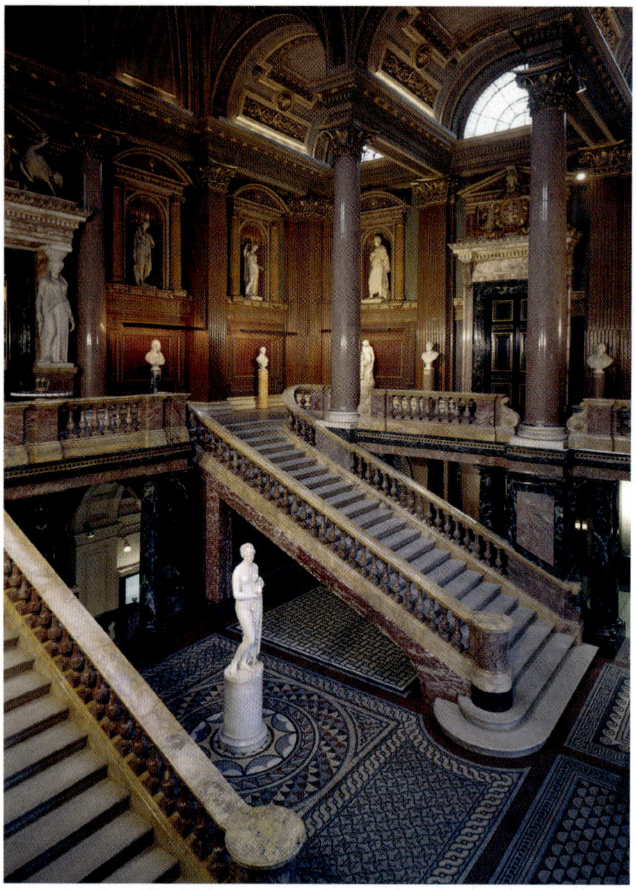

Figure 2 Fitzwilliam Museum, Cambridge: the Entrance Hall. *(© Fitzwilliam Museum)*

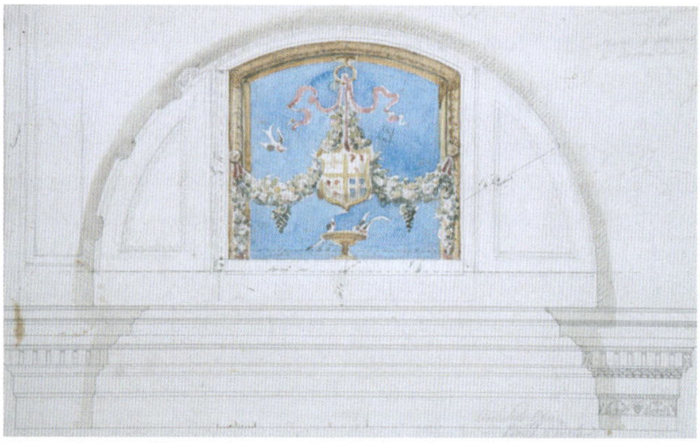

Figure 3 Fitzwilliam Museum, Cambridge: design for one of the windows by Charles Cockerell. *(© T. Curteis, by permission of the Fitzwilliam Museum)*

oration of the Entrance Hall and main galleries. He envisaged a hall with twin staircases rising to the upper gallery level (as they do now) but with a central staircase descending to the lower galleries. The areas on the north and south sides, which are now the descending staircases, were to be enclosed and used as offices. Above the staircase, the ceiling was to be a long barrel vault running east–west, with three small lanterns providing illumination. The ceiling above the upper landings was to be vaulted, as it is now, but with coffering rather than the lighter decoration that was eventually used. In October 1845, however, before his plans could be put into action, Basevi was killed falling from the west tower at Ely Cathedral.

The architect Charles Robert Cockerell (1788–1863) was appointed his successor and commissioned to complete the building and its internal decoration. While he based his plans for the decoration on Basevi's original design, Cockerell made a number of notable alterations, the most significant being the change from the barrel vault envisaged by Basevi to a single central lantern, decorated with herms and swags. Cockerell also redesigned the ceiling of the landing vaults, but retained the overall plan of the hall with the central descending staircase. While Basevi's designs were undoubtedly elaborate, it is very apparent from the surviving drawings that Cockerell's designs were very much more ornate (Fig. 3). When the accounts for the work already completed were made up in 1848, it was found that the cost was considerably in excess of that anticipated,[2] therefore the decoration of the Entrance Hall was put on hold. When the museum was opened to the public later that year, an alternative route was designed for entering the building. It is not clear how advanced the scheme of plastering and decoration was at this stage, although the analytical evidence suggests that little or none of the flat surface plaster or decorative stucco had yet been applied.[3]

Further funds became available in 1870, and the architect Edward M. Barry was approached to complete the Entrance Hall. Barry retained Cockerell's design for a central lantern, but made a significant change to the overall plan by replacing the proposed side offices with the descending staircases seen today. He also opened up the windows at the sides of the vaults so that they were completely glazed, rather than using the tripartite design envisaged by Cockerell, which just had central glazing. Barry's scheme is more restrained than Cockerell's, but still far from simple, incorporating large areas of polychrome paintwork, architectural stonework, ornate stucco, gilding and painted window glass, as well as employing mosaic floors, polished marble, alabaster and granite. The polychromy is entirely decorative with no figurative painting. Between the doors, the walls are divided into 12 bays by fictive porphyry pillars, each of which has a niche containing a reproduction of a classical figure sculpture (Fig. 4). The niches themselves are flanked by fictive Sienna marble columns supporting pediments decorated with stylised relief foliage. The centre is dominated by a highly ornate coved opening from which rises a lantern containing a series of herms that support the cupola (Fig. 5).

The doorways to the galleries on the north, south and west sides are elaborately decorated with marble and alabaster, and surmounted with ornate coats of arms. The entablature of the west doorway is supported by a pair of marble caryatids sculpted by Edward William Wyon. Basevi's original design included caryatids on all three doors, but this feature too was altered by Barry. Over the main entrance doorway, in the east wall, is an inscription commemorating the founding of the museum in 1816 by Richard, Viscount Fitzwilliam.

The Entrance Hall was finally completed in 1875, some 27 years after the museum was first opened to the public.

Original materials and technique

As with any conservation programme, the initial stage at the Fitzwilliam was a detailed investigation of the original materials and painting technique. One of the difficulties was that

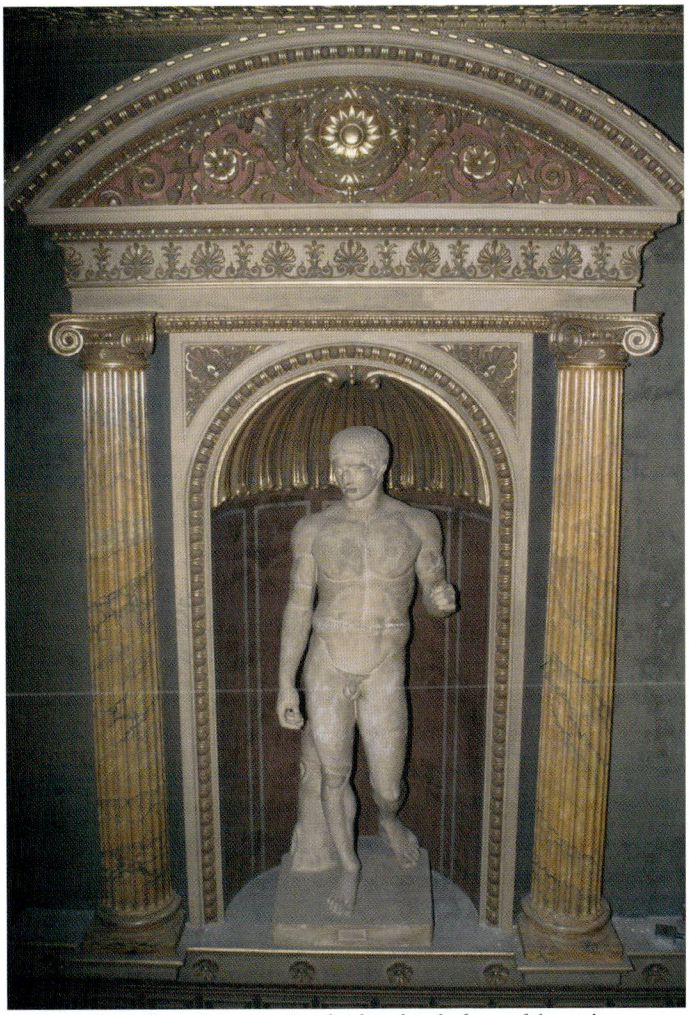

Figure 4 Fitzwilliam Museum, Cambridge: detail of one of the niches. *(© T. Curteis)*

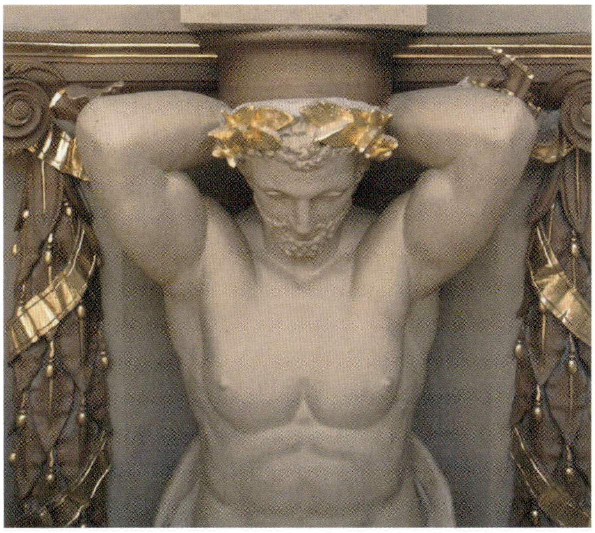

Figure 5 Fitzwilliam Museum, Cambridge: detail of a herm in the cupola. *(© T. Curteis)*

Figure 6 Fitzwilliam Museum, Cambridge: emerald green antiquing on part of a plaster moulding. *(© T. Curteis)*

detailed studies of schemes of this type are rare, and therefore little comparative material exists to allow new information to be put in context. Over the last 30 years, however, the field of architectural paint research has developed, and there is now considerable knowledge about original painting materials and techniques that allows schemes such as this to be understood in a historical context. Comparable analytical studies of plaster materials and techniques are unfortunately less common.

The main walls of the Entrance Hall are brick, with lime plaster on the internal walls and limestone cladding on the exterior. The ceiling is an elaborate lath-and-plaster construction supported on timber beams, and both the walls and the ceiling are entirely decorated with ornate plasterwork. The overall designs for the plasterwork would have been mapped out on drawings with scaled cartoons prepared of specific decorative details. Following the transfer of the design to the wall (either by measurement or by pouncing through pricked cartoons), the wet plaster would have been incised. The hand-modelled plasterwork would have been carried out directly on the flat work using nails, wire, wooden frames and, where necessary, armatures to support the deeper, heavier stucco ornamentation.

The pre-cast elements – which range from the large and complex pieces to smaller enriched architectural mouldings – would have been made with moulds taken from clay forms. While simpler areas of decoration would have been cast in a single-section mould, larger elements would have been constructed from a multi-sectioned 'piece' mould. Repetitive mouldings, such as those on the ceiling, were made up of multiple casts from the same mould, while some of the smaller elements would have been constructed using both hand-modelled plasterwork combined with pre-cast sections. Most cast elements were fitted *in situ* using a combination of small wooden pegs and scoring of the surfaces and sizing, before applying an adhesive plaster to the joint. Smaller cast ornaments were fixed directly with a plaster adhesive mix or with metal pins pushed up through the lathes. In some cases, large elements were not attached directly to the background plaster but were secured with wire to struts behind the lathes.

Paint analysis showed that a white-lead priming was applied directly over most areas of the plaster. A cream-coloured ground, consisting of lead white and yellow ochre, was then applied to all surfaces. The background grey was applied first, followed by the large areas of translucent bronzing. Bright emerald green lowlights were then dabbed in the hollows of the bronzed mouldings to give the appearance of age, although much of this 'antiquing' would have been invisible from the ground (Fig. 6).

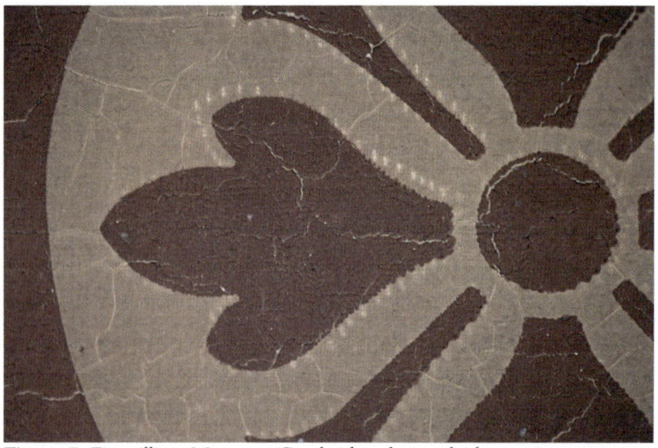

Figure 7 Fitzwilliam Museum, Cambridge: designs laid out using pouncing. *(© T. Curteis)*

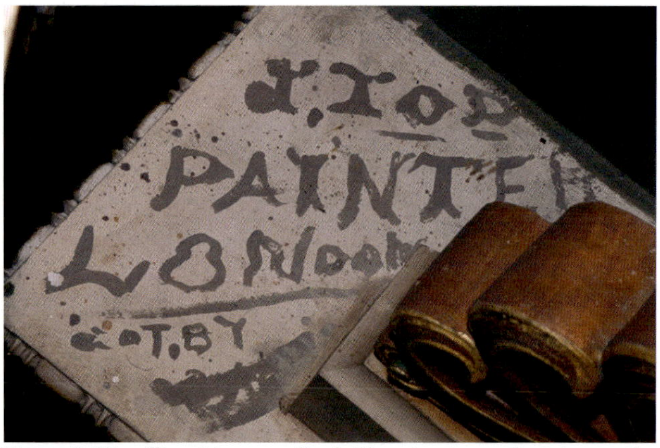

Figure 8 Fitzwilliam Museum, Cambridge: signatures of painters on the hidden upper surfaces. *(© T. Curteis)*

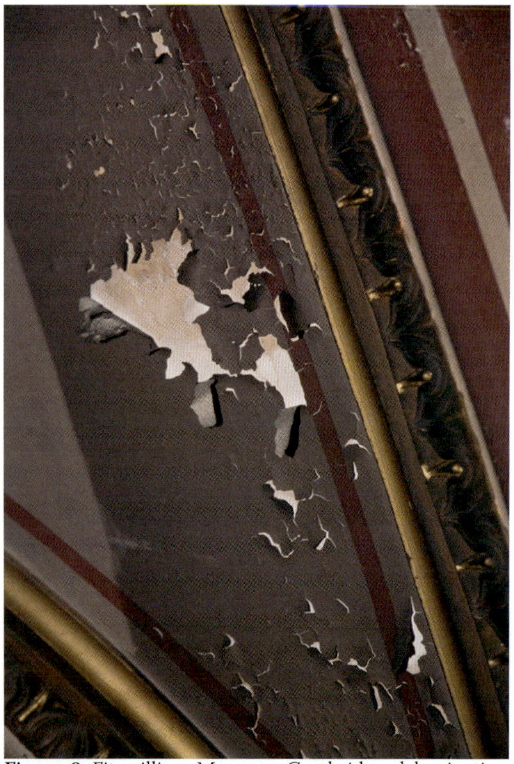

Figure 9 Fitzwilliam Museum, Cambridge: delamination and flaking of the paint layer. *(© T. Curteis)*

A fictive 'Carrara marble' skirting was painted at the same time as 'porphyry' and 'Sienna marble' pilasters. The strong background colours on the walls, the beds of the panels, and the ceiling were probably applied last. For these, two reds were used: vermilion and red iron oxide, mixed with lead white. The green walls were Brunswick green mixed with ochre, black and lead white, and the ceiling was Prussian blue. In the samples tested, the binding medium was found to be a drying oil. The gilding consisted of a coat of oil size tinted with yellow ochre, with pure gold leaf laid over the top. On the few areas where decorative motifs were painted on plain walls (such as in the upper part of the cupola), it appears that the design was laid out by pouncing through pricked cartoons (Fig. 7). Original pencil notes for colours and measurements were found on the upper walls throughout the hall and a number of signatures were also discovered (Fig. 8).

Condition before treatment and causes of deterioration

Much of the polychrome decoration was in relatively good condition although it had a dull and muted appearance after a century and a half of accumulated dirt and dust. The main cornice and the ceiling were covered with a thick veil of dirt, while the walls below had a more intermittent and strongly bonded dirt layer, possibly indicating that they had been partially cleaned before. In some areas, uneven patches of dark staining were observed, which appeared to follow the lines of the brushwork. Paint analysis showed that this was due to black dirt particles adhering to the surface, rather than to pigment discoloration. Infiltration of rainwater had resulted in delamination between the paint layer and the plaster substrate, causing significant flaking (Fig. 9). In the cupola, the level of delamination and flaking was significantly worse on the north side than elsewhere in the Hall as a result of its exposure to direct sunlight from the glass dome. Craquelure on the paint layer was very pronounced in this area, and infiltrating rainwater had dissolved the calcium sulphate component of the plaster, leaving honeycomb-like voids.

In most areas the plaster substrate was in good condition, although there were numerous historic hairline cracks associated with minor structural movement. More serious cracking was observed along the junction between the north and south walls and the corresponding vaults, apparently as a result of greater movement of the walls. In the structural engineer's opinion, this movement was historic. Although most of the cast plaster elements were stable, a number of the smaller sections were falling off where microbiological growth – initiated by the infiltration of water from a damaged lead roof – had weakened the animal-glue adhesive.

There was only one area of severe damage: on the west wall, the failure of the parapet gutter had caused rainwater to penetrate the brick structure, resulting in significant salt activity. This had caused delamination of the plaster substrate and severe flaking of the paint layer. Investigations showed that the problem was historic, however, and the gutter had long since been repaired.

Day-to-day use of the Entrance Hall by the many thousands of visitors had caused mechanical damage at the base of the walls. Damage to the plinths at the bases of the walls was also widespread, and evidence of previous repairs and crude repainting was found in numerous areas.

Conservation treatment

The treatment programme had two main aims: to stabilise the damaged areas of polychromy and to improve the overall appearance and presentation of the Entrance Hall.

Thanks to the generally good condition of the plaster substrate, the level of structural work was very limited. Small repairs were necessary where mechanical damage had occurred, and in the few areas of delamination between the plaster layer and the brick substrate a lime putty and brick-dust grout was used to re-establish acceptable adhesion. Small decorative elements that had become separated were reattached using Plextol B500 adhesive, while larger detached sections were secured using dowels to provide some mechanical strength and fixed in place with an epoxy resin.[4]

Readhesion of delaminating and flaking paint was more complex, requiring realignment of the individual flakes and application of a weak solution of Plextol B500 through an intervention layer of Japanese tissue. Although this approach was slow and painstaking, it was very successful in saving as much of the original paintwork as possible. While the reduction of the dirt layer was the largest operation, it was technically the most straightforward. All surfaces were first dusted with soft brushes and the loosened dirt was then carefully vacuumed away. Following this, Wishab sponges were used to clean the surfaces in more detail. The gilding and areas of marble were cleaned using a weak solution of ammonium bicarbonate. Retouching was limited, but where necessary it was carried out with watercolours, which can easily be removed if required in the future. The exception to this was the plinth at the base of the wall, which is subject to far greater mechanical damage. Here the retouching was carried out using powder pigments in a medium of Paraloid B72 acrylic resin.[5]

To make a permanent record of the condition before treatment, and to allow a more detailed analysis of the causes of deterioration, the principal deterioration types were documented on a series of line drawings and a photographic record was made. Not only did this allow the treatment itself to be recorded, but it established the condition in detail at that specific time, so that the extent of any future deterioration can be judged accurately (Fig. 10). The provision of interpretive material was considered to be an integral part of the project, giving the visiting public a greater understanding of the Entrance Hall itself as well as the conservation process. During the course of the work, temporary boards were displayed presenting basic information about the history and treatment. Regular talks were given to visitors and arrangements were made for students, conservators and other interested parties to be allowed on the scaffolding. Following the completion of the work, the project was published in the *Journal of Architectural Conservation*, and an illustrated booklet was produced with details of the history of the Entrance Hall and the conservation programme. Details were also included on the interactive portable audiovisual tour that the museum offers to visitors.

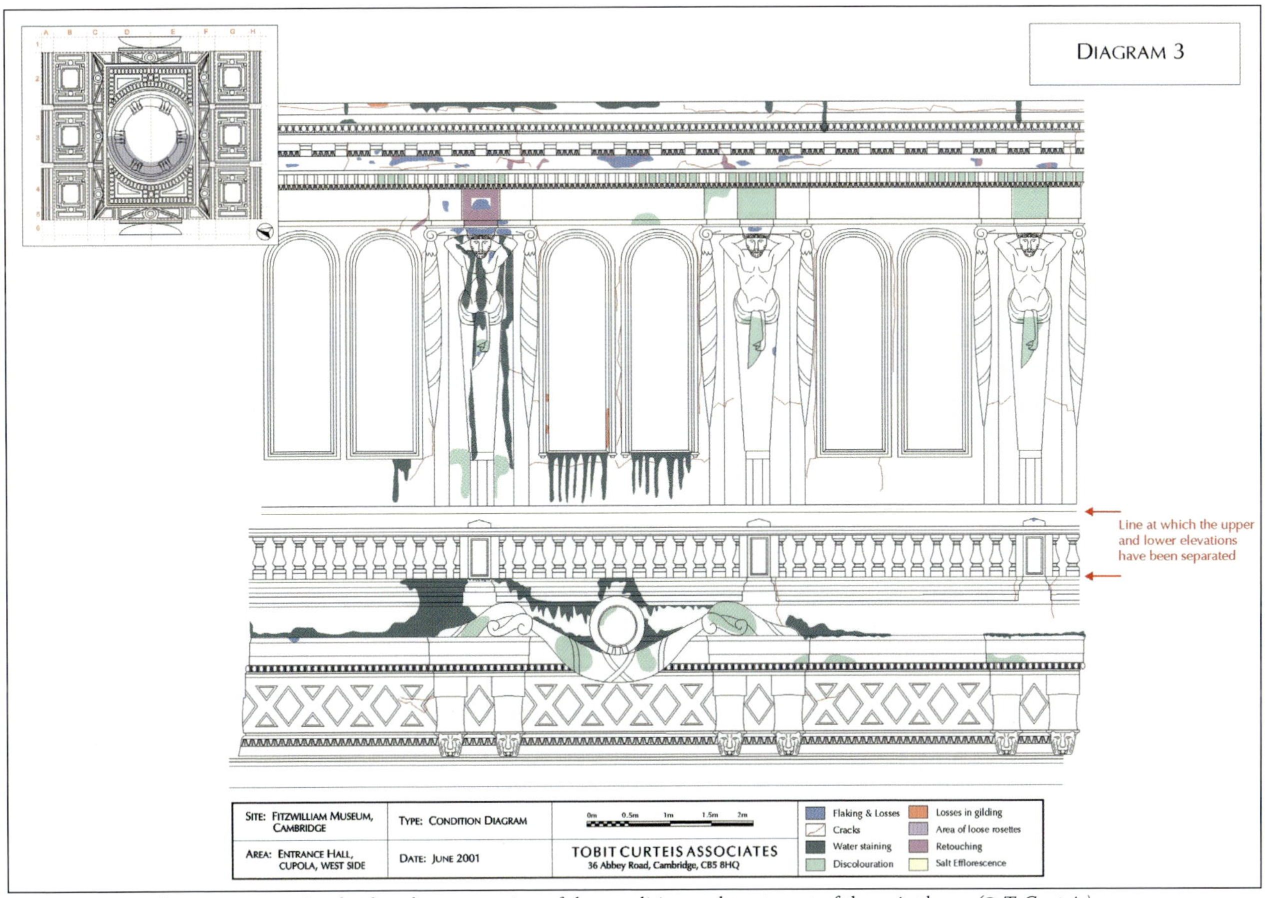

Figure 10 Fitzwilliam Museum, Cambridge: documentation of the condition and treatment of the paint layer. *(© T. Curteis)*

Enthusiastic feedback from all of these activities demonstrated the public's keen interest in the history of these buildings, and particularly in the conservation process. In an era when conservation is struggling for funding and public recognition (two things that are in fact interdependent), explaining and interpreting what we do is an extremely important and underutilised tool. The fact that such a high level of interest was shown in the conservation of a non-figurative 19th-century scheme demonstrates that it is the principles and the process of conservation, rather than simply the object, which is of interest to people. This reinforces the fact that we should be more circumspect before dismissing these later schemes as less worthy of conservation.

Other case studies

Blickling Hall, Norfolk

Generally, figurative painting has fared better than architectural polychromy, but this has not always been the case. Between 1859 and 1861 at Blickling Hall in Norfolk, a large scheme of decoration was undertaken by John Hungerford Pollen, a painter on the fringes of the pre-Raphaelite movement. This included figurative wall and ceiling paintings throughout the house, and, most importantly, the complete redecoration of the medieval Long Gallery (Figs 11 and 12).

The decorative scheme was commissioned by Pollen's friend from their university days at Oxford, the 8th Marquis of Lothian, who was an enthusiastic exponent of contemporary decorative tastes. Unfortunately the 11th Marquis, his great grandson, was unsympathetic to this sort of dramatic and colourful decoration, and in his 1930s redecoration of the house set about having it painted over or destroyed. The house is now under the stewardship of the National Trust, and in recent years the importance of Pollen's work has once again been recognised. Investigations are currently underway to examine how the surviving painting can be conserved, and whether the covered painting can be exposed or recreated.

St Michael's Church, Oxford

The Fitzwilliam Museum and Blickling Hall are both Grade 1 listed, and as such they enjoy considerable protection from the law. This is often not the case, however. One example of recent decoration that remains at serious risk is the scheme carried

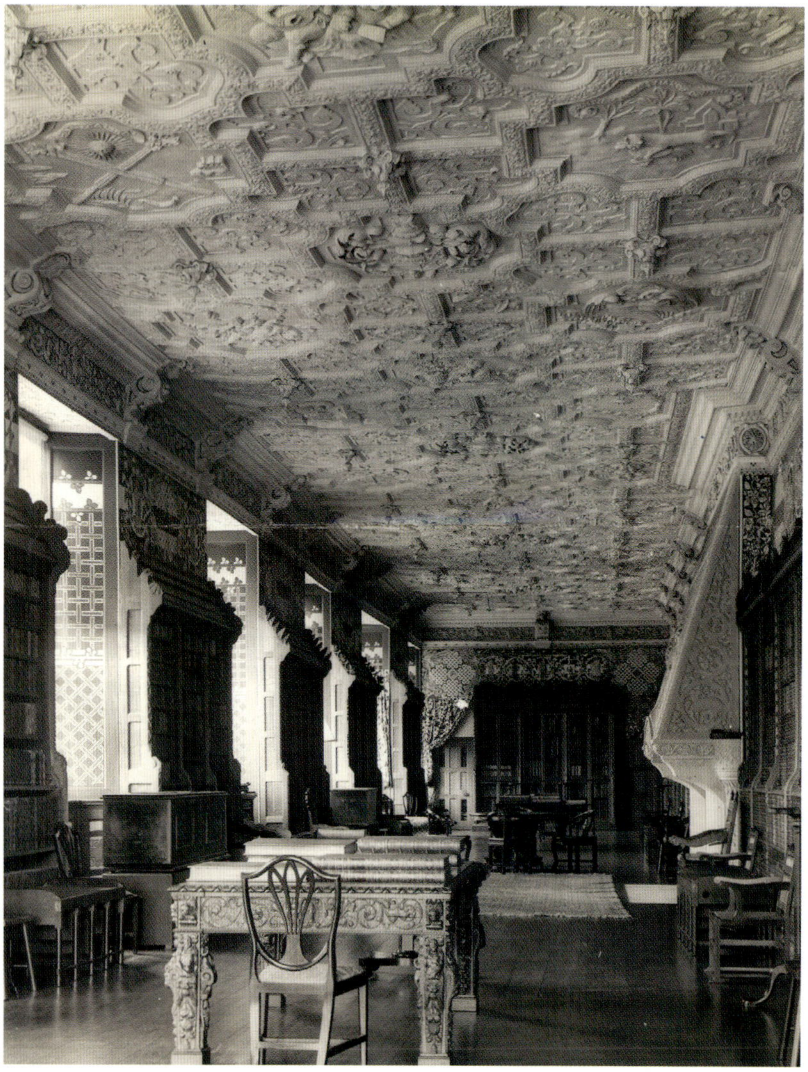

Figure 11 Blickling Hall, Norwich, Norfolk: view of the Long Gallery at Blickling in the early part of the 20th century. *(© Country Life Picture Library)*

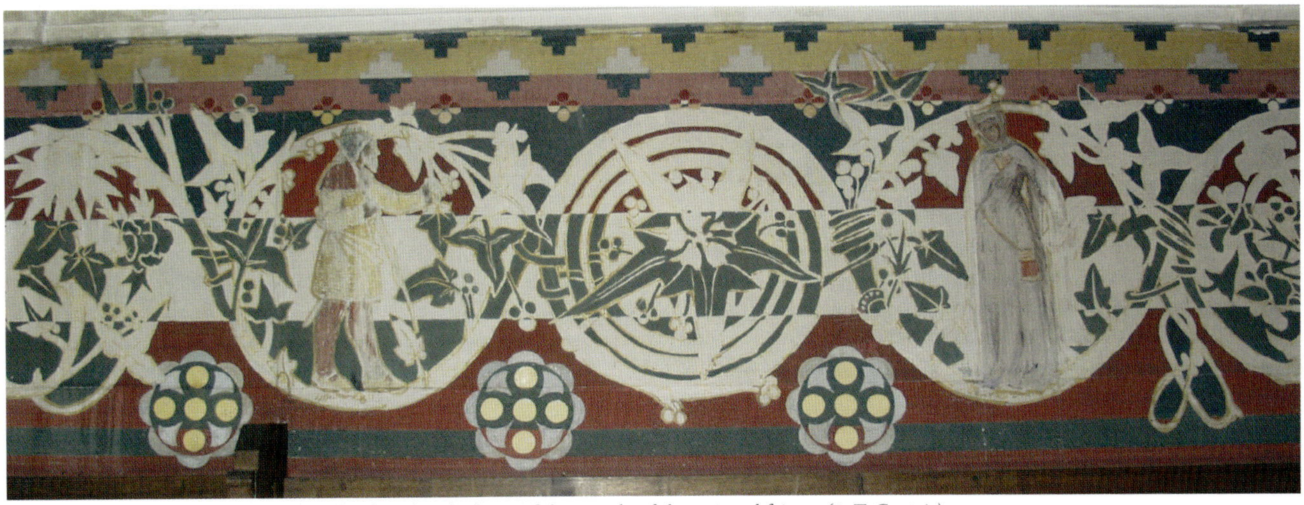

Figure 12 Fitzwilliam Museum, Cambridge: detail of one of the panels of the painted frieze. *(© T. Curteis)*

out by Leon Underwood at St Michael's Church, Oxford. St Michael's was built in 1954 by the architect Lawrence Dale, and the internal decorative scheme was regarded as an integral part of the original design. The most important pieces are found in the chancel, where an altar frontal painted with the figure of the dead Christ sits below a wall painting of the *Assumption* with trumpeting angels. High on the wall the figure of Christ floats above the city of Oxford in a stained glass window, also by Underwood (Fig. 13). The ensemble is an impressive combination of styles and media, and is integral to the structure of the building. In the north aisle a wonderfully contemporary *Annunciation* shows the Virgin asleep having dropped her knitting, while on the ground around lie the traditional iconographic symbols of the dog, the lilies and the glass. In addition the church is decorated with contemporary sculptures by John Bunting, the most significant of which are the *Stations of the Cross*.

A 1997 survey of the paintings showed that they were unstable and would require conservation at some future stage. Perhaps the greater risk was of inadvertent damage, however, either from day-to-day housekeeping or from alterations to the building fabric. Although under the faculty system the church is afforded a level of protection that would not be available for a secular building, in 1999 the parish applied for the church to be listed to provide a greater level of protection. Listing was rejected on account of the fact that 'the building is in a mixture of modern and Romanesque styles, which fails to conform to one element'. This total dismissal of the artistic content of the building was disappointing but not unusual when dealing with modern painting. The listing procedures are now being reviewed and in recent months there have been encouraging signs that such issues will be taken into account before these all-too-rare works of art are lost (see Introduction by Bowdler, pp. xvii–xx).

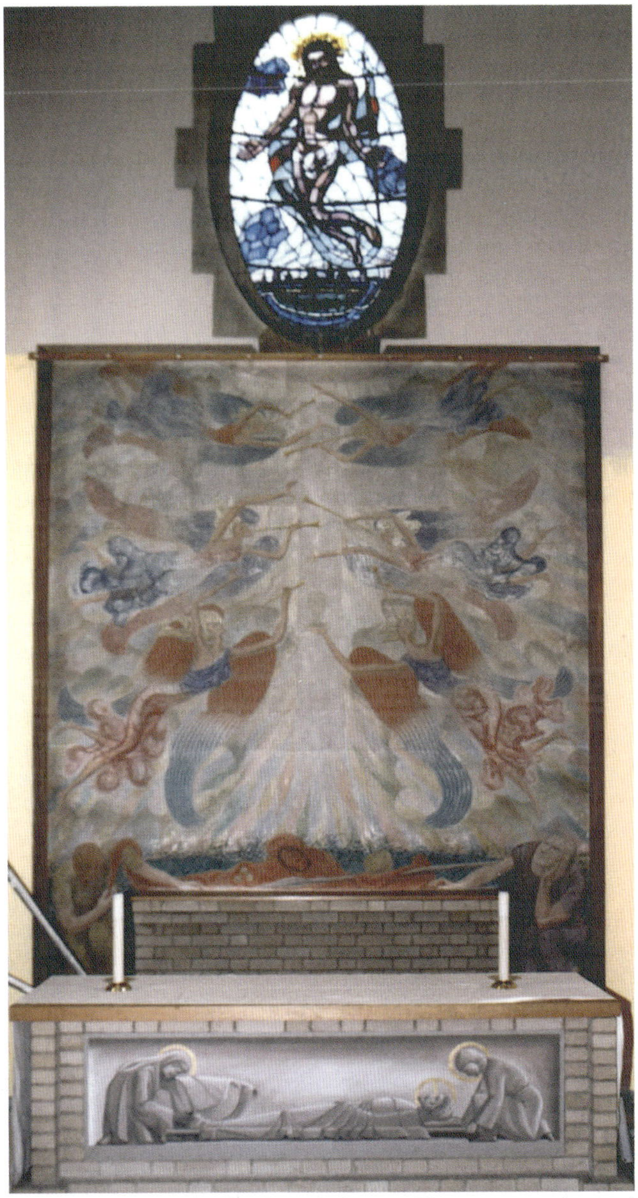

Figure 13 St Michael's Church, Oxford: view of the paintings and stained glass by Leon Underwood. *(© T. Curteis)*

Conclusions

There are a number of areas where the conservation of later polychromy differs from early decoration. First, schemes tend to be much larger than medieval wall paintings and this presents many practical challenges for project design. Another problematic area is the use of new painting materials and techniques. While research has been done on the deterioration of modern materials for artworks in some of the major museums, the body of research on *in-situ* paintings and polychrome decoration is limited. Therefore, from a technical point of view, the conservation of later painting can be particularly complex. However, because so many of the original records survive for later painting, the whole aspect of documentary research can also be considerably more fruitful than when working with medieval painting, where primary records so rarely survive. Similarly, the art history associated with many later paintings is only just starting to be written, and so the opportunity for new research is much greater.

Although the conservation of 19th- and 20th-century painted decoration is now regarded with less scepticism than it was only a generation ago, it is still often viewed as a less serious pursuit than the conservation of medieval polychromy. Certainly medieval polychromy is less common than recent decoration, and this endows it with a level of importance that is lacking in the more common later painting. But unless a more cautious approach is taken to later painting, it too will become as rare as its predecessor. While this might readdress the balance, we would have lost some important works of art in the process. The case at Blickling in particular shows our cyclical approach to decorative tastes, and reinforces the argument that we should think extremely carefully before destroying or repainting a decorative scheme simply because it is out of fashion.

The key to ensuring the successful conservation of later polychromy is having a client and conservator who are both aware of the importance of the artwork as well as a suitable statutory framework protecting against unnecessary damage. Obviously not all painted decoration created in the last two centuries justifies conservation, but it is important that, as a matter of course in any significant case, the merits of conservation are at least considered. Recent changes in the law have given important architectural paint finishes a similar level of protection to that of some physical structures, and the increasing influence of architectural paint research means that there is a general heightening of awareness that such schemes merit consideration. Recent indications that the significance of internal decoration will be more carefully considered when applications for listing are assessed are a welcome sign.

An encouraging postscript to the project at the Fitzwilliam is the fact that it was recently awarded the David Urwin Design Award, a prize presented biannually in Cambridge for the most successful historic building conservation projects. Since it is usually presented for the conservation of a building structure, the fact that the prize was awarded for the conservation of a 19th-century polychromy scheme was an acknowledgment that the wider conservation and building community is indeed beginning to recognise the significance of such work.

Notes

1. Details of the research and conservation programme at the Fitzwilliam can be found in Tobit Curteis Associates 2001 and Curteis 2002.
2. Willis and Clark 1886, p. 217.
3. Analysis of the paint cross-sections found a thin layer of coarse black dirt particles between the plaster and the paint in a number of samples. Although this dirt deposition must indicate a certain lapse of time, it cannot be the period between the opening of the building and Barry's decoration in 1870 because it occurs on both the flat plasterwork and the small mouldings, which were certainly part of Barry's design. Rather, it appears to relate to the interval between the completion of plasterwork and the start of painting.
4. Plextol B500 is an acrylic dispersion with good long-term chemical stability, commonly used as a conservation adhesive.
5. Paraloid B72 is an acrylic resin widely used in conservation and considered to be one of the most stable materials of its type.

References

Curteis T. 2002, 'The Entrance Hall of the Fitzwilliam Museum, Cambridge: a conservation approach to nineteenth-century architectural polychromy', *Journal of Architectural Conservation* 8(2), pp. 7–22

Tobit Curteis Associates 2001, *Conservation of the Polychromy in the Entrance Hall, Fitzwilliam Museum, Cambridge*, unpublished report

Willis R. and Clark J.W. 1886, *The Architectural History of the University of Cambridge, and of the Colleges of Cambridge and Eton, Vol. 3*, Cambridge University Press, Cambridge

The author

Tobit Curteis trained in the conservation of wall paintings at the Courtauld Institute of Art. Since 1992 he has run a practice specialising in the conservation of painted architectural surfaces and the identification and control of the causes of deterioration. He works in the UK and abroad for clients including English Heritage, the National Trust, the Council for the Care of Churches and the World Monument Fund.

Tracking historic attitudes towards wall painting conservation: Lord Leighton's frescoes at the V&A

Robert Gowing

Introduction

When research into the conservation history of any particular work of art is published, this tends to focus on the nature of deterioration, and on the methods and materials used in treatment. Often unexplored, but equally illuminating, is the decision-making process behind the physical treatment history. Providing information about developments in conservation practice, and the interrelationships between conservators and those who take responsibility for the care of works of art, the story of how and why works of art are treated is especially pertinent for wall paintings, where the stakeholders are so often many and diverse. Lord Leighton's monumental spirit frescoes at the Victoria and Albert Museum (V&A) offer an ideal case study of conservation decision-making.

The Leighton frescoes have had an extremely chequered and active conservation history: well over a dozen treatment campaigns recorded in only 100 years, involving a diverse array of historians, artists, restorers, scientists, curators and architects (Tables 1 and 2). The material published to date has documented the technical issues surrounding the seemingly endless problems of the paintings and the huge variety of methods, materials and approaches used in their treatment.[1] While this material has included aspects of decision-making, since museum and government interests were closely involved it is only through scrutiny of the massive documentary archives held by the V&A and English Heritage that a much bigger story emerges.[2] This story traces the continually changing role of the public sector and its influence on professional wall painting conservation in England.

1862–1886 Brief background: commissioning the frescoes

Frederic Lord Leighton's frescoes, in South Court of what was then the South Kensington Museum (now the V&A), were painted to decorate two facing lunettes in the upper galleries of the eastern side (Fig. 1). Leighton started the first of the two paintings, *The Industrial Arts as Applied to War*, in 1868, completing it in 1880. Shortly after this work began on the second fresco, *The Industrial Arts as Applied to Peace*, which was finished in 1886 (Figs 2 and 3).

Leighton had originally agreed to a £1,000 fee for *War*, but this eventually rose to £3,000; *Peace* cost a further £3,000.[3] Funds were provided by the Treasury with the approval of the Office of Works and the Board of Education, which in 1865 had been given overall responsibility of the museum buildings by the First Commissioner of Works, Acton Smee Ayrton.[4] From the beginning, responsibility for the frescoes was not entirely straightforward: as works of art, they formed part of the museum's collection (under the direction of the Board of Education, as the museum managers), but as integral components of a government building, they came under the umbrella of the Office of Works. Over the next century this dual ownership was to prove crucial to the ongoing care of the paintings.

1896–1922 The first repairs: making good the work of art

Less than ten years after the completion of Leighton's second mural, *Peace*, concerns were being raised within the museum about its condition: 'I beg leave to call your attention to the condition of the fresco, "Industrial Arts as applied to Peace" – What should you like to do to it?'[5] Initially, various internal museum staff examined, tested and even attempted minor interventions to address issues of flaking and changes in surface tackiness. At the same time James Ward, Leighton's assistant on the project, contacted the museum following a visit to express his own concern over the condition of *Peace*. In August 1897 the museum, through the Board of Education, commissioned Ward to restore this mural. While it was clearly considered an internal matter, one staff member is recorded as raising the issue of the Office of Works' ownership of the frescoes, even suggesting that the Office ought to be informed.[6]

Table 1 Summary of the recorded conservation interventions to the spirit fresco by Frederick Lord Leighton, *The Industrial Arts as Applied to Peace* (1880–86).

Date: Main conservator	Detailed examination of painting	Testing and analysis		Cleaning		Physical interventions		Coatings		Reports	
		Cleaning tests	Sample analysis	Vacuum and/ or dusting	Aqueous solutions	Surface/plaster repairs	Retouching	Spirit-fresco medium	Wax varnish	Type	Document
1896: Ward	✓						✓	Partial			
1897: Ward	✓			✓			✓			handwritten	annotated photograph
1901: Armstrong	✓	✓					✓			typed letter	annotated photograph
1902: Church	✓									typed letter	
1903: Church				✓	✓		✓			typed report	annotated photograph
1904: Sykes							✓			internal memo	
1904: Ward	✓			✓	✓		✓	partial		typed report	annotated photograph
1909: Cundall	✓			✓						internal memo	
1910: Ward				✓	✓		✓	total		typed report	
1912: Haines						minor				internal memo	sketches
1916: Haines						minor	✓			internal memo	sketches
1922: Art Room	✓					minor	✓			internal memo	sketches
1924/25: Jack/ Tristram	✓	✓	✓	✓	✓		✓		total	assorted formal reports	photos, sketches, drawings
1929: Office of Works					✓					internal memo	
1931: Office of Works	✓				✓					internal memo	
1941: Jack	✓				✓		✓		total	internal memo	
1951: Jack	✓	✓								internal memo	
1952: Jack/Blake				✓	✓				total	handwritten report	
1954: Jack	✓			✓	✓ (part)					handwritten reports	
1962: Stewart	✓									letter	
1994: Courtauld/ Rickerby	✓	✓								letter	
1995: Courtauld/Rickerby/V&A	✓		✓	✓	✓		✓			draft reports	full graphic documents and photos

Table 2 Summary of the recorded conservation interventions to the spirit fresco by Frederick Lord Leighton, *The Industrial Arts as Applied to War* (1868–80).

Date: Main conservator	Detailed examination of painting	Testing and analysis		Cleaning		Physical interventions		Coatings		Reports	
		Cleaning tests	Sample analysis	Vacuum and/ or dusting	Aqueous/ solvent solutions	Surface/plaster repairs	Retouching	Spirit-fresco medium	Wax varnish	Type	Document
1897: Ward	✓			✓						handwritten report	
1901: Armstrong	✓	✓								typed letter	
1902: Church	✓									typed letter	
1903: Church				✓	✓					typed report	
1904: Sykes							✓			internal memo	
1909: Cundall	✓									internal memo	
1912: Haines						minor	minor			internal memo	sketches
1922: Art Room	✓	✓								internal memo	
1924/25: Jack/Tristram	✓	✓	✓	✓	✓		✓		total	assorted formal reports	photos, sketches, drawings
1929: Office of Works					✓					internal memo	
1931: Office of Works	✓				✓					internal memo	
1933-35: Jack	✓					water damage	✓	partial		handwritten reports	sketches and diagrams
1938-40: Jack/Hampton	✓			✓		new plaster	✓		total	handwritten reports	sketches and diagrams
1951: Jack	✓	✓								internal memo	
1952: Jack/Blake				✓	✓				total	handwritten reports	
1954: Jack	✓			✓	✓ (part)					handwritten reports	
1962: Stewart	✓									letter	
1992: V&A	✓					facing				?	
1994: Courtauld/Rickerby	✓	✓								letter	
1995: Courtauld/Rickerby/V&A	✓		✓	✓	✓	✓	✓			draft reports	full graphic documents and photos

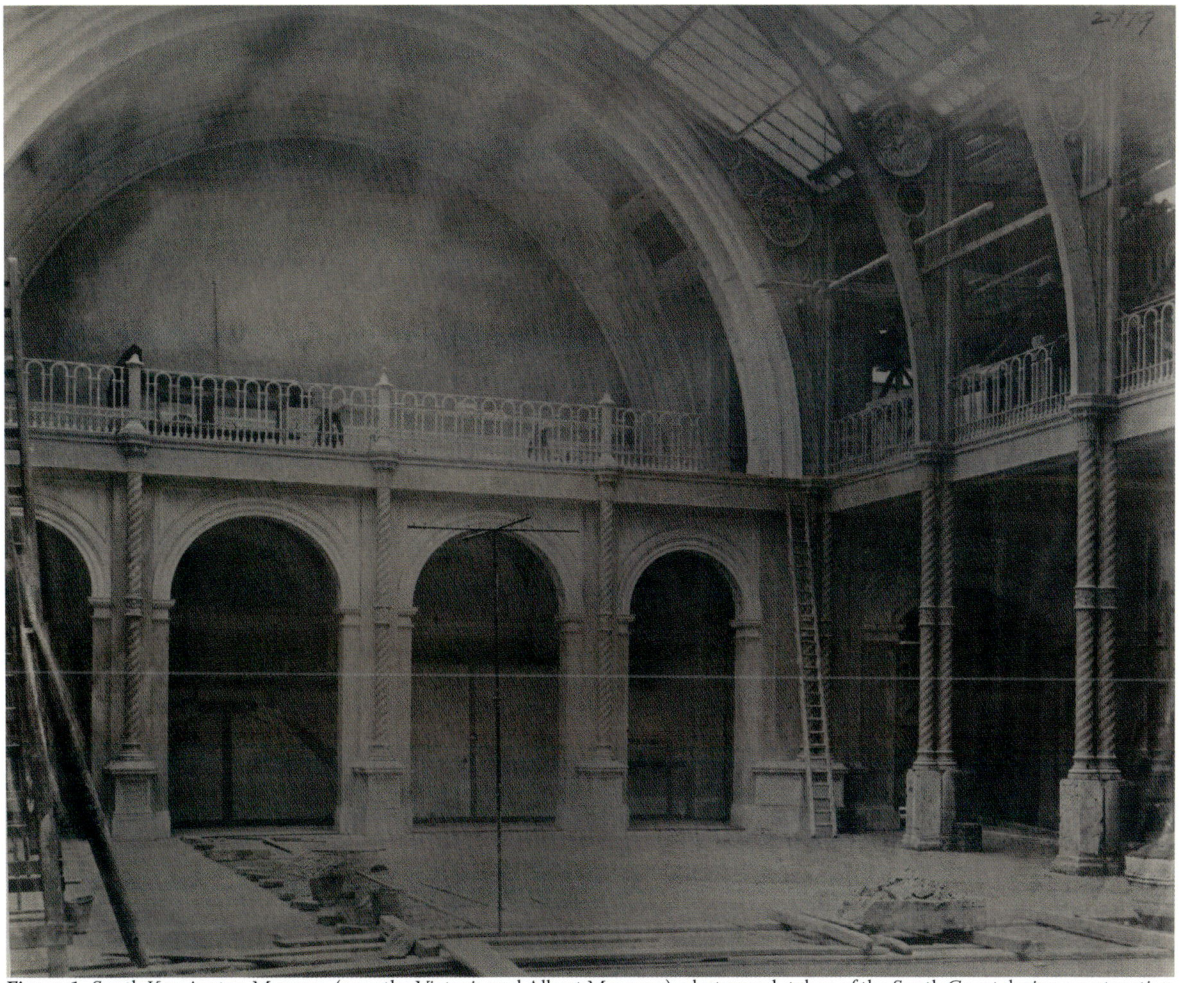

Figure 1 South Kensington Museum (now the Victoria and Albert Museum): photograph taken of the South Court during construction showing the eastern portion of the north end. *(© V&A Images/Victoria and Albert Museum)*

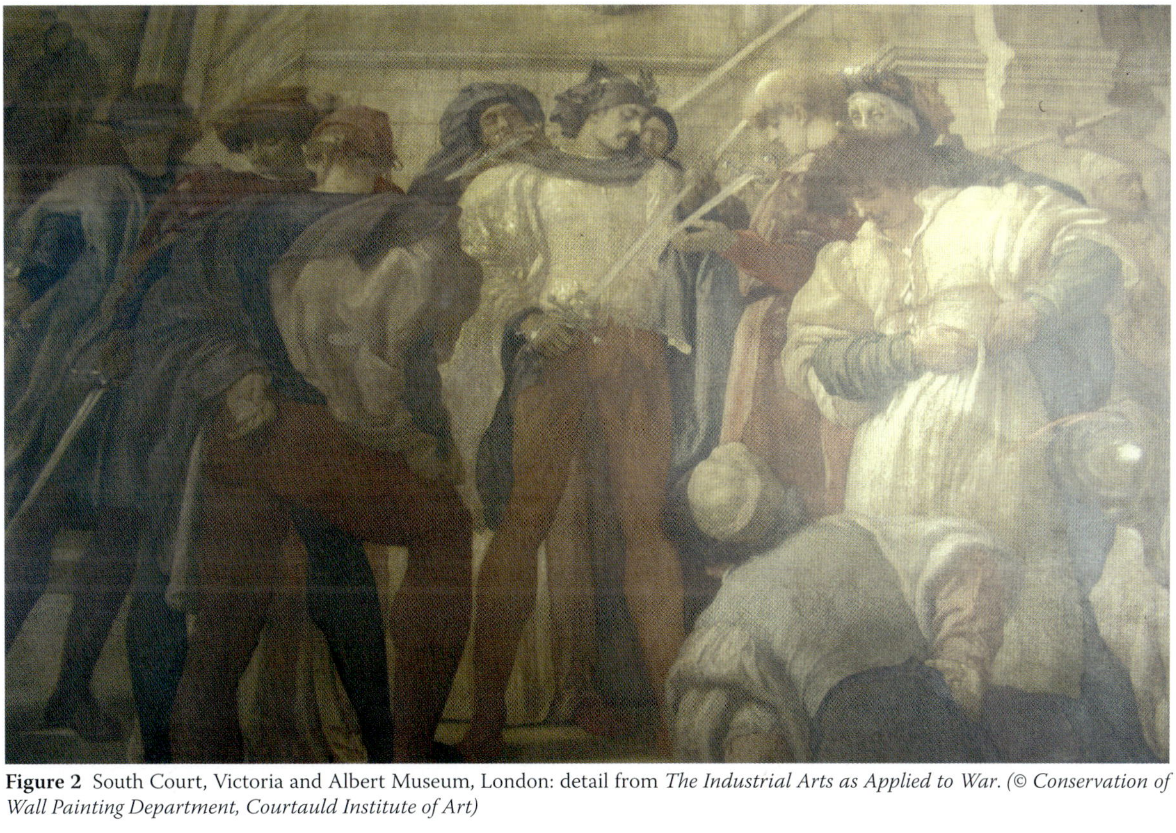

Figure 2 South Court, Victoria and Albert Museum, London: detail from *The Industrial Arts as Applied to War*. *(© Conservation of Wall Painting Department, Courtauld Institute of Art)*

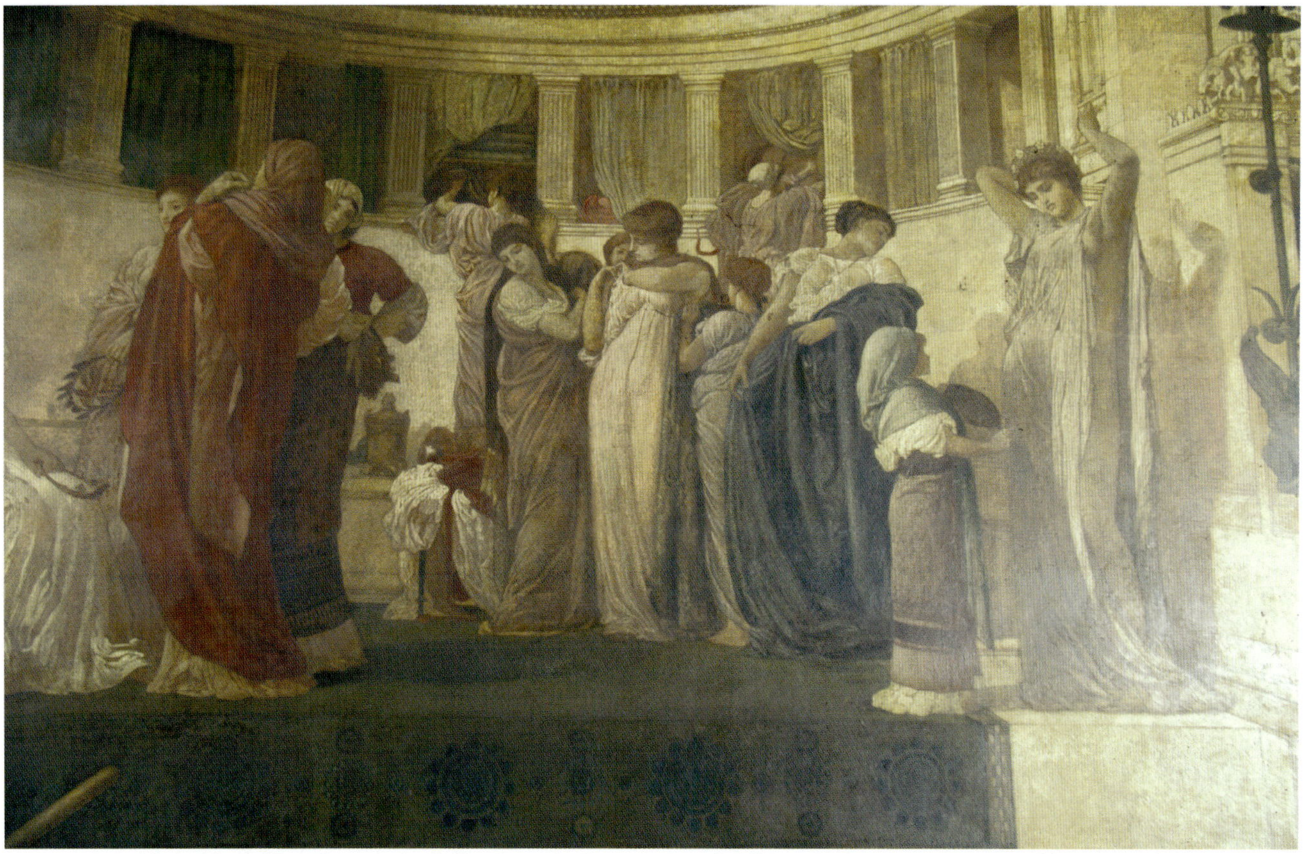

Figure 3 Detail from *The Industrial Arts as Applied to Peace. (© Conservation of Wall Painting Department, Courtauld Institute of Art)*

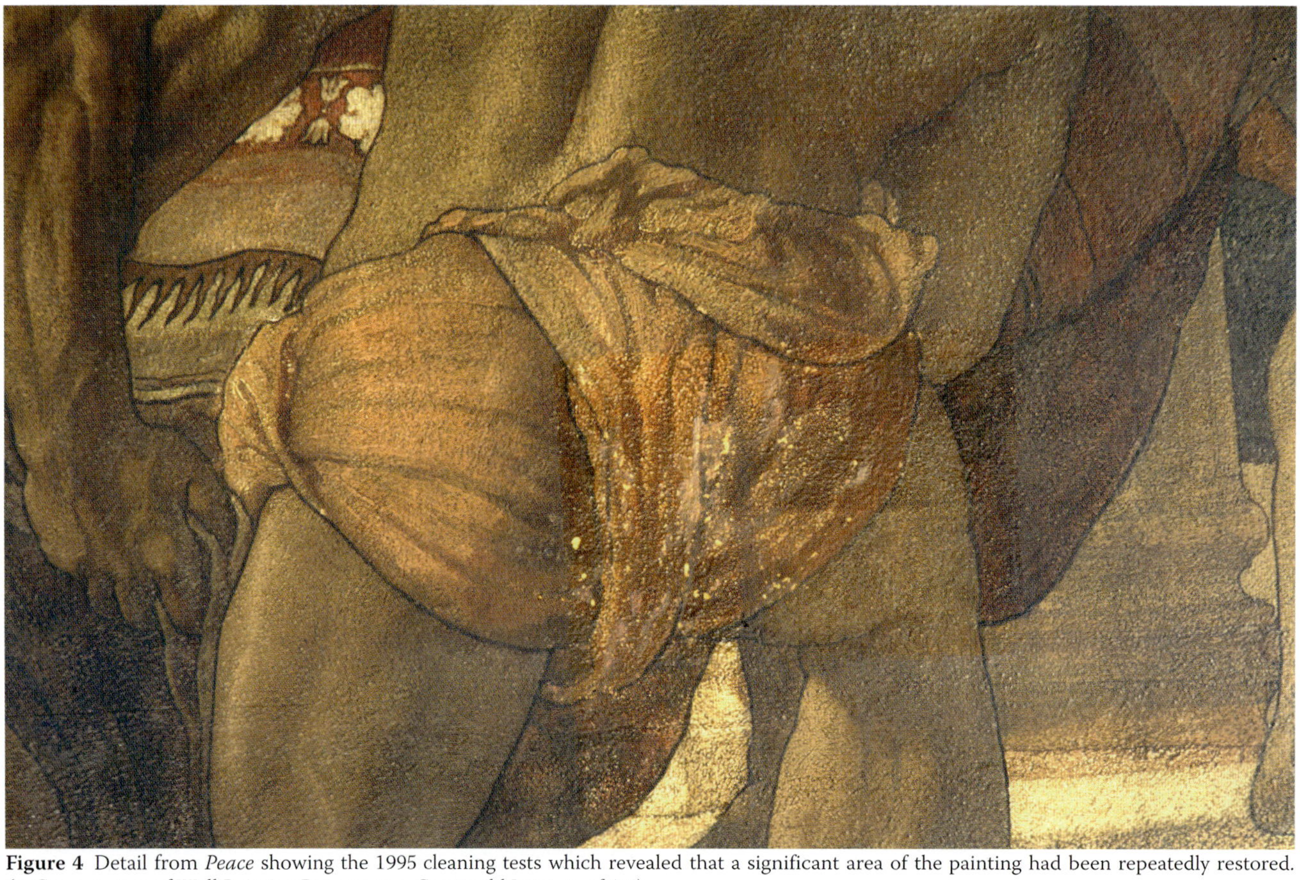

Figure 4 Detail from *Peace* showing the 1995 cleaning tests which revealed that a significant area of the painting had been repeatedly restored. *(© Conservation of Wall Painting Department, Courtauld Institute of Art)*

Ward's 1897 intervention, which concentrated on cosmetic restoration, is recorded in a clear and concise report with annotated graphic documentation. Sadly, results were short-lived. By 1902, Mr Cundall, the Officer in Charge of Paintings, had observed in a memo to the Director: 'For some years when the atmosphere is moist and warm the surface [of Peace] becomes "tacky" in places and recently it has become worse. It is apparently due to the wax which has been used, and which appears to be disintegrating.'[7] The possible jurisdiction of the Office of Works was again raised in a memo to the Director[8] on the basis that the frescoes form 'a part of the permanent building', but the Director instead requested a new condition report from Thomas Armstrong. The museum also looked outwards, requesting the advice of Sir William Richmond, Professor of Painting at the Royal Academy. In his response, Richmond admitted to a lack of understanding of Leighton's methods – in particular of his media – and he suggested that Professor Arthur Church from the Royal College of Art, the Government Chemist, should also be involved.

In July 1902, on receipt of Armstrong's invoice for his report (dated 5 December 1901), and assuming that Professor Church would need payment for his services, the Board of Education finally opted to inform the Office of Works, which duly accepted direct responsibility for the frescoes and eventually took charge of the investigations. Having commissioned a condition survey from Professor Church, the Office of Works then sanctioned him 'to be good enough to take such steps as he may consider necessary in the matter.'[9] Church made no reference to Armstrong or to his various treatment tests in his report, nor indeed to any of the previous treatments. Instead, he suggested his own set of trials. After these were completed, he treated both murals in the last months of 1902, undertaking further cleaning of *Peace* in May 1903.

Less than two months later, James Ward wrote to the Board of Education raising further concerns over condition. In his letter (dated 19 June 1903), Ward suggested that spirit fresco paintings required treatments of fixative every 7–10 years, and went on to suggest that, given his intimate knowledge of the frescoes, he should be entrusted to undertake the necessary work. Directed by the Office of Works, Ward carried out a two-month restoration of *Peace* in July and August 1904. Again, in Ward's detailed and illustrated report of his restoration, there are no references to previous treatments other than to the removal of a previous restoration that was found to have discoloured (Fig. 4).[10] He linked the ongoing deterioration of *Peace* to its location on an external wall, with cold and damp air behind causing condensation on the surface – something Leighton himself had been aware of and concerned about (Fig. 5). This hypothesis did not however appear to affect the treatment methods used, nor were there any specific recommendations for building works to mitigate adverse conditions.

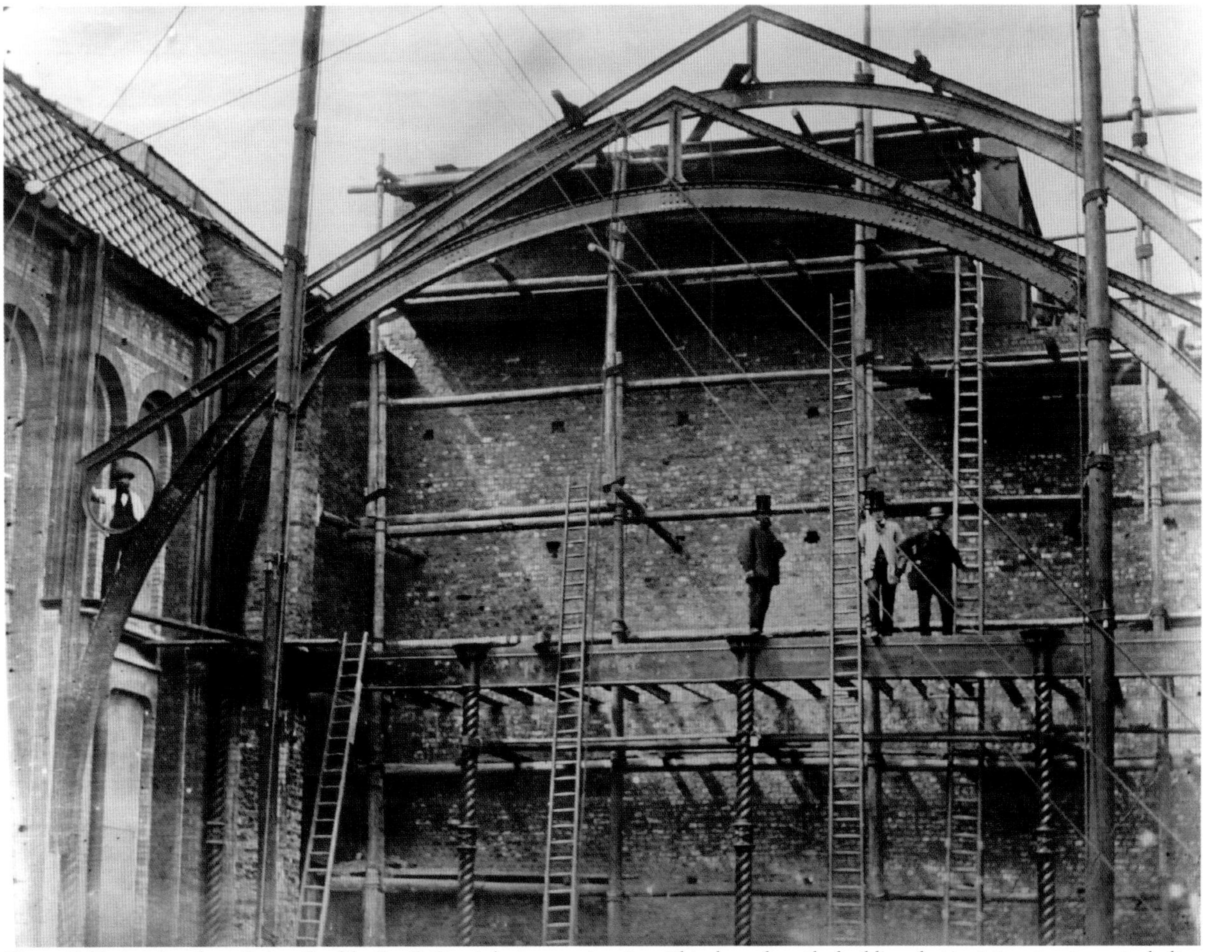

Figure 5 Photo taken from the south of the South Court during construction. This shows how the building abuts existing structures, including the east wall of the Sheepshanks Gallery (on the left), and the large end wall in brick. *(© V&A Images/Victoria and Albert Museum)*

In 1909, the Art Director of the Museum (by now renamed the Victoria and Albert Museum), H.M. Cundall, had arranged for the surface of both murals to be dusted using cotton wool. While this appears to have been done without Office of Works involvement, Cundall recommended that the Office should be contacted to address renewed deterioration of *Peace*.[11] After additional prompting, driven by increasing concerns over accelerated decay, the Office of Works directed Ward to re-treat the painting. It is of great significance that the Office ensured that a copy of Ward's prior report was made available to the museum, and desired that Ward's work be carried out in direct liaison with museum staff. For the first time, some explicit collaboration and cooperation was included.

The report of Ward's initial re-inspection (carried out in January 1910) was met with concern and scepticism by Cundall. Compiling a resumé of all previous reports – possibly the first such – Cundall challenged Ward's claim that 'all the parts which he had revived, and repainted, in 1904, are in perfectly sound condition'.[12] Cundall went on to query the reasons given by Ward for the glossy appearance of the surface, indicating that it differed from that suggested previously by Church and indeed from that in Ward's own 1904 report. How these concerns were expressed to Ward is not clear, though there do appear to have been informal meetings held on site.

Notwithstanding the concerns raised by the museum, the restoration of *Peace* by Ward in August 1910 focused on 'cleaning and reviving the colouring'.[13] That the painting's location on an external wall was making the painting more vulnerable to environmental fluctuations was again highlighted in Ward's report. By this stage, most of *Peace*'s surface had been subjected to a significant level of repainting, repeated surface cleaning, and it had received multiple applications of the spirit fresco medium (Figs 6 and 7 and Table 3).

Between 1910 and 1922, a number of localised repairs were made to specific areas of damage in both paintings, largely mechanical, again using restorers selected by the Office of Works. World War I successfully distracted minds from routine cleaning or repair, though some efforts were made to see if the frescoes could be protected from possible bomb damage: the files contain a lengthy debate over costs and supply of materials. As these had not been resolved before the end of the war, nothing was ever done.

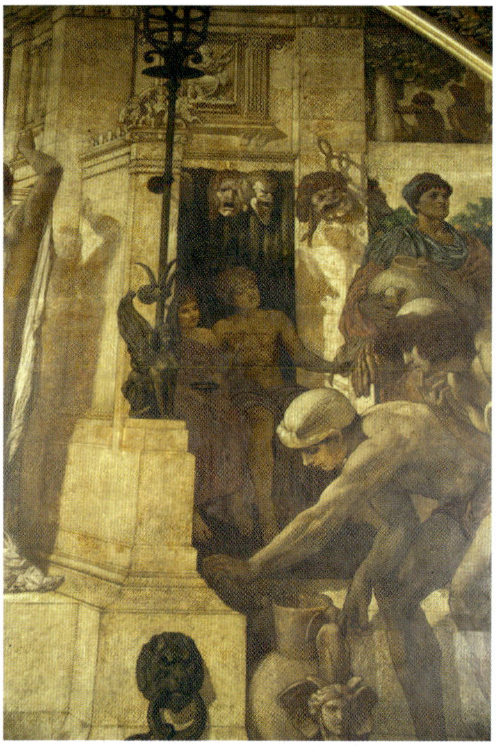

Figure 6 Detail of the mid section of *Peace*. *(© Conservation of Wall Painting Department, Courtauld Institute of Art)*

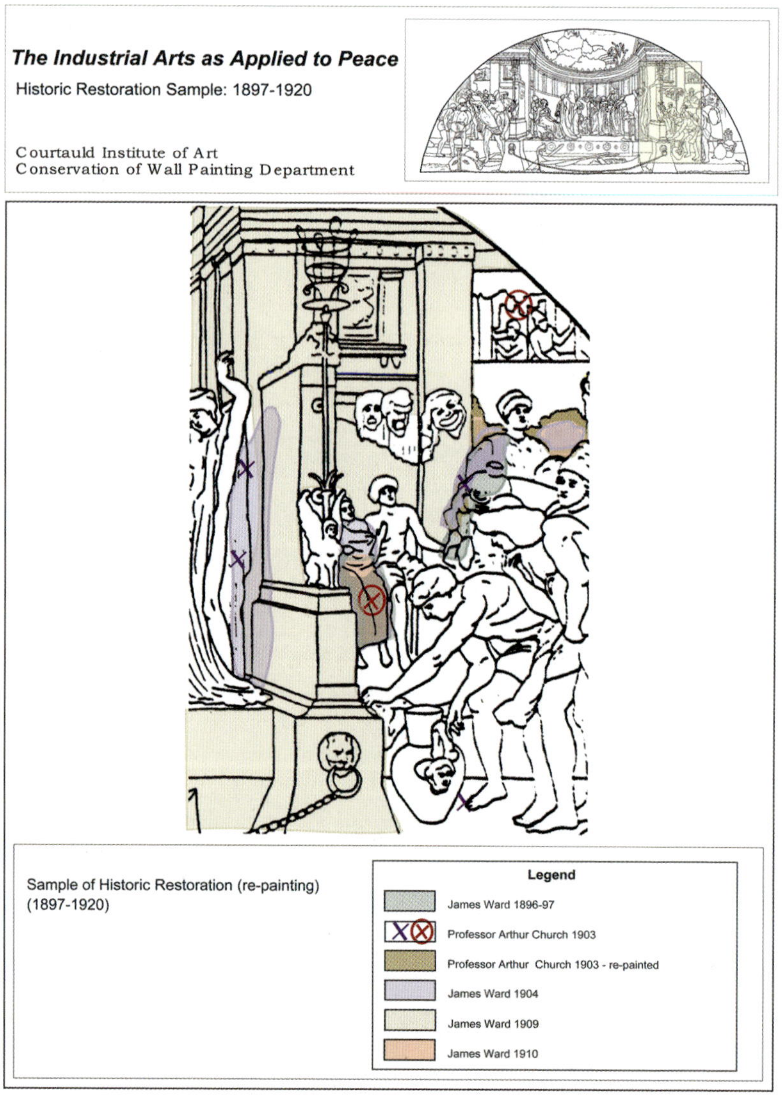

Figure 7 Graphic record showing the recorded restorations (1897–1920) to the area of *Peace* illustrated in Figure 6. *(© Conservation of Wall Painting Department, Courtauld Institute of Art)*

Table 3 Summary of the recorded restoration programmes undertaken to the spirit fresco by Frederick Lord Leighton, *The Industrial Arts as Applied to Peace* (1880–86).

	Interventions			Materials	
Date: Main conservator	Removal of loose pigment and/or original material	Retouching over original pigment	Replacing of previous retouchings	Spirit-fresco medium	Other materials
1896: Ward	✓	✓		✓	
1897: Ward	✓	✓		✓	
1901: Armstrong	✓	✓			✓
1902: Church					
1903: Church	✓	✓	✓	✓	
1904: Sykes					
1904: Ward	✓	✓	✓	✓	
1909: Cundall					
1910: Ward	✓	✓	✓	✓	
1912: Haines					
1916: Haines	✓			✓	✓
1922: Art Room	✓		✓	✓	✓
1924/25: Jack/Tristram	✓	✓	✓	✓	
1929: Office of Works					
1931: Office of Works					
1933-35: Jack					
1940: Jack					
1941: Jack	✓		✓	✓	
1995: Courtauld/Rickerby/V&A			✓		✓

1922–1926 Making sense of the issues: conservation by committee

In August 1922, the museum attempted to surface clean the paintings, an intervention that appears to have been internally guided and undertaken without wider consultation. This treatment proving unsuccessful, the V&A notified the Office of Works that the frescoes 'should be cleaned at the earliest opportunity'.[14] Despite this contact with the Office of Works, the museum also independently sought out James Ward.

A number of significant events then caused the focus and approach towards these troubled works to shift. Fate played a large hand, with the deaths of many of the original cast: Armstrong in 1911, Church in 1915 and Richmond in 1921. Ward was found to be in Africa, and although he was still interested in continuing his restoration work to the frescoes for a fee of £90, he wrote that he would be unable to return to England until summer 1924.[15] Then in early 1924, still abroad, he too died. Meanwhile the Office of Works was increasing in professional confidence, having recently worked on the condition problems of a number of murals at the House of Lords under the direction of the Office's architect Frank Baines, and with chemist Arthur Laurie.[16]

At this point, a correspondence began between V&A Director, Sir Cecil Harcourt Smith, and the Permanent Secretary at the Office of Works, Sir Lionel Earle. Harcourt Smith had pressed for Ward for the project, despite the potential delay, but Earle raised the issues of succession management and forward planning. Indeed he not only asked who else might be capable, but actually helped to arrange that a young E.W. Tristram should work with Ward on the frescoes as an apprentice (in a letter from Earle to Harcourt Smith of 8 March 1923, Tristram is identified as Professor Lethaby's assistant). Earle also suggested that a definitive report of methods of repair was needed to aid future care. The letters are here reprinted in their entirety as they beautifully demonstrate differences in attitudes towards the diagnostic understanding of the problems of Leighton's painting.

Letter to Sir Cecil Harcourt Smith from Sir Lionel Earle (26 March 1923)

Dear Harcourt Smith,
With reference to our correspondence on the question of the repair to the Leighton Frescoes, it seems to us that it would be advisable to go into this question very thoroughly, in view of the heavy cost of repairs in the past and of the bill which has to be faced now. It seems to be far from clear what the actual cause of the trouble is, and I think it is desirable that we should have some more exact data on the conditions which have to be contended with, and I think it may be advisable to consult Sir Robert Robertson, the Government Chemist.

Temperature records might be kept for a period of at least a year, both on the inside and outside wall faces, and, in addition, chemical analysis of any incrustations or flaking portions of the pigments could be made.

It might also be advisable that Mr Ward should give details of his process in order that they might be submitted to the Government Chemist for an expression of opinion. Do you see any objection to our taking up the matter on the lines I have indicated?
Yours sincerely,

Lionel Earle

Memo from Martin Hardie (V&A Keeper of Paintings) to Sir Cecil Harcourt Smith (2 April 1923)

Director,
I wonder whether Sir Lionel Earle knows Kipling's story of 'Pig', and how a poor civilian spent years in reduc-

ing Pig to five places of decimals for the honour of the service at the instigation of an Official who had to keep up the reputation of being 'earnest'.

The plaster is ordinary plaster – Leighton's colours ordinary pigments – with pastel here and there from previous restoration. No chemical analysis of incrustations or flaking portions will reveal more than that: and the fact remains that the colour crumbles off if touched, and that we have to do the best we can to keep it there.

Personally, in a matter of this kind, I have no faith in the Chemist, and would far rather trust Mr Ward, who has had practical experience (of the actual frescoes), or Mr Tristram who has made experiments in actual methods of fresco painting, besides studying examples all over the country. This Mr Noel Henton, or any Government Chemist, who can produce theories only, and know nothing of painting [sic].

However, if you think it advisable that we should act in accordance with Sir Lionel Earle's wishes, we can progress on the lines of 'Pig'; and send specimens of the pigment for him to forward to forward to the Government Chemist (and [?] temperature records on the wall faces): and we can also write to Mr Ward, explaining that the O of W would like him to supply details of his processes for submission to the Government Chemist 'for an expression of opinion' – before we can undertake to entrust the work to him.

Martin Hardie

The response to this memo:

Mr Hardie,
It rather looks as if Pig were likely to prove a simpler problem than pigment. If Kipling's hero had had a Government mathematician to refer to, the tale might have been longer.

To Sir L. Earle's plain question (in his last sentence) I can only say 'see no objection' even though I see no object – But before the Government Chemist embarks on his journey, I think he ought to be primed with the literature referred to in our letter of March 15. Personally, if this is done, I shall be surprised if he goes any further.

CJ 5 iv 23[17]

Resigned to the change in approach, Harcourt Smith suggested that a committee be formed (with himself as Chairman) to report to the President of the Board of Education. He proposed five other members: the Government Chemist Sir Robert Robertson, E.W. Tristram, Martin Hardie, a representative from the Royal Academy and one from the Office of Works. With the representative positions eventually filled by Sir David Murray and Office of Works architect A.W. Heasman, the first committee meeting was held on 5 December 1923, with 11 further meetings held up to March 1925.

In spite of the apparent scepticism of certain members, the minutes of the 12 formal committee meetings reveal all parties to have been serious and dedicated participants. Capitalising on their diverse backgrounds, they explored aspects of Leighton's original technique, the subsequent treatment and the possible causes for ongoing decay. The committee devised a systematic series of treatment tests, which was undertaken by the Office of Works supported by sampling and analysis of materials by the Office of the Government Chemist (Fig. 8). The *in-situ* testing was carried out by James Semple Jack (a draughtsman within Frank Baine's architectural team), under Heasman's supervision. Jack produced regular reports of his work, which at first centred on the efficacy of certain methods of cleaning and the removal of previous restorations (Fig. 9). These were presented to the committee by Heasman: Jack does not appear to have ever been invited to attend a formal committee meeting, though it is likely that he may have been present for some of the site visits.

By early 1924, much of the non-figurative areas of both paintings had been cleaned, and attention moved to the ongoing removal of previous restorations and the need for a 'preservative varnish'.[18] At this stage, Tristram suggested a wax varnish based on his previous work at Westminster Abbey, where he had treated a painting some 12 years before that remained in very good condition.[19] The committee agreed to allow him to carry out a small trial area, which they later approved. Within the Office of Works, however, there were rising concerns over Tristram's wax method, which was rapidly becoming routine for many high profile wall painting sites. In May 1924, Frank Baines wrote to Robertson regarding the proposed treatment of ceilings in Hampton Court:

> It is quite clear we had better leave the paintings [in Hampton Court] alone rather than use any system which would be found to have caused considerable harm to the paintings some years hence.
>
> We have got to bear in mind that the method adopted with the Leighton Frescoes by Professor Church and Mr Ward produced lamentable results, although both these gentleman were apparently convinced that they were preserving the panels. The ultimate effect of the treatment, however, is little short of disastrous, while the Gambier Parry treatment as used on one of the great ceilings at Greenwich Hospital has had absolutely disastrous results, and there would not appear to be very material difference between Mr Tristram's solution and that of Gambier Parry.[20]

Despite such concerns, Tristram's involvement in treating the paintings increased, and when Heasman determined that the figurative areas were a 'matter for an artist' and beyond the skills of Jack and his team, the committee agreed that Tristram should work directly with the team overseeing this aspect of the work, being paid by the Office of Works (Fig. 10).[21] Tristram and Jack worked together to complete the cleaning, restoration, and surface varnishing of *Peace* in advance of the final formal committee meeting held on 24 March 1925, at which they 'expressed their pleasure with the satisfactory result'. Final cleaning and varnishing of *War* was also approved at the same meeting, and this was completed by the end of October.

The final report from the committee was drafted by Hardie for circulation to all members, and on 26 February 1926, Eric Maclagan (who had replaced Harcourt Smith as Director in

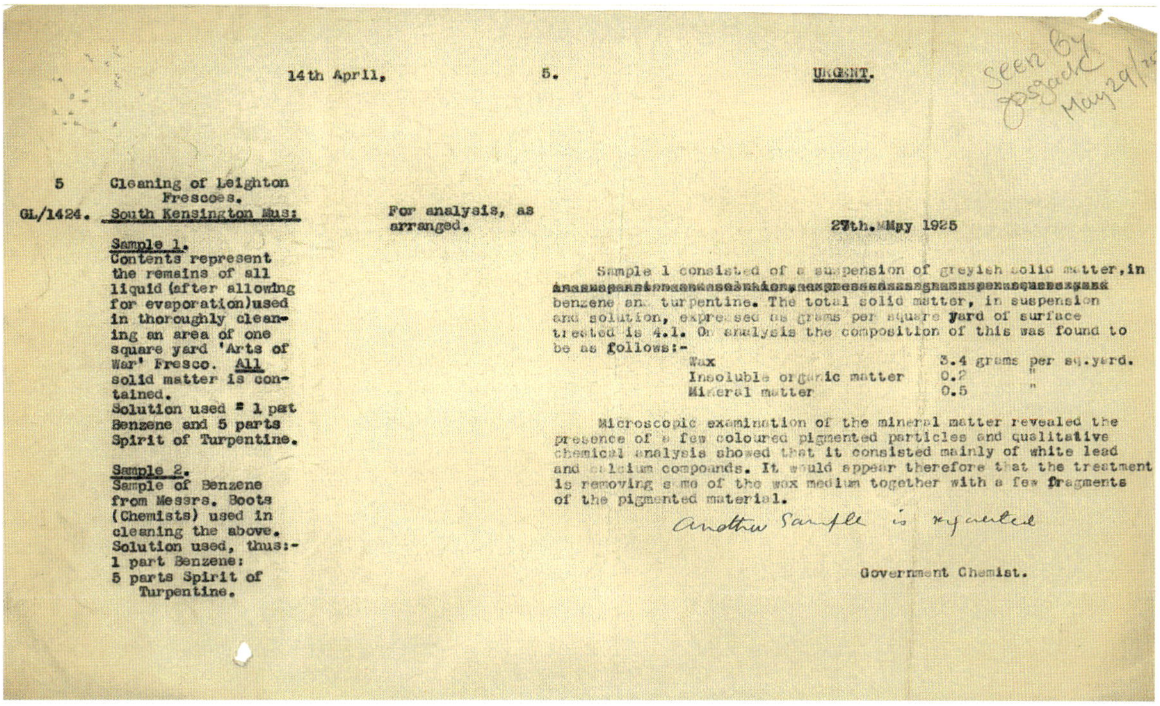

14th April, 5. URGENT.

Seen by J.S. Jack May 29/25

5 GL/1424. Cleaning of Leighton Frescoes. South Kensington Mus:

For analysis, as arranged.

Sample 1. Contents represent the remains of all liquid (after allowing for evaporation) used in thoroughly cleaning an area of one square yard 'Arts of War' Fresco. All solid matter is contained. Solution used = 1 part Benzene and 5 parts Spirit of Turpentine.

Sample 2. Sample of Benzene from Messrs. Boots (Chemists) used in cleaning the above. Solution used, thus:- 1 part Benzene: 5 parts Spirit of Turpentine.

27th. May 1925

Sample 1 consisted of a suspension of greyish solid matter, in benzene and turpentine. The total solid matter, in suspension and solution, expressed as grams per square yard of surface treated is 4.1. On analysis the composition of this was found to be as follows:-

Wax	3.4	grams per sq.yard.
Insoluble organic matter	0.2	"
Mineral matter	0.5	"

Microscopic examination of the mineral matter revealed the presence of a few coloured pigmented particles and qualitative chemical analysis showed that it consisted mainly of white lead and calcium compounds. It would appear therefore that the treatment is removing some of the wax medium together with a few fragments of the pigmented material.

Another sample is requested

Government Chemist.

Figure 8 Copy of the analytical report produced by the Government Chemist for the solution collected after cleaning during the major conservation programme 1923–5 (original held in English Heritage Registry File WP 019/0075). *(© English Heritage)*

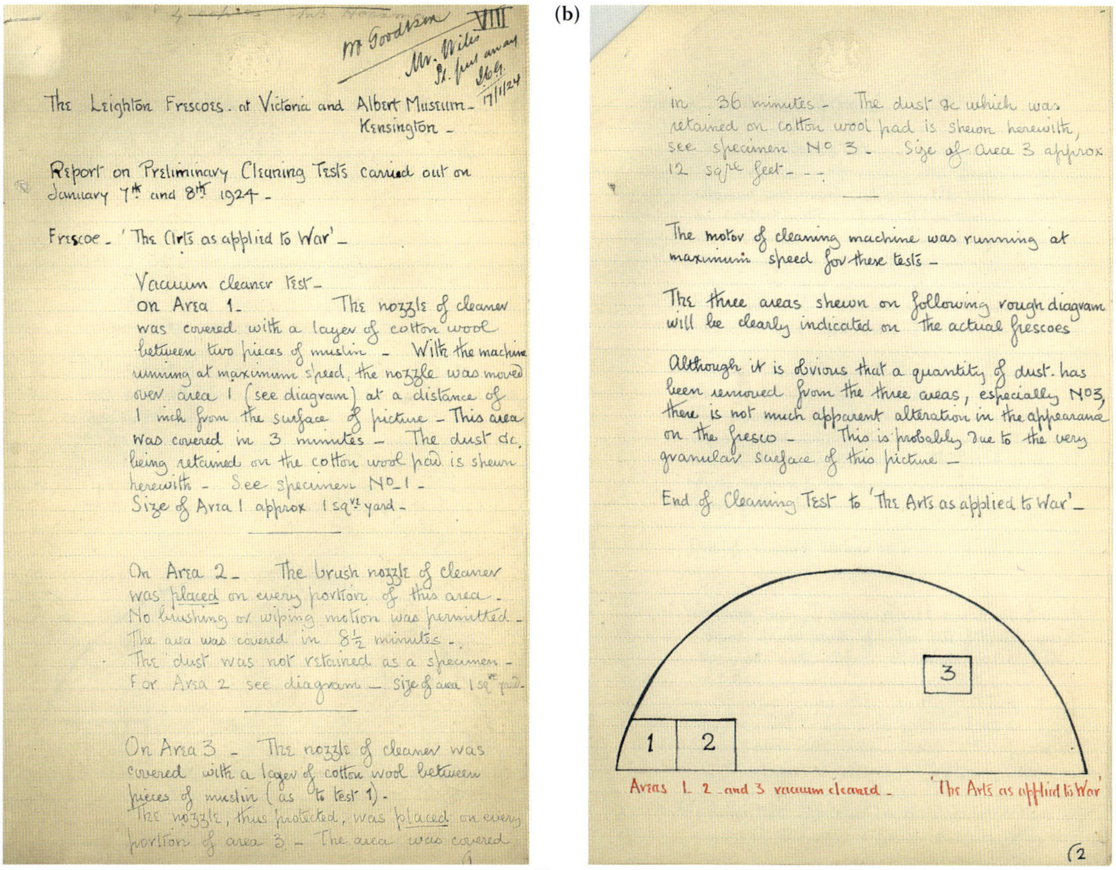

(a)

VIII

Mr Goodison

Mr. Wiles

The Leighton Frescoes. at Victoria and Albert Museum – Kensington –

Report on Preliminary Cleaning Tests carried out on January 7th and 8th 1924 –

Frescoe – 'The Arts as applied to War' –

Vacuum cleaner test –

On Area 1 – The nozzle of cleaner was covered with a layer of cotton wool between two pieces of muslin – With the machine running at maximum speed, the nozzle was moved over area 1 (see diagram) at a distance of 1 inch from the surface of picture – This area was covered in 3 minutes – The dust &c. being retained on the cotton wool pad is shewn herewith – See specimen No 1 – Size of Area 1 approx 1 sq. yard –

On Area 2 – The brush nozzle of cleaner was placed on every portion of this area – No brushing or wiping motion was permitted – The area was covered in 8½ minutes – The dust was not retained as a specimen – For Area 2 see diagram – Size of area 1 sq. yd.

On Area 3 – The nozzle of cleaner was covered with a layer of cotton wool between pieces of muslin (as to test 1) – The nozzle, thus protected, was placed on every portion of area 3 – The area was covered

(b)

in 36 minutes – The dust &c which was retained on cotton wool pad is shewn herewith, see specimen No 3 – Size of area 3 approx 12 sq. feet – –

The motor of cleaning machine was running at maximum speed for these tests –

The three areas shewn on following rough diagram will be clearly indicated on the actual frescoes

Although it is obvious that a quantity of dust has been removed from the three areas, especially No 3, there is not much apparent alteration in the appearance on the fresco – This is probably due to the very granular surface of this picture –

End of Cleaning Test to 'The Arts as applied to War' –

Areas 1 2 and 3 vacuum cleaned – 'The Arts as applied to War'

12

Figure 9 (a and b) Copy of the treatment trials report produced by J.S. Jack as part of the 1923–5 conservation programme. This report would have been presented to the committee by A.W. Heasman as representative of the HM Office of Works (original held in English Heritage Registry File WP 019/0075). *(© English Heritage)*

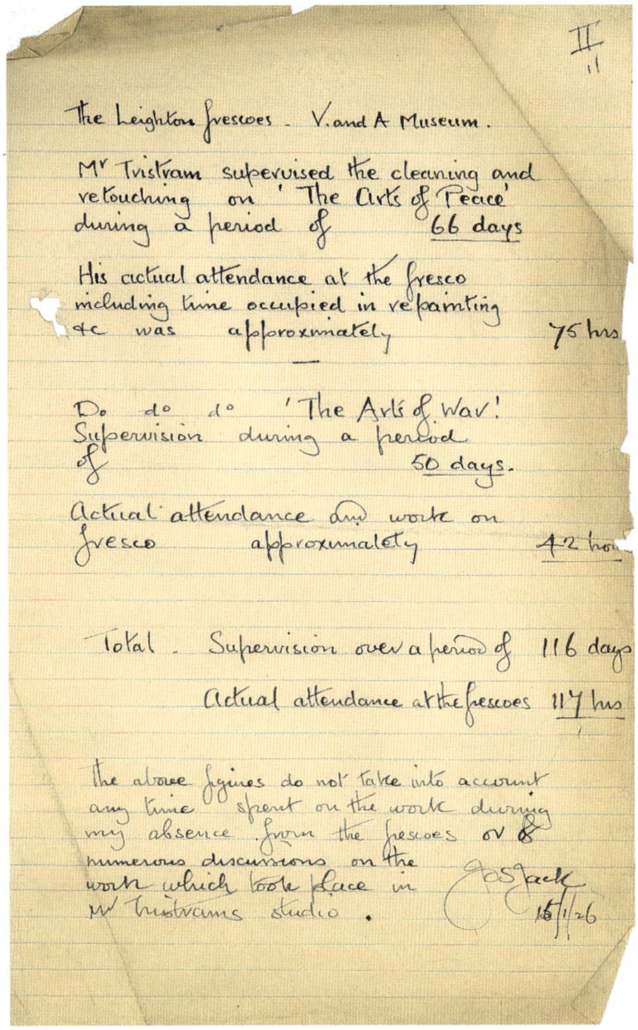
II
11

The Leighton frescoes . V. and A Museum.

Mr Tristram supervised the cleaning and retouching on 'The Arts of Peace' during a period of 66 days

His actual attendance at the fresco including time occupied in repainting &c was approximately 75 hrs

Do do do 'The Arts of War'
Supervision during a period of 50 days.

Actual attendance and work on fresco approximately 42 hrs

Total. Supervision over a period of 116 days
Actual attendance at the frescoes 117 hrs

The above figures do not take into account any time spent on the work during my absence from the frescoes or & numerous discussions on the work which took place in Mr Tristrams studio.

Jack
15/1/26

Figure 10 Copy of an internal record showing Professor E.W. Tristram's hours during the latter stages of the 1923–5 conservation programme when he was working in association with Jack (original held in English Heritage Registry File WP 019/0075). *(© English Heritage)*

1924) submitted the agreed version to Eustace Percy, President of the Board of Education. The report provided a comprehensive summary of the works. It included a detailed conservation history and appropriately drew attention to James Jack:

> We should like to put on record our appreciation of the careful and methodical work done by Mr Jack of the Office of Works. Mr Jack was responsible for the practical side of the cleaning processes. His intelligent workmanship, and his precise reports on the execution of his work, helped largely towards the achievement of a successful result.

Considerable discussion took place over whether the report should be published, and this split the committee: Harcourt Smith, Murray and Robertson all favoured publication, while Maclagan, Hardie, Heasman and Tristram all felt this was unnecessary and might provoke unwanted discussion and criticism in the Press. Unsurprisingly, Percy opted to support the decision not to publish, but agreed that the report remain available for publication should the need arise.[22]

1928–1945 Reactive repairs

Only three years after the final report (in August 1928), Hardie approached the Office of Works to have the surfaces of the paintings dusted; dusting was repeated three years later, this time with some input from Tristram to assess the efficacy of his protective wax varnish coating. Heasman's successor, N. de Normann, queried the rise in costs and the extent of the proposed cleaning. It was attributed to specialist involvement and the suggestion by Tristram that the surface wax might need to be renewed; in the event this aspect of the work was deferred.

The 1931 cleaning demonstrated that the paintings were subject to the routine but significant accumulation of dirt. The museum suggested that a maintenance and cleaning agreement be established, whereby 'the Office of Works should be asked to arrange to have the frescoes washed regularly every 18 months, without our having to make an application each time for the work to be done'.[23] In December 1931, a cyclical maintenance arrangement was agreed by de Normann with the proviso that the Keeper of Paintings be consulted on each occasion. In early 1933, before this system had been properly implemented, flaking and disruption of *War*'s plaster appeared, the cause thought to be a faulty asphalt roof. The V&A again looked outwards, recommending Tristram to the Office of Works for the repair work at a cost of £15. The success of the 1923–5 Leighton project, however, together with other high profile work on murals throughout the royal and government estates, had allowed Baines to fulfil his wish of establishing a dedicated in-house team of 'artist-restorers' at the Office of Works. Following Baines' departure in 1927, this team was led by Jack.[24] Therefore, responding to the V&A enquiry, the Office of Works Permanent Secretary, Patrick Duff, suggested Jack and his small team, citing his particular experience on the frescoes and the obvious savings of doing the work in-house. Writing to the museum's Director in September 1933, Duff stated: 'Apart from saving the Exchequer some money, there will also be this advantage, that we shall be able to establish in the Department some continuity of treatment which will not be the case if the work is always done by outsiders.'[25]

Such pragmatism prevailed. Initiating the treatment of *War*, the Office of Works found that a defective gutter was to blame for the damage and that water had completely saturated both the wall and the plaster. The project was scaled up and an area of both plaster and brick was removed and temporarily filled by a painted replica. Finally, in March 1940, just after the outbreak of war, Jack and his team instated a permanent plaster repair (see Fig. 14).

Taking over the cleaning routine established before the war, the team – now a part of the newly named Ministry of Works – surface cleaned both frescoes in 1941. Soon after this, however, the impact of the war on government priorities led to the very existence of an 'artist-restorers' team being questioned. Jack defended his team vehemently, charting the important early moves by Baines in 1923 to create an in-house service, and their continued treatment of mural paintings in the direct care of the Office of Works right up to the outbreak of war:

> It should be noted that up to that time [1939] the artists had repaired, cleaned, retouched, and preserved paint-

ings to the extent of approx 40,000 square feet of surface, besides carrying out a large variety of other artistic works in connection with ancient and historic buildings.[26]

Meanwhile within the V&A attention was focused on the safety and security of its collection. There were some attempts to determine a method of physical protection for the murals, but these were muted and soon overshadowed as the South Court was commandeered for use as a Royal Air Force canteen – much to the chagrin of museum staff (Fig. 11).

1945–1955 Attempts to recapture routine

Battling for its own professional survival, during the war years the Ministry of Works restoration team had been diverted to the recording of damaged buildings and to assisting art relocation and storage. As such, the Leighton frescoes were seemingly dropped from the team's agenda: indeed, both Physick and Ormond suggest that nothing much further happened to either mural following the war, citing the 1941 cleaning as the last known intervention. This was certainly not the case. The museum did in fact revisit its pre-war plans for periodic cleaning, as indicated in an internal memo of June 1947: 'After their exposure to so much dirt and the greasy steam from the canteen in the courts below during the war, it is now time they are examined afresh to see what treatment, if any, is required.[27]

The senior echelon within the museum appears to have had other priorities, and up to 1951 Leigh Ashton, the Director, annually deferred any action. In 1949–50, the Ministry of Works carried out building alterations, enclosing the eastern half of the South Court (the space between the two frescoes) to create a museum restaurant (Fig. 12). By inserting a false ceiling at the base of the two galleried recesses, and blocking the upper galleries with permanent partitions, the alterations left each mural isolated in its own narrow, dark corridor (spaces known today as Gallery 100 and Gallery 109).[28]

The necessary redecoration of these newly created spaces put renewed pressure on the museum to reconsider the condition of the murals. This finally led to a request from the museum to the Ministry of Works District Surveyor (H.T. Murrell), specifically asking whether Jack could inspect and clean the frescoes.[29] Jack and his team surveyed later that year, but cleaning was delayed until March 1952. Considering the future of the paintings, Jack returned to the notion of a regular cleaning programme, suggesting:

> Now that the frescoes are enclosed by the screens erected along the gallery edges they are no longer exposed to currents of air drifting up from the great exhibition court below and are probably not so liable to pick up heavy surface deposits. Perhaps under the

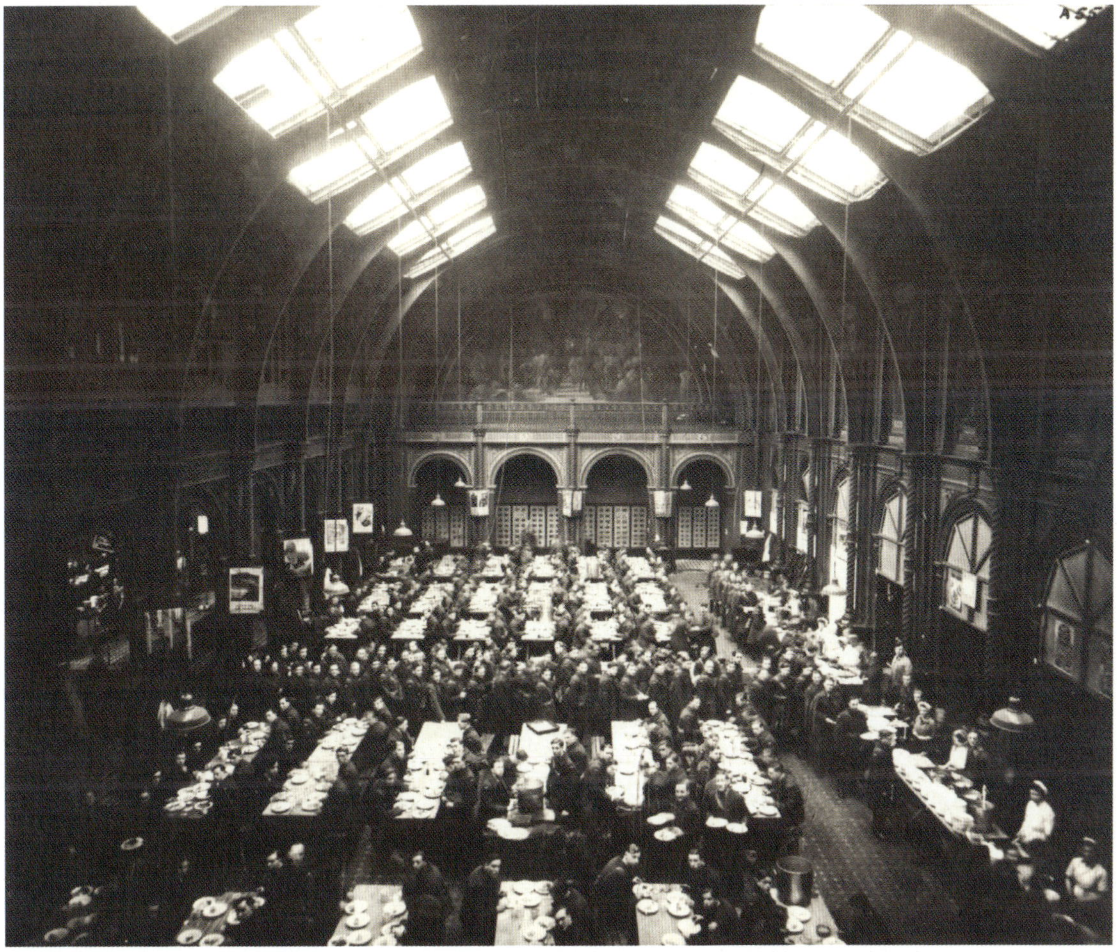

Figure 11 View northwards into the South Court (looking towards *War*), during World War 2 when the space was used as a Royal Air Force canteen. *(© V&A Images/Victoria and Albert Museum)*

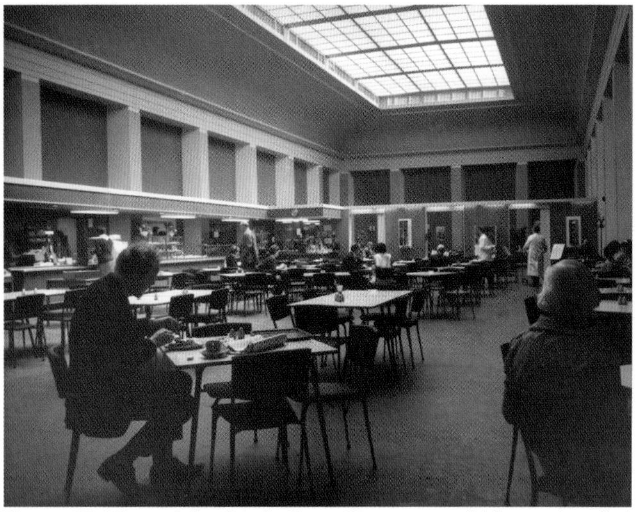

Figure 12 View of the South Court Restaurant, which was installed by the Ministry of Works c.1950. *(© V&A Images/Victoria and Albert Museum)*

> circumstances it would be sufficient to clean them every two years. If paintings such as these are attended to at regular interv-als then cleaning presents no difficulty and deterioration can be combated.[30]

This approach approved, Jack reported on a 'periodic' cleaning of the frescoes in December 1954. This was the last recorded intervention by Jack, who subsequently retired 'and died shortly after'.[31]

1955–1983 Decades of discussion

The remarkable thoroughness and clarity of record-keeping within the Ministry of Works Studio during Jack's regime seems not to have survived his departure. Researching the history of the studio, Barbara Bryant recently unearthed documents in the Public Records Office that indicate that the government had in fact put the workshop under renewed evaluation. The pressure to dismantle the studio, fought against by Jack since the outset of war and now renewed, placed significant strains on his successors. Despite protestations by the Earl of Huntingdon in the House of Lords (who argued on financial grounds for its retention), the number of permanent staff was reduced by half in 1955, severely limiting its capacity to undertake site projects.[32] These included the Leighton frescoes, for which the studio still accepted responsibility.

In an entry in the 'Lists of works in the London government buildings and royal palaces for the artists that required attention' (dated 12 May 1958), senior architect R.G. Wood described the Leighton frescoes:

> They are rather dirty. The Ministry is committed by agreement to periodic cleaning now overdue. The V&A Museum are pressing for early attention.
>
> Action: The paintings are badly lit and we are experimenting with the Engineers to improve illumination before taking action on the painted surfaces. This work could be entrusted to an outside firm if necessary.[33]

It is possible to glean from this a subtle form of deferral, and under the circumstances it seems unlikely that any intervention took place over the next few years.

While the Ministry of Works Studio was recovering from its latest (though certainly not its last) government review, the V&A was responding to the growing international momentum in conservation studies. In 1960 it transformed its Art Workshop into the V&A Conservation Department, to be led by Norman Brommelle.[34] Nevertheless, a number of letters from Brommelle to the studio acknowledged the ministry's ongoing commitment to the care of the frescoes (Fig. 13). While further correspondence in the later 1970s between the museum and the studio (which in 1970 had been transferred to the direction of the Department of the Environment) suggests that there was continued collaboration between the two in other areas of the museum, there is no recorded evidence to imply that any cleaning of the murals occurred during this time, or indeed in the intervening period up to 1983.

1983 onwards: major changes in roles and responsibilities

Direct government responsibility for the Leighton frescoes officially ceased with the creation (by the 1983 National Heritage Act) of the Historic Buildings and Monuments Commission for England, which established English Heritage and the parallel conversion of the major national museums into Non-Departmental Public Bodies (NDPB). Within English Heritage, the workshop survived as the Painting Conservation Studio. It concentrated its efforts on the substantial collection of easel and panels paintings held in English Heritage properties, alongside the conservation of English Heritage wall painting sites. Studio staff also continued to advise on non-English Heritage sites, but this role became linked to grant-related projects and statutory consultation.[35] By default, Leighton's frescoes, an integral part of both the building and the collection, finally became the direct responsibility of the V&A.

The problems of moisture ingress behind the upper corner of *War* were never entirely resolved (Fig. 14). At some point, museum staff applied facing tissue as a holding measure. In advance of the impending celebration of Leighton's centenary in 1994, the Conservation of Wall Painting Department at the Courtauld Institute of Art was invited to undertake the first re-examination of the murals for almost 40 years. Both parties accepted the compromised state of the frescoes and a limited programme of surface cleaning and localised repair was agreed, along with associated works to improve their presentation. The project also provided an opportunity to systematically review the physical history of the paintings, and clarify the overall extent of previous intervention.[36]

Despite its links to the Leighton frescoes, the English Heritage Painting Conservation Studio was not formally consulted during this work, nor was it involved in the centenary celebrations.

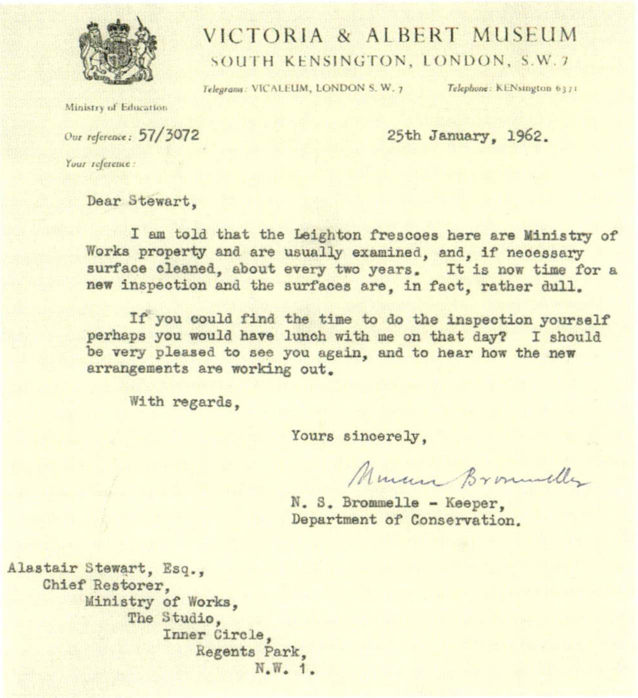
VICTORIA & ALBERT MUSEUM
SOUTH KENSINGTON, LONDON, S.W.7
Telegrams: VICALEUM, LONDON S.W.7 Telephone: KENsington 6371
Ministry of Education

Our reference: 57/3072 25th January, 1962.
Your reference:

Dear Stewart,

I am told that the Leighton frescoes here are Ministry of Works property and are usually examined, and, if necessary surface cleaned, about every two years. It is now time for a new inspection and the surfaces are, in fact, rather dull.

If you could find the time to do the inspection yourself perhaps you would have lunch with me on that day? I should be very pleased to see you again, and to hear how the new arrangements are working out.

With regards,

Yours sincerely,

N. S. Brommelle - Keeper,
Department of Conservation.

Alastair Stewart, Esq.,
Chief Restorer,
Ministry of Works,
The Studio,
Inner Circle,
Regents Park,
N.W. 1.

Figure 13 Copy of letter from Norman Brommelle to Alastair Stewart raising the issue of the Ministry of Works' responsibility for the care of the Leighton frescoes (original held in English Heritage Registry File WP 019/0075). *(© English Heritage)*

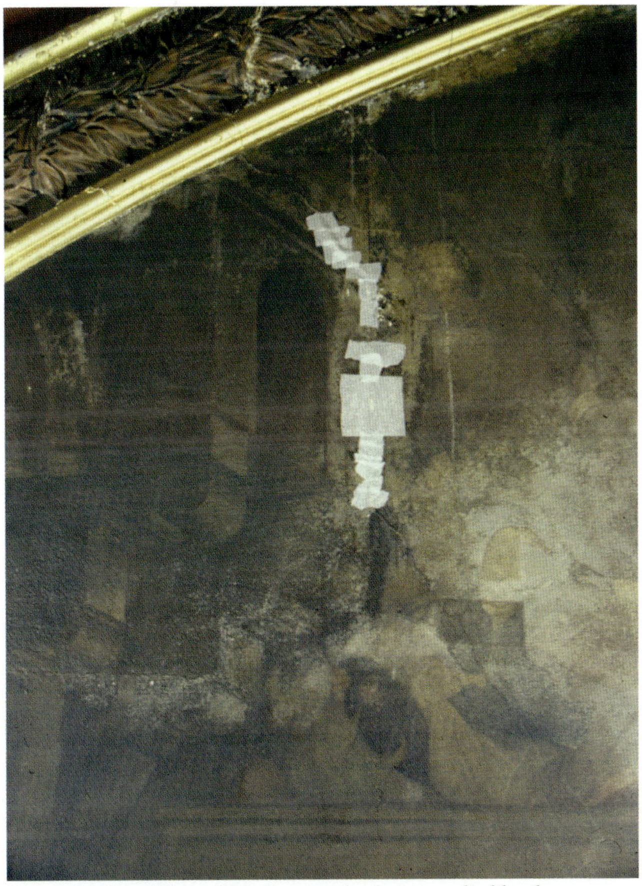

Figure 14 Detail from *War* showing the facing applied by the museum in the early 1990s to an area of lifting and flaking paint. This damage relates to water ingress behind the painting, first identified in the 1930s. A significant area of plaster (the outline of which can just be seen to the left of the facing) has been replaced. *(© Conservation of Wall Painting Department, Courtauld Institute of Art)*

Lessons learned and reflections on progress

Looking back at the decision-making processes surrounding the Leighton frescoes, we get an invaluable glimpse into the changing public-sector attitudes towards wall painting conservation over the last century. We can see conflicts arising over finance and misunderstandings as to levels of responsibility, the perils of not reviewing past records, and the challenges in maintaining appropriate continuity in the face of ever-changing agendas. We find scientific scepticism coupled with blatant prejudice, and see that attempts to establish a sustainable management strategy were repeatedly thwarted by bureaucracy and organisational metamorphoses (Fig. 15).

Most striking – and in many ways most pertinent to current circumstances – is the consistent absence of the reassessment of prior decisions and approaches, and indeed of a coordinated approach to allow lessons to be learned from these (Fig. 16). Such an avoidance of the lessons of history is all the more worrying in the present, when the numbers of practical conservators working directly in the public sector are rapidly reducing, and the emphasis is on 'outsourcing' to a competitive commercial market. English Heritage certainly continues to play a major part in influencing the conservation profession, but this influence is now largely directed towards the production and dissemination of national standards and guidance. One may indeed mourn the loss of what Frank Baines called his 'band of stalwart men', since their cogent and practical approach still offers a lesson for future decision makers.

Appendix: Key characters

South Kensington Museum/Victoria and Albert Museum

- Arthur Banks Skinner (1861–1911): Assistant Art Director 1896–1905; Art Director 1905–9
- Sir Cecil Harcourt Smith (1859–1944): Director 1909–24
- Sir Eric Maclagan (1879–1951): Director and Secretary 1924–45
- Sir Leigh Ashton (1897–1983): Director and Secretary 1945–55
- Mr Thomas Armstrong (1832–1911): Director of Art 1881–98
- Martin Hardie (1875–1952): Keeper of Paintings 1921–1935
- Herbert Minton Cundall (1848–1940): Keeper in Charge of Paintings 1891–1905; Senior Keeper 1905–10
- Mr Graham Reynolds (1914–): Keeper of Paintings 1959–74
- Norman Brommelle (1925–1989): Keeper of Conservation 1960–77
- Susannah Edmunds: Head of Paintings Conservation c.1994–2000

Government staff

- Acton Smee Ayrton (1816–1886): First Commissioner of Works 1869–73
- Sir William de Wiveleslie Abney (1843–1920): Principal Assistant Secretary, Board of Education 1899–1902 (Science Department)
- Sir Robert Morant (1863–1920): Permanent Secretary, Board of Education 1903–11
- Sir Lionel Earle (1866–1948): Permanent Secretary, HM Office of Works 1912–33; later Chairman of Ancient Monuments Board for England

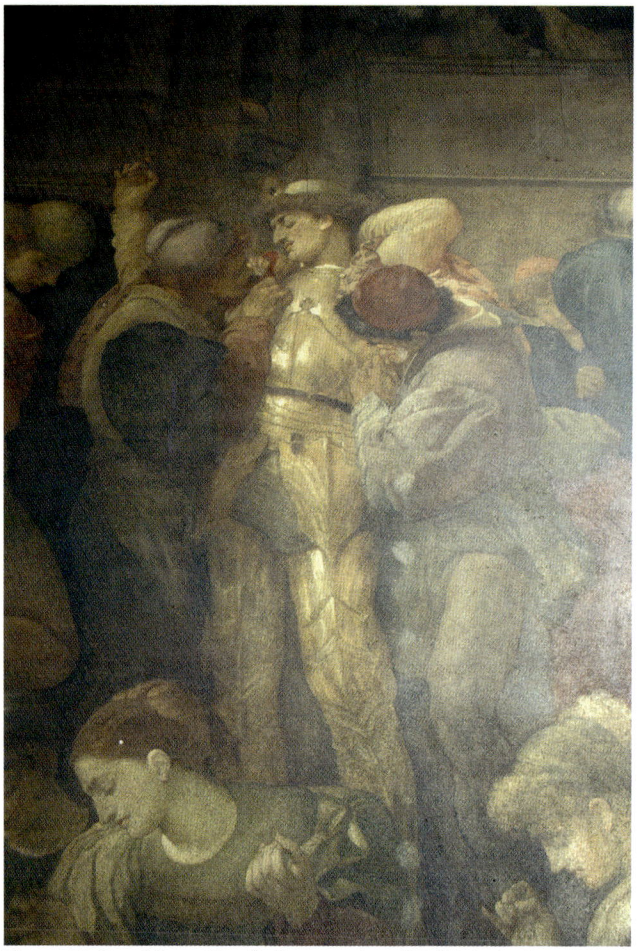

Figure 15 Detail from *War*. (*© Conservation of Wall Painting Department, Courtauld Institute of Art*)

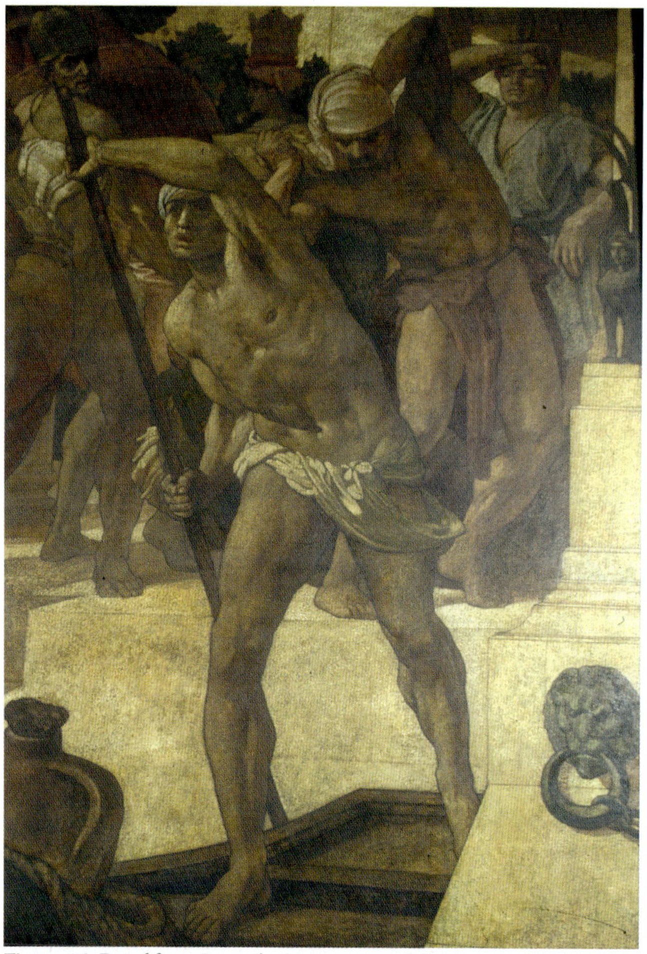

Figure 16 Detail from *Peace*. (*© Conservation of Wall Painting Department, Courtauld Institute of Art*)

- Sir Frank Baines (1877–1933): Director of Works in charge of Royal Palaces, Houses of Parliament, Public and Historic Buildings and Ancient Monuments 1914–27
- A.W. Heasman: Architect for Ancient Monuments (Office of Works)
- Sir Eric de Normann (1893–1982): Architect, Office of Works 1920–35; Deputy Secretary, Ministry of Works 1943–54; Chairman of Ancient Monuments Board for England 1955–64
- Mr Frederic James Edward Raby (1888–1966): Assistant Secretary in charge of Museums c.1939
- Sir Patrick Duff (1889–1972): Permanent Secretary, Ministry of Works 1933–41
- H.T. Murrell: District Surveyor, Ministry of Works

Royal Academy of Arts

- Sir Aston Webb (1839–1930): President RA 1919–24
- Charles Sims (1873–1928): Keeper RA Schools 1920–26
- Sir William Llewellyn (1858–1941): President RA 1928–38
- Sir William Richmond (1842–1921): RA 1895
- Sir David Murray (1849–1933): RA 1905

Specialists and conservator-restorers

- James Ward (1851–1924): artist; assistant to Leighton 1878–86; artist-restorer; Headmaster, Dublin Metropolitan School of Art 1907–18
- Professor Arthur Herbert Church (1834–1915) – Government Chemist; Professor of Chemistry, Royal Academy of Arts 1879–1911
- Sir Robert Robertson (1869–1949): Government Chemist 1921–36 assisted by Mr Nickolls (undertook *in-situ* microscopic examination)
- Mr Haines: private restorer
- Professor E.W. Tristram (1882–1952): RCA (assistant to Professor Lethaby), then Professor of Design 1925
- James F. Semple Jack (?–1955): Draughtsman, Office of Works from c.1913; head of artist-restorers team 1927–55
- W.H.D. Hampton: Restorer, Ministry of Works
- V.C. Hardingham: Restorer, Ministry of Works
- Alastair N. Stewart: Restorer, Ministry of Works; became Chief Restorer c.1955
- Stephen Rickerby: consultant conservator to the Conservation of Wall Painting Department, Courtauld Institute, from 1991

Acknowledgements

This research was driven by the 1995 conservation programme of the frescoes undertaken by the Conservation of Wall Painting Department at the Courtauld Institute of Art, and I am particularly grateful to Sharon Cather of the Courtauld for providing ongoing access to the material, and for her continuous support and encouragement in preparing this paper. Within the V&A, access to the archives was made possible by Susannah Edmunds and Lucia Scalisi. Lorinda Wong and Rachel Burch assisted me in the collation and cataloguing of this material undertaken as part of the initial Courtauld student project. Rachel Burch also assisted in producing the graphic material.

Notes

1. The primary publications that discuss the history of the Leighton frescoes are Ormond 1975 and Physick 1982. In addition, two further articles were published in association with the 1995 conservation: Rickerby and Barringer 1995 and Barringer 1996.
2. Examination of the documentary material was initiated as part of the programme of conservation undertaken in 1995 by the students on the Courtauld Institute of Art's Conservation of Wall Painting postgraduate course. This project was supervised by Stephen Rickerby, liaising with Susannah Edmunds and Lucia Scalisi from the V&A. Further archive files were later found at English Heritage in 1998 during the relocation of the Wall Painting Section to the headquarters' office on Savile Row.
3. See Physick 1982, pp. 74–5.
4. See Physick 1982, p. 12.
5. Memo from Museum Director Arthur B. Skinner to Art Director Thomas Armstrong, dated 19 June 1896 (V&A Nominal File).
6. Non-attributed memo from 'E.H.' dated 29 November 1897 (V&A Nominal File).
7. Internal memo dated 23 October 1901 (V&A Nominal File).
8. Internal memo dated 24 October 1901 (V&A Nominal File).
9. Letter to the Secretary of the Board of Education from Office of Works, 30 September 1902 (V&A Nominal File).
10. Ward's report is prepared as a letter to the Secretary of the Office of Works, 26 August 1904 (V&A Nominal File).
11. Memo to Cecil Smith, 12 September 1909 (V&A Nominal File).
12. Letter from Ward to the Office of Works 10 January 1910, and quoted in a memo from Cundall to Assistant Director Arthur Richmond, 14 March 1910 (V&A Nominal File).
13. Report by Ward presented as a letter to Secretary to the Office of Works, 22 August 1910 (V&A Nominal File).
14. Letter to Office of Works 8 August 1922, and associated memo to the Director from Martin Hardie 16 August 1922 (V&A Nominal File).
15. Letter from Ward to the Director 30 October 1922 (V&A Nominal File).
16. Bryant 2001.
17. All letters from V&A Nominal File. The story referred to by Hardie is one of the short stories by Rudyard Kipling, in *Plain Tales from the Hills*, first published in Calcutta and London in 1888. The story can be downloaded via www.gutenberg.org/etext/1858.
18. Minutes of the 5th meeting of the committee held on 17 March 1924 (V&A Nominal File).
19. Although the specific painting is not mentioned, it is most likely the large late medieval portrait panel of Richard II, located at the west end of the nave.
20. Copy from the Public Record Office held in the English Heritage Archive File.
21. Committee minutes from 18 June and 16 July 1924 (V&A Nominal File).
22. Memo to Hardie from Percy's private secretary, 26 February 1926 (V&A Nominal File).
23. Memo to Hardie from B.S. Long dated 16 October 1931 (V&A Nominal File).
24. Bryant 2001, p. 41.
25. V&A Nominal File, 21 September 1933.
26. Draft letter by Jack, March 1943 (English Heritage Archive File WP019/0075).
27. V&A Nominal File.
28. Physick 1982, p. 56.
29. Letter to Murrell from T.W.I. Hodgkinson, 19 May 1951 (English Heritage Archive File WP019/0075).
30. English Heritage archive memo to Mr Rotherwell from Jack, 20 March 1953, in response to a letter from Reynolds (English Heritage Archive File WP019/0075).
31. Memo to Rotherwell from Jack, 10 January 1955 (English Heritage Archive File WP019/0075). For details on Jack's death, see Bryant's working notes (English Heritage Registry File, *Painting Conservation Studio: History of the Studio Files*).
32. House of Lords Records Office 1952, report for 10 June 1952, *Preservation of Works of Art*, pp. 22–4.
33. English Heritage Archive File WP019/0075.
34. Webber 2005.
35. Gowing 2003.
36. No final conservation report has yet been produced, but a short summary of the project was published in the *V&A Conservation Journal* (see Rickerby 1995).

References

Barringer T. 1996, 'The Leighton Gallery at the V&A: the context, conservation and redisplay of the South Kensington frescoes' *Apollo* CXLIII(408), pp. 56–64

Bryant B. 2001, 'The Ministry and conservation: painting conservation in historic interiors under the Office and Ministry of Works, from c1923 to the 1950s', in A. Oddy and S. Smith (eds) *Past Practice – Future Prospects*, British Museum Occasional Paper No. 145, British Museum, London, pp. 39–44

English Heritage Registry File, *Victoria and Albert Museum, South Kensington, Greater London* (Wall Paintings, advisory file non-EH sites) (WP 019/0075)

English Heritage Registry File, *Painting Conservation Studio – History of the Studio Files*

Gowing R. 2003, 'Introduction – developing approaches to wall painting conservation in England', in R. Gowing and A. Heritage (eds) *Conserving the Painted Past: Developing Approaches to Wall Painting Conservation*, postprints of a conference organised by English Heritage, London 2–4 December 1999, James and James Science Publishers, London, pp. ix–xiii

Office of Works and Public Buildings 1912, *Report of the Inspector of Ancient Monuments for the Year Ending 31 March 1912*, HMSO, London

Ormond R. 1975, *Leighton's Frescoes*, Victoria and Albert Museum Brochure 6, Victoria and Albert Museum, London

Physick J. 1982, *The Victoria and Albert Museum: The History of its Building*, Phaidon-Christie, Oxford

Rickerby S. 1995, 'The conservation of Lord Leighton's spirit frescoes "War" and "Peace"', *V&A Conservation Journal* 17, pp. 9–10

V&A Nominal File, *Leighton*, Nominal File No. 100, Victoria and Albert Museum Registry

Webber P. 2005, 'Rising damp: a history of the Conservation Department', *V&A Conservation Journal* 50 [accessed online: www.vam.ac.uk]

The author

Robert Gowing has worked on wall painting conservation projects in England, Spain and Austria. He was employed by the Courtauld Institute as a research and teaching assistant prior to undertaking the post of Wall Painting Conservator at English Heritage. The Senior Wall Painting Conservator within the English Heritage Building Conservation and Research Team since 2002, he has specific responsibility for providing technical support at national level on projects involving the conservation of wall paintings, and he is active in the team's research and publications programmes. Within the professional conservation community, Robert was the Chair of the UKIC (now Icon) Stone and Wall Painting Group 2002–5. As part of the formation of the converged Institute of Conservation, he was asked to become Project Manager for the development and implementation of its new corporate identity and in December 2005 became a member of the Board of Trustees. Robert also sits on the International Advisory Board for the MA in Wall Painting Conservation course at the Courtauld Institute of Art.

Rex Whistler: a comparative study of three decorative schemes

Marguerite O'Leary

Introduction

Reginald John (Rex) Whistler was born in Kent in 1905 and died in action near Caen in 1944. In his short life Rex Whistler was remarkably productive, and demonstrated his versatility as an artist within several disciplines. Evident in his work is a natural ability to invent and to draw with an uninhibited dexterity. For Whistler, drawing was the purpose, the business and the pleasure of his everyday life. He examined the world that existed and recorded it, or in its place created another. The role of drawing in Whistler's work is fundamental and underpinned each discipline in which he worked.

In 1922 Whistler was accepted on probation by the Royal Academy Schools where, under Charles Simms, he spent an unsuccessful term. He failed and was considered not promising enough to remain. Subsequently however he met with Professor Henry Tonks of the Slade School of Art, where he was accepted and where he studied for the next three years. In Whistler's final year at the Slade, Tonks discouraged him from applying for a scholarship to the British School at Rome: nobody, he said, who won the scholarship had ever done anything afterwards. Undoubtedly Tonks was already aware of the prospect of the commission from the Tate, and intended to recommend him. Thus Whistler won his first major commission, the Tate Gallery restaurant scheme, at the age of only 20.

In total, Whistler carried out 14 mural and decorative schemes, both in private London residences and in remote country houses, and for each he made numerous rough sketches, designs and alternative proposals. He also completed some eight designs for murals that were not carried out. The setting and location of each particular project not only influenced the choice of subject, but also the manner in which it was painted. Many employ themes based on myth or invention, set in fantastical landscapes. These were influenced by 17th- and 18th-century painting, and make numerous references to Gothic ruins, Corinthian columns and grand façades. Occasionally in his mural paintings Whistler would cite actual buildings, and reconstruct them within his landscape. He was particularly influenced by the paintings of Poussin, Claude, Salvador Rosa, Watteau, Boucher and Canaletto, as well as the general architecture of Georgian England.

The Tate Gallery, London

On 19 April 1926, Whistler commenced work on the Tate Gallery restaurant scheme with the assistance of a fellow Slade student Nan West (West's involvement at the Tate seems to have only been in the preparatory and the final stages of painting). On entering the restaurant, it can be seen that the room is about 55ft long, with a doorway at the far end that leads to the restaurant kitchens. On the left is an external wall with a door and two windows, one of which is in an alcove. The wall to the right and both the main-entrance and kitchen-entrance walls are decorated with paintings on canvas. Little daylight is provided by the windows. A star-like arrangement of tungsten down-spots directs light around the room, and daylight fluorescent tubes around the edges light the mural directly.

The basis of the paintings is an imaginary group setting off on a journey of adventure through various continents, seeking out foods and meeting with strange beasts. They leave the palace at the left-hand corner of the main painting and reappear at various intervals throughout. The ambitious nature of a scheme of this scale played a substantial role in Whistler's future, as did the publicity and promotion it received. Further fame arose through collaboration with Edith Olivier: a story entitled *A Guide to the Duchy of Epicurania with Some Account of the Famous Expedition, In Pursuit of Rare Meats* was devised and later published on behalf on the Tate. The murals were partly based on the story, but as the paintings were never finished certain incidents do not appear.

Plas Newydd, Llangollen, Wales

In 1936 Whistler was commissioned to paint at Plas Newydd, home of the Marquess of Anglesey, promoted by the fact that he had already painted for other members of Lady Anglesey's

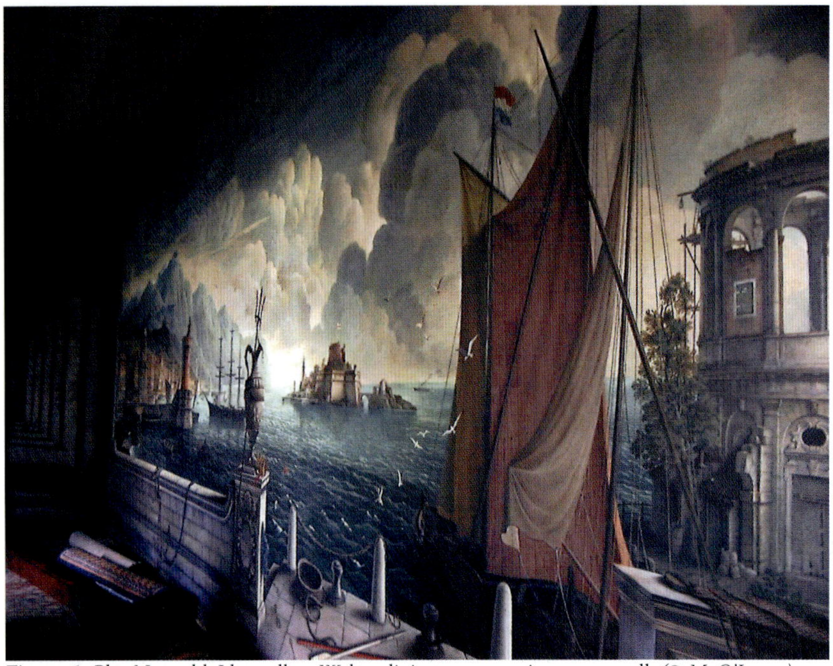

Figure 1 Plas Newydd, Llangollen, Wales: dining room, main canvas wall. *(© M. O'Leary)*

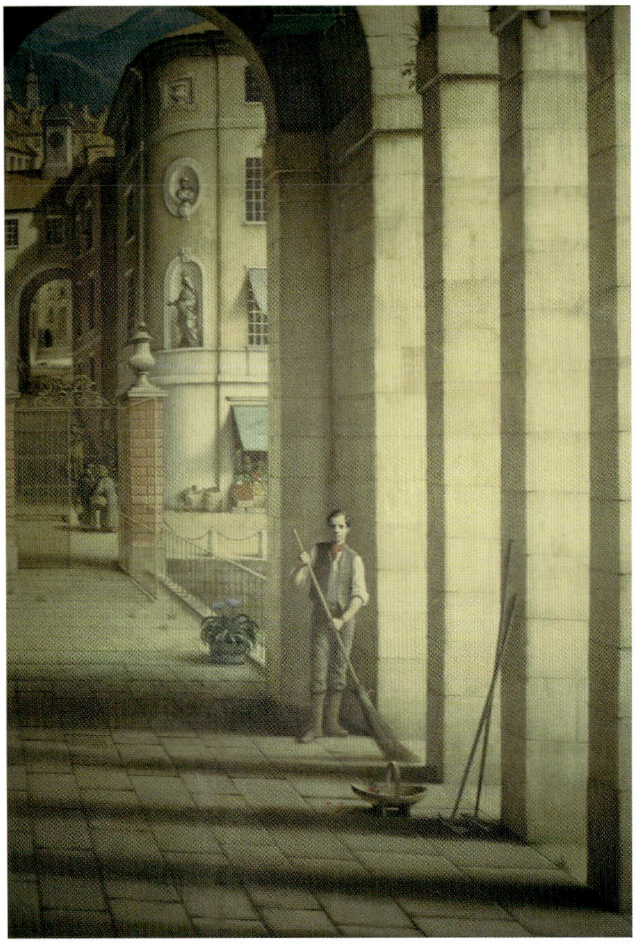

Figure 2 Plas Newydd, Llangollen, Wales: dining room, left end wall, detail of self-portrait. *(© M. O'Leary)*

family.[1] The main wall to be painted runs for approximately 47ft and faces four windows looking out onto the Menai Straits and the Snowdonian Mountains (Fig. 1). Laurence Whistler suggests that his brother 'resolved to answer it as a mirror – a mirror that transformed. He would answer it with another mountainscape-seascape, which could also be a townscape, the painted architecture breaking forward at the corner, onto the end walls.'[2]

A canvas measuring approximately 58ft, to cover the main wall and the end walls, was ordered from France. Whistler then hired a large studio from Alick Johnstone's scene-painting firm in Lambeth to accommodate the huge canvas. In the studio was a mechanism that allowed for raising and lowering the frame, which he illustrated in a letter to Lord Anglesey. The painting was taken to Plas Newydd in June 1937 when mostly complete. Two assistants worked with Whistler: Vic Bowen and C.W. Beretta (who was involved only when the painting was *in situ* at Plas Newydd).

The room is lit by two chandeliers and four windows facing south-east. The ceiling is painted to appear coffered, with repeated motifs in the centre of each, and the cornice is covered with gold leaf over which acanthus leaves have been drawn at the corners. The Christian names of the 6th Marquess and his wife are inscribed above trophies symbolising their family's history, painted on the chimney-pieces at either end of the room. Columns attached at either side of the chimney walls and the skirting are incorporated in the overall scheme. The main canvas depicts an imaginary view over a parapet wall of a harbour town and distant landscape. In the left arcade is a self-portrait – the largest figure painted – which is partly shadowed by the columns (Fig. 2). Behind are sunlit buildings and the distant mountains continued from the main wall. The right arcade makes a number of references to the family. According to the present Lord Anglesey, the cello was his when younger, the dogs were his sisters', and the glasses and cigarette are a reference to his mother, who was forever misplacing her spectacles.[3]

Mottisfont Abbey, Romsey, Hampshire

By the final stages of the Plas Newydd scheme in 1938, Whistler had already received another commission: the drawing room at

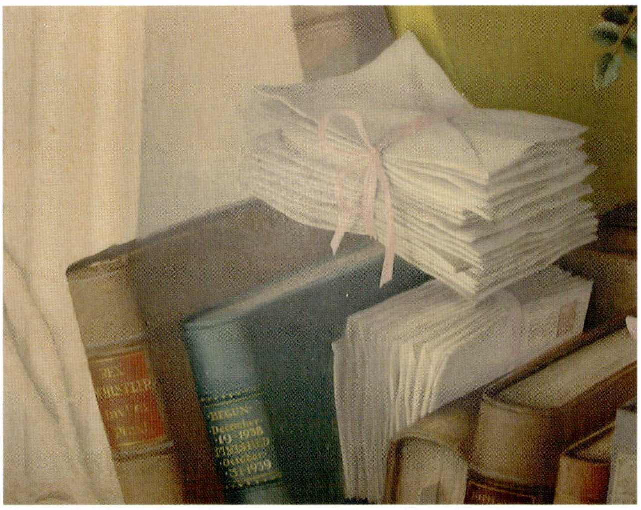

Figure 3 Mottisfont Abbey, Romsey, Hampshire: drawing room, detail of urn wall. *(© M. O'Leary)*

Mottisfont Abbey, from Mr and Mrs Gilbert Russell. Whistler made a number of drawings of alternative schemes for this room. His brother Laurence recalls that 'work began on countless sheets of paper in London'. It would seem Whistler originally intended a rather different scheme to that carried out. The proposal drawings indicate, for example, that in the spaces between the arches he intended to paint landscapes beneath a curtain, trophies all in gold, and, between the columns, statues in niches, along with other details. Laurence Whistler suggests that his brother wanted the drawing room to be 'colourful, diverse and suggestively mysterious', but Mrs Russell thought otherwise: 'no archways, no emphasis, nothing personal: all must be done in shallow relief'. The painter had intended this approach for the framework only.

As recorded on the painted spine of a book at the base of the urn on the west wall, Whistler worked on the Mottisfont scheme from 18 December 1938 into 1939 (Fig. 3). Again he had two assistants: Vic Bowen, who had already worked with him at Plas Newydd, and Percy Willats. The room is painted in *trompe l'oeil*, in the manner of Gothic Revival. At the centre of the east wall is a fireplace, painted to imitate green marble. On either side of this, trophies portray martial subjects. The trophy panels are separated and framed by slender columns on either side and arches above. Some decorative features are painted in shallow relief directly on the plaster wall, while others, painted on wood, project from the wall. The vaulted cove above is painted to simulate a decorative lattice filled with rosettes. A large Gothic design is painted on the ceiling: twisting vine leaves and a formal sun centre (Fig. 4).

Comparative analysis of materials and methods

The three decorative schemes examined incorporate a number of different supports. The Tate and Plas Newydd schemes are both painted on canvas and plaster. The Tate canvases are adhered to a board attached to studwork, while the Plas Newydd canvases are adhered directly to the plaster wall. The canvas ground in both schemes appears to be lead white and chalk. The greyish plaster preparation under the Tate painting comprises calcium carbonate, silica, alumina and a little iron oxide. The plaster of the Plas Newydd walls is also greyish, and incorporates calcium sulphate, silica, a small amount of iron oxide and alumina, followed by a skim of calcium sulphate. The scheme at Mottisfont Abbey is mostly painted on plaster; the reddish-brown plaster preparation includes calcium sulphate, silica and iron oxide, over which there is a skim of calcium sulphate.

The priming of the painted walls is different in each scheme. At the Tate there are numerous underlayers (which are perhaps associated with the previous wall paint); the lower layers consist mostly of variations of mixtures of lithopone, barium sulphate and calcium carbonate with iron-oxide-containing

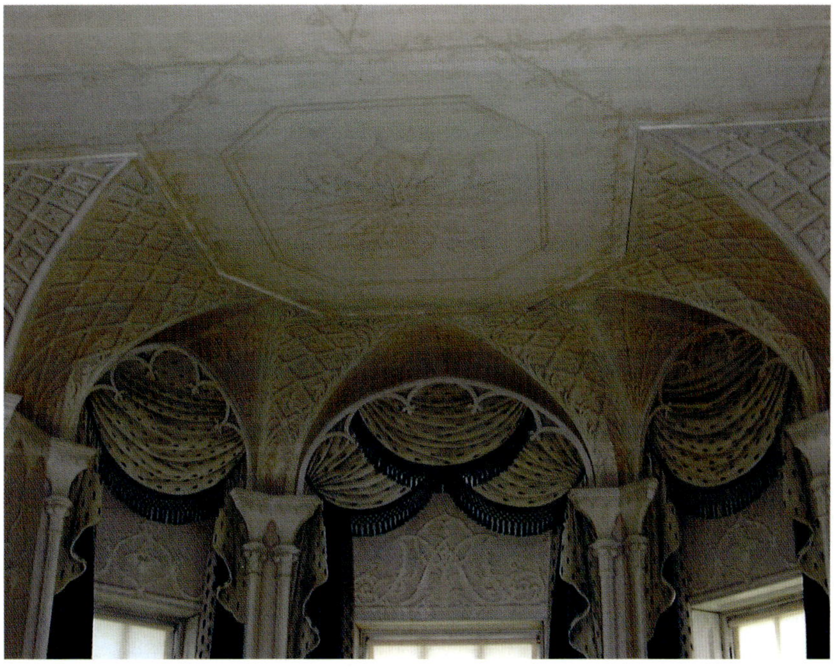

Figure 4 Mottisfont Abbey, Romsey, Hampshire: drawing room, ceiling. *(© M. O'Leary)*

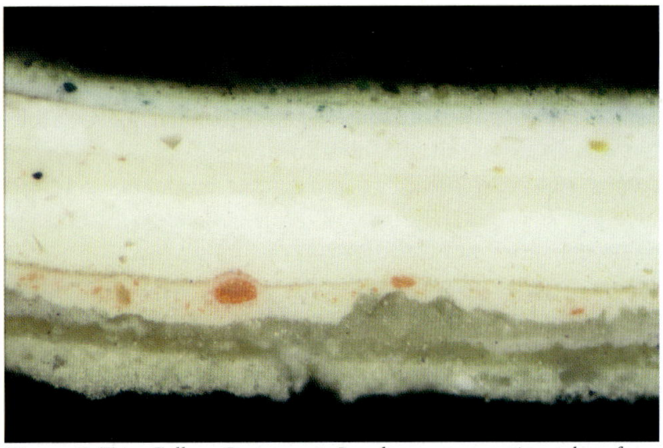

Figure 5 Tate Gallery Restaurant, London: cross-section taken from brown paint on the plaster wall. *(© M. O'Leary)*

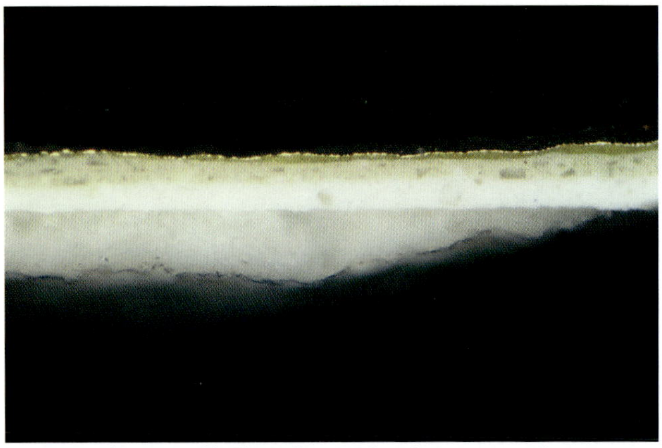

Figure 6 Plas Newydd, Llangollen, Wales: dining room. Cross-section taken from gold detailing on the plaster end wall. *(© M. O'Leary)*

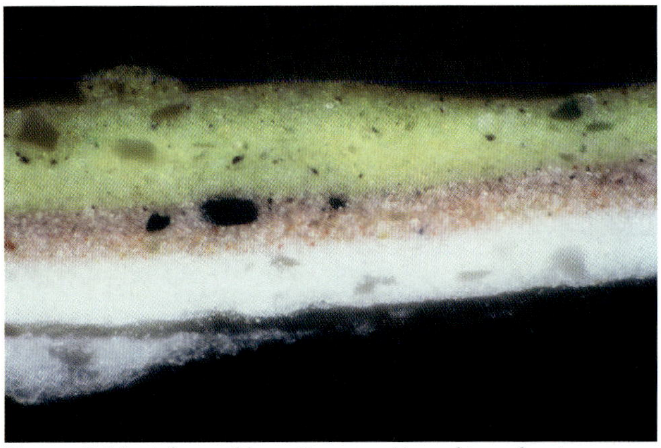

Figure 7 Mottisfont Abbey, Romsey, Hampshire: drawing room. Cross-section taken from the light green book painted on the urn wall. *(© M. O'Leary)*

pigments (Fig. 5). The Plas Newydd priming is a mixture of lithopone, silica and iron oxide (Fig. 6). The Mottisfont paintings have an extended lead-white priming, over which there is a thin organic layer containing a small amount of pigment (Fig. 7). An organic layer also is present in two samples from the Tate walls, but this is not consistent. There is no evidence of a similar organic layer in samples from Plas Newydd.

In terms of drawing there are distinct similarities of approach in each of the decorative schemes. In all three there are indications of pencil lines, and the drawing has been advanced with fluid paint during the painting process. The Tate canvases are squared, but not the plaster wall (Fig. 8). It has been suggested that the Plas Newydd design, and part of Mottisfont, were also transferred from squared drawings.

A similar range of pigments was used for both the Tate and Plas Newydd paintings. The Mottisfont range is more limited, but includes pigments found in both the other schemes. Examination of invoices from the artist's supply shop L. Cornelissen & Son, together with the contents of the paint-box at Plas Newydd, suggests that Whistler's palette did not alter a great deal. On the inside of the box a wide range of pigments is listed, many of which are not present. Gold has been incorporated in all three schemes, though unfortunately it is no longer visible at the Tate. The paint layers are generally thin (two or three layers), and applied over a white ground. Staining tests suggest that all the schemes are oil-based. The Tate and Mottisfont schemes are varnished with a thick (now discoloured) coating. At Mottisfont Abbey this is a spirit varnish based on copal with the addition of a drying oil. Plas Newydd is not varnished.

The scale of Whistler's decorative schemes demonstrates involved planning and foresight. Evident in the Tate and Plas Newydd paintings is Whistler's natural ability to create an imaginary landscape that successfully evokes a three-dimensional space. He punctuates the landscape with trees and architectural elements reminiscent of 17th- and 18th-century landscape painting, and there are implied narratives by virtue of the figure groups which, aside from anything else, add human interest. The level of finish at the Tate differs from wall to wall. The composition on plaster is roughly indicated by linear brushwork and the painting appears to have been left at the underpainting stage. Many elements are left unresolved and incomplete. To a certain extent the figurative elements throughout the Tate paintings lack the familiarity and the facility that Whistler demonstrates with the landscape. Professor Tonks noted that 'the hands which draw curves the most neatly are often not good at drawing the figure'.[4]

Many issues raised by the Tate paintings appear to have been reconsidered by the time Whistler came to paint the Plas Newydd scheme. The method of drawing with brown paint is taken up again in Plas Newydd, but is more refined and efficient. The main painted wall here is on a single piece of canvas, thus removing the difficulty presented by the series of joins in the main canvas at the Tate. In Plas Newydd the figures are less prominent. They create pockets of interest, but on the whole are less conspicuous. Moreover, in general terms, the scene is less animated and the treatment of the trees, for instance, is much less mannered than at the Tate.

The decorative scheme at Mottisfont combines *trompe l'oeil* and realism to great effect. The *trompe l'oeil* plasterwork is set in low relief and is kept subtle by being painted in pale shades of pink and green. The decorated cornice and columns give rhythm to the architectural space and serve as a framework for pictorial images (Fig. 9). Compared to Plas Newydd and the Tate, the scheme at Mottisfont seems almost stark. The richness and variation of the other schemes is lacking: it is entirely decorative and becomes tiring without the content displayed in the other schemes. The niche with the urn provides an area of emphasis to an otherwise mundane project, and this corresponds most closely with Whistler's other paintings (Fig. 10).

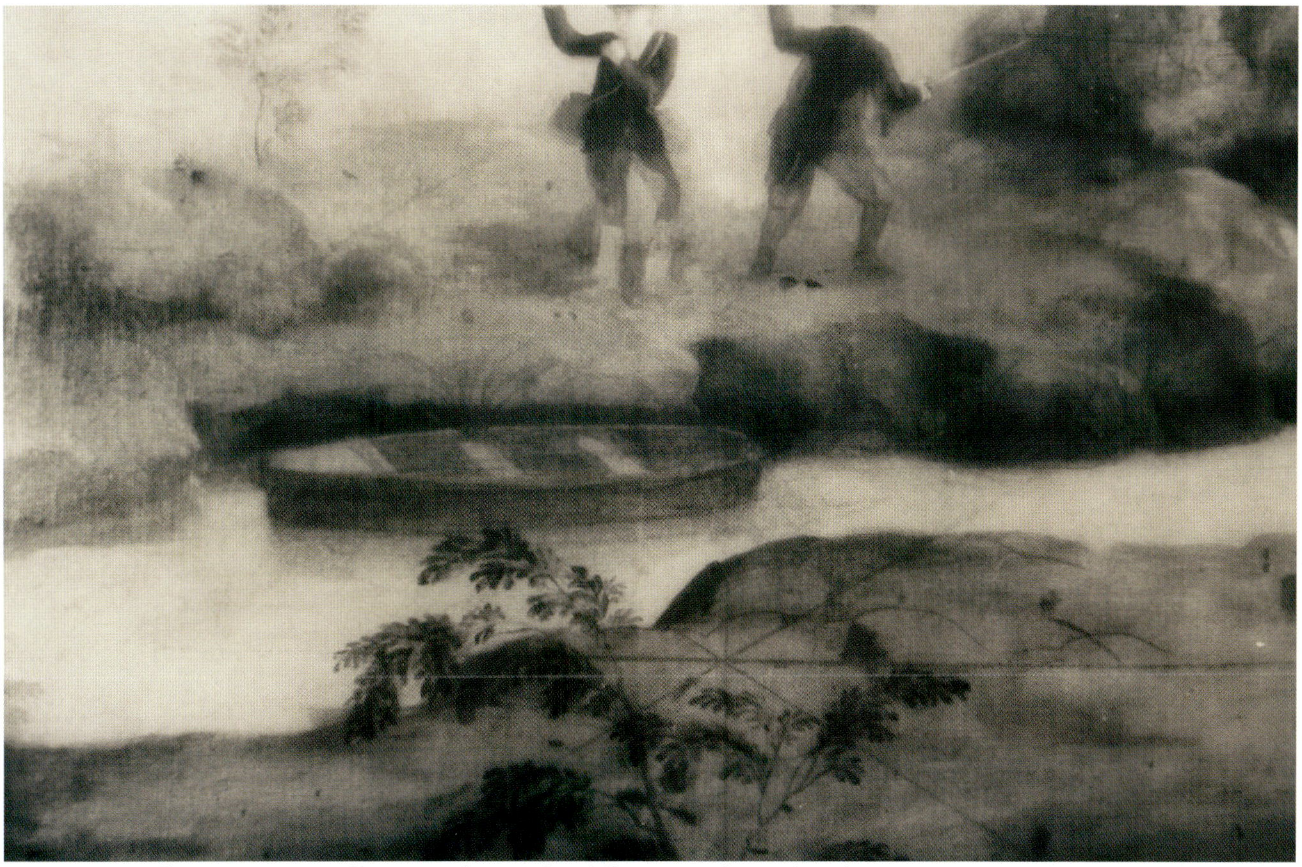

Figure 8 Tate Gallery Restaurant, London: image taken in infrared illumination. *(© M. O'Leary)*

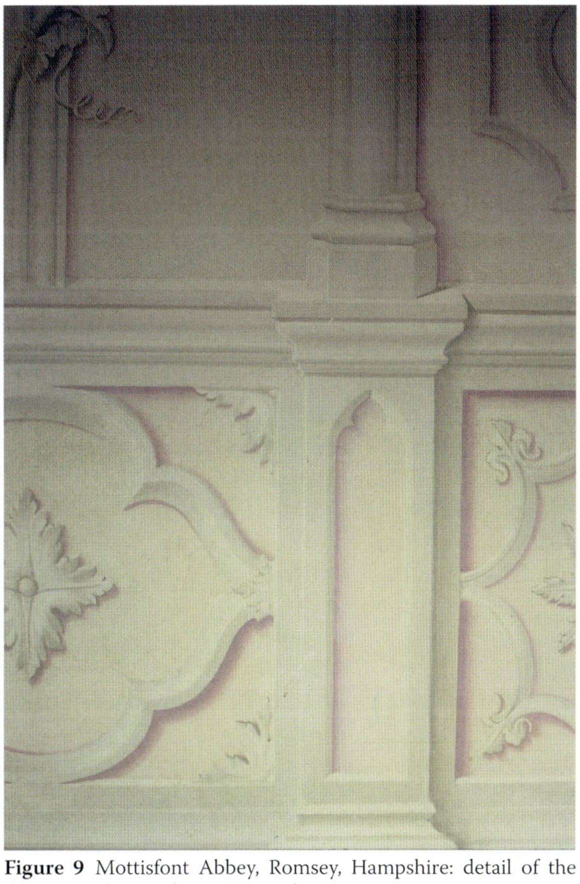

Figure 9 Mottisfont Abbey, Romsey, Hampshire: detail of the decorative design. *(© M. O'Leary)*

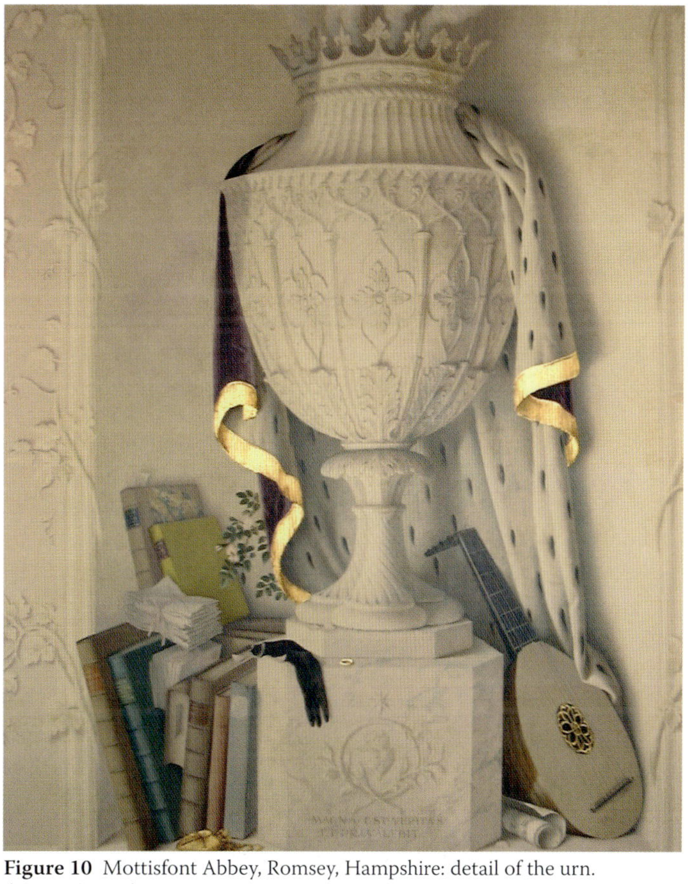

Figure 10 Mottisfont Abbey, Romsey, Hampshire: detail of the urn. *(© M. O'Leary)*

An important feature of Rex Whistler's work is the way in which he adapted painted schemes to their location and surroundings. Essentially he created an entirely individual and personal piece in each case. He incorporated the existing structure into each scheme, often embellishing it to great effect. The Tate murals reflect the function of the restaurant and create a visual impact for the diner. They commence about 4ft from the floor, and their colouring is kept light and cool. Other structural elements within the room are incorporated in the design, creating an effect of unity. Similarly at Plas Newydd, the location and the magnificent views from the house of the Menai Strait and the Snowdonian Mountains influenced the design. Another characteristic attribute of Whistler's work is the reference he made to details relevant to the employers: at Plas Newydd, trophies painted in grisaille on the chimney-pieces with names above symbolise the family's history, and again at Mottisfont he incorporated trophies symbolising subjects associated with Mottisfont Abbey including the family coat of arms (Fig. 11).

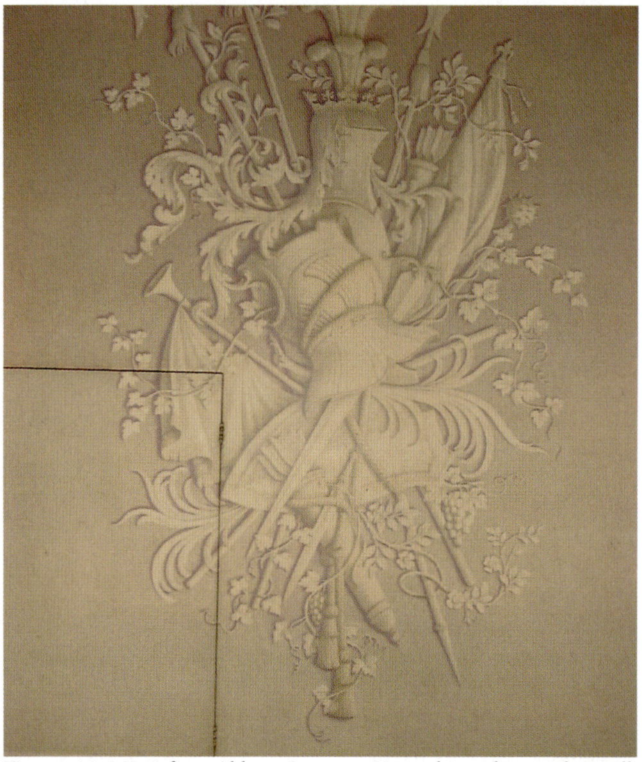

Figure 11 Mottisfont Abbey, Romsey, Hampshire: the trophy wall. *(© M. O'Leary)*

The present condition of the decorative schemes

The condition of Whistler's decorative schemes varies. The alterations and levels of deterioration observed in these three decorative schemes are influenced by a number of factors, and the implications for conservation are wide-ranging.

The Tate Gallery

The Tate scheme is coated with a substantial layer of dust and grime, much of which is embedded in the yellowed varnish. This has altered the surface appearance and darkened the overall painting. There is evidence of general wear in the paint where it has become translucent, revealing drawing and underpainting. The paintings on canvas have numerous blisters at the joins as a result of delamination from the board support (Fig. 12). In addition there are losses at the hardboard joints. Furthermore, there are numerous surface accretions, indentations and scratches. There is also an accumulation of retouching from several treatments over the years.

Problems associated with moisture play a large role and have affected the painting's appearance. In 1928 the Thames flooded the ground floor, causing immediate damage to the scheme, and probably initiating subsequent deterioration. In the 1940s, bomb damage to the external wall also affected the paintings. While the painting on the external wall is remarkably thin, it is applied over a thick complex structure that varies in its consistency. The hygroscopic nature of the structure is problematic due to the interchange of external and internal moisture. Evidence of organic biological infestation has also been observed in cross-section samples. Furthermore, the expansion and contraction of the entire wall structure seems to have resulted in large areas of the internal layering becoming dislocated, fracturing the paint.

More recently, infiltration of moisture from above has led to blanched streaks on the painting. These occur on an area left of the window alcove on the external wall, and appeared soon after the exterior of the building was cleaned. It would seem from examination of cross-sections that this is a surface coat phenomenon, which has led to an increase in light scatter. Examination of the paintings with ultraviolet (UV) illumination demonstrated that this particular area is not an isolated occurrence; drips are seen in other areas of the scheme and it has been suggested that this is also a disruption to the surface coating (Fig. 13).

Plas Newydd

The paintings at Plas Newydd have remained unvarnished, and the main painted canvas is in relatively good condition (Fig. 14). In the area that was reworked the surface appearance is 'hazed'. This may be the result of over-pigmentation and partial incompatibility of the media. Other constituents present in modern manufactured paints may have exacerbated the problem. The present Lord Anglesey recalls Whistler 'running out of Chinese white ... and dashing down to the harbour to where Captain Lilley was still at work and coming back with some very coarse white boat paint'. On the whole, the paint is well adhered and there appear to be only minor losses. There are, however, a number of scratches and small slits visible throughout. In addition to a series of blemishes, when lit by raking light separation of the canvas from the wall is apparent. This was noted when the canvases were initially adhered, and was subsequently treated with a syringe and hot iron. Problems associated with moisture have caused damage to the support, ground and upper layers. In the past, two leakages through the ceiling caused a hairline crack in the ceiling plaster, cornice and the plaster behind the canvas. On the surface of the

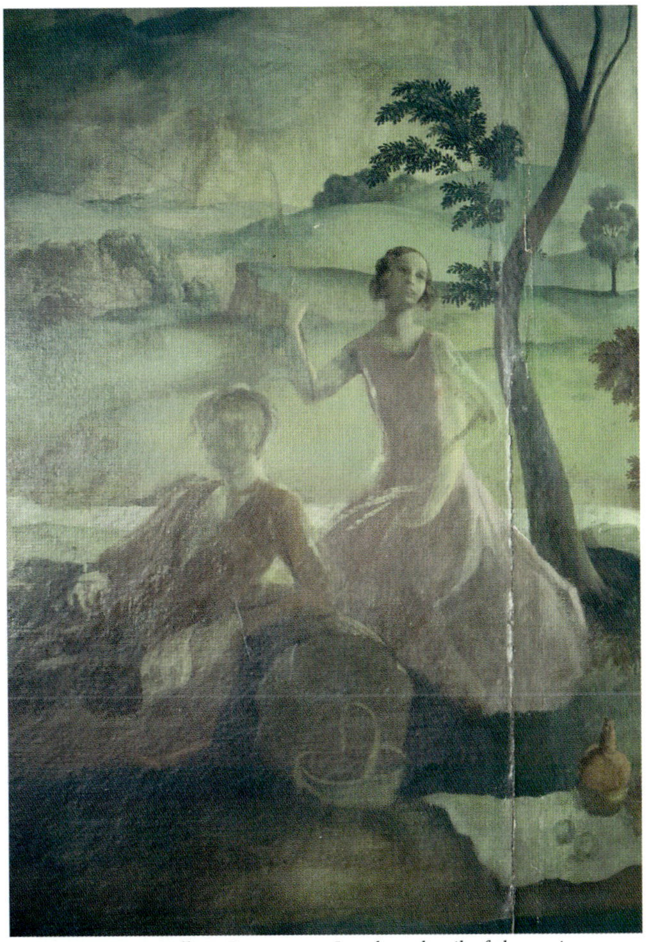

Figure 12 Tate Gallery Restaurant, London: detail of the main canvas wall join. *(© M. O'Leary)*

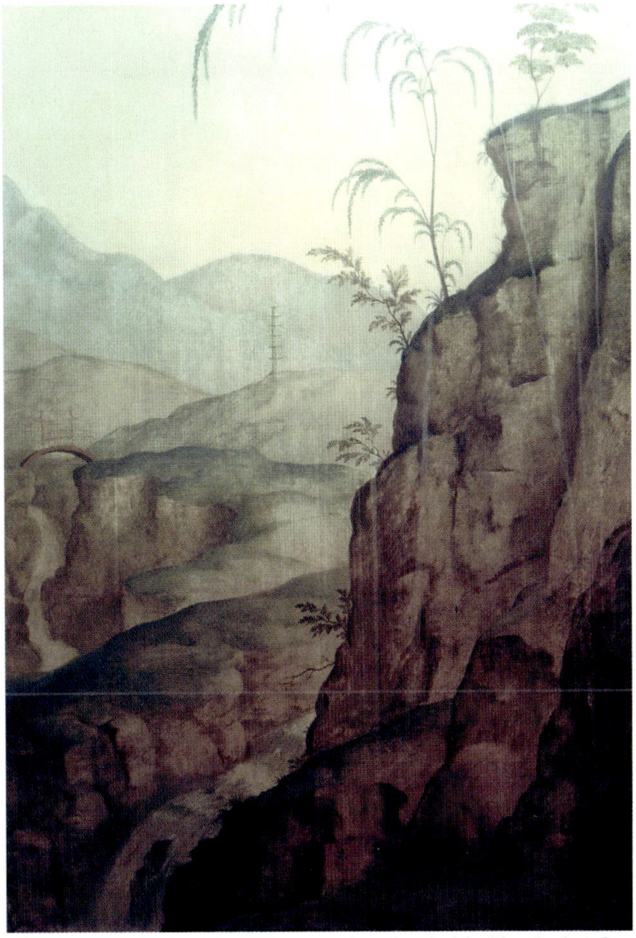

Figure 13 Tate Gallery Restaurant, London: detail of the blanched surface on the plaster wall. *(© M. O'Leary)*

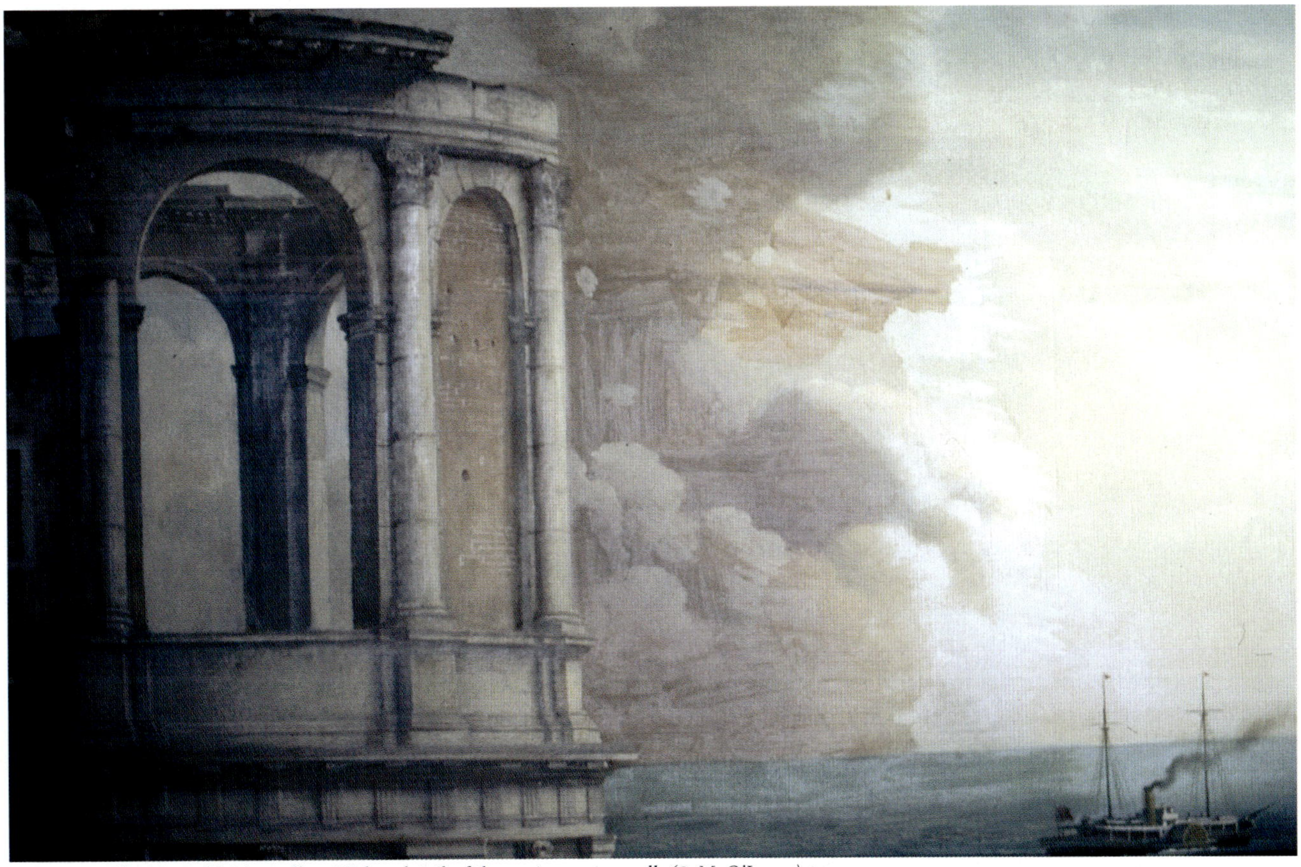

Figure 14 Plas Newydd, Llangollen, Wales: detail of the main canvas wall. *(© M. O'Leary)*

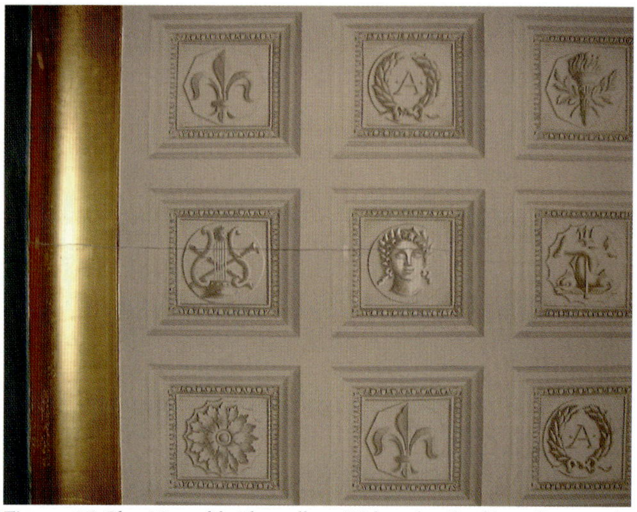

Figure 15 Plas Newydd, Llangollen, Wales: detail of a ceiling crack. *(© M. O'Leary)*

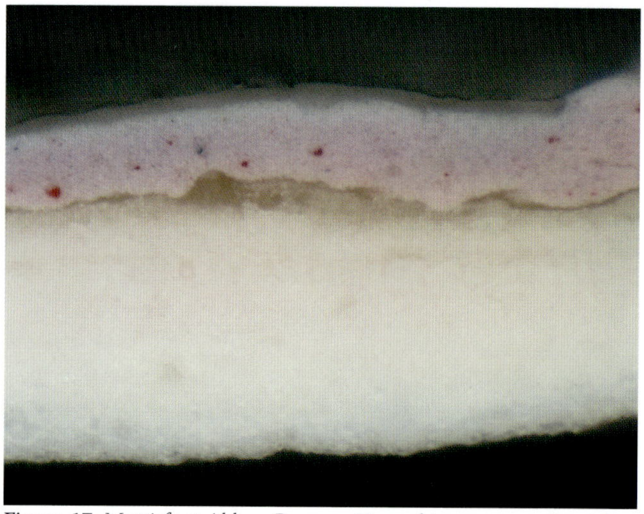

Figure 17 Mottisfont Abbey, Romsey, Hampshire: cross-section taken from a faded lake paint near the window. *(© M. O'Leary)*

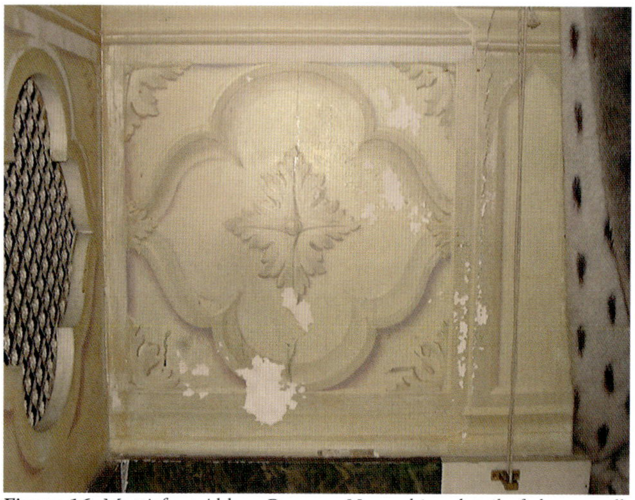

Figure 16 Mottisfont Abbey, Romsey, Hampshire: detail of alcove wall. *(© M. O'Leary)*

Figure 18 Mottisfont Abbey, Romsey, Hampshire: detail of the alcove wall. *(© M. O'Leary)*

canvas this has resulted in the expansion of the threads. The painted chimney-walls have a series of cracks, which are likely the result of their use and the nature of the rendering. The cumulative effect of years of vibrations also has contributed to the loss of paint and ground which may, however, have been weakened previously by other sources. The National Trust is currently monitoring the cracks.

Mottisfont Abbey

At Mottisfont an irregular varnish, applied over the painted scheme, has yellowed. This significantly alters the underlying hue. The painted trophies and the niche composition are in good condition. A number of wide fissures are evident elsewhere in the plaster, which have resulted in the localised flaking of the paint (Fig. 16). The areas most significantly damaged are the alcove walls. The architectural decorative elements throughout the scheme depend for their full effect on a mixture of lead white tinted by a small proportion of alizarin crimson, with the addition of a little Prussian blue and synthetic ultramarine. Lake pigments such as alizarin, based on animal or vegetable dyestuffs, may be expected to fade on exposure to light. It has been suggested that fading of the red pigment has occurred in areas exposed to direct sunlight, leaving the residual blue-grey colour (Fig. 17). The subtle gradations of pink-green throughout the scheme suggest, however, that some variations are deliberate. The action of light has certainly affected the durability and strength of the binding medium, leading to an embrittled surface and paint shrinkage. A significant amount of cleavage and loss of paint and ground from the plaster has occurred in the alcoves. This appears at the interface between the preparation and the lead-white priming. Much of the degradation in the alcoves is due to the destructive effects of UV light and heat, in addition to penetrating moisture (Fig. 18).

Conclusions

Becoming gradually more familiar with the painted schemes, it is apparent that there exist certain similar strands as well as distinct dissimilarities. While the principal supports are fairly standard (i.e. canvas or plaster) the grounds are different in each case. In addition, pigments such as viridian, yellow ochre, carbon black, lead white, vermilion, red lake, Prussian blue and a range of earth pigments are common to all. Unquestionably, the schemes are stylistically different but, despite this, the actual method of painting remains fairly constant: large thin areas that utilise the underlying ground, over which are occasionally more dense intricate patches. In all cases the drawing appears either directly on top of the ground as a sketched framework, subsequently strengthened and reinforced, or on top of a preliminary washing and mapping-out of the general distribution of forms. No doubt this was influenced to some degree by what was at hand and chalk, charcoal, pencil or fluid paint were used, depending on what stage the painting had reached and what function the drawn lines were to perform.

On balance, the support and its preparation, the structure of the actual buildings, and the requirements and function of the buildings themselves seem to have exerted a greater effect on the present condition of the paintings than the manner in which they were painted: a technique based on the application of thin paint with a sufficient binding medium ought not to be disastrous.

This project was conceived, principally, in response to the concern expressed by the National Trust about the deteriorating state of the Drawing Room at Mottisfont Abbey. Despite being monitored, neither this decorative scheme nor the paintings at Plas Newydd or the Tate Gallery have been subject to any serious holistic examination. Undoubtedly money, time and priority have played a significant role in this. Additionally Whistler is not a particularly famous artist, and modern wall paintings as yet rarely attract the same level of investigation as, for example, an equivalently sized Veronese.

In the space of a few short years we have witnessed the disappearance of established courses of study in mural painting at the most prestigious art schools in Britain. Much-coveted and long-established scholarships providing for periods of extended study have vanished, as well as any support structures or patronage for this type of work. Consequently mural painting has virtually atrophied from lack of use. In such a climate, surely existing large-scale modern schemes, including those of Rex Whistler, take on renewed significance.

Notes

1. Lady Anglesey's brother, the Duke of Rutland, had already commissioned a chimney-piece panel for Haddon Hall in Derbyshire in 1932–3. Her sister Lady Diana Cooper also commissioned Whistler to paint the Drawing Room at 90 Gower Street, London in 1935.
2. Whistler 1985.
3. Pers. comm., November 1999.
4. Tonks to Daniels (Hone 1939, p. 288).

References

Hampshire Record Office, file reference numbers: 13M63/ 428, 429, 439, 446

Hone J. 1939, *The Life of Henry Tonks*, Heinemann, London

National Trust 1996, *Plas Newydd Guidebook*, The National Trust, London

National Trust 1994, *Mottisfont Abbey Guidebook*, The National Trust, London

National Trust 1996, *Mottisfont Abbey Guidebook*, The National Trust, London

Plas Newydd Archives, box numbers 6M: 95–131, 267–291, 372–377

Saunders D. and Kirby J. 1994, 'Light induced colour change in red and yellow lake pigments', *National Gallery Technical Bulletin* 15, pp. 74–87

Spencer-Smith J. 1994, *Rex Whistler's War 1934–July 1944*, National Army Museum, London

Tate Gallery Archives, file temporary reference number: TG.PR.260

West Fitzhugh E. 1997, *Artists Pigments: A Handbook of their History and Characteristics*, National Gallery of Art, Washington DC

Whistler L. 1985, *The Laughter and the Urn: The Life of Rex Whistler*, Weidenfeld & Nicolson, London

The author

Marguerite O'Leary currently works as a paintings conservator at the London studio of Hamish Dewar.

More myth than mural: a study of the Hans Feibusch murals at South Civic Centre, Newport, South Wales

Kate Hunter and Elizabeth Holford[1]

Introduction

Few people are aware of the beautiful series of 20th-century wall paintings painted by Hans Feibusch (Fig. 1) and his assistant Phyllis Bray in the first floor atrium of Newport Civic Centre between 1961 and 1964. They are impressive not only for their scale, but for their use of colour and for the way they complement the architecture of the building. There are 12 panels depicting the history of Newport, South Wales. As this is a 20th-century commission, one could be forgiven for thinking that we should know everything about its inception and execution. Although some inescapable facts are available, however, many important questions remain unanswered.

The Newport Civic Centre, designed by T. Cecil Hewitt, was begun in January 1938 and halted by World War II (Fig. 2). Construction was resumed in 1950 and completed in 1964 with

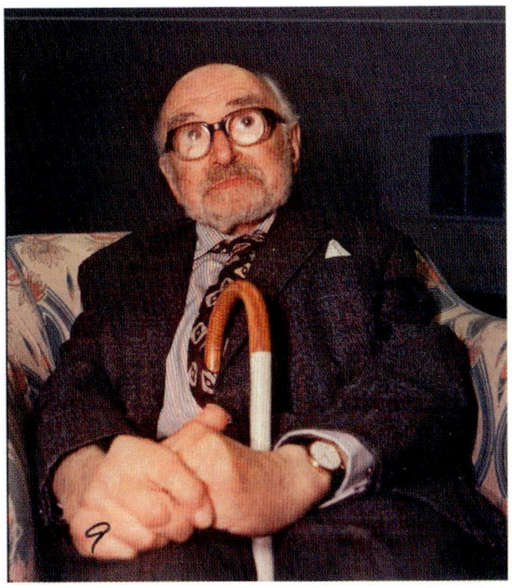

Figure 1 Hans Feibusch. *(© Newport City Council)*

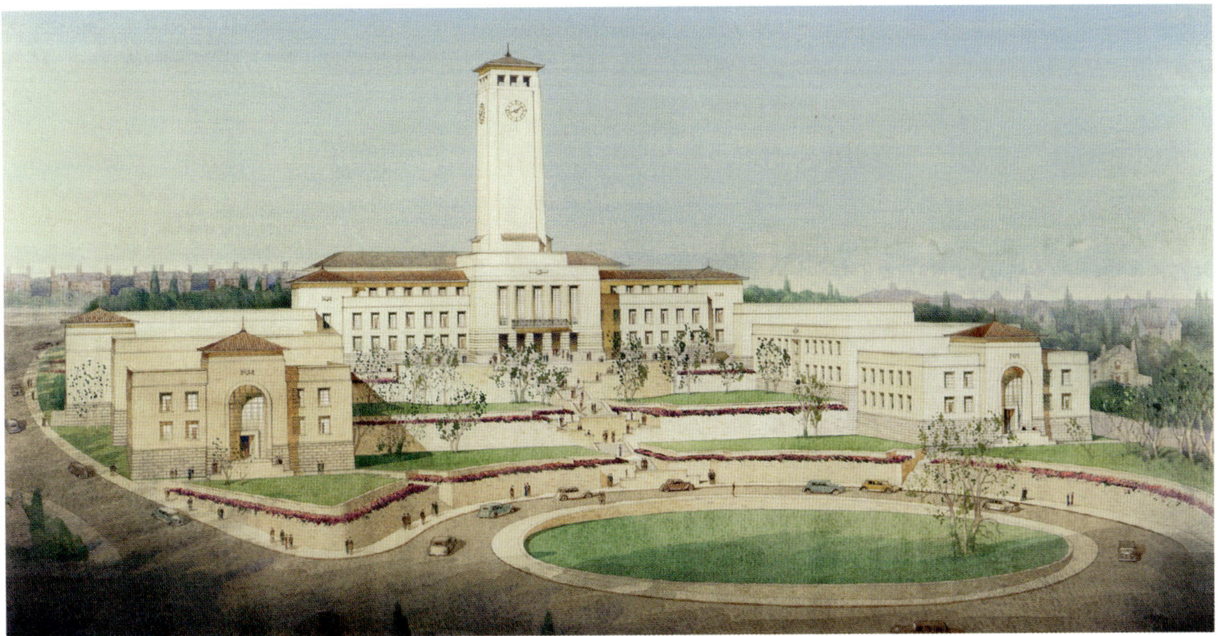

Figure 2 Proposed scheme for the Newport Civic Centre (watercolour on paper) by Cyril Fary (1888–1954) and Cecil Howitt (fl. 1920). *(© Newport Museum and Art Gallery, South Wales/Bridgeman Art Library)*

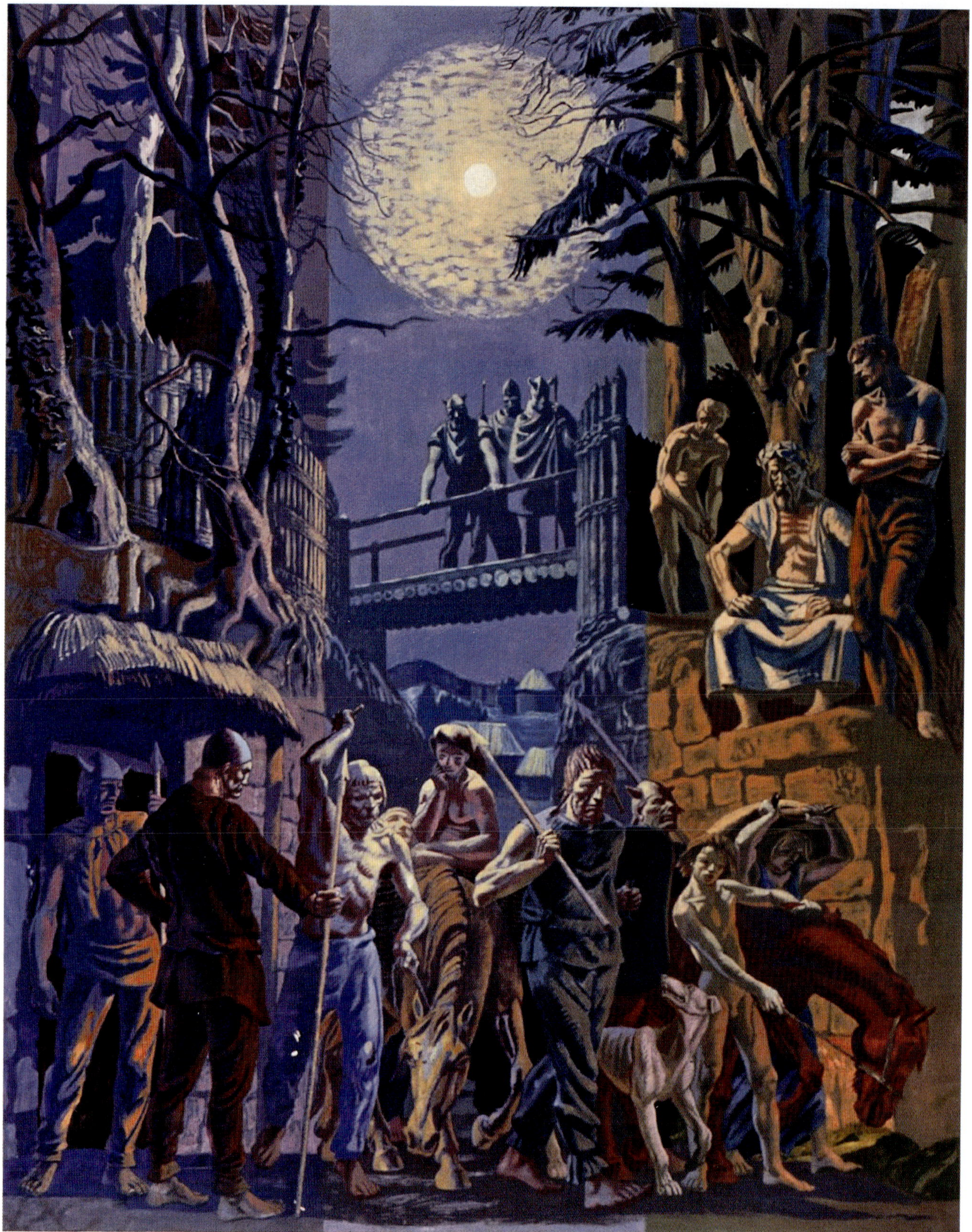

Figure 3 Civic Centre, Newport City Council, Newport, Wales: general view of *The Celtic Settlement of Newport*. (*© Downland Partnership Ltd.)*

the clock tower. It is, therefore, a 1930s building completed in the 1960s. The murals were funded with the assistance of the Edwin Austin Abbey Memorial Fund, and the painting was executed at the same time as the tower was being finished. The murals cost £10,041.9s.2d, of which £641. 9s. 2d was set aside for the materials.

We know that a competition was held to choose an artist, but we do not know the names of the other participants or who chose the winner. Feibusch may have left a clue as to the main people involved by including four members of Newport Town Council in his final mural: Jimmy Iles (the Town Clerk) and Aldermen Dolman, Cornforth and Tyack, who were mayors

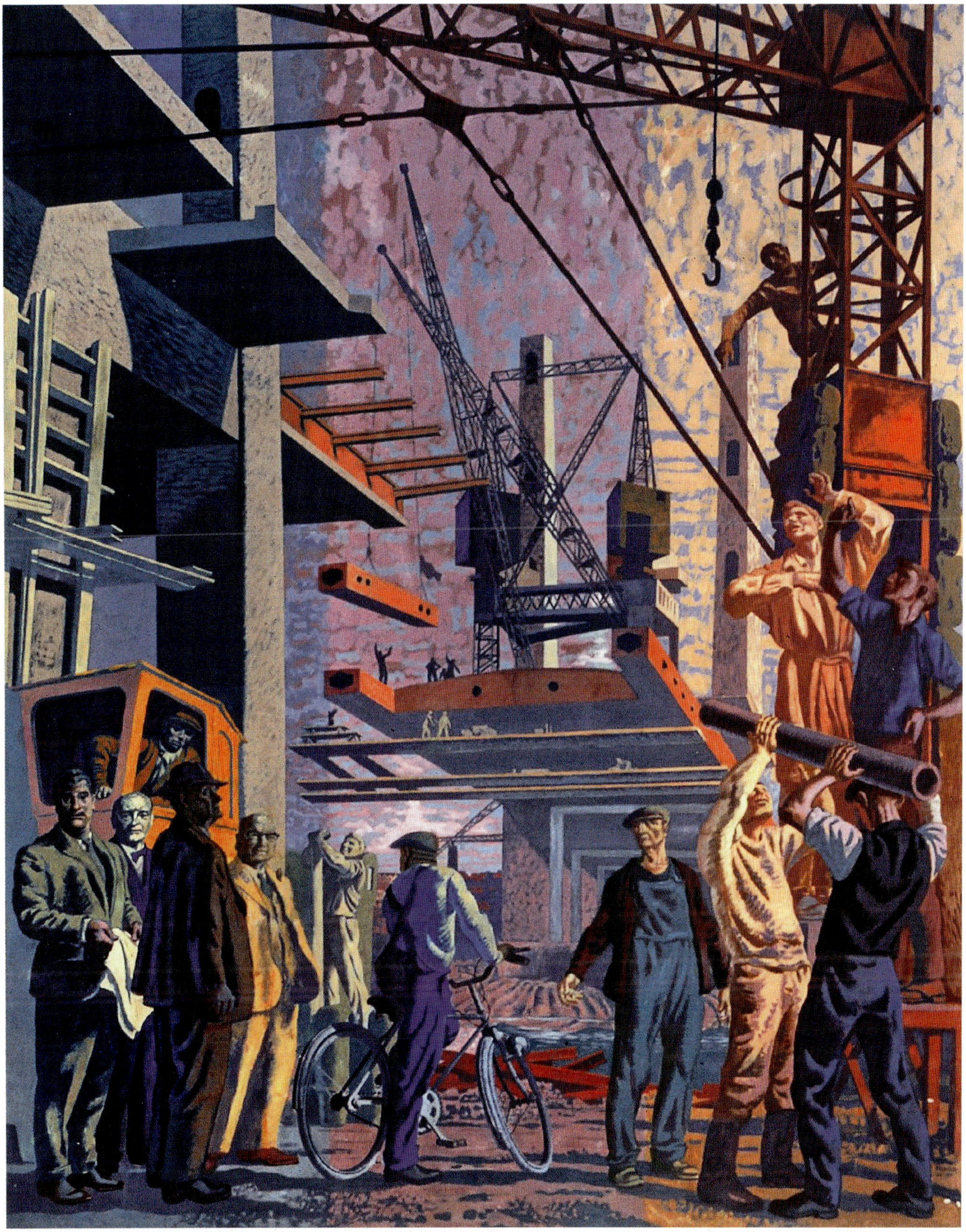

Figure 4 Civic Centre, Newport City Council, Newport, Wales: *The Building of the George Street Bridge*. (*© Downland Partnership Ltd.*)

during the period the murals were being painted. Edward Lycette, former owner of Llanwern steelworks, is not depicted, but must also have been important. Lycette would have had prior knowledge of Feibusch's work, and as one of the most important local employers in the region, it is highly probable that he influenced the commission. A 'Sunday artist', he also provided accommodation on his estate for Feibusch and Bray during the project.

The 12 murals that make up the project each measure 26ft high by 13–15ft wide. They illustrate the development of Newport, beginning with *The Celtic Settlement* (Fig. 3) and ending with *The Building of the George Street Bridge* (Fig. 4).

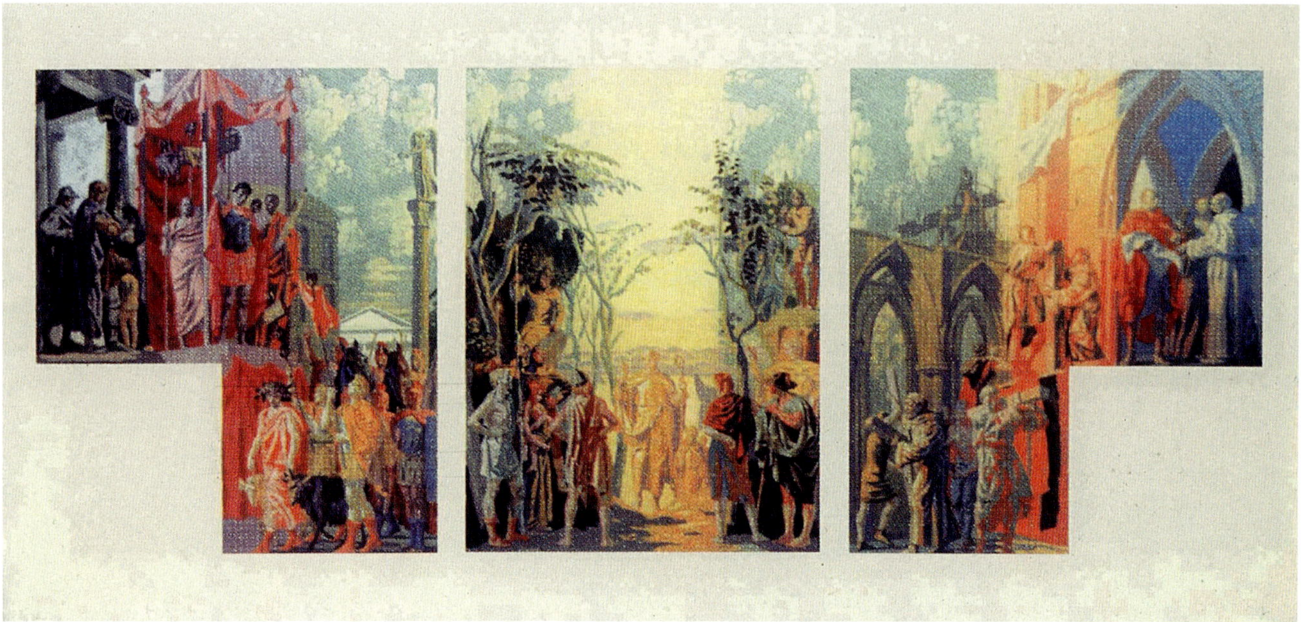

Figure 5 Civic Centre, Newport City Council, Newport, Wales: the entire north wall. *(© Newport City Council)*

This bridge over the Usk was finished in the same year as the murals, 1964. The link between these two murals, which form the beginning and end of the commission, is made by a half-height mural above a short flight of steps up into a meeting room. In this Feibusch manages to unite present-day Newport with its Celtic past, using the arms of the city.

The paintings

The paintings are an exercise in didactic social realism. Feibusch cleverly used the space both in terms of the locations of the openings in the walls and the fall of light from above. He made the most of the large atrium, enhancing its plain cubic structure with his paintings, which also complement the 1930s building style. During our time in Newport we came to admire Feibusch not only for his clever use of space but also his exciting use of colour. He uses colour to both link the different scenes in each panel, providing rhythm and continuity across the wall, and also to create a three-dimensional form by the juxtaposition of complementary colours.

Hans Feibusch had a background and training originally in Germany, and then in Italy and France, which acquainted him with mural paintings from the Renaissance and to later European painting (Fig. 4). In 1946 he wrote a book, *Mural Painting* (published by Adam and Charles Black). He records that his first and most impressive experience of mural painting resulted from a visit as a 'half-grown boy' to see Tiepolo's ceiling over the grand staircase in the Bishop's Palace in Würzburg. Feibusch studied in the Paris studio of Othon Friez and Andrá Lhôte, and participated in exhibitions at the Salon d'Automne and the Paris Indépendants. His experience made him sceptical of the style and aesthetics of this type of studio system. By the time he came to write his treatise on mural painting, he had united an understanding of traditional mural design and techniques with an understanding of post-war modernism. In his book he refers to mural painting as an extension of the building, stating that it 'always rises and falls with architecture'. He also describes how he liked to spend time in the space he was to decorate, to understand not only its function but also how it was used and lit.

The Newport cycle was designed so that each wall would carry three scenes (Fig. 5). Adjacent scenes articulate with each other by sharing coloured backgrounds, and the focal point and the only vanishing point are in the middle scene. They are painted as if lit from above, with light radiating out towards the corners, mirroring the actual lighting of the architectural space (by windows at the base of the tower). The corners of this space are always darker than the centre of the walls, and have doorways in each corner, above which the composition rises framing the central panels.

The figures are arranged on three vertical fields of colour (Fig. 6). Adjoining panels have the same colour field at the adjacent edge, so that the eye travels across the wall in an unbroken wave. Detail is kept to a minimum to avoid the wall becoming too fussy and can be read easily as a whole. The figure groups are always in the foreground and are oversized. The three-dimensional form of the figures is created entirely by the use of the contrasting colour to the colour field they are set against. They are accentuated by additively mixed highlights. The entire effect is of light emanating from the murals as through stained-glass windows or a photographic slide, or indeed through cinematic film. By recreating additive mixing, the murals appear to emit light, not absorb it.

Condition

Building structure

The building has a brick and steel core, externally faced with Portland stone and internally with cement render. The render has a thin gypsum skim and is painted with a lead-based paint. The 1930s style was continued in the final element – the mas-

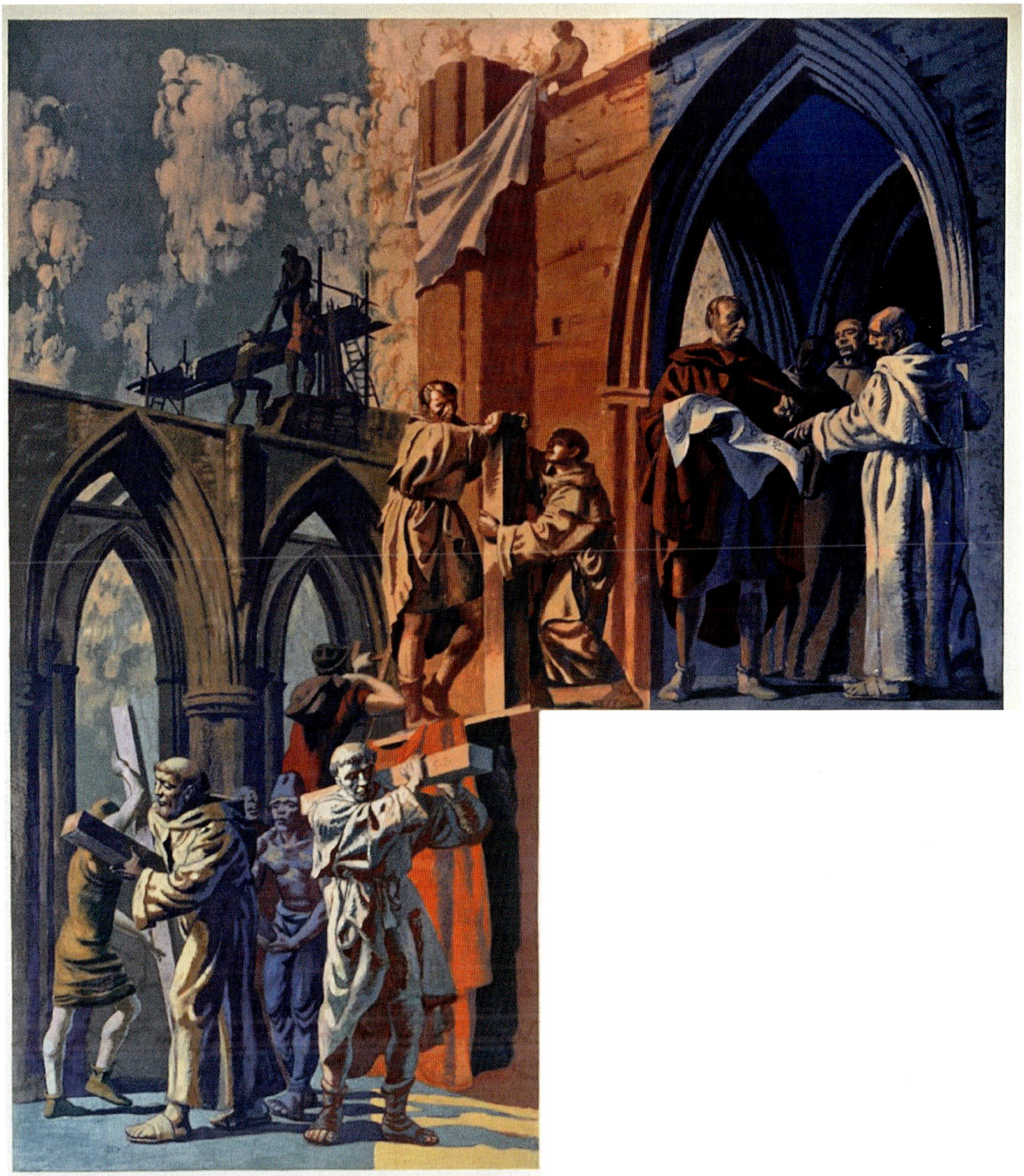

Figure 6 Civic Centre, Newport City Council, Newport, Wales: detail of the figure group from *The Building of Tintern Abbey*. *(© Downland Partnership Ltd.)*

sive clock tower that was being completed during the painting of the murals. This is constructed in steel and brick.

Since the building was completed in the mid-1960s there have been structural alterations, some of which have affected the walls on which the murals were painted. The north wall, which depicts *The Romans at Caerleon*, *The Coming of Christianity* and *The Building of Tintern Abbey*, had two small rooms adjoining. These have latterly been combined by removing the dividing wall to form one large Committee Room. Steel joists were cut into the reverse of the west wall – which carries the two large panels *The Building of the George Street Bridge* and *The Celtic Settlement* with their linking panel *The Arms of Newport* – to create a room behind. The entire building has been rewired for broadband, which involved drilling into the reverse of most of the walls carrying the murals.

Condition of the murals

The murals must have started to deteriorate soon after they were completed. There is evidence of several campaigns of conservation work, but only one of these has been documented (by Boulter in 1986). It is also recorded that the Direct Labour Force of Newport Town Council made several attempts at restoration, but they have left no details of the materials used. In the early 1990s the murals continued to peel and paint was being lost. The cause of the curling and peeling paint layers was not understood; it was thought that the materials used by Feibusch must have caused the deterioration.

Roger Cucksey, the Keeper of Art at the Newport Museum and Art Gallery, had expressed concern about the condition of the paintings: there were cracks all over the murals, the paint film was peeling back from these and had been lost in some areas. This process had obviously been continuing for some time. Under sustained pressure from both Roger Cucksey and Kate Hunter, then Keeper of Conservation, in February 2002 the City Council agreed to a photographic survey and a programme of conservation, with the aim of preserving the flaking paint film. The project was aided by the fact that Newport had put forward a bid to achieve city status.

Cliveden Conservation was asked to look at the murals in November 1998 and produced a condition report in February 1999. Its report identifies a very important element in the cycle of deterioration, namely that there is a single cement render, and that this was not sealed. As a result, the cracks in the render have caused the paint film to split, allowing moisture in the air to interact with soluble salts. An environmental monitoring programme showed that the heating in the winter and the lack of heating in the summer instigated a wetting and drying cycle that caused crystallisation of salts in the cracks, and this resulted in the curling of the paint. As curling exposed a greater area of render, so the process continued until areas of paint were dislodged. It was thought that the cracking was confined to the cement render and was due to its drying.

In 2000, Holford Conservation, on the initial request of Roger Cucksey, undertook a condition inspection and produced a report with conservation proposals. This material was revisited in 2002 and the revised proposals approved in 2003. Conservation work was carried out in two phases with a team of eight people working at any one time. This allowed the day-to-day business of the council to continue.

The first part of the conservation process – a fortunate spin-off from the Newport Ship Project – was rectified photography of each panel carried out by David Stevens of Downland Partnership Ltd. These scaled photographs should form the basis for any future monitoring programme. Cracks and the lost and lifting paint, as well as past interventions, were recorded. As a result of mapping the cracking, it became clear that there was another pattern over and above that of the drying cracks of the cement render. The secondary cracks were concentrated towards the corners of the cube of the atrium, and were more frequent at the top of the walls than at the bottom. A core sample[2] confirmed that there were cracks in the underlying brickwork, which had transferred to the render. There had been movement in the supporting masonry during the internal structural alterations, as well as with the sheer weight of the tower. These structural factors, combined with a 50% annual variation in the relative humidity, were the real causes of the paint loss, and not the nature of the paint itself.

Consequently, conservation will be a continuing necessity. A monitoring programme based on the accurate recording carried out using the rectified photography was identified as the way forward. The methods and materials used in the conservation programme would be dependent on a better understanding of Feibusch's technique.

Treatment

Understanding that the processes of decay were not static but dynamic demonstrated the need for a continuing treatment programme. Therefore, a suitable method of consolidation would have to allow for re-treatment. A monitoring document and a permanent archive would also need to be created.

Recording

The condition of the murals was recorded using overlays with the rectified photographs. This method of recording by hand on acetate sheets over the rectified photographs was faster and cheaper than using a computer (Fig. 7). The first overlay recorded the crack pattern, the location of lifting and flaking paint, the positions of the plumblines used by the artists to set out the fictive architecture, and the attachment holes for

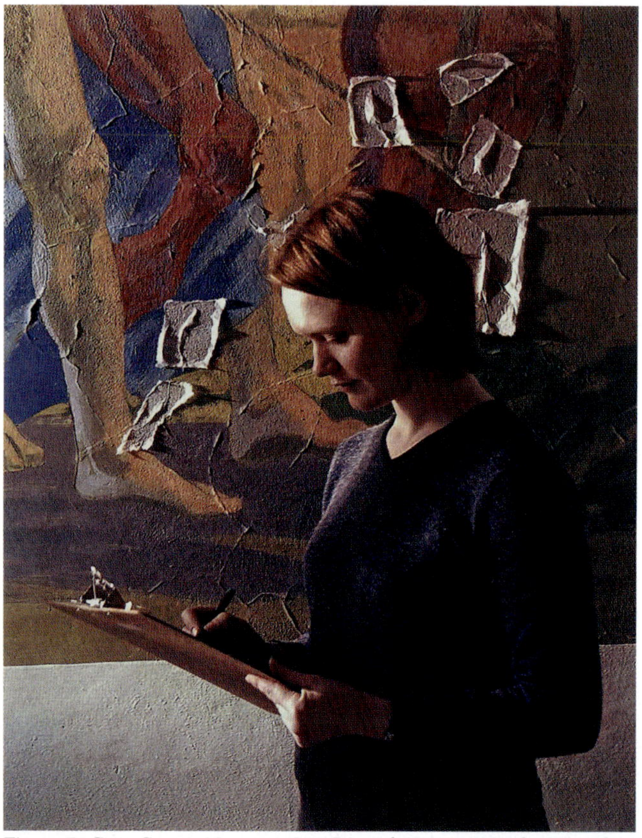

Figure 7 Civic Centre, Newport City Council, Newport, Wales: recording the crack pattern on *The Celtic Settlement*. (© *Newport City Council, photographer Rex Morton)*

the cartoons of the figure groups. The second recorded past interventions, oil-based retouching and cutting back, and the much larger areas of repainting using household paints. The third recorded our own interventions: where overpaint had been removed, flaking paint had been consolidated, and filling and final retouching had been undertaken. The overlays were subsequently scanned to create a digital file. Notes were made about each mural and all the information was combined in the final report, both digitally and in hard copy.

Details were photographed on both slide and print film. Using a black-out tent, areas were photographed under UV light to demonstrate the extent of the various phases of the (mainly undocumented) overpainting.[3] The house paint, which had a vinyl–resin binder, was found to give a lighter fluorescence, dark areas were oil paint retouching, and the original gave a mid-tone fluorescence.

Consolidation

Past attempts to fix the paint with polyvinyl acetate (PVA), or the use of retouching paint in oil or vinyl emulsion, had failed, so once recording was finished, a decision needed to be made about the best adhesive to use. Given that the tower is not going to become any lighter, the environment is unlikely show any signs of improvement, and the cement render will continue to effloresce, decay is likely to continue in spite of any conservation undertaken, therefore an adhesive had to be chosen that will allow the wall to be re-treated in the future. For this reason isinglass was selected; it has a low surface tension, high tack and a very low bulk, all of which make it ideal. It was injected and, where necessary, a piece of Japanese facing tissue was placed over the most brittle flakes using the same medium, and then removed after treatment. In the areas where the curling paint was most robust, an ingenious tool was devised[4] to supply radiant heat from a car cigarette lighter wired to a pressure switch mounted on a handle. The use of this device allowed us to avoid contact with the surface, which would have been polished by using hot spatulas.

Presentation

As time and cost were limited, only the most obtrusive and damaging areas of overpaint were removed using a mixture of acetone and iso-propyl alcohol. The losses were filled with gesso and retouched with watercolours. Finally the walls themselves and details of the conserved paintings were photographed.

Public awareness

During our time in the Civic Centre, it was clear that the council officers and the public were fascinated by our work. The general perception was that we were repainting the murals, as this practice had been so frequent. We therefore thought it prudent to create some illustrated panels explaining our work and the methods and materials employed. The constant enquiries were addressed by giving weekly talks, allowing more time to be dedicated to remedial conservation. We also suggested that the council could set up a webcam, which could be accessed from their website (although this suggestion was not taken up).

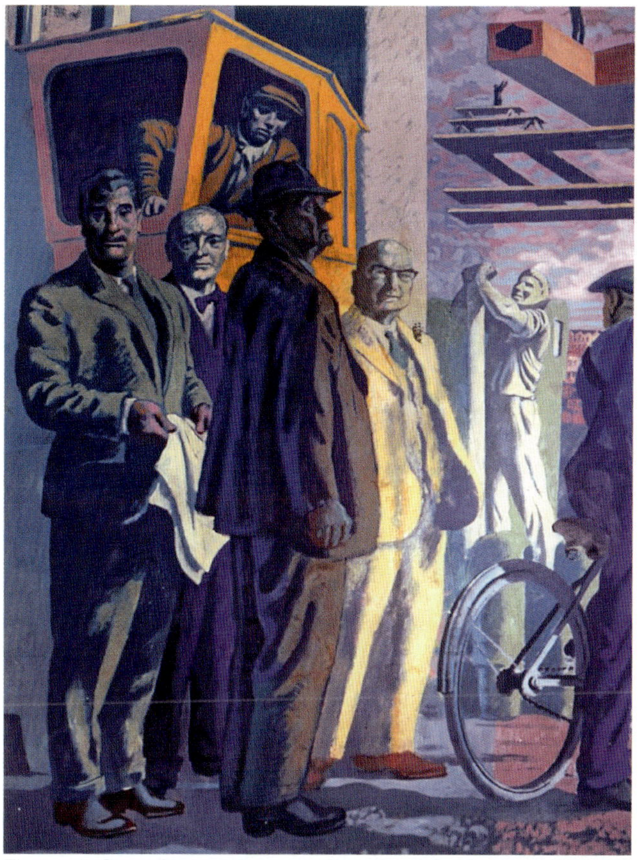

Figure 8 Civic Centre, Newport City Council, Newport, Wales: a detail from *The Building of the George Street Bridge*, completed in 1964, with portraits of those involved in the commission of the paintings. *(© C. Oldenbourg)*

We were able to identify the people illustrated in the final panel, *The Building of the George Street Bridge*: Town Clerk Jimmy Iles and Aldermen Dolman, Camford and Tyack, who were members of the original committee which chose and commissioned Hans Feibusch (Fig. 8).

Collection of anecdotal evidence

Anecdotal evidence was very important for piecing together the story of the murals. No record of alterations was available, although their effect on the walls could be seen. According to the resident engineer, there had indeed been alterations that would impact on the walls; in addition, he noted that the water tank was housed in the tower. Roger Cucksey made it his mission to rescue any material relating to the execution of the paintings. He made a film of the artist on his 90th birthday, inviting him back to Newport, and discovered and preserved some of his original cartoons, drawings and watercolours. After the death of Feibusch in 1989, his studio was acquired by the Pallant Art Gallery in Chichester. Some drawings of American soldiers that relate to the development of the Newport panel *The Coming of the Americans* were purchased for the Newport Museum and Art Gallery. Roger has managed to unite a body of material relating to the development

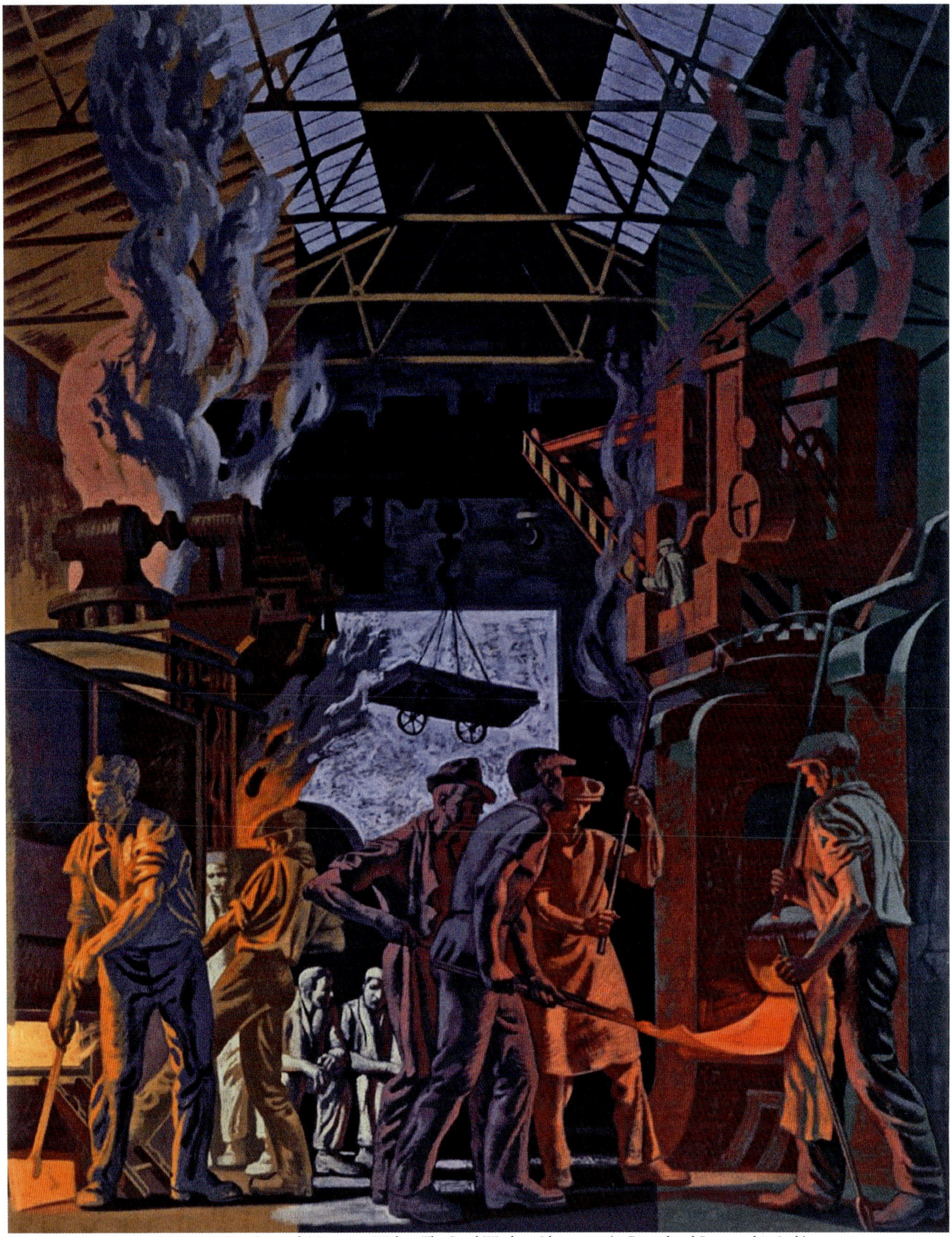

Figure 9 Civic Centre, Newport City Council, Newport, Wales: *The Steel Works – Llanwern. (© Downland Partnership Ltd.)*

of the compositional elements, allowing an understanding of the creative technique of the artist.

Since the paintings were only 40 years old, it was believed that there should be many people still living who may have witnessed the painting by Feibusch and Bray. To this end retired members of Unison (the relevant union organisation) were contacted, and a lunch was arranged in the Civic Centre to which a questionnaire was submitted. As a result of this meeting, some photographs came to light that had been taken by a past employee, photographer Gerry Powell, on behalf

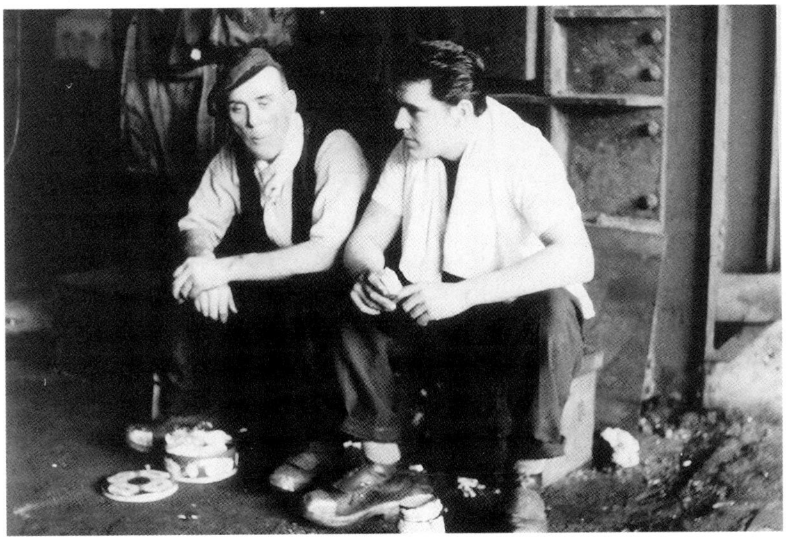

Figure 10 This photograph of a figure group, by Gerry Powell, was used for *The Steel Works – Llanwern* mural. *(© G. Powell)*

of Feibusch, to help him in his composition of the contemporary panels. Although some of the photographs for *The Building of the George Street Bridge* had been destroyed, the images that had been used in the composition of *The Steel Works – Llanwern* still existed (Figs 9 and 10). Along with the photographs, stories emerged about the artist's technique of transferring images, the painting medium he used, and the relative work carried out by Feibusch and Bray. It was particularly interesting to hear of the arguments that took place as a result of Feibusch using contemporary council employees for some of the historical figures.

Some of the recollections of the former Unison members were at odds with evidence both on the walls and in Feibusch's working drawings and watercolours. One of the stories was that his painting medium contained oil mixed with yoghurt, implying a type of casein. In his book Feibusch extols the virtues of using materials that are cheap and readily available, such as household paints.[5] There is also a newspaper cutting of him on top of the scaffolding with a row of yoghurt pots. It transpired that Feibusch was very fond of yoghurt, which he ate while working on the scaffolding, reusing the empty pots to mix his paints. In England in the early 1960s yoghurt was very unusual, so its presence was interpreted not as a foodstuff but as part of his painting technique. The paint analysis found no yoghurt, but showed that the paint was largely a household emulsion, full of chalk, and with an alkyd resin as the binder – an early use of alkyd resins.[6] From Feibusch's own records and from the materials found in his studio it was discovered that he used a household paint, known as Walpamur. Feibusch mentions using both Walpamur and another house paint, Stick B.[7] Walpamur was made by Halls Paints of Bristol (taken over by Crown Paints) and is still being manufactured under licence in Australia, although the binding medium has been changed. Traces of glue size and a small amount of linseed oil were also found. It would appear that Feibusch leached his oil paints and then added them to a household emulsion mixed up in the yoghurt pots.

Another myth about Feibusch's technique was dispelled, this time concerning the way he created the images and transferred them to the wall. His drawings were not squared up, and the full-size cartoons saved by Roger Cucksey were not squared up either. Nor was there evidence of squaring on the walls, in spite of the union members' recollections to the contrary. In his book, Feibusch writes that scaling up directly created awkward and sometimes bleak compositions, and that it was much better to work directly in the required scale.[8] The cartoons were backed with carbon paper, and a stylus was used to trace his figures onto the walls; any additions or alterations were made using pencil. Pinholes were found for attaching the cartoons to the wall, and for the use of plumblines for the architecture in the backgrounds.

Feibusch concentrated on the figure groups, which were transferred to the walls and painted by him after the three vertical colour fields had been painted. Bray would then paint the backgrounds, taking great care not to let the architectural features interfere with the figures. The evidence for this working method can be clearly seen on the walls.

Anecdotes also emerged regarding the artist himself. Feibusch was described as an agile man on the scaffolding for his 71 years, strong-willed with a fiery temper. He and Bray shared a cottage in Brockweir on the river Wye. Feibusch also liked to use appropriate members of staff as models for his figure groups. There are suggestions that it caused some friction when the portrait of Jimmy Iles appeared on the wall. He had commissioned Feibusch in the first instance, and the artist obviously admired him. His head appears to have been the original model for the head of David Gamm, who saved the life of Henry V at the battle of Agincourt. This painting is the centrepiece of the most important wall. Beneath the present head, a *pentimento* of this original portrait can be seen: when the elected members saw an unelected officer being immortalised on the wall, they made Feibusch change it, despite his protests.

This dispute may account for an extraordinary compositional change to this entire wall, which occurred about halfway through its painting. In the original gouache, the salmon-coloured central vertical section perfectly focuses the eye on the three protagonists (Fig. 11). On either side there are turquoise vertical bands, which are complementary and articulate with the panels on either side. In the finished painting, the central section is still salmon pink, but the sections to either side are mauve, which translates to the adjoining panels. Omitting

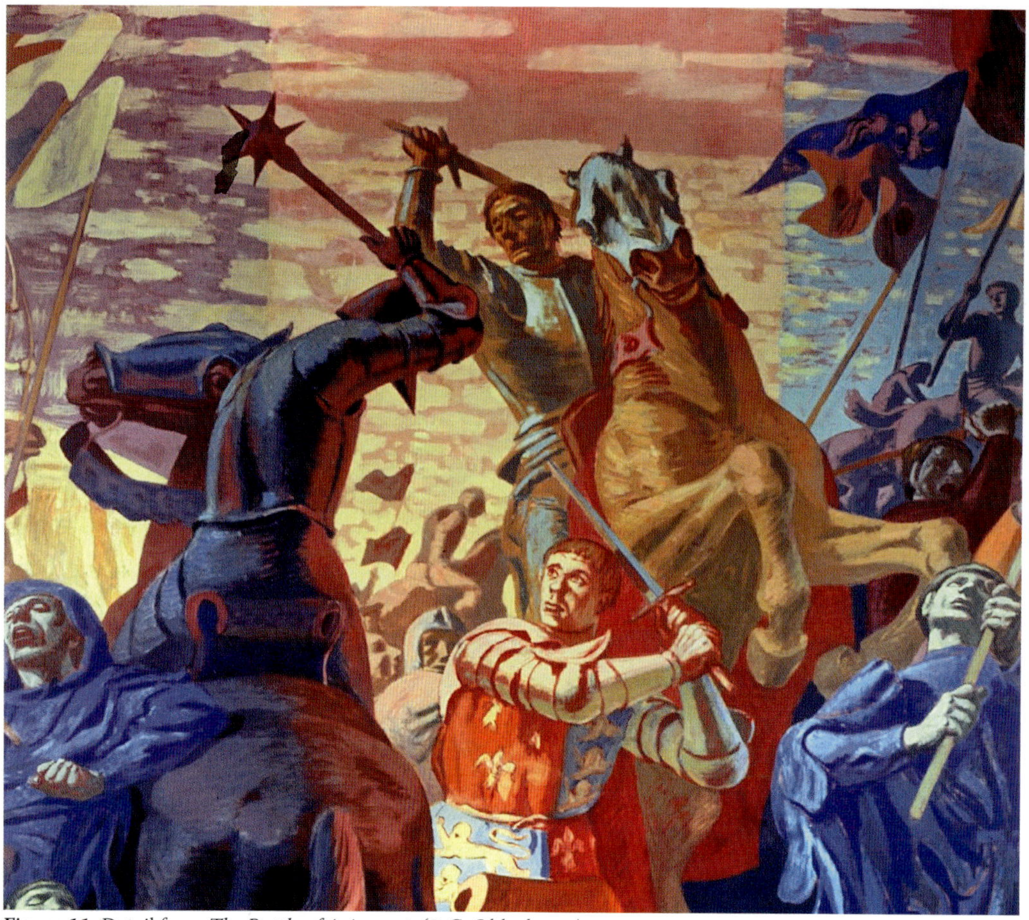

Figure 11 Detail from *The Battle of Agincourt*. (© C. Oldenbourg)

the complementary colour destroys the entire colour balance across the wall, and makes it the least effective area of painting. From the cross-sections, we can see that the left-hand and central panels had been finished when Feibusch returned and changed the whole colour arrangement. Why? Was he so annoyed at having to change the head of David Gamm that he was determined to reduce the impact of the entire wall?

This wall has also received the brunt of previous restoration. There is evidence of many campaigns, although only one has been documented: the 1985 campaign by Chris Boulter, a friend of Feibusch, who not only recommended him for the work but visited during the work. His only advice to Boulter seems to be a list of the pigments used. No advice was given about his medium or technique. We found some oil paint retouching that had darkened, and which had a very different texture from Feibusch and Bray's work. This retouching was 'painterly' and executed with prominent impasto, although the original was quite flat and painted in blocks of colour.

A later undocumented campaign carried out by the council's Direct Labour Force approached the wall much as a household decorator might. Lifting paint was cut back to a secure edge and then overpainted with matching household paint. Although the cutting back has caused much unnecessary loss, and the overpaint is copious, the texture and colour match quite well.

Future work

There are three aspects of the future maintenance of these mural paintings:

1. Amelioration of the environment in the central atrium: there are doors leading into the lower reception area, and although there are two sets, they are automatic and take a long time to close, so both can easily be opened at the same time. A revolving exterior door would avoid this. A floor-to-ceiling glass screen could be installed at a point where the current internal security barrier is located. The heating control could be improved, with more insulation on the large windows at the lower level of the tower. These windows should have UV filters and diffusing blinds. The conditions should at least be monitored.
2. Monitoring the condition of the mural paintings against the rectified photographs on a regular basis, for example once every five years: if no change is found, this period could be increased to every ten years. The same recording technique could be employed as that used during the conservation programme to record flaking.
3. Creation of a permanent archive in one location: this would aid future research into the materials and techniques, and could be combined with further evidence uncovered from existing but dispersed archives.

How can an archive containing all the relevant information from the different departments within a local authority be combined for current and future reference? There should be an archive that is solely dedicated to the object, which is separate from those in other local government departments. Documentation can be lost in deep storage or may be discarded after the statutory five years. If it were not for Roger Cucksey and Kate Hunter, much of the above information would be unknown or perhaps even destroyed, leaving a series of anecdotes to verify or refute the evidence found on the walls; only the fictions and none of the facts would be known. All information gained needs to be catalogued for future reference for conservators.

Conclusions

These works by Hans Feibusch are not only beautiful, but are also a rare example of 20th-century civic painting. Unfortunately, many of Feibusch's murals, painted under the patronage of Bishop George Bell and Maxwell Fry, have been destroyed or covered over. For these reasons alone, the Newport Cycle deserves to be better known to a wider public, in the same way as they are appreciated by the citizens of Newport.

The paintings are now safe and have been adequately recorded but there remains the question of their continuing well-being. The creation of a maintenance and monitoring programme was an essential part of the current conservation campaign. The recommended environmental ameliorations have yet to be carried out, but there is now an extensive archive to access for any future monitoring programme. There are more background images, including some not previously known. Much research has been undertaken to support the understanding of the methods and materials used by Hans Feibusch and the mechanisms of decay. All of this will aid future conservation and monitoring. There is still the question of where all this information should be kept. Experience has shown that this type of material can be too easily dispersed and forgotten. Publishing this paper is one way of ensuring that the existence of this collected information is known.

What does the future hold for these paintings? No archive has yet been established, and it is more difficult to obtain revenue funding for monitoring than a one-off capital grant. Staff will change – Kate Hunter has moved on to another post and Roger Cucksey will shortly retire. Jeff Knowles, the Civic Centre manager, has already retired, and many of the past members of Newport City Council who were involved in or observed the murals being painted are now deceased. The assumption is that contemporary works of art are fully documented but in fact, as this case demonstrates, more may be known about a medieval wall painting. Therefore, the evidence should be researched and anecdotal accounts need to be put into perspective.

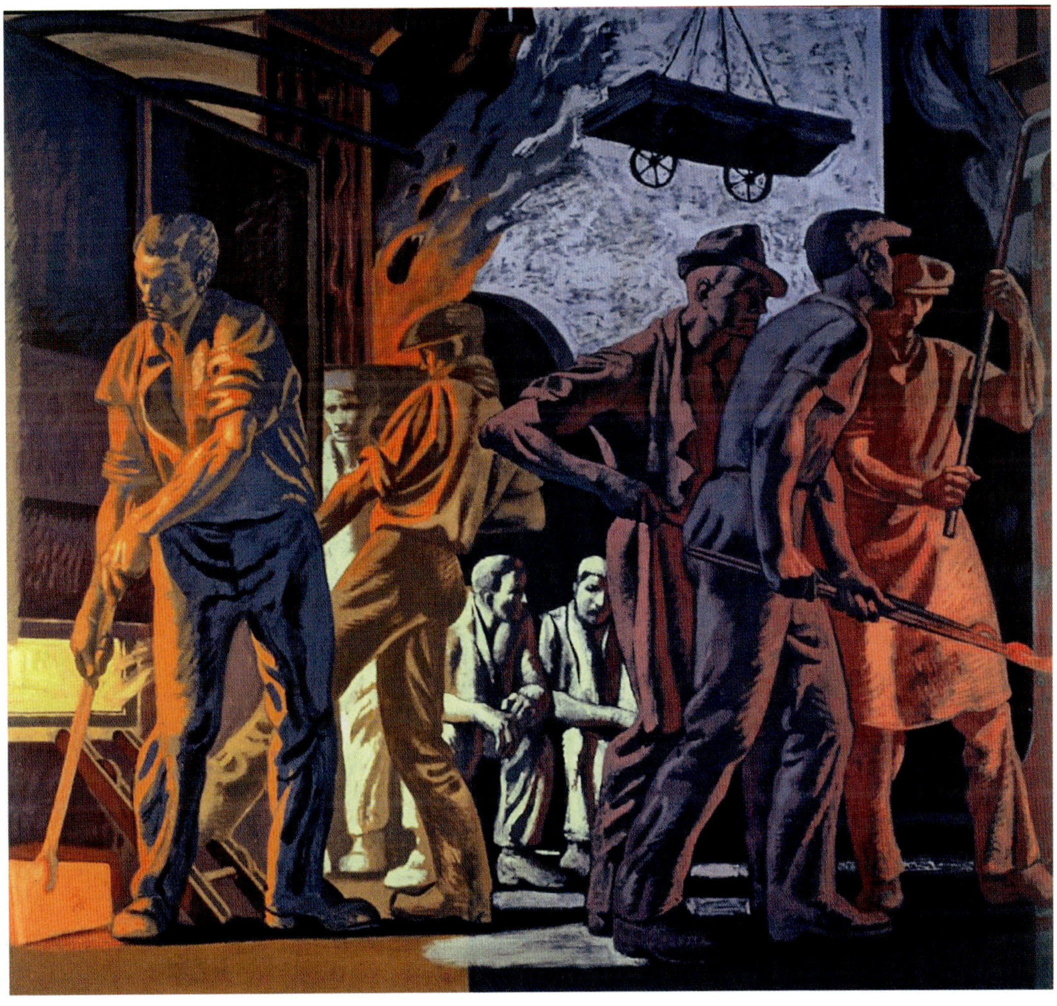

Figure 12 Civic Centre, Newport City Council, Newport, Wales: detail of the figures in *The Steel Works – Llanwern*. *(© C. Oldenbourg)*

An important work of art such as this deserves its own archive, which is accessible to all in the future. Indeed, there is a serious need for a central archive for 20th-century wall paintings, so many of which have disappeared.

Acknowledgements

The conservation team comprised Elizabeth Holford, Ian Thaden-Perrins, Christoph Oldenbourg, Teresa Smith, Carolyn Robinson, Paul Wooles, Marianna Bocedi, Christina Danielli, Anna Kettle, Sue Kelland, Patricia Claridge and Alexandra Winkles, a student from Dresden, and Isabel Roger-Jones, who was the documentation officer and processed all the images and information. Our thanks go to: Roger Cucksey, Curator, Newport Museum and Art Gallery; Ian Thaden-Perrins, painting conservator, for research and art historical notes; team member Christoph Oldenbourg; Dr Keith Hallam of Interfece Analysis Centre; Dr Brian W Singer, University of Northumbria; Catherine Hassell; David Stevens, Downland Partnership Ltd; and freelance photographer Rex Morton.

Notes

1. With additional research by Ian Thaden-Perrins.
2. Sample taken by Dr Keith Hallam of the Interface Analysis Centre, University of Bristol.
3. Photographs taken by Christoph Oldenbourg; black-out tent loaned by Aardman Animations.
4. By Christoph Oldenbourg.
5. Feibusch 1946.
6. Analyses carried out by Dr Brian Singer of the University of Northumbria using Fourier transform infrared (FTIR) analysis and gas chromatography–mass spectrometry (GC–MS).
7. Feibusch 1946.
8. *Ibid.*, 1946.

References

Bell G.K.A. 1883–1958, *The Correspondence and Diaries of George Kennedy Allen Bell*, archive collection held at the Lambeth Palace Library, London

Coke D. 1995, *Hans Feibusch: The Heat of Vision*, exhibition catalogue, Lund Humphries, London, in association with the Pallant House Gallery Trust, Chichester

Feibusch H. 1946, *Mural Painting*, Adam and Charles Black, London

Itten J. 1961, *The Art of Color: The Subjective Experience of Objective Rationale of Color*, Wiley, New York

Thaden-Perins I. and Holford E. In press. *The History of Newport Murals by Hans Feibusch*

Lambert T., *A Brief History of Newport*, www.localhistories.org/Newport.html [accessed June 2006]

Newport City Council *The Civic Centre Murals*, the Public Relations Officer and Printing Department of Newport Borough Council, Newport

The authors

- Elizabeth Holford worked for the Painting Conservation Section of the Department of the Environment before it became English Heritage. In 1978 she became a painting conservator for the Area Museum Council for the South West based at Bristol City Museum and Art Gallery. She took sabbaticals in 1985 to be the British Participant at the ICCROM Mural Painting Conservation Course and in 1998/9 completed an internship at the Opificio delle Pietre Dure, Florence. Between 1986 and 1989 she acted as a consultant to the Mural Painting Mission in Sri Lanka for the UNESCO Cultural Triangle Project. Since 1998 she has been a freelance conservator working on many wall painting projects and easel paintings based at her studio in Bristol.
- Kate Hunter worked for the Ancient Monuments Section of the Department of the Environment before it became English Heritage, at the Lincoln Archaeological Trust, Cardiff University and the National Museum of Wales. In 1992 she became Keeper of Conservation at Newport Museum and Art Gallery in South Wales, a post that involved a wide range of conservation responsibilities for a variety of materials and collections, including the Feibusch murals at Newport's Civic Centre. Since August 2004 she has been Leader for the Newport Ship Project.